THE ART OF URBANISM

THE ART OF URBANISM

How Mesoamerican Kingdoms Represented Themselves in Architecture and Imagery

WILLIAM L. FASH AND LEONARDO LÓPEZ LUJÁN
editors

PUBLISHED BY DUMBARTON OAKS RESEARCH LIBRARY AND COLLECTION,
WASHINGTON, D.C.
DISTRIBUTED BY HARVARD UNIVERSITY PRESS, 2009

Library of Congress Cataloging-in-Publication Data

Pre-Columbian Symposium, Dumbarton Oaks
(2005 : Museo del Templo Mayor, Mexico City, Mexico)
    The art of urbanism : how Mesoamerican kingdoms represented
themselves in architecture and imagery : 2005 Pre-Columbian Symposium,
Dumbarton Oaks, Museo del Templo Mayor, Mexico, D.F.,
7–9 October 2005 / William L. Fash and Leonardo López Luján, editors.
        p.   cm.
        Includes bibliographical references and index.
        ISBN 978-0-88402-344-9 (hardcover)
        ISBN 978-0-88402-378-4 (paperback)
1. Indians of Central America—Antiquities—Congresses.
2. Indians of Mexico—Antiquities—Congresses.
3. Indian art—Congresses.   4. Indian architecture—Congresses.
5. City and town life—Central America—History—Congresses.
6. City and town life—Mexico—History—Congresses.
7. Excavations (Archaeology)—Central America—Congresses.
8. Excavations (Archaeology)—Mexico—Congresses.
9. Central America—Antiquities—Congresses.
10. Mexico—Antiquities—Congresses.
I. Fash, William Leonard.   II. López Luján, Leonardo.   III. Title.
F1434.2.A7P74   2005
972'.01—dc22

                                              2008051088

Copyedited, designed, and typeset by Princeton Editorial Associates, Inc.,
Scottsdale, Arizona.

Cover illustration: Mexica sculpture of a figure dressed as a Toltec warrior.
Found in the Pasaje Catedral, Mexico City. Photograph by Michel Zabé.

www.doaks.org/publications

CONTENTS

FOREWORD

In September 2005 Dumbarton Oaks closed its Main House for two and a half years of renovations. The magnificent Music Room, the site of our symposia over the past forty years, was conserved, including a meticulous restoration of Armand Albert Rateau's ceiling inspired by the sixteenth-century Château de Cheverny near Paris. Despite the disruptions caused by renovations, Edward Keenan, then director of Dumbarton Oaks, felt it was important to continue the academic programs. This presented us with an opportunity to collaborate with our sister institutions both in Washington and abroad.

At the suggestion of William L. Fash, then chair of the Board of Senior Fellows in Pre-Columbian Studies, the 2005 Pre-Columbian Symposium was held at the Museo del Templo Mayor in Mexico City. The choice was a felicitous one for many reasons. Thirty years ago Eduardo Matos Moctezuma initiated excavations in the heart of Mexico City, reveal-ing the spectacular remains of the sacred center of the Aztec capital, Tenochtitlan. The excavations revolutionized our understanding of Aztec culture. Professor Matos, George Kubler, and Elizabeth Boone organized a conference at Dumbarton Oaks after the first four-year campaign of work, resulting in the volume *The Aztec Templo Mayor*, edited by Elizabeth H. Boone and published in 1987. Two of the original speakers at the 1983 con-ference, Eduardo Matos Moctezuma and Alfredo López Austin, were able to join us again, reflecting on the broader implications of Tenochtitlan's creation of a self-image.

A third speaker at the 1983 conference, Juan Román, director of the Museo del Templo Mayor, Instituto Nacional de Antropología e Historia, from 2000 to 2007, was our co-host for the 2005 symposium. Dumbarton Oaks remains indebted to Antropólogo Román and his excellent staff for their kind help with the organization of the event. I am also grateful to Edward Keenan for his support of this endeavor, particularly his warm words of welcome at the symposium in Mexico City. Thanks are also owed to Jai Alterman and Juan Antonio Murro for their generous help at the event, and Grace Morsberger and Emily Gulick for their assistance in the preparation of the present volume. Two anonymous outside reviewers offered thoughtful assessments and suggestions, and we are deeply grateful for those. I also thank the new director of Dumbarton Oaks, Jan Ziolkowski, for his numerous accomplishments within one short year, particularly his support of the publication program.

My greatest acknowledgments are reserved for William L. Fash and Leonardo López Luján, whose ideas and years of hard work were essential to the symposium and this volume. The topic, the art of urbanism and how the inhabitants of Mesoamerican centers represented themselves in art, architecture, and text, provides an innovative way to think about how the inhabitants of these cities and ritual centers conceptualized their world. It is a timely topic, for we have benefited greatly from recent advances in epigraphy, art history, anthropology, and archaeology. New discoveries in these fields have made new connections and a deeper understanding possible, as the contributions in this volume so eloquently demonstrate. It is with great pleasure that I thank both Bill and Leonardo for their vision.

Joanne Pillsbury
DIRECTOR OF STUDIES, PRE-COLUMBIAN PROGRAM
DUMBARTON OAKS

INTRODUCTION

William L. Fash

Leonardo López Luján

THIS VOLUME EXPLORES how the royal courts of several very powerful, iconic Mesoamerican centers represented their kingdoms in architectural, iconographic, and cosmological terms. The thorough investigation of the ecological contexts and environmental opportunities of urban centers throughout Mesoamerica now permits us to address the question of how ancient Mesoamerican cities defined themselves and reflected upon their physical—and metaphysical—place through their built environment. The participants in this symposium were asked to examine how a particular kingdom's public monuments were fashioned to reflect its geographic space, patron gods, and mythology, and how it sought to center the Mesoamerican world through its architectural monuments and public art. Specifically, how did each community leverage its environment and build upon its cultural and historical roots? How did its monuments signal its participation in Mesoamerican-wide exchanges of people, goods, and religious ideas? How were calendar rituals and other public events tied to particular places in both the center and the hinterlands, as Davíd Carrasco (1991) and his colleagues have shown for the Basin of Mexico?

Our responses to these questions are constructed from contemporary understandings of the built environment, its pictorial imagery, and specific hieroglyphic inscriptions that each royal court used to help define its identity and history to friend and foe alike. Each city had commonalities with its neighbors that were a product of shared ideology and the selective adoptions of ancient archetypes. Yet each showed innovations and symbol sets deriving from its own history that set it apart from those of its competitors and allies. We set out to explore enduring themes and historical changes in the art of urbanism across time and space, from the beginnings of complex society in proto-urban settings to its most complex and powerful expression in the late, great capital of Mexico-Tenochtitlan.

Mesoamericanist scholars have made tremendous headway on all of these themes in the nearly 30 years that elapsed between the 1976 Dumbarton

Oaks conference related to this subject (Benson 1981) and the one that took place in the Museo del Templo Mayor in the fall of 2005 that is the focus of the present volume. Of course, significant advances in method and theory have taken place over that time, not to mention an explosion of new information on the archaeology, architecture, and art of so many urban centers and their sustaining areas in the past three decades (see Houston 1998 and Kowalski 1999 for two excellent compendia). To prepare the reader for the divergent and yet complementary approaches taken by the various authors in this volume, we briefly review some of the key concepts and theoretical issues as we saw them at the time the conference took place.

CONTEMPORARY SCHOLARLY APPROACHES TO THE STUDY OF MESOAMERICAN URBANISM

The study of ancient Mesoamerican urbanism has made tremendous advances of late, with a recent series of important volumes chronicling scholarly understandings of a wide gamut of issues through time and space (Mastache et al. 2008; Sanders et al. 2003). Rather than focus on the still controversial question of defining precisely what constitutes an urban center, we sought instead to focus on how communities at various points in the process of urbanization represented themselves in the art and architecture of several iconic seats of power in ancient Mesoamerica. For the purposes of the present volume, we find Michael Smith's (2001) cogent discussion of the phenomenon of urbanization, in the *Oxford Encyclopedia of Mesoamerican Cultures*, provides some helpful definitions. Smith noted that several different conceptual approaches have been taken to study urbanization in ancient Mesoamerican communities. These included what he refers to as the ecological approach, the functional approach, the cosmovision approach, and the built-environment approach. We agree with his conclusion that even though "these views are sometimes seen as incompatible or mutually exclusive, each makes a contribution to our understanding of the ancient cities and towns of Mesoamerica" (Smith 2001: 291).

The ecological approach has most often been associated with the thinking and writings of William T. Sanders, who pioneered this framework in the Basin of Mexico in the 1950s and 1960s. In this paradigm urban centers are viewed as one means of adapting to the natural environment, and the driving questions are geared to understanding the relations between a local ecology and the kinds of communities that developed there (Sanders and Price 1968). This approach focused on what natural resources and advantages drove people to settle in an area; what means of subsistence supported the population; how settlements and diverse horticultural practices were distributed across the landscape; precisely how large, diverse, and tightly nucleated the central town or city became; and what kinds of economic specialization were practiced to support the people who lived there. Another key contribution of this approach has been the emphasis that Sanders placed on the energetics of transport in ancient Mesoamerica, where the lack of beasts of burden meant that all agricultural commodities and other goods had to be carried by people. For instance, one hypothesis is that because most food had to come from locations relatively close to a settlement, the size of urban centers was limited, and this restriction contributed to other features that appear to be common in Mesoamerican cities. These include relatively weak, decentralized rule; an emphasis on ritual functions; and poorly developed economic institutions relative to those known from other preindustrial urban societies.

Functional studies of urban societies made their first tentative steps in New World archaeology with the application of the settlement pattern approach (Willey 1953). Richard Fox's (1977) influential book *Urban Anthropology* broadened the scope of functional studies by considering noneconomic functions, such as administration and religion. His work also signaled that there were different kinds of towns and cities in Mesoamerica, ranging from modest craft production centers to towns and cities that combined ritual and political functions (including most of the Classic Maya and other urban centers in Mesoamerica), to large, densely nucleated imperial capitals focused on administration and trade. Teotihuacan and Mexico-Tenochtitlan have frequently been cited as the paramount exemplars of the densely nucleated imperial capital, with populations of more than 100,000 people who lived in wards ("barrios") devoted to particular class specializations and controlling vast areas of their hinterland through a variety of political and economic strategies. In the functional approach:

> An urban settlement is defined here as one whose activities and institutions (whether economic, political, religious, or cultural) affected areas outside of the settlement proper. Cities are large settlements with many urban functions that affect a larger hinterland, whereas towns are smaller settlements with fewer urban functions affecting a smaller region [Smith 2001: 291].

These definitions will serve the reader well for the purposes of this volume, since we are less concerned with the total numbers of people and their degree of nucleation or economic specialization than with how the different kinds of Mesoamerican kingdoms saw—and represented—themselves in their urban art and architecture.

The third vehicle for the study of Mesoamerican urbanism is the cosmovision approach, which emphasizes the symbolic role of cities as human replications of the cosmos, following the lead of the great urban geographer Paul Wheatley (1971). In Wheatley's view, people built cities in an attempt to replicate on earth the natural order they observed and charted in the sky, tying their most important sacred places to calendrical and astronomical phenomena. The 1976 Dumbarton Oaks conference *Mesoamerican Sites and World-Views* (Benson 1981) was in a very real way devoted to this approach, framed particularly by the question of urban place-making. Michael D. Coe and Elizabeth Benson stated in the preface that they had asked the contributors to the volume to focus their thinking along these lines:

> It is clear that ancient Mesoamerican sites were not randomly placed. The purpose of this conference was to explore questions of why these sites were placed where they were in the first place (what natural features may have determined the original choice of the site), how the sites might have been altered (how buildings were oriented, how earth was moved, how natural features like hills or streams were incorporated, featured, or modified), and what these activities and choices had to do with the cosmology and world view of the people who constructed the sites [Benson and Coe 1981: iii].

A seminal event in the history of Mesoamerican urban studies, place-making, and cosmovision was the discovery of the Coyolxauhqui Stone in 1978, leading to the subsequent intensive investigation of the Aztec Templo Mayor. A series of publications ensued from the academic conferences that took place in Mexico and the United States to explore the significance of the archaeological research that Eduardo Matos Moctezuma and his colleagues conducted there from 1978 forward. These conferences and related exhibitions both at the Museo del Templo Mayor and subsequently at museums around the world have had a dramatic effect on the scholarship devoted to cosmogony and urban planning in Mesoamerica. A particularly remarkable outcome was the conference organized by Davíd Carrasco and his Moses Mesoamerican Archive, which resulted in the influential volume *To Change Place: Aztec Ceremonial Landscapes* (Carrasco 1991). Most of the articles in the present volume make use of this cosmovision approach, albeit in the context of an ecological grounding and with functional interpretations.

A direct outgrowth of the work by archaeologists, anthropologists, ethnohistorians, and art historians in the Basin of Mexico was the ambitious exhibition and catalog *The Ancient Americas: Art from Sacred Landscapes*, assembled by the distinguished art historian Richard Townsend (1992). Townsend (1992: 38) gratefully acknowledged his inspiration from this group and its multidisciplinary approach to investigating sacred landscapes in the Pre-Columbian Americas, of which his own important work on Mt. Tlaloc formed an integral part (Townsend 1979, 1991). His early, indeed prescient, research *State and Cosmos in the Art of Tenochtitlan* (Townsend 1979) helped inspire many others to investigate the idea of ritual landscapes or sacred geography, which in Townsend's view was "an ancient principle, transmitted and adapted by a succession of societies over centuries or even millennia" in the Basin of Mexico (Townsend 1992: 39). This concept has been explored by archaeologists and other scholars all over the globe and was marvelously reconsidered in the important book *The Archaeologies of Landscape,* edited by Wendy Ashmore and Bernard Knapp (1999). Knapp and Ashmore (1999: 12) prefer to look at archaeological studies of ancient geography as encompassing other kinds of landscapes than the sacred alone. They define these as the constructed landscape, the conceptual landscape, and the ideational landscape, this last construed to be more inclusive than the tightly defined (and authority-driven) ideological constructs of ancient peoples.

The final perspective on urban studies of ancient Mesoamerica is the built-environment approach, which "applies insights from architectural design theory and environmental psychology to examine the dynamic interaction between human behavior and architecture" (Smith 2001: 292). Scholars who pursue this path seek to define not only why people build particular structures where they do (and decorate them accordingly), but also how those structures and the larger communities of which they form an integral part "influence behavior and perceptions by channeling the flow of people and providing clear visual signals about boundaries, interactions, and appropriate behavior." Eminent in this approach is the work of Amos Rapoport (2002), who noted that the built environment serves to organize space, time, meaning, and communication. Rapoport (2002: 473) distinguishes three levels of meaning in the built environment: a high level, concerned with cosmology and philosophy; a middle level, focused on identity, status, and power; and a lower level, which provides material clues for identifying specific uses for which particular settings are intended, including specific social situations and expected behaviors.

Most prominent among the Mesoamericanist scholars pursuing this approach is Wendy Ashmore (Ashmore 1989, 1991, 1992, 2002; Brady and Ashmore 1999; Ashmore and Sabloff 2002). Ashmore makes the insightful observation that "life histories of place" constitute a fascinating and productive new line of inquiry for scholars of ancient Mesoamerican cities. She cites work in Copan as one example of how the study of the use of particular spaces, through time, can yield insights into how "the act of rebuilding reflects at least leaders' decisions and dispositions to reproduce the social, political, and moral order" (Ashmore 2002: 1178).

Within the spatially complex place, the king's authority gains supernatural sanction, in part from where his portrait, residence, and public performances are situated (Ashmore 1989). In some Maya civic centers this mapped worldview is apparent fairly readily. At centers with more turbulent political history, marked by upheavals in royal succession and sometimes by conquest, the layouts are harder initially to read because we observe an unsorted palimpsest of decisions. When sorting by building program, evidence emerges for distinct decisions about place, some of which seem tied to shifts between competing dynastic lines (Ashmore and Sabloff 2002) [Ashmore 2002: 1178].

For the final phase royal architecture of Copan, Barbara W. Fash and the senior author laid out the conceptual map of rituals and the buildings that supported them in the Principal Group (Fash and Fash 1996). The life history of place there has been investigated by many able scholars who participated in the Copan Acropolis Archaeological Project, or PAAC (Andrews and Bill 2006; Andrews and Fash 1992; Bell et al. 2004; B. Fash 1992; B. Fash et al. 1992; W. Fash 1998; W. Fash et al. 1992; Sharer et al. 1999). Patricia McAnany (1995, 1998) has persuasively shown how the past conditions and guides the actions of the living, in both ritual and the creation of spaces for its performance, in ancient Maya communities. Rosemary Joyce and Julia Hendon (2000: 156) have explored how public settings imply "more hegemonic scales of performance," because highly visible performances were likely normative and fostered "a community with common experience, common social memories." Their thinking was much influenced by the work of Michael Herzfeld (1991: 10) regarding what he termed "monumental time," as opposed to "social time" that is merely the "grist of everyday experience." Monumental time "encounters events as realizations of supreme destiny, and it reduces social experience to collective predictability. Its main focus is on the past—a past constituted by categories and stereotypes" (Herzfeld 1991: 10).

FUNDAMENTAL MESOAMERICAN CONCEPTS OF URBAN COMMUNITIES: THE *ALTEPETL* AND TOLLAN

In our conversations (in Teotihuacan, and Tepoztlán, Morelos) leading up to our proposing the Art of Urbanism conference to Dumbarton Oaks in 2002, we agreed that for scholars to explore the links between Mesoamerican art and architecture and the natural environment through time and space, two emic terms would be of particular utility: the *altepetl*, or "watery hill," and Tollan, "Place of the Reeds," or bulrushes. All Mesoamerican peoples defined themselves in terms of sacred mountains, and it is also acknowledged that the Nahuatl concept of the *altepetl* had corresponding organizational structures in Oaxaca and the Maya lowlands (García Martínez 1998; Hirth 2003; Marcus 1983, 2000; Martin 2004).

In Late Postclassic Nahuatl culture every community was associated with a particular "hill of sustenance," or *altepetl* (literally, "water hill"). In sixteenth-century manuscripts, the *altepetl* is depicted as a bell-shaped hill with a pool of water inside, and the earlier, justly famous mural of Tepantitla in Teotihuacan depicts a very similar image, showing great antiquity for this foundational concept. James Lockhart (1993) defined the *altepetl* in terms of four basic elements: (1) a delineated territory of varying size; (2) an autonomous government; (3) a predetermined set of named constituent parts, including wards within the center and large and small outlying communities; and (4) a dynastic rulership. Xavier Noguez (2001) added that other common elements include a pyramid and a market. In terms of the cosmological significance of this concept, Alfredo López Austin (López Austin 1996; López Austin and López Luján 2009) has noted that a patron deity inhabited each "hill of sustenance." This deity (or deified ancestor) was both the creator and the protector of the group that had an affinity with him or her. In various contact period accounts, this titular deity sent his/her people on pilgrimages and bestowed a promised land on them at the end of their travels. In addition to providing them with water, the patron god rendered the land fertile and provided his/her people with the knowledge and the tools they needed for their various occupations. He or she protected them from attack and disease, yet also punished those subjects who abandoned traditions, failed to pay him or her proper homage, or committed moral transgressions. The deity could be worshiped on the hill that he or she had chosen as his/her residence or at a pyramid built in his/her honor for that purpose.

A working meeting of the Moses Mesoamerican Archive that took place in Copan, Honduras, in the summer of 2002 was an important preliminary step in the evolution of our thinking about the concept of the *altepetl* in ancient Mesoamerican place-making and urbanization. As part of the conference all of our colleagues visited not only the site center but also many of the sacred places that were incorporated in ancient ritual circuits in the Copan Valley. These included the outlying valley stelae, the ancient roads that linked the two largest urban wards or barrios with the civic-ceremonial center, several of the longest-lived residential compounds, the eastern plaza of the Principal Group that William T. Sanders (personal communications, 1981) had identified as the market, and the "named houses" of the Acropolis (Fash and Fash 1996), now represented in the Copan Sculpture Museum (Fash 2009). The paper that Karl Taube presented at this conference on the "Flowering Mountain" concept was subsequently published in *RES* (Taube 2005). The model of social integration that Carrasco (1991) and his colleagues had developed in *To Change Place* connected even the most distant communities and sacred places in the Copan kingdom or *altepetl*, whose own place-name may refer to it as a "three-mountain place."

Independently, in the context of a series of conferences on Mesoamerican urbanism coordinated by Sanders and his colleagues at the Pennsylvania State University, with Guadalupe Mastache, Robert Cobean, and their colleagues at the Instituto Nacional de Antropología e Historia (INAH), Kenneth Hirth (2003) was also formulating a model of Mesoamerican urbanism based on the *altepetl* concept. The reader is referred to his excellent chapter on this subject, which, among other important contributions, concluded that:

> From this perspective the *altepetl* or regional señorío and not the city was the primary geographic and organizational entity in Prehispanic Mesoamerica. The three primary components of these *altepetl* were the ruler, his supporting population, and the geographic territory that supported them. What is important in conceptual terms is that there is no separation between urban and rural space. The *altepetl* very often represents the community as a whole with no division between areas of settlement and their surrounding agricultural lands. . . .

> As a rule socio-political integration did not occur at the level of the urban communities. Instead, integration occurred at the level of the *altepetl* with urban communities occurring as a byproduct of regional political integration [Hirth 2003: 69, 79].

For the purposes of this volume, these considerations give added impetus to our goal of explaining how the ruling class of the towns and cities of Mesoamerica represented their place in the world and the ways in which both the supernatural and social forces in the hinterlands—as well as the urban wards—were reified and sanctioned in the built environment. Pred (1984) made the case that the conceptualization of place always involves appropriation and transformation of nature that is integral to the reproduction and transformation of society itself through both time and space. Place, therefore, is not merely a physical locus but is conceived of as all activities that occurred there and contributed historically to its creation and use.

The concept of Tollan, defined by the presence of swampy, verdant places, was of course appealing to the Culhua Mexica, whose own capital was surrounded by water. Yet archaeological investigations show that great capitals of earlier eras were also situated proximally to wetlands, with San Lorenzo, La Venta, El Mirador, and Teotihuacan being but a few prominent examples (Figure 1). "Tollan" is a term that resonates with meaning for all Mesoamericanist scholars. Associated first and foremost with the capital of the Toltecs, the name "Tollan" carries broader meanings that were applied to all large settlements where people were "thick as reeds." It is a reference to a civilized place, a place where the arts flourished, and one with a distinguished history. At the time of European contact, a series of Aztec texts identify Tollan as the first city, the cradle of maize agriculture, calendrics, writing, and artistry, and the shrine of the patron deity, Quetzalcoatl. The

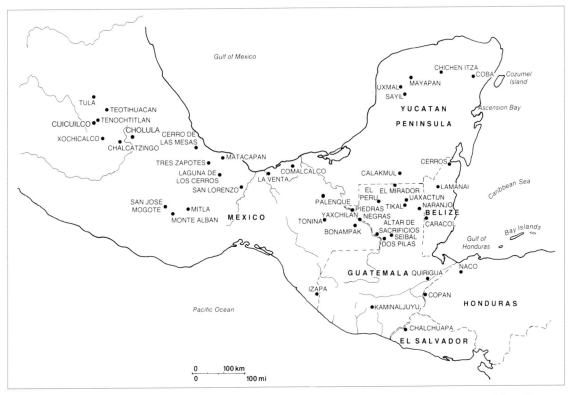

FIGURE 1. Map of Mesoamerica, showing sites mentioned in this volume.

Quiche Maya make similar associations in the *Popol Vuh*, citing Tollan as the first named city, where the first people of the present era created urban life. Writing flourished there and was then bestowed upon the Quiche and their neighbors in highland Guatemala.

For the peoples of Highland Central Mexico, the name is associated with great cities and states, both those that were active in their contemporary political landscape (Tollan Chollolan) and others belonging to bygone eras (Tollan Teotihuacan). Alfredo López Austin and Leonardo López Luján (2009) have recently argued that this concept was not tied merely to a historical individual and one particular site, but is a reflection of a deeper, Mesoamerican-wide concept of the origins of civilized urban life and, most particularly, of mercantilism and multiethnic polities in what they refer to as Zuyuan (López Austin and López Luján 2000). Because much of the discussion about Tollan goes back to the Primera Mesa Redonda de la Sociedad Mexicana de Antropología and Wigberto Jiménez Moreno's identification of Tula, Hidalgo, as the "Tollan" of the legendary Toltecs, we invited some of the leading authorities on the archaeology and ethnohistory of Late Postclassic Highland Mexico to hold forth at the conference. The documents and their concepts can be evaluated by in-depth considerations of the archaeological remains of many of the key sites in the narratives, including Mexico-Tenochtitlan and its Templo Mayor, Tula, Cholula, and Teotihuacan.

We can evaluate the emic notions expressed in numerous illuminating contact period manuscripts through an examination of the archaeological record of earlier cities, states, and civilizations to elucidate what principles and characters were integral to such concepts in the ancient Mesoamerican world. We take the same approach with other parts of Mesoamerica, with experts on the historical materials discussing the emic precepts, and archaeologists providing on-the-ground evaluations of the environment, organization, and history of prominent cities, states, and civilizations of note in both highland and lowland Mesoamerica. The discussion can now be profitably undertaken in emic terms in the Classic Period Maya lowlands, thanks to the decipherment of a glyph (read *pu*) for reed, or cattail, and its association with particular monuments and places (Stuart 2000). Both Tikal and Copan recorded this sign in their texts, which begs the question as to whether it is a concept imported from highland Mexico (as both these centers had extensive contacts with Teotihuacan) or one that is as indigenous to the Maya world as it was to the highlands. Perspectives from earlier kingdoms in Oaxaca and the Gulf Coast may prove useful in evaluating this question.

CHAPTER ORDERING AND THEMES

As archaeologists we of course have our own biases, and few readers will be surprised that we have organized the chapters in chronological order. We begin with the earliest known massive public architecture and art thus far known in Mesoamerica, at the Olmec center of San Lorenzo. Ann Cyphers and Anna Di Castro explore the first "watery hill of abundance," arguing that the island "hill" of San Lorenzo may well have represented an archetype for later kingdoms in Mesoamerica, the initial inspiration for the idea of a hill surrounded by water. Although the issue of whether San Lorenzo, and the Gulf Coast heartland Olmec culture more broadly, constituted a mother culture for the rest of Mesoamerica is not resolved in this volume, it is an important question for the topic at hand. Cyphers and Di Castro make a case for it in their chapter.

Many Middle Formative communities in Mesoamerica created major public works in architecture and art, from Teopantecuanitlan, Guerrero, in the west to Chalchuapa, El Salvador, in the east. Outside the heartland center of La Venta, few Middle Formative centers have as varied or as compelling sets of carved monuments as does the Highland site of Chalcatzingo, Morelos. David C. Grove and Susan D. Gillespie present a provocative discussion of how the rulers of the people of the Cerro legitimized their own social position through an explicit rendition of what made their space sacred and how the ruler was able to set himself up as the embodiment of both the center and the periphery. Grove and Gillespie argue thoughtfully and persuasively against the notion that later, Classic and Postclassic, patterns necessarily reflect the reasoning behind earlier practices or that one culture or place should be considered the inspiration for all subsequent cities or ideologies. For Chalcatzingo specifically, Grove and others have made the case that the two hills with the dramatic cleft between them were the reason that Early Formative agriculturalists decided to settle in an agriculturally marginal zone. Thus the geographic attributes of the locus selected for a center are inextricably linked to the vision of what makes that place sacred.

Few Mesoamerican capitals can rival Monte Albán in terms of its geographic setting or the level of effort expended to create a compelling master plan for its religious and political center. Joyce Marcus treats the reader to a masterful exposition of how a grand design was developed at Monte Albán and later imposed on a secondary center, that of San José Mogote. Through an analysis grounded in a broad regional survey, Marcus shows us what principles of organization Monte Albán's rulers and architects selected and the kinds of art, architecture, and hieroglyphic texts they commissioned through time. The discussion of the named mountains of the valley and the fact that each was considered to be a living being are pertinent for our considerations. As Marcus notes, the use of the hill sign to designate landmarks and place-names seems to have had its origin at Monte Albán at ca. 100 B.C. Marcus goes on to tentatively identify the original Zapotec name for Monte Albán itself. Monte Albán's use of prisoner scenes and martial imagery is analyzed in the context of the original conceptualization of the center and is contrasted to its later reformulation when the political power of the city declined. She shows that with the emergence of Oaxaca's first state, the new leaders residing at the capital became concerned with displaying symmetry and order, a tangible visual statement about their regime. Her comparison of Monte Albán to other cities stimulates a reassessment of both the Zapotec capital and other cities.

As the Zapotec were expressing their worldview and identity in the art and architecture of Monte Albán, the Late Preclassic Maya were developing extraordinary traditions of their own. The painted murals of San Bartolo, Guatemala, give us the most explicit as well as the most beautiful imaginable depiction of a Mesoamerican creation story, Maya style. William A. Saturno takes us through the narratives at San Bartolo to reveal how they visually, indeed quite graphically, represent the acts of creation carried out by gods and heroes in the mythological past. The murals also show how the sacrifices and the enthronement of the gods were mimicked by their flesh-and-blood followers, who sought to embody and dispense the power of the gods and their own royal ancestors. The clear parallels between aspects of the San Bartolo murals, dating to the first century B.C., and the much later accounts of the *Dresden Codex* and the *Popol Vuh* show the deep roots of much of this mythology. As Saturno has been at pains to point out, the artistic mastery exhibited in the San Bartolo murals indicates that there had already been many generations of master painters in the Maya world. Likewise the sophistication and clarity of the mythological and historical scenes clearly shows that the narratives they represent were also well established by the time San Bartolo's gifted artist set to work to adorn the interior of the Pinturas group.

For Cholula, Puebla, we are grateful to Gabriela Uruñuela y Ladrón de Guevara, Patricia Plunket Nagoda, and Amparo Robles Salmerón for their detailed descriptions and careful analysis of the beginnings of the art and architecture of what was to become one of the great archetypes of Mesoamerica, the Tlachihualtepetl or "Man-Made Mountain" of Cholula. This adobe structure was the largest of Mesoamerica; indeed, before its partial dismantling by the conquistadores, it was the largest single structure ever created in Mesoamerica. The great pyramid of Cholula underwent a series of transformations from its relatively humble beginnings in the first century A.D., after a major eruption of Popocatepetl. They argue that the pyramid came to represent the "smoking mountain" itself. Although the earliest painted murals have traditionally been interpreted as depicting grasshoppers, Uruñuela and her colleagues make a compelling case that they in fact represent a series of skulls and tied knots, perhaps representations of the ancestors. Springs emanate from the ceremonial area, and there is even the suggestion of a *xicalcoliuhqui* (spiral) in the plan of the central precinct. Small wonder that in later times Cholula was considered such a powerful place in cosmological and political terms.

For Cholula's contemporary and rival, the urban center of Teotihuacan, Mexico, it has long been noted that mural paintings from the city depict a "three-mountain place." Zoltán Paulinyi develops this observation by analyzing the representations of a mountain god in Teotihuacan art. The complexity of the imagery associated with this god suggests a mountain of importance with igneous aspects associated with a god who confers plant fertility. Through a detailed analysis of the imagery Paulinyi is able to show that this mountain god was likely tied to an ancestor—probably a patron of the Coyote Lords (previously referred to as an order of warriors in the literature). He makes the strong argument that this complex grows out of the Preclassic cult of mountain gods represented in braziers, such as those associated with Popocatepetl and its adjacent settlements to the south. The brazier/volcano associations are suggested by Uruñuela et al. here and in their masterful work at Tetimpa, and in the Basin of Mexico at Cuicuilco, as discussed by Eduardo Matos Moctezuma in his chapter at the end of this volume.

Of the man-made "mountains" of Teotihuacan, the Sun Pyramid has long been the subject of public admiration and scholarly inquiry. The chapter by William L. Fash, Alexandre Tokovinine, and Barbara W. Fash draws on that body of scholarship to propose a new set of meanings for the central temple-pyramid of the city. The Aztec appropriation of Teotihuacan artistic and architectural traditions, as analyzed by Leonardo López Luján (1989), serves as a point of departure for evaluating the ways in which the contemporary (Early Classic) and subsequent (Late Classic) Maya viewed and engaged with Teotihuacan. The archaeological, iconographic, and textual records found in the platform (Adosada) on the west side of the Sun Pyramid provide evidence for its function as the House of the New Fire. Textual and iconographic references to such a place, and to the investiture of Classic Maya kings there, provide important evidence for their argument. The Classic Maya and Aztec appropriations would seem to be indicators of the significance of this archetypal city in ancient Mesoamerican lore and about the art of urbanism.

The chapter by Barbara W. Fash focuses on the central role of watery places and water management in the public art and architecture of the Classic Maya centers. She ties the early work on water imagery by such scholars as Robert Rands and Dennis Puleston to real-world places and people through the detailed analysis of a complex of iconographic elements that represent the importance of water control and of the managers who wore the insignia of their lofty positions on their sleeves (or rather, in their headdresses). A relative of the Oaxaca "hill-sign" is manifested in Copan as a half-quatrefoil motif on prominent buildings, which Fash relates to places of origins, analogous to the Central Mexican concept of watery hills of abundance. The waterlily headdress, worn even by the later rulers of the site, are seen to indicate the central role of the provider of clean, sacred water, channeled to key reservoirs through sophisticated design and engineering of public architecture. This chapter closes with a discussion of the ways in which traditional descendant communities in Mesoamerica have kept such traditions alive, despite the fall of indigenous centralized political authority structures that followed the Spanish invasion.

Ripe with political competition in the wake of the collapse of Teotihuacan, the Epiclassic period saw an upsurge in regional centers that emphasized the role of warfare and sacrifice in the ideology of state domination. The Epiclassic center of El Tajín, Veracruz, is located in a physical setting quite different from the riverine environs of the Early and Middle Formative center of San Lorenzo. Rex Koontz argues that El Tajín represented itself as a "Flowering Maguey Mountain," in reference to the upland areas with which it was politically, economically, and ideologically linked. The site center was built around permanent springs, with the ballcourt situated so that it could be periodically flooded by them. The site of El Tajín is justly known for its many ballcourts and narrative sculptures, which Koontz persuasively argues indicate a great deal about the social identity of the individuals represented. He draws a strong link between a wind god and the ballgame, identifying a "flying impersonator" who is depicted both on the narrative reliefs and on ballgame yokes. His conclusion is that the flying impersonator represents a powerful political office associated with the "keeping of the cloth" of the king and ballcourt sacrificial rituals.

Chichen Itza was but one of four major Epiclassic Tollans, with Monte Albán, Tula, and Xochicalco being the others. This volume includes important essays on two of the archetypal ones, Tula and Chichen Itza. Both chapters explore the early architecture of each center, as well as the later buildings and styles for which they are most noted. In this volume Tula is explored first, followed by a reconsideration of Chichen Itza.

Alba Guadalupe Mastache, Dan M. Healan, and Robert H. Cobean draw on the research they have conducted over many decades in Tula, Hidalgo, with their colleagues Eduardo Matos Moctezuma and Richard Diehl. Their chapter clearly lays out the architectural and material cultural differences between the earlier capital of Tula Chico, and the later, more grandiose capital situated at some distance from the burned and abandoned original center. The marked change in grid alignment signals a new ruling order that likewise set about creating a grander stage for its public performances and political transactions. Mastache et al. argue that the central precinct of Tula Grande represents a deliberate appropriation of the layout of Tollan Teotihuacan, and they discuss the role of warfare as a central organizing theme in the public art of the new center. Carved images of Tezcatlipoca and a single-known instance of a representation of Quetzalcoatl provide archaeological evidence for each of these important deities in the final capital of Tula. The preponderance of butterfly warriors and martial and sacrificial imagery other than the feathered serpent so favored at the contemporary Tollans of Xochicalco and Chichen Itza certainly does seem to set Tula Grande apart. Also telling is the Late Postclassic image of Ce Acatl with his diagnostic calendric name, carved on a cliff face overlooking the capital—a reminder that the tale of this legendary hero was still vivid in the imagination and cosmology of the Aztec.

William M. Ringle and George J. Bey III explore the architecture and public art of the great capital Chichen Itza in both its earlier form and subsequent apogee. They find more evidence for continuity and overlap than for foreign invasion and takeover. It is abundantly clear that warfare was the predominant concern of this city and its rulers. The archaeological evidence shows that the cenote was primarily used for offering objects associated with the military orders of the city, rather than with the Chaac, as cited in so many of the later historical sources. Virtually the entire lithic assemblage from the cenote is projectiles, including atlatl points. Wooden atlatls have also been found in the cenote, and the fine ceramics and gold disks recovered from it also depict warriors. According to Ringle and Bey, Chichen's original program was a kind of neo-Teotihuacan version of militarism, which shifted to a more typically Toltec pattern during the mature Sotuta phase after A.D. 880. They argue that the hundreds of portraits of warriors do not carry elements of portraiture—despite the individual name glyphs and other personalized attributes—to convey a "disciplinary" individuality like that formulated by Michel Foucault. Chichen Itza, Monte Albán, Tula, and Xochicalco had truly become military capitals, to judge from the public art and spaces they created. For, as Ringle and Bey note, the audience is implied in the presentation. In the case of Chichen, the huge population, roads leading to the center, and enormous scale of the architecture meant that tens of thousands of people saw the images of the warriors and their ultimate supernatural patron, the feathered serpent.

The final chapters explore the ways in which Tula was emulated or directly copied in much later Mexico-Tenochtitlan, just as many authors have commented on the ways in which the center of Mayapan copied the form of the Castillo and other contemporary buildings at Chichen Itza. Leonardo López Luján and Alfredo López Austin explore the fascinating Tollan-Quetzalcoatl dyad in the political history of Mexico-Tenochtitlan. They provide exemplary documentation for important shifts in the ideological field during the evolution both of the Aztec Triple Alliance and its capital city. They chart an abandonment of both the charter of the Epiclassic Tollans (Zuyuanism) and the Triple Alliance that had sustained it in the Late Postclassic Valley of Mexico, during the reigns of Ahuitzotl and Motecuhzoma Xocoyotzin. The emulation of Tula and its warrior art in the House of Eagles replicated the forms of Tula architecture on a smaller scale, within a stone's throw of the Great Temple. López Luján and López Austin provide compelling new evidence for the observation of Octavio Paz that if Tula was a rustic version of Teotihuacan, then Mexico-Tenochtitlan was an imperial version of Tula. The arrival of Cortés brought the delusions of grandeur of the Culhua Mexica crashing down to earth. They had begun erecting Neo-Teotihuacan style shrines in their sacred center as if to claim it as part of their legacy, but the arrival of strangers heralded a breakdown of their claims to greater power. The crises that ensued brought them swiftly back to the reality of their need for their partners in the Triple Alliance and the ideological field that had given birth to the alliance.

Reflecting on these patterns and trends, Eduardo Matos Moctezuma traces the elements that became so prominent in the final version of Mexico-Tenochtitlan, the "heart of heaven," from its predecessors in the Central Highlands of Mexico. Going all the way back to Cuicuilco, Matos Moctezuma notes the presence of a single huge temple that served as the center of the community, and in which that community centered the world.

He also notes the vital role played by the old Fire God in Cuicuilco religion, as seen in the braziers that replicated the smoking volcanoes, whose massive eruptions would eventually put an end to the Basin of Mexico's first experiment in urban living. This same deity, still represented in basalt braziers, was equally well represented in Teotihuacan, which was carefully placed sufficiently far from the deadly volcanoes to create a stable (if more challenging) environment for urban life. Matos Moctezuma makes the case that the central building of Teotihuacan was at first the Pyramid of the Sun, but later the focus shifted to the Temple of the Feathered Serpent. He emphasizes the importance of the central building facing the west, the perceived need for access-controlling platforms surrounding them, and the presence of streams in their midst. Human sacrifice is an integral component of these pivotal buildings, as is life-death duality and an association of sacred mountains with caves. He finds some of the same elements at the later capital of Tula but also an important new one: a ballcourt blocking off the west side, with an associated *tzompantli* (skull rack). At the sacred precinct of Mexico-Tenochtitlan, all six elements are present, but two mountains (one representing fire/sun and the other water/caves) are fused, in a perpetual duality.

We now bring our introductory remarks to a close and allow the reader to form his or her own conclusions about the relationship of the ideology, imagery, and architecture of these distinguished Mesoamerican kingdoms to the physical landscape that gave them birth and nurtured them through several centuries of prosperous urban life. Davíd Carrasco's final essay provides the reader with the big picture regarding this volume's mission, its results, and his own reflections on the enduring theme of the cities of sacrifice in ancient Mesoamerica.

REFERENCES CITED

Andrews, E. Wyllys, and Cassandra R. Bill
   2006   A Late Classic Royal Residence at Copan. In *Copan: History of an
          Ancient Maya Kingdom* (E. Wyllys Andrews and William L. Fash,
          eds.): 239–314. School of American Research, Santa Fe, N.M.
Andrews, E. Wyllys, and Barbara W. Fash
   1992   Continuity and Change in a Royal Maya Residential Complex at
          Copan. *Ancient Mesoamerica* 3: 63–88.
Ashmore, Wendy
   1989   Construction and Cosmology: Politics and Ideology in Lowland Maya
          Settlement Patterns. In *Word and Image in Maya Culture: Explorations
          in Language, Writing and Representation* (William F. Hands and Don S.
          Rice, eds.): 272–286. University of Utah Press, Salt Lake City.
   1991   Site-Planning Principles and Concepts of Directionality among the
          Ancient Maya. *Latin American Antiquity* 2: 199–226.

1992 Deciphering Maya Site Plans. In *New Theories on the Ancient Maya* (Elin Danien and Robert J. Sharer, eds.): 173–184. University of Pennsylvania Museum of Archaeology and Anthropology, Philadelphia.

2002 Decisions and Dispositions: Socializing Spatial Archaeology. *American Anthropologist* 104(4): 1172–1183.

Ashmore, Wendy, and A. Bernard Knapp (eds.)

1999 *Archaeologies of Landscape: Contemporary Approaches.* Blackwell, Oxford.

Ashmore, Wendy, and Jeremy A. Sabloff

2002 Spatial Order in Maya Civic Plans. *Latin American Antiquity* 13: 201–215.

Bell, Ellen E., Marcello A. Canuto, and Robert J. Sharer (eds.)

2004 *Understanding Early Classic Copan.* University of Pennsylvania Museum of Archaeology and Anthropology, Philadelphia.

Benson, Elizabeth (ed.)

1981 *Mesoamerican Sites and Word-Views.* Dumbarton Oaks Research Library and Collections, Washington, D.C.

Benson, Elizabeth, and Michael D. Coe

1981 Preface. In *Mesoamerican Sites and Word-Views* (Elizabeth Benson, ed.): iii. Dumbarton Oaks Research Library and Collections, Washington, D.C.

Brady, James E., and Wendy Ashmore

1999 Mountains, Caves, Water: Ideational Landscapes of the Ancient Maya. In *Archaeological Landscapes: Contemporary Perspectives* (Wendy Ashmore and Bernard A. Knapp, eds.): 124–145. Blackwell, Malden, Mass.

Carrasco, Davíd (ed.)

1991 *To Change Place: Aztec Ceremonial Landscapes.* University of Colorado Press, Boulder.

Fash, Barbara W.

1992 Late Classic Architectural Sculpture Themes in Copán. *Ancient Mesoamerica* 3: 89–104.

2009 *The Copan Sculpture Museum: Ancient Maya Artistry in Stucco and Stone.* Peabody Museum of Archaeology and Anthropology, Cambridge, Mass.

Fash, Barbara W., William L. Fash, Sheree Lane, Rudy Larios, Linda Schele, Jeffrey Stomper, and David Stuart

1992 Investigations of a Classic Maya Council House in Copán, Honduras. *Journal of Field Archaeology* 19(4): 419–442.

Fash, William L.

1998 Dynastic Architectural Programs: Intention and Design in Classic Maya Buildings at Copan and Other Sites. In *Function and Meaning in Classic Maya Architecture* (Stephen D. Houston, ed.): 233–270. Dumbarton Oaks Research Library and Collection, Washington, D.C.

Fash, William L., and Barbara W. Fash

1996 Building a World-View: Visual Communication in Classic Maya Architecture. *RES* 29–30: 127–147.

Fash, William L., Richard V. Williamson, Carlos Rudy Larios, and Joel Palka
  1992 The Hieroglyphic Stairway and Its Ancestors: Investigations of
         Structure 10L-26. *Ancient Mesoamerica* 3: 105–115.
Fox, Richard
  1977 *Urban Anthropology: Cities in Their Cultural Settings*. Prentice-Hall,
         Englewood Cliffs, N.J.
García Martínez, Bernardo
  1998 El altépetl o pueblo de indios: Expresión básica del cuerpo político
         mesoamericano. *Arqueología Mexicana* VI(32): 58–65.
Herzfeld, Michael
  1991 *A Place in History: Social and Monumental Time in a Cretan Town*.
         Princeton University Press, Princeton, N.J.
Hirth, Kenneth G.
  2003 The *Altepetl* and Urban Structure in Prehispanic Mesoamerica. In
         El urbanismo en Mesoamérica—Urbanism in Mesoamerica (William T.
         Sanders, Alba Guadalupe Mastache, and Robert H. Cobean, eds.):
         57–84. Instituto Nacional de Antropología e Historia and Pennsylvania
         State University, Mexico City and University Park.
Houston, Stephen D. (ed.)
  1998 *Function and Meaning in Classic Maya Architecture*. Dumbarton Oaks
         Research Library and Collection, Washington, D.C.
Joyce, Rosemary A., and Julia Hendon
  2000 Heterarchy, History and Material Reality: "Communities" in Late
         Classic Honduras. In *The Archaeology of Communities. A New World
         Perspective* (Marcello A. Canuto and Jason Yaeger, eds.): 143–160.
         Routledge, London.
Knapp, Bernard A., and Wendy Ashmore
  1999 Archaeological Landscapes: Constructed, Conceptualized, Ideational.
         In *Archaeological Landscapes: Contemporary Perspectives* (Wendy Ash-
         more and Bernard A. Knapp, eds.): 1–30. Blackwell, Malden, Mass.
Kowalski, Jeff K. (ed.)
  1999 *Mesoamerican Architecture as a Cultural Symbol*. Oxford University
         Press, Oxford.
Lockhart, James
  1993 *The Nahuas after the Conquest: A Social and Cultural History of the Indians
         of Central Mexico, Sixteenth through Eighteenth Centuries*. Stanford
         University Press, Palo Alto, Calif.
López Austin, Alfredo
  1996 Los mexicas y su cosmos. In *Dioses del Mexico Antiguo* (Eduardo Matos
         Moctezuma, ed.): 21–43. Antiguo Colegio de San Ildefonso, México.
López Austin, Alfredo, and Leonardo López Luján
  2000 The Myth and Reality of Zuyuá. The Feathered Serpent and Meso-
         american Transformations from the Classic to the Postclassic. In
         Mesoamerica's Classic Heritage. From Teotihuacan to the Aztecs (Davíd
         Carrasco, Lindsay Jones, and Scott Sessions, eds.): 21–84. University
         Press of Colorado, Boulder.

2009 *Monte Sagrado/Templo Mayor: El cerro y la pirámide en la tradición religiosa mesoamericana*. Universidad Nacional Autónoma de México and Instituto Nacional de Antropología e Historia, México.

López Luján, Leonardo

2009 *La recuperación mexica del pasado teotihuacano*. Instituto Nacional de Antropología e Historia, Proyecto Templo Mayor, México.

Marcus, Joyce

1983 On the Nature of the Mesoamerican City. In *Prehistoric Settlement Patterns in the New World: Essays in Honor of Gordon R. Willey* (Evon Z. Vogt and Richard M. Leventhal, eds.): 195–242. University of New Mexico Press and Peabody Museum, Harvard University, Albuquerque and Cambridge, Mass.

2000 Toward an Archaeology of Communities. In *The Archaeology of Communities: A New World Perspective* (Marcello-Andrea Canuto and Jason Yaeger, eds.): 231–242. Routledge, London and New York.

Martin, Simon

2004 Preguntas epigráficas acerca de los escalones de Dzibanché. In *Los cautivos de Dzibanché* (E. Nalda, ed.): 105–115. Instituto Nacional de Antropología e Historia, México.

Mastache, Alba Guadalupe, Robert H. Cobean, Angel Garcia Cook, and Kenneth Hirth (eds.)

2008 *El urbanismo en Mesoamérica—Urbanism in Mesoamerica*, vol. 2. Instituto Nacional de Antropología e Historia and Pennsylvania State University, Mexico City and University Park.

McAnany, Patricia

1995 *Living with the Ancestors: Kinship and Kingship in Ancient Maya Society*. University of Texas Press, Austin.

1998 Ancestors and the Classic Maya Built Environment. In *Function and Meaning in Classic Maya Architecture* (Stephen D. Houston, ed.): 271–298. Dumbarton Oaks Research Library and Collection, Washington, D.C.

Noguez, Xavier

2001 Altepetl. In *The Oxford Encyclopedia of Mesoamerican Cultures: The Civilizations of Mexico and Central America* (Davíd Carrasco, ed.): I: 12–13. Oxford University Press, Oxford.

Pred, Allen

1984 Place as Historically Contingent Process: Structuration and the Time-Geography of Becoming Places. *Annals of the Association of American Geographers* 74(2): 279–297.

Rapoport, Amos

2002 Spatial Organization and the Built Environment. In *Companion Encyclopedia of Anthropology* (Timothy Ingold, ed.): 460–502. Routledge, New York.

Sanders, William T., and Barbara J. Price

1968 *Mesoamerica: The Evolution of a Civilization*. Random House, New York.

Sanders, William T., Alba Guadalupe Mastache, and Robert H. Cobean (eds.)

    2003   *El urbanismo en Mesoamérica—Urbanism in Mesoamerica*. Instituto
           Nacional de Antropología e Historia and Pennsylvania State Univer-
           sity, Mexico City and University Park.

Sharer, Robert J., William L. Fash, David W. Sedat, Loa P. Traxler, and
    Richard V. Williamson

    1999   Continuities and Contrasts in Early Classic Architecture of Central
           Copan. In *Mesoamerican Architecture as a Cultural Symbol* (Jeff K.
           Kowalski, ed.): 220–249. Oxford University, Oxford.

Smith, Michael E.

    2001   Urbanization. In *The Oxford Encyclopedia of Mesoamerican Cultures.
           The Civilizations of Mexico and Central America* (Davíd Carrasco, ed.),
           vol. 3: 290–294. Oxford University Press, New York.

Stuart, David

    2000   The Arrival of Strangers. Teotihuacan and Tollan in Classic Maya
           History. In *Mesoamerica's Classic Heritage. From Teotihuacan to the Aztecs*
           (Davíd Carrasco, Lindsay Jones, and Scott Sessions, eds.): 465–513.
           University of Colorado Press, Boulder.

Taube, Karl

    2005   Flower Mountain: Concepts of Life, Beauty, and Paradise among the
           Classic Maya. *RES* 45: 69–98.

Townsend, Richard F.

    1979   *State and Cosmos in the Art of Tenochtitlan*. Studies in Pre-Columbian
           Art and Archaeology 20. Dumbarton Oaks Research Library and
           Collection, Washington, D.C.

    1991   Tlaloc Project. In *To Change Place: Aztec Ceremonial Landscapes* (David
           Carrasco, ed.): 26–30. University Press of Colorado, Niwot.

    1992   (ed.) *The Ancient Americas: Art from Sacred Landscapes*. Art Institute of
           Chicago, Chicago.

Wheatley, Paul

    1971   *The Pivot of the Four Quarters*. Aldine, Chicago.

Willey, Gordon R.

    1953   *Prehistoric Settlement Patterns in the Virú Valley, Perú*. Government
           Printing Office, Washington, D.C.

EARLY OLMEC ARCHITECTURE AND IMAGERY

Ann Cyphers
Anna Di Castro

The task of approaching an understanding of the "world-view"
or cosmology of a vanished civilization from its material remains
ultimately requires nothing less than a holistic approach that
includes the examination of the "hard" archaeological data, on the
one hand, balanced by an attempt at understanding the mind and
spirit of the people, their ritual and religion [Carlson 1981: 144].

THE ABSENCE OF WRITTEN SOURCES for the Olmec civilization dictates the analysis of the natural and spatial order of this vanished culture from its material remains to discern the intricate relationship of symbolic meaning and social organization. Spaces, including their material contents, and human thoughts and actions form an interactive behavioral arena (Lawrence and Low 1990), which may be involved in the establishment and maintenance of social and political inequality (e.g., Ashmore 1989; Smith 1999). This volume, which emphasizes the coming together of archaeology and ethnohistory, promises important insights on this topic. Careful tracing of the tangible manifestations of cosmological ideas in the landscape may aid in understanding how ideology interrelated with social, economic, and political notions and actions in many archaeological sites, such as the first Olmec capital, San Lorenzo, Veracruz.

Set in the Preclassic milieu of Mesoamerica, the Olmec's complex development emerged in the sultry southern Gulf Coast lowlands. Its first capital, San Lorenzo, fluoresced during the Early Preclassic (ca. 1150–850 B.C.), followed by La Venta, Tabasco, in the late Early and Middle Preclassic (ca. 800–400 B.C.; Figure 1). Both centers participated in trade networks extending to distant regions. The Olmec culture is widely known for its stone monuments, which are emblematic of political power and contain intrinsic information regarding the ancient worldview. Their rulers, who were commemorated in colossal stone portraits, organized massive

FIGURE 1. Map of the southern Gulf Coast region showing the location of sites mentioned in the text. Drawing by Ann Cyphers.

construction projects and craft production and planned the transport of multiton stones from the neighboring Tuxtlas Mountains.

Since the beginning of Olmec archaeology, this society has been characterized as Mesoamerica's "mother culture" (Caso 1964; Coe 1965; Covarrubias 1957), an appellation subject to recent heated discussion. As a complex forerunner to later great civilizations, its contribution and impact on Mesoamerican ways of life and traditions have been outlined by a number of authors (Clark 1997; Clark and Perez 1994; Coe 1965, 1968; Coe and Diehl 1991; Diehl and Coe 1996; Lowe 1989; Tolstoy 1991) and questioned by others (Demarest 1989; Flannery and Marcus 2000; Grove 1989; Hammond 1988; Marcus 1989). With regard to cosmology, many studies point to the inception of fundamental beliefs in the Preclassic period (Coe 1972; Covarrubias 1957; Grove 1970; Reilly 1990, 1995; Schele 1995; Taube 1995, 1996) that persisted in later societies. Inquiries into the early expressions of several basic Mesoamerican cosmological concepts indicate that the Olmec and their contemporaries shared beliefs regarding the layered vertical cosmos, sacred mountains, cave entrances to the underworld, the sanctification of inanimate materials such as stone, and north-south and center-periphery dichotomies (see Angulo 1987; Cyphers 1997b, 1999; Grove 1970, 1972, 1987, 1999; Reilly 1994a, 1994b, 1999).

The present chapter on San Lorenzo follows this line of thinking and focuses on themes related to the built environment that include the San Lorenzo Island as a hill surrounded by water, the regional landscape as the horizontal cosmos, political centers and stone thrones, ritual performances involving stone monuments, and the cosmological referents for architecture and artifacts. Within these themes there is suggestive preliminary evidence obtained in regional and intrasite research that allows us to explore (1) the interaction of the natural environment with ideology and behavior and (2) the role of landscape in creating and legitimating inequality and the claim to authority.

SAN LORENZO ISLAND: A HILL SURROUNDED BY WATER

The lower Coatzacoalcos River drainage in southern Veracruz, Mexico, dramatically differs from its upper, hillier reaches in that it is a vast deltaic plain where wide, meandering rivers cut through immense wetlands. San Lorenzo sits on a natural ridge-shaped promontory that covers 2,200 ha (Figure 2) and rises to 50 m above the surrounding wetlands. Geomorphological studies indicate that this setting once was an island circumscribed by ancient rivers (Ortiz Pérez and Cyphers 1997) whose overall size (including promontory and wetlands) varied between 60 and 90 km^2 due to shifts in river courses over time. This setting constitutes San Lorenzo Island, the heart of the early Olmec world, because therein lived the greatest population density known in Early Preclassic Mesoamerica, with about 120 inhabitants/km^2 (Symonds et al. 2002: 66). The island's rich natural resources and its strategic position in a semiradial-shaped river system were unique environmental characteristics that enhanced its potential as a favorable location for the concentration of goods and services. In the center of the island, the San Lorenzo plateau formed the center and highest portion of this sprawling site that covers approximately 700 ha.

Recent research indicates that, following initial settlement ca. 1500 B.C., construction activities varied through time. Little is known about the earliest occupations because of the great depth at which they are found; nonetheless, there is a probable early stepped earthen platform approximately 1.6 m high that was built during the Bajío phase, 1350–1250 B.C. (Coe and Diehl 1980: 1: 106–109). Terrace construction began ca. 1150 B.C., and by 900–850 B.C., the site had a central core area (the top of the plateau) ringed by various levels of artificial terraces and a broad periphery lacking major landscape modification. Social and political stratification is echoed in the site's topography: the political elites were located atop the plateau,

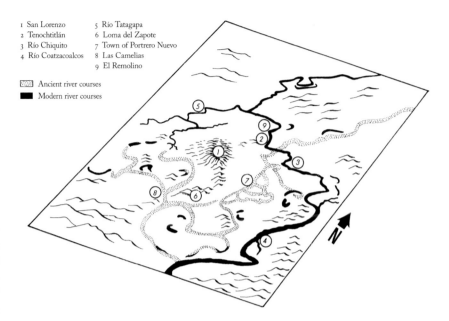

1 San Lorenzo   5 Río Tatagapa
2 Tenochtitlán   6 Loma del Zapote
3 Río Chiquito   7 Town of Portrero Nuevo
4 Río Coatzacoalcos   8 Las Camelias
                       9 El Remolino

▨ Ancient river courses
■ Modern river courses

FIGURE 2. Sketch map of San Lorenzo Island showing the location of archaeological sites and ancient and modern rivers. Drawing by Fernando Botas.

with diminishing status generally paralleling lower altitude or terrace and increasingly peripheral position.

Important architectural features in San Lorenzo Island are artificial earthen platforms (*islotes;* Figure 3), which are characteristically built in the alluvial plains. Each miniature island, ranging from 1 to 5 m high, is a haven of tierra firme rising from the watery surface of the plains. The initial construction of 47 Early Preclassic *islotes* in the wetlands north of San Lorenzo began as early as 1500–1150 B.C., indicating the key importance of the seasonal exploitation of this prime area of subsistence resource concentration.

Subsistence activities were conducted from these constructions, which protected the structures built on their upper surface from rising water levels and provided shelter for the people exploiting the natural resources of the floodplains. The planned construction of the *islotes* established rights to special spots in the island's floodplains as part of what appears to be a planned subsistence strategy designed to intensively exploit a specialized eco-niche for fishing, hunting, and collecting. Later in the Early Preclassic occupational sequence, the *islotes* also may have facilitated the practice of recession agriculture, which would have been conducted at the time of year when the higher lands were prepared for rainy season crops. Given their artificial character, the *islotes* were a critical part of the ancient landscape, because the nature of the Gulf Coast riverine lowlands demanded—since the onset of human occupation—the search for high ground, safe from flooding, for human habitation.

At the site level, the San Lorenzo plateau has been characterized as a sacred mountain (Bernal-García 1994) and has been considered a cosmo-

FIGURE 3. An artificial low mound (*islote*) located in the alluvial plain north of San Lorenzo. Photograph by Ann Cyphers.

logical template for variable architectural forms at other major Preclassic sites, such as La Venta and Chalcatzingo (Grove 1999). Settlement requirements in an environment where high ground is scarce may have been part of the inspiration for the concept of the sacred hill or mountain surrounded by water, which is applicable to the *islotes,* the island locations of San Lorenzo and La Venta (see Elzey 1991: 116), and other early sites on both the Gulf and Pacific coasts and elsewhere. The landscape model of the sacred hill encircled by water recalls the structure of Nahua cosmology in which horizontal space is conceived of as sky (*ilhuicatl*), the surface of the earth (*tlalticpac*), and a body of water circling the earth (*teoatl*); vertical space held the 13 heavens, the earth, and 9 levels of the underworld, with the hermaphroditic deity Ometeotl as the *axis mundi* (Léon-Portilla 1963).

Another perspective, provided by Robert Heizer (1968), focuses on a volcanic cone in the Tuxtlas Mountains, prominent on the coastal landscape and the source of sacred stone, as a natural model for the Great Pyramid at La Venta (Mound C-1). Notably, an elaborate human figure placed near the peak of the San Martin Pajapan volcano calls further attention to sacred landscape symbolism (Diehl and Coe 1996: 19–20; Schele 1995: 108).

THE REGIONAL LANDSCAPE: THE HORIZONTAL COSMOS

Geography conditions land travel in the immediate San Lorenzo area, because ridges and promontories provide the only perennial dry land rising from the floodplains. The convergence of three major rivers at San Lorenzo Island gave the capital a favorable natural position as a transportation node. In general, the characteristics of the natural environment conditioned the structure of the relationships of the hinterland centers with the capital. Such centers possessed monuments made of sacred stone that are a symbol of their place in the settlement system (Cyphers 2004b: 34–35). Lesser centers, located at important locations in the fluvial and settlement network (such as river confluences or high ground next to rivers), show the structure of the early Olmec world, where position on promontories above the floodplains near fluvial confluences is a basic principle in social and political spatial arrangements. Key natural junctures possess regulatory functions in the cultural domain such that settlement hierarchy is intertwined with the ceremonial landscape (Symonds et al. 2002).

Other key Olmec sites at this time were Laguna de los Cerros and La Venta. Laguna de los Cerros, located 55 km from San Lorenzo on the lower slopes of the Tuxtlas Mountains in the San Juan River drainage, once was considered a primary center; however, recent research suggests that it played a secondary role in the Olmec world (Borstein n.d. [2001]), one that included the procurement of nearby basalt and the manufacture of sculptural preforms (Cyphers and Borstein n.d.; Gillespie 1994; Medellín 1960). Initial insights into La Venta's regional developmental trajectory based on regional and site-specific research (González Lauck 1989, 1994, 1996; Mettner n.d. [2001]; Raab et al. 2000; Rust and Sharer 1988) indicate an Early Preclassic occupational component that was in no way equivalent to San Lorenzo.

The types and quantities of stone monuments at important Olmec sites have long been linked to site importance. The creation of sculptures containing sacred concepts was one outcome of early asymmetrical power relationships that enabled the use of costly nonutilitarian labor in the production and transport of the scarce imported resource (usually basalt) they are made of. Aspects of the belief system incorporated in their design helped structure the relationship between leaders and followers, as well as between elite and commoners. Within the corpus of stone monuments, the monolithic throne stands out in this regard, because it is an image used by rulers that incorporates symbols of hereditary rulership and lineage into its design (Coe 1968; Cyphers 1997b; Gillespie 1999; Grove 1973). Functioning at the center of the political scene, these hefty emblems of office and of the rulers that used them were outstanding material indicators of privileged social relations (compare Reilly 1995: 42–43). Particularly important are the large thrones, exclusive to the capital, because of their imagery related to cosmic ruler legitimation, sacred origins in the niche-cave, and divine ancestor figure and royal succession in the lateral bas-relief. Other thrones seem to be smaller replicas of the large ones but lack lateral bas-relief. And yet others, which are characteristically small and have a similar rectangular table-top form, lack the niche-cave and lateral bas-relief.

The ingenious design of large thrones shows the symbolism of cosmic

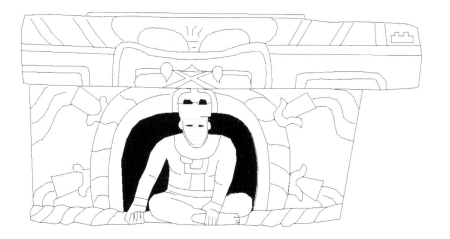

FIGURE 4. Altar 4 from La Venta, a monolithic stone throne, embodies the symbolism of the Olmec cosmos as a sacred mountain and cosmic monster. Drawing by Ann Cyphers.

and sociopolitical order (Figure 4). From top to bottom and from the inside out, each throne embodies a multivalent symbolism illuminating hierarchical and horizontal relations involved in actual and sacred geography, social organization, and the position of the ruler in the cosmos. The design recalls Aztec and Maya cosmology in several general ways, such as the layered symbolism, intrinsic metaphors, and profound concepts that eternally fuse the past, present, and future. Throne design revolving about the image of the Earth deity makes reference to the vertical structure of the cosmos, including the place of the ruler, the surface of the world or sky, and the underworld, which may be entered through the niche-cave (Grove 1973). The overall design of thrones alludes to a high place, such as a hill or mountain, and the vertical and horizontal structure of sociopolitical relations is embodied in it.

The spatially restricted distribution of stone thrones in the San Lorenzo hinterland, in conjunction with their particular characteristics, correlates favorably with the settlement hierarchy. Only large thrones with a frontal niche and lateral bas-relief are found at the capital, whereas small thrones lacking the niche and bas-relief are found at the secondary centers of Estero Rabón and Loma del Zapote. Estero Rabón's small throne, with an upper ledge identical to the one at Loma del Zapote, seems to be a metaphor for secondary political position. In the more distant hinterland, small and medium-sized thrones with frontal niches and ancestral figures from Laguna de los Cerros and La Venta suggest the existence of a regional hierarchy of hereditary rulers throughout the Early and Middle Preclassic. These monuments functioned not only as the emblems of major and lesser rulers but also were symbols of regional organization (Cyphers 2004b: 34–35).

Hieroglyphic inscriptions and settlement size have been used to infer the ancient worldview of quadrants in the Maya area (e.g., Marcus 1973). A similar approach may be attempted for the early Gulf Coast using Olmec-specific types of evidence. The cosmological significance of Early Preclassic settlement across the southern Gulf Coast perhaps may be inferred from what is known of relative site importance and the salient political symbols (i.e., thrones) they contain. San Lorenzo, the largest, most complex center at the time, offers large thrones with an ancestral figure, niche-cave, and lateral bas-relief, which are fundamental indicators of maximal ruler-ship. Lesser centers with smaller thrones are located on the landscape in the following way: Laguna de los Cerros to the northwest, La Venta to the northeast, Loma del Zapote to the south, and Estero Rabón to the southwest. It is tempting to interpret this cultural landscape in terms of an early notion of the four quadrants concept (e.g., Heyden 1981) in which the central place, located on a cosmologically charged hill surrounded by water, was considered the center of the Olmec universe. In addition, a four-quadrant concept has been inferred from Olmec iconography (see Reilly 1995; Schele 1995; Taube 2000).

RITUAL PERFORMANCES AND STONE MONUMENTS

Many stone monuments likely were moved repeatedly for different reasons. Each time a stone sculpture is moved or a display of weighty monuments is accommodated, there is a necessary conspicuous consumption of labor that reinforces, promotes, and proclaims elite ascendancy (Cyphers 1993, 1994; see also Ogburn 2005).

Evidence has been presented elsewhere for the Olmec's periodic use of stone monuments to physically re-create scenes imbued with mythological and historical meaning (Cyphers 1993, 1994, 1997b, 1999, 2004a). The vestiges of such scenes include: El Azuzul montage at Loma del Zapote with four in situ stone monuments, two nearly identical human figures and two felines, which is tantalizingly suggestive of the Hero Twin myth (see León and Sánchez 1991–92; Figure 5); the Loma del Zapote setting of a mutilated human figure, Monument 5, made in stone that was placed by a ceremonial structure containing at least one possible sacrificial victim and an adjacent ceremonial bath; and Monument 11 from Loma del Zapote, a decapitated and dismembered stone figure that must have been used in conjunction with an elevated surface, which makes it similar to the representation of the Olmec personage seated on the monster deity that is represented in Mural 1 of Oxtotitlan, Guerrero.

There is also the commemorative macro-scene of ancestral ruler portraits (see Beverido Pereau n.d. [1970]), composed of colossal heads made from thrones (see Porter 1989) that is located in the south-central sector of the San Lorenzo plateau (Figure 6). The space between the two lines of heads was not empty but rather contained numerous structures, such that it likely was not used for pageants. Although this spectacular setting

FIGURE 5.
Reconstruction of the
El Azuzul sculptural
scene from the Loma del
Zapote site. Drawing by
Fernando Botas.

could be characterized as a "processional arrangement" (Grove 1999: 277), the macro-scene, which was never completed because of the site's decline, seems to have been intended as a historical display of rulers, perhaps with spatial referents to their respective descent groups.

These examples appear to be unmistakable material manifestations of the dramaturgy of power (Cohen 1981) by which the ruling sector designs and controls social experience and interaction according to cosmological conventions in order to institute and sustain their power. Also, as energetically costly dynamic displays (see Ogburn 2005: 228), they reinforced sacred ideas for the same purpose (see Rick 2005: 75). The dramatization of mythical and historical events, as represented in these examples, is essential in the symbolic construction of authority (Bloch 1987). The making of

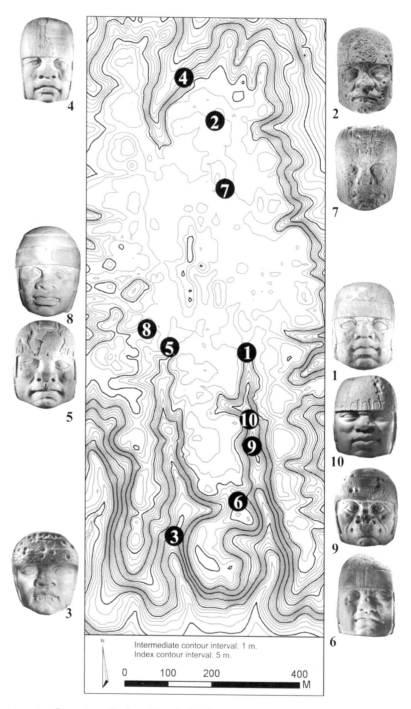

FIGURE 6. Location of colossal heads (sculptures are not to scale) on the San Lorenzo plateau. Topographic map by Timothy Murtha; colossal head photos by Brizio Martínez.

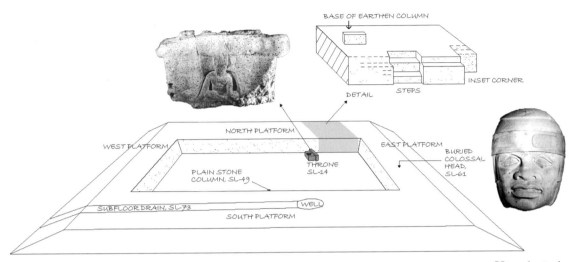

FIGURE 7. Hypothetical reconstruction of the Group E complex showing its design and the position of stone monuments. Drawing by Fernando Botas.

these scenes requiring commoner labor and the subsequent observation and participation of commoners in related events constituted a dazzling blend of emotion, cosmology, and power that served to legitimate inequality.

THE GROUP E ARCHITECTURAL COMPLEX

An area situated in the west central portion of the San Lorenzo plateau contains impressive early buildings (Cyphers et al. 2006), which, like sculptural scenes, were essential in shaping the dramaturgy of Olmec power. Group E's present-day topography, a gently rolling terrain punctuated by several lagoons, is unrelated to the Olmec construction there. The joint efforts of three projects—Brüggeman and Hers (1970), Coe and Diehl (1980), and the San Lorenzo Tenochtitlan Archaeological Project (SLTAP)—have revealed nearly 300 m² of a deeply buried architectural complex. Here, because of space limitations, we present only a summary of its characteristics; the forthcoming SLTAP report will present full details.

With a two-stage construction and continuous occupation sequence dating through the San Lorenzo phase (1150–850 b.c.), the large, low complex, composed of earthen platforms surrounding an interior sunken patio (Figure 7), was at least 75 m long on each side and rose about 4 m above the ancient ground surface (excluding the height of superstructures) in its final building phase. It is composed of northern, eastern, and southern platforms and the central sunken patio; the western section may have been destroyed by the post-Preclassic construction of Laguna 8 (Cyphers 1997a: 112). The complex stands out as a special area because of its large size; unusual construction style; central location within the site; and associated artifacts, including stone monuments. The following brief description of the complex outlines its principal characteristics and associated monuments.

The size, shape, and iconographic themes of four well-known large stone monuments in Group E indicate its special nature and cosmological meanings. The seat of a ruler or the throne, Monument 14 (or SL-14), exhibits the principle of divine descent via the sacred ancestor figure emerging from the cave-niche entrance to the underworld, the source of rain and mist (Grove 1973: 134). The lateral bas-relief figures tied with a rope to the frontal ancestor on this great throne may stand for ancestral rulers or kinsmen who were successors to the office of ruler. The rope may be interpreted as representing kinship (Grove 1973: 134–135, 1981: 66) rather than evidence of bound captives (Coe and Diehl 1980: 1: 392; Reilly 1995: 41). A colossal head, Monument 61, likely representing an ancestral ruler (Wicke 1971), also forms part of the setting. In addition, a 171-m-long basalt aqueduct (Coe and Diehl 1980: 1: 118–126; Krotser 1973) is located southwest of the colossal head and south of the throne. And finally, an unusual sculpture of a possible rain deity (Coe and Diehl 1980: 1: 363) shows a hollowed-out back, such that it may once have functioned as a standard-bearer (Cyphers 2004b: 112), an emblem heralding the identity of a ruler or elite group. The interlinked themes of rulership, ancestry, water, and the underworld in these monuments suggest that Group E had strong associations with one or several rulers.

The stone throne was positioned at the southern foot of the north platform (i.e., on the northern boundary of the sunken patio). This low sand-plastered rectangular building with at least one inset corner may have had a layout based on the quatrefoil motif, and its contour might have given such a shape to the adjacent patio. This platform measures about 7 m wide and more than 15 m long with a *talud* inclined at 15 degrees in its earliest construction phase; its south side is 1.25 m high, measured from the level of the patio. The base of a large earthen column (2 m × 2 m) is located on its upper surface, near the three plastered steps leading into the patio. Prior to the second and last construction episode, the superstructure was razed to the base of the column, and offerings were deposited on the floor of the adjacent sunken patio to the south. The second episode, beginning ca. 1000 B.C., increased the dimensions of the platform to about 9 m wide and 1.4 m high. The same east-west orientation as in the earlier episode was maintained along its length of more than 15 m. Along with numerous ceramic vessels, a chert biface was interred under the platform's floor.

The basal level of the sunken patio is higher than the ground surrounding the complex. Its enclosed design likely provided a restricted area for private ritual; public ritual was performed outside what must have looked like an acropolis with an interior sunken patio. The ritual destruction of both construction phases included the placement of offerings on the patio floors.

The east platform is associated with colossal head 8 (Monument 61).

Jürgen Brüggeman and Marie-Areti Hers (1970) thought that it had been interred in a large pit with mixed earthen fill, even though they did not detect its outline. The reanalysis of the 1970 excavations shows that the head had been placed in the interior of an earthen platform, perhaps as a ritual burial and shrine to commemorate an ancestral ruler, whose likeness was displayed in the colossal head portrait contained within it. Sealed by a red sand-plastered floor that made it invisible to observers, this powerful symbol may have symbolized the group collectivity associated with the complex.

The platform bordering the southern side of the sunken patio bears a more than 22.5-m-long superstructure. Monument 49, which rests on the floor of the sunken patio, marks its northern face. The basalt aqueduct (Coe and Diehl 1980: 1: 118–126, fig. 83; Krotser 1973), designated as Monument 73, is fed from a well and runs below the floor of this structure (Cyphers et al. 2006). Around 900 B.C., when the stone aqueduct ceased to function, the easternmost troughs were removed from their ditch, which was then filled with orange clay. This occurrence was simultaneous with other termination rites and the cessation of activity in the rest of the complex.

Offerings found in Group E may be compared to cosmological expressions in later societies, as, for example, the chert biface buried in the northern platform, which we mention only as one example of the symbolic content of the complex. It is reminiscent, for example, of the association of Flint (*tecpatl*) with North in the Aztec view of the world quarters (Ingham: 1971: 624); of the date, One Flint (Ce Tecpatl), the date of the creation of the world (Ixtlilxochitl 1952: 14) and the date associated with the war god Huitzilopochtli (Vaillant 1938: 556). In the Mayan area, the equivalent to *tecpatl* is *teij* (Mam), *tijax* (Quiche) and *etznab* (Yucatec Maya) (Soustelle 1951: 173). The day sign *etz'nab* is a year-bearer in the Campeche calendar and is associated with the West (Lacombe and d'Obrenovic 1968: 415; Tedlock 1982; Thompson 1960: 304). Jun Tijax (One Flint) was a major idol of the Cakchiquel group—corresponding to the patron deity Tojil, god of the sun, storm, war, and human sacrifice as well as a manifestation of Quetzalcoatl (Orellana 1981: 159, 162), who is the Thunderer and Mountain God of the modern Quiche (Tedlock 1990: 154). Whereas correlations of the meaning of Olmec objects and contexts with those of later civilizations requires caution, this example, which perhaps will be complemented by the ongoing interpretation of the other offerings, provides subtle and evocative links to later, well-documented concepts of the Mesoamerican world.

Group E's layout is reminiscent of later period architectural complexes, such as platforms bearing sunken plazas and temple groups. The thematically related monuments in the complex provide additional support for the interpretations of sunken patios as the symbolic access to a watery underworld in the Olmec belief system and in other Mesoamerican cultures (Bassie-Sweet 1996; Brown n.d.; Grove 1973, 1981; Reilly 1994a, 1994b). Concepts of sovereignty, ancestry, water, and the underworld are imbedded in the special construction style and artifact associations of the complex, which, as may be expected, lacks a typical domestic assemblage. Specialized public and private functions varied spatially in and around the complex, as exemplified by the northern platform's link to maximum regional leadership, the eastern platform's burial and veneration of an ancestral ruler, and the southern platform's connection to water. Perhaps it was a symbolic model of the Olmec universe, as in the interpretation of La Venta's Complex A, in which the enclosed court is conceived as an other-world and ancestral location (Reilly 1999), and its north-south symbolism may be part of another early template for site layouts (Grove 1999).

The Group E complex is one example of the early architectural and conceptual sophistication of the San Lorenzo Olmec. Oddly, the absence of adobe, lime plaster, and stone masonry in Olmec constructions is cited as evidence that they "lagged behind the highlands" (Flannery et al. 2005: 11219) in development. During the Early Preclassic period in the highlands, locally available materials, such as mud, lime, and stone, were employed in domestic and public buildings of relatively undifferentiated design, size, and function (e.g., Marcus 1989). In contrast, Group E's architecture, made merely of local mud and sand, stands out for its novel, large-scale design infused with overarching cosmological concepts and its highly specialized functions within the San Lorenzo site. If, indeed, the goal is to uncover, analyze, and interpret the sociopolitical institutions of different societies (Flannery and Marcus 2000: 33; Flannery et al. 2005: 11219), then a priori assumptions about building materials—as the diagnostics of outdated notions of culture lag or progress—will not achieve the aim. In the case of architecture, we suggest that labor investment, technological special-ization, social and political import, and ideological significance would be relevant points of departure for examining institutions.

The Group E architectural complex is directly related to such issues, because it is tangible evidence for the development of complex sociopoliti-cal institutions. In sum, its design appears to follow an early cosmological model validating the ruler's place in the universe, and as an emblem of asymmetrical power, it likely served as the official locus of at least one sovereign. Its internal segregation of symbolic, political, economic, and commemorative functions may also indicate its use by an elite politico-religious hierarchy.

THE COSMIC MONSTER

Numerous analyses indicate that an early model of the universe centered on an almighty cosmic creature with celestial and terrestrial aspects that include feline, serpent, and avian imagery (Angulo 1987; Coe 1968, 1972, 1989; Covarrubias 1957; Grove 1973, 2000; Joralemon 1971; Marcus 1989; Norman 1976; Piña Chan 1977, 1990; Quirarte 1976; Reilly 1995). These studies, although differing in specific details, suggest that this monster was the font of fertility, agricultural success, and the rulers' power. Its multi-faceted aspects denote the merging of sacred notions of earth and sky.

Some of the key iconographic elements related to the monster, as expressed in its frontal and lateral views (Grove 2000: 283; Reilly 1995: 36), or as *pars pro toto*, include: (1) the crossed bands, (2) the inverted U, and (3) the wing-paw-hand. Elements often labeled "fangs" and "flame eyebrows" also may be present. Each element has specific associations or meanings that have been inferred from their context and analogy with later cultures. The crossed-bands element has celestial connotations, including the sun and the clouds (Angulo 1987: 136; Ayala 1968: 92–93; Norman 1976: 33; Piña Chan 2002: 29; Piña Chan and Covarrubias 1964: 46). The inverted U refer-ring to the monster's jaws contains both celestial and terrestrial meanings (De la Fuente 1984: 152; Grove 2000; Norman 1976: 45–46; Quirarte 1977: 264; Reilly 1994a: 244; Taube 1995: 92; Urcid 2005: 53). The wing-paw-hand may be a referent to wind (Taube 1995: 85). Hence, principal concepts com-bined in the creature include the sky and earth, making it an integrative symbol of the ancient universe.

These symbols are explicitly represented in stone monuments as well as pottery vessels, the latter proposed as a medium for the interregional transmission of Olmec cosmological beliefs (Clark 1997; Blomster et al. 2005). But should these motifs be considered Olmec? One point of view regarding the presumed simultaneous emergence of the aforementioned cosmologically charged motifs in distant regions invokes multiple origins in a nebulous, ideological substratum shared by many peoples over a vast area (Demarest 1989; Grove 1989; Marcus 1989; Sharer 1989). In view of this difference of opinion, it is necessary to examine the earliest material evidence of these beliefs.

Where and when do these symbols first appear? According to Kent Flannery and Joyce Marcus (2000: 19), the site of Zohapilco in the Basin of Mexico allegedly has the earliest occurrence of the motifs on ceramic vessels, dating from 1350 B.C. Their use of Niederberger's (1976) Zohapilco ceramic data attempts to substantiate the primacy of the decorated ceramics outside the Gulf Coast but is invalid for several reasons. The Zohapilco sequence, as published, does not indicate (1) that all sherds of the types Tortuga Pulido, Volcán Pulido, Atoyac Gris Fino, Valle Borde Blanco, Pilli Blanco, and Paloma Negativo bear these motifs or (2) that the motifs in question occur between 1350 and 1250 B.C., given that Nevada phase decorations are reported as bands of parallel lines, slanting crossed lines, and punctuates (see Niederberger 1976: 116).

In addition, certain problems in the stratigraphic interpretation of the Zohapilco long trench raise doubts about the sequence itself, particularly regarding Nevada (1350–1250 B.C.) and Ayotla (1250–1000 B.C.) phase deposits (Di Castro and Cyphers 2006). In short, the definition of the Ayotla phase and part of the Nevada phase is based on redeposited strata that should be considered a single depositional event. Such dilemmas in stratigraphic interpretation may account for the fact that no other site in the central highlands has produced a column corroborating the early part of this sequence. Accordingly, the ceramic complexes of these phases appear widely divergent for the time frame. Some of the problems present in the Zohapilco ceramic sequence may be briefly illustrated with several incongruous horizon markers, such as pseudo-grater bottom bowls in the Ayotla phase, the advent of zoned cross-hatching on direct rim bowls, and the abundance of double-line-break rim motifs in the Nevada and Ayotla phases. These inconsistencies provoke considerable doubt about the viability of the published temporal position of Zohapilco's early decorated ceramics.

Now we turn to the San Lorenzo chronology. The sound sequence published by Michael Coe and Richard Diehl (1980) has been refined by later work. The most recent ceramic chronology for the San Lorenzo region is based on a sample of nearly 400,000 sherds and whole and partial vessels from numerous stratified deposits recorded at this and other hinterland communities (Cyphers n.d.). In this sequence, pottery vessels displaying explicit versions of the cosmic monster (Figure 8) are a temporal marker for the San Lorenzo B phase (1000–850 B.C.), whereas *pars pro toto* versions make their appearance in the San Lorenzo A phase, reaching their maximum frequency in the B phase (Figure 9). Motifs taking the form of crosses, inverted U shapes, and the wing-paw-hand element are characteristic of both San Lorenzo A and B phases (see also Coe and Diehl 1980: 1: 162–171; Figure 9).

Earth and sky symbolism appears in the ceramics of San Lorenzo since the Bajío phase (1350–1250 B.C.). Decoration in this phase includes fine-line incised S scrolls and fang-shaped elements suggestive of dragon's teeth (Figure 10). In the subsequent Chicharras phase (1250–1150 B.C.) fine-line incision of S scrolls and a few inverted U motifs (Figure 11) begin a popularity ascent that continues through the San Lorenzo A and B phases (1150–850 B.C.). In the San Lorenzo A and B phases the finely incised S scroll is associated with a woven element as well as a barb-shaped element.

The meaning of these elements, based on comparisons with later symbols, suggests conceptual links to the cosmic monster. Some scholars have called the S scroll on these vessels the *ilhuitl* (Coe and Diehl 1980: 1: 171), although it most likely is an early symbol for sky, or *ilhuicatl* (Houston

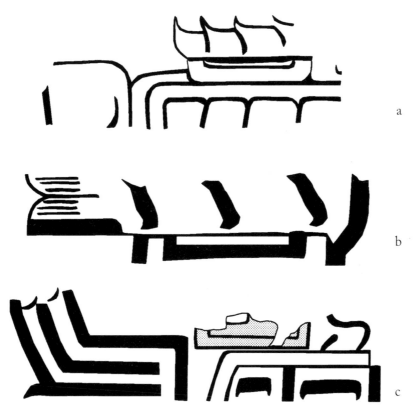

FIGURE 8. San Lorenzo B phase decorated ceramics showing the cosmic monster: (a) a scroll, likely part of a wing-paw-hand element, is located to the left of the head characterized by a flame eyebrow, U element for the eye and inverted U elements for the gums (redrawn from Coe and Diehl 1980: 1: fig. 140i); (b) representation lacking a mouth and showing featherlike elements in place of the wing-paw-hand element, U element for the eye, and diagonal lines in place of the flame eyebrow; (c) image with U element for the eye, anthropomorphic nose, inverted U elements forming the mouth, and wing-paw-hand element to the left of the head (redrawn from Covarrubias 1957: fig. 9). Drawing by Ann Cyphers.

and Taube 2000: 278). In Mayan hieroglyphs the S scroll is assigned the meaning of cloud (Taube 1995: 96). The woven or cross-hatched element may refer to earth (see, e.g., glyphs T526, T526:136; T526:88, and T526:246 in Montgomery 2002). The barb-shaped element takes the form of a slanting straight line ending in a small arc; we considered the possibility that it represents a blood-letting implement, such as a thorn, but its position near the S scroll suggests that it may be a symbol for wind or lightning. In sum, the vessels bearing these motifs transmit general messages related to earth and sky, similar to that of the cosmic monster.

To date, the available evidence indicates that earth and sky symbols

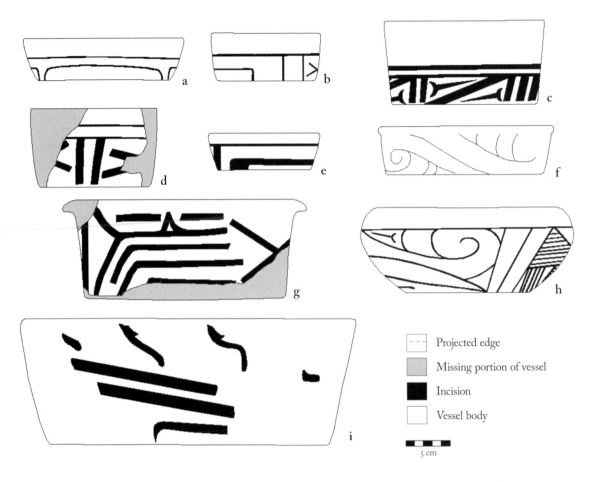

FIGURE 9. San Lorenzo A and B phase decorated ceramics from San Lorenzo showing earth and sky symbolism: (a, b, d, e) horizontal series of inverted U elements and crosses; (c) horizontal series of barb-shaped elements framed by horizontal and vertical lines; (f, h) S scrolls, barb-shaped element, and hatching; (g) wing-paw-hand element and cross; (i) *pars pro toto* representation. Drawing by Ann Cyphers.

have greater antiquity at San Lorenzo than at any other site. Before 1150 B.C., they are absent in early ceramics of Puebla, Morelos, and Oaxaca (e.g., Cyphers 1987; Flannery and Marcus 1994; MacNeish et al. 1970), as well as the Basin of Mexico. On the Pacific coast, the large spirals adorning *tecomate* forms since the Barra phase (1550–1400 B.C.) (Clark 1994), are unlike the S scroll; in addition, other evidence shows that this region did not share the proposed early ideology (Lesure 2000).

Ceramics with earth and sky symbols at San Lorenzo not only precede their appearance elsewhere, but also show up several centuries before such symbols are incorporated into monumental stone art. In distant regions, such ceramics appear after 1150 B.C., the time when San Lorenzo began

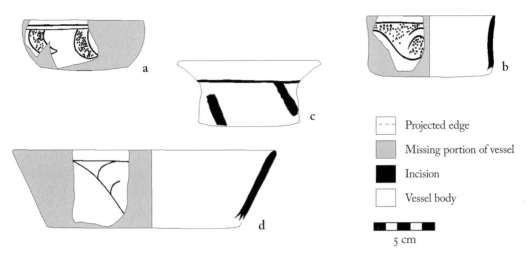

FIGURE 10. Bajío phase decorated sherds from San Lorenzo showing earth and sky symbolism: (a) fang-shaped elements with zoned punctuates (redrawn from Coe and Diehl 1980: 1: fig. 114e); (b) partial S scroll with zoned punctuates; (c) early wide band incision (redrawn from Coe and Diehl 1980: 1: fig. 114a); (d) stylized scroll representation. Drawing by Ann Cyphers.

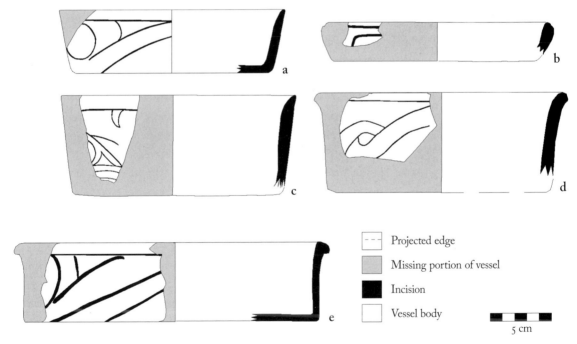

FIGURE 11. Chicharras phase decorated sherds from San Lorenzo showing earth and sky symbolism: (a, d, e) versions of the S scroll (compare with Figure 9d); (b) inverted U motif; (c) barb-shaped element and stylized scroll. Drawing by Ann Cyphers.

FIGURE 12. Ball player figurines from San Lorenzo characterized by an undisguised human face framed in a protective helmet. Photograph by Rogelio Santiago.

exporting its pottery (see Blomster et al. 2005). Consequently, we believe that it is appropriate to call these motifs "Olmec" and to assume that their initial dissemination emanated from the Gulf Coast homeland.

The purpose of these decorated ceramics at San Lorenzo was to provide information about the structure of the cosmos to a wide range of people. The common or everyday use of decorated ceramics with cosmologically charged motifs accomplished the dissemination of certain cosmological concepts throughout San Lorenzo's society. Such ceramics were the tangible manifestation of cosmology in the quotidian world where concepts could be contemplated, imagined, and transmitted to people of different ages and statuses (see Wengrow 2001: 176). Their use would have given food consumption and other activities a symbolic significance. By 1150 B.C., one of the functions of the decorated pottery at San Lorenzo was to infuse the society with the cosmological concepts necessary for the dramaturgy of Olmec power.

Turning to another medium for the conveyance of cosmological ideas, clay figurines, we note that Karl Taube (1995: 100) relates the Olmec Rain Deity to masked anthropomorphic ballplayer figurines at San Lorenzo that were reported by Coe and Diehl (1980: 1: 269), and John Clark (1997: 223) believes that such figurines were representations of rulers metaphorically linked to creation cosmology through the ritual game. The ballplayer figurines at San Lorenzo, both in the SLTAP collections and those reported previously (Coe and Diehl 1980), shed light on the relationship of the cosmic monster to this important Mesoamerican ritual.

There are two general groupings of ballplayer figurines that may be indicative of types of ballgame (see Cohodas 1991) or teams of players with differing sponsorship. Both wear round pectorals, likely concave iron-ore mirrors, and

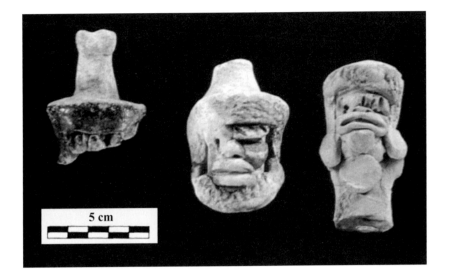

FIGURE 13. *Tuerto* figurines from San Lorenzo showing two different eye treatments: the black painted helmet/headdress with conical element and typical round pectoral adornment. Photograph by Rogelio Santiago.

thick protective belts. One shows an undisguised human face, whereas the other wears a mask with anthropo-zoomorphic features. The figure with a human face wears an encompassing helmet that leaves exposed a small portion of his countenance (Figure 12; see also Coe and Diehl 1980: 1: fig. 332). The other representation is called the "one-eyed god" by Coe and Diehl (1980: 1: 270) and is an important link to Olmec cosmological notions.

We hesitate to refer to this second kind of figurine as a deity, given the problems in distinguishing supernatural beings from deity impersonators (see Ekholm 1991: 248), so we call them *tuertos*, which simply means a being with one good eye (Figure 13). The *tuertos* show two different kinds of eyes: the right eye is formed by a round application with central punctuate, identical to the eyes of clay dogs and other quadrupeds, and the left eye is an elongated application with multiple slashes (perhaps closed). These male ballplayer figurines with a tripod support (indicating their upright display) wear a distinctive square headdress topped by a conical element. They have black painting on the headdress and also sometimes on the eyes and body. The mouth is extraordinarily large and down-turned, similar to the monster depicted in Monument 104 from San Lorenzo, which shows faint traces of vertical black painted lines on its face (see Cyphers 2004b: 176).

In iconographic representations from later times the color black, the canine eye, the conical headdress, the mirror pectoral, and the ballgame equipment would be associated with one of the four Tezcatlipocas, Quetzalcoatl, whose aspects are linked to the sky, earth, wind, water, and sustenance. In the case of the *Tuerto* figurines, which are by far the most frequent ballplayer image at San Lorenzo, we propose that their supernatural elements may derive from the cosmic monster, a divine being with multiple aspects that is part of the ideological bedrock out of which are distilled major deities of later Mesoamerican cultures, such as Quetzalcoatl.

Like the decorated ceramics with earth and sky symbolism, the *tuertos* appear to have played a role in ritual reenactment designed to reinforce the Olmec worldview.

To sum up, we contrast the use of important cosmological icons in ceramic and stone artifacts. When they occur in monumental stone sculpture, these symbols were not available to all social sectors; even within the elite, the largest monuments were associated only with rulers. When displayed in large stone thrones, the meaning of these elements and motifs relates to divine origins, sacred ancestors, and ruler legitimation; in sculptures of lesser size, sacred elements were given the form of wearable status symbols for the elite, such as the pectoral containing a cross and U elements in headdresses. The motifs' sacred meaning, when represented in the common medium of pottery vessels, was united with the practical function of containers that were used by all social sectors.

John Rick's (2005) cohesive-devotional and manipulative models (recognized as stereotyped and polar, respectively, by Rick) of religious leadership, when framed in the context of the early Olmec of San Lorenzo, suggest insights regarding the operation of religious beliefs on various levels. In the conservative, cohesive-devotional model, authorities participate in a belief system broadly shared across the society, whereas in the manipulative model leaders skillfully utilize religious concepts to gain power and privilege. The evidence presented in this chapter suggests that certain ceramic objects complemented system-serving leadership, because they reflect sacred concepts that were widely shared in the society. The willful, or self-serving, manipulation of religious concepts appeared when the office of ruler was formalized, as seen in stone monuments. The hierarchical ordering of descent groups defined in relation to one another by their genealogical proximity to divine ancestral origins was the model for the ritual and decision-making structure. The production and use of common objects imbued with sacred meaning increased over time, suggesting that a continuing emphasis on widespread, shared beliefs was perceived as aiding the preservation of social cohesion during times of political instability.

Finally, a similar pattern appears among distant groups of highland country cousins, subsequent to contact with the Olmec. Sacred motifs on objects made of common materials helped disseminate a set of beliefs that fomented social and political differentiation. Later, ideological manipulation by self-serving leaders is exemplified by the emulation of Olmec stone monuments and architecture.

CLOSING COMMENTS

It may never be known whether the ancient inhabitants of San Lorenzo viewed themselves, their architecture, and imagery in the same fashion as later civilizations, but a number of lasting Mesoamerican concepts closely implicated in later sociopolitical developments can be perceived in their material culture. In our survey of selected material expressions of the Olmec worldview at San Lorenzo that are relevant to the theme of this volume, the archetypal model involving a hill emerging from the watery surface of the underworld seems to underlie aspects of settlement patterns, the design of thrones, and the Group E architectural complex at San Lorenzo. In addition, it is intimately involved with the interwoven cosmological notions of sky and earth personified as the prototypical cosmic monster. The archaeological data presented here illustrate the innovative character of the Olmec built environment with its inherent cosmological and political "reciprocal metaphors" (Houston 1998: 348), as was typical of later Mesoamerican capitals.

At San Lorenzo, these qualities helped create and maintain a clear differentiation between the descendants of sacred ancestors and the rest of the population (see Coe 1972). Messages sent out on all social levels confirmed and reiterated the cosmologically based social order. The social fabric was impregnated with messages of divine domination and subordination, privilege and obligation, and power and duty, and the rulers' political aspirations found spiritual justification for the perpetuation of their divine authority. From everyday activities to ruler-sponsored ceremonies, sensorial perception was continuously saturated with cosmological concepts imbedded in the design and operation of the first Olmec center.

Preliminary evidence regarding San Lorenzo's iconographic, architectural, and cosmological blueprint and its social consequences contrasts strongly with that of the Olmec's contemporaries. The dissemination of sacred concepts to distant regions fostered a common platform for communication between groups of differing traditions. The translation and acceptance of Olmec sacred concepts by these societies included fusion with local beliefs, thus giving shape to a composite heritage that would enrich the cosmologies of later civilizations.

Acknowledgments

SLTAP research has been generously supported by the Instituto de Investigaciones Antropológicas and the Dirección General de Asuntos del Personal Académico of the Universidad Nacional Autónoma de México, the American Philosophical Society, the Consejo Nacional de Ciencia y Tecnología, the National Endowment for the Humanities, the National Geographic Society, and the Foundation for the Advancement of Mesoamerican Studies. Field research was kindly authorized by the Consejo de Arqueología del Instituto Nacional de Antropología e Historia. Numerous property owners and townspeople of Tenochtitlan and surrounding communities can never be thanked enough for supporting our work. We bow to the SLTAP team in deep appreciation of their dedicated efforts in the field and lab.

REFERENCES CITED

Angulo V., Jorge
    1987 The Chalcatzingo Reliefs: An Iconographic Analysis. In *Ancient Chalcatzingo* (David C. Grove, ed.): 132–158. University of Texas Press, Austin.

Ashmore, Wendy
    1989 Construction and Cosmology: Politics and Ideology in Lowland Maya Settlement Patterns. In *World and Image in Maya Culture: Explorations in Language, Writing and Representation* (William F. Hanks and Don S. Rice, eds.): 272–298. University of Utah Press, Salt Lake City.

Ayala Falcón, Maricela
    1968 Relaciones entre textos y dibujos en el Códice de Dresde. *Estudios de Cultura Maya* VII: 85–113.

Bassie-Sweet, Karen
    1996 *At the Edge of the World*. University of Oklahoma Press, Norman.

Bernal-García, María Elena
    1994 Tzatza: Olmec Mountains and the Ruler's Ritual Speech. In *Seventh Palenque Round Table 1989* (Merle G. Robertson and Virginia M. Fields, eds.): 113–124. Pre-Columbian Art Research Institute, San Francisco.

Beverido Pereau, Francisco
    n.d. San Lorenzo Tenochtitlán y la civilización olmeca. Master's thesis, Facultad de Antropología, Universidad Veracruzana, Xalapa, 1970.

Bloch, Maurice
    1987 The Ritual of the Royal Bath in Madagascar: The Dissolution of Death, Birth and Fertility into Authority. In *Rituals of Royalty, Power and Ceremonial in Traditional Societies* (David Cannadine and Simon Price, eds.): 271–297. Cambridge University Press, Cambridge.

Blomster, Jeffrey P., Hector Neff, and Michael D. Glascock
    2005 Olmec Pottery Production and Export in Ancient Mexico Determined through Elemental Analysis. *Science* 307: 1068–1072.

Borstein, Joshua
    n.d. Tripping over Colossal Heads: Settlement Patterns and Population Development in the Upland Olmec Heartland. Ph.D. dissertation, Department of Anthropology, Pennsylvania State University, University Park, 2001.

Brown, A. Kathryn
    n.d. Investigations of Middle Preclassic Public Architecture at the Site of Blackman Eddy, Belize. Electronic document, http://www.famsi.org/reports/brown/brown96.htm. Foundation for the Advancement of Mesoamerican Studies, Crystal River.

Brüggeman, Jürgen, and Marie-Areti Hers
1970 Exploraciones arqueológicas en San Lorenzo Tenochtitlán. *Boletín del INAH* 39: 18–23.

Carlson, John
1981 A Geomantic Model for the Interpretation of Mesoamerican Sites: An Essay in Cross-Cultural Comparison. In *Mesoamerican Sites and World-Views* (Elizabeth P. Benson, ed.): 143–216. Dumbarton Oaks Research Library and Collection, Washington, D.C.

Caso, Alfonso
1964 ¿Existió un imperio olmeca? *Memoria de El Colegio Nacional* V(3): 11–60.

Clark, John E.
1994 Antecedentes de la cultura olmeca. In *Los olmecas en Mesoamérica* (John E. Clark, ed.): 31–41. Citibank, México.
1997 The Arts of Government in Early Mesoamerica. *Annual Review of Anthropology* 26: 211–234.

Clark, John E., and Tomás Perez
1994 Los olmecas y el primer milenio de Mesoamérica. In *Los olmecas en Mesoamérica* (John E. Clark, ed.): 261–275. Citibank, México.

Coe, Michael D.
1965 The Olmec Style and Its Distributions. In *Handbook of Middle American Indians*, vol. 3: *Archaeology of Southern Mesoamerica*, part 2 (Gordon R. Willey, ed.): 739–775. University of Texas Press, Austin.
1968 *America's First Civilization*. American Heritage Publishing, New York.
1972 Olmec Jaguars and Olmec Kings. In *The Cult of the Feline: A Conference in Pre-Columbian Iconography* (Elizabeth P. Benson, ed.): 1–18. Dumbarton Oaks Research Library and Collection, Washington, D.C.
1989 The Olmec Heartland: Evolution of Ideology. In *Regional Perspectives on the Olmec* (Robert J. Sharer and David C. Grove, eds.): 68–82. Cambridge University Press, Cambridge.

Coe, Michael D., and Richard A. Diehl
1980 *In the Land of the Olmec.* 2 vols. University of Texas Press, Austin.
1991 Reply to Hammond's "Cultura Hermana: Reappraising the Olmec." *Review of Archaeology* 12(1): 30–35.

Cohen, Abner
1981 *The Politics of Elite Culture: Exploration in the Dramaturgy of Power in a Modern African Society.* University of California Press, Berkeley.

Cohodas, Marvin
1991 Ballgame Imagery of the Maya Lowlands: History and Iconography. In *The Mesoamerican Ballgame* (Vernon L. Scarborough and David R. Wilcox, eds.): 251–288. University of Arizona Press, Tucson.

Covarrubias, Miguel
1957 *Indian Art of Mexico and Central America.* Alfred A. Knopf, New York.

Cyphers, Ann
1987 Ceramics. In *Ancient Chalcatzingo* (David C. Grove, ed.): 200–251. University of Texas Press, Austin.
1993 Escenas escultóricas olmecas. *Antropológicas* 6: 47–52.

1994 Olmec Sculpture. *National Geographic Research and Exploration* 10(3): 294–305.

1997a La arquitectura olmeca en San Lorenzo Tenochtitlán. In *Población, subsistencia y medio ambiente en San Lorenzo Tenochtitlán* (Ann Cyphers, ed.): 91–118. Instituto de Investigaciones Antropológicas, Universidad Nacional Autónoma de México, México.

1997b La Gobernatura en San Lorenzo: Inferencias del arte y patrón de asentamiento. In *Población, subsistencia y medio ambiente en San Lorenzo Tenochtitlán* (Ann Cyphers, ed.): 227–242. Instituto de Investigaciones Antropológicas, Universidad Nacional Autónoma de México, México.

1999 From Stone to Symbols: Olmec Art in Social Context at San Lorenzo Tenochtitlán. In *Social Patterns in Pre-Classic Mesoamerica* (David C. Grove and Rosemary A. Joyce, eds.): 155–182. Dumbarton Oaks Research Library and Collection, Washington, D.C.

2004a Escultura monumental olmeca: Temas y contextos. In *Acercarse y mirar, Homenaje a Beatriz de la Fuente* (María Teresa Uriarte and Leticia Staines, eds.): 51–74. Instituto de Investigaciones Estéticas, Universidad Nacional Autónoma de México, México.

2004b *Escultura olmeca de San Lorenzo Tenochtitlán.* Instituto de Investigaciones Antropológicas and La Coordinación de Humanidades, Universidad Nacional Autónoma de México, México.

n.d. La cerámica de San Lorenzo Tenochtitlán.

Cyphers, Ann, and Joshua Borstein

n.d. *Laguna de los Cerros.*

Cyphers, Ann, Alejandro Hernández-Portilla, Marisol Varela-Gómez, and Lilia Grégor-López

2006 Cosmological and Sociopolitical Synergy in Preclassic Architectural Complexes. In *Water Management and Ideology* (Lisa Lucero and Barbara W. Fash, eds.): 17–32. University of Arizona Press, Tucson.

Demarest, Arthur

1989 The Olmec and the Rise of Civilization in Eastern Mesoamerica. In *Regional Perspectives on the Olmec* (Robert J. Sharer and David C. Grove, eds.): 303–344. Cambridge University Press, New York.

Di Castro, Anna, and Ann Cyphers

2006 Iconografía de la cerámica olmeca. *Anales del Instituto de Investigaciones Estéticas* 89: 29–58.

Diehl, Richard A., and Michael D. Coe

1996 Olmec Archaeology. In *The Olmec World: Ritual and Rulership* (Art Museum, ed.): 10–25. Art Museum of Princeton University, Princeton, N.J.

Ekholm, Susanna M.

1991 Ceramic Figurines and the Mesoamerican Ballgame. In *The Mesoamerican Ballgame* (Vernon L. Scarborough and David R. Wilcox, eds.): 241–249. University of Arizona Press, Tucson.

Elzey, Wayne

1991 A Hill on a Land Surrounded by Water: An Aztec Story of Origin and Destiny. *History of Religions* 31(2): 105–149.

Flannery, Kent V., and Joyce Marcus

1994 *Early Formative Pottery of the Valley of Oaxaca, Mexico.* University of Michigan Museum of Anthropology, Memoir 27. Ann Arbor.

2000 Formative Mexican Chiefdoms and the Myth of the "Mother Culture." *Journal of Anthropological Archaeology* 19: 1–37.

Flannery, Kent V., Andrew K. Balkansky, Gary M. Feinman, David C. Grove, Joyce Marcus, Elsa M. Redmond, Robert G. Reynolds, Robert J. Sharer, Charles S. Spencer, and Jason Yaeger

2005 Implications of New Petrographic Analysis for the Olmec "Mother Culture" Model. *Proceedings of the National Academy of Sciences USA* 102: 1219–11223.

De la Fuente, Beatriz

1984 *Los hombres de piedra: Escultura olmeca.* Universidad Nacional Autónoma de México, México.

Gillespie, Susan D.

1994 Llano del Jícaro: An Olmec Monument Workshop. *Ancient Mesoamerica* 5: 231–242.

1999 Olmec Thrones as Ancestral Altars: The Two Sides of Power. In *Material Symbols: Culture and Economy in Prehistory* (John E. Robb, ed.): 224–253. Center for Archaeological Investigations, Southern Illinois University, Carbondale.

González Lauck, Rebecca

1989 Recientes investigaciones en La Venta, Tabasco. In *El Preclásico o Formativo, avances y perspectivas* (Martha Carmona, ed.): 81–90. Instituto Nacional de Antropología e Historia, México.

1994 La Zona del Golfo en el Preclás: La Etapa olmeca. In *Historia antigua de México* (Linda Manzanilla and Leonardo López Luján, eds.), I: 279–321. Instituto Nacional de Antropología e Historia and Instituto de Investigaciones Antropológicas, Universidad Nacional Autónoma de México, México.

1996 La Venta: An Olmec Capital. In *Olmec Art of Ancient Mexico* (Elizabeth P. Benson and Beatriz de la Fuente, eds.): 73–81. National Gallery of Art, Washington, D.C.

Grove, David C.

1970 *The Olmec Paintings of Oxtotitlan Cave, Guerrero, Mexico.* Studies in Pre-Columbian Art and Archaeology 6. Dumbarton Oaks Research Library and Collection, Washington, D.C.

1972 El Teocuicani: 'Cantor Divino' en Jantetelco. *Boletín del INAH* (serie 2) 3: 35–36.

1973 Olmec Altars and Myths. *Archaeology* 26: 128–135.

1981 Olmec Monuments: Mutilation as a Clue to Meaning. In *The Olmec and Their Neighbors* (Elizabeth P. Benson, ed.): 49–68. Dumbarton Oaks Research Library and Collection, Washington, D.C.

1987   Comments on the Site and Its Organization. In *Ancient Chalcatzingo* (David C. Grove, ed.): 420–433. University of Texas Press, Austin.

1989   Olmec: What's in a Name? In *Regional Perspectives on the Olmec* (Robert J. Sharer and David C. Grove, eds.): 8–16. Cambridge University Press, New York.

1999   Public Monuments and Sacred Mountains: Observations on Three Formative Period Sacred Landscapes. In *Social Patterns in Preclassic Mesoamerica* (David C. Grove and Rosemary Joyce, eds.): 255–299. Dumbarton Oaks Research Library and Collection, Washington, D.C.

2000   Faces of the Earth at Chalcatzingo: Serpents, Caves, and Mountains in Middle Formative Period Iconography. In *Olmec Art and Archaeology in Mesoamerica* (John E. Clark and Mary E. Pye, eds.): 277–295. National Gallery of Art, Washington, D.C.

Hammond, Norman

1988   *Cultura hermana:* Reappraising the Olmec. *Quarterly Review of Archaeology* 9(4): 1–4.

Heizer, Robert F.

1968   New Observations on La Venta. In *Dumbarton Oaks Conference on the Olmec* (Elizabeth P. Benson, ed.): 9–36. Dumbarton Oaks Research Library and Collection, Washington, D.C.

Heyden, Doris

1981   Caves, Gods and Myths: World-View and Planning in Teotihuacan. In *Mesoamerican Sites and World-Views* (Elizabeth P. Benson, ed.): 1–40. Dumbarton Oaks Research Library and Collection, Washington, D.C.

Houston, Stephen D.

1998   Classic Maya Depictions of the Built Environment. In *Function and Meaning in Classic Maya Architecture* (Stephen D. Houston, ed.): 333–372. Dumbarton Oaks Research Library and Collection, Washington, D.C.

Houston, Stephen D., and Karl Taube

2000   An Archaeology of the Senses: Perception and Cultural Expression in Ancient Mesoamerica. *Cambridge Archaeological Journal* 10(2): 261–294.

Ingham, John M.

1971   Time and Space in Ancient Mexico: The Symbolic Dimensions of Clanship. *Man* (new series) 6(4): 615–629.

Ixtlilxochitl, Fernando de Alva

1952   *Obras históricas.* Editorial Leyenda, México.

Joralemon, Peter D.

1971   *A Study of Olmec Iconography.* Studies in Pre-Colombian Art and Archaeology 7. Dumbarton Oaks Research Library and Collection, Washington, D.C.

Krotser, Ramón

1973   El agua ceremonial de los olmecas. *Boletín del INAH* 2: 43–48.

Lacombe, Charles, and Frai Michel d'Obrenovic

1968   Project "XOC": Some Keys to Maya Hieroglyphics. *Journal of Inter-American Studies* 10(3): 406–430.

Lawrence, Denise L., and Setha M. Low
  1990 The Built Environment and Spatial Form. *Annual Review of Anthropology* 19: 453–505.
León, Ignacio, and Juan Carlos Sánchez
1991–92 Las Gemelas y el Jaguar del sitio El Azuzul. *Horizonte* (año 1) 5–6: 56–60.
León-Portilla, Miguel
  1963 *Aztec Thought and Culture: A Study of the Ancient Nahuatl Mind.* University of Oklahoma Press, Norman.
Lesure, Richard
  2000 Animal Imagery, Cultural Unities, and Ideologies of Inequality in Early Formative Mesoamerica. In *Olmec Art and Archaeology in Mesoamerica* (John E. Clark and Mary E. Pye, eds.): 193–215. National Gallery of Art, Washington, D.C.
Lowe, Gareth W.
  1989 The Heartland Olmec: Evolution of Material Culture. In *Regional Perspectives on the Olmec* (Robert J. Sharer and David C. Grove, eds.): 33–67. School of American Research, Cambridge University Press, Cambridge.
MacNeish, Richard S., Frederick A. Peterson, and Kent V. Flannery
  1970 *The Prehistory of the Tehuacán Valley,* vol. 3: *Ceramics.* University of Texas Press, Austin.
Marcus, Joyce
  1973 Territorial Organization of the Lowland Classic Maya. *Science* 180: 911–916.
  1989 Zapotec Chiefdoms and the Nature of Formative Religions. In *Regional Perspectives on the Olmec* (Robert Sharer and David C. Grove, eds.): 148–197. School of American Research, Cambridge University Press, Cambridge.
Medellín, Alfonso
  1960 Monolitos inéditos olmecas. *La Palabra y el hombre* 16: 75–97.
Mettner, Brett E.
  n.d. Ceramic Raw Material and Pottery Variability from La Venta, Tabasco, Mexico: A Test for Zonal Complementarity. Master's thesis, Department of Anthropology, University of Kansas, Topeka, 2001.
Montgomery, John
  2002 Dictionary of Maya Hieroglyphs. Electronic document, http://www.famsi.org/mayawriting/dictionary/montgomery/.
Niederberger, Christine
  1976 *Zohapilco. Cinco milenios de ocupación humana en un sitio lacustre de la Cuenca de México.* Colección Científica No. 30, Arqueología. Instituto Nacional de Antropología e Historia, México.
Norman, V. Garth
  1976 *Izapa Sculpture.* Papers of the New World Archaeological Foundation 33. Brigham Young University, Provo, Ut.

Ogburn, Dennis

 2005 Dynamic Display, Propaganda, and the Reinforcement of Provincial
    Power in the Inca Empire. *Archaeological Papers of the American
    Anthropological Association* 14: 225–239.

Orellana, Sandra L.

 1981 Idols and Idolatry in Highland Guatemala. *Ethnohistory* 28(2): 157–177.

Ortiz Pérez, Mario Arturo, and Ann Cyphers

 1997 La geomorfología y las evidencias arqueológicas en la región de San
    Lorenzo Tenochtitlán, Veracruz. In *Población, subsistencia y medio ambi-
    ente en San Lorenzo Tenochtitlán* (Ann Cyphers, ed.): 31–54. Instituto de
    Investigaciones Antropológicas, Universidad Nacional Autónoma de
    México, México.

Piña Chan, Román

 1977 *Quetzalcoatl, serpiente emplumada.* Fondo de Cultura Económica,
    México.

 1990 *Los olmecas: La cultura madre.* Lunwerg Editores, Barcelona-Madrid.

 2002 *El lenguaje de las Piedras. Glífica olmeca y Zapoteca,* Fondo de Cultura
    Económica, México.

Piña Chan, Román, and Luís Covarrubias

 1964 *El pueblo del jaguar (Los olmecas arqueológicas).* Consejo para la plane-
    ación e instalación del Museo Nacional de Antropología, México.

Porter, James

 1989 Olmec Colossal Heads as Recarved Thrones: "Mutilation," Revolution,
    and Recarving. *RES* 17–18: 23–30.

Quirarte, Jacinto

 1976 The Relationship of Izapan-Style Art to Olmec and Maya Art. In
    Origins of Religious Art and Iconography in Pre-Classic Mesoamerica
    (Henry B. Nicholson, ed.): 73–86. UCLA Latin American Studies
    Series 31. University of California at Los Angeles.

 1977 Early Art Styles of Mesoamerica and Early Classic Maya Art. In *The
    Origins of Maya Civilization* (Richard E. W. Adams, ed.): 249–283.
    University of New Mexico Press, Albuquerque.

Raab, L. Mark, Matthew A. Boxt, Katherine Bradford, Brian A. Stokes, and
    Rebecca B. González Lauck

 2000 Testing at Isla Alor in the La Venta Olmec Hinterland. *Journal of Field
    Archaeology* 27(3): 257–270.

Reilly, F. Kent, III

 1990 Olmec Iconographic Influences on the Symbols of Maya Rulership:
    An Examination of Possible Sources. In *Sixth Palenque Round Table
    1986* (Merle G. Robertson, ed.): 151–166. University of Oklahoma Press,
    Norman.

 1994a Cosmología, soberanísmo y espacio ritual en la Mesoamérica del
    Formativo. In *Los olmecas en Mesoamérica* (John E. Clark, ed.): 239–259.
    Citibank, México.

 1994b Enclosed Ritual Spaces and the Watery Underworld in Formative
    Period Architecture: New Observations on the Function of

La Venta Complex A. In *Seventh Palenque Round Table 1989* (Merle G. Robertson and Virginia M. Fields, eds.): 125–135. Pre-Columbian Art Research Institute, San Francisco.

1995 Art, Ritual and Rulership in the Olmec World. In *The Olmec World, Ritual and Rulership* (Art Museum, ed.): 27–45. Art Museum of Princeton University, Princeton, N.J.

1999 Mountains of Creation and Underworld Portals: The Ritual Function of Olmec Architecture at La Venta, Tabasco. In *Mesoamerican Architecture as a Cultural Symbol* (Jeff K. Kowalski, ed.): 14–39. Oxford University Press, New York.

Rick, John W.

2005 The Evolution of Authority and Power at Chavín de Huántar, Peru. *Archaeological Papers of the American Anthropological Association* 14: 71–89.

Rust, William F., III, and Robert J. Sharer

1988 Olmec Settlement Data from La Venta, Tabasco, Mexico. *Science* 242: 102–104.

Schele, Linda

1995 The Olmec Mountain and Tree of Creation in Mesoamerican Cosmology. In *The Olmec World, Ritual and Rulership* (Art Museum, ed.): 105–117. Art Museum of Princeton University, Princeton, N.J.

Sharer, Robert J.

1989 The Olmec and the Southeast Periphery of Mesoamerica. In *Regional Perspectives on the Olmec* (Robert J. Sharer and David C. Grove, eds.): 247–271. Cambridge University Press, New York.

Smith, Adam T.

1999 The Making of an Urartian Landscape in Southern Transcaucasia: A Study of Political Architectonics. *American Journal of Archaeology* 103: 45–71.

Soustelle, Jacques

1951 Book Review of *The Two Crosses of Todos Santos: Survivals of Mayan Religious Ritual* by Maud Oakes. *Man* 51: 172–173.

Symonds, Stacey, Ann Cyphers, and Roberto Lunagómez

2002 *Asentamiento prehispánico en San Lorenzo Tenochtitlán*. Instituto de Investigaciones Antropológicas, Universidad Nacional Autónoma de México, México.

Taube, Karl A.

1995 The Rainmakers: The Olmec and Their Contribution to Mesoamerican Belief and Ritual. In *The Olmec World, Ritual and Rulership* (Art Museum, ed.): 83–103. Art Museum of Princeton University, Princeton, N.J.

1996 The Olmec Maize God: The Face of Corn in Formative Mesoamerica. *RES* 29–30: 39–81.

2000 Lightning Celts and Corn Fetishes: The Formative Olmec and the Development of Maize Symbolism in Mesoamerica and the American Southwest. In *Olmec Art and Archaeology in Mesoamerica* (John E. Clark and Mary E. Pye, eds.): 297–337. National Gallery of Art, Washington, D.C.

Tedlock, Barbara
    1982   *Time and the Highland Maya*. University of New Mexico Press,
            Albuquerque.
Tedlock, Dennis
    1990   From Voice and Ear to Hand and Eye. *Journal of American Folklore*
            103(408): 133–156.
Thompson, J. Eric S.
    1960   *Maya Hieroglyphic Writing*. University of Oklahoma Press, Norman.
Tolstoy, Paul
    1991   Reply to Hammond's "Cultura Hermana: Reappraising the Olmec."
            Review of Archaeology 12(1): 36–39.
Urcid, Javier
    2005   Knowledge, Power, and Memory in Ancient Oaxaca. Electronic docu-
            ment, http://www.famsi.org/zapotecwriting/zapotec_text.pdf.
Vaillant, George C.
    1938   A Correlation of Archaeological and Historical Sequences in the
            Valley of Mexico. *American Anthropologist* 40: 535–573.
Wengrow, David
    2001   The Evolution of Simplicity: Aesthetic Labour and Social Change in
            the Neolithic Near East. *World Archaeology* 33(2): 168–188.
Wicke, Charles
    1971   *Olmec: An Early Art Style of Precolumbian Mexico*. University of Arizona
            Press, Tucson.

PEOPLE OF THE *CERRO*

Landscape, Settlement, and Art at Middle Formative Period Chalcatzingo

David C. Grove
Susan D. Gillespie

THE DIFFERENT WAYS IN WHICH Mesoamerican cities of the Classic and Postclassic periods situated themselves in their natural and built landscapes and represented themselves in architectural, iconographic, and cosmological terms were unquestionably based on conditions inherited from the past. A small glimpse of the more venerable legacies can be obtained in the archaeological records of the Early and Middle Formative periods (1700–500 B.C.), the time of the earliest evidence of village- or town-sized settlements, some of them with public art, architecture, and anthropogenic transformations to the natural landscape. This chapter discusses some of those legacies manifest at the central Mexican site of Chalcatzingo, Morelos.

Chalcatzingo was founded in the Early Formative and apparently became a regional center during that period. The site reached its zenith during the late Middle Formative (Cantera phase, 700–500 B.C.), at which time Olmec-like stone carvings were created and displayed there (e.g., Grove 1984, 1987; Grove and Angulo 1987). Some of that art took the form of carved stone stelae erected adjacent to precocious stone-faced rectangular platform mounds in the village. In addition, the community was situated at the base of two dramatic mountains (Figure 1), one of which has Cantera phase bas-reliefs executed directly on its exposed rock faces. Chalcatzingo thus provides an excellent early example of the integration of art and architecture in two contiguous but distinct contexts: the settlement and the surrounding natural landscape.

This chapter discusses the integration of mountains, as natural landscape features, with the built environment of the village in the coalescence of a sense of place, as a means to examine "the ways in which citizens of the earth constitute their landscapes and take themselves to be connected to them" (Basso 1996: 54). We consider how the people of Chalcatzingo

FIGURE 1. The twin *cerros* of Chalcatzingo: Cerro Delgado (left) and Cerro Chalcatzingo (right). View is to the east. Photo by David C. Grove.

viewed their relationships to mountains in general and to the twin *cerros* in particular, and how they represented this identification of their community in such media as monumental architecture and stone art.

LEGACIES

It is not our intention here to seek out the origins of Classic and Postclassic symbolic motifs or architectural forms in the Formative period. As Moore (1995: 51) has observed, archaeologists are frequently motivated to construct narratives of "origins," but such narratives are misleading because they are determined "not by their beginnings but by their endings." For example, even if such icons as "Coatepetl" or "Tollan" are identified at widespread Mesoamerican cities in the Postclassic or even Classic period, it would nevertheless be presumptuous for us to assume that they are all the same phenomenon and that their origins must lie in some homogenous shared belief system deep in the Formative period. To make such an assumption would be to ignore other avenues of investigation, and variability in the Formative period would be played down by seeking only the origins of forms recognizable by their similarities to much later manifestations.

An example of this potential problem is the symbolic relationship claimed between man-made pyramids and sacred mountains. "Architectural mimicry" equating mounds with mountains is a common phenomenon worldwide (Knapp and Ashmore 1999: 2–3). The idea that "Mesoamerican pyramids were universally understood to replicate mountains" (Reilly 1999: 18) may have been the case for the later periods, but there is less basis for this symbolic reading further back in time, especially back to the Formative period when the earliest mounds were erected. In particular, as Joyce (2004: 8, emphasis in original) notes, "it is difficult to be comfortable with the assumption that *from the beginning* Mesoamerican monumental architecture was fully realized as an intentional effigy of sacred mountains." Using evidence from Formative Honduras, Joyce argues, on the contrary, that the intentions of the builders of the earliest platforms were likely quite different, perhaps no more than simply to elevate a space for certain activities. The probable unintended consequences of such building would have been to spatially segregate some actions in highly visible and ultimately more restricted places. However, once it came into existence, such monumental architecture became "irrevocably a part of the traditional knowledge" of Mesoamerican peoples (Joyce 2004: 23).

Rather than look for familiar categories of architectural or landscape features, we seek to examine the specific media and contexts by which the inhabitants of Chalcatzingo represented themselves and their sense of place. These media were material manifestations of their cosmology, the ordering principles that provide "a classification of the world and a set of prescriptions for correct action towards the world in both its human and non-human elements" (Gosden 1999: 77). Although we have argued for temporal and spatial diversity in the forms and expressions of cosmologies across Mesoamerica (e.g., Gillespie 1993; Grove 1999, 2000), we nevertheless recognize the existence of foundational concepts that characterize cosmologies on a virtually pan-Mesoamerican scale (see, e.g., Gossen 1986; Hunt 1977; Monaghan 2000). They helped to shape a *longue durée*, a structural history that is distinctively Mesoamerican, as the products of countless generations of intentional actions, transformations, historical contingencies, and unintended consequences. The cosmology of Chalcatzingo's inhabitants was influenced by their particular setting; however, they engaged in various activities to modify that setting, resulting in a dynamic series of historical processes whereby their sense of place, and their relationships to one another and to that place, changed over time.

TWO FUNDAMENTAL CONCEPTS IN MESOAMERICAN LANDSCAPES

We begin by considering two very basic concepts of Mesoamerican worldview, drawing especially from ethnography. The first is that features of the natural landscape had sacred qualities (monism and pantheism). The second is that the most fundamental sociospatial distinction was that between center and periphery (concentricity). Our intention in discussing these concepts is not simply to project their existence back into Formative period central Mexico, but to use them as a starting point to investigate how Chalcatzingo's inhabitants conceived, lived, and represented their place in the world.

Monism and Pantheism

Mesoamerican religion (or metaphysics more generally) is characterized as "monistic," in the sense that "reality is a unified whole, with a single divine principle responsible for the nature of the cosmos" (Monaghan 2000: 26). Put more simply, the universe is God, and everything within the universe partakes of the sacred (Monaghan 2000: 27; Sandstrom 2003: 56). The concept of deity is therefore pantheistic (Hunt 1977: 55; Monaghan 2000: 27; Sandstrom and Sandstrom 1986: 275–280), with "multiple manifestations of a single unity of being" (Hunt 1977: 55). All of the world is infused with this spirit or power, making animate that which modern Westerners consider inanimate (see, e.g., Hanks 1990: 86–87; López Austin 1993: 114, 135; Marcus 1983: 345; Monaghan 1995: 127–128; Spores 1983: 342; Vogt 1969: 369–371, 1981: 133). Spirit is not diffuse but assumes the form of individual, if fluid, entities—deities, ancestors, souls, winds, guardian spirits, mischievous beings (e.g., *chaneques*), and so forth. These animates are typically anchored in particular places, although they can move from place to place and can accumulate in both places and objects (Gillespie and Joyce 1998: 291).

As Sandstrom (1991: 241) described for the conceived landscape of a contemporary Nahua village in Veracruz:

> The landscape surrounding the village . . . is literally alive with aspects of spirit. Every hill, valley, spring, lake, stream, section of river, boulder, plain, grove, gorge, and cave has its proper name and associated spirit. . . . The features that figure most prominently in Nahua religion are the hills and mountains that are abundant in the region. Called *santo tepemej,* a mixed Spanish-Nahuatl phrase meaning "sacred hills," they are living entities that are the dwelling places of the seed and rain spirits associated with crop growth, and of the powerful spirits that guard over humans. . . . The hills are ranked according to size and importance, and each has a special place in village mythology.

It seems probable that Mesoamerican peoples of the Paleo-Indian and Archaic periods would have viewed their physical surroundings in the same way that Sandstrom describes. However, the Formative period witnessed the earliest compelling archaeological evidence for the treatment of prominent natural features as sites for ritual activity, as sacralized places where one could commune with the divine. For example, the wooden busts, rubber balls, and green stone celts placed in the waters of the spring at the base of the Cerro Manatí (e.g., Ortiz and Rodríguez 1994, 1999) near San Lorenzo, Veracruz, suggest that both the spring and the hill were venerated by Olmec peoples. Another Olmec example is the "Señor de San Martín

Pajapan," a large basalt anthropomorphic statue that had been laboriously hauled to the summit of the San Martín Pajapan volcano (Blom and La Farge 1926: 44–46, figs. 41–43; Medellín Zenil 1968). A third example is the Middle Formative period bas-relief carvings on the Cerro Chalcatzingo that are described below.

A monistic orientation to the universe renders moot such common Western distinctions as natural/supernatural (Monaghan 2000: 27) or sacred/profane. It similarly calls into question the analytical division typically made between nature/culture or natural/built environments. Even man-made structures, including mundane domestic architecture, and portable objects are dwelling places or surficial forms of animate spirit entities (e.g., Grove and Gillespie 2002). A more useful distinction would be that between the visible and invisible worlds (following Dwyer 1996). This terminology is not meant to privilege sight above other senses; "invisible" could include that which is intangible or imperceptible (to most persons) except perhaps as a wind, a smell, a feeling of awe or dread, or a luminous presence. Invisible beings are immaterial, but they can be manifest in material ways: "they assume the forms, or inhabit the bodies, of particular physical entities such as individual rocks, plants, animals, or persons" (Dwyer 1996: 163).

Dwyer's (1996) study of the spatial relationships of the invisible and visible worlds of three New Guinea societies demonstrated that in those societies with more intensified agricultural production and greater modification of the landscape, the "invisible world" had been moved to specific circumscribed places. Social differentiation, such as gendered division of labor, was also more pronounced in such societies. This situation presented a contrast with the coextensive existence of the invisible with the visible world in the case of simple horticulturalists, among whom spirits permeated all of the landscape and were regularly encountered in daily activities. Similar actions intended to mark—or even bound—the anchorage points of certain portions of the spirit world (deities, ancestors, or souls) seem to have occurred with the rise of complex society in Mesoamerica, alongside the development of new kinds of social status differences. Our analysis of Chalcatzingo's landscape takes into account the marking of certain places as associated with greater access to the invisible spirit world.

Concentricity

Dualism of a specific form—complementary opposition—is often highlighted as a fundamental axiom of Mesoamerican cosmologies (e.g., Gossen 1986: 6). Manifest on the spatial plane, given the egocentric orientation typical of Mesoamerican cosmography, such dualism is expressed in the division between center and periphery as the most basic sociospatial distinction (Gillespie and Joyce 1998: 282). Center and periphery, whose relationship is sometimes verbally expressed as town versus forest, implicate each other in concentric or nested scales of reference (see Vogt 1993: 11 on scaling). One's center is one's house, neighborhood, community, even polity, whereas the periphery could range in scale from the house yard to the untamed wilderness beyond the ken of most village inhabitants. The center is the place of inhabited space, daily activities, moral and physical order, and harmony, whereas the periphery is amoral, disorderly, and even chaotic and dangerous. On the temporal plane, the center is the time of the everyday and mundane, but the periphery may represent timelessness, past (including the mythological past), or future (see, e.g., Gossen 1974: 29–30; Hanks 1990: 306–307; Sandstrom 1996: 163; Taggart 1983: 55–56; Watanabe 1992: 62–63).[1]

Complementary opposition is based on the same holistic principle of monism—both aspects of the duality are parts of an encompassing whole—but as such it also has the potential for hierarchy. Not only will the two aspects be of unequal value (Lévi-Strauss 1963: 139), although both are needed for the whole to exist, but one of them may also encompass the other (its contrary) and therefore be hierarchically superior (following Dumont 1980: 240). More specifically, in certain respects or contexts the center may encompass its periphery. This dualistic encompassing quality has been best described regarding the most important inhabitant of any center—its ruler (chief or king). Persons of "power" (power in the nonsecular sense described above) are able to "concentrate opposites" in their person, notably as male and female, or mother and father (Anderson 1972: 14). More particularly, someone who claims sovereign power has to be both "above and beyond society and thus counterposed to it" while simultaneously incorporating the society (Sahlins 1985: 91). They must represent and encompass both center and periphery.

The proper place of such a person is a center in a political (not necessarily geographic) sense. Although we cannot argue that Chalcatzingo was a city or urban settlement, it was certainly a center, and it marked itself as such, as shown below. Centers have been broadly defined as loci "in a society where its leading ideas come together with its leading institutions to create an arena in which the events that most vitally affect its members' lives take place" (Geertz 1977: 151). In the Javanese case described by Geertz (1977: 157–159), which has a similar concentric worldview, the court was a copy of the cosmos and the larger realm a copy of the court, with the king at the center thereby summing up the whole in his person—court, realm, and cosmos. In Mesoamerica there is similar evidence that landscape features from the periphery (geographic and/or temporal) were replicated in centers, for example, in the form of pyramids named as mountains. An exemplar is the Aztec Templo Mayor (see the chapters by Eduardo Matos Moctezuma, and Leonardo López Lujan and Alfredo López Austin). This pyramid was explicitly named and adorned as Coatepetl (Serpent-Hill), a reference to a mountain known from myth, distant in both space and time from the original builders of that pyramid, which formed the center of Tenochtitlan and was said to be its first edifice. In this and parallel cases, the center encompasses both its spatial and temporal peripheries at the locus of the concentration of power in the form of tutelary deities in their temples and divine kings in their palaces. The king may also undertake activities to draw the periphery into his center (Geertz 1977) or interact with categories of persons (warriors, merchants, or vassals) who operate on the periphery on his behalf (Gillespie and Joyce 1998).

With these fundamental principles in mind, we now turn more specifically to consider how the inhabitants of Chalcatzingo materialized their sense of place and community self-identity in architecture and artworks.

CHALCATZINGO: LANDSCAPE, SETTLEMENT, AND ART

The Larger Landscape of Eastern Morelos

Rather than examine Chalcatzingo in isolation, we begin with its positioning in the Amatzinac valley in eastern Morelos. Three tall hills rise abruptly and dramatically from the broad flat floor at the center of the Amatzinac valley and dominate the surrounding landscape. Two of those hills, Cerro Chalcatzingo and Cerro Delgado (see Figure 1), tower above the settlement of Chalcatzingo at their western base. An equally imposing hill, Cerro Jantetelco, lies a few kilometers to the north, and at the north end of the Amatzinac valley is one of Mexico's tallest and most magnificent volcanos, Popocatepetl (Figure 2). Of this still smoking volcano, sixteenth-century chronicler Fray Diego Durán (1971: 255) said, "[i]n olden times this mountain was hallowed by the natives as the most important among the mountains, especially by those who lived in its vicinity or on its slopes." He went on to describe in some detail the special ceremonies and offerings made to this and other mountains in the central Mexican highlands. Similar ceremonies are still carried out today to venerate mountains (e.g., Albores and Broda 1997; Monaghan 1995: 107–109; Sandstrom 2003; Vogt 1999).

Durán (1971: 257–258) also mentioned other important mountain shrines near Popocatepetl, including one called Teocuicani:

> On the southern side of the volcano, in the region of Tetelan, Ocuituco, Temoac, Tzacualpan, and other towns, there is a hill to which the entire country journeyed with its offerings, sacrifices, and prayers. This [hill] was called Teocuicani, which means Divine Singer. . . . On this mountain stood the best-constructed building in

FIGURE 2.
The Amatzinac valley looking north from the top of Cerro Chalcatzingo. Cerro Delgado is in the foreground, Cerro Jantetelco is in the upper center, and Popocatepetl volcano is in the background. Photo by David C. Grove.

the entire area. This was called Ayauhcalli, which means Mansion of Rest and Shade of the Gods.

Heyden and Horcasitas (in Durán 1971: 258 footnote) have noted that "Ayauhcalli" more literally means house of mist or Mist House.

The towns of Tetela, Ocuituco, Temoac, and Zacualpan are all situated in the northern Amatzinac valley. It is therefore possible that Teocuicani could have been Cerro Chalcatzingo, and Ayauhcalli (Mist House) the modest Postclassic shrine unearthed there in 1972 (Arana 1987: 395, Fig. 24.14; Grove and Angulo 1973: 25–26). Perhaps Mist House could even have been a Postclassic reference to the famed Middle Formative period El Rey image carved high on Cerro Chalcatzingo, which includes scroll motifs that are often interpreted as mist (see below). However, it seems more likely that the hill mentioned by Durán's informants as Teocuicani (Divine Singer) is Cerro Jantetelco, because that mountain has a natural hole near its summit that whistles or "sings" in the wind (Grove 1972: 36).

The Twin Cerros of Chalcatzingo

From an ecofunctional perspective, it is difficult to explain why the Amatzinac valley saw the development of a major regional center. The vast majority of the population of Formative period Morelos was situated in the agriculturally rich and well-watered river valleys in the west and center of the state. In contrast, eastern Morelos and the Amatzinac valley are far less fertile and verdant. For much of its course the valley's lone river runs in a deep *barranca*, where access to its waters is restricted and arable river bottomlands are lacking (Angulo 1987: 157; Grove 1987: 420, 431; Grove et al. 1987: 8–9). Although the foothill slopes occupied by the Formative period settlement of Chalcatzingo were perhaps somewhat better for agriculture than many areas elsewhere in the Amatzinac valley (Grove 1987: 420), the setting pales in comparison to the richness of central and western Morelos.

We suggest, as have others before (e.g., Angulo 1987: 155–156; Cook de Leonard 1967: 63–66; Grove 1987: 431–432), that the special character of the two hills that dominate the valley and are visible from great distances in all directions—Cerro Chalcatzingo and Cerro Delgado—may have been a factor in both the decision to settle there and in the site's rather early fluorescence as a center. Not only are the hills visually compelling, but also these two granodiorite masses stand side-by-side as if conjoined, separated only by a large V-shaped cleft (see Figure 1). In Mesoamerican worldview, clefts or similar openings into the earth were considered portals to the other world of invisible spirits that exists on the spatiotemporal periphery of everyday existence in the center (Vogt 1981). In later creation myths split mountains were the source of the first corn or the first humans (e.g., Freidel et al. 1993: 111, 138–139).

However, we cannot assume a specific meaning of the cleft cerros as the "Split Hill" of later mythology. As Barnes (1999: 101) observed:

> any particular landscape feature may be attributed with different meanings by different viewers, or indeed by a single viewer at different moments. . . . Nevertheless, some landscape features may be intentionally and explicitly "marked" as to what their intended meaning is in specific systems of thought. . . . Explicit "marking" of landscape attributes is a method of extending meaning among inhabitants and contributes to the development of a shared acknowledgment of such meanings even if not all inhabitants adopt them as their own.

In the case of Chalcatzingo, there is compelling archaeological evidence for such marking or inscribing of both natural and human-made features in the landscape. More than 36 stone monuments and bas-relief carvings have been recorded there, a quantity exceeded in the Early and Middle Formative periods only at the Gulf Coast Olmec centers of San Lorenzo and La Venta.

The carved stone art at Chalcatzingo occurs in spatially and thematically distinct groups on Cerro Chalcatzingo and in the village (Figure 3). Interestingly, no such bas-relief art occurs on Cerro Delgado. Instead, simple painted pictographs are abundant in the niches of that smaller hill (Apostolides 1987). Although most of those paintings are of uncertain age,

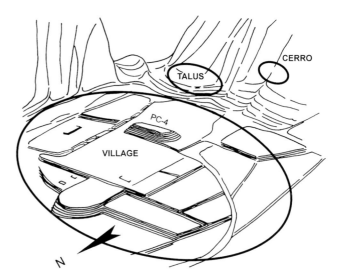

FIGURE 3. Schematic view of the site of Chalcatzingo showing the three areas of stone artworks (circled) and the location of Middle Formative period mound PC Structure 4. The 70-m-long PC-4 mound provides approximate scale. Drawing by David C. Grove.

this situation poses an interesting dichotomy, suggesting that the two mountains were perceived differently. As for the sculptures, they form three groupings: the Cerro Chalcatzingo carvings, the talus carvings, and the village carvings. The first two are both within view of the village area. Significantly, each group has a different iconographic theme (Grove 1984: 49–68, 109–122, 1999: 258–263). Although their specific iconographic readings remain speculative, those general themes evoke the dichotomy of center and periphery and the conception of a living landscape.

Cerro Chalcatzingo Carvings

This group of six bas-reliefs occurs on exposed rock faces high on the mountainside (Figure 3), where the images are positioned on both sides of the mountain's natural rainwater drainage channel. The first report on these reliefs (Guzmán 1934) called attention to their general theme of rain and agricultural fertility, and that interpretation has since been reiterated by many scholars. Five of the reliefs (Monuments 6/7, 8, 11, 14, 15) are small (about 0.3–0.6 m^2) and depict the same basic scene: a small lizardlike animal crouched atop a recumbent S-shaped scroll and beneath a rain cloud with falling raindrops (Angulo 1987: figs. 10.1–10.6; Grove and Angulo 1987: 117–119; Figure 4). Squash plants are carved below three of the small animals.

Immediately adjacent to those smallish reliefs is the famous El Rey (Monument 1), a very large bas-relief carving covering an area of about 8.5 m^2 and depicting a personage seated in a large recumbent U-shaped niche (Figure 5). That niche, a vertically sectioned quatrefoil, represents a cave (Angulo 1987: 135–141; Cook de Leonard 1967: 66; Gay 1972: 38–45; Grove 1968: 486–487, 2000: 279–283; Grove and Angulo 1987: 115–117; Guzmán

FIGURE 4. Monument 14, a small lizardlike animal beneath a rain cloud with falling raindrops. A squash plant is depicted at the base of the scene. Photo by David C. Grove.

1934: 238–243; Figure 6a). Rain clouds with falling raindrops hang over the cave-niche, and scrolls emanate from the niche's opening, suggesting the mist that naturally emanates from caves (see the above comments on Mist House). The niche's quatrefoil form also creates a Oaxaca-like mountain glyph (Grove 2000: 279–283; Reilly 1994: fig. 15.18; Figure 6b,c). The U-shaped niche thus seems to signify a cave in a mountain, a portal to the invisible world.

In addition, the presence of an eye and outcurved fang motifs on the quatrefoil niche show it to also be the profile face of a zoomorphic entity. Because outcurved fangs denote the sky realm in Mesoamerican iconography (incurved fangs mark the earth or underworld; see Grove [2000: 281–282] for a complete iconographic argument), the combined motifs indicate that the El Rey personage sits in a "sky-mountain cave" or in the interior of a mountain, a reading that is reiterated by the actual elevated mountainside location of the carving. The zoomorphic sky-mountain cave is identifiable as a serpent (Grove 2000: 279–281), and it may be enticing to interpret that symbolism as indicating that Cerro Chalcatzingo was conceived as a "Serpent-Hill"—an early "Coatepetl." However, serpent imagery is common in Mesoamerican depictions of the various portals to the otherworld, especially caves, mountains, and trees (Gillespie 1993). Thus there is not

FIGURE 5. El Rey (Monument 1), depicting a personage seated in a cave. Rain clouds with falling raindrops appear above the cave, and mistlike scrolls emanate from the cave mouth. Photo by David C. Grove.

sufficient reason to suggest that the serpent face signifies the hill rather than the cave as an opening.

Plant motifs sprout from the exterior corners of the mountain/cave glyph and appear elsewhere in the scene. Given the later mythological association of primeval maize with "Split Hill," it might be assumed that these plants are maize. However, Angulo (1987: 139–140) has convincingly argued that the plants resemble the bromeliads that abound on the rock faces of Cerro Chalcatzingo and flourish with the first rains. The presence of bromeliads in the El Rey image indicates to us that the U-shaped sky-mountain cave is not a generic representation of a mythological place but is more likely Cerro Chalcatzingo itself.

The El Rey personage is an elaborately dressed human figure with no mask or apparent supernatural characteristics (Grove 1987: 427). Triple raindrop motifs adorn his kilt, and similar triple raindrop groups, paired quetzal birds, and two bromeliad representations occur with the headdress.[2] The last motif apparently reiterates the person's association with Cerro Chalcatzingo.

The basic rain and fertility aspects of the scene are almost universally accepted, but there have been several different interpretations of the type

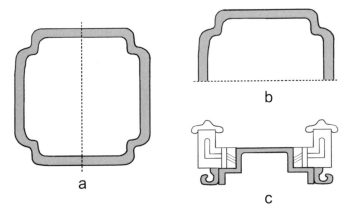

FIGURE 6. Quatrefoil motif: (a) a vertically sectioned quatrefoil (compare left half to Monument 1); (b) half-quatrefoil, horizontally sectioned; (c) Oaxaca mountain glyph (Building J, Monte Albán). Drawing by David C. Grove.

of character represented by the personage. Bernal (1969: 139) and more recently Brady and Ashmore (1999: 129–130) have interpreted the personage in the cave-niche as depicting a living ruler. The latter authors suggest that through the relief the ruler associated himself directly with water control, rainmaking, and fertility. They propose that water gushing down the mountainside next to this relief, channeled through the human-modified terraces below, would have served as a "hierophany, a manifestation of the sacred," linking the mountain, rainfall, agricultural fertility, and rulership in a predictable fashion following the rhythms of nature (Brady and Ashmore 1999: 129). In their interpretation, the portrait as a representation is integrated with the natural environment.

Based on the setting of the personage in the sky-mountain cave, making him a denizen of the invisible world, others have identified him as a rain deity (Gay 1972: 38), or have compared him to Postclassic deities such as Tlaloc—who was associated with earth, caves, and rain—and Tepeyollotl (Heart of the Mountain; e.g., Angulo 1987: 140–141). Those Postclassic deity concepts reiterate the Mesoamerican worldview that a mountain is a living thing, animated by its resident spirits. Although this fundamental concept was shared from at least the Formative onward, the notion of deity need not have been constant. We believe it may be more appropriate to consider the personage as an ancestral spirit. Many indigenous peoples today, as in Pre-Hispanic times, believe that ancestors live in mountains (e.g., Vogt 1969). Those spirits, as Sandstrom observed (see quote above), are associated with rain and plant growth, and they guard over humans. Perhaps the El Rey personage was such an ancestral spirit, a guardian of Cerro Chalcatzingo and the benefactor of the Formative period community situated at the base of that sacred mountain. It is conceivable that even as a communal ancestral spirit, El Rey may have been more personally claimed as ancestor by one of Chalcatzingo's chiefly houses (following Gillespie 1999).

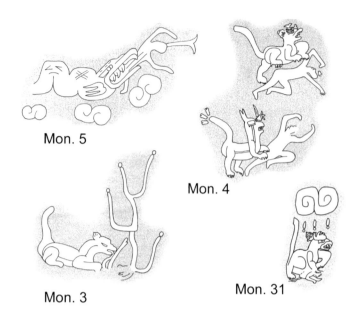

Mon. 5

Mon. 4

Mon. 3

Mon. 31

FIGURE 7. Monuments 3, 4, 5, and 31. Drawings by David C. Grove.

In summary, the carvings high on Cerro Chalcatzingo identify the mountain and its ancestral spirit, and relate that spirit and the mountain to rain, water, and fertility. Thematically they are carvings of the periphery, and significantly, they are situated on the periphery of the village.

Talus Carvings

A second and distinctly different group of five carvings is executed on boulders and stone slabs on the talus slope at the foot of the mountain (see Figure 3). They are all relatively large carvings (up to 4.5 m²) and are arranged across the talus in a general east-west line. Four of the five reliefs depict supernatural zoomorphic creatures dominating generalized human figures (Figure 7). The easternmost of the group is Monument 5, a large reptilian-like creature partially grasping a human figure in its mouth. Monument 4 depicts two felines with extraordinary features pouncing with claws extended onto two prone humans. Monument 3 is a recumbent feline (puma) beside a cactuslike symbol. In a damaged area of the bas-relief Angulo (1987: 144, fig. 10.15) identified what seems to be a human figure in a pose suggesting that the puma is dominating the human. Nearby is Monument 31 showing a snarling feline atop a prone human figure. Monument 2, the westernmost relief of the five, is different and is best described as depicting a ritual involving four human actors (Figure 8), three standing or walking and one seated. The standing figures are masked and wear tall headdresses. One figure's headdress incorporates symbols adorning the head of the upper feline of Monument 4 (see Figure 7). That correspondence suggests that the

FIGURE 8. Talus Monument 2, a ritual scene with three standing masked figures and a seated figure. The headdress of the second person from the right contains symbols also adorning the head of the upper feline in Monument 4 (see Figure 7). Drawing by Barbara W. Fash.

ritual scene in Monument 2 was related in some manner to the mythological events displayed by the other monuments in the sequence.

These carvings at the foot of the *cerro* show mythical scenes that would have been significant to the cosmogony and religious life of the people of Chalcatzingo. They are thematically comparable to mythologies of other societies and of later Mesoamerican peoples that relate the domination of humans by supernatural animal beings in primordial times. They are also themes outside of the norm of everyday life and moral order, themes of a peripheral state of being, and they occur on the periphery of the site.

Village Carvings

The third area with monumental stone artworks is the Formative period village area (see Figure 3). Monuments in this zone include a tabletop altar-throne (Monument 22), a decapitated seated statue (Monument 16), and nearly a dozen stelae (Grove 2005; Grove and Angulo 1987).[3] That is the largest number of carved stelae known for any Middle Formative Mesoamerican site, including the Olmec centers of San Lorenzo and La Venta. As noted above, many of those stelae were spatially associated with stone-faced platform structures, and almost all of them depict an individual dressed personage, male or female. The stelae and other carvings from the village area manifest concepts associated with rulership (Grove 1984: 49–68), a theme appropriate for the center—the place of moral, social, and cosmic order.

Also situated in the settlement area is a large earthen platform mound, designated Plaza Central Structure 4 (PC-4; see Figure 3). Measuring approximately 70 m long, 29 m wide (upper surface), and about 8 m tall, PC-4 is the largest known Middle Formative mound in the Morelos–Basin

FIGURE 9. Monument 9, a quatrefoil-shaped serpent face with a hollow mouth. The stone is 1.8 m tall and 1.5 m wide. Drawing by David C. Grove and David Hixson.

of Mexico region. It is significant that the richest elite burials recovered during the Chalcatzingo Project excavations, perhaps those of the village's leaders, were found buried beneath the mound's upper surface (Merry de Morales 1987: 100). In addition, Monument 9, a large stone slab carved with a bas-relief image, had apparently been erected and displayed on top of the platform mound (Grove 1984: 49–50, 1999: 262, 2000: 285; Grove and Angulo 1987: 124; Figure 9).

The bas-relief carving of Monument 9 depicts a full frontal view of the quatrefoil supernatural serpent face, with sprouting bromeliads, that in profile view forms the cave motif of El Rey (Monument 1) high on the mountainside (Grove 2000: 289–291; Reilly 1994: fig. 15.18). Based on the carving's close similarities to Monument 1, Grove (1999: 264, 2000: 289–291) has suggested that Monument 9 was erected atop the massive PC-4 mound to identify the mound as a sacred mountain. The bromeliad motifs on Monument 9 would further indicate that the mound represents Cerro Chalcatzingo. Significantly, the inner mouth area of the monument's large serpent face was hollowed out, creating a quatrefoil-shaped hole that passes through the entire stone slab (Angulo 1987: 141; Grove 1984: 50). Thus the serpent's mouth on this artwork is an actual opening, which suggests that people and objects could have passed through that open mouth and so entered the realm of the invisible, associated with the past and with access to primordial power (Gillespie 1993: 75). Such persons or objects would therefore have been positioned in the same sacred location as that of the El Rey personage high on the mountainside.

Because of its similarities to Monument 1, Monument 9 is highly significant for understanding the mediation of center and periphery, the role of mountains as access to the sacred—the world of invisible spirits and power—and the encompassment of the periphery by the center. The placement of Monument 9 on the massive PC-4 mound in the village center may have marked this structure as sharing in the meanings ascribed to Cerro Chalcatzingo, a landscape feature of the periphery. In other words, the periphery was replicated, in miniature, in the center, as represented by PC-4 and Monument 9. Beyond these material representations, it is not hard to imagine practices that would have actively mediated between center and periphery. For example, ritual processions likely occurred from the village center to Cerro Chalcatzingo and the talus slope carvings, thereby transcending the division between the visible and invisible worlds, past and present, the quotidian and the extraordinary. These processions were channeled by the placement of the carvings on the hillside, the talus slope, and the center (see Grove 1999: 260, 2005). Access to the invisible world was thereby becoming circumscribed.

PEOPLE OF THE *CERRO*

In presenting this case for the use of mounds and sculptures to represent Chalcatzingo to its inhabitants as a center, it is important to reiterate the historical context of these media. Although the artworks and their spatial arrangement—integrating the mountains with the settlement—can be shown to manifest fundamental axioms of Mesoamerican cosmology—pantheism and concentricity—they were created at a specific historical juncture.

The Middle Formative (starting in 900 B.C.) was a time of great change in Mesoamerica. Modifications to the landscape were becoming more common and intensive. This was the time of the earliest mound architecture, which within a few hundred years had become an essential feature of Mesoamerican centers. At Chalcatzingo the major anthropogenic changes to the landscape included the Barranca phase (900–700 B.C.) terracing of the slopes at the base of the twin *cerros* (Grove 1987: 421). That dramatically changed landscape would have transformed the referential frames for peoples' daily interactions and activities, and the increased categorization of space would have produced in tandem increasing social differentiation (Love 1999: 144). Not surprisingly, the Middle Formative also witnessed increasing sociopolitical complexity and the material marking of certain persons as having special status, including greater access to the invisible world (e.g., Grove and Gillespie 1992a, 1992b).

Although it is possible that the Cantera phase carvings merely made more explicit, in graphic form, concepts that were already being activated in more ephemeral media, we consider the likelihood that these sociopolitical changes were part of the motivation for new forms of expression. In particular, there is no evidence that in the Early Formative period, when PC-4 was erected, it was intended to symbolize a mountain. This platform was rebuilt and enlarged several times over 500 years (Prindiville and Grove 1987: 63, fig. 6.2). Its low height, flat top, and rectangular shape do not resemble a mountain. Nevertheless, sometime after 700 B.C. that signification was materially marked, minimally in the form of Monument 9. It was also during that time (the Cantera phase) that chiefly individuals were buried in PC-4, positioning their bodies in the same kind of sacred space as that of El Rey, the ancestral figure depicted in the Monument 1 relief.

Once the carvings were made, they changed the visible landscape to an anthropogenic one now inscribed with specific symbolic content, promulgating certain meanings and silencing potential others (see Barnes 1999: 102). As with the change in land forms and architecture, the system of material references that the community members used to guide their daily interactions had been transformed. The delineation of certain sacred places would have been coordinated with the delineation of social units (following Vogt 1981: 133). The claim to encompassing cosmic hierarchy in the center associated with PC-4 (a claim likely made specifically by chiefly houses) would have been paralleled by claims to the apex of sociopolitical hierarchy.

Significantly, these kinds of changes were happening elsewhere in Mesoamerica (e.g., Love 1999). At least one other Middle Formative mound was apparently intentionally marked as a mountain: the 30-m-tall earthen mound (C-1) at the Olmec center of La Venta. Heizer (1968: 1520, figs. 2–9) had argued that C-1 was built to replicate the volcanic cones in the Tuxtlas Mountains, the source of the basalt used for many of La Venta's stone carvings. However, he made that hypothesis based on the appearance of the mound after millennia of erosion. Nevertheless, whatever its ultimate form (González Lauck 1988; Graham and Johnson 1979), this pyramid had probably been built in stages over a long period of time and thus it is impossible to assert the intent of its original builders. However, four large Middle Formative period stelae (Monuments 25/26, 27, 88, 89) were erected in a line in front of the pyramid's southern base (Drucker et al. 1959: 204–209, figs. 59, 60; González Lauck 1996: 76). The bas-relief carving on each stela is identical: a large frontal face with outcurved sky fangs. Grove (1999: 264, 286, 2000: 289–292) has suggested that those are sky-mountain faces that marked La Venta's Mound C-1 as a mountain.

The relationships evident between La Venta and Chalcatzingo based on the similarities in their respective carvings (Grove 1987: 427–429, 1989: 130–139) further demonstrate the important role of historical contexts in interpreting evidence of a materialized cosmology. As we stated at the start of this chapter, it is too simple to assume that a homogeneous corpus of symbols existed in Mesoamerica from the Formative period on; instead, the likelihood of multiple and changing meanings must be investigated. Thus it is possible that elite residents of both Chalcatzingo and La Venta took a preexisting mound, within a preexisting frame of reference, and gave it a new or embellished signification. With the erection of Monument 9 on the massive mound at Chalcatzingo, the villagers formally represented themselves, in the media of art and architecture, as the People of the *Cerro*.

NOTES

1. In a previous article, Grove (1999) discussed the basic center/peripheral thematic distributions and differences at Chalcatzingo, La Venta, and San Lorenzo. In this chapter we focus more specifically on details at Chalcatzingo.

2. Similar triple-raindrop motifs occur on the headdress of the seated personage in the niche on La Venta's Altar 5, and paired quetzal birds also occur on La Venta Monument 19 (Grove 1989: 133–137, figs. 7.7–7.9).

3. Consolidation work by the Instituto Nacional de Antropología e Historia in 2005 on the site's Classic period ballcourt and plaza area adjacent to the PC-4 mound revealed three Cantera phase monuments buried in Classic period fill, including two stelae sections (Monuments 35 and 37; Córdova Tello and Meza Rodríguez 2007: 64–65). In addition, over the years Grove has recorded several probable in situ stela bases at the site; thus the total number of stelae certainly exceeded a dozen.

REFERENCES CITED

Albores, Beatriz, and Johanna Broda (eds.)

    1997   *Graniceros: Cosmovisión y meteorología indígenas de Mesoamérica.* El Colegio Mexiquense and the Instituto de Investigaciones Históricas, Universidad Nacional Autónoma de México, México.

Anderson, Benedict R. O'G.

    1972   The Idea of Power in Javanese Culture. In *Culture and Politics in Indonesia* (Claire Holt, Benedict R. O'G. Anderson, and James Siegel, eds.): 1–69. Cornell University Press, Ithaca, N.Y.

Angulo V., Jorge

    1987   The Chalcatzingo Reliefs: An Iconographic Analysis. In *Ancient Chalcatzingo* (David C. Grove, ed.): 132–158. University of Texas Press, Austin.

Apostolides, Alex

    1987   Painted Art. In *Ancient Chalcatzingo* (David C. Grove, ed.): 171–189. University of Texas Press, Austin.

Arana, Raul Martín

    1987   Classic and Postclassic Chalcatzingo. In *Ancient Chalcatzingo* (David C. Grove, ed.): 387–399. University of Texas Press, Austin.

Barnes, Gina L.

    1999   Buddhist Landscapes of East Asia. In *Archaeologies of Landscape: Contemporary Perspectives* (Wendy Ashmore and A. Bernard Knapp, eds.): 101–123. Blackwell, Malden, Mass.

Basso, Keith H.

    1996   Wisdom Sits in Places: Notes on a Western Apache Landscape. In *Senses of Place* (Steven Feld and Keith H. Basso, eds.): 53–90. School of American Research Advanced Seminar Series. School of American Research Press, Santa Fe, N.M.

Bernal, Ignacio

    1969   *The Olmec World.* University of California Press, Berkeley.

Blom, Frans F., and Oliver La Farge

    1926   *Tribes and Temples,* vol. 1. Middle American Research Institute, Tulane University, New Orleans.

Brady, James E., and Wendy Ashmore

    1999   Mountains, Caves, Water: Ideational Landscapes of the Ancient Maya. In *Archaeologies of Landscape: Contemporary Perspectives* (Wendy Ashmore and A. Bernard Knapp, eds.): 124–145. Blackwell, Malden, Mass.

Cook de Leonard, Carmen
    1967 Sculptures and Rock Carvings at Chalcatzingo, Morelos. *Contributions of the University of California Archaeological Research Facility* 3: 57–84.
Córdova Tello, Mario, and Carolina Meza Rodríguez
    2007 Chalcatzingo, Morelos: Un discurso sobre piedra. *Arqueología Mexicana* 87: 60–65.
Drucker, Philip, Robert F. Heizer, and Robert J. Squier
    1959 Excavations at La Venta, Tabasco, 1955. Bureau of American Ethnology Bulletin 170. Smithsonian Institution, Washington, D.C.
Dumont, Louis
    1980 *Homo Hierarchicus: The Caste System and Its Implications* (Mark Sainsbury, Louis Dumont, and Basia Gulati, trans.). University of Chicago Press, Chicago.
Durán, Fray Diego
    1971 [ca. 1570] *Book of the Gods and Rites and the Ancient Calendar* (Fernando Horcasitas and Doris Heyden, eds. and trans.). University of Oklahoma Press, Norman.
Dwyer, Peter D.
    1996 The Invention of Nature. In *Redefining Nature: Ecology, Culture and Domestication* (Roy Ellen and Katsuyoshi Fukui, eds.): 157–186. Berg, Oxford.
Freidel, David, Linda Schele, and Joy Parker
    1993 *Maya Cosmos: Three Thousand Years on the Shaman's Path.* William Morrow, New York.
Gay, Carlo T. E.
    1972 *Chalcacingo.* International Scholarly Book Services, Portland, Ore.
Geertz, Clifford
    1977 Centers, Kings, and Charisma: Reflections on the Symbolics of Power. In *Culture and Its Creators: Essays in Honor of Edward Shils* (Joseph Ben-David and Terry Nichols Clark, eds.): 150–171. University of Chicago Press, Chicago.
Gillespie, Susan D.
    1993 Power, Pathways, and Appropriations in Mesoamerican Art. In *Imagery and Creativity: Ethnoaesthetics and Art Worlds in the Americas* (Dorothea S. Whitten and Norman E. Whitten, Jr., eds.): 67–107. University of Arizona Press, Tucson.
    1999 Olmec Thrones as Ancestral Altars: The Two Sides of Power. In *Material Symbols: Culture and Economy in Prehistory* (John E. Robb, ed.): 224–253. Occasional Paper 26. Center for Archaeological Investigations, Southern Illinois University, Carbondale.
Gillespie, Susan D., and Rosemary A. Joyce
    1998 Deity Relationships in Mesoamerican Cosmologies: The Case of the Maya God L. *Ancient Mesoamerica* 9: 279–296.
González Lauck, Rebecca
    1988 Proyecto arqueológico La Venta. *Arqueología (Revista de la Coordinación Nacional de Arqueología)* 4: 121–165.

1996   La Venta: An Olmec Capital. In *Olmec Art of Ancient Mexico* (Elizabeth
       P. Benson and Beatriz de la Fuente, eds.): 73–81. National Gallery of
       Art, Washington, D.C.

Gosden, Chris
   1999   *Anthropology and Archaeology: A Changing Relationship.* Routledge,
          London.

Gossen, Gary H.
   1974   *Chamulas in the World of the Sun: Time and Space in a Maya Oral Tradi-
          tion.* Harvard University Press, Cambridge, Mass.
   1986   Mesoamerican Ideas as a Foundation for Regional Synthesis. In *Symbol
          and Meaning beyond the Closed Community: Essays in Mesoamerican Ideas*
          (Gary H. Gossen, ed.): 1–8. Institute for Mesoamerican Studies, State
          University of New York, Albany.

Graham, John A., and Mark Johnson
   1979   The Great Mound of La Venta. *Contributions of the University of
          California Archaeological Research Facility* 41: 1–5.

Grove, David C.
   1968   Chalcatzingo, Morelos, Mexico: A Re-appraisal of the Olmec Rock
          Carvings. *American Antiquity* 33: 468–491.
   1972   El Teocuicani: "Cantor Divino" en Jantetelco. *INAH Boletín* (Epoca II)
          3: 35–36.
   1984   *Chalcatzingo: Excavations on the Olmec Frontier.* Thames and Hudson,
          London and New York.
   1987   Comments on the Site and Its Organization. In *Ancient Chalcatzingo*
          (David C. Grove, ed.): 420–433. University of Texas Press, Austin.
   1989   Chalcatzingo and Its Olmec Connection. In *Regional Perspectives on the
          Olmec* (Robert J. Sharer and David C. Grove, eds.): 122–147. School of
          American Research Advanced Seminar Series. Cambridge University
          Press, Cambridge.
   1999   Public Monuments and Sacred Mountains: Observations on Three
          Formative Period Sacred Landscapes. In *Social Patterns in Pre-Classic
          Mesoamerica* (David C. Grove and Rosemary A. Joyce, eds.): 255–299.
          Dumbarton Oaks, Washington, D.C.
   2000   Faces of the Earth at Chalcatzingo: Serpents, Caves, and Mountains
          in Middle Formative Period Iconography. In *Olmec Art and Archaeol-
          ogy in Mesoamerica* (John E. Clark and Mary Pye, eds.): 277–295.
          Center for Advanced Study, National Gallery of Art, Washington,
          D.C.
   2005   Los monumentos de la Terraza 6 de Chalcatzingo, Morelos. *Arqueología
          (Revista de la Coordinación Nacional de Arqueología)* (Epoca II) 35: 23–32.

Grove, David C., and Jorge Angulo V.
   1973   Chalcatzingo, un sitio excepcional en el Estado de Morelos. *INAH
          Boletín* (Epoca II) 4: 21–26.
   1987   A Catalog and Description of Chalcatzingo's Monuments. In *Ancient
          Chalcatzingo* (David C. Grove, ed.): 114–131. University of Texas Press,
          Austin.

Grove, David C., and Susan D. Gillespie

1992a   Archaeological Indicators of Formative Period Elites: A Perspective from Central Mexico. In *Mesoamerican Elites: An Archaeological Assessment* (Diane Z. Chase and Arlen F. Chase, eds.): 191–205. University of Oklahoma Press, Norman.

1992b   Ideology and Evolution at the Pre-State Level: Formative Period Mesoamerica. In *Ideology and Pre-Columbian Civilizations* (Arthur A. Demarest and Geoffrey W. Conrad, eds.): 15–36. School of American Research Advanced Seminar Series. School of American Research Press, Santa Fe, N.M.

2002   Middle Formative Domestic Ritual at Chalcatzingo, Morelos. In *Domestic Ritual in Ancient Mesoamerica* (Patricia Plunket, ed.): 11–19. Cotsen Institute of Archaeology Monograph 46. University of California at Los Angeles, Los Angeles.

Grove, David C., Kenneth G. Hirth, and David E. Bugé

1987   Physical and Cultural Setting. In *Ancient Chalcatzingo* (David C. Grove, ed.): 6–13. University of Texas Press, Austin.

Guzmán, Eulalia

1934   Los relieves de las rocas del Cerro de la Cantera, Jonacatepec, Morelos. *Anales del Museo Nacional de Arqueología, Historia, y Etnografía* (Epoca 5) 1: 237–251.

Hanks, William F.

1990   *Referential Practice: Language and Lived Space among the Maya.* University of Chicago Press, Chicago.

Heizer, Robert F.

1968   New Observations on La Venta. In *Dumbarton Oaks Conference on the Olmec* (Elizabeth P. Benson, ed.): 9–36. Dumbarton Oaks, Washington, D.C.

Hunt, Eva

1977   *The Transformation of the Hummingbird: Cultural Roots of a Zinacantecan Mythical Poem.* Cornell University Press, Ithaca, N.Y.

Joyce, Rosemary A.

2004   Unintended Consequences? Monumentality as a Novel Experience in Formative Mesoamerica. *Journal of Archaeological Method and Theory* 11: 5–29.

Knapp, A. Bernard, and Wendy Ashmore

1999   Archaeological Landscapes: Constructed, Conceptualized, Ideational. In *Archaeologies of Landscape: Contemporary Perspectives* (Wendy Ashmore and A. Bernard Knapp, eds.): 1–30. Blackwell, Malden, Mass.

Lévi-Strauss, Claude

1963   *Structural Anthropology* (Claire Jacobson and Brooke Grundfest Schoepf, trans.). Basic Books, New York.

López Austin, Alfredo

1993   *The Myths of the Opposum: Pathways of Mesoamerican Mythology* (Bernard R. Ortiz de Montellano and Thelma Ortiz de Montellano, trans.). University of New Mexico Press, Albuquerque.

Love, Michael

    1999   Ideology, Material Culture, and Daily Practice in Pre-Classic Meso-america: A Pacific Coast Perspective. In *Social Patterns in Pre-Classic Mesoamerica* (David C. Grove and Rosemary A. Joyce, eds.): 127–153. Dumbarton Oaks, Washington, D.C.

Marcus, Joyce

    1983   Zapotec Religion. In *The Cloud People: Divergent Evolution of the Zapotec and Mixtec Civilizations* (Kent V. Flannery and Joyce Marcus, eds.): 345–351. Academic Press, New York.

Medellín Zenil, Alfonso

    1968   El dios jaguar de San Martín. *INAH Boletín* 33: 9–16.

Merry de Morales, Marcia

    1987   Chalcatzingo Burials as Indicators of Social Ranking. In *Ancient Chalcatzingo* (David C. Grove, ed.): 95–113. University of Texas Press, Austin.

Monaghan, John

    1995   *The Covenants with Earth and Rain: Exchange, Sacrifice, and Revelation in Mixtec Sociality.* University of Oklahoma Press, Norman.

    2000   Theology and History in the Study of Mesoamerican Religions. In *Supplement to the Handbook of Middle American Indians* (Victoria Reifler Bricker, ed.), vol. 6: *Ethnology* (John Monaghan, ed.): 24–49. University of Texas Press, Austin.

Moore, Henrietta

    1995   The Problems of Origins: Poststructuralism and Beyond. In *Interpreting Archaeology: Finding Meaning in the Past* (Ian Hodder, ed.): 51–53. Routledge, London.

Ortiz, Ponciano, and Ma. del Carmen Rodríguez

    1994   Los espacios sagrados olmecas: El Manatí, un caso especial. In *Los Olmecas en Mesoamérica* (John E. Clark, ed.): 69–91. Citibank, México.

    1999   Olmec Ritual Behavior at El Manatí: A Sacred Space. In *Social Patterns in Pre-Classic Mesoamerica* (David C. Grove and Rosemary A. Joyce, eds.): 225–254. Dumbarton Oaks, Washington, D.C.

Prindiville, Mary, and David C. Grove

    1987   The Settlement and Its Architecture. In *Ancient Chalcatzingo* (David C. Grove, ed.): 63–81. University of Texas Press, Austin.

Reilly, F. Kent, III

    1994   Cosmología, soberanismo y espacio ritual en la Mesoamérica del Formativo. In *Los Olmecas en Mesoamérica* (John E. Clark, ed.): 239–259. Citibank, México.

    1999   Mountains of Creation and Underworld Portals: The Ritual Function of Olmec Architecture at La Venta, Tabasco. In *Mesoamerican Architecture as Cultural Symbol* (Jeff Karl Kowalski, ed.): 14–39. Oxford University Press, New York.

Sahlins, Marshall

    1985   *Islands of History.* University of Chicago Press, Chicago.

Sandstrom, Alan R.

 1991 *Corn Is Our Blood: Culture and Ethnic Identity in a Contemporary Aztec Indian Village.* University of Oklahoma Press, Norman.

 1996 Center and Periphery in the Social Organization of Contemporary Nahuas of Mexico. *Ethnology* 35: 161–180.

 2003 Sacred Mountains and Miniature Worlds: Altar Design among the Nahua of Northern Veracruz, Mexico. In *Mesas and Cosmologies in Mesoamerica* (Douglas Sharon, ed.): 51–70. Museum Papers 42. San Diego Museum of Man, San Diego, Calif.

Sandstrom, Alan R., and Pamela Effrein Sandstrom

 1986 *Traditional Papermaking and Paper Cult Figures of Mexico.* University of Oklahoma Press, Norman.

Spores, Ronald

 1983 Mixtec Religion. In *The Cloud People: Divergent Evolution of the Zapotec and Mixtec Civilizations* (Kent V. Flannery and Joyce Marcus, eds.): 342–345. Academic Press, New York.

Taggart, James M.

 1983 *Nahuat Myth and Social Structure.* University of Texas Press, Austin.

Vogt, Evon Z.

 1969 *Zinacantan: A Maya Community in the Highlands of Chiapas.* Belknap Press of Harvard University Press, Cambridge, Mass.

 1981 Some Aspects of the Sacred Geography of Highland Chiapas. In *Mesoamerican Sites and World Views* (Elizabeth P. Benson, ed.): 119–138. Dumbarton Oaks, Washington, D.C.

 1993 *Tortillas for the Gods: A Symbolic Analysis of Zinacanteco Rituals.* University of Oklahoma Press, Norman.

 1999 Communicating with the Mountain Gods among the Modern Maya. *Pre-Columbian Art Institute Newsletter* 30: 11–14.

Watanabe, John M.

 1992 *Maya Saints and Souls in a Changing World.* University of Texas Press, Austin.

THREE

HOW MONTE ALBÁN REPRESENTED ITSELF

Joyce Marcus

THE THEME OF THIS VOLUME is how the people of different Mesoamerican cities viewed themselves, and my specific assignment is to describe the city of Monte Albán (Figure 1). This task is difficult, because unlike some Aztec cities, no relevant written records from Monte Albán exist. What can be done is to suggest how Monte Albán represented itself—the principles of organization its rulers and architects selected, and the kinds of art, architecture, and hieroglyphic texts they commissioned through time. In the process of reviewing such information, I (1) describe how a "Grand Plaza" design was developed at Monte Albán and later imposed on at least one second-tier settlement; (2) argue that Monte Albán saw itself as the capital of a militaristic, expansionist state early in its history, but later as more of a religious and elite center; (3) suggest what the ancient name of Monte Albán might have been; and (4) compare Monte Albán with other ancient cities.

MONTE ALBÁN'S ARCHITECTURE

Shortly after 500 B.C., when at least 2,000 people abruptly moved to the top of a mountain in the center of the Oaxaca Valley, they probably had no master plan for converting a mountaintop into an orderly city with a symmetrical layout. Instead, the new residents simply built themselves houses and began work on a defensive wall. They also selected areas for at least three public buildings, choosing locations that take advantage of natural stone outcrops to form the core of those monumental structures (Acosta 1965; Caso et al. 1967; Flannery and Marcus 1983a: fig. 4.3).

The three known Monte Albán I (500–100 B.C.) public buildings do not seem to form a coherent plan, although there might be other buildings still buried that complement those already discovered (Figure 2). However, by 100 B.C. the outlines of a master plan had begun to appear.

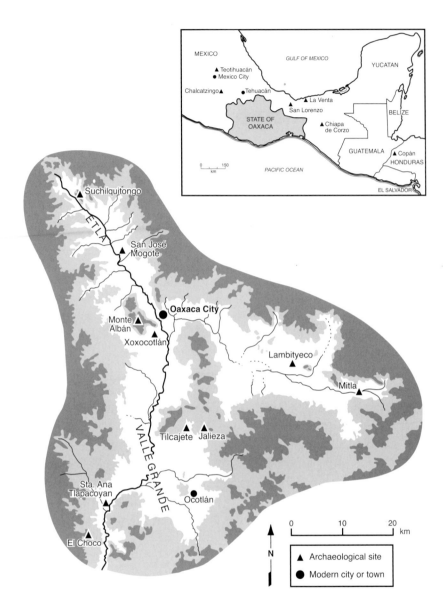

FIGURE 1. Maps showing (top) the state of Oaxaca in Mexico and (bottom) the Valley of Oaxaca. Drawn by Kay Clahassey.

"Grand Plaza" Design of the Zapotec Capital

An old *Official Guide*, published by the Instituto Nacional de Antropología e Historia (INAH), suggests that Monte Albán's Great Plaza "can best be seen at sunset" and "conveys an impression of unrivaled majesty and calm beauty" (INAH 1968: 8). How did the Zapotec convey both unrivaled majesty and calm beauty? They did so in at least three ways: (1) by leveling a huge area delimited by impressive monumental structures, (2) by controlling access to that open space, and (3) by creating the overall semblance of

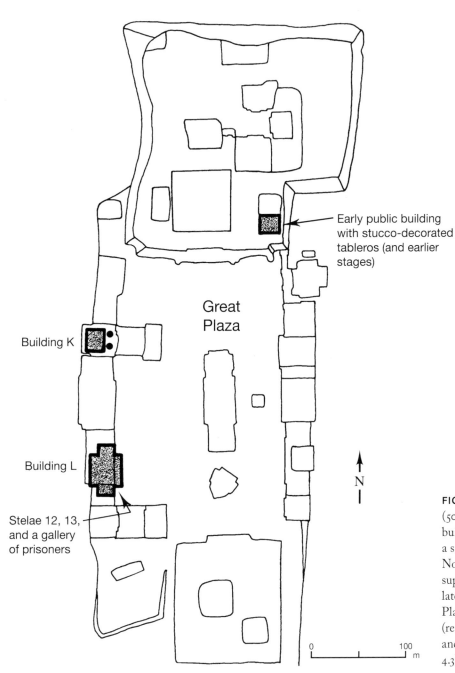

Great
Plaza

Early public building
with stucco-decorated
tableros (and earlier
stages)

Building K

Building L

Stelae 12, 13,
and a gallery
of prisoners

N

0   100
                        m

FIGURE 2. Three Period I
(500–100 B.C.) public
buildings—K, L, and
a structure below the
North Platform—shown
superimposed on what
later became the Great
Plaza at Monte Albán
(redrawn from Flannery
and Marcus 1983a: fig.
4.3).

perfect symmetry. This apparent symmetry is what many tourists first note
when they enter the Great Plaza (Figure 3).

The ancient architects imposed order on what had been a mountaintop
of irregular rock outcrops and depressions. To create the Great Plaza during Monte Albán II (100 B.C.–A.D. 200), the architects leveled off an area
300 m × 200 m and paved it with white plaster. As they proceeded, they
removed rock outcrops or covered them with structures to hide them from

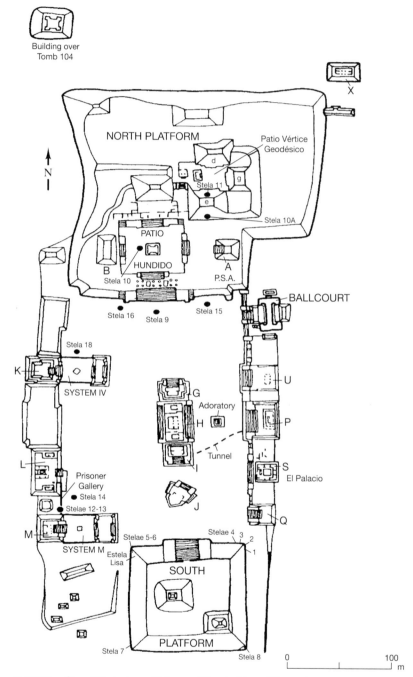

FIGURE 3. Simplified plan of Monte Albán's Great Plaza, showing that the central spine of structures (G, H, I, and J) was not equidistant from both the western and eastern sides of the plaza. The ancient architects created extensions called System IV and System M to make the western flank of structures seem closer to the central spine (adapted from Flannery 1983: fig 4.12).

view. Cores of natural rock still exist inside the North and South Platforms at opposite ends of the plaza, and despite their appearance, the immense stairways of the North and South Platforms are neither perfectly aligned nor symmetrical. In the middle of the Great Plaza, architects opted to leave a series of natural outcrops, using them as the core of a string of buildings (G, H, I, and J) that supported temples and altars. Not surprisingly, that decision ensured that the central spine does not correspond exactly to the midline of the Great Plaza.

An even more glaring lack of genuine symmetry is seen in the rows of structures built over outcrops on the sides of the Great Plaza. The western row of buildings (from K to M) and the eastern row (from the ballcourt to Q) were not equidistant from the central spine. In fact, the west flank is roughly 120 m from the central spine, whereas the east flank lies 60 m away. The ancient architects solved this problem of asymmetry "with a solution worthy of Le Corbusier," as Ignacio Bernal so aptly stated six decades ago (Bernal n.d. [1946]: 8). The architects decided to construct temples midway between the western row of buildings and the central spine, and to connect those temples to the western row of buildings. These extensions to the western row of buildings were called *sistemas* by Alfonso Caso (1938); thus, System IV includes Building K and its temple, whereas System M includes Building M and its temple. These extensions—walls, courtyards, altars, and temples—not only made the Great Plaza look symmetrical, but also allowed the architects to cover earlier (Monte Albán I) constructions with new buildings.

Symmetry, Master Plans, and Architects

Why did Monte Albán's master planners go to such lengths to achieve symmetry, and what does such a layout imply about a city? A symmetrical layout suggests order, perhaps even a new political order that establishes urban policies. In Middle Kingdom Egypt, for example, the city of Thebes was considered the model for a city and was often referred to as *the* city because its layout was a grid that had been imposed to create order. Egyptologist Barry Kemp states that "for the Middle Kingdom we can speak of urbanization as a policy of the state, achieved by laying out pre-planned settlements which in their rigid grid-plans reflected an intense bureaucratic control of society" (Kemp 1991: 202).

Master plans can also be implemented by rulers with new religious beliefs, as happened in Egypt during the reign of Akhenaten. Five years into his reign, Akhenaten decided to build an entirely new royal city at a new location. He did so to honor Aten, the Sun Disk, and he called his new city Akhetaten, "The Horizon of the Aten." This ruler began to describe himself with the phrase "he who lives on *maat*," an epithet that formerly had been the prerogative of gods, as *maat* meant "truth," "justice," and "the correct order of the universe." The limits of Akhenaten's new city were recorded on stelae, placed to delimit an area 16 km × 13 km. Similar boundary stelae are known for the ancient Maya; for example, the twelfth ruler of Copan set up "boundary stelae" that probably established various mountain shrines as stopping places in the ruler's ceremonial circuit.

Estimates of Akhetaten's population are 20,000–40,000, making this Egyptian city comparable in size to Richard Blanton's (1978) estimate for Monte Albán at its peak. Akhenaten, who lived in a fortified palace at the north end of Akhetaten, emerged occasionally to descend in splendor to the central city. It is not hard to imagine the Zapotec ruler descending from his palace on the North Platform at Monte Albán to visit the buildings in the Great Plaza.

The Egyptian data also suggest that planning can reflect and reinforce the dichotomy of chaos and order. The Egyptians believed that chaos could be beaten back by a ruler who could create a master plan. To be sure, a master plan implies not only a master planner but also a master architect. For one of Egypt's pyramids—the Step Pyramid—we actually know the names of the planner and his architect. It was the ruler Djoser who charged the legendary architect Imhotep with building the Step Pyramid. In hieroglyphic texts Imhotep is honored as the "seal bearer of the King of Lower Egypt."

The Zapotec must have had their Imhoteps, but sadly, we know neither the names of the rulers who created the master plan nor the names of the architects who carried it out. Providing those names was not a major concern of those who commissioned Zapotec texts. All that can be inferred is that the Zapotec and Egyptians were similarly concerned with symmetry and order.

Models

Some ancient states, like Rome, left plans of whole cities. For the Zapotec, however, only miniature models of individual buildings have been recovered. Some of these models are made of baked clay, whereas others are stone. One ceramic model, painted red on cream, shows an open-air temple with pairs of columns on each side instead of walls and a giant macaw emerging from the center of the floor (Figure 4). The roof of this temple, which includes an abbreviated sky glyph, slopes downward. This remarkable Monte Albán II ceramic model was found in Offering 1, deeply buried below Building B on Monte Albán's North Platform (Caso and Bernal 1952: fig. 502 bis). The model is not fanciful, as a similar open-air temple (Building II) has been excavated at Monte Albán. According to Ignacio Bernal, it was a "small temple with five pillars in the front and five in the back. . . . It never had side walls and in fact was open to the four winds" (Bernal 1985: 54). On the south side of this open-air temple excavators found the entrance to a tunnel that appears to have been in use only during Monte Albán II (see Figure 3). This tunnel allowed priests to move between buildings on the central spine and those on the east side of the Great Plaza without being seen.

FIGURE 4. Ceramic model depicting an open-air temple with a giant macaw emerging from the floor, found in Offering 1, deeply buried below Building B on the North Platform at Monte Albán. Height 49.5 cm. Drawn by John Klausmeyer from a painting in Caso and Bernal (1952: fig. 502 bis).

Of the models made of stone, some appear to depict temple or tomb facades that honored an ancestor (Easby and Scott 1970; Marcus and Flannery 1996: 223; Marquina 1951). The hieroglyphic names of these ancestors (given as day-names from the 260-day calendar) were usually carved on the exterior of the building—in the doorway, above the door lintel, and even on the rooftop. One model honors an individual whose name, 3 E (Caso 1928), appears inside the temple doorway (Figure 5).

Another model shows a deified ancestor who holds a copal bag in his left hand and possibly copal in his right (Figure 6; see also Batres 1902: plate XXV). This individual's name, 1 L, is carved on the top of the stone model and thus can only be seen when looking down at the roof (this name, 1 L, is the same as that of the sacrificial victim depicted on Monument 3 at San José Mogote, a man who died hundreds of years earlier; see Marcus and Flannery 2004).

By including a hieroglyphic name such as 1 L on the outside of a temple or tomb, the architect ensures that the commemorated individual will not be forgotten, because the exterior of his temple and tomb continue to evoke his name and memory (Easby and Scott 1970: fig. 165; Marquina 1951: foto 151). In the doorway, we see a bird diving downward, perhaps the kind of bird who brought messages from the deceased to their living descendants. Similarly, the facade of Tomb 104 at Monte Albán features one large urn that depicts an elaborately attired ancestor who sports a nose plug, pectoral, and headdress honoring Cociyo, or Lightning. This urn was set within a recessed niche (Caso 1938: fig. 92; Marcus and Flannery 1996: fig. 251); such framing draws attention to this ancestor's portrait. That these kinds of frames can be associated with ancestors is also seen on stone models; for example, see Figure 6, where framing elements flank the stairway and the bust of an ancestor named 1 L. Setting ancestors within a frame is also seen on the facade of Tomb 6 at Lambityeco, a site in the eastern arm of the Valley of Oaxaca. Tomb 6 was reopened at various times between A.D. 650 and 750. Over the entrance are modeled faces of an ancestral pair, a man named 1 L and a woman named 10 J or 10 Maize (Figure 7); in front of the entrance archaeologists found urns and vessels placed there on different occasions (Lind 2003; Lind and Urcid 1983; Miller 1995; Rabin 1970: 12, fig. 18). Several

FIGURE 5. Stone model of a flat-roofed temple or tomb dedicated to the memory of 3 E, whose hieroglyphic name is given in the entryway. The architectural detail known as double scapulary decorates the platform. Drawn by John Klausmeyer.

FIGURE 6. Stone model of a temple or tomb showing the three-dimensional bust of 1 L, whose name is given on the roof (not shown). In the doorway is a descending bird that may be the messenger that transmitted information between 1 L and the descendants of 1 L. Double scapulary elements decorate the upper zone of the structure, flanking the bust of 1 L, and they also flank the stairway of the platform. Drawn by John Klausmeyer.

FIGURE 7. Portraits of an ancestral marital pair named 1 L and 10 J, each set into a "picture frame." The portraits were located above the entrance to Tomb 6 at Lambityeco. Drawn and painted by John Klausmeyer.

vessels depict Cociyo, the supernatural being most closely associated with the Zapotec elite (Caso and Bernal 1952; Marcus 1983a, 2006).

Placing ancestors within a frame was also used by the ancient Maya (for example, on Stela 1 at Ek' Balam, Mexico) and could be used to indicate ascending generations and marital pairs, as seen on Stela 11 at Yaxchilán, Mexico, where Bird Jaguar's parents are framed by hieroglyphic texts that supply their names (Marcus 1992b: figs. 9.16, 11.5). The Maya ruler Bird Jaguar commissioned this monument not only to show his parents sitting above him (where they serve to legitimize him) but also to show himself standing above kneeling prisoners (demonstrating his military prowess, which fulfills one of the prerequisites for taking office). Still another Maya example of framing ancestors can be seen on Stela 40 at Piedras Negras, Guatemala, where Ruler 4 kneels above his mother's final resting place. Her cavelike tomb is shown as a quatrefoil cartouche that frames her head and torso, which rest on top of a bier or throne (Morley 1937: plate 135b).

Carving the name of a ruler or deified ancestor on the facade of a tomb or temple was, of course, not the only way that the Zapotec could honor someone. Another was to place a vessel carved with that individual's name in a dedicatory cache below a temple floor. Such a cache was found by Alfonso Caso below a temple floor in Building I on the central spine of the Great Plaza (Figures 3, 8). This Monte Albán III cache included a Cociyo urn containing 24 greenstone figurines in Teotihuacan style and a large cylindrical (putative drinking) vessel, carved with the hieroglyphs 3 J (3 Maize), containing a beautifully polished jade figurine. Although this Building I cache could be interpreted in various ways, it is possible that the vessel records the name of a revered royal ancestor, 3 Maize, honored by the dedication of a new temple and by an offering of 24 figurines from Teotihuacan. This interpretation would be bolstered if the Building I temple had borne the hieroglyphic name 3 Maize on its facade, as seen on some of the stone models (Figure 9).

These building models are important because they reveal details of

FIGURE 8. The hill, now called Monte Albán, that had to be leveled to create a Great Plaza. The plaza's diverse structures (temples, tombs, palaces, and ballcourt) housed specialized personnel that administered this Zapotec capitol. Drawn by John Klausmeyer.

FIGURE 9. Pottery vessel with the name 3 J (3 Maize), found in a cache below the floor of a temple in Building I, Monte Albán. Redrawn by John Klausmeyer from Caso et al. (1967: fig. 273e).

Zapotec temples and tombs that are rarely recovered archaeologically. They show that Zapotec tombs and temples might have flat roofs, be decorated with double scapulary motifs on platforms (Figure 10) or upper facades (Figure 11), have cloth and feather curtains hanging in the doorway to ensure privacy (Figure 12), and display the names of royal ancestors on their facades or elsewhere (see Figures 5, 6). These details in the models indicate some of the ways Zapotec structures were viewed by their occupants. Although these stone and ceramic models have not been found in primary contexts, it is possible that offerings were made in front of such models if they were set up in the patios and tombs of noble residences. If several such models were to be found in situ, they would enhance our understanding of their function.

Zapotec architects were, of course, not the only ones to create models of temples and shrines dedicated to ancestors. Such models are also known for the ancient Maya and Egyptians. At the Maya site of Copan, Honduras, stone models representing shrines were carved to honor ancestors and supernatural patrons. Short hieroglyphic texts on these models

FIGURE 10. Temple platform at Monte Albán showing three levels or tiers, each decorated with the architectural decoration called double scapulary (from Marcus and Flannery 1996: fig. 266).

FIGURE 11. Stone model showing double scapulary above the doorway and cornice (see Figure 10, which shows this architectural detail on one of several buildings at Monte Albán); this kind of double scapulary is similar to that framing the ancestral pair depicted on the outside of Tomb 6 at Lambityeco in Figure 7. Drawn by John Klausmeyer.

FIGURE 12. Stone model of a structure that shows a curtain closing off its doorway. The double scapulary above the cornice on this model can be compared with the rectangular elements that frame the portraits on the outside of the Zapotec tomb shown in Figure 7. Drawn by John Klausmeyer.

FIGURE 13. Stone model of a shrine that honors the deity and spirit companion of Yax Pasaj, the Maya ruler of Copan, Honduras. Drawn by Kay Clahassey from Andrews and Fash (1992: fig. 16) and Freidel et al. (1993: fig. 4.4).

refer to companion spirits or ancestors and describe the shrine as the venue where that spirit could come to rest. The front of the shrine usually has a recessed doorway in which the ancestral spirit or patron is placed (Figure 13). Examples of such miniature shrines have been found in association with a "conjuring temple" (Copan's Structure 10L-29), a place where the spirit of an ancestor or supernatural patron (Chaak) was invoked (Andrews and Fash 1992: figs. 16, 17; Freidel et al. 1993: 188–190). From Chaak, the sixteenth ruler of Copan received supernatural power (and such help may have been needed, because he did not inherit the throne from his father; Andrews and Bill 2005: 293). The facade of the conjuring temple (Structure 10L-29) displayed cloud scrolls and ancestor cartouches, had niches for offerings, and showed traces of soot and burning on its floor where incense burners had been placed.

The Egyptians also carved stone shrines (called *naos*) with niches; they placed a divine statue inside that recessed area (Kemp 1991: 88; Figure 14). These Egyptian statues were placed in a position similar to the urn set into a niche on the facade of Tomb 104 at Monte Albán (Marcus and Flannery 1996: fig. 251). In our small sample of three societies—Zapotec, Maya, and Egyptian—there seems to have been independent, but parallel, invention of miniature stone models that depict temples, shrines, and tombs as well as the ancestors, spirits, or patrons to whom such buildings were dedicated.

How State Emergence Affected Monte Albán's Master Plan

As early as 100 B.C., Oaxaca society was organized as a state, and an expansionist one at that. As a result, the rulers during Monte Albán II believed that the time was right to embark on an impressive campaign of public construction. They had by that time already subjugated local enemies, incorporated rival polities, and established colonies as far away as the Cañada de Cuicatlán and the Valley of Sola de Vega (Balkansky 2002; Marcus and Flannery 1996: 195–207; Spencer and Redmond 2001a,b).

Virtually every archaeologically recoverable institution of Monte Albán II reflects a state level of political organization. At this time there were some 518 communities in the Valley of Oaxaca, with an estimated population of 41,000 (Kowalewski et al. 1989). Several attributes of the settlement system indicate that the entire Valley of Oaxaca was then under the control of a state whose capital was Monte Albán. The central region of the Valley of Oaxaca, populated during Late Period I with 155 satellite communities, had been reduced to 23 such communities. In other words, Monte Albán no longer needed to concentrate thousands of farmers, warriors, and laborers within 15 km of the city, because its rulers could now count on the support of the entire valley.

During this period Monte Albán itself occupied 416 ha with a population estimated at 14,500, and it administered a four-tiered hierarchy of settlements. Ranked below the capital were six towns with estimated populations of 1,000–2,000 people. All these Tier 2 sites lay between 14 and 28 km of Monte Albán, less than a day's trip. Even the fourth largest of these Tier 2 towns, San José Mogote, covered 60–70 ha and had several public buildings. Tier 3 of the political hierarchy consisted of at least 30 places, each occupying 5–10 ha, with populations estimated at 200–700 persons. Some of these smaller towns include public buildings. Tier 4 consisted of

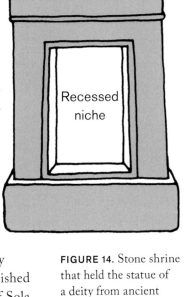

FIGURE 14. Stone shrine that held the statue of a deity from ancient Egypt (redrawn from Kemp 1991: fig. 31). Compare this Egyptian shrine to the Maya shrine in Figure 13.

more than 400 small villages with estimated populations of fewer than 200 people.

Diversification of Building Types at Monte Albán

By Period II at Monte Albán, the Great Plaza had assumed much of the form seen today, featuring the multifunctional North Platform; many two-room temples; a ballcourt; adoratorios; and the arrowhead-shaped Building J, with its hieroglyphic inventory of more than 40 places claimed by Monte Albán as the limits of its territory. The sheer variety of institutions and specialized personnel represented by these discrete building types, combined with the evidence for a four-tier administrative hierarchy, suggests that Monte Albán had become the capital of a territorial state. As impressive as its Great Plaza was, Monte Albán controlled access to it by narrowing the openings at each corner, allowing the public to enter only when permitted by the ruling elite. The Great Plaza was a spectacular place but a private one except on special occasions. Let us now look at a series of its functionally distinct buildings.

Colonnaded Two-Room Temple   Prior to Late Monte Albán I (Period Ic), all temples in the Valley of Oaxaca consisted of one room. During Late Monte Albán I, a second room was added to the temple, converting it from a generalized religious structure to the yohopee or "House of the Vital Force" described in sixteenth-century Spanish accounts. The oldest fully exposed two-room temple is Structure 16 of San Martín Tilcajete, excavated by Charles Spencer and Elsa Redmond (2004: fig. 5). The addition of a second room is significant, and it was probably done to accommodate full-time priests who lived in the inner room of the temple. Spanish eyewitness accounts of later Zapotec temples relate that although high priests (*uijatao*) had comfortable residences, coming and going as they saw fit, the minor priests (*bigaña*) never left the temples. Ethnohistorical data suggest that rulers ordered such temples to be built and underwrote the cost of construction as acts of royal piety. In some cases, before a new temple could be built, it was necessary to perform a ritual of sanctification. This rite converted secular to sacred ground, often requiring the burial of costly or labor-intensive offerings below the temple floor (Caso 1938; Marcus and Flannery 1994, 2004).

Why did Monte Albán build so many contemporaneous temples? Some possibilities are that (1) each temple was dedicated to a different ancestor, deity, or function; (2) different neighborhoods in the city had exclusive privileges in and access to specific temples; or (3) each noble lineage was responsible for constructing and maintaining its own temple in the city.

One Monte Albán II temple, located atop Building X to the northeast of the North Platform at Monte Albán (see Figure 3), was reached by a stuccoed stairway running the length of the south side of the building. The inner, higher, and more sacred room of this two-room temple had a plastered basin (*tlecuil*) set in the floor; it also had a masonry offering box in the back of the room, at the midline of the temple (Marcus 1978). The basin and offering box probably relate to the receipt of offerings and the bloodletting of sacrificial animals performed by the priests occupying the inner room.

Such temples were the most numerous type of public building at Monte Albán, and unlike Building X, most faced toward the rising or setting sun. Indeed, it would appear that the reason the long axis of the Great Plaza ran north-south was to allow the temples lining both sides to have their doorways facing east or west when they opened onto the Plaza (see Figure 3). Below one of the temples in the Building I sequence, Caso found an offering consisting of Monte Albán II pottery, a necklace of marine shell, flower-shaped jade earspools, two mosaic masks (one of jade and turquoise, the other of pyrite and shell), and a bone carved in the shape of a chess pawn; these objects were found in a typical Monte Albán II offering box. There were also bird bones below and around the box, perhaps the remains of sacrificed birds.

Adoratory Between Buildings P and H of the Great Plaza, and directly in front of the stairway of Building H, lies a sunken adoratory (see Figure 3). This multilevel construction is set in a large rectangular recessed area in such a way that its upper surface is roughly level with the stucco floor of the plaza (Figure 15). Here excavators discovered an important multiple burial (Burial XIV-10) to the east of the adoratory. At least five individuals lay on a flagstone floor that runs partly under the adoratory. They were associated with multiple jade necklaces, flower-shaped jade earspools, masks and pectorals of jade, pearls, conchs, and other marine shells. Most of the individuals seem to be young people. One wore as his pectoral a magnificent bat mask that has long been considered a masterpiece of Zapotec art. The bat mask is composed of 25 separate pieces of jade, which, when fitted together, form the face of a man disguised as a bat; the mask's eyes and teeth are made from marine shell (Marcus and Flannery 1996: following p. 32). Most Oaxaca specialists believe that the individuals in this multiperson burial were sacrificial victims associated with an event of some importance that involved the adoratory. Like some sacrificial victims in later Mesoamerican societies, they may have been elaborately dressed and adorned to impersonate or stand in for deities or legendary figures.

Tunnel under the Great Plaza During Monte Albán II, the architects of Monte Albán constructed a tunnel below the Great Plaza that links

FIGURE 15. Adoratory to the east of the central spine of buildings in the Great Plaza of Monte Albán. A multiperson sacrificial burial and a jade bat mask were both found here.

Building P with the buildings on the central spine (see Figure 3). Jorge Acosta (1974) found four Period II offerings inside the tunnel and suggested that the tunnel was used only during that period. The function of these tunnels is not known, but perhaps they were used to allow a priest to stand in a Building P temple, perform a rite, and then disappear into the tunnel, only to reappear in one of the temples on the central spine. If the attendees of this rite had no knowledge of the tunnel, such a disappearing and reappearing act would have been quite impressive, perhaps adding more mystery to the movements of the priests. There were such secret passageways at Monte Negro (Acosta and Romero 1992: fig. 41) and San José Mogote (Marcus and Flannery 1996: fig. 203).

North and South Platforms   Two immense platforms fill the space at the north and south ends of the Great Plaza. The North Platform supported a sunken court, or Patio Hundido (Figure 16); royal residences and temples; and several areas where private royal rituals and administrative decisions could have been made. In contrast to the diversity of structures and activity areas on the North Platform, the South Platform seems to have been devoted mainly to religious rituals. Both monumental platforms had wide, steep, impressive stairways, making those structures more

FIGURE 16. Sunken patio on the North Platform at Monte Albán. This photo was taken near the spot where Stela 10A was found.

forbidding to those standing below on the Plaza floor and perhaps indicating that these platforms were restricted to royalty and state-sponsored ceremonies.

Replication of the Master Plan at San José Mogote

Settlement pattern studies show that during Monte Albán II, five second-tier administrative centers existed that ranked below Monte Albán. These secondary centers had diverse layouts, but the northernmost, San José Mogote, had a Great Plaza laid out on the Monte Albán model (Figure 17, left). The plazas at Monte Albán and San José Mogote had ballcourts in the shape of a capital I (Figure 17, right). San José Mogote, however, never had more than one ballcourt, and Monte Albán eventually came to have at least seven (Flannery and Marcus 1983b).

Mound 8 at San José Mogote, which forms the northern limit of its Main Plaza, corresponds to the North Platform at Monte Albán (Marcus and Flannery 1996: figs. 200–202). Mound 8 also supported a governmental structure with a sunken patio, reached by climbing a wide stairway and passing through a colonnaded portico (Figure 18). Monte Albán's portico, however, had a double row of six columns, whereas that in San José Mogote

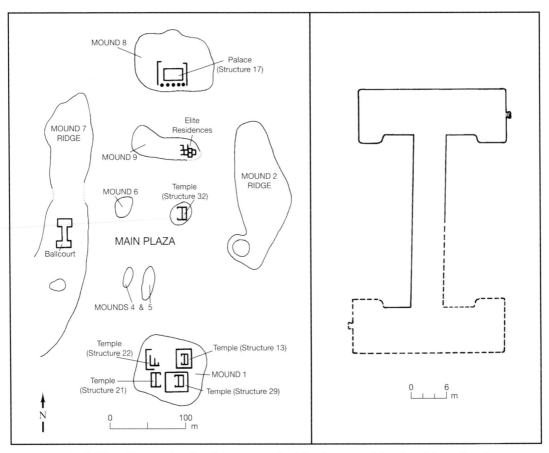

FIGURE 17. (left) Main Plaza at San José Mogote and (right) a drawing of San José Mogote's ballcourt.

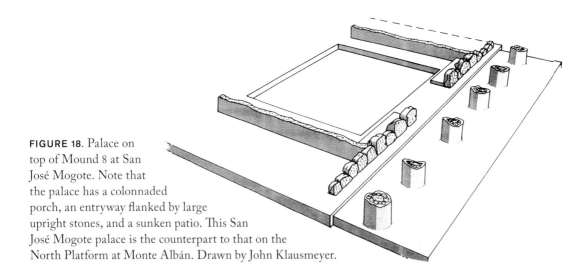

FIGURE 18. Palace on top of Mound 8 at San José Mogote. Note that the palace has a colonnaded porch, an entryway flanked by large upright stones, and a sunken patio. This San José Mogote palace is the counterpart to that on the North Platform at Monte Albán. Drawn by John Klausmeyer.

had a single row of six columns. Monte Albán's sunken patio was 50 m across and 4 m deep; San José Mogote's was 20 m across and shallower. Both structures were probably used as places for governmental assembly.

Both Monte Albán and San José Mogote had two-room temples along both sides of the plaza, as well as temples placed on natural rises in the plaza. San José Mogote had at least 10 temples in Monte Albán II (Marcus 1999: 71); Monte Albán may have had twice that many. Was anything notable missing at San José Mogote? Yes. Although it had Monte Albán's plaza plan, San José Mogote lacked the official scribes and hieroglyphic texts. Monte Albán evidently was the only place in the valley entitled to commission scribes to write texts at this time. Even though secondary centers like Dainzú did carve ballplayers and other human and animal figures (Bernal 1968), Monte Albán had a near monopoly on hieroglyphic texts.

MONTE ALBÁN'S ART AND WRITING
FROM PERIODS I THROUGH IV

Monte Albán I

All the evidence from settlement pattern data and from excavations at such places as Tilcajete and San José Mogote suggests that the founders of Monte Albán came from the northern and central parts of the valley during a time of interregional conflict. These founders chose Monte Albán as a defensible redoubt, and they built 3 km of defensive wall. Monte Albán was not the only site in the Valley of Oaxaca concerned with defense. Indeed, during Period I more than a third of the valley's population had moved to defensible sites. Monte Albán's concern with military activity is evident not only from its defensible location and defensive wall but also from its carving of 320 monuments of slain enemies, originally set in the facade of Building L (Figure 19).

That display, reminiscent of prisoner galleries from later Maya cities, once contained 80 percent of the carved monuments known from Monte Albán. Presumably to intimidate their rivals at such places as Tilcajete, the leaders of Monte Albán had created the largest propaganda display in the history of the Valley of Oaxaca. A remnant of that display, now buried under Building L, preserves four rows of these slain enemy stones in their original position (Batres 1902). Each stone shows a single male victim, stripped naked, eyes closed, mouth open, and some even feature scrolls of blood that indicate genital mutilation. Most victims are shown sprawling in awkward positions, as they would look to an observer standing over them as they lay on the ground. Had they been displayed horizontally, so that anyone could step on the corpses (as the Maya did with "prisoner staircases"), their correct meaning would have been clear even to the

FIGURE 19. Wall of carved slabs, located between Structures L and M at Monte Albán, constructed in Period I to display a Gallery of Prisoners.

nineteenth-century explorers who first reported them. That the slabs were placed in vertical positions in a wall led early observers to misinterpret them as "dancers." These carvings imply that Monte Albán, at that time, saw itself as the undisputed victor in a series of wars for control of its valley, celebrating the mutilated corpses of its enemies (Marcus 1974).

Monte Albán II

By Monte Albán II, Monte Albán was so preeminent that its rulers did not feel compelled to intimidate their rivals with propaganda displays of hundreds of slain victims. Instead, the Monte Albán II leaders chose to list the names of those regions that represented the limits of the 30,000 km^2 territory over which they claimed authority (Marcus 1992a: fig. 10, 1998: fig. 3.3). The names of these places were displayed on stones set in the most unusual building ever erected in the Great Plaza. Building J was built in the shape of an arrowhead and oriented at an oblique angle that contrasts with the north-south, east-west orientations of other public buildings on the Plaza (Caso 1938). Building J may have functioned both as a war memorial and as a territorial map listing 40 or more places up to 150 km distant that were brought into Monte Albán's sphere either by colonization, conquest, political pressure, or alliance by royal marriage.

Monte Albán III

Political propaganda, military victory, and strategic political alliance continue to be themes during Monte Albán III. The South Platform of Monte

FIGURE 20. Stela 1, Monte Albán, shows (left) the Zapotec ruler atop his throne and (right) two columns of hieroglyphs. Height 2.08 m.

Albán serves as an example. Between A.D. 200 and 500, a Zapotec ruler named 12 Jaguar was inaugurated at Monte Albán. His inauguration rites apparently included the rededication of that huge platform at the south end of the Great Plaza. At least nine stelae (eight of them carved) were set into the base of the South Platform. Six of the stelae display captives with their arms tied behind their backs, and judging by their costumes, it is likely that some were elite captives. They may include prisoners taken by the ruler during military campaigns carried out to prove his military prowess and may have been destined to be sacrificed at his inauguration; later Maya and Aztec rulers were often required to demonstrate such military prowess before they were inaugurated (Marcus 1992b: 353–434). The front of Stela 1 depicts the ruler seated on his magnificent throne, wearing a jaguar costume and holding a staff of office (Figure 20).

Dedicatory offering boxes were placed under three of the corners of the South Platform, often directly below the carved stones. Each box contained 10 spiny oyster shells, 10 tent olive shells, and 7 jade beads (Acosta 1958–59: 27). Similar Classic period offerings of spiny oyster shells and jade beads have been found at Teotihuacan, which makes it all the more interesting that references to Teotihuacan ambassadors were carved on the underside of Stela 1. One of the four ambassadors, 9 Monkey, departs from a temple decorated in Teotihuacan style (Figure 21). A more elaborate ambassadorial scene was carved on the underside of the Estela Lisa, a stone set in the northwest corner of the South Platform. On this stela, the ambassador leaving a Teotihuacan-style temple is also named 9 Monkey (Figure 22). These Teotihuacan ambassadors are shown arriving at a place called Hill of 1 Jaguar (Guie Yobi Beche in Zapotec). Later in this chapter I suggest that Hill of 1 Jaguar was possibly the ancient name for the hill

FIGURE 21. Underside of Stela 1 at Monte Albán. At c is a Teotihuacan-style temple, associated with footprints and the hieroglyphic name 9 Monkey, the name of the Teotihuacan ambassador depicted on the Estela Lisa (see Figure 22). Drawn by Kay Clahassey.

FIGURE 22. Carved stone (known as the Estela Lisa) found associated with the South Platform at Monte Albán. A Zapotec ruler is shown receiving ambassadors from the site of Teotihuacan. At e is the Zapotec ruler wearing a mask and elaborate headdress. Separating him from the procession of Teotihuacan ambassadors is the hieroglyph "Hill of 1 Jaguar," possibly the name for the South Platform or the hill on which the Great Plaza sits. At a is 9 Monkey and a set of footprints leaving from a Teotihuacan-style temple. Drawn by John Klausmeyer.

that was leveled to create Monte Albán's Great Plaza. At this time, Monte Albán represented itself as a place so important that Teotihuacan would send ambassadors to attend the inauguration of its rulers.

Monte Albán IIIb–IV

Monuments carved during Monte Albán IIIb–IV (A.D. 600–900) show less concern with military activity. During this period public construction was waning at Monte Albán itself, while sites elsewhere in the Valley of Oaxaca were busy building. Monuments of this era tend to concentrate on genealogy, social ties, and rituals. In fact, establishing one's dynastic credentials and ritual ties seems to have been more important than boasting of one's conquests. Particularly common are two kinds of carved stones—ritual slabs and genealogical registers. Genealogical registers are usually divided into two or three zones (registers), each depicting relatives and/or royal marital pairs from different generations.

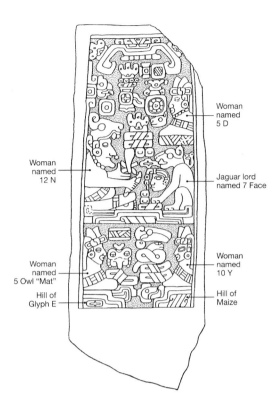

Woman named 5 D

Woman named 12 N

Jaguar lord named 7 Face

Woman named 5 Owl "Mat"

Woman named 10 Y

Hill of Glyph E

Hill of Maize

FIGURE 23. Stela 10A, found south of Temple e and northeast of the sunken patio on the North Platform of Monte Albán. Height: 2.76 m. Drawn by Kay Clahassey and modified by John Klausmeyer from Urcid et al. (1994: fig. 20).

Although few carved stones from Period IIIb–IV have been recovered at Monte Albán itself, one of them was a stela (here called Stela 10A; Figure 23) found south of the Patio Vértice Geodésico, on the steps of Temple e (see Figure 3). This area on the North Platform—described as the most private and least accessible place at Monte Albán based on ekistic (traffic flow) studies (Blanton 1978: 61–63)—includes three temples that delimit a patio. Stela 10A seems to show three generations. The earliest, at the bottom, includes two women sitting on hill signs, each representing a distinct town. The middle register shows an old woman named 12 N and a deified/metamorphosed lord named 7 Face. The upper register shows just one person, a woman named 5 D whose nickname includes two glyphs—Caso's Glyph E and Glyph G (Urcid et al. 1994). It is likely that this 2.7-m-tall monument was commissioned by 5 D to provide her genealogy and dynastic credentials. To legitimize herself, 5 D used the middle register to feature her elderly mother and deceased father (perhaps a former ruler who, in death, metamorphosed into a jaguar lord) and the lowest register to honor two aunts or grandmothers who came to Monte Albán from different towns.

Not far from Stela 10A, another carved stone, designated Stela 10 by Alfonso Caso (1928: 92–93), was discovered on the floor of the sunken court of the North Platform (see Figure 3). Like Stela 10A, Stela 10 seems to depict more women than men, and both stelae show multiple genera-

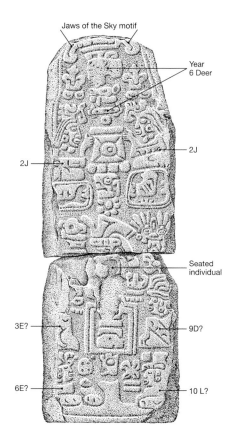

FIGURE 24. Stela 10, found in the sunken patio, North Platform, Monte Albán. Height: 2.92 m. Drawn by Mark Orsen.

tions. At the bottom of Stela 10 are two remote ancestors (Figure 24). The hieroglyphic name of the person on the left may be 6 E and that of the person on the right may be 10 L. Above them are two seated individuals (regarded as men by Caso), named 3 E and 9 D. At the center is a seated individual. Near the top are two people (regarded as women by Caso), both associated with the same hieroglyphic name, 2 J (Caso 1928: fig. 55). Above are the Jaws of the Sky, a motif referring to noble descent (Marcus 1992b: 84, 208, 238; 2002: fig. 7.22).

These two stones, Stelae 10 and 10A, may have been carved at about the same time and perhaps displayed near each other. Since these stelae stood more than 2.7 m high when intact, they may have been visible to everyone occupying the North Platform. Perhaps because there were so many competing dynasties at several sites, the Zapotec of this period at Monte Albán and elsewhere invested considerable energy in carving genealogical records (Marcus 1983b).

These records were commissioned by the descendants of local dynastic founders to show their connections to noble ancestors. To demonstrate their ties to those ancestors, they constructed multigenerational family tombs that were kept accessible so that additional family members could be added, new offerings inserted, and murals and friezes repainted or altered.

Thus the final magnificence of some royal tombs should be credited not only to the original occupant but also to the heirs who added offerings, repainted murals, and commissioned new genealogical stelae in which they were included (Marcus 2003; Miller 1991, 1995). It is clear that by this period Monte Albán was seen as a place where deceased rulers and noble couples gave legitimacy to their living descendants—even if some of their remote ancestors had come to Monte Albán from other towns.

During Period IIIb–IV, Monte Albán's political power and regional influence began to decline. It was therefore an era in which new patterns of elite interaction were established. Many communities, once subject to Monte Albán's authority, were now free to forge their own alliances and even to carve their own monuments and use Zapotec hieroglyphic writing. The monopoly on texts had been broken. New centers were aided in their self-promotion by Monte Albán's loss of this monopoly on writing. Many rival centers acquired the necessary authority, scribes, and stone carvers to create texts. Elite families throughout the valley could now commission monuments to record their genealogies and document political and ritual events. Many former secondary or tertiary centers had become heads of their own local polities, including Cuilapan, Jalieza, Lambityeco, Matatlan, Mitla, Suchilquitongo, Xoxocotlan, and Zaachila (Marcus 1983b, 1989, 2006). Each of these centers had a chance to move up in the political hierarchy if it chose the right strategy.

Instead of commissioning huge monuments, like those previously displayed in the Great Plaza, the new Zapotec elite at Monte Albán (and elsewhere in the Valley of Oaxaca) commissioned smaller slabs that depicted local nobility, gave the names of their relatives, and showed them participating in diverse rituals. When found in situ, most of these monuments were in or near temples and tombs. Unlike the vertical propaganda of the Monte Albán I Prisoner Gallery—which presented information designed to impress followers and intimidate enemies—the monuments of Period IIIb–IV conveyed horizontal propaganda, that is, information commissioned by nobles to be read principally by other nobles (Marcus 1992b: 10–12). During this era of changing politics, horizontal linkages between elites became as important as the vertical links between elites and commoners had been.

Nobles also bonded with other nobles by inviting them to participate in funerals, weddings, and other ritual ceremonies. Possibly relevant to the latter is a carved stone found in association with Structure III, a temple on top of the South Platform, which shows an elaborately dressed figure holding an apparent leaf of *toloache* (*Datura* sp.), a hallucinogenic plant used by the Zapotec to induce visions (Marcus and Flannery 1978: 74). The date of the rite involving this plant may be given above an ancestor cartouche, which may contain the image of an ancestor (Figure 25).

FIGURE 25. Stone slab, from the South Platform of Monte Albán, showing a person holding a leaf of *toloache* (*Datura* sp.), a hallucinogenic plant known to induce visions. Drawn by Kay Clahassey and redrawn by John Klausmeyer from Winter (1989: 33).

Although ethnohistorical documents suggest that *toloache* was used to induce visions and communicate with ancestors, no paleobotanical remains of *toloache* have been found so far.

Zapotec monuments dating to A.D. 600–900 often show royal couples, family genealogies, and sacred rituals conducted by the elite. The variety of scenes includes incense burning; food sharing; offering precious items, such as strands of jade beads; and the drinking of ritual beverages, possibly pulque and chocolate. By making a heavy investment in horizontal propaganda and horizontal links such as exchange, marriage, social alliance, funerary ritual, and commemoration of shared ancestors, the Zapotec seem to have developed techniques for preventing elite competition from escalating into warfare. Monte Albán had to invest in social and ritual ties because it no longer had the power to impose its will on all of its neighbors.

TERMS USED BY THE ANCIENT ZAPOTEC FOR "CITY" AND FOR MONTE ALBÁN

The name of the city we call Monte Albán is not given in any ethnohistorical document. However, there is some evidence indicating how the Zapotec conceptualized cities and mountains. According to the Spanish priest Juan de Córdova (1942 [1578]), the Zapotec term for "city" or "populated place" was *queche*. A capital was called *quechecoqui* (city + hereditary lord) and considered the primary town where the ruler resided. Another Zapotec term was *quechetaonabiy*, or "great walled city." Both terms (*quechecoqui* and *quechetaonabiy*) may have been applied to Monte Albán, but there is no way to confirm this suggestion.

Long before Monte Albán became an urban center, it seems likely that the hill itself had a Zapotec name. This tradition of naming individual hills is evident in the Valley of Oaxaca. Examples include Gui binii, a mountain south of Tlacolula; Gui dolaii, a sacred mountain north of Mitla; Guie ngola ("old rocky hill"), a mountaintop fortress near Tehuantepec; Gui gaa, a mountain south of Mitla, now called Nueve Puntas (Nine Points or Nine Peaks); Gui gotz, a mountain northwest of Mitla; Guilá Naquitz, a white cliff south of Díaz Ordaz; and Gui run, a mountain east of Mitla.

Mountains in Oaxaca seem to have had multiple functions, serving as sacred landmarks, natural territorial boundaries, refuge areas, defensible promontories, and ritual altars. The Zapotec considered mountains to be living, sacred beings. Like the highland Tzotzil Maya of Zinacantán (Vogt 1969), today's Zapotec anthropomorphize mountains, labeling them with the same terms used for the human body. In Zapotec, the summit of a

FIGURE 26. Pair of pottery vessels commemorating the noble marital pair named (left) 1 Jaguar and (right) 2 Maize. Drawn by John Klausmeyer.

mountain is called its head; the sides are its ribs; the front is its face; the back is its back; and the base of the hill is its foot (Robert MacLaury, personal communication, June 1978). Regarding mountains as sacred, living landmarks was a widespread belief in Mexico, and so was the custom of using a hill sign to designate places. Indeed, the Zapotec may have been the first to use a hill sign to designate landmarks and place names (Caso 1947; Marcus 1992a).

Monte Albán extends over more than one hill. It comprises the main hill (the location of the Great Plaza) and a series of nearby hills, today called El Gallo, Atzompa, Mogotillo, and Monte Albán Chico. Each hill may once have had its own name in Zapotec. It is possible that the main hill of Monte Albán took its name from a legendary marital pair, two primordial founders named Lord 1 Jaguar and Lady 2 Maize.

This venerated couple is honored on numerous ceramic vessels whose shape suggests that the vessels were used for ritual drinking. Paired gray ware beakers bearing the carved and excised names 1 Jaguar and 2 Maize have been found together in caches and tombs. Although they usually occur as a matching pair of vessels (Figure 26), on some occasions the two vessels are joined together. It is likely that 1 Jaguar and 2 Maize were the Zapotec equivalent of the primordial Mixtec founding couple, both called 1 Deer.

In addition to beakers recording the names 1 Jaguar and 2 Maize, one carved stone from the South Platform at Monte Albán shows the place called Hill of 1 Jaguar in association with a Zapotec ruler (see Figure 22). This Hill of 1 Jaguar was the destination for ambassadors from Teotihuacan, and might refer to the hill on which the South Platform and Great Plaza sit.

As for the names of the other hills comprising Monte Albán, only a few clues have been found. One of these is the carving of a trilobed heart set inside a hill sign. This glyph appears on Stela 8 in the South Platform and

FIGURE 27. Possible names for either the entire city of Monte Albán or specific locations within the city: (top) Hill of Trilobed Heart, carved on the upper surface of Stela 8, Monte Albán (redrawn from Marcus 1992b: fig. 10.12); (bottom) Hill of Trilobed Heart, carved on Lápida 44, Building J, Monte Albán (redrawn from Caso 1947: fig. 49).

on a slab set into the wall of Building J (Figure 27). This glyph, perhaps "Hill of the Heart" or "Hill of Sacrifice," may have belonged to one of the other hills constituting Monte Albán, but this is no more than speculation.

COMPARING MONTE ALBÁN TO OTHER CITIES

Other than the secondary center of San José Mogote, there are few sites whose layout resembles closely that of Monte Albán. A Late Classic center in Veracruz that does show important similarities is Cuajilote. Like Monte Albán, Cuajilote has a "Great Plaza" layout with the long axis running north-south (Wilkerson 1993: fig. 22). The Great Plaza at Monte Albán is roughly 300 m from north to south, whereas that at Cuajilote is about 350 m along the same direction. The east-west dimension for the Great Plaza at Monte Albán is about 200 m; that at Cuajilote is about 60 m (Figure 28).

Both Great Plazas have a major ballcourt and a multifunctional set of structures at their northern ends, and an immense temple platform closing off the southern end. Both also have a line of structures along the midline of the Plaza, although the three at Cuajilote seem to be equidistant (roughly 90 m apart), whereas those at Monte Albán (Buildings G, H, and I) form a nearly contiguous block. This difference, however, may reflect the

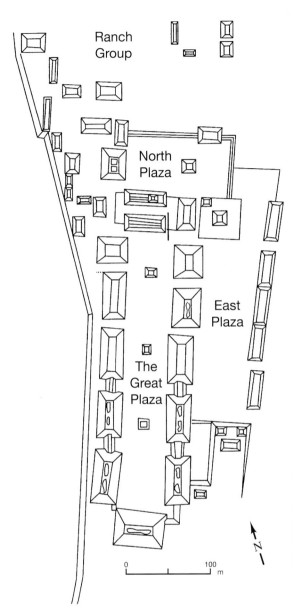

FIGURE 28. Layout of the Great Plaza of Cuajilote, Veracruz, which shares some of the planning principles evident in the Great Plaza at Monte Albán. Adapted by Kay Clahassey from Wilkerson (1993: fig. 22).

desire to have each midline building take advantage of natural outcrops at Monte Albán. At both sites, the western and eastern flanks of the Great Plazas reveal many temples whose doorways faced toward either the rising or the setting sun.

In both cities, limiting access to the plazas seems to have been a major concern. At Cuajilote a set of structures or walls prevented people from entering the Plaza from the south; these features also occur along the southern half of the western and eastern lines of structures. Such concern with restricting access to the Great Plaza would suggest that commoners were to be allowed in only for certain events. Furthermore, the linear sequence of temples suggests the possibility of a ceremonial circuit around the Great Plaza, one in which rulers and/or priests proceeded in prescribed fashion from one building to the next. The same kind of ceremonial circuit may have been conducted at Monte Albán.

CONCLUSIONS

Over time Monte Albán grew dramatically in both population and monumentality. Such growth was neither uniform nor gradual. One spurt took place between 100 B.C. and A.D. 200, when Monte Albán's growth was accompanied by an enormous increase in the types and numbers of monumental buildings and by the implementation of a "Grand Plaza" design.

Why did the Zapotec choose this time to impose a master plan on what had been a rocky and irregular mountaintop? The timing seems to have been intimately related to the process of state formation and the establishment of a new political order. With the emergence of Oaxaca's first state, the new leaders residing at the capital evidently became concerned with displaying symmetry and order, a tangible statement about their regime. They went beyond imposing this master plan at the capital; indeed, not too much later they were able to impose it on at least one second-tier settlement, San José Mogote.

Once a master plan is imposed it may be easier to add to that template than to create a new one. In the case of Monte Albán, the imposition of a master plan may indicate several motives: perhaps the initial Zapotec state (1) needed legitimization and chose this plan as part of a policy of political propaganda; (2) wanted to emphasize orderliness and a new beginning; and/or (3) wanted to conduct new kinds of rites in a huge plaza. Later rulers and regimes did not dramatically alter the master plan, but instead invested more labor into building larger palaces, tombs, and monumental temples to venerate noble ancestors.

I close on a cautionary note. We should never forget that Mesoamerica's earliest towns and cities were abandoned long before the Spaniards arrived, so there are no eyewitness Western accounts. We cannot fully comprehend the self-representations of these sites, as we can with ethnohistorically known cities, such as Tenochtitlan or Tlatelolco. Our views of Olmec centers, or even such Classic cities as Monte Albán and Teotihuacan, can only be based on inferences from archaeological remains. We should never delude ourselves into believing that we can fully understand how these people saw their world. Thus in this chapter I have simply shown how Monte Albán developed a "Grand Plaza" design and inferred how the ancient Zapotec represented themselves in art, architecture, and writing over time.

REFERENCES CITED

Acosta, Jorge R.
1958–59 Exploraciones arqueológicas en Monte Albán, XVIII temporada. *Revista Mexicana de Estudios Antropológicos* 15: 7–50.
1965 Preclassic and Classic Architecture of Oaxaca. In *Handbook of Middle American Indians* (Robert Wauchope and Gordon R. Willey, eds.), vol. 3: 814–836. University of Texas Press, Austin.
1974 Informe de la XIV temporada de exploraciones en la zona arqueológica de Monte Albán, 1945–1946. *Cultura y Sociedad* 1(2): 69–82.

Acosta, Jorge R., and Javier Romero
1992 *Exploraciones en Monte Negro, Oaxaca: 1937–38, 1938–39 y 1939–1940.* Instituto Nacional de Antropología e Historia, México.

Andrews, E. Wyllys, and Cassandra R. Bill
2005 A Late Classic Royal Residence at Copán. In *Copán: The History of a Maya Kingdom* (E. Wyllys Andrews and William L. Fash, eds.): 239–314. School of American Research Press, Santa Fe, N.M.

Andrews, E. Wyllys, and Barbara W. Fash
1992 Continuity and Change in a Royal Maya Residential Complex at Copan. *Ancient Mesoamerica* 3: 63–88.

Balkansky, Andrew K.
2002 *The Sola Valley and the Monte Albán State: A Study of Zapotec Imperial Expansion.* University of Michigan Museum of Anthropology, Memoir 36. Ann Arbor.

Batres, Leopoldo
1902 *Exploraciones en Monte Albán.* Inspección y Conservación de la República Mexicana. Calle Gante, México.

Bernal, Ignacio
1968 The Ball Players of Dainzu. *Archaeology* 21: 246–251.
1985 *Official Guide to the Oaxaca Valley.* INAH/Salvat Mexicana de Ediciones, México.
n.d. La cerámica preclásica de Monte Albán. Master's thesis, Escuela Nacional de Antropología e Historia, México, 1946.

Blanton, Richard E.
1978 *Monte Albán: Settlement Patterns at the Ancient Zapotec Capital.* Academic Press, New York.

Caso, Alfonso
1928 *Las estelas zapotecas.* Monografías del Museo Nacional de Arqueología, Historia y Etnografía. Publicaciones de la Secretaría de Educación Pública. Talleres Gráficos de la Nación, México.
1938 *Exploraciones en Oaxaca, quinta y sexta temporadas, 1936–1937.* Instituto Panamericano de Geografía e Historia, Publicación 34. México.
1947 Calendario y escritura de las antiguas culturas de Monte Albán. In *Obras Completas de Miguel Othón de Mendizábal,* vol. 1: 5–102. Talleres de la Nación, México.

Caso, Alfonso, and Ignacio Bernal
    1952   *Urnas de Oaxaca*. Memorias del Instituto Nacional de Antropología e Historia 2. México.

Caso, Alfonso, Ignacio Bernal, and Jorge R. Acosta
    1967   *La cerámica de Monte Albán*. Memorias del Instituto Nacional de Antropología e Historia 13. México.

Córdova, Fray Juan de
    1942 [1578]   *Vocabulario en lengua zapoteca* (Wigberto Jiménez Moreno, ed.). Instituto Nacional de Antropología e Historia, México.

Easby, Elizabeth K., and John F. Scott
    1970   *Before Cortés: Sculpture of Middle America*. New York Graphic Society, Metropolitan Museum of Art, New York.

Flannery, Kent V.
    1983   The Development of Monte Albán's Main Plaza in Period II. In *The Cloud People* (Kent V. Flannery and Joyce Marcus, eds.): 102–104. Academic Press, New York.

Flannery, Kent V., and Joyce Marcus
    1983a   The Earliest Public Buildings, Tombs, and Monuments at Monte Albán, with Notes on the Internal Chronology of Period I. In *The Cloud People* (Kent V. Flannery and Joyce Marcus, eds.): 87–91. Academic Press, New York.
    1983b   San José Mogote in Monte Albán II: A Secondary Administrative Center. In *The Cloud People* (Kent V. Flannery and Joyce Marcus, eds.): 111–113. Academic Press, New York.

Freidel, David, Linda Schele, and Joy Parker
    1993   *Maya Cosmos: Three Thousand Years on the Shaman's Path*. William Morrow, New York.

Instituto Nacional de Antropología e Historia
    1968   *Monte Albán. Mitla. Official Guide*. Fifth ed. in English. Instituto Nacional de Antropología e Historia, México.

Kemp, Barry J.
    1991   *Ancient Egypt: Anatomy of a Civilization*. Routledge, London and New York.

Kowalewski, Stephen A., Gary M. Feinman, Laura Finsten, Richard E. Blanton, and Linda M. Nicholas
    1989   *Monte Albán's Hinterland*, part II: *Prehispanic Settlement Patterns in Tlacolula, Etla, and Ocotlán, the Valley of Oaxaca, Mexico*. University of Michigan Museum of Anthropology, Memoir 23. Ann Arbor.

Lind, Michael
    2003   Lambityeco—Tomb 6. In *Homenaje a John Paddock* (Patricia Plunket, ed.): 45–66. Universidad de las Américas, Cholula, Puebla, México.

Lind, Michael, and Javier Urcid
    1983   The Lords of Lambityeco and Their Nearest Neighbors. *Notas Mesoamericanas* 9: 78–111.

Marcus, Joyce
    1974   The Iconography of Power among the Classic Maya. *World Archaeology* 6: 83–94.

1978   Archaeology and Religion: A Comparison of the Zapotec and Maya. *World Archaeology* 10: 172–191.

1983a   Zapotec Religion. In *The Cloud People* (Kent V. Flannery and Joyce Marcus, eds.): 345–351. Academic Press, New York.

1983b   Changing Patterns of Stone Monuments after the Fall of Monte Albán, A.D. 600–900. In *The Cloud People* (Kent V. Flannery and Joyce Marcus, eds.): 191–197. Academic Press, New York.

1989   From Centralized Systems to City-States: Possible Models for the Epiclassic. In *Mesoamerica after the Decline of Teotihuacan: A.D. 700–900* (Richard A. Diehl and Janet C. Berlo, eds.): 201–208. Dumbarton Oaks, Washington, D.C.

1992a   Dynamic Cycles of Mesoamerican States. *National Geographic Research & Exploration* 8: 392–411.

1992b   M*esoamerican Writing Systems.* Princeton University Press, Princeton, N.J.

1998   The Peaks and Valleys of Ancient States: An Extension of the Dynamic Model. In *Archaic States* (Gary M. Feinman and Joyce Marcus, eds.): 59–94. School of American Research Press, Santa Fe, N.M.

1999   Early Architecture in the Valley of Oaxaca: 1350 B.C.–A.D. 500. In *Mesoamerican Architecture as a Cultural Symbol* (Jeff Karl Kowalski, ed.): 58–75. Oxford University Press, Oxford.

2002   Carved Stones from the Sola Valley. In *The Sola Valley and the Monte Albán State: A Study of Zapotec Imperial Expansion* (Andrew K. Balkansky, ed.): 103–121. University of Michigan Museum of Anthropology, Memoir 36. Ann Arbor.

2003   Monumentality in Archaic States: Lessons Learned from Large-Scale Excavations of the Past. In *Theory and Practice in Mediterranean Archaeology: Old World and New World Perspectives* (John K. Papadopoulos and Richard M. Leventhal, eds.): 115–134. Cotsen Institute of Archaeology at the University of California at Los Angeles, Los Angeles.

2006   Identifying Elites and Their Strategies. In *Intermediate Elites in Pre-Columbian States and Empires* (Christina M. Elson and R. Alan Covey, eds.): 212–246. University of Arizona Press, Tucson.

Marcus, Joyce, and Kent V. Flannery

1978   Ethnoscience of the Sixteenth-Century Valley Zapotec. In *The Nature and Status of Ethnobotany* (Richard I. Ford, ed.): 51–79. University of Michigan Museum of Anthropology, Anthropological Papers 67. Ann Arbor.

1994   Ancient Zapotec Ritual and Religion: An Application of the Direct Historical Approach. In *The Ancient Mind* (Colin Renfrew and Ezra B.W. Zubrow, eds.): 55–74. Cambridge University Press, Cambridge.

1996   *Zapotec Civilization: How Urban Society Evolved in Mexico's Oaxaca Valley.* Thames and Hudson, New York.

2004   The Coevolution of Ritual and Society: New [14]C Dates from Ancient Mexico. *Proceedings of the National Academy of Sciences, USA* 101: 18257–18261.

Marquina, Ignacio

    1951 *Arquitectura prehispánica*. Memorias del Instituto Nacional de
           Antropología e Historia 1. México.

Miller, Arthur G.

    1991 The Carved Stela in Tomb 5, Suchilquitongo, Oaxaca, Mexico. *Ancient
           Mesoamerica* 2: 215–224.

    1995 *The Painted Tombs of Oaxaca, Mexico: Living with the Dead.* Cambridge
           University Press, New York.

Morley, Sylvanus Griswold

    1937 *The Inscriptions of Peten,* vol. V, part 1. Carnegie Institution of Washington Publication 437. Washington, D.C.

Rabin, Emily

    1970 The Lambityeco Friezes: Notes on Their Content, with an Appendix on C_{14} Dates. *Boletín de Estudios Oaxaqueños* 33.

Spencer, Charles S., and Elsa M. Redmond

    2001a The Chronology of Conquest: Implications of New Radiocarbon Analyses from the Cañada de Cuicatlán, Oaxaca. *Latin American Antiquity* 12: 182–202.

    2001b Multilevel Selection and Political Evolution in the Valley of Oaxaca, 500–100 B.C. *Journal of Anthropological Archaeology* 20: 195–229.

    2004 Primary State Formation in Mesoamerica. *Annual Review of Anthropology* 33: 173–199.

Urcid, Javier, Marcus Winter, and Raúl Matadamas

    1994 Nuevos monumentos grabados en Monte Albán, Oaxaca. In *Escritura Zapoteca Prehispánica: Nuevas Aportaciones* (Marcus Winter, coordinador; Javier Urcid, Raúl Matadamas, Damon E. Peeler, and Benjamín Maldonado, eds.): 2–52. Centro del Instituto Nacional de Antropología e Historia, Oaxaca, México.

Vogt, Evon Z.

    1969 *Zinacantán: A Maya Community in the Highlands of Chiapas.* Harvard University Press, Cambridge, Mass.

Wilkerson, S. Jeffrey K.

    1993 Escalante's Entrada: The Lost Aztec Garrison of the Mar del Norte in New Spain. *National Geographic Research and Exploration* 9: 12–31.

Winter, Marcus C.

    1989 *Oaxaca: The Archaeological Record.* Minutiae Mexicana, México.

CENTERING THE KINGDOM, CENTERING THE KING

Maya Creation and Legitimization at San Bartolo

William A. Saturno

THE EXAMINATION OF THE WALL PAINTINGS at San Bartolo, Guatemala, not only allows a discussion of how and how well early Maya artists painted—that is, the raw materials they used, the techniques they practiced, and the skills they required—but also illuminates more broadly the society in which they participated and the importance of their works for illustrating and even defining the roles of individuals and institutions in that society. At a glance, the quality of the painting at San Bartolo indicates the level of mastery possessed by those responsible for its production. The flowing calligraphy of the line work and the control of paint and plaster indicate both a long-established tradition of wall painting in the Maya lowlands and a cohort of well-trained artists at work at San Bartolo by the beginning of the first century B.C. By examining the specific narrative of the San Bartolo murals in addition to their architectural context, I consider which stories were selected for painting, by whom they were likely selected, where they were destined to be exhibited, and for what audience and what purpose they were ultimately intended. In doing so, this chapter discusses how, through the work of artists, early Maya kings both envisioned and voiced the role they saw themselves playing in Preclassic Maya society.

SAN BARTOLO AND THE PRECLASSIC PERIOD

Research carried out since the mid-1970s has dramatically altered current ideas about the size and complexity of Preclassic lowland Maya centers. It is now known that such features as formal ceremonialism, craft specialization, and urbanism were already well established in the lowlands during Preclassic times. In many instances, however, these associations have been hard-won, as Preclassic materials were often deeply buried beneath later constructions (Ringle 1999: 183). This was the case with the initial discovery of monumental architecture dating to the Late Preclassic at Uaxactun, Guatemala (Ricketson and Ricketson 1937), as well as with subsequent materials encountered beneath the North Acropolis at Tikal, Guatemala (Coe 1965). A few sites—namely, Cerros, Belize (Robertson and Freidel 1986; Scarborough 1991); Cuello, Belize (Hammond 1991); Komchen, Mexico (Andrews and Ringle 1992), and El Mirador, Guatemala (Dahlin 1984; Matheny and Matheny 1990)—were largely free of the overburden restricting insight into early patterns of community organization. Nonetheless, traditional models for the rise of lowland Maya civilization have originated from decades of archaeological investigation at sites illustrating gradual evolutionary trajectories in which descriptions of Preclassic architecture and artifacts as "simpler," "formative," and "developmental" carried with them clear evolutionary implications (e.g., Coe and Coe 1956: 372; Smith 1937: 3).

Coupled with abundant and spectacular Classic period remains, this circumstance fostered a bias that Maya civilization developed in the lowlands only by ca. A.D. 300, much later than their highland counterparts, suggesting external origins in addition to a slow pace. "Such an isolated region as the Petén would hardly have witnessed the beginnings of Maya civilization, which might rather be expected in parts of the Maya area where the stimulus of contact with other cultures should have quickened development—Central Chiapas seems ideal" (Thompson 1954: 50).

The work on the North Acropolis at Tikal was perhaps the first to challenge these notions, as the farther down they excavated, "the elaborateness and Classic appearance of the discovered structures were no less apparent." In fact "things were not getting simpler or cruder or increasingly formative" (Coe and McGinn 1963: 26). More recently, investigations in the "Mirador Basin" have revealed abundant Middle and Late Preclassic architectural remains and other manifestations of complex society. In fact, some of the largest constructions in Mesoamerica come from this time and region, and settlement surveys at several sites have shown Late Preclassic occupations eclipsing Early and Late Classic densities (Hansen 1998). In addition, recent research has conveyed a greater appreciation for the sophistication and antiquity of early Maya ritual, deities, and art (e.g., Bauer 2005; Fields 1991; Freidel 1990; Freidel and Schele 1988; Hammond et al. 1992, 1999; Laporte and Fialko 1990, 1995; Ringle 1999; Saturno et al. 2005). Nonetheless, biases persist, and evidence opposing traditional models can often be regarded as simply epiphenomenal. It is hard to consider El Mirador as representative. Its sheer size illustrates both its exemplary urban nature and its uniqueness compared to anything found in the lowlands. It is a sample of one, and it is decidedly not average.

The site of San Bartolo, by comparison, appears more commonplace. It has only a few truly monumental structures that clearly indicate a certain degree of complexity, yet the site is easily dwarfed by the architectural mass of El Mirador. Despite its reduced geographic extent, San Bartolo in the Late Preclassic still possesses many of the characteristics one would expect to find at a large Classic center, specifically, a well-differentiated residential hierarchy and clearly defined monumental ceremonial spaces. Moreover, its polychromatic narrative murals and painted hieroglyphic texts largely resolve the once-lamented shortcomings of both the missing agent in lowland Preclassic art and "the absence of a mechanism to ensure the stable transmission of central leadership over generations" that long hindered discussions of the developing institutions of governance (Freidel and Schele 1988: 550).

The Classic Maya are widely recognized for their masterful polychrome vases, and the few murals that survive indicate that fine narrative painting was not limited to small portable objects but also appeared on stucco walls in elaborate compositions of brilliant polychrome. In contrast to the comparatively limited format provided by vases or stone monuments, wall surfaces provide a nearly infinite canvas for artistic narrative. Discovered in 1946, the murals of Structure 1 at Bonampak, Chiapas, are by far the most famous murals known from the Classic Maya (Ruppert et al. 1955). The three rooms of Structure 1 have provided unique insights into Classic Maya courtly life, ritual, warfare, and astronomy (Lounsbury 1982; Miller 1986; Staines Cicero 1998). For the Early Classic period (A.D. 250–600), murals are known from Tikal; Uaxactun; and Río Azul, Guatemala, appearing both on temple walls and in painted tombs (Adams 1999; Coe 1990: fig. 175; Laporte and Fialko 1990: figs. 3.18–3.21; Smith 1950: figs. 45–47). Although there are a good number of murals known for the Classic Maya, much of our understanding of Late Preclassic Maya art and iconography derives from stucco sculpture on buildings and stone bas-reliefs, with the great majority of the latter deriving from the Guatemalan highlands and neighboring Pacific coastal region. The stone sculpture from Kaminaljuyu, Guatemala; Takalik Abaj, Guatemala; Izapa, Chiapas; and other Late Preclassic sites is strongly curvilinear and evokes a painterly tradition. However, for the Late Preclassic period, very few painted scenes are known from either ceramics or murals. The stucco masks from Structure 5C-2nd at Cerros are elaborately painted, but this polychrome is limited to ornamenting the stucco sculpture (see Freidel 1985). At Tikal, excavations in the North Acropolis revealed Late Preclassic mural paintings on the walls of Structure 5D-Sub.10-1st and Burial 166, but unfortunately in both cases the murals were poorly preserved (see Coe 1990: figs. 32, 34). Without a doubt, the newly discovered murals at San Bartolo constitute by far the most important corpus of painted scenes known from the Late Preclassic Maya period. To date, approximately 15 m of the mural surface has been exposed, revealing more than 40 interacting figures. Not only are the murals well preserved, but they are also of exceptional quality in both composition and skill of execution. Brilliantly painted in a rich array of colors, the murals

FIGURE 1. Plan map of the ruins of San Bartolo, showing four main architectural complexes from east to west: Saraguates, Pinturas, Ventanas, and Jabalí. Drawing by T. Garrison and R. Griffin, courtesy of Proyecto San Bartolo.

are extremely refined and detailed. They offer an unparalleled opportunity to evaluate how early lowland Maya kingdoms used the fine arts to both represent and define their place in the world, physical and metaphysical, that surrounded them.

Until March 2001, the ruins of San Bartolo were unknown to archaeologists, resulting in all but a few of its structures suffering years of illicit excavation by looters. San Bartolo is best characterized as a small Maya center whose monumental construction phases were concentrated in the period from 400 B.C. to A.D. 100. There are numerous indications in the palynological record that the area around San Bartolo was much wetter during its main occupation (Nicholas Dunning, personal communication, April 2006). Trees, water, limestone, and mud (as well as the food to support laborers and artisans) must have been in abundance, given the explosion of building seen beginning in the fourth century B.C. That the Maya depleted these local resources by the first century A.D. is evident from the decreasing thickness of plaster surfaces and the overall abandonment of the site around this time.

The site, located in a currently uninhabited region of the northeastern part of the Department of Petén, Guatemala, covers an area of approxi-

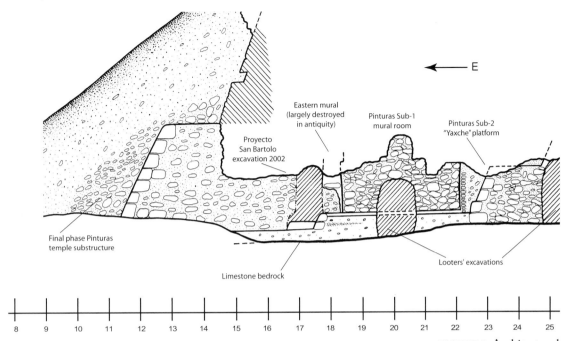

Eastern mural
(largely destroyed
in antiquity)

Pinturas Sub-1
mural room

Pinturas Sub-2
"Yaxche" platform

Proyecto
San Bartolo
excavation 2002

Final phase Pinturas
temple substructure

Looters' excavations

Limestone bedrock

E

8 9 10 11 12 13 14 15 16 17 18 19 20 21 22 23 24 25

FIGURE 2. Architectural profile of looters' trench and tunnel into the rear of the Pinturas Complex, showing the mural room abutted to the Yaxche platform and buried by the final-phase construction. Scale bar is in meters. Drawing by H. Escobedo and R. Ozaeta, courtesy of Proyecto San Bartolo.

mately 1 km^2 and is comprised of more than 130 stone structures organized around four principal architectural groups (Figure 1). The largest of the groups is associated with the pyramid, Structure 20, named Las Ventanas ("The Windows") because of the preserved masonry windows in its final-phase superstructure. The group consists of a large number of residential mounds, a "palace" structure, a large central plaza, and a small ballcourt likely forming the administrative center of San Bartolo's growing Preclassic population. In addition a causeway leads from the southern end of the central plaza and extends more than 200 m toward a limestone quarry and an area of seasonal swamps to the south.

A second architectural group, Las Pinturas, named after the paintings found in it, lies approximately 500 m to the east of Las Ventanas, facing west. The central structure, Structure 1, is part of a triadic group and stands more than 26 m high. It is pierced by numerous looters' excavations, the largest of which were concentrated in its posterior. The principal looters' excavation (Figure 2) began as an axial trench of the final-phase substructure; however, after finding the preserved basal terrace the looters converted to tunneling. The east-west looters' tunnel continues for more than 40 m to the west, occasionally branching to both north and south in a vain search for tombs.

At present, at least seven stages of construction are evident in Pinturas, all of which date through radiocarbon and ceramic evidence to the Preclassic. The final completed building episode began in the waning years of the first century B.C., when the penultimate constructions in the group were filled in to make a stable base for Structure 1. In 2006 the remnants of additional construction were uncovered at the base of Structure 1 where the beginnings of an expanded platform had been initiated but had never reached the first terrace.

ARCHITECTURE OF PINTURAS SUB-I

To interpret the mural in the Pinturas Complex, an understanding of its architectural context is as important as the imagery itself. The building that houses the murals was one of multiple structures added to the rear of the large ceremonial complex now known as Las Pinturas as part of its penultimate completed building phase. Pinturas Sub-I, as the mural room was originally designated, is a rectangular masonry building (Figure 3) placed atop a low (60 cm) red platform. Its vertical exterior walls rise 1.5 m and were decorated with painted human figures amid swirling red volutes at the building's corners and surrounding its five doorways. Above the vertical walls begins a cornice and slightly angled facade of painted and modeled stucco relief just over a meter in height. This facade is currently preserved only on the structure's north side, though it would have extended to its eastern and southern sides as well when the building was in use. The main entry to the building was from its eastern side, where a single step rises in front of the 2.6-m-wide central doorway. Two smaller (1.3 m) doorways were located on either side of the central one just beyond the extent of the step. In addition two other doorways were placed toward the rear of the building at its northwest and southwest corners. All five doorways are relatively low (1.4 m), meaning that the average-sized Maya would likely have had to stoop or kneel to enter the space.

The interior is characterized by vertical plaster walls that rise to a height of 1.4 m before stepping inward, where a vault spring might be expected. However, in the absence of a vault the walls continue to rise vertically approximately 1 m to the ceiling. The spring, or medial molding, visually divides the room into vertical halves. The underside of the molding is painted red—beneath it a geometric skyband extends around the lower walls and above it the narrative of the mural unfolds.

During the 2005 field season a second contemporary building was discovered to the north of Pinturas Sub-I, forcing a redesignation of the original mural room as Pinturas Sub-IA, with the new building being called Pinturas Sub-IB (Figure 4). Pinturas Sub-IB was also largely dismantled during the same building episode that buried Sub-IA; in fact only the western side of the building remains. From what is left, however, some important comparisons can be made with its better-preserved neighbor. Sub-IB was a two-roomed structure on a 1.5-m-high red platform with stucco masks flanking its single south-facing stairway. The exterior, like

FIGURE 3.
Reconstruction of the interior of Pinturas Sub-IA. The west wall mural is illustrated at the rear of the room, and the north wall mural is shown at right. Arrows indicate the choice to proceed north or south when entering along the building's centerline. Drawing by H. Hurst, courtesy of Proyecto San Bartolo.

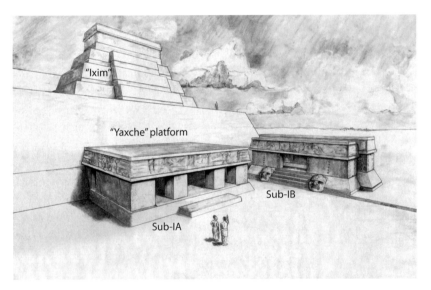

FIGURE 4.
Reconstruction of the rear of the Pinturas Complex during its penultimate completed phase. Sub-IA and Sub-IB are shown attached to the Yaxche platform. The rear of the Ixim pyramid is shown atop Yaxche. Drawing by H. Hurst, courtesy of Proyecto San Bartolo.

that of Sub-IA, was decorated with human figures and red volutes at its corners, though with the addition of an exterior skyband circling the building beneath the cornice. Any modeled stucco decoration was destroyed during the building's burial. The interior space was divided into two rooms; the rear one was reached by ascending an internal red-painted step that mimicked the form of the exterior platform. The walls are well preserved and are unpainted except for the underside of the medial molding, which, as in Sub-IA, was painted red. All plaster above the medial molding was removed before burial; however, the prevalence of mural fragments painted by different hands throughout the final-phase construction fill raises the likelihood that Sub-IB may have been decorated with interior murals as well.

The orientation of Sub-IB and its relation to Sub-IA raises the intriguing possibility that a third structure (Sub-IC?) might be located farther to the south, partially enclosing a small plaza in front of Sub-IA. With or without the presence of a third structure, Sub-IA and Sub-IB form a somewhat restricted ceremonial area that is distinct from the public, front side of the Yaxche platform, where the main Pinturas Pyramid rises as the central building in a triadic group. A stairway found at the rear (northwest) corner of the Yaxche platform may provide the means for connecting the relatively private rituals of the mural complex with those more public displays performed on the pyramid's front.

The mural building (Pinturas Sub-IA) directly abuts the eastern (rear) face of the Yaxche platform, and this placement likely contributed to the room's truncated useful life, and ironically, to the mural's preservation. When seen from the exterior, the building was designed to have no western wall but rather to have its northern and southern walls integrate directly into the sloping base of the Yaxche platform. From the interior of the room, it was imperceptible, as the vertical interior western wall concealed the platform's face behind its thin veneer of masonry and stucco, joining the northern and southern interior walls at right angles. However, the weight of the fill between the sloping platform and interior west wall was structurally untenable, moving down the slope where its horizontal component was redirected at the base of the interior west wall. There it began to undercut the thin wall's stability, causing it to crack and bow markedly into the interior space. Large portions of the plaster from the lower west wall had already delaminated from the underlying masonry and been removed from the structure before the room was filled in.

The building's flat roof may have been another contributing factor to the structure's termination. It is clear from areas of water damage and calcium carbonate accretion that predate the room's destruction that water repeatedly permeated the roof. In addition, the expansive interior space (4.2 m × 9.5 m) of the single-roomed structure was the result of using five large horizontal beams running north-south to carry the majority of the flat masonry roof's load. The five beam sockets are clearly identifiable along the top of the western mural where the wall plaster lips up to the different fill material present in the sockets. Four of the roof beams would have been easily supported, one on each side of the northern and southern doorways, respectively, but the load carried by the central roof beam would have been supported directly above the wide central doorway, possibly leading to further structural complications.

The mural room's five doorways and open floor plan provide for multiple ways to both see and interact with the painted narrative, and though in terms of its organization, the mural "reads much like an unfolded screenfold codex" (Taube et al. n.d.), it is unclear where the beginning of the story is to be found. One could conceivably enter and exit through the central doorway (following either a clockwise or counterclockwise circuit of the entire room) just as easily as one could enter from the southwest corner and exit through the northwest corner (having walked only along the west wall). Though counterclockwise ritual movement is well documented during later periods and to the present, it cannot be presumed to have been the sole or even main path of ritual action in the room without further evidence. The artists consistently designated divisions in the overall narrative by placing individual characters back to back, creating visual breaks in the painted program, where participants in the same narrative segment either face each other or a common protagonist. This arrangement has the effect of focusing the eye of the observer toward the center of a segment by clearly defining its borders. Despite the utility of this convention for identifying individual scenes, it is less useful for establishing the broader flow of the entire piece. There are ten instances in the preserved portion of the mural of characters placed back to back, creating eleven individual scenes of varying length and complexity. Though some associations can be drawn between scenes by the presence of repeating characters, the specific sequential relationship between scenes is more difficult to establish with any degree of certainty.

Elsewhere the mural narrative has been presented in a primarily linear fashion, moving from left to right both as a function of nomenclature (the figures appearing in the mural are numbered and described from left to right) and as one possible interpretation of the intended reading order (Saturno 2006; Saturno et al. 2005; Taube et al. n.d.). The interpretation given here relies on both linear and concentric visual syntaxes (Freidel 1985; Freidel and Schele 1988) to present an alternative view. It should be stated at the outset, however, that the specific iconographic evidence for the identification of individual characters in the narrative is discussed in greater depth in other publications (e.g., Saturno et al. 2005; Taube et al. n.d.) and is only briefly dealt with in the following descriptions.

Entering through the building's main doorway, the first thing the viewer sees is the west wall. Overhead, at the very center of that wall, the central roof beam penetrates the painted surface directly between the southward-facing Principal Bird Deity, as first identified and labeled by Lawrence Bardawil (1976), and the northward-facing Maize God, reinforcing the visual break established by their back-to-back placement. Directly beneath the beam, three birds with song scrolls emanating from their beaks fly to the left, away from the back of the Maize God, further highlighting the division. Moving to the left, the Principal Bird Deity is the focus of the narrative, appearing five times along the southern half of the wall. Moving to the right, the Maize God enjoys the central role, similarly being shown repeatedly. Thus upon entering the room along its centerline (see Figure 3) the viewer is immediately confronted with a decision that affects the story being told, and it is likely that at different times different choices would have been made. For the purposes of the current presentation, I follow the birds south before returning to the centerline and picking up the narrative of the Maize God.

BOUNDING THE WORLD

The southern half of the west wall mural illustrates a quadripartite vision of the Maya cosmos in which four very similar scenes show a Young Lord, akin to the Classic period Hun Ahaw or the sixteenth-century K'iche Maya Hunahpu, engaged in sacrificial bloodletting before the Principal Bird Deity perched in a tree. Following Karl Taube (Taube et al. n.d.), the repeated appearance of these individuals engaged in similar acts of sacrifice likely indicates the consecutive display of world directions, as is commonly seen in Mesoamerican representations of cosmogenesis. The San Bartolo scenes recall both page 1 of the Codex Fejérváry-Mayer (where the dismembered Tezcaltipoca is cast bleeding to the trees at the four corners of the world) and pages 49–53 of the Codex Borgia (where the world trees sprout from the bodies of sacrificed goddesses). In all instances divine sacrifice is associated with the establishment of an ordered world. Moreover, the maintenance of that order is understood as the responsibility of all humanity through similar ritual action, but most importantly through the blood sacrifice of kings.

The San Bartolo version of this archetypical Mesoamerican story begins with the emergence of a cleft serpent-headed skyband from the roof beam along the upper edge of the mural (Figure 5). The Principal Bird Deity descends out of the cleft sky amid dark cloud scrolls. Immediately beneath the monstrous bird is the date 3 IK in a red dripping cartouche very similar in form to that on Kaminaljuyu Stela 10. To the left of the date is a short painted text that likely describes the event. Unfortunately, the early form of the writing and its poor state of preservation render its details difficult to decipher. To the left of the text a dancing duck-billed dwarflike figure gestures upward toward the descending bird. A thin black line, like the song scrolls of the three birds behind this creature, swirls above him, likely indicating that he, too, is singing and perhaps even calling the Principal Bird Deity down from the sky. As the scene continues to the left the Principal Bird Deity alights in the first of four trees, whose branches splay outward under his great weight,

Here the bird is seen in his most resplendent form. Covered in jewels, he grasps the tree's round calabash fruit in his enormous talons and holds a bicephalic serpent in his monstrous beak. His wings are rotated in opposite directions, displaying the symbols k'in and ak'bal, day and darkness, along with stone projectile points among his feathers. His tree rises out of a field of scented blossoms; its twisted trunk blooms with both flowers and

FIGURE 5. San Bartolo west wall mural, illustrating the blood sacrifice of the Young Lord. The Principal Bird Deity is descending out of the sky and landing in a calabash tree. Painting by H. Hurst, courtesy of Proyecto San Bartolo.

fruit, consistent with Maya conceptions of an abundant floral paradise associated with the east, where the sun is reborn each day (Taube 2004).

The humility of Young Lord's costume stands in contrast to the resplendence of the great mythic bird before him and belies the boldness of his actions in the scene. With only a cloth belt around his waist, knots tied at his knees and ankles, a woven collar about his neck, and a crossed headband and false beard framing his face, he stands facing the Principal Bird Deity. As he stands among the flowers in front of the world tree, he runs a sharpened branch through his phallus, releasing great gouts of blood in perhaps the earliest and most graphic display of genital self-sacrifice in the Maya world. It is a sacrifice repeated three more times as the viewer moves southward along the wall following the mythic bird's descent from the floral paradise of the east to the watery underworld realm of the west.

FIGURE 6. San Bartolo west wall mural, illustrating the blood sacrifice of the Young Lord and the offering of a turkey to the Principal Bird Deity. Drawing by H. Hurst, courtesy of Proyecto San Bartolo.

In the next scene (Figure 6) much of the second tree and bird were destroyed in antiquity when the Maya built a retaining wall to stabilize the rubble used to fill the room. Only one of the Principal Bird Deity's wings, no longer bearing the k'in or ak'bal, and its beak are visible. It is clearly still perched in a tree, though the foliage is distinct, and he still clutches a two-headed serpent in his mouth. One of the jewels that sat on his brow as he both descended from the sky and alit in the first tree, however, is seen here detached and floating in front of him dripping blood from its base, perhaps hinting at the mythic bird's slow loss of status through the sacrifices offered by the Young Lord.

For this second sacrifice the Young Lord does not stand among flower blossoms but instead is shown with his feet floating just slightly above the ground line of the mural. Thus standing in mid-air, with a pair of birds tied

FIGURE 7. San Bartolo west wall mural, illustrating the blood sacrifice of the Young Lord and the offering of a deer to the Principal Bird Deity. Drawing by H. Hurst, courtesy of Proyecto San Bartolo.

to a woven basket on his belt, he again offers his blood in sacrifice, though this time accompanied by a sacrificed turkey as well. The turkey is bent backward over a wooden tripod, and three stones are piled on its open belly, releasing black and red volutes that swirl upward toward the Principal Bird Deity. The costume of the Young Lord is little changed from the first scene, though he does wear a star element in his headdress that identifies him with the short painted text above and behind him, likely adding specificity to the directional aspects of the narrative (Taube et al. n.d.).

The narrative continues with the Principal Bird Deity perched in the branches of the third directional tree, his wings spread wide, but with the two-headed serpent in his beak missing one of its heads (Figure 7). The dismembered head floats nearby with blood pouring down from both ends of the severed neck. The Young Lord stands in front of the tree, this time with feet firmly on the ground and a small deer trussed to his belt. His costume and method of sacrifice are little changed, though he no longer wears knots about his knees and stubble is visible for the first time on his chin, emerging from beneath his false beard. Between the Young Lord and the Principal Bird Deity is a sacrificed deer, again placed on the wooden tripod with three stones placed in its open belly. Black and red volutes swirl upward as black and red blood drips down.

The fourth tree (Figure 8) sprouts from the saurian head of the earth monster with black water flowing over the scutes of its back. The limited preservation of the mural in the southwest corner of the room restricts what can be said about the state of the Principal Bird Deity, as only his talons and tail are preserved among the foliage of the final tree. Similarly, only the one head of the formerly bicephalic serpent is preserved, and only the legs of the Young Lord are visible, this time covered in large black spots.

FIGURE 8. San Bartolo west wall mural, illustrating the blood sacrifice of the Young Lord and the offering of a fish to the Principal Bird Deity. Drawing by H. Hurst, courtesy of Proyecto San Bartolo.

FIGURE 9. San Bartolo mural fragments, illustrating the dead Principal Bird Deity on the back of the Young Lord. Drawing by H. Hurst, courtesy of Proyecto San Bartolo.

The fin of a fish can just be made out behind him, likely tied to his waist, but what is clear is that the fourth autosacrificial offering takes place in the water and is accompanied by a fish placed on the tripod. In this instance five stones have been piled on the upturned fish, and red and black volutes rise, but little if any blood flows from the fish itself.

Interestingly, a group of eleven mural fragments bearing a similar patina to the southwest corner of the mural room was uncovered in excavations between Pinturas Sub-IA and Sub-IB. These fragments depict the spotted legs and arms of the watery Young Lord (Figure 9). He holds his tree branch in his hand but is not engaged in autosacrifice. More importantly he carries the dead Principal Bird Deity attached to his back, raising the intriguing possibility that the final defeat of the mythic bird may have taken place as the narrative continued on the now-destroyed south wall mural.

Immediately on seeing the excavated west wall mural, Taube noted the remarkable similarity, despite being separated by approximately 1,500 years, between the narrative of the paintings and that of the New Year's Pages

(pages 25–28) of the Dresden Codex. These pages illustrate the erection of four directional world trees, accompanied by the scattering of blood and offerings of incense in the east, turkey in the south, deer in the north, and fish in the west (Taube et al. n.d.).

The four San Bartolo scenes not only illustrate the organization of the world through the creation of the four cardinal directions but also perhaps give insight into other four-part Maya taxonomies. The sacrifices take place first in a field of blossoms in the floral paradise closely associated with the east, followed by sacrifices in the air, on the ground, and in the water (the last often associated with the underworld and the west). In addition the sacrifices themselves demonstrate a quadripartite division of classes of sustenance: fragrant blossoms can be seen as the "symbolic 'food' of gods and ancestors" whereas turkey, deer, and fish can be understood as foods from sky, forest, and stream (Taube et al. n.d.: 19). Thus sacrifice not only orders the cosmos east, west, north, and south, but it also defines the categories of its division as paradise, underworld, land, and sky; floral, aquatic, animal, and avian.

In traditional Maya thought the trees bounding the four-sided world reflect the socially constructed space of temple, plaza, house, and field, in stark contrast to the chaotic growth of the untamed forest (Taube 2003). In this way the Young Lord, through his sacrifice, organizes the cosmos around the propitiation and perhaps piecemeal humbling of the preeminent symbol of the supernatural wilds, the Principal Bird Deity. The Young Lord's method is related to that of contemporary Preclassic (e.g., Izapa)— as well as Classic and Postclassic—versions of Hun Ahaw/Hunahpu, who shoot this monstrous bird out of the sky. By extension the actions of Maya kings and commoners alike recall this conquest through the expansion of the civilized domain to the figurative four corners of kingdoms (as well as the material corners of house platforms and milpas).

Note that the narrative being portrayed was, given its evident geographic and temporal extent, a widely known one at the time it was painted. Thus the artists at San Bartolo are illustrating episodes of a familiar creation epic rather than inventing one de novo. In this way, the mural is being painted not to tell the story, but rather to show it in relation to the rest of the artistic program of the room. The episode of creation resulting in the four-sided world and the commensurate defeat of the Principal Bird Deity was painted to be seen within the architectural space where it is located and can be readily viewed as both an independent passage and in relation to the other passages discussed below. Thus although the simile of the screenfold codex remains accurate, perhaps it can be further refined by thinking of the painting as something akin to an edited volume compiled around a common theme rather than as a tale to be read from start to finish. Each chapter is still comprehensible when read out of its intended order, and

FIGURE 10. San Bartolo west wall mural, illustrating the Maize God being reborn with the harvest out of the turtle-shaped quatrefoil earth. He dances and plays music between seated water deities. Drawing by H. Hurst, courtesy of Proyecto San Bartolo.

when they are read together must be seen as the assembled segments of the mythology best suited to the mural program's purpose.

CENTERING THE KING

Moving north from the room's centerline reveals a very different composition. Rather than a linear progression of repeated scenes in which only certain details change, the viewer is presented with a series of concentric narratives involving the cycle of maize, the world center, and the coronation of kings. In deference to this concentric arrangement, rather than describe the scenes from left to right or right to left, I instead move from the center outward, highlighting the series of concentric pairings.

At the very center of a symmetrical composition the Maya Maize God dances and plays music in the quatrefoil turtle-earth (Figure 10). The Maize God has a turtle carapace suspended around his neck and strikes it as a drum with the taloned foot of a bird while he raises his other hand to sound the subsequent beat. The symbolic relationship between the turtle shell drum, rain-making, and thunder—as noted by Eduard Seler (1990–98, V: 281) where "the turtle shell is a natural drum . . . the thunder the celestial drum"—is reinforced by the Maize God's audience of Maya water deities. To his left Chaak the rain god sits cross-legged on a masonry throne, listening with his hand outstretched; to the Maize God's right the god of terrestrial water similarly gestures from his cushion (Taube 1992: 56–59; Taube et al. n.d.). The entire scene takes place in the quatrefoil cave motif, perhaps best known from the Olmec-era relief sculpture at Chalcatzingo, Mexico, where the lobed sides of the quatrefoil both symmetrically frame the action and designate its location as within the earth (see, e.g., Grove and Gillespie, this volume). That the cave is located within the turtle-shaped earth is shown by placing clawed feet at the four clefts on the cave's lobed exterior, accompanied by a prominently beaked head extending to the left in an undulating current of water.

FIGURE 12. San Bartolo west wall mural,
showing the death of the Maize God as he
dives into a current of water. Drawing by
H. Hurst, courtesy of Proyecto San Bartolo.

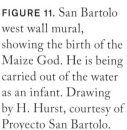

FIGURE 11. San Bartolo
west wall mural,
showing the birth of the
Maize God. He is being
carried out of the water
as an infant. Drawing
by H. Hurst, courtesy of
Proyecto San Bartolo.

Images of the Maize God emerging from within the turtle-shaped earth
are common in Classic Maya art (see, e.g., Robicsek and Hales 1981; Taube
1985, 1988; Quenon and le Fort 1997). In the San Bartolo mural, one of the
earliest and most explicit depictions of this mythic episode, the Maize God
carries a basket on his back, held by a tumpline across his forehead, which
suggests that he is carrying the harvest of corn with him as he dances out of
the earth (Taube et al. n.d.: 50). It is interesting that this part of the mural
was intentionally defaced before its burial: the repeated blows of a stone ax
blade are still visible in the mural plaster—perhaps, as suggested by Karl
Taube (personal communication, April 2004), physically opening the turtle
shell to symbolically allow the maize harvest to emerge.

On either side of the turtle there are paired images of the Maize God.
On the left he is seen at his birth, as an infant being carried in the arms of
another deity striding through water (Figure 11). The infant Maize God,
whose appearance bears a striking similarity to Olmec versions of the same
deity, is clearly identifiable by his sinuous cranium, slanted eye, pronounced
upper lip, and curved fang (Taube 1996). On the right he is shown in death,
a snake coiled around his waist, diving downward into a black current of
water (Figure 12). The cycle of maize—its metaphoric birth, death, and
emergence out of the quatrefoil center of the turtle earth as the harvest—

FIGURE 13. San Bartolo west wall mural, illustrating the Maize God dressed as a bird at the world center in front of the fifth tree and crowning himself king atop a wooden scaffold. Drawing by H. Hurst, courtesy of Proyecto San Bartolo.

thus occupies the central portion of the composition and provides and an interesting contrast with the southern scenes that depict the four-part creation of an ordered cosmos. The boundaries of civilized space, symbolized by the forest and inhabited by mythical beasts, are distinct from the center, where order is dependent both literally and metaphorically on the agricultural cycle and those who maintain it.

Moving outward yet again there appear a pair of coronations and two scenes illustrating the role of the crowned kings as the world center. On the left (Figure 13), the Maize God, elaborately dressed in jaguar-skin leggings, sits upon a wooden scaffold draped with a jaguar pelt. Three jade belt celts and a sacrificed jaguar hang suspended from a tree placed atop the scaffold behind the seated god. In front of the scaffold, the Maize God dressed in the same costume (including a feathered cape and tail of a bird) hands himself the foliating head of the Principal Bird Deity as his crowning jewel.

To the left of the scaffold the Maize God appears yet again, in the same costume as in his coronation scene. He holds a spear in his hand and offers an unknown (eroded) sacrifice, completing the creation of the four-sided world through the establishment of the world center in the form of the fifth tree. This tree is different from the four on the southern half of the west wall, as its branches reach upward unburdened of the weight of the Principal Bird Deity; it supports only a simple toucan. By establishing the tamed world center, the Maize God reinforces the notion that the world center is governed by order and that order is founded in agriculture.

To the right of the maize cycle is seen a parallel coronation likely featuring a human Ahaw (Figure 14). The Ahaw sits on a woven cushion atop a wooden scaffold with his hands clasped around a sacred bundle. Behind

FIGURE 14. San Bartolo north and west wall murals, illustrating the five-part division of the world. A Maya Ahaw is being born from a gourd centered among babies, and the coronation of the Ahaw takes place atop a wooden scaffold. Drawing by H. Hurst, courtesy of Proyecto San Bartolo.

him a woven mat symbol and a sacrificed jaguar hang from a tree placed on the scaffold. In front of the scaffold an attendant wearing a bird headdress and an elaborately woven cape climbs a ladder to place a trefoil crown, symbolic of foliating maize, on the Ahaw's head. Between the two figures a painted text ending in the glyph AHAW likely provides his full title.

Behind the scaffold, actually on the room's north wall, the birth of five babies out of an exploding gourd is depicted (for a more complete description see Saturno et al. 2005; van Akkeren 2006). Importantly the individual emerging from the center of the gourd wears the same helmet and belt as the Ahaw seated on the scaffold, showing him to be the center of a mythic quadripartite birth in much the same way as the Maize God is shown centering the four-part creation at the fifth tree. In this way, the artistic narrative, as well as its very composition, serves to establish parallels between divine and royal action and reinforces the connection between the world center, civilization, corn, and the king. This connection is given further import through the use of symbols, such as the Maize God, that extend back into the distant past through iconic similarity with more ancient civilizations.

Again the stories of the Maize God that are illustrated by the artists on the west wall of Sub-IA would likely be ones well known to most viewers. The central tenets of Maize God mythology were well established throughout Mesoamerica long before the murals were painted (Taube 1995), and the iconographic familiarity with the cannons of Mesoamerican art evident in the paintings themselves (e.g., quatrefoil, skybands, the Principal Bird Deity, Maize God, Hun Ahaw) is a clear indication that San Bartolo did not exist in a cultural vacuum. That said, if we accept the proposition that the mutual inclusion of these well-known stories in this particular room at the beginning of the first century B.C. was intentional, we are still left with questions about the intent of the mural and its audience.

CENTERING THE KINGDOM

Considering the entirety of the west wall, in addition to the proposed extension of its narrative onto the north and south walls, there are four main actors: the Principal Bird Deity, Hun Ahaw, the Maize God, and the Ahaw. The first three are seen throughout Maya art as symbols of the fourth. Maya Ahaws accede to the throne wearing the crossed headband of Hun Ahaw, often show themselves wearing the ornaments of the defeated Principal Bird Deity, and depict themselves in death as the Maize God. The compilation of well-known narrative episodes along with the parallel coronation of a historical Ahaw has clear implications for legitimizing both the early Maya institution of kingship as well as the individual king. Interestingly enough, the best-known example of a Maya mural depicts the historical legitimization of the heir to the throne of Bonampak from the late eighth century A.D. The historical events at Bonampak are all shown beneath a geometric skyband, above which sit various deities and constellations. In contrast, at San Bartolo all of the action—including the coronation of the historical Ahaw—takes place above the skyband in the realm of the gods. In this way the Ahaw ties his legitimacy not to his mortal ancestry but to his direct association with the divine. The early Maya Ahaw is shown to be the inheritor of the divine qualities of the deities who bring about creation and order. The Maya Ahaw is a hunter, following Hun Ahaw, whose actions as a gatherer of flowers and a hunter of fowl, game, and fish tame the frontiers of his newly established domain through sacrifice and pave the way for further domestication of the natural environment through agriculture. The Maya Ahaw is both farmer and king, following the Maize God, who brings order through agriculture to the world center and crowns himself on the scaffold. The Maya Ahaw is shown as the stable center around which the kingdom, farms, and forests all revolve. The painters at San Bartolo compose a work of art that establishes and justifies the institution of kingship in familiar ideological terms, likely at the behest of the individual king that commissioned the architectural complex. However, the intended audience for this justification remains largely unresolved.

Note that although the murals of Pinturas Sub-IA are currently unique in the Maya lowlands, because of their early date and state of preservation, they were clearly part of a long-established painting tradition. Additional paintings in both contemporary and earlier architectural phases have been found throughout the Pinturas complex. The collapsed remains of the final-phase temple included both interior painted fragments as well as modeled and painted exterior stucco. Along the front side of the Ixim pyramid a cache of some 8,000 interior mural fragments that are contemporary with the Sub-IA murals was uncovered, presumably from the collapsed or destroyed temple at the top of the pyramid. Tunneling deeper within the Pinturas complex has led to the discovery of other buildings with painted decoration that substantially predate the Pinturas Sub-IA murals (Saturno et al. 2006). One example of this earlier painting comes from the Ixbalamque or Sub-V building phase, dating to the early third or late fourth century B.C. and includes both hieroglyphic text and the Maya Maize God.

Excavations outside the Pinturas complex at San Bartolo have failed to uncover evidence of painted buildings. In fact the largest ceremonial structure at the site, Las Ventanas, seems to have been unpainted throughout its roughly 500 years of continuous construction. Thus the Pinturas complex, though not the largest architectural complex at the site, may well have been regarded as the site's material manifestation of the figurative world center throughout its long occupation, continuously decorated with symbols of agricultural fertility and tied to the very notion of rulership at the site.

That said, the presence of contemporary narrative murals from Ixim has implications for the potential audience of the Sub-IA murals. Because the Ixim murals presumably originated at the top of the pyramid, they would be considerably less accessible than those painted at the bottom of the rear of the pyramid. Indeed, a cursory glance at the fragments from Ixim confirms that they were far more finely painted, with a broader palette and the inclusion of more textual material, befitting their placement at the temple top. Although the location of Sub-IA on the rear of the platform may be considered less public than Ixim, it is nonetheless far more accessible. Thus Sub-IA may no longer be considered the sole or even primary repository for narrative mural painting, and the question of its possible audience becomes even more intriguing.

At present the analysis of the Ixim fragments and their original architectural context is in its initial stages, but it can be said with confidence that the viewership permitted to the top of Ixim would stand in stark contrast with that of Sub-IA with its low central step and wide central doorway. Its well-designed narrative of the ideological foundations of governance is also a topic best suited to a broad audience. The presence of incised and crudely painted graffiti on both the interior and exterior of Sub-IA suggests the addition of graphic elements by nonartists as part of the ritual use of the space or perhaps as a result of visitation by a more general audience. One intriguing possibility is that the mural room was intended as an accessible location to be educated in the ideological foundations of Maya rule, where a Maya king commissioned his artists to produce art illustrating the very foundations of his reign for an audience that would grow up to support his successors.

The specific audience intended for a 2,100-year-old mural is unlikely to be resolved with any degree of certainty, but the murals of Sub-IA illustrate the clear desire of the early Maya kings as patrons of the fine arts to be represented to any and all audiences in mythologically familiar terms as the rightful heirs to those responsible for bringing the world out of chaos and into settled, agricultural, civil order. This artistic emphasis is markedly different from Maya political art of later periods, where an emphasis on genealogy and historical action belies both a substantially different audience and a substantially different society.

REFERENCES CITED

Adams, Richard E. W.
    1999   *Río Azul: An Ancient Maya City.* University of Oklahoma Press, Norman.
Andrews, E. Wyllys, V, and William M. Ringle
    1992   Los Mayas tempranos en Yucatán: Investigaciones arqueológicas en Komchén. *Mayab* 8: 5–17.
Bardawil, Lawrence
    1976   The Principal Bird Deity in Maya Art: An Iconographic Study of Form and Meaning. In *The Art, Iconography, and Dynastic History of Palenque,* part III (Merle Green Robertson, ed.): 195–209. Precolumbian Art Research, Robert Louis Stevenson School, Pebble Beach, Calif.
Bauer, Jeremy R.
    2005   Between Heaven and Earth: The Cival Cache and the Creation of the Mesoamerican Cosmos. In *Lords of Creation: The Origins of Sacred Maya Kingship* (Virgina Fields and Dorie Reets-Budet, eds.): 28–29. Scala, London.
Coe, William R.
    1965   Tikal, Guatemala and Emergent Maya Civilization. *Science* 147(3664): 1401–1419.
    1990   *Excavations in the Great Plaza, North Terrace, and North Acropolis of Tikal.* Tikal Report 14, 6 vols. University Museum, University of Pennsylvania, Philadelphia.
Coe, William R., and Michael D. Coe
    1956   Excavations at Nohoch Ek, British Honduras. *American Antiquity* 21: 370–382.
Coe, William R., and John J. McGinn
    1963   Tikal: The North Acropolis and an Early Tomb. *Expedition* 5(2): 24–32.
Dahlin, Bruce H.
    1984   A Colossus in Guatemala: The Preclassic Maya City of El Mirador. *Archaeology* 37(3): 18–25.
Fields, Virginia M.
    1991   The Iconographic Heritage of the Maya Jester God. In *Sixth Palenque Round Table 1986* (Merle G. Robertson and Virginia M. Fields, eds.): 167–174. University of Oklahoma Press, Norman.

Freidel, David A.

1985 Polychrome Facades of the Late Preclassic Period. In *Painted Architecture and Polychrome Monumental Sculpture in Mesoamerica* (Elizabeth H. Boone, ed.): 5–30. Dumbarton Oaks, Washington, D.C.

1990 The Jester God: The Beginning and End of a Maya Royal Symbol. In *Vision and Revision in Maya Studies* (Flora S. Clancy and Peter D. Harrison, eds.): 67–76. University of New Mexico Press, Albuquerque.

Freidel, David A., and Linda Schele

1988 Kingship in the Late Preclassic Maya Lowlands: The Instruments and Places of Ritual Power. *American Anthropologist* 90(3): 547–567.

Hammond, Norman (ed.)

1991 *Cuello: An Early Maya Community in Belize.* Cambridge University Press, Cambridge.

Hammond, Norman, Amanda Clarke, and Francisco Estrada Belli

1992 Middle Preclassic Maya Buildings and Burials at Cuello, Belize. *Antiquity* 66: 955–964.

Hammond, Norman, Sheena Howarth, and Richard R. Wilk

1999 *The Discovery Exploration and Monuments of Nimli Punit, Belize.* Research Reports on Ancient Maya Writing 40. Center for Maya Research, Washington, D.C.

Hansen, Richard

1998 Continuity and Disjunction: The Pre-Classic Antecedents of Classic Maya Architecture. In *Function and Meaning in Classic Maya Architecture* (Stephen Houston, ed.): 49–122. Dumbarton Oaks Research Library and Collection, Washington, D.C.

Laporte, Juan Pedro, and Vilma Fialko

1990 New Perspectives on Old Problems: Dynastic References for the Early Classic at Tikal. In *Vision and Revision in Maya Studies* (Flora S. Clancy and Peter D. Harrison, eds.): 33–66. University of New Mexico Press, Albuquerque.

1995 Un reencuentro con Mundo Perdido, Tikal, Guatemala. *Ancient Mesoamerica* 6(1): 41–94.

Lounsbury, Floyd G.

1982 Astronomical Knowledge and Its Uses at Bonampak, Mexico. In *Archaeoastronomy in the New World* (Anthony Aveni, ed.): 143–158. Cambridge University Press, Cambridge.

Miller, Mary Ellen

1986 *The Murals of Bonampak.* Princeton University Press, Princeton, N.J.

Quenon, Michel, and Genevieve le Fort

1997 Rebirth and Resurrection in Maize God Iconography. In *The Maya Vase Book,* vol. 5 (Justin Kerr, ed.): 884–902. Kerr Associates, New York.

Ricketson, Oliver G., Jr., and Edith B. Ricketson

1937 *Uaxactun, Guatemala.* Carnegie Institution of Washington Publication 477. Carnegie Institution of Washington, Washington, D.C.

Ringle, William M.

    1999   Pre-Classic Cityscapes: Ritual Politics among the Early Lowland
            Maya. In *Social Patterns in Pre-Classic Mesoamerica* (Rosemary Joyce
            and David C. Grove, eds.): 183–223. Dumbarton Oaks Research
            Library and Collection, Washington, D.C.

Robertson, Robin A., and David A. Freidel (eds.)

    1986   *Archaeology at Cerros, Belize, Central America*, vol. 1: *An Interim Report.*
            Southern Methodist University Press, Dallas.

Robicsek, Francis, and Donald M. Hales

    1981   *The Maya Book of the Dead: The Ceramic Codex.* University of Virginia
            Art Museum, Charlottesville.

Ruppert, Karl, J. Eric S. Thompson, and Tatiana Proskouriakoff

    1955   *Bonampak, Chiapas, Mexico.* Carnegie Institution of Washington Pub-
            lication 602. Carnegie Institution of Washington, Washington, D.C.

Saturno, William A.

    2006   The Dawn of Maya Gods and Kings. *National Geographic* January:
            68–77.

Saturno, William A., David Stuart, and Boris Beltrán

    2006   Early Maya Writing at San Bartolo, Guatemala. *Science* 311: 1281–1283.

Saturno, William A., Karl A. Taube, and David Stuart

    2005   *The Murals of San Bartolo, El Petén Guatemala*, part 1: *The North Wall.*
            Ancient America 7. Center for Ancient American Studies, Barnards-
            ville, N.C., and Washington, D.C.

Scarborough, Vernon

    1991   *The Settlement System in a Late Preclassic Maya Community.* David
            Freidel, series ed. Archaeology at Cerros, Belize, Central America III.
            Southern Methodist University Press, Dallas.

Seler, Eduard

1990–98   *Collected Works in Mesoamerican Linguistics and Iconography*, 6 vols.
            (Frank E. Comparato, general ed.). Labyrinthos, Culver City, Calif.

Smith, A. Ledyard

    1950   *Uaxactun, Guatemala: Excavations of 1931–1937.* Publication 588.
            Carnegie Institution of Washington, Washington, D.C.

Smith, Robert E.

    1937   A Study of Structure A-I Complex at Uaxactun, Peten, Guatemala. In
            Contributions to American Archaeology 3, no. 19: 189–231. Publication 456.
            Carnegie Institution of Washington, Washington, D.C.

Staines Cicero, Leticia (ed.)

    1998   *La Pintura mural prehispánica en México, II, Area Maya: Bonampak*, 2
            vols. Universidad Nacional Autónoma de México, México.

Taube, Karl

    1985   The Classic Maya Maize God: A Reappraisal. In *Fifth Palenque Round
            Table 1983* (Merle G. Robertson, ed.): 171–181. Pre-Columbian Art
            Research Institute, San Francisco.

    1988   A Prehispanic Katun Wheel. *Journal of Anthropological Research* 44:
            183–203.

1992   *The Major Gods of Ancient Yucatan.* Studies in Pre-Columbian Art and
       Archaeology 32. Dumbarton Oaks, Washington, D.C.

1995   The Rainmakers: The Olmec and Their Contribution to Mesoamerican
       Belief and Ritual. In *The Olmec World, Ritual and Rulership* (Michael
       Coe, ed.): 83–103. Art Museum, Princeton University, Princeton, N.J.

1996   The Olmec Maize God: The Face of Corn in Formative Mesoamerica.
       RES: Anthropology and Aesthetics 29–30: 39–81.

2003   Ancient and Contemporary Maya Conceptions about the Field and
       Forest. In *Lowland Maya Area: Three Millennia at the Human-Wildland
       Interface* (Arturo Gomez-Pompa, Michael F. Allen, Scott Fedick, and
       J. Jimenez-Moreno, eds.): 461–492. Haworth Press, New York.

2004   Flower Mountain: Concepts of Life, Beauty and Paradise among the
       Classic Maya. *RES: Anthropology and Aesthetics* 45: 69–98.

Taube, Karl A., William A. Saturno, and David Stuart

n.d.   *The Murals of San Bartolo, El Petén Guatemala,* part 2: *The West Wall.*
       Ancient America 10. Center for Ancient American Studies, Barnards-
       ville, N.C., and Washington, D.C.

Thompson, J. Eric

1954   *The Rise and Fall of Maya Civilization.* University of Oklahoma Press,
       Norman.

Van Akkeren, Ruud

2006   *Tzuywa: Place of the Gourd.* Ancient America 9. Center for Ancient
       American Studies, Barnardsville and Washington, D.C.

CHOLULA

FIVE

Art and Architecture of an Archetypal City

Gabriela Uruñuela y Ladrón de Guevara
Patricia Plunket Nagoda
Amparo Robles Salmerón

A STUDY OF THE ART AND ARCHITECTURE of Pre-Columbian Cholula, Mexico, constitutes a many-faceted challenge. First inhabited 3,000 years ago, Cholula (Figure 1) is the oldest continually occupied settlement in the New World. When the Spaniards arrived, it was a complex metropolis and one of Mesoamerica's main pilgrimage centers, prompting Gabriel de Rojas (1927 [1581]: 162) to compare it to Rome among the Christians and Mecca among the Moors. However, its uninterrupted habitation to the present has resulted in the burial of most of the ancient vestiges beneath centuries of later building activity. This circumstance has produced two major currents in its archaeology: grand projects focused on the Great Pyramid that offer few data about the remainder of the site and constant rescue work responding to the development of modern infrastructure, where extensive excavation rarely occurs.

The contrast between the fragmented archaeological information and the descriptions bequeathed by the conquistadores (e.g., Cortés 1928 [1519–26]; Díaz del Castillo 1956 [1517–21]; Motolinía 1969 [1858]) and other early chroniclers (de Rojas 1927 [1581]) has favored the ethnohistorical perspective as the referent for ancient Cholula. The panorama becomes still more nebulous when, as one goes back in time, the support provided by written sources is diluted until it disappears, making it difficult to visualize the site's characteristics prior to the sixteenth century and even more so to define when it can be considered a city and whether it represented an archetype. Furthermore, its long occupation requires that this chapter's discussion be limited to a specific time span to avoid painting a homogeneous picture that, by ignoring the diachronic component, would prove too superficial for what was a dynamic and complex history. Thus our temporal selection

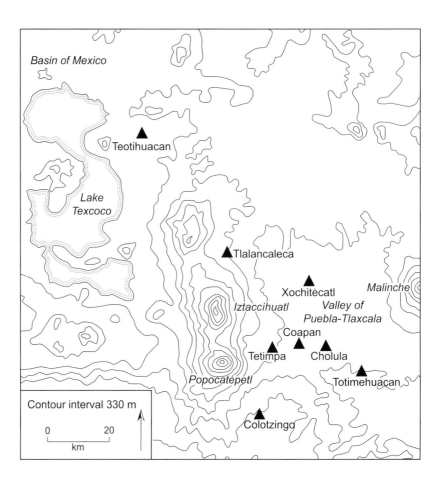

FIGURE 1.
Archaeological sites
mentioned in the text.

is based on two criteria: "begin at the beginning" and employ the firsthand
knowledge we have gathered over the past few years.

The Tetimpa Project was designed to evaluate the impact of Popocatepetl's eruptions on the Pre-Hispanic population of the Puebla Valley.
Besides documenting villages buried by those events (Plunket and Uruñuela 1998), we are exploring the relationships between the consequences
for the affected communities and the development of Cholula, which would
become a preeminent regional center at the beginning of our era. Because
few areas remain in which extensive explorations can be undertaken to
obtain a broad view of the site, one of the only opportunities still available
to address this problem is the information that can be recovered from the
Great Pyramid, the Tlachihualtepetl ("man-made mountain"). As the most
representative monument of a good part of Cholultecan history, this structure can serve as a barometer for inferring the fortune of the settlement of
which it formed part and of the society that created it.

Although from 1931 to 1971 the Tlachihualtepetl was subject to intensive
research, the plans resulting from more than 10 km of excavated tunnels
(de la Luz and Contreras n.d. [1968]) were misplaced. Hence, to understand

its origin and development, we are remapping the construction sequence and obtaining samples for radiometric dating. Having now finished with the earliest substructures, we decided to use these findings and restrict our discussion to the first centuries A.D.

Because the theme of this volume is the art of urbanism, it would seem logical to start this discussion by determining whether, for the selected time period, Cholula can be considered a city. Dozens of studies have focused on defining this term. Traditional arguments privilege a typological approach in which urbanism is determined by a series of attributes, framed since the mid-twentieth century by the Weberian consideration (Weber 1958: 81) that cities are autonomous corporate communities, spatially and socially bounded by those that surround them. Employing a list of criteria that cannot be applied cross-culturally has multiple limitations (Blanton 1976: 250); consequently, more recent perspectives favor the functional aspect regarding managerial and administrative services that a center provides to adjacent towns, because cities are considered to be the resulting seat of institutions developed to create and integrate regional socioeconomic systems (e.g., Blanton 1981; Marcus 2000; Smith 1989).

In either case, the few data available for Cholula during the first and second centuries A.D. hinder both the identification of a trait inventory and the detection of the range of functions offered. However, those centuries witnessed important changes in local history that for the first time allow us to perceive Cholula as a leading regional player. Thus in effect it is better to examine the site's context for that time; describe the emergence of its monumental art and architecture according to the evidence from the Great Pyramid; highlight the differences we have detected with respect to the known information; and, finally, discuss whether that evidence concurs with what one would expect of a city and if it is pertinent to consider this case an archetype. Therefore, perhaps a more appropriate title for our chapter might be: "Cholula: The Beginning of Monumental Art and Architecture of an Archetypal City?"

There have been previous efforts to interpret the iconography and other data from Cholula linked to this theme (e.g., McCafferty 1996, 2001), but we prefer to perform an exercise that, with solid foundations, attempts to impose order on the disjointed facts. Although we only address the Great Pyramid's first stages, we hope that this first step will benefit colleagues interested in the enigmatic Cholula.

CHOLULA PRIOR TO THE GREAT PYRAMID

The earliest archaeological evidence in Cholula goes back to the beginning of the Middle Formative, with a few radiometrically dated contexts (Table 1) at the Universidad de las Américas (UDLA) campus (Figure 2) corresponding

TABLE 1. Radiocarbon dates for Formative and Early Classic Cholula

Lab and specimen number	Years B.P.	Context	Intercept (cal)	1σ (cal)	2σ (cal)
Beta 188355	2,800 ± 100	UDLA, charred material, bell-shaped pit[1]	930 B.C.	1055–830 B.C.	1260–795 B.C.
GX 2256	2,645 ± 110	UDLA, charred wood, Pit 6[2]	804 B.C.*	901–765 B.C.*	1010–412 B.C.*
Beta 188353	2,030 ± 70	Rancho de la Virgen, charred material, adobe wall, middle phase of Structure 2, Pit 5[3]	40 B.C.	115 B.C.–A.D. 55	195 B.C.–A.D. 115
Beta 188352	2,010 ± 80	Rancho de la Virgen, charred material, adobe wall, last phase of Structure 2, Pit 5[3]	5 B.C.	100 B.C.–A.D. 75	195 B.C.–A.D. 140
I 17627	1,890 ± 80	San Gabriel, charred material, hearth on top of platform[4]	A.D. 125*	A.D. 59–235*	41 B.C.–A.D. 268* and A.D. 273–336*
Beta 188344 (AMS)	1,920 ± 50	Great Pyramid, carbonized seed, bell-shaped pit (Pit 2) in front of Structure 1[5]	A.D. 80	A.D. 45–130	30 B.C.–A.D. 225
Beta 188345 (AMS)	1,910 ± 50	Great Pyramid, carbonized bean, sandy fill between adobes of Structure 1[5]	A.D. 85	A.D. 55–135	5 B.C.–A.D. 230
Beta 188343 (AMS)	1,870 ± 50	Great Pyramid, carbonized bean, bell-shaped pit (Pit 1) in front of Structure 1[5]	A.D. 130	A.D. 80–225	A.D. 45–250
Beta 188346 (AMS)	1,850 ± 50	Great Pyramid, carbonized maize kernel, sandy lens, fill of Structure 1[5]	A.D. 140	A.D. 95–235	A.D. 60–260
Beta 162997 (AMS)	1,810 ± 40	Great Pyramid, charred material, fill of Structure 1[5]	A.D. 230	A.D. 140–250	A.D. 110–330
Beta 188342 (AMS)	1,790 ± 50	Great Pyramid, carbonized bean, bell-shaped pit (Pit 1) in front of Structure 1[5]	A.D. 240	A.D. 155–265 and 290–325	A.D. 115–385
Beta 212349 (AMS)	1,960 ± 40	Great Pyramid, Structure 2, fourth level, wood support of Los Chapulincitos *tablero*	A.D. 50	A.D. 10–80	A.D. 40–120
Beta 188348 (AMS)	1,930 ± 50	Great Pyramid, charred material, Structure 2, north face, seventh level (Chapulines mural, east section) between clay plaster and base of *tablero*[5]	A.D. 75	A.D. 30–120	B.C. 40–A.D. 215
Beta 212346 (AMS)	1,910 ± 40	Great Pyramid, Structure 2, fourth level, charred roof beam from portico	A.D. 90	A.D. 60–130	A.D. 20–220
Beta 188350 (AMS)	1,980 ± 50	Great Pyramid, charred material directly on top of seventh level, north face of Structure 2 (Chapulines mural, west section)[5]	A.D. 30	40 B.C.–A.D. 75	80 B.C.–A.D. 120
Beta 212347 (AMS)	1,880 ± 40	Great Pyramid, charcoal inside a vessel, inaugural offering under north staircase of Structure 3	A.D. 120	A.D. 80–150	A.D. 50–230
Beta 188347 (AMS)	1,820 ± 40	Great Pyramid, carbonized maize kernel, trash lens, fill over west side of Structure 2 (core of Structure 3)[5]	A.D. 225	A.D. 135–245	A.D. 95–265 and 290–325
Beta 188349 (AMS)	1,760 ± 40	Great Pyramid, charred material directly on top of seventh level, north face of Structure 2 (Chapulines mural, west section) (core of Structure 3)[5]	A.D. 255	A.D. 235–340	A.D. 155–390
Beta 162998	1,700 ± 60	Great Pyramid, charred material, fill over west side of Structure 2 (core of Structure 3)[5]	A.D. 370	A.D. 250–410	A.D. 220–450
Beta 188351 (AMS)	1,930 ± 50	Great Pyramid, charred material directly on top of seventh level, north face of Structure 3 (west section of the *tableros lisos*)[5]	A.D. 75	A.D. 30–120	40 B.C.–A.D. 215

Sources: (1) López et al. (n.d. [2004]); (2) Mountjoy and Peterson (1973); (3) López, A. et al. (n.d. [2002]); (4) Plunket and Uruñuela (2002a); (5) Plunket and Uruñuela (2005).

Note: cal, calibrated; UDLA, Universidad de las Américas.

*Calibrated by Radiocarbon Calibration Program Rev 4.3 (Plunket and Uruñuela 2005).

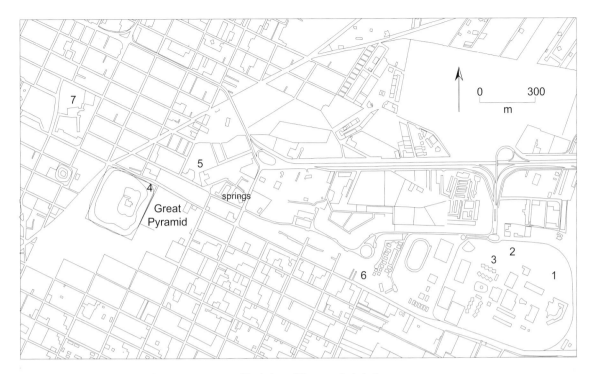

FIGURE 2. Early evidence for occupation in Cholula: 1, Universidad de las Américas (UDLA) campus; 2, early ceramics from the swamp; 3, early ceramics from bell-shaped pits; 4, La Conejera; 5, Rancho de la Virgen; 6, Terminal Formative platforms at UDLA; and 7, Monastery of San Gabriel.

to ceramics from the bottom of a swamp (Mountjoy and Peterson 1973: 62) and from bell-shaped pits on its shores (López et al. n.d. [2004]). However, in spite of numerous rescue and salvage operations, traces of occupation outside the area of the Great Pyramid before the first century A.D. are scarce and isolated (e.g., Caskey n.d. [1988]; Hernández et al. n.d. [1998]).

As for the Tlachihualtepetl itself, Middle and Late Formative materials have been reported from strata beneath its initial foundations (Müller 1978: 14, 15; Noguera 1954: 199–203, 290–292). Some come from La Conejera (Figure 2)—not part of the Great Pyramid itself, but a structure covered by later additions to its northeast corner—excavated by Luz Campos in the 1950s (Noguera 1956). Associated with other partially explored contemporary buildings, this platform—more than 9 m on a side and 2 m high—has sloping walls (*taludes*) crowned by a plain panel (*tablero*) and supports a room—3.5 m north–south by 4.5 m east–west—with mud-plastered adobe walls. Noguera (1956: 214, 216, 217) identified the ceramics in the fill as El Arbolillo I, and Zacatenco I and II, dating its construction to Zacatenco III–Ticomán or perhaps Teotihuacan I, although he mentions indications of a substructure.

Thus, prior to the Common Era, nothing suggests that Cholula prevailed over neighboring communities like Coapan, Colotzingo, Totimehuacan, or Xochitecatl, which all had formal public architecture by the Late Formative. In fact, only the La Conejera group might indicate that Cholula belonged to this category of major sites.

About the middle of the first century A.D., Popocatepetl produced a 20- to 30-km-high eruptive column whose collapse blanketed with pumitic lapilli an area extending 25 km east of its crater (Panfil n.d. [1996]: 16). It buried villages like Tetimpa, located 15 km from Cholula on the eastern flank of the volcano (see Figure 1) and occupied since 800 B.C., which had grown to become a dispersed settlement covering more than 3 km², with about 3,000 inhabitants. Based on the Volcanic Explosivity Index that describes on a scale of 0 to 8 the size of eruptions (Pyle 2000: 263–264), this event was a level 6 (Siebe 2000: 61), a major catastrophe—like Krakatoa in 1883—of the kind that only occurs globally about once every century, is highly explosive, and is 100 percent fatal to those in its vicinity (Simkin and Siebert 2000: 259).

The consequent abandonment of Tetimpa is well documented (e.g., Plunket and Uruñuela 2003; Uruñuela and Plunket 2003), but many other places were also affected, and in western Puebla-Tlaxcala major sites near the slopes, like Colotzingo (Uruñuela 1989), Coapan (Uruñuela n.d. [1981]), Xochitecatl (Serra Puche and Palavacini 1996; Spranz 1970b), and Tlalancaleca (García Cook 1981), were deserted. Indeed, the volcanic activity even had repercussions to the west of the Sierra Nevada in the Basin of Mexico, where the southeastern sector underwent severe depopulation (Sanders et al. 1979: tables 16, 17), perhaps provoked by pyroclastic flows that resulted in massive migrations (Plunket and Uruñuela 2006; Siebe 2000: 61). Thus during the late first century A.D., the abandonment of extensive areas near the volcano and an apparently generalized demographic decrease in the Puebla Valley (Dumond 1972: 115; García Cook 1981: 263) contrast with the accumulation of evidence for occupation in Cholula that, from this time onward, would definitely have monumental architecture.

FIRST-CENTURY STRUCTURES OUTSIDE THE TLACHIHUALTEPETL

The eruption precedes the construction of the Great Pyramid, the best-known early building in Cholula, although other structures accompanied its beginnings. At the Rancho de la Virgen (see Figure 2), one block northeast of the Great Pyramid, archaeological testing revealed adobe architectural remains 1.80 to 3.50 m below the surface (López et al. n.d. [2002]). Two dates (see Table 1) associated with a 1.60-m-high platform, erected in three stages on sterile clay overlying the *tepetate* (water-alluviated tuff), situate it no later than the start of the second century A.D., because it is sealed by Early Classic materials. Another platform, 67 cm high, with two building phases—including a limestone reinforced step and *alfarda* from the later stage—was sealed by a layer lacking cultural remains, but it was built on the same sterile clay as the first platform, suggesting that the two structures are contemporaneous. Mountjoy and Peterson (1973) documented similar constructions on the UDLA campus (see Figure 2).

Those buildings seem relatively minor, but adjacent to the Monastery of San Gabriel (see Figure 2), 450 m northwest of the Great Pyramid, we recorded a 12-m-wide staircase with at least 13 steps on the east facade of a large platform. The platform is covered by the sixteenth-century edifice and by the Instituto García de Cisneros (Plunket and Uruñuela 2002a). Carbon from a hearth on top of this structure (Plunket and Uruñuela 2005) places it between the first and third centuries A.D. (see Table 1).

PROYECTO CHOLULA

At the Great Pyramid, the known information comes from the three stages of the Proyecto Cholula, a gigantic undertaking whose planning involved a masterly deployment of talent and ability and whose execution required an enormous amount of work. Unfortunately, that effort was unbalanced by a brief and often contradictory dissemination, aggravated by the disappearance of much of the field data required to faithfully trace not only the archaeological sequence but also the project's own history.

The first intervention began under Ignacio Marquina in 1931 through the initiative of José Reygadas, Director of Monuments for the Secretary of Education (Marquina 1939: 52, 57, 1970a: 33). Until 1934, Emilio Cuevas was in charge of excavations, subsequently Marino Gómez (Marquina 1939: 57, 63), and then in the 1950s Luz Campos, the latter's widow (Noguera 1956: 213). The exploration started on the northeast corner of the Great Pyramid—where ancient structures had been cut by a newly built road—with tunnels that followed staircases and building contours to reveal their form and dimensions (Marquina 1939: 59, 1970a: 33). The complex superpositioning of those buildings abutting some of the early phases of the Great Pyramid motivated a change in strategy, leading to the direct intervention of the massive platform by way of two principal intersecting tunnels along its north-south and east-west axes and numerous branches; this work continued until 1956, by which time there were 8,000 m of tunnels (Marquina 1970a: 33). Stratigraphic pits were made between 1932 and 1936 to sequence the occupation periods (Noguera 1954: 12). Apart from specific documents on ceramics or burials (e.g., Müller 1978; Noguera 1937, 1954; Romero 1935), this first stage generated only two comprehensive publications: a preliminary article in 1939 (Marquina 1939), and a book chapter in 1951 (in Marquina 1990) that summarized in 15 pages the first 20 years of work.

The effort then languished until 1965, when Eusebio Dávalos, director of Instituto Nacional de Antropología e Historia (INAH), assigned Miguel Messmacher to renew the project with an anthropological perspective and a regional scope. The work at the Great Pyramid primarily investigated the platforms that extend on the south side of it (Marquina 1970a: 33–34; Messmacher 1967: 12–14). This second stage was highly conflicted and culminated with the director's resignation in mid-1967 (Marquina 1970a: 33–34). According to Messmacher's (1967) preface to the only volume that compiled some of the results obtained from 1966 to 1967, the problems were such that project members had to fund the publication themselves.

Upon Messmacher's departure, Marquina (1970a: 33–34) returned as director. Although exploration at this time concentrated on the Great Pyramid's exterior (south, east, and west fronts), tunnels were lengthened and new ones were excavated (Marquina 1970a: 36). The researchers also addressed topographic recording, under Eduardo Contreras, to correlate data from the three stages of fieldwork (Marquina 1970a: 35), but neither the plans from the tunnels nor the corresponding field notes arrived at the Technical Archive of INAH. The general information from this season was documented in one publication in 1970 (Marquina 1970b) that collects the results up to that point of this stage that ended abruptly in 1971 and in a brief chapter in a book (Marquina 1975). Only the human remains were the object of later analysis and diffusion (López et al. 1976, 2002). The local press (García 1971a, 1971b) attributed the sudden demise of the research to pressure from landowners who demanded payment of back rent from 1965 at current prices: the UDLA had recently moved to Cholula, and as a consequence land values had rapidly appreciated, so that the debt was exorbitant. If indeed the case, it seems only fair that now this institution, through archival research and the remaking of lost plans, is attempting to reconstruct the puzzle left behind.

ON MARQUINA'S TRAIL

Establishing a possible link between the beginnings of monumental architecture in Cholula and the consequences of the volcanic eruption in the first century A.D. requires precise information on the initial phases of the construction of the Great Pyramid. McCafferty (1996) attempted to correlate its construction sequence using data published by the Proyecto Cholula, but we considered that their schematic and often contradictory nature, the impossibility of consulting the original plans, and the lack of radiometric dating were obstacles that needed to be overcome before proposing interpretations. Therefore we decided to map with a total station the

FIGURE 3. Collapsed tunnel in the Great Pyramid.

tunnels and the architecture they exposed and to obtain carbon samples to reconstruct the chronology. We have to date completed the study of more than 2 km of tunnels, corresponding to the earliest buildings.

This work has not been simple. Certain tunnels were sealed or refilled by earlier researchers, and others collapsed during the 1999 earthquake (Figure 3). Some tunnels indicated in the documents do not exist—perhaps they were planned but not executed—whereas others that do exist are not recorded. Marquina's team protected the floors with dirt that had to be removed to define their contours, and the tests they made to solve interpretative problems were back-filled and needed to be relocated by detecting differences in the compaction of the surfaces, so that we could reopen and register them. To add to these difficulties, electrical power only remains functional in a section of the north-south central tunnel and in part of Los Chapulines Murals. Notwithstanding, we have recovered detailed data that were only schematically known and others that were never published. This effort allows us to present a model of the Great Pyramid that is a bit different from the traditional version; we first describe briefly the latter in order to contextualize the modifications that we offer.

CONSTRUCTION SEQUENCE OF THE GREAT PYRAMID ACCORDING TO MARQUINA

Having assembled the information from his diverse publications, we conclude that Marquina (1939, 1970a, 1990) viewed the Great Pyramid as the

outcome of seven major construction stages, although only five of these
affected the platform itself. He places Stage I in the first or second century
A.D. (Marquina 1990: 129) and subdivides that stage into parts A and B.

For Marquina, in Stage IA (Figure 4) the 17- to 18-m-high lime-plastered
adobe structure had an approximately square plan, 113 m east-west by 107
m north-south, oriented 24° east of astronomical north (Marquina 1970a:
36–39, 1990: 118, 120–121). It has a basal platform of five levels with sloping
walls, each about 2.5 m high; on the fifth—whose west side is T-shaped in
plan view—two more levels rise after a 6-m-wide landing, forming a 43-m
square "plaza" on the surface of the seventh (Marquina 1939: 60, 1970a:
36–39, 1990: 120–121). Centered on the top of this plaza is a precinct, 19 m
square, delimited by wide, low walls with *taludes* on both faces (Marquina
1970a: 36–39, 1990: 120–121), although sometimes these limits are mentioned only for the east and west sides of this area, where no other remains
crowned the building (Marquina 1939: 60). The structure is accessed by a
west stairway flanked by *alfardas* and superimposed on the steep *taludes;*
wide landings interrupt the stairs, creating, in ascending order, sets with
10, 11, 10, 9, 8, 17, and 12 risers, the last set being narrower than the others
(Marquina 1939: 60, 1970a: 36–39, 1990: 120–121, 124).

Marquina (1970a: 39) indicates that Building IA was covered by various
structures, but that only the one over the north side is clear. He designates
it IB (see Figure 4), and it corresponds to the addition of several levels of
stepped *taludes*, each about 3 m high. The top two of these levels support
decorated *tableros* interrupted by a wide gap at the center; the *tablero* wraps
around to the south on the east and west sides of the seventh level, while on
the sixth it folds to the south on the west but to the north on the east side,
where it terminates abruptly (Marquina 1939: 60, 1970a: 33, 39, 1990: 121).

Stage IB was covered by Stage II or C (see Figure 4), a pyramid stepped on all four sides with recessed corners. Formed by nine levels, each with sets of between 11 and 13 steps separated by 2-m-wide landings, it measures 180 m square and rises 35 m before culminating in a surface 90 m on a side; although the main access must have been on the now-destroyed west facade, on the north there is a narrow superimposed staircase with various segments of 11 steps and another with 52 (Marquina 1970: 39, 1990: 121–122).

Stage III or D (see Figure 4) corresponds to additions abutting the northeast corner (Marquina 1990: 123). There are another two substructures of the monument between stages II and IV, for which Marquina (1970: 41, figs. 5, 6, 7) simply indicates a length of 350 m on a side, designating both substructures by E.

Dismantled prior to the Spaniards' arrival, Stage IV (see Figure 4) is the last building phase of the Great Pyramid. Marquina (1990: 123–124) envisions it as a platform 400 m on a side and some 25 m high supporting on its posterior—eastern—part a 200 m square, 37-m-high platform, giving a total height of 62 m, not including the temple that might have surmounted it. The dating of Stages II through IV is very vague, and Marquina (1990: 129) merely establishes that they must have been built between Teotihuacan II and Tula.

The final building phase, or Stage V (see Figure 4), corresponds to later structures around the base or on part of the Great Pyramid's platform (Marquina 1990: 124).

OUR MODIFICATIONS

Summary of the Construction Sequence

Reconstructing the morphology of the Great Pyramid is complicated. The buildings have undergone significant settling, some during their uselife and others from the enormous overburden that has compressed and deformed them (Marquina 1939: 60). A space can be displaced by as much as 2 m, confounding the correlation of constructive features. In addition, there are large sections without tunnels, and the architectural complexity does not always allow us to make projections from existing data. Even so, we have obtained information that Marquina obviously also had by the end of the Proyecto Cholula but never disseminated, and we can compare it with the established version of the Great Pyramid (Figure 5) derived from the schematic published plans that are essentially based on evidence from the project's earliest interventions.

Although much mapping remains to be done, we have detected at least eight construction stages (Figure 6) affecting the entire platform, not including partial enlargements or abutting additions. This result contrasts

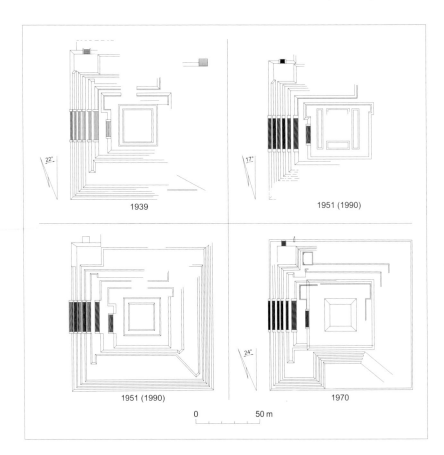

FIGURE 5. Marquina's (1939, 1951 [1990], 1970a) versions of the Edificio de los Chapulines.

with the five stages (I, II, E, E, and IV) identified by Marquina, and compels us to change the nomenclature. Here we review our proposed sequence, still making numerical reference to the constructive stages while proposing new names for those we have defined well to date.

Marquina (1990: 118) suspected that his Stage I was the result of super-positions. In effect (Table 2), underneath it we recorded an earlier building that we label Structure 1 or Edificio de la Olla (see Figure 6); its dimensions are unknown, because it is only evident in a 53-m-long tunnel whose excavation was never documented. The tunnel cuts 2 m into the *tepetate* in front of the west facade of Marquina's Stage I and then rises and penetrates its base from west to east. Some 18 m from the beginning of the tunnel and 14 m east of the edge of Marquina's Stage I, the tunnel perforates the west *talud* of the Edificio de la Olla (Figure 7); it continues 33 m farther inside its core formed of adobe *cajones* filled with *tepetate*, clay, and sand lenses, terminating inside a hollowed-out *cajón* known locally as "La Olla" (cf. McCafferty 2001: 286). Three dates from the core, and three from Pre-Hispanic pits excavated in front of the structure into the *tepetate* on which it is built—these pits were filled with sand when the surface was leveled for construction—suggest that the Edificio de la Olla was erected toward the end of the first or the beginning of the second century A.D. (see Table 1). Those dates are a bit later than we expected, because excellent contexts from the building that covers the Edificio de la Olla are contemporary with or earlier than these dates. The tunnel to La Olla has been often visited by groups involved in esoteric rites, who burn different substances there, and it may be that these rituals slightly contaminated the samples exposed in the tunnel walls. Therefore, considering the solid dates from the next structure, we think that the Edificio de la Olla was erected during the first century A.D.

Marquina's Stage I—which is what most interests us here and to whose detailed description we return later—is thus the second version of the monument, our Structure 2 or Edificio de los Chapulines (or for brevity, Los Chapulines; see Table 2 and Figure 6). As mentioned above, Marquina divides his Stage I into parts A and B, but for reasons we will submit when we describe it, we consider both of his substages to be just one phase with a dual facade (meaning principal side), one to the north and the other to the west. Carbon incrusted between the plaster and the body of the seventh-level *tableros*, a charred roof beam from a portico in a sealed tunnel, and wood that supports a *tablero* on the fourth level all rendered dates indicating that Los Chapulines was constructed ca. A.D. 100 (see Table 1).

Structure 3 (Edificio de los Tableros Lisos) covers Los Chapulines and in many ways replicates its form, including the north *tableros* (Figure 8) and the dual facade, but the *tableros* are undecorated, and a large elevated plaza is created on the west (see Figure 6); the west facade of Los Tableros Lisos is not exposed, but the plaza extends 71 m from the edge of the earlier Edificio de los Chapulines. Thus, Los Tableros Lisos marks a change to privilege the west side, something that would be maintained in subsequent versions of the monument, as is apparent in later models that show an elevated plaza in that direction (Figure 9). Los Tableros Lisos, constructed with adobe *cajones* filled with adobe, *tepetate,* and clay, has not been reported before, although it covered the entire monument and was subject to various evident modifications (Figure 10). Eliminating a sample that corresponds to older

TABLE 2. Correlation between our proposal and Marquina's constructive sequence

Marquina	Tetimpa Project
	Structure 1 (Edificio de la Olla)
Stage IA	Structure 2
Stage IB	(Edificio de los Chapulines)
	Structure 3 (Edificio de los Tableros Lisos)
Stage II or C	Structure 4 (Edificio Escalonado)
	Structure 5
Stage E (1)	Structure 6
Stage E (2)	Structure 7
Stage V	Structure 8

FIGURE 6. West-east profile of the construction sequence proposed by the Tetimpa Project (modified from Marquina 1970a: 37, fig. 6). Dotted lines indicate unconfirmed dimensions. Our additions to Marquina's proposal are: Structure 1, the morphology of Structure 2, Structure 3, and Structure 5.

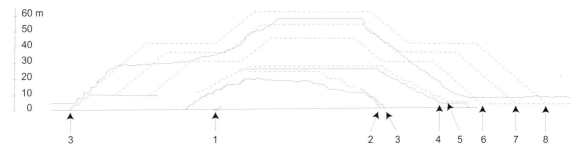

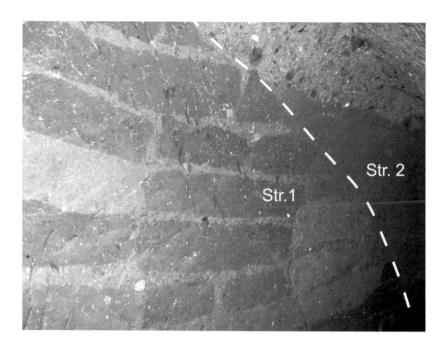

FIGURE 7. West *talud* of Structure 1 (Edificio de la Olla) in tunnel profile. Although it lacks its plaster finish, the arrangement of the *adobes* marks the difference between Structures 1 and 2.

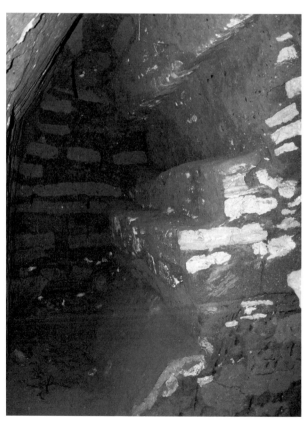

FIGURE 8. Section of the north *tableros* of Structure 3 (Edificio de los Tableros Lisos) exposed in a tunnel. Photo by Aurelio López.

FIGURE 9. Late domestic patio on south side of the Tlachihualtepetl with a model of the pyramid showing an elevated west plaza.

FIGURE 10. Floors and *taludes* (arrows) of Structure 3 (Edificio de los Tableros Lisos) and its renovations, which have been cut by the tunnels in the north facade.

material (Beta 188350 in Table 1), four more dates from its core—two from the north side and two from the west—plus another on charcoal inside a vessel from an offering under the north staircase, suggest that Los Tableros Lisos sealed Los Chapulines during the second century A.D. (see Table 1).

One date (Beta 188351) from the fill covering the first version of Los Tableros Lisos is identical to the one from beneath the plaster of Los Chapulines (Beta 188348), indicating that it is older, reincorporated carbon, so we still do not know the time of closure for this edifice. Los Tableros Lisos and its enlargements were sealed by the stone—mainly limestone—and clay core of the pyramid stepped on all four sides (Marquina's Stage II and our Structure 4 or Edificio Escalonado). This is superimposed by Structure 5, which duplicates the lower structure's form and materials and has not been reported before (see Figure 6 and Table 2).

Structure 5 was covered by another, again employing an adobe core; for us this is the sixth, and should correspond to one of Marquina's E structures (1970a: figs. 5–7), the other E being the seventh. Finally, the last Pre-Hispanic construction is our Structure 8 and Marquina's Stage IV (see Figure 6 and Table 2). Because we have concentrated on the earliest buildings, it is even possible that there are other unreported structures built after our Edificio Escalonado.

Architecture of the Edificio de los Chapulines

We now return in detail to Los Chapulines to present the deviations from Marquina's description that our study has revealed. To begin with, we have joined Marquina's substages IA and IB into a single phase: a small test made by the Proyecto Cholula demonstrates that the north *alfarda* of IA's stairway rests on the end of the *tablero* of IB on the sixth level of the pyramid, and at the same time the north *alfarda* of IA on the seventh level is set back to the south (Figure 11), as if the stairway were adjusted to the turn of the *tablero* of IB on the west facade and not the other way around. Although from its first publication Marquina (1939: 60) alleged that the *tableros*—IB—were later than Stage IA, farther on in the same article (1939: 62) he mentions that the section with the *tableros* is the earliest part of the building. In later interpretations Marquina (1970a: 33, 39) never returned to that idea. We think that the *tableros* are part of the original plan; in fact, they were placed first and then followed by the stairway, but simply as a matter of steps in the construction process of a design that included both from the beginning. This procedure resulted in a platform with a dual facade, one on the west and a more elaborate one on the north (see Figure 11).

The building technique used on Los Chapulines is highly unsystematic. Its core is formed by *cajones* made of adobes of diverse dimensions and materials and filled with *tepetate*, clay, and/or sand. This core was overlain with a support layer of variably sized limestone on the *taludes*, steps, *alfardas*,

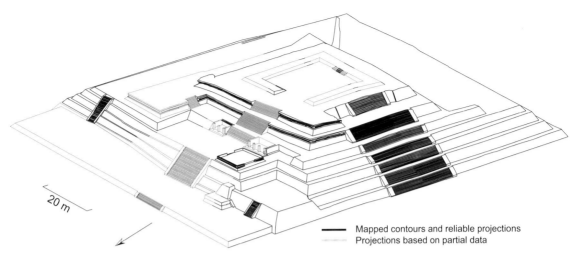

Mapped contours and reliable projections
Projections based on partial data

20 m

FIGURE 11. Northwest view of Structure 2 (Edificio de los Chapulines) according to our reconstruction. Major deformations are shown; dotted lines indicate hypothetical projections.

and *tableros*, and on the angles joining *taludes* and landings; the stone can be arranged diagonally, horizontally, or, on occasion, not be there. On top, or on a foundation layer of *tepetate* or mud on the horizontal surfaces, or directly on the fill, a 3- to 8-cm-thick gray clay mortar with small volcanic inclusions is placed, finished with polished mud. The inconsistency and the plasticity of the materials employed created problems from the beginning, and subsided zones filled and patched with flooring are fairly common.

The Edificio de los Chapulines is 17.24 m high. Rather than being a pyramid in the sense of those at Teotihuacan, its seven levels create a play of volumes and terraces, lacking symmetry but balanced by the distribution of solid and open spaces, that recalls a southern Mesoamerican acropolis. Unfortunately, the tunnels do not always cross the center of the terraces to see whether these supported other buildings.

To facilitate comprehension of the modifications we propose for the Edificio de los Chapulines, we proceed in ascending order. The first level, 107.41 m east-west by at least 130 m north-south, includes a large (at least 16 m north-south by approximately 106 m east-west) unreported plaza on the north (Figure 12, a). Access to it must have been from the north, but there is no tunnel to verify this hypothesis. Curiously, the northern section of an earlier *talud-tablero* platform (including an *alfarda* on its west face) remained exposed (Figure 12, b) on the west part of this plaza.

Two stairways rise from that plaza. One, 2.7 m wide with 17 steps flanked by 56-cm-wide *alfardas*, is in the northwest (Figure 12, c). Marquina (1939) recorded it as ascending to the first level, or adjoined descending from its base to an unknown surface (Marquina 1990: 120), but in reality it ascends the second level to a terrace—15 m north-south by 18.5 m east-west—on the northwest corner (Figure 12, d), created by a recess of the third and fourth levels; a tunnel crosses the center of this terrace and shows that it does not support a building. The other stairway (Figure 12, e) is in the northeast section and either does not appear on Marquina's plans (Marquina 1970a,

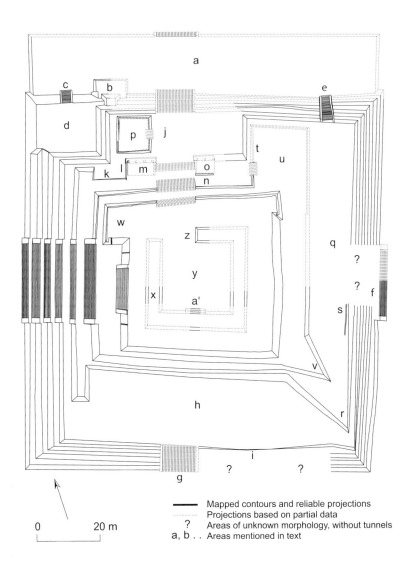

FIGURE 12. Plan of Structure 2 (Edificio de los Chapulines). Major deformations are shown; dotted lines indicate hypothetical projections. See text for a discussion of the lettered elements.

0   20 m

——— Mapped contours and reliable projections
.... Projections based on partial data
?   Areas of unknown morphology, without tunnels
a, b . . Areas mentioned in text

1990: 120) or is shown as isolated (Marquina 1939). This 3-m-wide stairway with narrow 40-cm *alfardas* and at least 33 steps (its upper part is destroyed), rises from the first level plaza and leads to a terrace on the fifth.

We found two other previously undocumented elements on the first level. A stairway on the east face (Figure 12, f) was partially destroyed by a Los Tableros Lisos *talud*, but its south *alfarda* and remains of three steps are visible. Although it seems to be symmetrical with the main west staircase, it does not appear in the corresponding upper level tunnels; we cannot determine whether it just ascended the first level, or it continued to at least the terrace on the fifth level and its absence in other tunnels derives from the deformation of this sector.

Dismantled on the south face, another stairway (Figure 12, g) is evidenced by the abrupt ending of the first-level *talud* in a straight cut, 41.6 m from the southwest corner. That cut is aligned with the west side of the dismantled stairway on the sixth and seventh levels on the north facade. There are no upper level tunnels appropriate to verify it, but it would make sense if this south stairway led to the fourth-level terrace.

Besides the already mentioned access to the second-level northwest corner terrace, we detected no major differences from Marquina's plans on the second and third levels.

The fourth level creates two large flat spaces. One—which appears on Marquina's 1939 and 1951 (1990) plans but not on the last version of 1970— is an ample terrace (Figure 12, h) along the south side—89 m east-west by 20.5 m north-south—and the *talud* that descends from it to the third level turns at the center into a vertical face (Figure 12, i), suggesting a complex morphology for the lower levels, but no tunnels go down farther into this section to confirm this idea. The other flat space (Figure 12, j), well documented on the northwest, is a terrace that probably extends to the northeast. To the south of it the north *talud* of the fifth level converts into a vertical surface (Figure 12, k); adjoined to it is a wall (Figure 12, l) running north—4.83 m long and conserved up to a height of 1.85 m—at the end of which abuts a 54-cm square limestone pillar preserved up to 1.22 m that could be part of a gallery or portico extending to the east (Figure 12, m); the pillar rises from a 21-cm-high base, with sloping sides constructed of well-dressed volcanic rock. A tunnel in the northeast section of the fourth level exposes a roof—including a 5.62-m-long beam (Figure 12, n)—and the fill of a burned room that again abuts the vertical face of the fifth level, which might represent another portico (Figure 12, o), such that both would flank the north access of the fifth level.

In the northwest section of the fourth level of the north terrace, the horizontal surface extends in front of the gallery at least 12 m farther north, to support Los Chapulincitos, a platform that is 11 m square and 1.2 m high (Figure 12, p). Originally the west *talud* of this platform rose directly from the west end of the terrace, which descended vertically to the third level; later, a *talud* creating a 2-m-wide landing in front of Los Chapulincitos covered that vertical face. Remains of a decorated *tablero* on the platform's west side are interrupted at the center by a plastered vertical section. The *tableros* framing the west side could be taken as an indication that this may have been the main facade, but the absence of an original landing and the narrowness of the one that was added plus the lack of a stairway suggest otherwise. Access instead might be from the east, where the *talud* is abruptly broken toward the center, suggesting a dismantled stairway. Although the west *tablero* only wraps around the south for about 3 m, it does not formally end but rather is broken; considering this break and that the north face and northeast corner of the platform are not exposed, it is highly probable that there were *tableros* decorating all four sides, particularly as the fill covering the base of Los Chapulincitos includes much limestone rubble that could come from the destroyed *tableros*. Hence, perhaps the segment dividing the north and south parts of the west *tableros* is a matter of the general design, but we have too few conserved elements to reconstruct this design.

The fifth level creates a terrace (Figure 12, q) on the east, which is accessed via the stairway ascending from the first level in the northeast section. Although this terrace does not appear on Marquina's (1970a) last plans, it is implied on those of 1939 and 1951 (Marquina 1990) to support the northern projection of the sixth level, but it must continue much farther north, given the location of the stairway. The terrace extends along the east side—91.83 m—and would have had a north front of 33.5 m, which, by supporting the sixth-level projection, would be reduced to 11.5 m east-west of open space east of the latter. Its southeast corner (Figure 12, r) forms a strange acute angle—also shown in Marquina's (1990) 1951 version— connecting with the 1-m-wide south landing. An east-west tunnel cuts the middle of the terrace, exposing a 60-cm-wide bench (Figure 12, s) between it and its descending *talud* that slopes down 26 cm to the west, creating a sunken space. No more tunnels explore this area, but the bench implies that even on this side the monument has a complex morphology.

As for the sixth level, changes in the fill show that there was a previously unreported stairway without *alfardas* in the 12.15-m gap between the *tableros* of the north facade—on the sixth and seventh levels—but it was dismantled. This destruction and the partial removal of the *tablero* frames (fragments of which are incorporated in the fill on the fourth level) perhaps reflect acts of desecration or termination for this stage of the monument, as reported for other sites (e.g., Manzanilla 2003: 96; Sharer et al. 1999). Another previously undocumented stairway—again lacking *alfardas*—is evident in the fill at the north end of the *tablero* on the sixth level's east side, suggesting that another *tablero* (Figure 12, t) should flank it to the north, in a section lacking tunnels. If so, it is likely that this *tablero* subsequently turns east and then south, perhaps terminating parallel to the seventh level *tablero* on that side, because the sixth-level *talud* exposed farther south no longer has a *tablero*. The top of the northeast projection of the sixth level would generate a terrace (Figure 12, u) more than 16 m wide. Narrowing a bit more than half—to 7.61 m—to surround the seventh level, this terrace extends along the entire east side—71.86 m—joining the south landing in an angular southeast corner (Figure 12, v) similar to that of the fifth level.

On the seventh level, an asymmetrical prolongation of the *tablero* forms a small terrace (Figure 12, w) on its northwest corner—10.5 m north-south by 12.46 m east-west—producing a landing 6 m wide south of it, in front of the west stairway, between the sixth and seventh levels (not the fifth and sixth, as noted by Marquina [1970a: 36]). On the surface of the seventh level a 5-m-wide, 1-m-high wall with *taludes* on both sides (Figure 12, x), plastered and lacking any trace of postmolds or superstructures, delimits

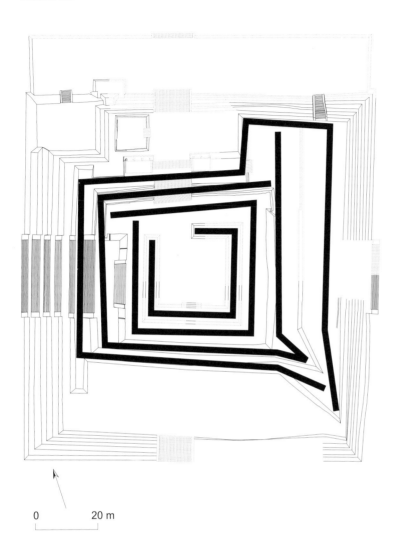

0   20 m

FIGURE 13. The arrangement of open spaces (heavy lines) from the seventh to the fourth levels suggests a conch shell or a *xicalcolhiuqui*.

a central quadrangular space (Figure 12, y) about 20 m on a side. The only exposed corner of the wall (Figure 12, z) reveals an opening on the north that is aligned with the eastern side of the staircase between the *tableros*, suggesting that access to the precinct was from this direction. But because no other corners are exposed, it is also possible that instead of a continuous wall there were independent platforms, as one of Marquina's (1990: 119) proposals shows, although usually he illustrates an entirely enclosed area (Marquina 1939, 1970a, 1990: 120). Three unreported steps (Figure 12, a') ascend the inside of the perimetric wall on the south; these reiterate the idea that entry was from the north and suggest that the top of the wall constituted a circulation area.

Although the distribution of the monument's volumes seems disorganized, in an overall view the disposition of the larger flat spaces at diverse elevations provides balance and seems to follow a circular clockwise pattern, which, aided by the diagonal projection of the southeast part of the *taludes* on the fifth and sixth levels, gives the impression (Figure 13) of a

FIGURE 14. Frame and molding of the *tablero* (east end of west section on seventh level). Photo by Víctor Blanco.

FIGURE 15. Chapulines mural, west section on sixth level. Photo by Víctor Blanco.

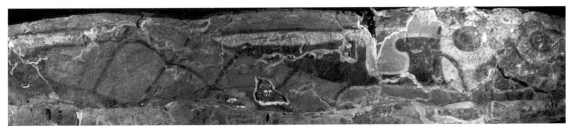

FIGURE 16. Skull (right) and segmented element (left), east section on seventh level. Photo by Víctor Blanco.

conch shell or of a *xicalcolhiuqui* (at least from the seventh to the fourth levels, for which we have relatively complete or reconstructible contours).

The Murals of the Edificio de los Chapulines

Besides its complex architecture, the Edificio de los Chapulines is distinctive because of its painted embellishment. The sixth- and seventh-level *tableros*—which have projecting moldings above and below the Teotihuacan-like frame (Figure 14)—display the Los Chapulines murals (Figure 15), executed on a fine clay plaster in red, green, yellow, and white on a black background (Marquina 1939: 60–61, 1970a: 33, 39, 1990: 121). Following Alfonso Caso, Marquina (1939: 61, 1970a: 39) describes them as formed by equidistant motifs along the *tablero*, representing insects—maybe butterflies—facing front and exhibiting antennae, as their bodies intertwine with one another.

To us they are a series of skulls crowned with knots, separated by segmented diagonal elements that could recall caterpillar bodies, but their lower edge is rounded, whereas the upper has crests (Figure 16). The skulls are not identical, most are red but some are yellow, and the way the features are expressed varies (Figure 17), so that they may not be the product of a single hand. According to our reconstruction, the mural should continue on the *tablero* after the dismantled staircase of the sixth-level northeast projection.

The same theme is repeated on the badly preserved *tableros*—not described by Marquina—of Los Chapulincitos (see Figure 12, p) on the northwest of the fourth-level north terrace. A frame surrounds the *tablero* that exhibits skulls—here with ear ornaments (Figure 18)—painted in the same colors as the large murals but on very thinly plastered wood; the segmented body is here substituted by a simple curvilinear motif. A plain lower molding juts out below the frame, while an upper recessed larger molding (about 24 cm high) incorporates reliefs of polychromed volutes on a base of clayey *tepetate* (Figure 19). It is likely that the four sides of this platform originally displayed *tableros*. None of the murals was carefully executed, but the colors—still brilliant after two millennia—would have provided an ostentatious north facade.

FIGURE 17. Skull, west section on seventh level. Photo by Víctor Blanco.

FIGURE 18. Detail on south side of Los Chapulincitos mural. Although poorly preserved, the teeth and flanking ear ornaments are visible. Photo by Víctor Blanco.

DISCUSSION

To decide whether, during the life of the Edificio de los Chapulines (during the second century A.D.), Cholula can be classified as a city requires confronting the existing information with one's understanding of this term. In light of the vast literature that discusses this subject, it is perhaps advisable to examine the social inferences that can be gleaned from the available data, so that the reader can decide whether these agree with his/her definition of a city.

Starting with the materials used to build the Great Pyramid, the nearest outcrops of limestone are more than 10 km from Cholula (Von Erffa et al.

FIGURE 19. South section of Los Chapulincitos mural, showing the modeled volutes on the upper recessed frame. Photo by Víctor Blanco.

1976: fig. 8). This rock was utilized as support for over 6,000 m² of *taludes*, breaks, *alfardas, tableros,* and stairs, indicating that Cholula had ample access to resources outside its immediate surroundings.

We cannot estimate the size, the morphology, or hence the density of Cholula for those times. Although neighboring the Great Pyramid—both to the northeast (at the Rancho de la Virgen and UDLA) and to the northwest (under the Monastery of San Gabriel)—formal constructions existed, their monumentality does not seem comparable, and we do not know how they might be related to the ancient settlement's layout, because the intermediate areas are unexplored. However, the Edificio de los Chapulines alone has an approximate volume of 119,934 m³, which, in addition to the extraction, transport—thousands of trips if one considers the traditional individual load of 23 kg (Hassig 1985: 32)—and placement of the limestone, implies the manufacture, movement, and arrangement of thousands of adobes for the *cajones,* and the extraction, hauling, and unloading of tons of *tepetate,* clay, and sand to fill them. Simply in terms of the basic materials employed in that building, Cholula must have had access to enough people to extract—or produce—and transfer them.

One also should consider specialization. No workshops have been excavated, but the variation in size and composition of the adobes used contemporaneously testifies to the existence of different manufacturing loci. Additionally, the specialization required for the architecture, engineering, and embellishment of the Great Pyramid, as well as the administrative, political, and religious apparatus associated with its creation, are unmatched at neighboring sites, because settlement patterns after the first century A.D. suggest a ruralization of the valley with the abandonment of many places and the increasing scarcity of settlements with public structures (García Cook 1981: 263–264).

In terms of scale and design, perhaps with the exception of Totimehuacan (Spranz 1996), no nearby second-century A.D. sites have buildings of dimensions comparable to the Great Pyramid, show such an investment in materials selected to resist the passage of time, or exhibit such a complex configuration that reflects both a planned effort by the elites and their ability to mobilize and direct labor. If control over a wide area, the existence of a huge workforce engaged in public construction, the presence of specialists of distinct categories, the ability to plan and administer a preeminent monumental constructive enterprise in the regional religious hierarchy, and the implicit social inequality—all of which distinguish the site from its neighbors—can be judged as indicative of a city, then we can consider Cholula as such for those times.

But was Cholula an archetype? And an archetype of what type of city? An archetype is an original pattern from which copies are made. How the patterns arose in emergent urban centers has been discussed from various perspectives. The materialist approach sees cities developing to concentrate a range of specialized functions within a wider territory and considers their form and arrangement to result from political strategies that seek to increase efficiency and create economies of scale (Prem 1991; Smith 2003; Trigger 2003: 120–121). The ideological position visualizes urban centers as cosmological models, replicas of a vertical and horizontal cosmic geometry, created to harmonize supernatural and social forces (e.g., Ashmore and Sabloff 2003; Carrasco 1999: 30–31; Reilly 1999; Wheatley 1971). A third view (Smith 2003: 223) considers the possibility that much of what seems to reflect cosmological planning may in fact be the product of fortuitous growth and pragmatic decisions. We consider these perspectives to be complementary, not contradictory. Economic functions, political decisions, and fortuitous growth all mold cities; however, the ideological expression of power, both terrestrial and supernatural, is articulated by public architecture.

Cholula had traits that identify it as a sacred place and allowed such

an identification to persist through time, like the replica that the Great
Pyramid itself makes of Popocatepetl and the existence of springs near
the ceremonial area. But lacking a plan of the urban arrangement, or reasonable knowledge about its monumental architecture, we must limit our
discussion to the Edificio de los Chapulines and consider whether it corresponds to an original model, what its design might reflect, and whether
others imitated it.

During the second century A.D., the Great Pyramid could be regarded
as an archetype in the sense that, as a whole, its complex design seems
to have been an original creation. However, with certain adjustments, its
builders had embraced and combined earlier features. One of these was
the *talud-tablero* that for centuries had formed part of the Sierra Nevada
traditions (García Cook 1981: 262; Plunket and Uruñuela 2002c) and that
would be adopted by Teotihuacan in a slightly different version. Another
instance is the curious precinct that crowns the Edificio de los Chapulines,
which perhaps has parallels at both Totimehuacan and Xochitecatl. At
Totimehuacan, a 1.5-m-wide wall with *taludes* on both sides encloses a
precinct on the surface of the penultimate constructive phase; calibrating
to 2σ the only radiocarbon date (2150 ± 125 B.P. or 200 ± 125 B.C. [HV1151])
from overlying fill (Spranz 1970a: 33) provides a range of 408 B.C.–A.D. 123,
so that the feature in question could be prior to or contemporaneous with
Los Chapulines. As for Xochitecatl, vestiges of a wall that might be similar
were recorded in test pits in Structure X04 (Spranz 1970b) or "Pirámide
de las Flores" (Serra Puche and Palavacini 1996); the only date (2300 ±
55 B.P. or 350 B.C. ± 55 [HV4429]) that Spranz (1996: 145) obtained from
a test excavation offers a 2σ range of 475–203 cal B.C., in accordance with
the 750- to 350-B.C. placement given by Serra Puche and Palavacini (1996:
46–49) for the building, which would make it earlier than Los Chapulines.

Besides merging features from regional traditions, the builders of Los
Chapulines must have used age-old ideas regarding the natural and social
order of things: a world divided into quadrants and a center, each associated with particular characteristics. What remains of its artistic program
suggests that this conceptual structure was used to create the first phases
of the Great Pyramid: the facade, embellished with *tableros* displaying
animated skulls emerging from a black ground, faces north, the direction
later cultures linked to the region of the dead (León-Portilla 1963: 57), thus
linking the primordial message of the edifice with the underworld.

The Great Pyramid was situated near a spring (see Figure 2) that flowed
into swampy land to the northeast, generating the image of a mountain
emerging from water that is central to the Mesoamerican place of creation
(Reilly 1999: 37). In Cholula, however, the Great Pyramid probably represents a specific feature of the sacred geography: the volcano that serves as
a backdrop to the west, and which perhaps explains the second facade of

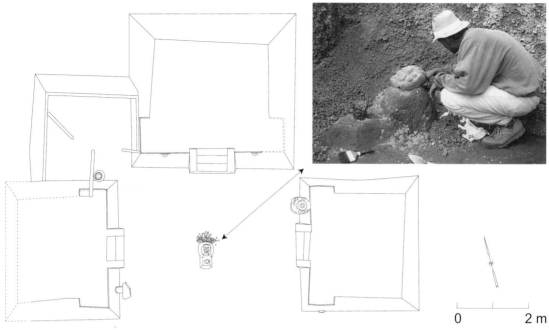

(above) **FIGURE 20.** House plan at Tetimpa, with volcano shrine at patio center. Dashed lines indicate our reconstruction.

FIGURE 21. *Talud-tablero* platform shrine (front) at center of domestic patio, Tetimpa.

Los Chapulines facing that direction. At Tetimpa, the ritual center of each house was marked by a shrine evoking Popocatepetl, the living volcano, the original brazier (Plunket and Uruñuela 2002b). Many of these shrines are effigies of the volcano (Figure 20), but some already have replaced that icon with a *talud-tablero* platform (Figure 21), as is found in later patios of Cholula and Teotihuacan, showing that these societies based themselves on earlier traditions as they constructed larger and more elaborate cosmological representations. In a number of Mesoamerican cities, the myth of Coatepec, the Serpent Mountain, provided the archetype for their sacred precincts (Schele and Mathews 1998: 38). There are no direct indications of this concept in Los Chapulines. However, clearly the Great Pyramid replicates Popocatepetl in the constructed landscape, and on one of Tetimpa's volcano shrines, the crowning sculpture is in effect a serpent, perhaps in an early expression of Coatepec. Elsewhere (Plunket and Uruñuela 2002b) we have proposed that Tetimpa's houses were designed as simple cosmological models where the shrines marked the center connecting the underworld, the earth, and the heavens. As a recipient of ancient traditions, perhaps the Great Pyramid was erected as a gigantic version of those same specifications.

We do not know whether the pattern of Edificio de los Chapulines was imitated, although several of its noteworthy features—the *tableros* with exterior moldings, the murals with bands of skulls, the mud reliefs, and the building's singular architectural design that rotates with balanced asymmetry—do not appear to have been duplicated elsewhere. But how many of these characteristics are actually exclusive to it and how much is supposition stemming from our lack of information about contemporary sites must remain subject to further debate. A dual facade also has been recorded for the second and third centuries A.D. on one of Totimehuacan's main platforms, one facing the plaza to the south and the other facing west (Spranz 1970a: 33). This dual facade and the use of older features (e.g., the *talud-tablero* and the enigmatic upper precinct) suggest that perhaps what seem to be unique elements of Los Chapulines had a more extensive previous or contemporary existence that is not apparent due to a paucity of research on Puebla's major architecture of this time.

But why was there a rapid increase in monumental building in Cholula during the second century A.D.? What accelerated the processes involved in promoting ideological principles via public exhibition? Our tentative answer is that the first-century volcanic eruption led to dramatic changes in western Puebla—community displacement and territorial reorganization—and some of the resulting sociopolitical adjustments must have contributed to the constructive program of the Great Pyramid.

According to Hirth (2003: 57), conferring fundamental importance to the region in which a city develops allows one to postulate that, in Mesoamerica, urban centers were a secondary product of a larger political system, specifically, for the time of the Conquest, the *altepetl*. Without trying to extend this type of organization back to the dawn of our era, a regional approach facilitates an understanding of Cholula's increased complexity as a function of the problem of population resettlement caused by a natural disaster. Its public buildings must have been designed as instruments to regulate the reconfigured society's behavior, attitudes, and

emotions, and to legitimate authority and governmental power (Cowgill 2004: 528).

Cholula's incorporation of refugees—and the implied social remodeling—would have required new practices and institutions to reorganize the sociopolitical system as groups from diverse villages were integrated into one more complex settlement. The role of natural disasters in the collapse of cities has been widely commented on (e.g., Thera [Hoffman 1999], Pompeii [Scarth 1999], and Cuicuilco [Siebe 2000]), but in this case it would be the disaster, the abrupt population increase in Cholula, and the consequent sociopolitical reforms this demanded that motivated the conformation of a city.

The challenges faced might be similar to cases in which the dynamics of synoikism led to the relocation of village populations, combining them to create cities in a process of outright urban revolution (Marcus and Flannery 2001: 169–189): suddenly accommodate masses of new arrivals, arrange their incorporation and reorganize the division of labor, assure the supply of resources, reestablish social capital—hierarchies and social ties—for the immigrants, and create a new social cement for the heterogeneity of assembled local identities. But a fundamental difference is that synoikism

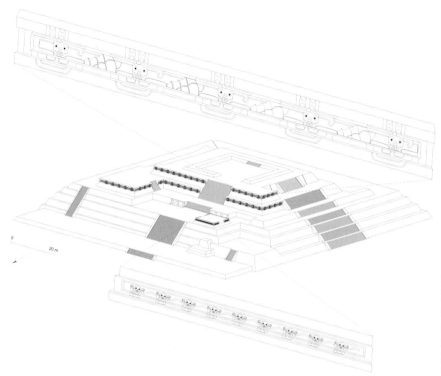

FIGURE 23. Our isometric reconstruction of Structure 2 (Edificio de los Chapulines), seen from the northwest. Major deformations have been eliminated.

implies a forced yet directed relocation and thus previous planning by its leaders. Because the volcanic catastrophe (Figure 22) was the prime mover that occasioned the displacement of communities and their agglutination to develop a city, Cholula's peculiarity is that its institutions would have been obliged to organize into more complex forms without preparation; more immediate decisions would have been necessary in the process, thereby exponentially multiplying risks in the management of problems.

The constructive inconsistency of Los Chapulines perhaps indicates little former experience with architecture on that scale, diverse work groups that may not have shared the same standards or abilities, and/or hasty construction. Population growth is as much a reflection of changes in social structure as a cause of those changes (Blanton 1981: 398). In Cholula's case, the incorporation of migrants would have led to organizational reconfigurations, and perhaps the ambitious enterprise of erecting the Great Pyramid resulted from a confluence of the sudden abundance of refugee labor, the need to integrate them into a new social core and develop new political agendas, the ideological need to reorder human-divine relations after a catastrophe of enormous proportions, and the need to create symbols that could serve both to legitimate authority and to provide shared referents for a heterogeneous society.

The same lack of refinement is apparent in the execution of the murals in Los Chapulines, but their thematic insistence on skulls (Figure 23), a gigantic *tzompantli* on a scale and of a brilliance visible from a distance, more than favor quality seems to be an effort in mass communication referring to the underworld. That subject could be understood and shared by the diverse groups of immigrants for whom, if the evidence recovered from Tetimpa is representative of other contemporary villages, the veneration of ancestors was a deeply rooted tradition (Plunket and Uruñuela 2002b; Uruñuela and Plunket 2002, 2003). The murals do not allude to particular individuals; they are general references that perhaps would be more efficient in providing an adequate social cement for a mixed population in which the prior importance of genealogies recognized at the village level would have to be rearranged in the conformation of a new society.

Acknowledgments

We thank William Fash, Leonardo López Luján, and Joanne Pillsbury for the invitation to share part of our work in Cholula with our colleagues, and David Carrasco and two anonymous reviewers for their comments, which improved our text.

As part of the Tetimpa Project, our research at the Great Pyramid was authorized by the Consejo Nacional de Arqueología of INAH. In particular we thank Joaquín García-Bárcena for his continual support during his tenure as president. Consejo Nacional de Ciencia y Tecnología, Foundation for the Advancement of Mesoamerican Studies, Inc., and UDLA provided indispensable funding.

Martín Cruz, administrator of the archaeological zone, and custodians Aurelio Mendoza, Lupe Ramírez, Odilón Xihuitl, Alberto García, and Cruz Villa—several of whom worked for the Proyecto Cholula—offered us their unconditional help and valuable oral history. Pepe Ramírez was very generous with his time and knowledge of the documents in the Archivo Técnico of INAH. Aurelio López and Manuel Vera of UDLA collaborated many times in the mapping. To all of them, our sincere thanks for helping us follow Marquina's footsteps.

REFERENCES CITED

Ashmore, Wendy, and Jeremy A. Sabloff
   2003   Interpreting Ancient Maya Civic Plans: A Reply to Smith. *Latin American Antiquity* 14(2): 229–236.
Blanton, Richard E.
   1976   Anthropological Studies of Cities. *Annual Review of Anthropology* 5: 249–264.
   1981   The Rise of Cities. In *Archaeology* (Jeremy A. Sabloff, ed.): 392–400. Handbook of Middle American Indians, Supplement I (Victoria R. Bricker, general ed.). University of Texas Press, Austin.

Carrasco, Davíd

   1999 *City of Sacrifice: The Aztec Empire and the Role of Violence in Civilization.*
       Beacon Press, Boston.

Caskey, Charles R.

   n.d. Two Archaeological Discoveries at Cholula, Puebla, Mexico. M.A.
       thesis, Departamento de Antropología, Universidad de las Américas,
       Cholula, Mexico, 1988.

Cortés, Hernando

   1928 [1519–26] *Five Letters, 1519–1526* (J. Bayard Morris, trans.). Billing and
       Sons, Guildford, U.K.

Cowgill, George L.

   2004 Origins and Development of Urbanism: Archaeological Perspectives.
       Annual Review of Anthropology 33: 525–549.

Díaz del Castillo, Bernal

   1956 [1517–21] *The Discovery and Conquest of Mexico 1517–1521* (Alfred P.
       Maudslay, trans.). Kingsport Press, Kingsport, Tenn.

Dumond, Don E.

   1972 Demographic Aspects of the Classic Period in Puebla-Tlaxcala.
       Southwestern Journal of Anthropology 28: 101–130.

García, María de los Angeles

   1971a En peligro las excavaciones de Cholula. Quieren aumentar precios a los
       terrenos rentados por Antropología. *El Sol de Puebla*, April 17, Puebla.

   1971b Paralizadas las obras del Plan Cholula. En peligro los monumentos que
       han sido descubiertos. *El Sol de Puebla*, April 29, Puebla.

García Cook, Angel

   1981 The Historical Importance of Tlaxcala in the Cultural Development of
       the Central Highlands. In *Archaeology* (Jeremy Sabloff, ed.): 244–276.
       Handbook of Middle American Indians, Supplement I (Victoria
       Bricker, general ed.). University of Texas Press, Austin.

Hassig, Ross

   1985 *Trade, Tribute, and Transportation: The Sixteenth-Century Politi-
       cal Economy of the Valley of Mexico.* University of Oklahoma Press,
       Norman.

Hernández, Gilda, Nicolás Quintana, Gabriela Uruñuela, and Patricia Plunket

   n.d. Informe Sondeo UA98B: Area para instalación de un sistema de riego.
       Informe técnico al Consejo Nacional de Arqueología, Instituto Nacional
       de Antropología e Historia. Archivo Técnico del INAH, México, 1998.

Hirth, Kenneth

   2003 The Altepetl and Urban Structure in Prehispanic Mesoamerica. In *El
       urbanismo en Mesoamérica*, vol. I (William T. Sanders, Alba Guadalupe
       Mastache, and Robert Cobean, eds.): 57–84. Instituto Nacional de
       Antropología e Historia and Pennsylvania State University, México.

Hoffman, Susanna M.

   1999 After Atlas Shrugs: Cultural Change or Persistence after a Disaster. In
       The Angry Earth: Disaster in Anthropological Perspective (Anthony Oliver-
       Smith and Susanna M. Hoffman, eds.): 302–325. Routledge, London.

León-Portilla, Miguel
  1963 *Aztec Thought and Culture.* Translated by Jack Emory Davis. University
        of Oklahoma Press, Norman.
López, Aurelio, Soledad Talavera, Araceli Rojas, Gabriela Uruñuela, and
        Patricia Plunket
  n.d. Rescate arqueológico UA-03a. Informe técnico de campo y análisis de
        materiales al Consejo Nacional de Arqueología, Instituto Nacional de
        Antropología e Historia. Archivo Técnico del INAH, México, 2004.
López, Aurelio, Soledad Talavera, Gabriela Uruñuela, and Patricia Plunket
  n.d. Sondeo arqueológico Rancho de la Virgen 2002. Informe técnico de
        campo al Consejo Nacional de Arqueología, Instituto Nacional de
        Antropología e Historia. Archivo Técnico del INAH, México, 2002.
López, Sergio, Zaid Lagunas, and Carlos Serrano
  1976 *Enterramientos humanos de la zona arqueológica de Cholula, Puebla.*
        Colección Científica 44. Instituto Nacional de Antropología e
        Historia, México.
  2002 *Costumbres funerarias y sacrificio humano en Cholula prehispánica.*
        Universidad Nacional Autónoma de México, México.
de la Luz, Leobardo, and Eduardo Contreras
  n.d. Proyecto Cholula. Temporada 1968. Sección de Topografía. Archivo
        Técnico del INAH, México, 1968.
Manzanilla, Linda
  2003 The Abandonment of Teotihuacan. In *The Archaeology of Settlement
        Abandonment in Middle America* (Takeshi Inomata and Ronald W.
        Webb, eds.): 91–101. University of Utah Press, Salt Lake City.
Marcus, Joyce
  2000 On the Nature of the Mesoamerican City. In *The Ancient Civilizations
        of Mesoamerica* (Michael E. Smith and Marilyn A. Masson, eds.):
        49–82. Blackwell, Oxford.
Marcus, Joyce, and Kent V. Flannery
  2001 *La civilización zapoteca: Cómo evolucionó la sociedad urbana en el valle de
        Oaxaca.* Fondo de Cultura Económica, México.
Marquina, Ignacio
  1939 Exploraciones en la pirámide de Cholula, Pue. In *Vigésimo Congreso
        Internacional de Americanistas. Actas de la primera sesión, celebrada en
        la Ciudad de México en 1939,* Tomo II: 52–63. Instituto Nacional de
        Antropología e Historia, Secretaría de Educación Pública, México.
  1970a Pirámide de Cholula. In *Proyecto Cholula* (Ignacio Marquina, ed.):
        31–45. Serie Investigaciones 19. Secretaría de Educación Pública,
        Instituto Nacional de Antropología e Historia, México.
  1970b (ed.) *Proyecto Cholula.* Serie Investigaciones 19. Secretaría de Educación
        Pública, Instituto Nacional de Antropología e Historia, México.
  1975 Cholula, Puebla. In *Los pueblos y señoríos teocráticos: El periodo de las
        ciudades urbanas,* primera parte (Eduardo Matos Moctezuma, ed.):
        109–122. México, panorama histórico y cultural, vol. VIII
        (Ignacio Bernal, general ed.). Secretaría de Educación Pública,
        Instituto Nacional de Antropología e Historia, México.

1990   *Arquitectura prehispánica.* Versión facsimilar de la edición de 1951, aumentada con el apéndice de la edición de 1964. Instituto Nacional de Antropología e Historia, Secretaría de Educación Pública, México.

McCafferty, Geoffrey G.

1996   Reinterpreting the Great Pyramid of Cholula, Mexico. *Ancient Mesoamerica* 7: 1–17.

2001   Mountain of Heaven, Mountain of Earth: The Great Pyramid of Cholula as Sacred Landscape. In *Landscape and Power in Ancient Mesoamerica* (Rex Koontz, Kathryn Reese-Taylor, and Annabeth Headrick, eds.): 279–316. Westview Press, Boulder, Colo.

Messmacher, Miguel

1967   *Cholula. Reporte preliminar.* Editorial Nueva Antropología, México.

Motolinía, Fray Toribio de Benavente

1969 [1858]   *Historia de los indios de la Nueva España.* Editorial Porrúa, México.

Mountjoy, Joseph, and David Peterson

1973   *Man and Land at Prehispanic Cholula.* Vanderbilt University Publications in Anthropology 4. Vanderbilt University, Nashville.

Müller, Florencia

1978   *La alfarería de Cholula.* Secretaría de Educación Pública, Instituto Nacional de Antropología e Historia, México.

Noguera, Eduardo

1937   *El altar de los cráneos esculpidos de Cholula.* Talleres Gráficos de la Nación, México.

1954   *La cerámica arqueológica de Cholula.* Editorial Guaranía, México.

1956   Un edificio preclásico en Cholula. In *Estudios antropológicos publicados en homenaje al Dr. Manuel Gamio:* 213–224. Dirección General de Publicaciones, Universidad Nacional Autónoma de México, México.

Panfil, Maria

n.d.   The Late Holocene Volcanic Stratigraphy of the Tetimpa Area, Northeast Flank of Popocatépetl Volcano, Central Mexico. M.S. thesis, Department of Geosciences, Pennsylvania State University, College Park, 1996.

Plunket, Patricia, and Gabriela Uruñuela

1998   Preclassic Household Patterns Preserved under Volcanic Ash at Tetimpa, Puebla. *Latin American Antiquity* 9: 287–309.

2002a   Antecedentes prehispánicos. In *Cholula, un vínculo de sabiduría y fraternidad:* 19–27. Universidad de las Américas, Puebla, Cholula.

2002b   Shrines, Ancestors and the Volcanic Landscape at Tetimpa, Puebla. In *Domestic Ritual in Ancient Mesoamerica* (Patricia Plunket, ed.): 31–42. Cotsen Institute of Archaeology Monograph 46. University of California, Los Angeles.

2002c   Antecedentes conceptuales de los conjuntos de tres templos. In *Ideología y política a través de materiales, imágenes y símbolos. Memoria de la Primera Mesa Redonda de Teotihuacan* (María Elena Ruiz Gallut, ed.): 529–546. Instituto Nacional de Antropología e Historia, Universidad Nacional Autónoma de México, México.

2003 From Episodic to Permanent Abandonment: Responses to Volcanic Hazards at Tetimpa, Puebla, Mexico. In *The Archaeology of Settlement Abandonment in Middle America* (Takeshi Inomata and Ronald W. Webb, eds.): 13–27. University of Utah Press, Salt Lake City.

2005 Dating Cholula. Electronic document, http://www.famsi.org/reports/02042/index.html, accessed June 3, 2005.

2006 Social and Cultural Consequences of a Late Holocene Eruption of Popocatepetl in Central Mexico. *Dark Nature, Quaternary International* 151: 19–28.

Prem, Hanns J.

1991 ¿Conceptos cosmológicos o racionalidad política en la organización territorial del México Central? In *América: Religión y cosmos* (Joaquín Muñoz, ed.): 214–239. Cuartas Jornadas de Historiadores Americanistas, Junta de Andalucía, Diputación Provincial de Granada, Sociedad de Historiadores Mexicanistas, Santa Fé, Granada.

Pyle, David

2000 Sizes of Volcanic Eruptions. In *Encyclopedia of Volcanoes* (Haraldur Sigurdsson, ed.): 263–269. Academic Press, San Diego.

Reilly, F. Kent III

1999 Mountains of Creation and Underworld Portals. In *Mesoamerican Architecture as a Cultural Symbol* (Jeff Karl Kowalski, ed.): 14–39. Oxford University Press, Oxford.

de Rojas, Gabriel

1927 [1581] Descripción de Cholula. *Revista Mexicana de Estudios Históricos* I(6): 158–170.

Romero, Javier

1935 Estudio de los entierros de la Pirámide de Cholula. *Anales del Museo Nacional de Antropología, Historia y Etnografía*, Epoca 5, tomo 2. Secretaría de Educación Pública, Talleres Gráficos de la Nación, México.

Sanders, William T., Jeffrey R. Parsons, and Robert S. Santley

1979 *The Basin of Mexico: Ecological Processes in the Evolution of a Civilization.* Academic Press, New York.

Scarth, Alwyn

1999 *Vulcan's Fury: Man against the Volcano.* Yale University Press, New Haven, Conn.

Schele, Linda, and Peter Mathews

1998 *The Code of Kings: The Language of Seven Sacred Maya Temples and Tombs.* Scribner, New York.

Serra Puche, Mari Carmen, and Beatriz Palavacini

1996 Xochitécatl, Tlaxcala, en el periodo Formativo (800 A.C.–100 D.C.). *Arqueología* 16: 43–57.

Sharer, Robert J., Loa P. Traxler, David W. Sedat, Elen E. Bell, Marcello A. Canuto, and Christopher Powell

1999 Early Classic Architecture beneath the Copan Acropolis: A Research Update. *Ancient Mesoamerica* 10: 3–23.

Siebe, Claus
   2000   Age and Archaeological Implications of Xitle Volcano, Southwestern
          Basin of Mexico-City. *Journal of Volcanology and Geothermal Research*
          104: 45–64.
Simkin, Tom, and Lee Siebert
   2000   Earth's Volcanoes and Eruptions: An Overview. In *Encyclopedia of
          Volcanoes* (Haraldur Sigurdsson, ed.): 249–261. Academic Press, San
          Diego.
Smith, Michael E.
   1989   Cities, Towns and Urbanism: Comment on Sanders and Webster.
          American Anthropologist 91: 454–460.
   2003   Can We Read Cosmology in Ancient Maya City Plans? Comment on
          Ashmore and Sabloff. *Latin American Antiquity* 14: 221–228.
Spranz, Bodo
   1970a *Die Pyramiden von Totimehuacan, Puebla (Mexico)*. Franz Steiner Verlag,
          Wiesbaden.
   1970b Investigaciones arqueológicas en el cerro Xochitécatl, Tlaxcala.
          Temporada 1969/70. *Comunicaciones* 1: 37–38.
   1996   Totimehuacan und Xochitecatl: Zwei Plätze in Puebla und Tlaxcala,
          Mexiko, in Präklassischer Zeit. *Tribus* 45: 138–150.
Trigger, Bruce G.
   2003   *Understanding Early Civilizations*. Cambridge University Press, New
          York.
Uruñuela, Gabriela
   1989   Investigaciones arqueológicas en Colotzingo, Puebla. *Notas Meso-
          americanas* 11: 110–119.
   n.d.   El sitio arqueológico de San Francisco Coapan. Laboratorio de
          Arqueología, Universidad de las Américas, Puebla, Cholula, 1981.
Uruñuela, Gabriela, and Patricia Plunket
   2002   Lineages and Ancestors. The Formative Mortuary Assemblages of
          Tetimpa, Puebla. In *Domestic Ritual in Ancient Mesoamerica* (Patricia
          Plunket, ed.): 21–30. Cotsen Institute of Archaeology Monograph 46.
          University of California, Los Angeles.
   2003   Testimonios de diversos tipos de abandono en Tetimpa, Puebla. *Trace*
          43: 84–96.
Von Erffa, Axel, Wolfgang Hilger, Klaus Knoblich, and Richard Weyl
   1976   Geología de la cuenca alta de Puebla-Tlaxcala y sus contornos.
          Comunicaciones 13: 99–106.
Weber, Max
   1958   *The City*. Free Press, New York.
Wheatley, Paul
   1971   *The Pivot of the Four Quarters: A Preliminary Enquiry into the Origins
          and Character of the Ancient Chinese City*. Edinburgh University Press,
          Edinburgh.

SIX

A MOUNTAIN GOD
IN TEOTIHUACAN ART

Zoltán Paulinyi

THE TEOTIHUACAN PANTHEON has several deities who so far have not been the subject of any systematic investigation. One of them is the deity on a mural in the Denver Art Museum (Figure 1), who also appears on a fragment of a mural in the Musées Royaux d'Art et d'Histoire in Brussels (Figure 2), which, in its original state, appears to have been practically identical to the first. The two murals have received little attention, appearing only in some exhibition catalogs and accompanied by brief remarks.

Reviewing the scant historiography of the two murals in chronological order shows that the Denver mural was first published in the Dallas Museum of Fine Arts (1950) catalog under the title of "Goddess of Agriculture." Three decades later the first, and anonymous, commentary appeared regarding this mural in another catalog that laconically notes that it represents an agricultural deity, probably Xochipilli, god of spring and flowers, and proposes its possible provenience as Tetitla, Teotihuacan (Denver Art Museum 1981: 126–127). This comment was probably based on the branches with flowers held by the deity. Séjourné (1962) has proposed the existence of Xochipilli at Teotihuacan—despite the god's belonging to the much later Nahua tradition—but this conjecture has not been confirmed by later research. No reason is given for the supposed origin at Tetitla.

The mural fragment (Figure 2) located since 1948 in the Musées Royaux d'Art et d'Histoire in Brussels (Sergio Purini, personal communication, March 2003), was published in two catalogs of that exhibition—in German and French—together with comments by two different authors. In the first catalog Thieme (1986) mentions the frontal yellow face with facial painting and headdress. He states that the headdress is of an unknown type, and for that reason one cannot tell who the personage represented is, although the ear ornament indicates high status. He observes that the left hand is holding a plant as a scepter and that a bundle of plumes rises from behind the head. He does not mention, however, that at the edge of the headdress, in fact, there appear two different bundles of plumes and another of strips

FIGURE 1. Mountain God on the Denver mural (from Berrin and Pasztory 1993: no. 41). Reproduced with the permission of the Denver Art Museum.

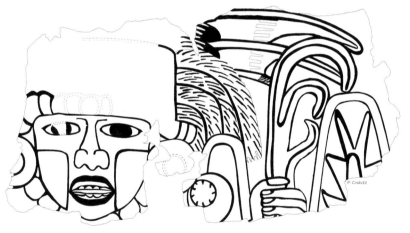

FIGURE 2. Mountain God on the Brussels mural (after Bankmann 1988: no. 121). Drawing by Paulina Chávez.

of coyote skin. He describes the enclosed serrated figure located to the right as a star-shaped symbol. Finally he concludes that the personage might be a vegetation god, although he does not explain why it would be a god and not a goddess.

In the second catalog Bankmann (1988) describes the face with its facial painting and high headdress, the bundle of long plumes, the ear ornament and necklace fragments, and the hand that holds a plant or branch. The author calls attention to the existence of an analogous complete mural that had been shown in the Dallas Museum of Fine Arts in 1950, which appears to represent the same personage in a similar manner. This analogous mural that he mentions is obviously the Denver mural. In this mural Bankmann notes a sequence of arched shapes in front of the personage. He recognizes the same shape located between the face and the hand on the Brussels fragment and another arched shape with the enclosed serrations to the right of the hand (see Figures 1, 2). He identifies all these arched figures as the Teotihuacan mountain motif and declares that in the analogous mural the head, as well as the two hands that hold branches of flowers, rise out of the mountain peaks. The author concludes that the personage represented in the two murals is possibly a mountain and vegetation goddess. Bankmann—with the help of an analogy to the other complete mural—goes further in the interpretation of the Brussels fragment than does Thieme, although he is also mistaken on several points: the female gender of the deity is an arbitrary interpretation that is not supported by argument, the shape with the enclosed serrations is different from the hill motif, and there is not one bundle of plumes but rather two in the headdress. Nor does he mention the strips of coyote skin.

Later Pasztory (Berrin and Pasztory 1993: no. 41) in a brief comment interprets the deity of the Denver mural as a manifestation of the Teotihuacan "Great Goddess." The only argument she presents is that the personage has a mouth with visible teeth, which in her opinion would be an attribute of the "Goddess." In passing she mentions that the deity rises from forms that suggest hills and that its hands hold objects similar to branches with flowers.

My recent analysis of the history of the "Great Goddess" in Teotihuacan studies has led me to the conclusion that this deity never really existed, and instead is an entity artificially created by researchers during the 1980s and 1990s, based on several different images and iconographic clusters that, for the greater part, differ radically from one another.[1] In place of this megagoddess, it seems that there actually existed several different deities, among them two or three were feminine, as well as the deity that is the subject of this work (Paulinyi 2006a, 2007a,b). Regarding this last deity I argued at the time that one of its attributes excludes the possibility of interpreting it as the "Great Goddess" or any other feminine deity, since it wears a version of the helmet headdress of high-ranking Teotihuacan lords. I have attempted to demonstrate that Pasztory's attributing the mouth with visible teeth as a characteristic of the "Goddess" is the error of a faulty chain of reasoning (Paulinyi 2006a: 3–5, 13).

In this chapter I analyze the Denver mural together with the Brussels fragment, in both of which the deity is given a great richness of attributes, although the figure is found in a simple symbolic context. Following this analysis, I examine a new abstract image of the same deity that I have detected in the rich context of the Atetelco (Teotihuacan) murals. In this manner I attempt to grasp the essence of the deity and establish its position within both the pantheon and the social fabric of Teotihuacan. Throughout this analysis I must also inquire into other related areas of Teotihuacan iconography not yet investigated.

THE TWIN MURALS

The Denver mural has been extensively restored; nevertheless there is no reason to doubt its authenticity. On one hand, as Pasztory (Berrin and Pasztory 1993: no. 41) observes, the mural follows the Teotihuacan artistic canon. On the other hand there exists the Brussels fragment—undoubtedly authentic—which is almost identical to the corresponding part of the Denver mural. The only major difference is in the details of the plant scepter (to avoid unecessary complications, this common term will be used for the two different plant motifs of these murals). One cannot exclude the possibility that some minor details and the present-day colors of the Denver mural might not be completely faithful to the original; nevertheless this possibility is not important from the point of view of this analysis, which focuses on what is essential in the iconography of the mural.

Both murals were probably looted during the 1940s from a single unidentified Teotihuacan building—and perhaps from the same architectural space. As stated above, the Tetitla residential compound has been mentioned as the place of origin for the complete mural but without any proof. The two murals must have formed part of a repeated sequence of the same image with small differences, a characteristic of Teotihuacan mural painting. Here I describe the Denver mural and its deity, taking the Brussels fragment into account when necessary, and then attempt an interpretation.

The deity is shown on a red background as a frontal bust, the torso of which is made up of two horizontal rows, one over the other, of five chest-high and two shoulder-high arched shapes, the whole approximating a trapezoidal form (see Figure 1). These are correctly identified by Bankmann (1988) as the Teotihuacan mountain motif. They are green with a red border and a green or red circle in the center. The head rises in the center of the upper row, substituting for two of these motifs in the center, and its yellow hands come out from the upper row as well. The yellow face of the deity shows a half-open mouth and bears green painting on the cheeks. It wears large circular orange and green ear ornaments and a fine necklace that has two rows of round beads (green in the center, orange on the sides) above a row of large red circles, each of which has a green center with a notched border. The deity wears an intricate and singular headdress. Its red, nearly rectangular, base (already referred to here as a helmet headdress) is made up of small round elements, in this case arranged in five vertical rows, with the lower strip slightly turned out and composed of smaller round elements.

In the Brussels fragment the details in this nearly rectangular base are not recognizable, except for the previously mentioned characteristic strip.

Other elements rise from the main body of the headdress. A bundle of strips with rows of short lines (strips of coyote skin) fall on each side. On top of the main body of the headdress appears a small red half-oval with an undulating edge, and above that is a yellow vertical shape with a notched edge. Behind these elements rises a broad vertical crest of feathers (in two tones of green) that reaches the upper edge of the painting and is flanked on both sides by three horizontal yellow bands, each crossed by a broad vertical red band. Each horizontal band shows a row of recumbant V-shaped figures pointing toward the outer edge of the mural.

On the lower part of the crest of vertical green feathers there are two quadripartite diamond shapes in yellow and red, arranged symmetrically. Outside the crest both diamond shapes abut a somewhat elongated fig-shaped motif in two tones of green. Below the diamond shapes and on the nearly rectangular main body of the headdress there is, on each side, a horizontal bundle of short red feathers, with dark lengthwise lines at the tips and crosswise within. From behind each bundle extend two horizontal feathers in two tones of green, interrupted on both sides by the flowery branches held in the hands of the deity. On the Brussels mural fragment, however, the feathers continue, passing behind the scepter. The explanation for this difference may be that in the Denver mural there are flowers on the other side of the scepter.

In the Denver mural, the two branching plant scepters consist of curved parallel strips painted yellow and green, made up of four and two branching elements, respectively, if one counts the central stalk. These, with one exception, curve upward. Three yellow or red flowers, represented in profile, hang down from each branch. The plant scepter of the Brussels mural is also composed of two parallel strips (yellow and possibly green), but it has no flowers, is not as long, and has three branches (counting the stalk), of which the upper two curve downward (see Figure 2). In the Denver mural—between each plant scepter and the border of the mural—there is a yellow diagonal strip that is saw-toothed on its lower edge. On each of these strips there are three concentric circular shapes, the lower of which is identical to the elements in the third row of the necklace of the god. The yellow strip and the circles appear not to be part of the scepter. On the right edge a half-oval, striped in two tones of green, originates from one of the circles previously mentioned.

In the lower half of the mural, on both sides of the deity, a cluster of shapes appears. Counting from the lower part upward, there are a yellow horizontal band, saw-toothed on its upper edge; two bands of dark green; and one red band. These last three bands are also horizontal and separated by three narrower yellow strips. Above these, on the level of the deity's

FIGURE 3. Image of a mountain consisting of multiple mountain motifs (from Seler 1915: fig. 178).

hands and his branches, there is a large arched shape painted in red and green. This shape is different from the arched motifs of the bust of the deity, not only in its coloring but also in its greater size, in its saw-toothed interior, and in the absence of a central circle.

THE MOUNTAIN GOD

The iconography of the deity on these murals is complex and corresponds to no other known Teotihuacan deity, although it does have points in common with several of them. There is little doubt that these images represent a separate deity with a character of its own.

The body of the deity is the nucleus of the mural. His head replaces the central portion of the upper row of mountain motifs, and at the same time crowns the trapezoidal group of the two rows of these motifs, thus producing an overall pyramidal form whose outline is barely interrupted by the hands. In this way, the anthropomorphic parts of the body and the mountain motifs fuse into a single harmonious and indivisible unit, which constitutes the essence of the representation of this deity. In Teotihuacan art the mountain motif scarcely ever appears by itself (Langley 1986: 331), but instead, three or more of them form pyramidal clusters, and the typical representation of a mountain is a grouping of this type (Figure 3). There also exist linear sequences of mountain motifs and sometimes more realistic images of mountains with a curvilinear contour, which are not built up of the motifs just mentioned. The personage on the mural—which in his elemental form is a mountain with head and hands—in all probability is a mountain deity. His pyramidal form is exceptionally complex. Since its base line is made up of five mountain motifs, not including the head of the god, the body would have had five rows, diminishing in length, one above the other in a 5-4-3-2-1 sequence. This complexity suggests a mountain of importance, although this Mountain God, judging by his rare appearance in Teotihuacan art, must not have belonged in the ranks of the great deities of the Teotihuacan pantheon.

Among the known Teotihuacan deity images, there is no analogue for the combination of mountain and anthropomorphic motifs. However, for some relationship between a deity and a mountain, or several mountains in general, consider the Rain God and the Butterfly-Bird God. Representations of the Teotihuacan Rain God, or rather—taking into account the hierarchic multiplicity that one sees in its art—the rain gods, show that they live in the interior of the mountains and in an aquatic world below the surface of the earth. In the well-known Tepantitla mural, below the image of a goddess, the emblem of the Rain God appears in a cave as a fountain of water and seeds, in an exuberant aquatic environment (Paulinyi 2007b). There are also two noteworthy images, one from Tiquisate, Guatemala (Hellmuth 1978: fig. 16), and one from the island of Jaina (Delgado et al. 1965: 57), in which the Teotihuacan Rain God appears in a mountain cave. In the first case the mountain is surrounded by four minor rain gods. Nevertheless, in Teotihuacan art the rain gods do not appear with the body of a mountain. The Butterfly-Bird God, which, according to my interpretation, is a solar god of vegetation fertility (Paulinyi 1995, 2006b), is commonly found represented together with a triple or multiple mountain. In other words, neither the Rain God nor the Butterfly-Bird God offers an exact iconographic analogue, but the rain gods, who live in the body of the mountains, seem to be closely related to the deity examined here.

The plant scepters held in the hands that rise from the depths of the mountain are key to the essence of the deity: he should possess the powers that assure plant fertility. The yellow saw-toothed strips that begin at the scepters, and those located at the lower edge of the mural, may be symbols of fire, or representations of the emission of light or heat (cf. von Winning 1977: fig. 1b). This saw-toothed strip appears at times in aquatic images on stylized waves, apparently expressing the brightness of the water's surface. In the border of the "Coyote Portico" murals (Portico 1 of the White Patio in Atetelco), there is a clear analogue for these scepters: the plant branch held is similar to that of the Brussels fragment (presented later in Figure 13).[2] Elsewhere a similar object with two curving branches appears with the Rain God (Figure 4). Because the plant branch is one of the more outstanding attributes of the Mountain God, this possible connection with the Rain God suggests again that it may be wise to look within the context surrounding the Rain God for the place occupied by the Mountain God in the Teotihuacan supernatural world.

FIGURE 4. Rain God with a curved object in hand (from Cabrera Castro 1996: fig. 1).

FIGURE 5. Dignitary with helmet headdress (from Scott 2001: plate 132d). Photo by Sue Scott.

The nearly rectangular base of the deity's headdress, composed of rows of smaller elements, is the helmet headdress, a recurring insignia of power among the great dignitaries of the city (Figure 5). As mentioned above, this headdress shows that the sex of the deity is masculine. The helmet itself is the central and most important part of the headdress and consequently must be of considerable importance among the attributes of the god. This raises a question as to why the god should possess a version of this type of headdress, which would more appropriately correspond to a high-ranking mortal. I shall return to the problem later.

The two quadripartite diamond shapes placed on the headdress of the god in the Denver mural also frequently form part of the iconography of the Teotihuacan Butterfly-Bird God censers. In these cases, the quadripartite diamond shape is the main element of the blunt end of a certain type of dart, which appears arranged in clusters (Figure 6), and is almost never represented other than on censers. Considering that diamond-shaped eyes are symbols of the Old Fire God (von Winning 1977: 13–14), there can be little doubt that the diamond shapes on the headdress carry some igneous meaning. The two fig-shaped motifs found with diamond motifs are difficult to interpret within Teotihuacan iconography. The only thing that might be mentioned is that the ear-spools and ear-pendants of figures of the enigmatic personage traditionally called the Fat God have a similar shape (see von Winning 1987, 1: 141–145). However, I cannot say with any assurance that they are the same object.

In Teotihuacan art, bundles of strips with rows of short lines represent coyote (or wolf?) skin (cf. Latsanopoulos n.d.; Figure 7). The presence of strips of coyote skin in the headdress of the Mountain God is again reminiscent of the Atetelco White Patio murals, where there are headdresses with

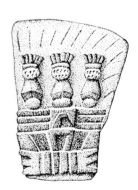

FIGURE 6. Quadripartite diamond shape on the blunt end of darts, in the upper portion of a cluster of symbols (from von Winning 1977: fig. 13b).

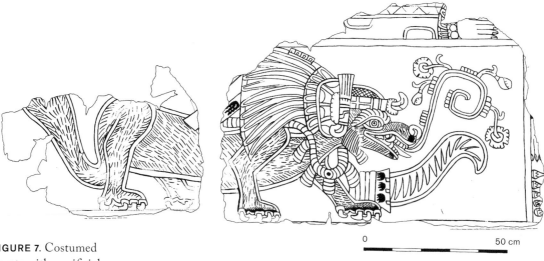

FIGURE 7. Costumed coyote with sacrificial knife, displaying aquatic symbols in the speech volute and in the aquatic band of the upper frame. Drawing by Saburo Sugiyama (from C. Millon 1988a: fig. V.12).

FIGURE 8. Supernatural butterfly with strips hanging from its antenae (from Séjourné 1966a: fig. 93).

similar bundles of coyote tails, as well as strips of flayed coyote skin around the figures of the Coyote Lords in the Coyote Portico. (Regarding the use of the term "Coyote Lords," see the following section.) The significance of the headdress element in the form of a half-oval with an undulating edge is not understood, but it may indicate a connection with representations of coyotes that appear finely dressed as high-ranking personages. In one of these representations one finds the same motif indicated in the head-dress of a coyote. At the right paw of the coyote there is a large obsidian knife, which suggests that this figure is performing the role of sacrificial

FIGURE 9. Triple cluster of obsidian blades next to a person bearing a sacrificial knife (from Conides n.d. [2001]: fig. 57c).

priest (see Figure 7). This coyote—and by extension, any coyote similarly attired—may well be an incarnation of the Coyote Lords.

The horizontal bands in the upper border of the Denver mural appear on headdresses of both supernatural beings and offerants (Berrin and Pasztory 1993, no. 158; Scott 2001: plate 79h, I; Séjourné 1966a; von Winning 1977: figs. 3d, 5f, j; Figure 8). The similarities between these bands with their series of V-shaped motifs and the paper strips and sheets of paper that appear in ceremonial contexts in the Postclassic codices, seem to indicate that in Teotihuacan art these bands refer to the same object (see Anders et al. 1991: 23, 34, 36, 37; Seler 1963: 18, 65, 68, 69). Accordingly, the horizontal bands in the upper part of the headdress of the Mountain God may correspond to ritual strips of paper.

As seen below, the large arched shape with saw-toothed interior, which is found on both sides of the god and constitutes an important part of its symbolic surroundings, has exact and recurring analogues in the White Patio at Atetelco, in the border of the murals of the Coyote Lords, where in that same patio, this shape appears associated with the Rain God.

Although it seems to be a large leaf (C. Millon 1988b: 214), it is my opinion that Cabrera Castro (1995: 207) and Headrick (n.d. [1996]) are correct in identifying this motif as a knife and obsidian blade, respectively. It often appears centered between curved obsidian blades, which are shaped like the typical Teotihuacan sacrificial knife and also have a saw-toothed interior (Figure 9). It is for these reasons that the motif with its saw-toothed interior on the twin murals should be interpreted as a stylized image of a straight, broad obsidian blade. Versions of this cluster of obsidian blades—which is often seen in headdresses—are at times associated with the Rain God (C. Miller 1973: fig. 193; Figures 10, 11) and more often with personages related to him, as those who wear the eye rings of this god while making a sacrifice (see Figure 9). It would appear then that this symbol is another tie to both the Rain God and the Coyote Lords. I shall return to this motif below, in the context of the Atetelco murals.

Summing up the analysis of the god of the two murals, I have estab-

FIGURE 10. Rain God bearing triple cluster of obsidian blades as a headdress (after Eduardo Matos Moctezuma 1990: fig. 120). Drawing by Paulina Chávez.

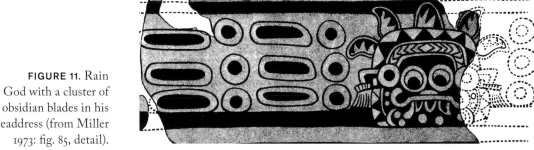

FIGURE 11. Rain
God with a cluster of
obsidian blades in his
headdress (from Miller
1973: fig. 85, detail).

lished the following observations. This is a mountain god that confers plant
fertility and possesses some igneous aspect that cannot at this point be
specified. Although its iconography shows points in common with several
deities, the basic concept of the deity and those attributes that can be interpreted lead principally toward the Rain God. Nevertheless, even though
this deity is related to the Rain God, he is not identical to the latter, because
he does not have the same facial features and diagnostic attributes. Instead,
the iconography of the two are associated in a less direct way, through the
sharing of some of the less notable or nonrecurring characteristics of the
Rain God. In any case, the god in question appears to have a limited field
of action that is inseparable from the bulk of a mountain. For this reason,
when I point out its relationship with the Rain God, I am thinking rather
of the minor rain gods in the hierarchy of supernatural beings. Finally,
the Mountain God shows a notable affinity with the iconography of the
Coyote Lords and with the murals in the White Patio at Atetelco. At times
a correspondence is shared by the three figures—the Mountain God, the
Rain God, and the Coyote Lords.

THE MOUNTAIN GOD AND THE COYOTE LORDS

Analysis of the Atetelco White Patio (Figure 12) calls first for a close examination of an important image repeated in the border of the Coyote Lords
murals in Portico 1 of the White Patio (Figure 13) and then an examination
of its broader context—a general consideration of the murals of Portico 1
and the White Patio.[3] Comparing the image of Figure 13 (and of Figure 12)
with that of the deity of the twin murals (see Figures 1, 2), I show that in
the first two a cluster of elements appears that is key to the representation
of the Mountain God in other murals, although these elements form a new
constellation and employ a more abstract visual language.

Figure 13 shows a central curvilinear shape, from which a hand with a
fringed wristband (in other instances two hands) emerges, holding a plant
scepter, which immediately evokes the Mountain God. Whereas C. Millon

FIGURE 12. White Patio, Atetelco, Teotihuacan: view of Portico 1 (from Kubler 1967: fig. 8).

FIGURE 13. Mountain God of Portico 1, White Patio, Atetelco (from Villagra Caleti 1971: fig. 18).

FIGURE 14.
Representation of
inverted mountains in
the upper portion of
a mural of Portico 2,
North Patio, Atetelco.
Here the figure is
shown inverted from
its original orientation
(from Cabrera Castro
1995: fig. 18.18).

(1988b: 214–215) and Headrick (n.d. [1996]) come to the conclusion that
it is the entrance to a cave as portal to the supernatural world, Cabrera
Castro (1995: 207) points out its likeness to a mountain. I agree that it is
a mountain, because its outline is identical to that of the mountain that
appears in the murals excavated in the North Patio of Atetelco (Figure
14). These murals represent a symbolic landscape (curiously enough, upside
down) with plants and unidentified objects, in which a mountain with
an undulating outline appears repeatedly with sacred attributes—obsidian
knives in the border and a front-facing bird within it (see Cabrera Castro
1995: 249; Taube 2000: 9). The two interpretations of cave or mountain are
not necessarily mutually exclusive: a cave is a doorway to the interior of a
mountain, and in principle, the central part of the image in Figure 13 could
be interpreted to be a cave. However, although no systematic studies have
been made of cave representation in Teotihuacan (and Teotihuacan-style)
art, in some cases, such as the Tlalocan mural of Tepantitla and a vessel
from Escuintla (Hellmuth 1978: fig. 16), the shape seems more apt to be an
arched doorway (Paulinyi 2007b).

Thus we have an image that is visually proximate, and conceptually
identical, to that of the Mountain God of the twin murals—a living
mountain, or rather, a mountain god. As was mentioned in the previous
section, the three-pronged scepter held by a hand with a fringed wristband
(see Figure 13) is very similar to the plant scepter in the Brussels mural.
In Teotihuacan iconography, hands wearing fringed wristbands indicate
masculine sex (Paulinyi 2006a: 2), as does the helmet headdress of the deity
on the twin murals. In the center of the mountain are the familiar diamond

FIGURE 15. Fire symbols in the form of concentric diamond shapes (from von Winning 1977: figs. 5f, j).

shapes, although this time arranged concentrically. In Teotihuacan art sometimes similar fire symbols are found built up of concentric diamond shapes (Figure 15). Shining saw-toothed bands emanate from the mountain's diamond shapes. The same bands appear in the Denver mural. Five plants with protuberances grow around the outline of the mountain—a new motif not seen previously. As discussed below, it appears on the crisscrossed strips representing coyote skin on the mural itself, a motif identified by Angulo Villaseñor (1972: 50) as the grass later called *malinalli* by the Nahuas.[4]

The border or frame that surrounds the mural consists of four horizontal bands situated on both sides of the mountain (see Figure 13). The first broad band (from bottom to top) is covered by the same arched motifs with saw-toothed interiors that appear on each side of the Mountain God on the Denver mural. I have shown these to be obsidian blades. This time, a larger number of them appear, arranged horizontally in several rows and overlapping one another. The third band is a series of short feathers, a stylized version of the short red feathers in the bundles of the helmet headdress of the Denver mural god.

From all of the analogies presented, I conclude that Figure 13 is a new image of the Mountain God, one that more clearly reveals the nature of the deity. As already seen, in the Denver mural the god wears diamond motifs in his headdress—although they are quadripartite there—and the shining saw-toothed bands appear apart from the body, thus offering only a limited field of interpretation. In Figure 13, however, the two fire motifs form the nucleus of the mountain, thus constituting a concentric grouping, and it is precisely from this nucleus of fire that the hand (or hands) emerges with the plant scepter. This arrangement suggests that the Mountain God's fire is the source of its ability to confer plant fertility.

Taken as a whole, the murals in Portico 1 provide the nucleus of the broader context for an in-depth analysis of the Mountain God of the White Patio. In the upper murals of Portico 1 are the Coyote Lords (e.g., Figure 16); in the lower murals are coyotes, which, because of their headdresses, are probably metaphors or zoomorphic alter-egos of the Coyote Lords (Figure 17). Regarding the term "Coyote Lords," several authors have

FIGURE 16. Coyote Lord from Portico 1, White Patio, Atetelco (from Villagra Caleti 1971: fig. 17).

FIGURE 17. Coyotes from Portico 1, White Patio, Atetelco (from Villagra Caleti 1971: fig. 16).

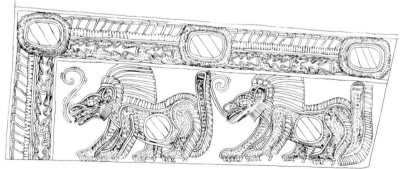

spoken in general of warriors and even of the order of the coyote or canine warriors on the Atetelco murals (Cabrera Castro 2002; Headrick 2007: 72–89; Latsanopoulos, n.d.; C. Millon 1988b; von Winning 1987, I: 86–88). However, although the warrior character of the figures is clear, it is obvious that they represent personages of high rank, as indicated by the complexity, richness, and various specific components of their apparel—for example, a shoulder ornament shared with the Lords with Tasselled Headdress (C. Millon 1988a: 118), who were possibly the city's rulers (Paulinyi 2001). For these reasons, I believe it is more accurate to call them Coyote Lords.

FIGURE 18. Front-facing personages with bundles of coyote tails in their headdresses, Portico 3, White Patio, Atetelco (from Cabrera Castro 1995: fig. 18.7).

In the three upper murals of Portico 1 the images of the Mountain God surround and accompany the Coyote Lords; thus it is probable that this god and these lords are interrelated. The lords appear as warriors wearing coyote garments and carrying darts. Flames emanate from their coyote skin–covered bodies and from the objects held in their hands, as they do from the crisscrossed strips of flayed coyote skin that frame each of the lords within a diamond-shaped space. Fire appears as the common denominator between the lords represented with flames and the deity that has within it the shining concentric diamond shapes. On the strips of coyote skin each pair of flames alternates with the plant observed next to each representation of the Mountain God in the frame for the mural. In this way, the strips of coyote skin constitute a close link between the god and the lords wearing coyote skins, underlining their mutual association.

At this point the image of the Mountain God on the twin murals takes an added significance, reinforcing and extending the connection sketched out above. The strips of coyote skin from the headdress, just as noted above, show an affinity with the iconography of the Coyote Lords. On the points of their headdresses, as well as in the ornaments worn on their back, can be found the same feathers that were observed in the headdress of the god of the twin murals.

The other two porticos of the White Patio offer close analogies regarding the strips of coyote skin in the headdress of the god of the twin murals; these analogies, in turn, establish a link with the Rain God. In Portico 3 (Figure 18), in the border of the lower murals it is possible to make out a series of unidentifed front-facing personages who, in addition to wearing the Rain God's eye rings, display two bunches of coyote tails on their headdresses. In Portico 2, which is the principal portico of the White Patio, there appear, in the lower murals, richly costumed coyotes that are devouring human hearts in the company of net jaguars. This takes place under the indirect supervision of the Rain God, whose head appears sequentially in the border of the upper murals of Portico 2 (Figure 19). This head wears two bunches of coyote tails in its headdress, the same as the personage in Portico 3, and is found inserted between interlaced bands, one

FIGURE 19. Rain God with bundles of coyote tails in his headdress, Portico 2, White Patio, Atetelco (after Stone 1989: fig. 3, detail).

of which is covered by the same broad blades of obsidian already seen in the border of the upper murals of Portico 1.[5] In short, the Mountain God and the Coyote Lords are closely joined, and apparently the Mountain God is the special deity of the Coyote Lords. The first indication of this relationship arises during the analysis of the twin murals, but it becomes apparent through examining the Atetelco murals. Nevertheless, the twin murals and those of the White Patio at Atetelco suggest that this link somehow had to do with a third party: the Rain God.

THE COYOTE LORDS AND THE RAIN GOD

There are questions to answer. It is not yet clear who the Coyote Lords are, nor what kind of fire is emitted from their bodies. The evidence given here indicates that the flames emitted by the Coyote Lords come from lightning and that they formed one of the groups of nobles under the protection of the Rain God.

These images of the Coyote Lords giving off flames are not unique in Teotihuacan and Teotihuacanoid art. In a previous paper (Paulinyi 2001: 14–18) I proposed that there were other high-ranking personages— with tasselled headdresses, helmet headdresses, or dressed as feathered jaguars—emitting flames, each one of them clearly linked to the Rain God (Hellmuth 1987: fig. 14; Figures 20, 21). A detailed analysis establishes that the Rain God is the source of the flames in every case, and these personages are considered to be lords with magic powers who were able to carry lightning on their bodies (cf. Figure 22). Because two of the images of the lords giving off flames bear arms (e.g., Figure 20), I argued that Teotihuacanos could have considered lightning a supernatural weapon. In that interpretation, I proposed the possibility that the flame-bearing personages from Atetelco, dressed as coyotes and armed, might also have been connected to the Rain God.

Apart from this argument, there is other evidence that leads to the same

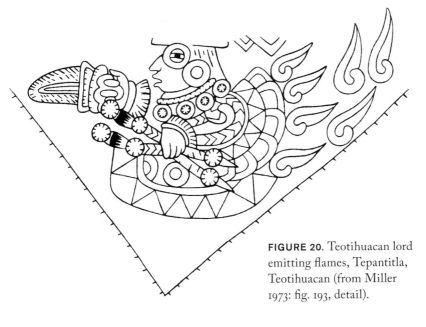

FIGURE 20. Teotihuacan lord emitting flames, Tepantitla, Teotihuacan (from Miller 1973: fig. 193, detail).

FIGURE 21. Personage dressed as a feathered jaguar. Drawing by Saburo Sugiyama (from Pasztory 1988b: fig. VI.15).

conclusion. These same Coyote Lords in Portico 1 wear the eye rings worn by the Rain God. In a context of coyotes and net jaguars, the Rain God in the main portico of the White Patio wears a headdress with coyote tails; in Portico 3 the front-facing personage with the Rain God's eye rings wears coyote tails on his headdress.

The shoulder ornament characteristic of these Coyote Lords has its parallel in the images of nobles linked to the Rain God: there are two groups of warrior lords in Portico 3 at Atetelco—one in the *talud* and the

FIGURE 22. Rain God with his lightning scepter. Drawing by Saburo Sugiyama (from Pasztory 1988b: fig. VI.1).

other in the *tablero*—who display the eye rings of the Rain God (see Figure 18). The same type of shoulder ornament is displayed by the Lords with Tasselled Headdress at Techinantitla, by the Red Tlaloques located below the images of the Lords with Tasselled Headdress at Tepantitla, and also by sacrificial Priests of the Rain God (Conides n.d. [2001]: figs. 47b, 57c; Garcia Cisneros 1969: no. 2; C. Millon 1988a: 118; Paulinyi 2001: 8, 18–21; von Winning 1984: fig. 18; see also Figure 9). Clara Millon (1988a) proposed that this ornament might express the coyote aspect of those personages, whereas I have pointed out that it is not the exclusive attribute of that group. After examining the cited images again, it now seems reasonable to me to propose that the shoulder ornament must have belonged to different nobles, or groups of nobles, all having links to the Rain God.

The disk with bands across it on the belly of the coyotes in Portico 1 (see Figure 17) forms part of the iconography of the nobles of the Rain God. For example, it appears as a pectoral on the symbolic personage wearing the Rain God's tasselled headdress (Figure 23). The disk also appears on the breast of a Lord with Tasselled Headdress (Conides and Barbour 2002: fig. 6). A figure with the eye rings of the Rain God wears the disk as a pectoral (see Figure 9), and it appears again on the shield of a high-ranking dignitary wearing identical eye rings and a helmet-type headdress (Figure 24), where it is located just above a band that at times forms part of the headdress of the Rain God (Séjourné 1959: fig. 127a, 1966a: fig. 41; von Winning 1987 1, VII: fig. 11d).[6]

Considering this evidence, it is not surprising, then, to see that among the four high-ranking dignitaries making offerings around the image of the Rain God on the well-known Calpulalpan bowl—a scene in which a Lord with Tasselled Headdress is playing the principal role—that the

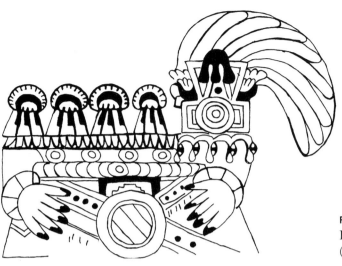

FIGURE 23. The "coyote disk" of the Sacred Hands mural at Tetitla, Teotihuacan (after Villagra Caleti 1971: fig. 15, detail).

FIGURE 24. Dignitary with the "coyote disk" on his shield (from Paulinyi 2001: fig. 19).

symbol accompanying a dignitary with a helmet headdress should be a coyote (Figure 25). Similarly, the Coyote Lords of Atetelco are accompanied by coyotes on the lower murals of Portico 1. The Lords with Tasselled Headdress form the highest ranking group of Teotihuacan nobles, which was a group under the protection of the Rain God (C. Millon 1973, 1988a; Paulinyi 2001). If this reasoning is correct, then the coyote lord on the Calpulalpan vessel is very probably a representative of another group of high-ranking nobles also under the protection of the Rain God. According to the arguments presented above, the Coyote Lords on the Atetelco murals should correspond to this group.

Although I have proposed that the flames scattered by the Teotihuacan lords were indications of their supernatural military capacity (Paulinyi 2001)—without, however, excluding other possible aspects of their magical

FIGURE 25. The
Calpulalpan bowl (from
Linné 1942: fig. 128).

power—at this point, I broaden that interpretation in another direction. Another aspect of the fire of the lightning is shown in images linked to water, fertility, and plants. The most important evidence in favor of this linkage, represented in two murals, is an individual of high rank dressed as a feathered jaguar whose hands emit flames. He bears no arms, and his speech volute is charged with aquatic and vegetation symbols (Pasztory 1988b: plate 32, figs. 6.15, 6.17; see Figure 21). Similarly, elsewhere a Coyote Lord appears with two flames on his body, unarmed and with flowers in his speech volute (Figure 26). On more than one occasion, coyotes costumed as persons (possibly incarnations of the Coyote Lords) appear with water and vegetation symbols both on their bodies and in their speech volutes (Figures 7, 27). There is also a coyote sitting in a vessel of water—a symbol of the world of water and earth (Berlo 1984: 103–105; Paulinyi 1995: 87–90). Accompanying it there are several sacrifice symbols and, in its speech volute and on its claw, aquatic and fertility symbols (Cabrera Castro 1995: fig. 18.19).[7]

What relationship can lightning have with water and plants? At Teotihuacan, lightning represents the feared weapon of the Rain God, but above all, it is the source of water and rain, and consequently of plant life. Regarding this latter aspect of lightning, in some images water flows as stylized waves from the lightning scepter of the god (Juárez Osnaya et al. 1995: figs. 13–17; R. Millon 1988: fig. IV, 21a–c; see Figure 22). If the Teotihuacan lords did, in fact, claim control over lightning, it was probably used in a manner similar to the power of the Rain God, with the two functions mentioned here: as a supernatural weapon and as the generating source of the rain.

According to this explanation, it is very likely that in Portico 1 of the White Patio, the flames of the Coyote Lords, as well as the strips of coyote

FIGURE 26. Coyote Lord, unarmed and with flames (from Séjourné 1966b: fig. 135).

FIGURE 27. Costumed coyote with water symbols (from Miller 1973: 367).

skin, all correspond to the fire of lightning. If that is so, owing to this close relationship between the Coyote Lords and the Mountain God, it is likely that both share the same divine fire and that the fire within the image of the god is lightning. In addition, in the murals with the Coyote Lords, fire has the two aspects of lightning mentioned here: martial, as in the warrior figures of the Coyote Lords; and fertility, as in the images of the Mountain God.

THE RAIN GOD AND THE MOUNTAIN GOD

The nature of the Mountain God is complex. He is a mountain deity, probably having the powers of the rain gods; but at the same time, he is the protecting deity of the Coyote Lords.

If not only the Mountain God but also—as argued in the previous section—the Rain God were each a tutelary god of the Coyote Lords, these lords were probably under the protection of two gods of different rank, each corresponding to one of two different levels in the

Teotihuacan pantheon. The Rain God, the tutelary god of Teotihuacan, is the more important of the two. It appears that he was closely connected to several groups of Teotihuacan nobility, among them, that of the Coyote Lords. These several groups of nobles seem to have made up the dominant segment of the Teotihuacan elite, which was headed by the Lords with Tasselled Headdress. The second protective deity is the Mountain God, who is of much more limited importance and has his own iconographic features. He is dedicated specifically to his Coyote Lords.

Each deity appears in the White Patio of Atetelco in its appropriate place and role. The Rain God rises from the top of the main portico, in a clear but nonexclusive relationship to the coyote complex. This nonexclusivity is demonstrated by the presence of net jaguars next to the coyotes and of persons of high rank above them who are also not Coyote Lords. In contrast, the Mountain God is located in a portico off to one side and is alone with his Coyote Lords, forming a small, exclusive universe without the participation of other actors.

To complete the portrait of the Mountain God, let us take one last look at one of his attributes. It is noteworthy that the god represented on the twin murals shows similarities to a dignitary, as if the god were the dignitary's divine image. Most important of all, above his anthropomorphic face he wears a version of the helmet headdress of the high-ranking dignitaries, and as noted above the Coyote Lord in the Calpulalpan bowl bears another version of the same headdress. Other attributes of the deity may belong to a god as well as to a high-ranking mortal, for example, the bundles of strips of coyote skin, the ear ornaments, and necklace of round beads in the Denver mural and the fringed wristbands in the Atetelco mural. For these reasons, the Mountain God might have been considered an ancestral leader or founder of the group of Coyote Lords.

The archaeological and iconographic evidence corroborates the existence of mountain deity worship in the valley of Mexico and its adjacent valleys, at least from the early years A.D. (e.g., Plunket and Uruñuela 1998). Worship of these deities is one of the oldest and most enduring phenomena in the religious tradition of the Central Highlands. The Mountain God discussed here is the first discovered as such in Teotihuacan art, reaffirming the archaeological evidence that indicates that, in that era also, mountain worship was practiced. Perhaps this god is only one representative of a larger group of mountain deities in the Teotihuacan pantheon, with others still unknown.

It is striking that the outline sketched out here for the Mountain God is similar to the essential characteristics of the tutelary deities of Postclassic socioethnic groups in the Central Highlands. These deities usually lived in the interior of mountains near those they protected, and although they may not have belonged to the rain gods proper, they also played the role of a local rain deity (López Austin 1973: 61–65). The existence of a hierarchy among tutelary gods similarly characterizes these centuries. If my analysis of the Mountain God is valid, then this deity is an important example of sociohistorical continuity between Teotihuacan and the Postclassic world, in spite of the many centuries that separate them.

Acknowledgments

This study was made under Fondecyt Project No. 1020764, for which I am the grantee. I thank Helena Horta for her meticulous correction of the original Spanish text; Linda Manzanilla for her bibliographic assistance; Damon and Marjorie Peeler for the English translation; Sergio Purini for sending data on the Brussels mural fragment; and finally, Carol Robbins, who helped me identify the earliest publication on the Denver mural.

NOTES

1. The most relevant works that propose the existence of the "Great Goddess" are Berlo (1992) and Pasztory (1988a, 1992, 1997).

2. The scepter of the Brussels mural appears in the updated version of the list of Teotihuacan notational signs by Langley (2002: no. 232), although it was not included in the original version (Langley 1986). I am of the opinion that it is only one component of the Mountain God's costume and that its inclusion is not justified.

3. The White Patio murals of Atetelco have been the subject of various interpretations from different points of view. Based on these murals, von Winning (1987, 1, VI: 73–76, VII: 86–88) considered Atetelco a place associated with warriors recently initiated into military orders. C. Millon's (1988b: 212–216) analysis revolves around coyote symbology. Headrick (2007: 72–102; n.d. [1996]) essentially attempts to reconstruct the basic structure of the Teotihuacan state based on this cluster of murals. Cabrera Castro (2002) examines its martial aspects and those of human sacrifice.

4. There is the possibility that the malinalli plants that appear along the outline of the mountain may indicate a place name. One of the most important mountains near Teotihuacan is today called Cerro Malinalco ("mountain where malinalli grows"). This mountain had the same Nahua name during the colonial period (Gamio 1922, 1, II: facing page 384), and one may suppose that it comes from the Pre-Hispanic period. Nevertheless, it is not certain that the Mountain God was the god of this mountain, because many centuries passed between the fall of Teotihuacan and the Spanish conquest, and the language of the inhabitants of Teotihuacan is unknown. Further, it is possible the malinalli plants do not refer to the name of the mountain but rather have some different connotation. Despite these difficulties, I leave the question open for future study.

5. According to C. Millon (1988b: 213) the headdresses mentioned above include coyote tails, whereas Cabrera Castro (2002: 146, 147) speaks of strips of coyote skin. I share the opinion of Millon, because the rounded end and the dark spot on the end of these objects are characteristics that are also found on the coyote tail in the White Patio (see Figure 17).

6. Nevertheless, these "coyote disks" are not exclusively the iconography of the Rain God and his lords: they also form a cluster of symbols that Langley (1986: 103–107) calls the "core cluster," which is related to butterfly representations. In my opinion, this cluster belongs to the Butterfly-Bird God. Although the iconography of these two deities shares several points, an attempt to explain this commonality is beyond the scope of this chapter.

7. For arguments in favor of an interpretation of the motif as a vessel, see Taube (1983: 112–113) and Berlo (1984: 82, 87, 103–105). Cabrera Castro (1995: 249–250) is of the opinion that they are broad volutes coming out of the upper part of a pedestal.

REFERENCES CITED

Anders, Ferdinand, Marteen Jansen, and Luis Reyes García
  1991   *El Libro del Cihuacoatl, Homenaje para el año del Fuego Nuevo: Libro explicativo del llamado Códice Borbónico.* Códices Mexicanos III. Sociedad Estatal Quinto Centenario, Akademische Druck- und Verlagsanstalt, and Fondo de Cultura Económica, Madrid, Graz, and México.

Angulo Villaseñor, Jorge
  1972   Reconstrucción etnográfica a través de la pintura mural. In *XI Mesa Redonda de la Sociedad Mexicana de Antropología. Teotihuacan, el valle de Teotihuacan y su contorno:* 43–63. Sociedad Mexicana de Antropología, México.

Bankmann, Ulf
  1988   Fragment d'une peinture murale. No. 121 in *Les Aztèques—Trésors du Mexique ancien.* Musées Royaux d'Art et d'Histoire, Brussels, catalog. Philip von Zabern, Mainz am Rhein.

Berlo, Janet C.
  1984   *Teotihuacan Art Abroad: A Study of Metropolitan Style and Provincial Transformation in Incensario Workshops.* BAR International Series 199. British Archaeological Reports, Oxford.

  1992   Icons and Ideologies at Teotihuacan: The Great Goddess Reconsidered. In *Art, Ideology and the City of Teotihuacan* (Janet C. Berlo, ed.): 129–168. Dumbarton Oaks Research Library and Collection, Washington D.C.

Berrin, Kathleen, and Esther Pasztory (eds.)
  1993   *Teotihuacan: Art from the City of the Gods.* Thames & Hudson and Fine Arts Museums of San Francisco, San Francisco.

Cabrera Castro, Rubén
  1995   Atetelco. In *La Pintura mural prehispánica en México I: Teotihuacán, Tomo I, Catálogo* (Beatriz de la Fuente, coord.): 203–258. Universidad Nacional Autónoma de México, Instituto de Investigaciones Estéticas, México.

  1996   Caracteres glíficos teotihuacanos en un piso de La Ventilla. In *La Pintura mural prehispánica en México I: Teotihuacán, Tomo II, Estudios* (Beatriz de la Fuente, coord.): 401–428. Universidad Nacional Autónoma de México, Instituto de Investigaciones Estéticas, México.

2002   La expresión pictórica de Atetelco, Teotihuacan. Su significado con el militarismo y el sacrificio humano. In *Ideología y política a través de materiales, imágenes y símbolos. Memoria de la Primera Mesa Redonda de Teotihuacan* (María Helena Ruiz Gallut, ed.): 137–164. Universidad Nacional Autónoma de México, Instituto de Investigaciones Antropológicas, Instituto de Investigaciones Estéticas–Instituto Nacional de Antropología e Historia, México.

Conides, Cynthia Alexandria
   n.d.   The Stuccoed and Painted Ceramics from Teotihuacan, Mexico: A Study of Authorship and Function of Works of Art from an Ancient Mesoamerican City. Ph.D. dissertation, Department of Art History, Columbia University, New York, 2001.

Conides, Cynthia Alexandria, and Warren Barbour
   2002   Tocados dentro del paisaje arquitectónico y social en Teotihuacan. In *Ideología y política a través de materiales, imágenes y símbolos. Memoria de la Primera Mesa Redonda de Teotihuacan* (María Helena Ruiz Gallut, ed.): 411–430. Universidad Nacional Autónoma de México, Instituto de Investigaciones Antropológicas, Instituto de Investigaciones Estéticas–Instituto Nacional de Antropología e Historia, México.

Dallas Museum of Fine Arts
   1950   *Pre-Columbian Art: Loan Exhibition of Objects Illustrating the Cultures of Middle American Civilizations before Their Conquest by Cortez.* Catalog. Dallas Museum of Fine Arts, Dallas.

Delgado, Agustin, Carlos Zaldivar Weyer, and Enrique Moreno de Tagle
   1965   *El arte de Jaina.* Artes de México XXI, no. 60. Instituto Cultural Domecq, México.

Denver Art Museum
   1981   *Major Works in the Collection.* Catalog. Denver Art Museum, Denver.

Gamio, Manuel
   1922   *La población del valle de Teotihuacan. El medio en que se ha desarrollado, su evolución étnica y social. Iniciativas para procurar su mejoramiento,* 3 vols. Dirección de Antropología–Secretaría de la Agricultura y Fomento, México.

García Cisneros, Florencia
   1969   *Surrealism in Pre-Columbian Art.* Cisneros, New York.

Headrick, Annabeth
   2007   *The Teotihuacan Trinity: The Sociopolitical Structure of an Ancient Mesoamerican City.* University of Texas Press, Austin.
   n.d.   The Teotihuacan Trinity: Unmasking the Political Structure. Ph.D. dissertation, Department of Art and Art History, University of Texas, Austin, 1996.

Hellmuth, Nicholas
   1978   Teotihuacan Art in the Escuintla, Guatemala Region. In *Middle Classic Mesoamerica: A.D. 400–700* (Esther Pasztory, ed.): 71–85. Columbia University Press, New York.

Juárez Osnaya, Alberto, and Elizabeth Carmen Avila Rivera
  1995 Totómetla. In *La Pintura mural prehispánica en México I: Teotihuacán,
        Tomo I, Catálogo* (Beatriz de la Fuente, coord.): 347–360. Universidad
        Nacional Autónoma de México, Instituto de Investigaciones Estéticas,
        México.

Kubler, George
  1967 *The Iconography of Art of Teotihuacan.* Studies in Pre-Columbian Art
        and Archaeology 4. Dumbarton Oaks Research Library and Collec-
        tion, Washington, D.C.

Langley, James C.
  1986 *Symbolic Notation of Teotihuacan. Elements of Writing in a Mesoamerican
        Culture of the Classic Period.* BAR International Series 313. British
        Archaeological Reports, Oxford.
  2002 Teotihuacan Notation in a Mesoamerican Context: Likeness, Concept
        and Metaphor. In *Ideología y política a través de materiales, imágenes y
        símbolos. Memoria de la Primera Mesa Redonda de Teotihuacan* (María
        Elena Ruiz Gallut, ed.): 275–301. Universidad Nacional Autónoma
        de México, Instituto de Investigaciones Antropológicas, Instituto
        de Investigaciones Estéticas–Instituto Nacional de Antropología e
        Historia, México.

Latsanopoulos, Nicolas
  n.d. De lobos y coyotes: Notas sobre los grandes cánidos en Teotihuacan. In
        Arquitectura y urbanismo: Pasado y presente de los espacios en Teotihuacan
        (María Elena Ruiz Gallut and Jesús Torres Peralta, eds.). Instituto
        Nacional de Antropología e Historia, Memorias de la Tercera Mesa
        Redonda de Teotihuacan (2002), México. (in press).

Linné, Sigvald
  1942 *Mexican highland cultures. Archaeological researches at Teotihuacan, Calpu-
        lalpan and Chalchicomula, in 1934–1935.* New Series 7. Ethnographical
        Museum of Sweden, Stockholm.

López Austin, Alfredo
  1973 *Hombre-dios. Religión y política en el mundo náhuatl.* Serie de Cultura
        Náhuatl. Monografías 15. Universidad Nacional Autónoma de México,
        Instituto de Investigaciones Históricas, México.

Matos Moctezuma, Eduardo
  1990 *Teotihuacan. La metrópoli degli dei.* Editoriale Jaca Book, Milan.

Miller, Arthur G.
  1973 *The Mural Painting of Teotihuacan.* Dumbarton Oaks Research Library
        and Collection, Washington, D.C.

Millon, Clara
  1973 Painting, Writing and Polity in Teotihuacan, Mexico. *American
        Antiquity* 38: 294–314.
  1988a A Reexamination of the Teotihuacan Tassel Headdress Insignia. In
        *Feathered Serpents and Flowering Trees: Reconstructing the Murals of
        Teotihuacan* (Kathleen Berrin, ed.): 114–134. Fine Arts Museums of San
        Francisco, San Francisco.

1988b   Coyote with Sacrificial Knife. In *Feathered Serpents and Flowering Trees: Reconstructing the Murals of Teotihuacan* (Kathleen Berrin, ed.): 207–217. Fine Arts Museums of San Francisco, San Francisco.

Millon, Rene

1988   Where Do They All Come From? The Provenance of the Wagner Murals from Teotihuacan. In *Feathered Serpents and Flowering Trees: Reconstructing the Murals of Teotihuacan* (Kathleen Berrin, ed.): 78–113. Fine Arts Museums of San Francisco.

Pasztory, Esther

1988a   A Reinterpretation of Teotihuacan and Its Mural Painting Tradition. In *Feathered Serpents and Flowering Trees: Reconstructing the Murals of Teotihuacan* (Kathleen Berrin, ed): 45–77. Fine Arts Museums of San Francisco, San Francisco.

1988b   Feathered Feline and Bird Border. In *Feathered Serpents and Flowering Trees: Reconstructing the Murals of Teotihuacan* (Kathleen Berrin, ed.): 185–193. Fine Arts Museums of San Francisco, San Francisco.

1992   Abstraction and the Rise of a Utopian State at Teotihuacan. In *Art, Ideology and the City of Teotihuacan* (Janet C. Berlo, ed.): 281–320. Dumbarton Oaks Research Library and Collection, Washington, D.C.

1997   *Teotihuacan. An Experiment in Living.* University of Oklahoma Press, Norman and London.

Paulinyi, Zoltán

1995   El pájaro del Dios Mariposa de Teotihuacan: Análisis iconográfico a partir de una vasija de Tiquisate, Guatemala. *Boletín del Museo Chileno de Arte Precolombino* 6: 71–110.

2001   Los señores con tocado de borlas: Un estudio sobre el Estado teotihua-cano. *Ancient Mesoamerica* 12: 1–30.

2006a   The "Great Goddess" of Teotihuacan: Fiction or Reality? *Ancient Mesoamerica* 17: 1–15.

2006b   El Dios Mariposa—Pájaro y sus acompañantes zoomorfos en los murales del Patio 1 del Palacio del Sol, Teotihuacan. *La Pintura Mural Prehispánica en México. Boletín Informativo* XII(24–25): 47–54.

2007a   La tierra como ser viviente en el arte teotihuacano. *Indiana* 24: 317–337.

2007b   La diosa de Tepantitla en Teotihuacan: Una nueva interpretación. *Cuicuilco* 41: 243–277.

Plunket, Patricia, and Gabriela Uruñuela

1998   Preclassic Household Patterns Preserved under Volcanic Ash at Tetimpa, Puebla, Mexico. *Latin American Antiquity* 9: 287–309.

Scott, Sue

2001   *The Corpus of Terracotta Figurines from Sigvald Linné's Excavations at Teotihuacan, Mexico (1932 and 1934–35) and Comparative Material.* Monograph Series 18. National Museum of Ethnography, Stockholm.

Séjourné, Laurette

1959   *Un palacio de la ciudad de los dioses (Teotihuacan).* Instituto Nacional de Antropología e Historia, México.

1962 Interpretación de un jeroglífico teotihuacano. *Cuadernos Americanos* 124(5): 137–158.

1966a *Arqueología de Teotihuacán: La cerámica.* Fondo de Cultura Económica, México.

1966b *El lenguaje de las formas de Teotihuacán.* Mancero, México.

Seler, Eduard

1915 Die Teotihuacan-Kultur des Hochlands von Mexico. In *Gesammelte Abhandlungen zur Amerikanischen Sprach- und Altertumskunde,* vol. V: 405–485. Behrend & Co., Berlin.

1963 *Comentarios al Códice Borgia,* 3 vols. Fondo de Cultura Económica, México.

Stone, Andrea J.

1989 Disconnection, Foreign Insignia, and Political Expansion: Teotihuacan and the Warrior Stelae of Piedras Negras. In *Mesoamerica: After the Decline of Teotihuacan, A.D. 700–900* (Richard A. Diehl and Janet C. Berlo, eds.): 153–186. Dumbarton Oaks Research Library and Collection, Washington, D.C.

Taube, Karl

1983 The Teotihuacan Spider Woman. *Journal of Latin American Lore* 9(2): 107–189.

2000 *The Writing System of Ancient Teotihuacan.* Ancient America 1. Center for Ancient American Studies, Barnardsville, N.C.

Thieme, Wolf-Günter

1986 Fragment einer Wandmalerei. No. 121 in *Glanz und Untergang des Alten Mexico,* 2 vols. Musées Royaux d'Art et d'Histoire, Brussels, catalog. Philip von Zabern, Mainz am Rhein.

Villagra Caleti, Agustín

1971 Mural Painting in Central Mexico. In *Handbook of Middle American Indians* (Robert Wauchope, general ed.), vol. 10: *The Archaeology of Northern Mesoamerica,* part 1 (Gordon Ekholm and Ignacio Bernal, eds.): 135–156. University of Texas Press, Austin.

Von Winning, Hasso

1977 The Old Fire God and His Symbolism at Teotihuacan. *Indiana* 4: 7–61.

1984 Insignias de oficio en la iconografía de Teotihuacán. *Pantóc* 8: 5–54.

1987 *La iconografía de Teotihuacán: Los dioses y los signos,* 2 vols. Universidad Nacional Autónoma de México, México.

THE HOUSE OF NEW FIRE AT TEOTIHUACAN AND ITS LEGACY IN MESOAMERICA

William L. Fash

Alexandre Tokovinine

Barbara W. Fash

THE ARTISTIC, TEXTUAL, AND ARCHAEOLOGICAL legacies of the Basin of Mexico provide abundant evidence for the central place of one city in its collective imaginary (Boone 2000a). From its foundation early in the current era until the arrival of the Spanish invaders, Teotihuacan—the "Place Where Men Became Gods"—was the city whose art, architecture, and ideology most inspired others. It became an archetypal city to its contemporaries both in the Basin of Mexico and far beyond the Central Highlands. Even after the city was sacked and burned in 550 C.E. (López Luján et al. 2006), it was the source of inspiration to its successor civilizations in Highland Mexico. The Toltecs of Tula (Mastache et al., this volume) and their later admirers, the Culhua Mexica of Mexico-Tenochtitlan (López Luján and López Austin, this volume), consciously evoked its buildings and their symbolism. Teotihuacan was the locus of the first monumental archaeological project carried out by the government of Mexico, undertaken to celebrate the centennial of Mexico's independence. It continues to be visited by pilgrims each year on the vernal equinox. This chapter explores some of the uses and meanings of the central monument of Teotihuacan and its magnetic power for ancient and contemporary Mesoamerican cultures.

AZTEC CONCEPTIONS AND USES OF TEOTIHUACAN

Elizabeth Boone's close reading of relevant sixteenth-century manuscripts and maps enabled her to show that the Aztec understanding of Teotihuacan—that "Venerable Place of Beginnings" as she insightfully put it—was broad and multifaceted:

The sources show us how the Aztecs venerated Teotihuacan as the place where the Fifth Sun was created, where the gods first sacrificed themselves, and where the future warriors first showed their valor by risking their lives for the sun. They knew the ancient Teotihuacan to be the place where government as they knew it was established, where rulers were installed for the first time, where the first laws were made, and where the Chichimecs divided themselves and distinguished themselves as Acolhua, Mexica, Chalca, etc. [Boone 2000a: 387].

Boone (2000b: 16) also noted that in Late Postclassic Highland Mexico, the making of New Fire corresponds with the founding of new polities. As noted below this datum is of great importance in understanding the art of urbanism at Teotihuacan and beyond.

In her classic *American Antiquity* article about the artificial cavern beneath the Sun Pyramid at Teotihuacan, Doris Heyden (1975: 139) noted that the *Relación Geográfica* of the Teotihuacan Valley "tells us that the priests of 'Montesuma, the lord of Mexico-Tenochtitlan, with the said Montesuma came to offer sacrifices (in Teotihuacan) every twenty days' . . . apparently continuing or reviving the ancient tradition of pilgrimages to the shrine." She cited Bernadino de Sahagún's sixteenth-century informants:

> Offerings were made at a place named Teotihuacan. And there all the people raised pyramids for the sun and for the moon. . . . And there leaders were elected, wherefore it is called Teotiuacan [place where lords or gods are made]. And when the rulers died, they buried them there. Then they built a pyramid over them . . . those who made them at that time were giants [Heyden 1975: 137].

Heyden emphasized the testimony of Sahagún's (1950–82) informants that Teotihuacan was known as a place for the investiture of kings in office, an observation that has been cited often by many scholars since her influential article was published.

The archaeological evidence has illuminated how the Aztecs practiced what they preached regarding the primacy of this archetypal city. In his monograph on "La recuperación Mexica del pasado Teotihuacano," Leonardo López Luján (1989) catalogued the various strategies the Mexica employed to appropriate the greatness of Teotihuacan in their sacred precinct of Tenochititlan. These included the use of a grid, copying architectural forms, decorating buildings with polychrome painting, imitating Teotihuacan styles in their stone sculpture, and making offerings of Teotihuacan objects. The evidence indicates that the Mexica concern with Teotihuacan only manifested itself in the reign of Motecuhzoma Ilhuicamina (1440–1469), once they had begun to dominate the Central Highlands of Mexico. The pilgrimages of Motecuhzoma Xocoyotzin to the ruins of Teotihuacan every 20 days commented on in the *Relación Geográfica* indicate that the emperor himself felt a strong need to connect his kingdom to this powerful font of Mesoamerican civilization. As their domain rivaled or surpassed that of Teotihuacan, the Mexica began the process of shifting their focus from Tula to Teotihuacan (López 1989; Matos Moctezuma and López Luján 1993). This shift signals their understanding of the power of association with the most awe-inspiring ancient city in the Basin of Mexico.

In the present chapter we explore how and why earlier Mesoamerican kingdoms sought to legitimize themselves through their associations with Teotihuacan. Some of the same appropriation strategies that López Luján documented for the later Tenochca were also practiced by some of the Classic Maya kingdoms. We agree that some Early Classic Maya rulers were invested in office in rituals associated with an "Origins House" related to Teotihuacan (Stuart 2000, 2004; Taube 2004a). In contradistinction to earlier studies, however, we believe that we can identify the Teotihuacan temple at which several Classic Maya kings performed ceremonies, were invested in office, and were given powerful insignia of office and royal titles. We provide archaeological, iconographic, and epigraphic evidence in support of the hypothesis that the investiture of Classic period rulers took place at the Sun Pyramid, in conjunction with New Fire Ceremonies. This finding helps to explain why rituals performed by Maya kings at this locus became central to legitimation strategies at several Maya kingdoms, in what Tokovinine (n.d. [2008]) refers to as master narratives at those sites. We begin with a review of pertinent scholarship regarding the meaning and uses of the central monument of Teotihuacan.

THE SUN PYRAMID, THE STORM GOD, AND THE ORIGINS HOUSE

For the past quarter century, Teotihuacan specialists have argued that the Sun Pyramid at Teotihuacan (Figure 1), the name given it by Late Postclassic Nahuatlatos, was in fact closely associated with water deities by its original builders and users. Both Berlo (1992) and Millon (1992) interpreted this monument as a temple to the Storm God (Tlaloc, to the later Aztecs), based on the evidence for water channels in the long artificial cave found beneath it. More recently, the investigations of the Sun Pyramid directed by Eduardo Matos Moctezuma (1995) demonstrated that the pyramid was surrounded by a canal or moat, likely filled with water, further strengthening the association of this monument with water deities.

Matos Moctezuma (1995: 314) went so far as to suggest that the Sun Pyramid came to symbolize the *altepetl* or "water hill" of ancient Teotihuacan. All of the aforementioned authors made reference to the dis-

FIGURE 1. Sun Pyramid and Adosada Platform (foreground), showing access door to the artificial cave beneath, Teotihuacan, Mexico. Photo by Barbara Fash.

covery by Leopoldo Batres (1906: 22; Figure 2) of a series of child burials at the corners of the final construction stage of the Sun Pyramid. Heyden (1975: 141, 154) noted that child sacrifices are related to the water deity Tlaloc, who lived in caves as well as on mountaintops, and that Durán describes Tlaloc as "God of Rain, Thunder, and Lightning. . . . The name means Path under the Earth or Long Cave." Millon (1992) and his colleagues (Millon and Drewitt 1963) recovered important data from the artificial cave found beneath the pyramid that was investigated by Jorge Acosta; the latter's untimely death prevented him from publishing the results of his own work. Access to this orifice was provided by a portal in the frontal platform ("Adosada") affixed to the base of the west side of the pyramid. The artificial cave has been interpreted both as the dwelling place of Tlaloc and a "place of emergence," such as signaled in later Mesoamerican origins stories (Kowalski 1999). Sload (2008) recently conducted an exhaustive review of the literature on this theme, corroborated by comparative analyses of Maya practices, and concluded that the primary meaning of this feature was indeed as a place of emergence, or Origins House.

Ongoing investigations of the Adosada platform by Alejandro Sarabia, director of the Archaeological Zone of Teotihuacan, will no doubt provide fresh insights into its uses through time. Sarabia (personal communication, February 2008) generously provided us with a photograph of a stone sculp-

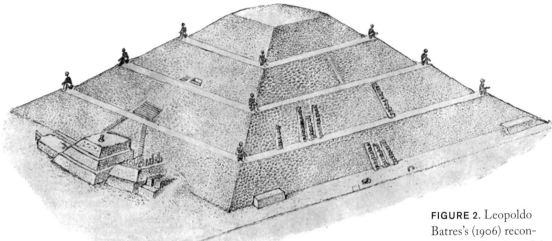

FIGURE 2. Leopoldo Batres's (1906) reconstruction drawing of the Sun Pyramid, with child burials (shown as seated figures) at the corners and a stone brazier on the central Adosada platform.

ture of the face of the Storm God, surrounded by *chalchihuitl* (water) signs that he recently discovered in his excavations there. Significantly, large *chalchihuitl* signs (signifying "precious," "greenstone," and "water") were the most abundant sculptures that adorned the *tableros* (vertical panels) of the Adosada, likely forming the frames of the *tableros* (Batres 1906: figs. 16, 17).

We consider the evidence adduced by scholars for links between the Teotihuacan Storm God and the Sun Pyramid—especially the exterior decoration of the Adosada and its portal to the artificial cave beneath the pyramid—to be compelling and persuasive. All lines of evidence mentioned above lead us to concur that this artificial cave was associated by its makers with the Storm God, among other constellations of meanings. Its role as a place of emergence or Origins House seems quite secure in Mesoamerican scholarship.

SOLAR AND ASTRONOMICAL ASSOCIATIONS OF THE SUN PYRAMID

Like Millon (1981, 1992), we consider it unwise to simply ignore the insistence of the sixteenth-century sources on the Sun Pyramid as the temple, indeed perhaps even the birthplace, of the Fifth Sun. There are several compelling lines of evidence that indicate strong solar associations with Teotihuacan's largest monument. We respect and support Saburo Sugiyama's powerful arguments regarding the pyramid's central position in the city, its solar eclipse cycle cosmogony, and the sight-lines associated with solar observations that tie the pyramid to other units of calendrical and astronomical reckoning and were noted by earlier scholars (Sugiyama 1993, 2005, n.d.; cf. Heyden 1975).

Of great interest for our purposes here is the relationship between the orientation of the Sun Pyramid and the movements of not only the sun but also the Pleiades:

> The city's east-west direction of all constructions was related to the astronomical movements of the sun and [the] Pleiades, as has been documented by detailed archaeoastronomical studies (Aveni 1980; Dow 1967; Drucker 1977; Malmstrom 1978; Millon 1981, 1993). The sun set on the western horizon exactly following the direction of the city's east-west axis on August 12 and April 29. These two dates separate a year into two periods lasting 105 and 260 days, the latter of which coincides perfectly with the ritual calendar. August 12 was also important as the legendary day of the beginning of time, presumably in 3114 BC for the Maya. The Pleiades, well recorded as an important constellation in Mesoamerica, was also centrally related to the city's east-west axis, as this important star cluster set on the same spot on the western horizon at Teotihuacan around 18 May when the sun passes the zenith at noon (Aveni 1980; Millon 1981, 1993: 35) [Sugiyama n.d.: 9].

The association with the Pleiades is particularly important for our analysis. When the later Aztecs practiced their New Fire Ceremony at the completion of each cycle of 52 years (*tonalpoalli*) to celebrate the renewal of the calendar and the continuation of the Fifth Sun, the key event in the cosmic drama was the moment when the Pleiades passed the zenith (cf. Caso 1937). When this occurred, the priests of the four quarters knew that the sun would live on, so the New Fire was ignited over the chest of the sacrificial victim offered to the sun on this occasion. The depiction of this ritual in the Codex Borbonicus (Anders et al. 1991; Figure 3) shows each of the four priests carrying a bundle of sticks signifying years (a *xiumohlpilli* or *atado de años*). Three-dimensional Aztec stone representations of these bound bundles of sticks have been recovered in numerous excavations in Mexico City. In the Borbonicus rendition, the crossed bundles approximate very closely the version depicted in Classic Maya hieroglyphic inscriptions, glyph T600, in the Thompson (1962) catalog (Figure 4).

Another compelling argument for solar associations with the Sun Pyramid is the way the ancient Teotihuacanos themselves labeled this monument with architectural sculpture. During their excavations at the Teotihuacan Xalla compound in 2002, Leonardo López Luján and William Fash examined stone mosaic sculptures arranged in front of the Adosada platform of the Sun Pyramid. López Luján pointed out that three of them were depictions of the bundle of years or *xiumohlpilli*. He subsequently published his own drawing of the most complete example (López Luján 2002: fig. 17; see the glyphs in Figure 4). These three sculptures derive from the interior of the

FIGURE 3. Page 34 of the Codex Borbonicus (modified from Anders et al. 1991: 34). Drawing by Alexandre Tokovinine.

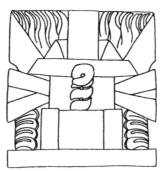

FIGURE 4. (Left) T600 (TE'-NAAH) hieroglyph. Drawing by David Stuart. (Right) Adosada New Fire glyph. Drawing by Francisco Carrizosa.

temple at the summit of the Adosada, along with square columns (or dadoes) bearing a variant of the same motif, according to the excavator (Batres 1906: 26, 61, 81; Figure 5; cf. Coggins 1987; Von Winning 1979).

In assessing the relative significance of the exterior and interior decoration of Teotihuacan buildings, Kubler (1973: 24) likened the exterior facades to billboards, which give a general sense of the meaning of the structure. Kubler surmised that the sculptures (including the dadoes) and mural paintings on the interior of the structure provide the most secure evidence for the rituals performed inside the building. In terms of practices in the interior of the central platform of the Adosada, Batres (1906: 26, 65, 71) very clearly records having found a large cylindrical stone censer or brazier there, resting on a stone masonry platform. He made a point of illustrating the location of it in the center of the Adosada platform in his rendition of the Sun Pyramid (Batres 1906: 109; see Figure 2). In Figure 5b it can be

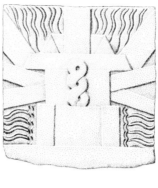

a

FIGURE 5. Three
types of sculptures
from the Adosada
platform, showing
the twisted cord of
the New Fire inside
a temple: (a) "name-
tag" glyph; (b) stone
brazier; and (c) carved
column. Drawings by
Alexandre Tokovinine.

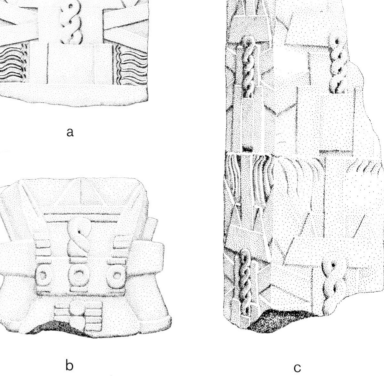

b

c

seen that this brazier's central icon is that of a twisted cord as a fire-making
sign, with the knotted sign of sacrificial offerings below (Coggins 1987;
Taube 2000b: fig. 10.14c; Von Winning 1979). This iconography labels the
censer as the place where fire was made, as part of sacrificial offerings. Its
placement inside a building that was decorated with dadoes and wall panels
that show temples where the New Fire was lit signals that the censer was
used in such rituals inside the Adosada itself.

To his credit, Batres (1906: 25) argued that the iconography of all these
sculptures linked the Adosada to the New Fire Ceremony. These sculptures
and Batres's interpretations have received scant attention in the ensuing
century. However much we might lament the lack of recovery of carbon or
other behavioral residues from the floor of the Adosada's central temple,
the archaeological context of the three sets of *xiumohlpilli* sculptures is
secure. Given Kubler's abovementioned observations, there is no reason to
refute Batres's inferences regarding the rituals that took place there. The
three large *xiumohlpilli* signs were originally painted (Batres 1906: 11) and
would appear to be name tags, such as are shown prominently elsewhere in
Teotihuacan writing (Taube 2000a). They all label the central platform of

FIGURE 6. Stone mosaic sculpture of a supernatural feline from the Xalla compound, sharing characteristics of the "jaguar-serpent-bird" identified by Kubler (1967). Drawing by Fernando Carrizosa.

the Adosada as the House of New Fire. Given the flames shown emerging from the house in the explicitly name-tagging glyph, we can see that it was considered the house where the crossed bundles of years were burned. In later Aztec practice this would be the House of New Fire, where the bundles representing the 52 years of the Calendar Round were burned as each such cycle drew to completion.

Note also the recent article by Sugiyama and López Luján (2007) in which they note that the principal burial (5C) of the three dignitaries laid to rest in the Pyramid of the Moon, without evidence of sacrifice, bore a jadeite pectoral with the symbol of the *xiumohlpilli*. They consider this symbol the paramount one of rulership at Teotihuacan. Thus the use of this symbol on the Adosada, at the foot of what is clearly the central temple in the city, is of signal importance. The historical, archaeological, and iconographic registers are consonant with one another: rulership was tied to the rituals that took place at the Adosada of the Sun Pyramid.

The other prominent element in the iconography of the Adosada platform is a large supernatural feline that repeated on the exterior facades of the platform (Batres 1906: 23–24). Barbara Fash noted a minimum of nine heads of large cats in the groups of sculptures at the Adosada and the site museum, and there may well have been many more. A more elaborate version of this cat was found in excavations at the Xalla compound (Manzanilla and López Luján 2002; Figure 6), which combines celestial as well as terrestrial aspects and displays goggle eyes (cf. Kubler 1967 on the jaguar-serpent-bird). This deity may be a Teotihuacan version of the Classic Maya deity referred to as the Jaguar God of the Underworld, which Stuart (1998) demonstrated was the Classic Maya Fire God. Such a role would be consistent with the fire, solar, and underworld associations of the Adosada. It bears emphasizing that Batres (1906: 12) noted that there were black spots on the Adosada feline sculptures that he found, securing their identification as jaguars ("*tigres*"), not pumas.

We close this discussion by citing the evidence for rituals that took place in the cave beneath the pyramid, which Millon et al. (1965) note involved fire, water, shell, and fish. This duality of fire and water, of course, was to be repeated in the subterranean offerings of the later Templo Mayor (López Luján 1994). As discussed below, at least one Classic Maya kingdom also repeated this pattern on its central, iconic temple-pyramid. Taken together we maintain that there are excellent reasons to retain the Nahua interpretation of this monument as the Sun Pyramid, but with strong Storm God, water, and place-of-emergence associations, as adumbrated by the scholarship of Teotihuacan experts cited above.

When viewed as a complex, the cosmogony of the Sun Pyramid at Teotihuacan clearly reflects observation of the solar, *tonalpoalli*, and eclipse cycles; the setting of the Pleiades on the day of solar zenith; the New Fire Ceremony; the Storm God and his home in the "long cave"; and the pyramid itself as a sacred mountain. The clear association of the alignment of the Sun Pyramid to the setting of the Pleiades and to the sun at zenith on May 18 suggests that concepts similar to those that prevailed among the later Mexica were at work in Classic Teotihuacan. This combination is unique in the city, made all the more compelling when we consider that the pyramid was deliberately placed at the very heart of the metropolis. This unique and powerful cosmogony, we believe, made the Sun Pyramid the focus of pilgrimages by rulers from near and far, including as far away as the southeasternmost capital of the Classic Maya realm. Our reading of the Adosada and its function and meaning can be corroborated by archaeological, epigraphic, and iconographic data from the lowland Maya area. The comparative studies also strongly suggest that the Adosada and the Sun Pyramid served as the locus where Maya kings were invested in office. This conclusion is fully in keeping with Boone's (2000b) discussion of the New Fire and investiture of kings in the Basin of Mexico.

STORM GOD, SOLAR, AND NEW FIRE ASSOCIATIONS OF TEMPLE 16 IN COPAN, HONDURAS

Turning now to the practices of Classic Maya appropriations of Teotihuacan ideology, prestige, and power, we return to a point made at the 2000 Moses Mesoamerican Archive conference held in Copan (B. Fash and W. Fash

2000). The great western stairway leading to the temple atop the final version of the central pyramid of the Copan Acropolis, Structure 10L-16 (Temple 16), contained iconic representations of both the Sun God and the Storm God, in a sense presaging the later Postclassic Twin Temples of Huitzilopochtli and Tlaloc (B. Fash and W. Fash 2000). The lowermost icon is that of a large and dramatic depiction of the Teotihuacan Storm God, surrounded by 30 stone human skulls with circular markings that indicate holes drilled into their temples, clearly a representation of a skull rack. At the foot of the stairs is Altar Q, which depicts the founder of the Copan dynasty wearing the goggles of the Teotihuacan Storm God. A stone Tlaloc jar was found that mimicks the Tlaloc mask (W. Fash and B. Fash 2000: 452, fig. 14.6). Above the Storm God panel on the stairs was a large outset solar panel, from which emerged the figure of the founding king, K'inich Yax K'uk' Mo' (Agurcia and Fash 2005; B. Fash and W. Fash 2000; W. Fash and B. Fash 2000; Taube 2004a). We now believe there was a compelling link between the two cultural expressions that we were not aware of at the time of the 2000 Copan conference: the Sun Pyramid and the Adosada at Teotihuacan.

Taube (2004a) subsequently noted that the founder is not only depicted as the Sun God, he is simultaneously represented as a Fire God, on the Copan Temple 16 stairway outsets and the earlier buried versions of this temple. We believe that his research makes Temple 16's similarities with the Adosada and the Sun Pyramid at Teotihuacan (and the Huitzilopochtli side of the much later Templo Mayor) all the more striking, and indicates that we should take a closer look at the explicit iconography of the final phase of Copan Temple 16.

At the top of Temple 16's dramatic staircase was a third outset panel, with a bound captive emerging from the jaws of an earth monster. Mountain signs forming the panel's lower border are reminiscent of those found in Teotihuacan mural art. Taube (2004a) and Ramos (n.d.) showed that the imagery on both the Temple 16 stairway and temple deliberately invoked Teotihuacan in Copan's past, specifically in the person of the dynastic founder. Stuart (2000, 2004, 2006) previously made this point for Structure 26 and its Hieroglyphic Stairway and Temple. We concur that Temple 16 was labeled by a T600 glyph on its facade and in the text of Altar Q as a *wite' naah*, originally translated as "origins house," or "crossed bundles building" by Stuart (2000). Susan Milbrath (1999: 194–197) read T-600 as "New Fire," and Taube (2004a: 268) presciently concluded that Altar Q shows the Founder passing along the New Fire to all of his successors.

We differ with Taube in that we believe that rather than merely constituting an evocation of a foreign past, the final phase of Temple 16 at Copan is that dynasty's re-creation of the Sun Pyramid and the Adosada of Teotihuacan. Like the Sun Pyramid and the Adosada, Temple 16 at

Copan was associated directly with the Sun God, jaguars (Fash 1991: 169–170), the Storm God, sacred mountains, the bundle of years, and the New Fire Ceremony. Taube was right to emphasize that Temple 16 was the central, tallest temple in ancient Copan, for the Sun Pyramid was also the tallest and most central temple in the city of Teotihuacan. Just as the Classic Maya hieroglyphic texts that cite a deity called "Eighteen Heads of the Serpent" have been interpreted as references to the Feathered Serpent Pyramid at Teotihuacan by Stuart (2000, 2004) and Taube (2000b, 2004a), we believe that the "crossed bundles building" cited on the texts of Altar Q and Temple 16 of Copan refer directly to the Adosada platform of the Sun Pyramid in Teotihuacan. In the light of this new reading, we now review the citations of the pilgrimage of K'inich Yax K'uk' Mo' to the Wite' Naah or "crossed bundles building" on Altar Q, and the glyph from the facade of the temple that carried the same sign, to evaluate our hypothesis.

THE CLASSIC MAYA "WITE' NAAH" SIGN AND ITS ASSOCIATIONS WITH THE FOUNDING OF THE COPAN DYNASTY

David Stuart has long held that Altar Q signals a vital message regarding the dynastic founder of Copan and the evocation of Teotihuacan in the origins of the dynasty (Stuart 2000, 2004, 2006; Stuart and Schele 1986). Stuart noted that the text begins by stating that the founder took part in a ritual performed at a named house ("naah") or building, specified by the T600 sign. This sign depicts two crossed bundles identifiable as bundles of firewood (Taube 2004a: 272–273, fig. 13.4; see Figure 4) and a round object with two dots and a horizontal line underneath (or occasionally three dots) that could be a representation of a mirror/hearth (see Taube 2000b: 317–323). Taube previously argued that this combination seems to evoke the theme of fire rituals and fire-making across Mesoamerica. The Altar Q event saw the founder *ch'am K'awiil* ("take the K'awiil"), a representation of the Lightning God that was the patron of Maya kings. The glyph that named the structure where the enthronement took place was originally labeled the "founder's sign" by Schele (1992), but Stuart (2000) later transcribed the glyph as the *wite' naah*, and glossed it as the "crossed bundles building" (2000: 492–493). In his subsequent, more detailed, analysis, Stuart (2004: 236) offered the literal translation "Tree-Root House," perhaps best conveyed by the term "Origin House" (Stuart 2004: 237).

Upon taking the K'awiil, or Lightning God insignia, at the Wite' Naah, the Copan king was apparently transformed. For in the next event, three days after he had grasped the insignia of the Lightning God, his name has changed from Quetzal Macaw Lord to Sun-Faced New Quetzal Macaw, or K'inich ("Sun-Faced" or "Sun-Eyed") Yax K'uk' Mo' (Stuart 2004: 233).

While the taking of the K'awiil is generally associated with accession to rulership, Stuart concludes that in the case of Altar Q, the *ch'am K'awiil* passage means much more:

> Rather, it carries the sense of a more significant or pronounced political change, where a ruler receives the divine symbols or sacred charters associated with rulership. . . . On Copan's Altar Q the initial passage thus records how K'uk' Mo' Ajaw assumed some new, divinely sanctioned stature—perhaps but not limited to his accession to rulership [Stuart 2004: 233].

This idea recalls Boone's observations, quoted above, that Teotihuacan was the place where laws were first laid down and kings were invested in office, and that New Fire Ceremonies (in later times) were associated with the creation of new polities. In the recent multidisciplinary research on the Mapa de Cuauhtinchan 2, led by Davíd Carrasco, it was noted that the New Fire Ceremony was performed at two vital times: when the Chichimecs left the cave of Chicomoztoc and when they arrived at the foot of the cave where the Eagle and Jaguar resided, in Cuauhtinchan (Carrasco and Sessions 2007: 2). This finding was examined by numerous other scholars in the exhaustive analysis of this document, and it is clear that New Fire Ceremonies were not only undertaken at the end of the 52-year cycle. In summing up all the uses of this ceremony in Highland Postclassic Mexico, Olivier (2007: 301) noted that New Fire Ceremonies were conducted at the birth of a people when leaving a place of origin, the transformation of a people when passing through that place, the foundation of a city or seigniorial domain, the foundation of a new house or temple, the accession to power of a new authority, or the foundation of a new lineage after a conquest.

ADOSADA PLATFORM AS THE WITE' NAAH

Both the iconographic and the phonetic readings of the T600 sign emphasize the crossed bundles of wood, the most literal rendering possible of a building devoted to New Fire Ceremonies. After traveling for 153 days from the Origin House, K'inich Yax K'uk' Mo' returns to his kingdom in the Copan Valley, and thereupon the K'awiil "rests his legs," according to the text on Altar Q. Although Stuart (2000: 491–492) originally suggested that the Wite' Naah "Origin House" signified a Teotihuacan temple, subsequently—perhaps at the urging of his Mayanist colleagues— he allowed that said temple could have been either at Teotihuacan or at Tikal (Stuart 2004: 239). A single glyphic element of the T600 sign was found among the sculpture fragments fallen from Temple 16, as noted by

Taube (2004). It is a small sign, and its original placement is unknown, but Taube and Stuart both believe that it labels Temple 16 itself as a Wite' Naah. We agree, but again, posit that it is a Copan rendition of the original, archetypal Wite' Naah: the Sun Pyramid at Teotihuacan.

We believe that the symbolism of the eighth-century Copan Structure 10L-16 and the text of Altar Q replicate and directly reference the meanings associated with the Early Classic Sun Pyramid, its Adosada platform, and the cave with water beneath it. The T600 sign substitutes for the *xiumohlpilli* sculptures on the Adosada, which we believe were associated with New Fire Ceremonies that took place there. The grasping of the K'awiil would be associated with the Storm God associations of the cave, in which said god resided in Teotihuacan. What better place for the "God of the Long Cave" to live and be revered? After three days of rituals, Copan's founder donned the goggles of the Storm God and assumed the titles "New" and "Sun-Faced," reflecting his newly won status together with the eclipse and other solar associations of the Sun Pyramid. In another effort to duplicate Teotihuacan customs, Altar Q's citation of the events that we propose took place at the Adosada and the Sun Pyramid are only referred to in Calendar Round dates (used at Teotihuacan; Coggins n.d. [1975], 1979a, 1979b; López Luján et al. 2000). Later in the text a Distance Number ties the early events in the Calendar Round to the Long Count and the life and times of the sixteenth king of Copan, who commissioned and dedicated this "stone of K'inich Yax K'uk' Mo'" in honor of his kingdom's founder.

Of the Sun Pyramid Heyden (1975: 139) noted "Millon et al. suggested that Teotihuacan had a strong religious attraction early in its history (1967:38) and that pilgrimages to the shrine area, an ancient tradition in Mexico, may have played a part in the building of the pyramid (1965:36)." Evocation of Teotihuacan imagery and references to K'inich Yax K'uk' Mo' in association with Wite' Naah are common in Late Classic Copan monuments and architecture, particularly after its resurgence from a hiatus caused by a defeat in a war against Quirigua (Fash 1992; W. Fash and B. Fash 2000; Fash 2002; Stuart 2000, 2004, 2006). Quirigua inscriptions also mention the visit of K'inich Yax K'uk' Mo' to Wite' Naah as an event related to the foundation of the Quirigua dynasty. The founder is also given the titles of "man of Wite' Naah" (CPN Altar B'), "Wite' Naah *ch'ajoom*" (CPN, Stela J, Temple 11 hieroglyphic step and northwest panel; QRG, Stela F), and "Wite' Naah lord" (CPN, Stela 12). Finally, Copan and Quirigua inscriptions refer to K'inich Yax K'uk' Mo' by his Copan emblem glyph, "holy T756d lord" (CPN Altar B', Stela 11, Stela 12; QRG Zoomorph P). It is clear that his association with the Wite' Naah is central to his image, identity, and legacy for his successors. It was, in the parlance of our times, his claim to fame. The identification of the Wite' Naah as the Sun Pyramid helps to explain why.

FIGURE 7. Mosaic sculptures from the lower part of the south facade of Copan Structure 10L-29. Drawing by Barbara Fash.

WITE' NAAH AND *TONALPOALLI* ICONOGRAPHY ON COPAN TEMPLE 29

A scant 30 m southeast of Altar Q in Copan is Structure 10L-29, considered to be the royal ancestor shrine of the residential zone of Ruler 16, Yax Pasaj Chan Yopaat (Andrews and Bill 2006; Andrews and Fash 1992). As a product of the careful recording and re-articulation of the hundreds of fragments of sculpture that fell in antiquity, Barbara Fash and Jodi Johnson were able to deduce that there were originally 10 large solar niches that adorned the facades of this L-shaped building (Fash 2009). Most interesting and utterly unique among those facades was the south one, which faced toward the ruler's domicile, Structure 10L-32. There, three identical large composite glyphs were placed beneath the solar niche and ancestor, with a most unusual configuration of signs (Figure 7).

The central element of all three glyphs was the same T600 sign found on Altar Q. Above and below the New Fire sign were carved Mexican Year signs, long associated with the *tonalpoalli;* the glyphs combine the sign for the New Fire Ceremony with two Calendar Round glyphs. On realizing how these elements were configured in 1991, B. Fash wondered whether they might not represent a calendrical reference to the dedication date of the building they adorned. Six Calendar Rounds, or 312 years, from the time of the pilgrimage of K'inich Yax K'uk' Mo' to Teotihuacan in 426 C.E. would bring us forward to 738 C.E. Based on architectural stratigraphy and Cassandra Bill's careful control of ceramic chronology, Andrews and Bill (2005) place the construction of Structure 10L-29 to just before the accession of Ruler 16. Six Calendar Rounds would be the exact number that had been completed by the time Structure 10L-29 was built. In like manner, the Distance Number (340 years) on the top of Altar Q is only an

FIGURE 8. Stone mosaic facade sculpture from Structure 5, Río Amarillo, Copan Valley, Honduras. Photograph by Rick Frehsee.

approximate or short-hand reference to the number of (20-year, or *katun*) cycles elapsed between the return of K'inich Yax K'uk' Mo' to Copan and the dedication of the altar itself.

The association of Copan Structure 10L-29 with the pilgrimage of the founder, the Adosada and its meaning and associations, and the Mesoamerican-wide Calendar Round lead us to suggest that the final king of Copan who resided in Structure 10L-32 was visually reminded, on a daily basis, of the legendary power of Teotihuacan and its importance in the origins and legitimation of the Copan dynasty. A cadet lineage of the royal line that resided in the 30-km-distant site of Río Amarillo also emblazoned this symbol on its facades (Figure 8), as well as the Wite' Naah glyphs (Saturno n.d. [2000]; Stuart 2000, 2004).

OTHER CASES OF CLASSIC MAYA DYNASTIES REFERRING TO THE WITE' NAAH

The foundation of the Copan dynasty is not the only example of references to Wite' Naah embedded in master narratives evoking essential, formative events in the histories of Classic Maya royal courts. In one way or another, the underlying context of these particular narratives is the interaction between Classic Maya polities and Teotihuacan during the Early Classic period. Key events in this interaction happened in the last quarter of the fourth century A.D., when an individual named Ochk'in K'awiil Sihyaj K'ahk' ("West-Lightning-Fire-Is-Born") became the overlord of many Maya kings, including the rulers of Tikal, one of the most ancient and powerful Classic Maya dynasties (Stuart 2000). Although the origins of Sihyaj K'ahk' and the nature of the hegemony that he established are still debated by archaeologists (e.g., Braswell 2003), there can be no doubt that it coincided with the peak of the Teotihuacan traits in Classic Maya architecture, imagery, and writing (Coggins n.d. [1975]; Cowgill 2003; Laporte and Fialko 1990; Taube 2000b). Recent investigations at the site of La Sufricaya, Guatemala, reveal that Teotihuacan influence during that period extended even to small secondary political centers governed by nonroyal families (Estrada Belli et al. 2009). As Taube (2000b) and Nielsen (2006a) suggest, fire-making, calendrical rituals, and the foundations of the new political order seem to be the prevalent and interrelated messages of the Classic Maya monuments produced in the wake of Sihyaj K'ahk's arrival in 378 and the accession of the new Tikal lord at the Wite' Naah. As noted above, there is a close iconographic association between the T600 sign, year bundles, and the sculptural themes associated with the Adosada platform.

Early Classic Citations of the Wite' Naah

Just as in the case of Copan kings, other Late Classic Maya rulers singled out the Teotihuacan connection as one of the narratives defining the identity of their dynasties. The emphasis on Teotihuacan origins is evidenced in the Late Classic monuments and buildings at Tikal (Grube and Martin 2000: 29–37; Haviland 1992; Stuart 2000: 489–490). In fact, the very last Tikal inscribed stela (Stela 11:C14) evokes the Wite' Naah (Jones and Satterthwaite 1982: fig. 16). The Wite' Naah was the location of pre-accession rituals and of the final accession ceremony of the new Tikal ruler installed by Sihyaj K'ahk' (Stuart 2000). Tikal Stelae 4 and 31 depict that new king, Yax Nuun Ahiin, as a young Teotihuacan warrior. According to the text on Tikal Stela 31 (Jones and Satterthwaite 1982: fig. 52), 283 days after the death of his predecessor, Yax Nuun Ahiin "ascended to the Wite' Naah." He "descended from the Wite' Naah" in 61 days. Some 261 day later, Yax Nuun Ahiin acceded to kingship at the Wite' Naah and "took twenty-eight provinces" under the eye of his liege, Sihyaj K'ahk'.

The inscriptions on the monuments from Tres Islas (Stelae 1 and 2) and Piedras Negras (Panel 2, the Obregon wooden box) suggest that other Early Classic Maya kings also acceded to kingship at the Wite' Naah (Stuart 2000: fig. 15.25; Tomasic and Fahsen 2004: 802–808). Piedras Negras Panel 2 depicts several figures dressed as Teotihuacan warriors—the local king faces six kneeling lords from nearby polities, including Yaxchilan and Bonampak. Its text informs us that the Early Classic ruler of the site Yat Chan Ahk received a helmet from "Kaloomte' of the West," Tajoom Uk'ab Tuun, in A.D. 510. The text on a recently discovered wooden box reveals that Tajoom Uk'ab Tuun was also a "Wite' Naah lord" and that Yat Chan Ahk traveled for 155 days—about the same time it took for K'inich Yax K'uk' Mo' to get from the Wite' Naah to Copan (Anaya Hernández et al. 2002; Skidmore 2002; Zender n.d.).

Late Classic Citations of the Wite' Naah

During the Late Classic Period, although there were no more travels to the Wite' Naah or other new events involving this place as a real geographic location (Figure 9), the list of royal families associating themselves with the Wite' Naah became longer. For instance, the seventh-century Kanu'l lords from Calakmul acquired the title of "those of Wite' Naah" (Prager 2004). However, by the beginning of the seventh century A.D., the original Wite' Naah was a place of the past: archaeological evidence indicates that Teotihuacan burned to the ground in A.D. 550 (López Luján et al. 2006). As no doubt the New Fire Ceremonies continued to be performed after the

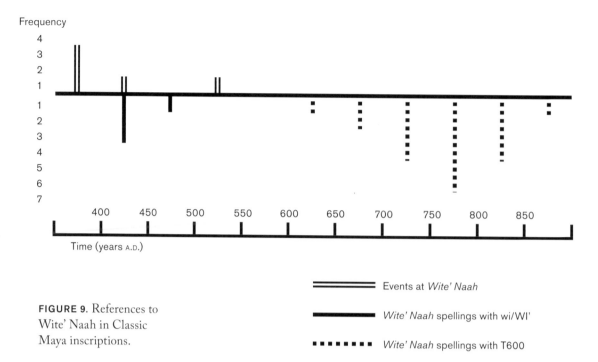

FIGURE 9. References to
Wite' Naah in Classic
Maya inscriptions.

fall of Teotihuacan, perhaps other cities aspiring to establish themselves as
the new primary location of the Wite' Naah used the symbolism on their
buildings and the master narrative in their texts.

The Wite' Naah was not the only location mentioned in association with
Teotihuacan imagery, individuals "from the west," and the Early Classic
political order. In the text on the famous Tikal Marker (Laporte and Fialko
1995), Yax Nuun Ahiin's father "Spearthrower Owl," who, as Stuart (2000:
485–490) suggested, might be the Teotihuacan ruler, is called Jo' No[h]
Wits kaloomte'. The same inscription refers to the "War Serpent" deity
or Waxaklajuun Ubaah Kan—the most prominent Teotihuacan-inspired
icon in Classic Maya art (Taube 2000b)—as Jo' No[h] Wits Waxaklajuun
Ubaah Kan. Therefore, Jo' No[h] Wits ("Five Great Mountains"; see Figure
10c) seems to be a highly important place, possibly the name for the city of
Teotihuacan itself.[1]

The Wite' Naah Glyph

These considerations bring us back to the question of the literal translation
and the meaning of "Wite' Naah." The first important point to consider is
the chronological distribution of the two different spellings of *wite' naah:*
wi/WI'-TE'-NAAH; and T600-TE'-NAAH (Figure 10a,b). As seen in
Figure 9, all wi/WI'-TE'-NAAH spellings can be traced to the times
before the burning of Teotihuacan. There are no examples of the T600 sign

a   b.   c   d

FIGURE 10. Teotihuacan places cited in Classic Maya hieroglyphic texts: (a) Early Classic Wite' Naah (TIK St 31:E15); (b) Late Classic Wite' Naah (YAX Ln 25:G2); (c) Jo' No[h] Wits (Tikal Marker:A4); (d) Nikte' Wits (carved bone, Burial 116, Tikal). Drawings by Alexandre Tokovinine.

in the Maya inscriptions from that period. There seems to be a hiatus in references to Wite' Naah some time between A.D. 500 and 650. Beginning with the second half of the seventh century A.D., Wite' Naah returns to Classic Maya inscriptions, but the spelling is T600-TE'-NAAH. The text on Yaxchilan Lintel 25 (Figure 10b) seemed to provide a phonetic clue to its reading (wi-T600-TE'-NAAH), suggesting that T600-TE'-NAAH and wi-TE'-NAAH likely corresponded to the same combination of words (Stuart 2004: 236–239). At a time when Teotihuacan is a ghost town, an enduring and powerful symbol of a once glorious past, the T600 sign seems to be a Maya innovation, simultaneously adopted in script and in iconography. Its appearance coincides with a renewed emphasis on the connections between Teotihuacan and the Classic Maya dynasties. Although the true motives for this innovation may never be known, one possible intention might be to stress the conceptual connection between the word and its association with Teotihuacan. Calligraphic innovations of this kind peak during the Late Classic period.

Although there can be little doubt that the spellings T600-TE'-NAAH and wi-TE'-NAAH correspond to the same combination of words, the phonetic value of the T600 sign is not necessarily wi or WI'. The glosses *wi' te' naah* proposed by Stuart (2004) cannot be translated as a "tree-root house." That should have been *uwi'il te' naah*. Therefore, the more metaphorical translation of *wi' te' naah* as "origin house" is open to discussion. The literal translation of *wi' te' naah* results in a combination of words like "root/origin tree/wood house." Moreover, wi in wi-TE' could be an underspelling. We may reconstruct a consonant between wi and TE'. Given that we are dealing with a potentially non-Maya concept, the underspelled word could be foreign. All the available spellings use the logogram TE', indicating that *te'* in this context is a separate word. Therefore the only thing that is certain about the spelling is that it refers to a kind of "house" for/of/with a certain kind of "trees" or "wood," which is spelled with wi/WI' or with T600.

In the Late Classic, just as Copan scribes and carvers adopted the T600 sign, they emphasized that K'inich Yax K'uk' Mo' was a Wite' Naah "period-ending priest" by using the *ch' ajoom* title, referring to "one who

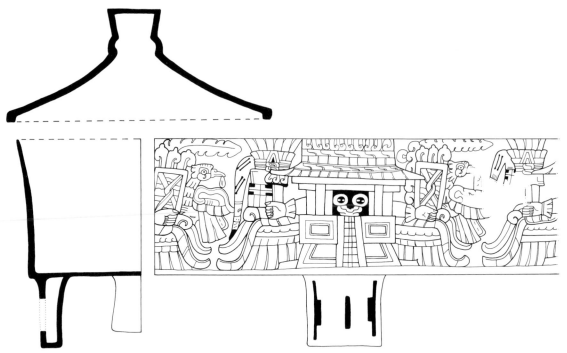

FIGURE 11. Figure of K'inich Yax K'uk' Mo' inside a temple with fire, from the Teotihuacan style painted stucco vessel from the Margarita tomb in Copan, Honduras. Drawing by Barbara Fash.

drops" copal at period-ending ceremonies. His association with the 9.0.0.0.0 period ending (in A.D. 435) is attested in numerous inscriptions both during and after his lifetime and by direct archaeological evidence in the burning that took place in the Motmot tomb in conjunction with the rituals he and his son/successor undertook on that date (Fash and Fash 2004; Fash et al. 2004). Note also the strong similarity in the depiction of the House of New Fire at the Adosada, with the portrait of K'inich Yax K'uk' Mo' found on the iconic Early Classic vessel found in the Margarita tomb at Copan, considered to be the final resting place of his spouse (Figure 11). It bears noting that her grave also contained two Teotihuacan mirrors, which Nielsen (2006b) suggests were part of the toolkit of the founder. Finally, the most compelling epigraphic evidence for the Hunal tomb being that of K'inich Yax K'uk' Mo' is the shell pectoral that is labeled as *yuh wite'* [*naah ajaw*] ("the necklace of the Wite' [Naah lord]"; Stuart 2004: 232). The pectoral constitutes direct evidence that the founder labeled himself and his possessions based on this association.

CONCLUSIONS

The Wite' Naah master narrative involves three place names—Jo' Noh Wits, Wite' Naah, and Nikte' Wits—and one deity—Waxaklajuun Ub'aah Kan (Eighteen Heads of the Serpent)—all located somewhere in the west, approximately 150 days away from the Maya lowlands. Jo' Noh Wits (Five

Great Mountains) seems to be the most general place-name and possibly the ancient Maya name for Teotihuacan. Nikte' Wits (Flower Mountain) is mentioned as a location where Eighteen Heads of the Serpent is conjured. The Wite' Naah, proposed here as the Adosada, is the place where visiting Maya lords acceded to kingship.

In summarizing the Mexica's attitudes toward the past, Matos Moctezuma and López Luján (1993: 162) state that although the Teotihuacan past was mythologized, "their indirect descent from Toltec people made them feel that they belonged to a world in which they had become masters." We believe that a similar mentality prevailed among some of the Late Classic Maya dynasties that sought to justify their own exalted status, in part, through the recitation of a storied past that linked them to the great Tollan-Teotihuacan. "Thus, the Mexicas could instill fear in their enemies and legitimate their hegemony, thanks, among other things, to their authority emanating from the Templo Mayor, the precinct that concentrated the power of deities of war and water, as well as of the ancestors" (Matos Moctezuma and Lopez Luján 1993: 163). This duality held sway from much earlier times in Mesoamerica, as seen from the deities of war and water at Structure 10L-16 in Copan and, we conclude, from the Sun Pyramid at Teotihuacan.

For the Sun Pyramid, we follow Kubler's (1973: 24) thesis that the meaning of a Teotihuacan building and of the rituals that took place in it was spelled out most clearly by its interior decoration. The three different expressions carved in stone of fire being set to the bundles of years, including on a large central brazier labeled with the twisted cord (Batres 1906), leave no doubt that the Adosada of the Sun Pyramid was built, labeled, and used as the House of New Fire of Early Classic Mesoamerica. Maya kings took pride in saying that they were invested in office at the Wite' Naah and even boasted of how many days it took for them to return to their homeland from that storied edifice. The Late Classic kings went to great pains to make the iconography and even their script very clear on this point, particularly at the many sites whose rulers claimed their investiture at the Wite' Naah as a master narrative. This helps explain why the rulers of Tikal, Copan, Piedras Negras, Yaxchilan, Calakmul, and Tres Islas were all so keen on legitimating themselves in image, word, and deed even as their own political orders were about to follow in the footsteps of that of Teotihuacan.

In broader terms, the Sun Pyramid and the other two great temples at Teotihuacan made it the Tollan par excellence for its citizens, tributaries, and allies. The process that Carrasco (1982) described as "Tollanization" can be documented in the archaeology, art, and epigraphy of the broader Early Classic Mesoamerican world. In terms of self-representation, Matos Moctezuma (1995) believes that the Sun Pyramid and its surrounding canal filled with water was a representation of the *altepetl* of Teotihuacan. We are more persuaded by the arguments of Tobriner (1972), seconded by Aveni (2000) and Kowalski (1999), that the Moon Pyramid was Teotihuacan's "water mountain," and that is why their city was laid out from that point of reference. The superb investigations by Saburo Sugiyama and his colleagues (Sugiyama and Carballo n.d.; Sugiyama and López Luján 2007) have revealed that the Moon Pyramid was built before all others and was clearly associated with female aspects, water, and offerings of animals (recalling Maya beliefs of animals residing in sacred mountains; Vogt 1969). The Sun Pyramid, by contrast, was centrally located and centrally important in terms of a place of emergence, the duality of sun and rain, and the practice of New Fire Ceremonies at the installation of rulers and the founding of new political orders. The renewal of the sun and the world that took place there were symbolic of the new beginnings of urban life that took root after the explosion of Popocatepetl and the creation of a new cosmological and political order at Teotihuacan. With time, the pyramid came to be associated with the beginning of time though its temples, ballcourts, and cosmogony (Uriarte 2006). Appropriately, the millions of solar worshippers who flock to the Sun Pyramid every vernal equinox ascend a pyramid where New Fire Ceremonies renewed the solar cycle and political orders in ancient times.

Acknowledgments

WLF and BWF thank Leonardo López Luján and Linda Manzanilla for the opportunity to participate in the Xalla Archaeological Project in Teotihuacan (2000–2002), and they thank Leonardo for the chance to work with him and with Laura Filloy on interesting questions regarding Teotihuacan and the Maya. They also thank Davíd Carrasco for his generosity in inviting us to participate in recent Moses Mesoamerican Archive conferences, where we have learned so much from so many different kinds of scholars working on interrelated issues in various parts of Mesoamerica. All three authors acknowledge and thank our many friends and colleagues working in Copan for the past three decades, some of whom have contributed significantly to the questions we address here.

NOTE

1. In addition, Late Classic Tikal inscriptions (Grube and Martin 2000: 28; Taube 2004b: fig. 17d) mention that Waxaklajuun Ubaah Kan was "conjured" at Nikte' Wits ("Flower Mountain"; see Figure 10d) four days after Sihyaj K'ahk' embarked on his campaign. We wonder whether that was the consecration of the Waxaklajuun Ubaah Kan effigy that subsequently entered Tikal according to the text on the Tikal Marker. If so, Nikte' Wits is another location in Teotihuacan or its vicinity.

REFERENCES CITED

Agurcia Fasquelle, Ricardo, and Barbara W. Fash
2005 The Evolution of Structure 10L-16, Heart of the Copan Acropolis. In *Copan: The History of an Ancient Maya Kingdom* (E. Wyllys Andrews and William L. Fash, eds.): 201–237. School of American Research Press, Santa Fe, N.M.

Anaya Hernández, Alfonso, Stanley Guenter, and Peter Mathews
2002 An Inscribed Wooden Box from Tabasco, Mexico. *Mesoweb Report*. Electronic document, http://www.mesoweb.com/reports/box/index.html, accessed April 2008.

Anders, Ferdinand, Marteen Jansen, and Luis Reyes García
1991 *El Libro del Cihuacoatl, Homenaje para el año del Fuego Nuevo: Libro explicativo del llamado Códice Borbónico.* Códices Mexicanos III. Sociedad Estatal Quinto Centenario, Akademische Druck- und Verlagsanstalt, and Fondo de Cultura Económica, Madrid, Graz, and México.

Andrews, E. Wyllys, and Cassandra Bill
2005 A Late Classic Royal residence at Copan. In *Copan: The History of an Ancient Maya Kingdom* (E. Wyllys Andrews and William L. Fash, eds.): 239–314. School of American Research Press, Santa Fe, N.M.

Andrews, E. Wyllys, and Barbara W. Fash
1992 Continuity and Change in a Royal Residential Complex at Copan. *Ancient Mesoamerica* 3(1): 63–88.

Aveni, Anthony F.
1980 *Skywatchers of Ancient Mexico.* University of Texas Press, Austin.
2000 Out of Teotihuacan: Origins of the Celestial Canon in Mesoamerica. In *Mesoamerica's Classic Heritage: From Teotihuacan to the Aztecs* (Davíd Carrasco, Lindsay Jones, and Scott Sessions, eds.): 253–268. University Press of Colorado, Boulder.

Batres, Leopoldo
1906 *Teotihuacán ó la ciudad sagrada de los Toltecas.* Imprenta de Hull, México.

Berlo, Janet C.
1992 Icons and Ideologies at Teotihuacan: The Great Goddess Reconsidered. In *Art, Ideology, and the City of the Gods* (Janet C. Berlo, ed.): 129–168. Dumbarton Oaks Research Library and Collection, Washington, D.C.

Boone, Elizabeth
2000a Venerable Place of Beginnings: The Aztec Understanding of Teotihuacan. In *Mesoamerica's Classic Heritage: From Teotihuacan to the Aztecs* (Davíd Carrasco, Lindsay Jones, and Scott Sessions, eds.): 371–395. University Press of Colorado, Boulder.
2000b *Stories in Red and Black: Pictorial Histories of the Aztecs and Mixtecs.* University of Texas Press, Austin.

Braswell, Geoffrey E. (ed.)
2003 *The Maya and Teotihuacan: Reinterpreting Early Classic Interaction.* University of Texas Press, Austin.

Carrasco, Davíd

  1982   *Quetzalcoatl and the Irony of Empire: Myths and Prophecies in the Aztec Tradition.* University of Chicago Press, Chicago.

Carrasco, Davíd, and Scott Sessions

  2007   Introduction: An Interpretive Journey through the Mapa de Cuauhtinchan No. 2. In *Cave, City, and Eagle's Nest: An Interpretive Journey through the Mapa de Cuauhtinchan No. 2* (Davíd Carrasco and Scott Sessions, eds.): 1–24. University of New Mexico Press, Albuquerque.

Caso, Alfonso

  1937   ¿Tenían los teotihuacanos conocimiento del tonalpohualli? *El México Antiguo* 4: 131–143.

Coggins, Clemency C.

  1979a A New Order and the Role of the Calendar: Some Characteristics of the Middle Classic Period at Tikal. In *Maya Archaeology and Ethnohistory* (Norman Hammond and Gordon R. Willey, eds.): 38–50. University of Texas Press, Austin.

  1979b Teotihuacan at Tikal in the Early Classic Period. In *Actes du XLIIe Congrès International des Américanistes, Congrès du Centenaire, Paris, 2–9 Septembre 1976,* vol. 8: 251–269. Société des Américanistes, Paris.

  1987   New Fire at Chichen Itza. In *Memorias del Primer Coloquio Internacional de Mayistas, 5–10 de agosto de 1985:* 425–484. Universidad Nacional Autonoma de México, México.

  n.d.   Painting and Drawing Styles at Tikal: An Historical and Iconographic Reconstruction. Ph.D. dissertation, Department of Fine Arts, Harvard University, Cambridge, Mass., 1975.

Cowgill, George L.

  2003   Teotihuacan and Early Classic Interaction: A Perspective from Outside the Maya Region. In *The Maya and Teotihuacan: Re-Interpreting Early Classic Interaction* (Geoffrey E. Braswell, ed.): 315–335. University of Texas Press, Austin.

Dow, James W.

  1967   Astronomical Orientations at Teotihuacan, a Case Study in Astro-Archaeology. *American Antiquity* 32: 326–234.

Drucker, Richard D.

  1977   A Solar Orientation Framework for Teotihuacan. A paper presented at the XV Mesa Redonda of the Sociedad Mexicana de Antropología, Guanajuato, Mexico.

Estrada Belli, Francisco, Alexandre Tokovinine, Jennifer Foley, Heather Hurst, Gene Ware, David Stuart, and Nikolai Grube

  2009   A Maya Palace at Holmul, Peten, Guatemala and the Teotihuacan "Entrada": Evidence from Murals 7 and 9. *Latin American Antiquity* 20(1): 228–259.

Fash, Barbara W.

  1992   Late Classic Architectural Sculpture Themes in Copan. *Ancient Mesoamerica* 3(1): 89–104.

  2009   *The Copan Sculpture Museum: Maya Artistry in Stucco and Stone.* Peabody Museum Press, Cambridge, Mass. (in press).

Fash, Barbara W., and William L. Fash

    2000   Named Houses and Sacred Mountains in the Ancient Kingdom of Copan. A paper presented at the Moses Mesoamerican Archive Conference on Sacred Mountains in Mesoamerica, Copan, Honduras, August 2–6.

Fash, William L.

    1991   *Scribes, Warriors and Kings: The City of Copán and the Ancient Maya.* Thames and Hudson, New York.

    2002   Religion and Human Agency in Ancient Maya History: Tales from the Hieroglyphic Stairway. *Cambridge Archaeological Journal* 12(1): 5–19.

Fash, William L., and Barbara W. Fash

    2000   Teotihuacan and the Maya: A Classic Heritage. In *Mesoamerica's Classic Heritage: From Teotihuacan to the Aztecs* (Davíd Carrasco, Lindsay Jones, and Scott Sessions, eds.): 433–464. University Press of Colorado, Boulder.

    2004   La ciudad de Copán, Honduras: Arte y escritura Mayas. *Arqueología Mexicana* 11(66): 64–69.

Fash, William L., Barbara W. Fash, and Karla Davis-Salazar

    2004   Setting the Stage: Origins of the Hieroglyphic Stairway Plaza on the Great Period Ending. In *Understanding Early Classic Copan* (Ellen E. Bell, Marcello A. Canuto, and Robert J. Sharer, eds.): 65–83. University of Pennsylvania Museum of Archaeology and Anthropology, Philadelphia.

Grube, Nikolai, and Simon Martin

    2000   Tikal and Its Neighbors. In *Notebook for the XXIVth Maya Hieroglyphic Forum at Texas* (Linda Schele, Nikolai Grube, and Simon Martin, eds.), part II: 1–78. University of Texas at Austin, Department of Art and Art History, College of Fine Arts and Institute of Latin American Studies, Austin.

Haviland, William A.

    1992   From Double Bird to Ah Cacaw: Dynastic Trouble and the Cycle of Katuns at Tikal, Guatemala. In *New Theories on the Ancient Maya* (Elin C. Danien and Robert J. Sharer, eds.): 71–80. University Museum, University of Pennsylvania, Philadelphia.

Heyden, Doris

    1975   An Interpretation of the Cave beneath the Pyramid of the Sun in Teotihuacan, Mexico. *American Antiquity* 40(2): 131–147.

Jones, Christopher, and Linton Satterthwaite

    1982   *The Monuments and Inscriptions of Tikal: The Carved Monuments.* University Museum, University of Pennsylvania, Philadelphia.

Kowalski, Jeff K.

    1999   Natural Order, Social Order, Political Legitimacy, and the Sacred City: The Architecture of Teotihuacan. In *Mesoamerican Architecture as a Cultural Symbol* (Jeff K. Kowalski, ed.): 76–109. Oxford University Press, Oxford and New York.

Kubler, George

    1967   *The Iconography of the Art of Teotihuacan.* Studies in Pre-Columbian Art and Archaeology 4. Dumbarton Oaks Research Library and Collection, Washington, D.C.

1973 Iconographic Aspects of Architectural Profiles at Teotihuacan and in Mesoamerica. In *Iconography of Middle American Sculpture* (Samuel Lothrop, ed.): 24–39. Metropolitan Museum of Art, New York.

Laporte, Juan Pedro, and Vilma Fialko C.

1990 New Perspectives on Old Problems: Dynastic References for the Early Classic at Tikal. In *Vision and Revision in Maya Studies* (Flora S. Clancy and Peter D. Harrison, eds.): 33–66. University of New Mexico Press, Albuquerque.

1995 Un reencuentro con mundo perdido, Tikal, Guatemala. *Ancient Mesoamerica* 6: 41–94.

López Luján, Leonardo

1989 *La recuperación Mexica del pasado Teotihuacano.* Instituto Nacional de Antropología e Historia, Proyecto Templo Mayor, México.

1994 *The Offerings of the Templo Mayor of Tenochtitlan.* University Press of Colorado, Niwot.

2002 The Aztecs' Search for the Past. In *Aztecs* (Eduardo Matos Moctezuma and Felipe Solís Olguín, eds.): 22–29. Royal Academy of Arts, London.

López Luján, Leonardo, Laura Filloy, William L. Fash, Barbara W. Fash, and Pilar Fernandez

2006 The Destruction of Images in Teotihuacan: Anthropomorphic Sculpture, Elite Cults and the End of a Civilization. *RES* 49/50: 12–39.

López Luján, Leonardo, Hector Neff, and Saburo Sugiyama

2000 The 9-Xi Vase: A Classic Thin Orange Vessel Found at Tenochtitlan. In *Mesoamerica's Classic Heritage: From Teotihuacan to the Aztecs* (Davíd Carrasco, Lindsay Jones, and Scott Sessions, eds.): 219–249. University Press of Colorado, Boulder.

Malmstrom, Vincent H.

1978 A Reconstruction of the Chronology of Mesoamerican Calendrical Systems. *Journal for the History of Astronomy* 9: 105–116.

Manzanilla, Linda, and Leonardo López Luján

2002 17, Mythological Feline. In *Aztecs* (Eduardo Matos Moctezuma and Felipe Solís Olguín, eds.): 405. Royal Academy of Arts, London.

Matos Moctezuma, Eduardo (ed.)

1995 *La Pirámide del Sol, Teotihuacan: Antología.* Artes de México para el Instituto Cultural Domecq, México.

Matos Moctezuma, Eduardo, and Leonardo López Luján

1993 Teotihuacan and Its Mexica Legacy. In *Teotihuacan: Art from the City of the Gods* (Kathleen Berrin and Esther Pasztory, eds.): 156–165. Thames and Hudson, London and New York.

Milbrath, Susan

1999 *Star Gods of the Maya: Astronomy in Art, Folklore, and Calendars.* University of Texas Press, Austin.

Millon, René F.

1981 Teotihuacan: City, State, and Civilization. In *Supplement to the Handbook of Middle American Indians, Volume One: Archaeology* (Victoria R. Bricker and Jeremy Sabloff, eds.): 198–243. University of Texas Press, Austin.

1992 Teotihuacan Studies: From 1950 to 1990 and Beyond. In *Art, Ideology, and the City of Teotihuacan* (Janet C. Berlo, ed.): 339–429. Dumbarton Oaks Research Library and Collection, Washington, D.C.

1993 The Place Where Time Began: An Archaeologist's View of What Happened in Teotihuacan History. In *Teotihuacan: Art from the City of the Gods* (Kathleen Berrin and Esther Pasztory, eds.): 16–43. Thames and Hudson, Fine Arts Museum of San Francisco, San Francisco.

Millon, René F., and Bruce Drewitt

1963 Earlier Structures within the Pyramid of the Sun at Teotihuacan. *American Antiquity* 26(3): 371–380.

Millon, René, Bruce Drewitt, and James A. Bennyhoff

1965 *The Pyramid of the Sun at Teotihuacán: 1959 Investigations.* Transactions of the American Philosophical Society, new series, vol. 55, part 6. American Philosophical Society, Philadelphia.

Nielsen, Jesper

2006a The Coming of the Torch: Observations on Teotihuacan Iconography in Early Classic Tikal. In *Maya Ethnicity: The Construction of Ethnic Identity from Preclassic to Modern Times: Proceedings of the 9th European Maya Conference, Bonn, December 10–12, 2004* (Frauke Sachse, ed.): 19–30. Verlag Anton Saurwein, Markt Schwaben.

2006b The Queen's Mirrors: Interpreting the Iconography of Two Teotihuacan Style Mirrors from the Early Classic Margarita Tomb at Copan. *PARI Journal* 6(4): 1–8.

Olivier, Guilhem

2007 Sacred Bundles, Arrows, and New Fire: Foundation and Power in the Mapa de Cuahutinchan No. 2. In *Cave, City, and Eagle's Nest: An Interpretive Journey through the Mapa de Cuauhtinchan No. 2* (Davíd Carrasco and Scott Sessions, eds.): 281–313. University of New Mexico Press, Albuquerque.

Prager, Christian

2004 A Classic Maya Ceramic Vessel from the Calakmul Region in the Museum zu Allerheiligen, Schaffhausen, Switzerland. *Human Mosaic* 35: 31–40.

Ramos Gómez, Jorge H.

n.d. The Iconography of Temple 16: Yax Pasaj and the Evocation of a "Foreign" Identity at Copan. Ph.D. dissertation, Department of Anthropology, University of California, Riverside, 2006.

Sahagún, Bernardino de

1950–82 *Florentine Codex: General History of the Things of New Spain*, 12 vols. (Arthur J. O. Anderson and Charles E. Dibble, trans.). School of American Research and University of Utah Press, Santa Fe, N.M., and Salt Lake City.

Saturno, William A.

n.d. In the Shadow of the Acropolis: Río Amarillo and Its Role in the Copán Polity. Ph.D. dissertation, Department of Anthropology, Harvard University, 2000.

Schele, Linda
  1992 The Founders of Lineages at Copán and Other Maya Sites. *Ancient Mesoamerica* 3(1): 135–144

Skidmore, Joel
  2002 New Piece of Precolumbian Wooden Box. *Mesoweb Report.* Electronic document, http://mesoweb.com/reports/box/piece.html/.

Sload, Rebecca
  2008 The Pyramid of the Sun as a Place of Emergence. An electronic paper presented at the 73rd Annual Meeting of the Society for American Archaeology, Vancouver, B.C., April.

Stuart, David S.
  1998 "The Fire Enters His House": Architecture and Ritual in Classic Maya Texts. In *Function and Meaning in Classic Maya Architecture: A Symposium at Dumbarton Oaks, 7th and 8th October 1994* (Stephen D. Houston, ed.): 373–425. Dumbarton Oaks Research Library and Collection, Washington, D.C.
  2000 "The Arrival of Strangers": Teotihuacan and Tollan in Classic Maya History. In *Mesoamerica's Classic Heritage: From Teotihuacan to the Aztecs* (Davíd Carrasco, Lindsay Jones, and Scott Sessions, eds.): 465–513. University Press of Colorado, Boulder.
  2004 The Beginnings of the Copan Dynasty: A Review of the Hieroglyphic and Historical Evidence. In *Understanding Early Classic Copan* (Ellen E. Bell, Marcello A. Canuto, and Robert J. Sharer, eds.): 215–248. University of Pennsylvania Museum of Archaeology and Anthropology, Philadelphia.
  2005 A Foreign Past: The Writing and Representation of History on a Royal Ancestral Shrine at Copan. In *Copan: The History of an Ancient Maya Kingdom* (E. Wyllys Andrews and William L. Fash, eds.): 373–394. School of American Research Press, Santa Fe, N.M.

Sugiyama, Saburo
  1993 Worldview Materialized in Teotihuacan, Mexico. *Latin American Antiquity* 4(2): 103–129.
  2005 *Human Sacrifice, Militarism, and Rulership: Materialization of State Ideology at the Feathered Serpent Pyramid, Teotihuacan.* Cambridge University Press, Cambridge and New York.
  n.d. Teotihuacan City Layout as a Cosmogram: Architectural and Measurement-Unit Study at the Moon Pyramid and Beyond. A paper presented at the 73rd Annual Meeting of the Society for American Archaeology, Vancouver, B.C., April 2008.

Sugiyama, Saburo, and David Carballo (eds.)
  n.d. *Excavations at the Moon Pyramid, Teotihuacan.* University of Oklahoma Press, Norman (in preparation).

Sugiyama, Saburo, and Leonardo López Luján
  2007 Dedicatory Burial/Offering Complexes at the Moon Pyramid, Teotihuacan: A Preliminary Report of 1998–2004 Explorations. *Ancient Mesoamerica* 18: 127–146.

Taube, Karl A.

2000a *The Writing System of Ancient Teotihuacan*. Ancient America 1. Center for Ancient American Studies, Barnardsville, N.C.

2000b The Turquoise Hearth: Fire, Self Sacrifice, and the Central Mexican Cult of War. In *Mesoamerica's Classic Heritage: From Teotihuacan to the Aztecs* (Davíd Carrasco, Lindsay Jones, and Scott Sessions, eds.): 269–340. University Press of Colorado, Boulder.

2004a Structure 10L-16 and Its Early Classic Antecedents: Fire and the Evocation and Resurrection of K'inich Yax K'uk' Mo'. In *Understanding Early Classic Copan* (Ellen E. Bell, Marcello A. Canuto, and Robert J. Sharer, eds.): 265–296. University of Pennsylvania Museum of Archaeology and Anthropology, Philadelphia.

2004b Flower Mountain: Concepts of Life, Beauty, and Paradise among the Classic Maya. *RES* 45: 69–98.

Thompson, J. Eric S.

1962 A *Catalog of Maya Hieroglyphs*. University of Oklahoma Press, Norman.

Tobriner, Stephen

1972 The Fertile Mountain: An Investigation of Cerro Gordo's Importance to the Town Plan and Iconography of Teotihuacan. In *Teotihuacan: XI Mesa Redonda*, vol. 2: 103–115. Sociedad Mexicana de Antropología, México.

Tokovinine, Alexandre

n.d. The Power of Place: Political Landscape and Identity in Classic Maya Inscriptions, Imagery, and Architecture. Ph.D. thesis, Department of Anthropology, Harvard University, Cambridge, Mass., 2008.

Tomasic, John, and Federico Fahsen

2004 Exploraciones y excavaciones preliminares en Tres Islas, Petén. In *XVII Simposio de Investigaciones Arqueológicas en Guatemala, 2003, Museo Nacional de Arqueologia y Etnologia* (Juan Pedro Laporte, Barbara Arroyo, Héctor L. Escobedo, and Héctor E. Mejía, eds.): 794–809. Ministerio de Cultura y Deportes, Instituto de Antropología e Historia, Asociación Tikal, Guatemala City.

Uriarte, María Teresa

2006 The Teotihuacan Ballgame and the Beginning of Time. *Ancient Mesoamerica* 17(1): 17–38.

Vogt, Evon Z.

1969 *Zinacantan: A Maya Community in the Highlands of Chiapas*. Belknap Press of Harvard University Press, Cambridge, Mass.

Von Winning, Hasso

1967 The "Binding of the Years" and the "New Fire" at Teotihuacan. *Indiana* 5: 15–32.

Zender, Marc

n.d. Mexican Associations of the Early Classic Dynasty of Turtle Tooth I. A paper presented at the 31st Annual Maya Meetings, Austin, Tex., March 2007.

EIGHT

WATERY PLACES AND URBAN FOUNDATIONS DEPICTED IN MAYA ART AND ARCHITECTURE

Barbara W. Fash

WATER AND AGRICULTURE were two vital elements that shaped the ancient Maya visual concept of an urban environment at its foundations. Proper control and management of these resources were fundamental for sustaining an urban zone (Fash and López Luján, this volume; Roys 1934; Sanders 1973). Recognizing the importance of these fundamentals in the art of urbanism brings together an understanding of ancient Maya technological achievements with their creative depictions, which were made to capture the essence of their built environments. As both functional and spiritual resources, water and its dualistic counterpart, fire, and their extremes, floods and droughts, were commonly featured in Maya urban art and ideology from the onset of the Maya civilization. These elements were perpetuated into much later times, as witnessed in the dual temples dedicated to fire and water deities in Mexico-Tenochtitlan (Broda et al. 1987). Water symbolism in particular is important in urban contexts, because widespread ritual activities that were closely tied to the functional use and control of water significantly shaped the ancient economic, political, and sacred landscapes, which are the focus of this chapter. Furthermore, water appears to have had a particularly significant role in uniting social groups around its maintenance, access, and ritual activities (Fash 2005; Fash and Davis-Salazar 2006; Vogt 1976, 1993).

In Mesoamerican dualism, the notion of a complementary sky and earth dates back to the origins of complex society. As early as the first artistic representations in Mesoamerica the celestial storm deity is differentiated from the jaguar deity that represents the earth; both deities are depicted as distinct on vessels from the Early Preclassic period. Apparently it was not sufficient to appease the rain deities, Tlaloc, Cocijo or Chaak, but it was also necessary and important to manage rainwater from the moment it fell to earth. This sense of responsibility led the sovereign Mexica Ahuitzotl to dedicate a new water channel for the great capital of Tenochtitlan. The channel, however, flooded the capital, causing a disaster in his kingdom, during which he sustained a mortal wound only to die a few days following the dedication. The history of Ahuitzotl is a reminder that the success of all the great urban centers of the Americas depended strongly on reliable water sources, food sources, and waste systems.

Today the Anishinabe of northwest Ontario describe the essential role water continues to play in their daily life, a characteristic of indigenous cultures throughout the Americas:

> Water is our lifeblood: it is the lifeblood of Mother Earth, and the essence of life. In many indigenous cultures, as men tend the sacred fire, women are considered the caretakers of water. Many aboriginal societies are located around bodies of water because our gatherings and family activities depend on it. Water provides a subsistence base for us and the activities that sustain us. Water is a key component to our sense of community, our sense of identity, our spiritual ways, and our livelihood [Stephens 2006: 1].

Urban environments depend on reliable sources and management programs for food, water, and waste disposal. Without efficient delivery of these basic needs the urban environment will seize up, become unhealthy, and eventually cease to exist. This grim fact of urban life became all too familiar during the 2005 flooding devastation in New Orleans from Hurricane Katrina. In today's world of running faucets, massive agricultural irrigation, and swimming pools, it might seem that developed society has come to take these precious resources and services for granted; ancient Mesoamerican urban dwellers most probably did not. Whether settlement was grid-oriented or organic, small or massive, this chapter shows that water considerations were integral to the founding and sustainability of a city.

Today the symbolic meaning or power of modern water delivery systems are rarely celebrated. Yet, in the not so distant past buildings and public spaces constructed to control water were embellished with sculptures to acknowledge a city's progressive nature. For example, the early American sculptor William Rush ornamented Philadelphia waterworks with stone sculptures from 1809 to 1825 (Garvan 1987). Rush's sculptures were commissioned to commemorate the city's artistic ingenuity coupled with its scientific expertise. By decorating waterworks constructed to harness nature for the benefit of the city, the sculptures testified to the civic governmental success and enhanced the urban structure. Such efforts to ornament landmarks evoke civic and sacred pride while animating the urban space with symbolism (Amundson n.d.).

Similarly, we might expect that in representations of urban Maya art there would be tributes to water resources and celebrations of human mastery over its control. In fact ancient Mesoamerican city environments utilized the nature and power of water, mountains, maize, and the divine ruler to visually define their urban landscapes and city conceptions (Brady and Ashmore 1999; Dunning 1992, 1995, 2003; Dunning et al. 2002; Fash 2005; Knapp and Ashmore 1999; Lucero 1999, 2006; Lucero and Fash 2006; Puleston 1976, 1977; Schele and Mathews 1998; Schele and Miller 1986; Stark 1999; Taube 1996).

Research including ancient water management facilities, settlement patterns, shrines, and water-related imagery associated with both the built environment and sacred places permits scholars to assess how people were once integrated around this vital element of the natural and social worlds. It effectively integrates all four approaches to urbanism described by Fash and López Luján in this volume's Introduction. Previous works emphasize that the Maya built environment mimics the surrounding landscape, revealing that constructed waterholes and reservoirs went beyond a purely practical purpose. Such features were often purposefully situated for symbolic purposes, such as at Tikal, Guatemala, where they corresponded to the four cardinal directions from the epicenter (Ashmore n.d.; Scarborough 1996: 305). Water pools seem to have been considered as mirror-like reflective portals to the underworld, where rituals, divination, and sacrifices were performed (Brady and Ashmore 1999; Coggins 1992; Scarborough 1998; Taube 1992a). Scarborough (2003b) makes a strong case for ballcourts to be another component of the replicated landscape, featuring their low-lying water-retention characteristics.

These considerations of the fundamental importance of water management in the Maya lowlands find echo in the public works at great urban centers of Highland Mesoamerica as well. Scholars of Teotihuacan, Mexico, have long appreciated that the channeling of the Río San Lorenzo and the Río San Juan was critical in the initial layout of the great metropolis and in its long-term success as a large, densely nucleated urban center (Palerm 1961, 1973; Sanders 1965, 1976). The San Juan was diverted 2.5 km from its original course running southeast, in a westerly direction directly through the city center, and from there it was channeled to the spring-fed fertile lands that constituted the agricultural heartland of the ancient city (Sugiyama 1993: 110). Saburo Sugiyama (1993) has explored the cosmological and cosmogonic aspects of this great feat of hydraulic engineering, noting that the river divides the upper (northern) part of the site from the Ciudadela and lower, southern parts of the city. He associates the city south of the river with the underworld and the iconography of the Feathered Serpent Pyramid with the watery realm of creation where time began.

In efforts to elucidate how urbanism was potentially conceived and depicted in Maya art and architecture, this chapter explores a pattern of water symbolism and its interpretation, which builds on my Copan,

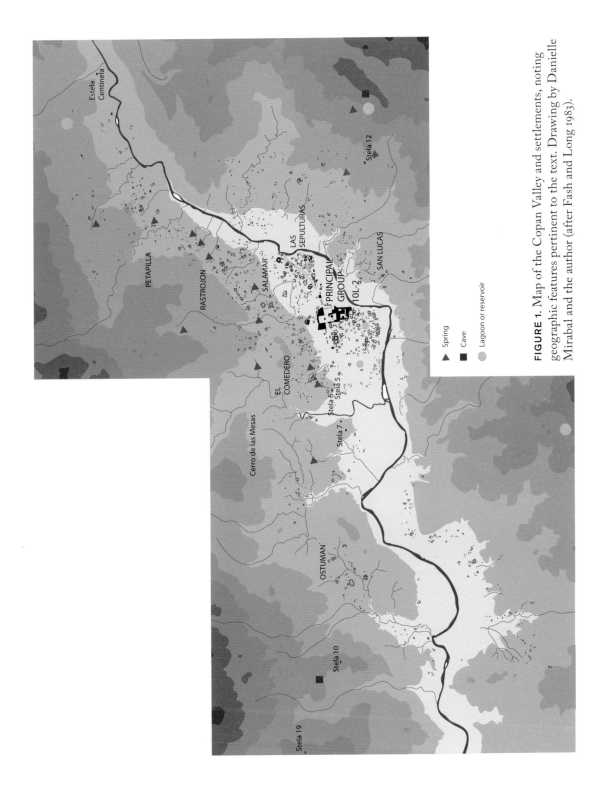

FIGURE 1. Map of the Copan Valley and settlements, noting geographic features pertinent to the text. Drawing by Danielle Mirabal and the author (after Fash and Long 1983).

Spring ▲
Cave ■
Lagoon or reservoir ●

FIGURE 2. Water plants and symbolism from Palace House, Palenque, Mexico (after Maudslay 1889–1902).

Honduras, research by comparison with similar iconography and research at other Maya and more distant Mexican sites (Figure 1). In early societies the nature of water as a fundamental resource with both benevolent and malevolent aspects, with life-giving and life-taking properties, reinforced its spiritual potency. Water's birthing and nurturing characteristics most commonly become naturally linked with female roles, fertility, and growth, whereas its opposites, fire and solar heat, generally become associated with male qualities (as in the Anishinabe quote above). For the ancient Maya, solar and fire rituals were closely associated with ancestor worship and fiery resurrection (Baudez 1988, 1994; Taube 2004). For example, at Copan, the Temple 22 facade is covered with watery cave and mountain symbolism, whereas Structure 16 is quite the opposite, replete with fire symbolism and ancestor images. William Fash suggested these dualistic structures at Copan were precursors to the twin temple complex at Tenochtitlan, of Huitzilopochtli and Tlaloc (Fash et al., this volume).

Founding rituals at Maya sites also appear to have involved fire and water. As these activities become better understood, often from later inscriptions recalling the events, some archaeological investigations may actually confirm aspects of those practices with physical evidence (Stuart 2004, 2005a). For example at Copan, smudging from fires via small cut-stone tubes or psychoducts is evident from the earliest Acropolis structures, and water channels crisscrossed the nascent urban landscape (Sharer et al. 1992). Copan's first dynastic ruler K'inich Yax K'uk' Mo's ability to harness natural resources was no doubt an important quality for a ruler to demonstrate as he planned and laid out the new dynastic center.

Palenque, Mexico, is a water-rich zone, as are Copan and numerous other Maya sites, yet the imaginative and creative ways the Otolum River and water cascades were channeled and incorporated into the site design, and the iconography reflecting this core aspect, distinguish it from other realms (Barnhart n.d. [2001]; French 2001, 2007; French et al. 2006). New hieroglyphic interpretations emerging from recent finds at Palenque propose that the well-known Triadic deities of the Cross Group were born of a progenitor in a mythological act at a watery place called Matawil (Stuart 2005b). Although the gender and exact identification of the progenitor is still open to debate,[1] there can be no doubt but that the water associations with the birth of patron gods were also essential to the mythical narrative and the ideological foundations of Palenque's built environment. As such, water birds, water plants, crocodiles, the fused "Starry-Deer-Crocodile" creature, turtle shells, shells, maize, and water bands all proliferate in the art of both Copan and Palenque (Figure 2).

WATER POWER AND ITS REPRESENTATION IN ANCIENT MESOAMERICA

Control of water is a complex undertaking. It requires engineering skills, environmental awareness, and foresight to deal with the agricultural and personal needs of a community (Lucero 2006; Roys 1934; Scarborough 1993, 2003a). Puleston and Puleston (1971) noted "the necessity of orga- nizing labor to carry out large public projects such as the construction of reservoirs may well have been a catalyst for the development of social stratification and the conceptualization of the state." More recently a strong interest to continue research into understanding the variety of human- engineered water systems designed and managed throughout the Maya area has led scholars to the realization that every site incorporated a suitable system into its original planning (Ashmore 1984; Beach and Dunning 1997; Brown 2006; Chase and Chase 1998; Culbert et al. 1990; Dahlin et al. 1980; Davis-Salazar 2003; Doolittle 1990; Dunning et al. 1999; Fash 2005; Fedick and Ford 1990; Ford 1996; French 2001, 2007; Gliessman et al. 1983; Gunn et al. 2002; Hansen 1991; Harrison 1993; Harrison and Turner 1978; Healy et al. 1983; Kunen 2004, 2006; Kunen et al. 2000; Luzzadder-Beach 2000; Matheny 1978; Ortloff 1997; Pope and Dahlin 1989; Price 1971; Rice 1996; Scarborough 1993, 1996, 1998, 2003a; Scarborough and Valdez 2003; Scarborough et al. 1994; Siemens 1978; Siemens and Puleston 1972; Turner et al. 1983; Valdés 1998).

Research in other parts of Mesoamerica, such as the highlands and lowlands in Mexico, reveals the ways that the ruling elites were involved in water management and agricultural production as a means of acquiring political power through agricultural intensification and landscape modifi- cation (Adams 1980; Angulo Villaseñor 1987, 1993; Armillas 1985; Coe and Diehl 1980; Cortés Hernández 1989; Cyphers 1997; Heyden 2000; Neely 2001; Nichols 1982, 1987; Nichols and Frederick 1993; Palerm 1955, 1961, 1973; Parsons 1991; Sanders 1965, 1976; Spencer 2000; Woodbury and Neely 1972). Aztec water management at Tenochtitlan rose to new levels with extensive raised fields, or *chinampas*, and a complex causeway network providing a massively engineered system to support the Aztec empire. With the advent of Spanish colonization, these Mesoamerican systems were permanently altered (Carballal Staedtler and Flores Hernández 1989, 2006; Carrasco 1999; Gillespie 1989; Rojas et al. 1974).

Numerous scholars have shown that ancient Mesoamerican cities and ceremonial complexes were conceived as architectural replicas of the sacred landscape, a concept extensively used in the chapters in this volume (Benson 1985; Broda et al. 1987; Dunning 1995; Fash and López Luján, this volume; Grove 1987, 1999; Heyden 1981, 2000; Schele and Mathews 1998). Temple-pyramids were human-made mountains that provided an axis of communication with the gods and ancestral spirits (Heyden 1981, 2000; Stuart 1997). Courtyards surrounding them collected rain runoff that created shallow, watery ponds that mimicked natural valley depressions (Hansen 1991; Scarborough 1993, 1996). Evidence of the importance of water management in neighboring cultures encourages scholars not only to look for cosmological and functional equivalents in the iconography and architecture among the ancient Maya but also to question why they would not be present (Fash 2005). At Copan and other Maya sites, temples identi-fied by their iconography as sacred mountains symbolized the important water source and mountain of sustenance. As Fash and López Luján explain (this volume), the Postclassic Nahuatl term for the same was *altepetl*, which literally translates as "mountain of water" or "mountain filled with water" (Bierhorst 1985; Broda et al. 1987: 93; López Austin 1973, 1997; Stark 1999). As a concept it was applied broadly to define a village or community and offers a basis to explain the social unity that developed around the need to control these resources. A fine iconographic example at Copan in the form of a Classic Period structure, given the field name Indigo, appears to be purposefully decorated with imagery drawing attention to its water-diversion functions (Fash 2005). Sacred water collected on its plastered roof was channeled into internal pyramidal drains and out the mouths of an earth and water deity. A similar theme continues in the latest version that covered Indigo, the well-known Temple 22, which is decorated with *tuun wits*, or mountain deities, and water birds (Fash and Fash 1996; Schele and Freidel 1990).

At Copan's Principal Group, the multiple-plaza design of the Acropolis provided a threefold catchment system that utilized the East Court, the West Court, and the Court of the Hieroglyphic Stairway. It is believed that the smooth plaster temple surfaces channeled water into the plazas and diverted it via drains in a southerly direction to the reservoir in the densely populated urban area (Fash 2005; Fash and Davis 2006). Although the ancient site of Copan is located along the river, during the rainy sea-son early inhabitants probably relied on reservoirs, in addition to natural springs, for potable water.[2] To the northwest of the residences composing Group 9N-8, or Las Sepulturas, is a large rectangular depression, one of several in the valley that was investigated by Karla Davis-Salazar. She found supporting evidence that it was an ancient reservoir for this large residential zone (see Davis-Salazar 2003: fig. 1). Once rainwater and runoff

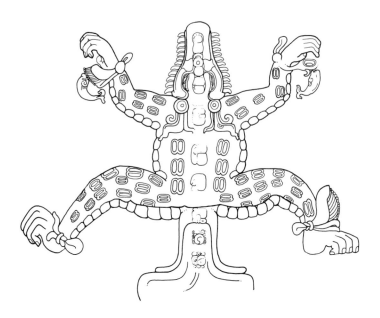

FIGURE 3. Aquatic symbolism on the top surface of Altar T, Copan, Honduras. Drawing by the author (after Maudslay 1889–1902).

were retained in reservoirs, clean sources of drinking water and aquatic resources could have been continually available year round.

Roberts Rands's (1955) and Dennis Puleston's (1976, 1977) Maya subsistence studies called attention to aquatic flora and fauna iconography and water symbolism. They associated these motifs with sluggish streams, rivers, ponds, *aguadas* (natural seasonal water sinks), swamps, and river floodplain environments, specifically mentioning the crocodile and waterlily motifs on Copan's Altar T as evidence for developed water technology at the site (Figure 3). Maudslay (1889–1902) and Spinden (1913) illustrated aquatic elements, water lilies and water birds, which appear frequently on facade sculpture and freestanding monuments at Copan and Palenque, suggesting the importance water locales held for the Classic Maya, who cultivated and venerated this environmental biodiversity. Indeed, the name Tollan, or "Place of the Reeds," which was at the core of founding sacred cities throughout Mesoamerica, is descriptive of a lagoon or aquatic environment. Jeannette Sherbondy (1992) uses the term "ethnohydrology" in her ethnographic studies in Peru to explain a combination of regional hydraulic sensibility and ritual formulas, which ensured the continuity of the water supply over time. This fused focus on water and community wellbeing appears similar to modern Maya situations, suggesting that it was a long-standing tradition from ancient times (Faust et al. 2004).

ICONOGRAPHY OF WATER MANAGEMENT

In two previous articles I described three iconographic elements found throughout Copan that I believe represent key aspects of water management

FIGURE 4. Waterlily headdress on Stela N, Ruler 15, Copan, Honduras. Drawing by the author.

10 cm

FIGURE 5. A stepped motif with infixed *tuun* sign on a painted stucco vessel believed to signify a cave dripwater feature, from a burial near Structure 10L-41, Copan, Honduras. Photo by the author.

and rituals in ancient times (Fash 2005; Fash and Davis-Salazar 2006). These key elements—the waterlily headdress, the stepped *tuun* symbol, and the half quatrefoil niche—occur at many Maya sites (Figures 4–6). I proposed that when worn by rulers and nobles, the waterlily headdress explicitly relates to a social structure of water-management duties and the wearer's divine ritual role of ensuring fertility and sustenance. As such, it may be the specific headdress of regional water masters, who helped conceive and design the built environments. Waterlily headdresses donned by nobles on the Bonampak, Mexico, murals, stelae at Machaquila, Guatemala, the Del Rio throne at Palenque, and a combination of these motifs on vessels from Tikal hint that the underlying water template for urban design was not only widespread throughout the Maya area, but that rulers and nobles also specifically sought to link their roles with the nurturing and female qualities associated with water features (Figures 7–9).

Epigraphers have identified hieroglyphs in the inscriptions of Palenque and Copan, further supporting this role. In some cases rulers are described as impersonators of an entity called Ha'-?-EK' 1_WITZ' or Water Serpent, whose name (witz') actually occurs in Copan Ruler 12's name (Stuart 2007). The Water Serpent (also known as the Waterlily Serpent and Waterlily

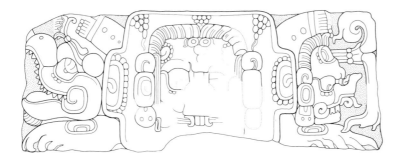

FIGURE 6. Quatrefoil (Altar W') and half quatrefoil (Structure 8N-66S) motifs, Copan, Honduras. Drawings by the author.

FIGURE 7. Figure wearing a waterlily headdress, Bonampak murals. Drawing by the author (after Hurst in Miller 2002).

A

1

2

3

4

B

1

2

3

4

FIGURE 8. Ruler donning a waterlily headdress and standing over a half quatrefoil symbol marked with an Imix glyph, designating a water place name, Stela 4, Machaquila. Drawing by Ian Graham. Courtesy of the Corpus of Maya Hieroglyphic Program, Peabody Museum.

Monster), well known to be depicted as a long-snouted beast wearing a tied waterlily blossom and pad headdress, is associated with the number 13, and the spirit of rivers and standing bodies of water or *nahb* (Bassie-Sweet 1996: 81; Fash 2005: 122–123; Schele and Miller 1986: 46; Taube 1992b: 59; Thompson 1970: 136; Wisdom 1940: 394). As the animate form of water emerging from the mountains, akin to the Chor'ti' belief in *chichans* (Wisdom 1940), the Water Serpent appears to have been the icon worn by ruler, priests, and nobles to signal this important association (Fash 2005: 123).

María Teresa Uriarte emphasizes the role of the water-lily as both a primordial water plant and a solar symbol at Teotihuacan (Uriarte 2006). She proposes that its appearance with Tlaloc and association with ballgames renders it a symbol of the beginning of time. The Maya seem to have also designated this meaning to the waterlily. I agree with Sugiyama (1993) that water management features were essential components from the beginning for the city layout at Teotihuacan. I would add that the ideological foundations and initial urban planning at Maya sites, such as Copan, also included water symbolism and water management.

Thompson (1952) and later Bassie-Sweet (1996) have shown that water dripping in a cave is considered extremely sacred and pure. Still today it is collected for the preparation of ritual drinks and healing potions (Vogt 1969, 1993). The symbol for a dripwater stone is the *tuun* sign, a grape-like cluster that adorns the heads of *wits* (mountain deities) found on both facades and stelae and at least one vessel at Copan (Fash 2005; see Figure 5).

Quatrefoil and half quatrefoil motifs are understood to represent portals in general, most frequently caves, as well as the opening to waterholes. They have been interpreted as representing *nahb*, or waterlily places (Houston et al. 2005; Schele and Grube 1990). Mountains and toponyms are proposed to be depicted as half quatrefoil cartouches (a quatrefoil at the horizon) at Copan, where they appear on several residential structures with motifs or figures inside them, possibly designating named places and shrines visited on ritual circuits (Fash 2005; see Figure 6). At Palenque they are carved on Pacal's sarcophagus with human personages within (Figure 10). Other examples are found at Monte Albán and Acanceh, Mexico (see Marcus, this volume). The Structure 1 facade of Acanceh combines *pu* or cattail reed signs, truncated mountain motifs depicted as half quatrefoils, and water motifs to denote a lush environment (Miller 1991; Stuart 2000; Taube

FIGURE 9. Painted pottery figure wearing a waterlily headdress and seated on a jaguar throne, surrounded by quatrefoil and half quatrefoil signs, Tikal, Guatemala. Drawing by the author.

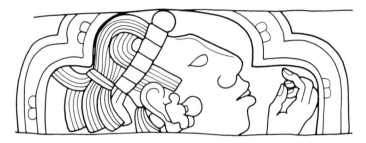

FIGURE 10. Half quatrefoil cartouche on Pacal's sarcophagus at Palenque, Mexico. Drawing by the author (after Robertson 1993).

2004; von Winning 1985). The cattail reeds are of course found in swampy areas (*nahb*). They alternate with the animal figures framed with mountain signs that may refer to places associated with the water/mountain complex and associated communities. Altogether these motifs suggest a reference to Tollan or various urban landscapes as individual Tollans, the fertile Mesoamerican place of origin, which later forms the nucleus of the Nahuatl *altepetl* concept.

The magnificent Preclassic murals from San Bartolo, Guatemala, depict an accession scene on the west wall (Saturno et al. 2005; Saturno, this volume). Key figures in the scene are seated facing one another inside a quatrefoil motif in the form of a turtle's shell. Water flows beneath the scenes, and caves figure prominently in the mythical narrative. This scene may be not simply an origin myth unfolding but the physiographic back-drop for the site's founding event, a sort of necessary precondition for the event depicted.

Following the model that Mesoamerican sites were generally laid out in four quadrants in conjunction with the cardinal directions (Coggins 1980), it may be there were four directional locations of significance in ancient Copan that may have been shrine areas (see Figure 1). Water, caves, or simple openings in the earth seemed to play a role in the selection of these sacred locales and ancient shrines. Ritual offerings of jade, ceramics, and sculpture fragments were left during ancient ritual visits to fissures and natural features near Stela 12 along the eastern ridge and a lagoon (La

Laguna) on the southern rim (Nuñez Chinchilla 1966), potentially the southern shrine area. Two other directional shrines associated with caves and water sources in the mountains were likely marked by Stela 10 in the west and Stela 12 in the east. A northern shrine was located on the top of Cerro de las Mesas, a locale that is marked today by a cross and has been the destination of the May 3, Day of the Cross ceremony, which celebrates the return of the rainy season. A geographic study of the valley noted small depressions that filled with water at the mountain's summit (Turner et al. 1983).

WATER AND SOCIAL ORGANIZATION

In earlier treatments of this subject (Andrews and Fash 1992; Fash 2005; Fash and Davis-Salazar 2006), I proposed that water management roles were revealed on the sculptured facades from Copan's large residential sectors at Group 9N-8, Las Sepulturas, east of the Principal Group, and Group 10L-2, El Cementerio, south of the main Acropolis. In both cases the dominant building facades are adorned with carved figures wearing waterlily headdresses (Figure 11). In the case of the Structure 9N-82, the central figure wears the waterlily headdress and is flanked by two seated figures wearing maize headdresses (Fash 1988). Following the ethnographic model described by Vogt (1969, 1981) for Zinacantan, Chiapas, Mexico, the figures depicted with maize headdresses were interpreted as representatives of agriculturally based lineage groups, or *snas*, from this valley sector; the more important central figure wearing the waterlily headdress perhaps represented the head of a larger waterhole group incorporated by several lineages. It is not difficult to picture the head of the waterhole group carrying out duties similar to those of the modern-day Zinacantan water managers (Fash 2005; Fash and Davis-Salazar 2006). At Copan's Late Classic royal residence, Group 10L-2, all the figures on the most prominent plaza building, Structure 10L-32, wear waterlily headdresses. This display suggests that the royal males in this group were analogous to regional water masters and perhaps had jurisdiction over the nearby reservoir. Part of their duties may have been overseeing the conceptualization and engineering design of the sacred precinct, making the ruling dynasty of Copan the largest corporate group of water managers, but also those most responsible for the well-being of the urban landscape's continued viability. Structure 41, the neighboring long residential building, is adorned with dripwater elements, further suggesting that water purity and fertility were important concerns of the royal residential compound (Figure 12; see Andrews and Bill 2005).

Such a complex organization unified by water-management activities may have exercised a direct role in the central government of the city during

FIGURE 11. Facade figures wearing the waterlily headdress, Group 10L-2, Structure 10L-32 and Group 9N-8, Structure 9N-82, Copan, Honduras. Drawing by the author.

the seventh and eighth centuries A.D. The collapse of the ruling elite in A.D. 822 most likely also signaled the eventual disintegration of the managed water systems, a model Lucero (2006) also posits for the Maya area as a whole. If true, the site core would likely have been abandoned in favor of rural sites with more accessible and safer water.

The proposed waterhole social units, inclusive of the smaller lineage-based agricultural groups, would have been drawn together by their common use of a water source or management of an urban system, such as a reservoir. Such waterhole groups would have reinforced territorial boundaries by the groups' shared participation in a belief system that required ceremonial offerings to the waterhole spirits and ancestral patrons in conjunction with maintenance of the waterhole and related shrines. Although the population was diverse and changing, water management in local communities was potentially a cohesive force and created local identity.

Maya place names often include a water or cave reference, such as "black hole," or *ch'en,* providing other clues to water's ubiquitous nature in the Maya landscape (Stuart and Houston 1994). These features most likely became the reference points for communities and residential settlements centered on waterholes, possibly the cohesive feature for clusters called *sian otot* among the Chorti Maya (Fash 1983). My model goes a step further to propose that the central council house, or *popol nah* (Fash et al. 1992), was the ancient sociopolitical organization for Copan Valley that unified the waterhole groups into a governing body at the site's core (Fash 2005). Outlying residential facades labeled with stepped half quatrefoil niches and their interior icons might identify the group's water-related toponym and ancestral patron. Similar cases existed at other non-Maya sites, such as Xochicalco, Mexico, where water toponyms figure prominently on the most decorated structure at the site (Wilkerson 1999; Figure 13).

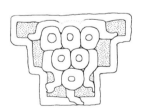

FIGURE 12. Stepped *tuun* sign from Structure 41, Copan, Honduras. Drawing by the author.

FIGURE 13. Water toponym at Xochicalco. Photo by the author.

CONTINUING TRADITIONS AS SOURCES FOR MODEL BUILDING

Corporate systems functioning today among the living Maya show continuity in many realms since the time of the conquest, suggesting that similar levels of managerial systems may have been well developed at the peak of Maya civilization. John L. Stephens (1841: 404) noted during his journey through Yucatan that water was the most valuable possession. Landowners who invested much time and many resources in procuring water and maintaining tanks and reservoirs were in a position of power over the native population. The Yucatecan model of Farriss (1984) identifies the waterhole as essentially the base point for defining the geographic boundaries of a given community and the saints associated with that water source.

Indigenous groups have tenaciously held on to the cave and water ceremonies in an effort to sustain their religious beliefs, unite communities around common economic goals, and ensure the continual availability of water. Scarborough (1998) has amply explored the role of ecology and ritual

FIGURE 14.
Decorated water
shrine near Malinalco,
Morelos, Mexico.
Photos by the author.

among the ancient Maya, whose continuity from ancient times is apparent in the rituals and festivals that numerous contemporary communities throughout Mesoamerica maintain as a link to sacred springs and water catchment systems. These activities help to safeguard the purity of community resources, control water rights, and protect the sacred environment. Continuity is documented for example in Nahua villages today (Hersch Martínez et al. 2004). In places as far removed from Copan as Guerrero, Mexico, Zinacantan, Chiapas, and highland Guatemala, towns also celebrate May 3 as a water festival that has carried over from ancient times, while simultaneously continuing to adapt their water installations to meet modern needs (Figure 14).

CONCLUSIONS

Early Maya rulers used water management as a key component of their core belief systems and basis for political hierarchy, making themselves the pivotal figures in the centering of a site. This process involved spiritual and cosmological beliefs tied to water and water rituals revolving around waterhole or reservoir groups as social units. It is proposed that from this social network water masters were selected to operate in the larger political organization, representing their lineage or "house" groups and joining rulers to invoke their ancestral deities in the sacred geography, thereby legitimating their power and unifying their local communities. The urban design thus became a mirror of the natural landscape, with water engineering becoming an important function for ensuring this vital resource's availability for the polity's growing communities. Copan's first dynastic ruler, K'inich Yax K'uk' Mo', may have initiated the triadic plaza/*nahb* configurations as cosmological symbols in the built environment, which later evolved into a massive Acropolis construction that embodied those symbolic features through time.

These water motifs and architectural complexes encourage us to view the ancient Maya urban landscape in light of its hydraulic functions. In contrast to the grid structure of Teotihuacan, Maya cities' organic structures took form through such technological developments as adapting to hilly or mountainous terrain, arid landscapes, or verdant tropical environments. Water sources and/or cosmic directionality and quadrants were important factors that organized the organic city growth. By studying visual depictions of water in urban environments, it becomes apparent that similar ideological concepts of cities and places were transposed from these varied geographies. Today's concerns over elite corporate brokerage of water rights and water associations can be enlightened by understanding these uses of water management by the ancient Maya ruling elite as a source of political power and social organization.[3]

In addition to reservoirs and lagoons, springs in the hillsides were most likely well protected and cleaned by the communities who used them in ancient times. Architectural facade iconography reveals a sacred connection to the springs by association of toponyms and patron saints of the water sources. This feedback system ensured that those who claimed water rights from a particular source would stay unified in efforts to preserve it. Although Lucero (2006) suggests that ancient water-related ritual festivals were promoted by leaders to legitimate inequality, it appears that what were perhaps less extravagant community rituals are the ones that are preserved today and maintain a focus on the importance of clean, accessible water sources.

Collapse of water systems can play a major role in the eventual cessation of urban functions. If there is power to be found in water management, those seeking it will manipulate it and devise a system for their own benefit. Although this behavior may in part rest on altruistic intentions to meet everyone's water needs, it ultimately fails when the power structure collapses. If today's community hydraulic systems are supported by water protection and community celebrations, which include monuments decorated with festive regalia, it is because the people believe it will help to ensure the system's sustainability by providing community identity and equal opportunities for access to water rights. It may be revealing that in twenty-first-century developed countries, water celebrations and veneration of water sources are virtually nonexistent. It is only in rural indigenous communities that we find these quiet ritual activities still persevering in the face of monumental global changes.

NOTES

1. Stuart (2005b: 181) favors a male maize deity progenitor, but I suggest there may be a female/male duality at work. Following Karen Bassie-Sweet's (personal communication, March 2005) interpretations, the maize plant is female in its ripe (fruit-giving) phase and "bone" (or dried-regenerative) phase, and the growing plant stalk is the male component. I think there is room for interpreting the progenitor as a female maize entity. Given that women are closely connected to watery places across the Americas, it seems likely there could be a fertilization process being described that involves both female and male roles.

2. Miller (1988: 161–162) proposed that the East Court was envisioned as an underwater place because of the large conch shells that adorned the Reviewing Stand on the south side of Temple 11. Although the court had a water-control function, I suggest that these sculptures do not so much label it as a watery place but rather as a performance area where drums and conch-shell trumpets mark the parameters. I also propose that the large columnar sculptures decorated with masks, which as far as I know have eluded identification, may actually be representations of the tall Maya *pax* drum, later known as the *huehuetl* in Postclassic Mexico, to make a complete musical ensemble.

3. See Hunt (1988), Hunt and Hunt (1976), and Mabry (1996) for additional perspectives.

REFERENCES CITED

Adams, R. E. W.
    1980   Swamps, Canals, and the Location of Ancient Maya Cities. *Antiquity* 54: 206–214.
Amundson, Jhennifer A.
    n.d.   Roman Triumph and American Technology: Sculpture for Architecture and Republicanism in Philadelphia. A paper presented at a symposium titled "More than Just a Pretty Face: Architectural Sculpture in Context," at the 90th Annual Meeting of the College Art Association, New York, February 2002.

Andrews, E. Wyllys, V, and Barbara W. Fash

1992 Continuity and Change in a Royal Maya Residential Complex at Copán. *Ancient Mesoamerica* 3: 63–88.

Andrews, E. Wyllys, and Cassandra R. Bill

2005 A Late Classic Royal Residence at Copán. In *Copan: The History of an Ancient Maya Kingdom* (E. Wyllys Andrews and William L. Fash, eds.): 239–314. School of American Research Press, Santa Fe, N.M.

Angulo Villaseñor, Jorge

1987 El sistema Otli-apantli dentro del área urbana. In *Teotihuacan: Nuevos datos, nuevas síntesis, nuevos problemas* (Emily McClung and Evelyn Rattray, eds.): 267–274. Serie Antropológica 72. Instituto de Investigaciones Antropológicas, Universidad Nacional Autónoma de México, Arqueología, México.

1993 Water Control and Communal Labor during the Formative and Classic Periods in Central Mexico (ca. 1000 BC–AD 650). In *Economic Aspects of Water Management in the Prehispanic New World* (Vernon L. Scarborough and Barry L. Isaac, eds.): 17–69. JAI Press, Greenwich, Conn.

Armillas, Pedro

1985 Tecnología, formaciones socio-económicas y religión en Mesoamérica. In *Mesoamérica y el centro de México* (Jesús Monjaraz-Ruíz, Rosa Brambila, and Emma Pérez Rocha, eds.): 25–40. Instituto de Antropología e Historia, México.

Ashmore, Wendy

1984 Classic Maya Wells at Quiriguá. *American Antiquity* 49: 147–153.

n.d. The Idea of a Maya Town. A paper presented at the conference titled "Structure and Meaning in Human Settlements" at the Annual Penn Maya Weekend, University of Pennsylvania, Philadelphia, October 2000.

Barnhart, Edwin E.

n.d. The Palenque Mapping Project: Settlement and Urbanism at an Ancient Maya City. Ph.D. dissertation, Department of Anthropology, University of Texas, Austin, 2001.

Bassie-Sweet, Karen

1996 *At the Edge of the World: Caves and Late Classic Maya World View.* University of Oklahoma Press, Norman.

n.d. Maya Gods of Renewal: Part I. Manuscript.

Baudez, Claude F.

1988 Solar Cycle and Dynastic Succession in the Southeast Maya Zone. In *The Southeast Classic Maya Zone* (Elizabeth Boone and Gordon R. Willey, eds.): 125–148. Dumbarton Oaks, Washington, D.C.

1994 *Maya Sculpture of Copán: The Iconography.* University of Oklahoma Press, Norman and London.

Beach, Timothy, and Nicholas Dunning

1997 An Ancient Maya Reservoir and Dam at Tamarindito, El Petén, Guatemala. *Latin American Antiquity* 8: 20–29.

Benson, Elizabeth P.

    1985 Architecture as Metaphor. In *Fifth Palenque Round Table 1983* (Merle G. Robertson and Virginia M. Fields, eds.): 183–192. Pre-Columbian Art Research Institute, San Francisco.

Bierhorst, John

    1985 *A Nauhatl-English Dictionary and Concordance to the Cantares Mexicanos.* Stanford University Press, Stanford, Calif.

Brady, James E., and Wendy Ashmore

    1999 Mountains, Caves, Water: Ideational Landscapes of the Ancient Maya. In *Archaeologies of Landscape: Contemporary Perspectives* (Wendy Ashmore and A. Bernard Knapp, eds.): 124–145. Blackwell, London.

Broda, Johanna, Davíd Carrasco, and Eduardo Matos Moctezuma

    1987 *The Great Temple of Tenochtitlán, Center and Periphery in the Aztec World.* University of California Press, Berkeley.

Brown, Clifford T.

    2006 Caves, Karst, and Settlement at Mayapán, Yucatán. In *In the Maw of the Earth Monster* (James Brady and Keith Prufer, eds.): 373–402. University of Texas Press, Austin.

Carballal Staedtler, Margarita, and Maria Flores Hernández

    1989 Las calzadas prehispánicas de la Isla de México. Algunas consideraciones acerca de sus funciones. *Arqueología* 1: 71–80.

    2006 Water Control Technology in the Basin of Mexico during the Postclassic Period. In *Precolumbian Water Management: Ideology, Ritual and Power* (Lisa Lucero and Barbara W. Fash, eds.): 155–170. University of Arizona Press, Tucson.

Carrasco, Pedro

    1999 *The Tenochca Empire of Ancient Mexico: The Triple Alliance of Tenochtitlan, Tetzcoco, and Tlacopan.* University of Oklahoma Press, Norman.

Chase, Arlen F., and Diane Z. Chase

    1998 Scale and Intensity in Classic Period Maya Agriculture: Terracing and Settlement at the "Garden City" of Caracol, Belize. *Culture and Agriculture* 20(2/3): 60–77.

Coe, Michael D., and Richard A. Diehl

    1980 *In the Land of the Olmec.* University of Texas Press, Austin.

Coggins, Clemency C.

    1980 The Shape of Time: Some Political Implications of a Four-Part Figure. *American Antiquity* 45: 727–739.

    1992 Dredging the Cenote. In *Artifacts from the Cenote of Sacrifice, Chichen Itza, Yucatan: Textiles, Basketry, Stone, Bone, Shell, Ceramics, Wood, Copal, Rubber, Other Organic Materials, and Mammalian Remains:* 9–13. Memoirs of the Peabody Museum of Archaeology and Ethnology, vol. 10, no, 3. Harvard University, Cambridge, Mass.

Cortés Hernández, Jaime

    1989 Elementos para un intento de interpretación de desarrollo hidráulico de Tajín. *Arqueología* 5: 175–190.

Culbert, T. Patrick, Laura J. Levi, and Luis Cruz
    1990   Lowland Maya Wetland Agriculture: The Rio Azul Agronomy
           Program. In *Vision and Revision in Maya Studies* (Flora S. Clancy and
           Peter D. Harrison, eds.): 115–124. University of New Mexico Press,
           Albuquerque.

Cyphers, Ann
    1997   La arquitectura Olmeca en San Lorenzo Tenochtitlán. In *Población,*
           subsistencia y medio ambiente en San Lorenzo Tenochtitlán (Ann Cyphers,
           ed.): 91–117. Instituto de Investigaciones Antropológicas, Universidad
           Nacional Autónoma de México, México.

Dahlin, Bruce H., J. Foss, and M. E. Chambers
    1980   Project Akalches: Reconstructing the Natural and Cultural History
           of a Seasonal Swamp: Preliminary Results. In *El Mirador, El Petén,*
           Guatemala: An Interim Report (Ray T. Matheny, ed.): 37–58. Papers
           of the New World Archaeological Foundation 45. Brigham Young
           University, Provo, Utah.

Davis-Salazar, Karla
    2003   Late Classic Maya Water Management and Community Organization
           at Copan, Honduras. *Latin American Antiquity* 14: 275–299.

Doolittle, William E.
    1990   *Canal Irrigation in Prehistoric Mexico: The Sequence of Technological*
           Change. University of Texas Press, Austin.

Dunning, Nicholas P.
    1992   *Lords of the Hills: Ancient Maya Settlement in the Puuc Region, Yucatan,*
           Mexico. Prehistory Press, Madison, Wis.
    1995   Coming Together at the Temple Mountain: Environment, Subsis-
           tence, and the Emergence of Classic Maya Segmentary States. In *The*
           Emergence of Classic Maya Civilization. Acta Mesoamericana 8 (Nikolai
           Grube, ed.): 61–70. Verlag von Flemming, Möckmühl, Germany.
    2003   Birth and Death of Waters: Environmental Change, Adaptation, and
           Symbolism in the Southern Maya Lowlands. In *Espacios Mayas: Usos,*
           representaciones, creencias (Alain Breton, Aurore Monod Becquelin, and
           Mario Humberto Ruz, eds.): 49–76. Universidad Autónoma de México,
           México.

Dunning, Nicholas, Sheryl Luzzadder-Beach, Timothy Beach, John Jones,
           Vernon L. Scarborough, and T. Patrick Culbert
    2002   Arising from the Bajos: Anthropogenic Change of Wetlands and
           the Rise of Maya Civilization. *Annals of the Association of American*
           Geographers 92: 267–283.

Dunning, Nicholas, Vernon L. Scarborough, Fred Valdez, Jr., Sheryl Luzzadder-
           Beach, Timothy Beach, and John G. Jones
    1999   Temple Mountains, Sacred Lakes, and Fertile Fields: Ancient Maya
           Landscapes in Northwestern Belize. *Antiquity* 73: 650–660.

Farriss, Nancy
    1984   *Maya Society under Colonial Rule.* Princeton University Press, Prince-
           ton, N.J.

Fash, Barbara W.
    2005 Iconographic Evidence for Water Management at Copán, Honduras.
          In *Copán: History of an Ancient Maya Kingdom* (E. Wyllys Andrews and
          William L. Fash, eds.): 103–138. School of American Research Press,
          Santa Fe, N.M.
Fash, Barbara W., and Karla Davis-Salazar
    2006 Copan Water Ritual and Management: Imagery and Sacred Place.
          In *Precolumbian Water Management: Ideology, Ritual, and Power* (Lisa
          J. Lucero and Barbara W. Fash, eds.): 129–143. University of Arizona
          Press, Tucson.
Fash, Barbara W., William L. Fash, Rudy Larios, Sheree Lane, Linda Schele,
          Jeffrey Stomper, and David Stuart
    1992 Investigations of a Maya Council House from Copán, Honduras.
          Journal of Field Archaeology 19: 419–442.
Fash, William L.
    1983 Deducing Social Organization from Classic Maya Settlement Patterns:
          A Case Study from the Copán Valley. In *Civilization in the Ancient
          Americas, Essays in Honor of Gordon R. Willey* (Richard Leventhal and
          Alan Kolata, eds.): 261–288. University of New Mexico Press, and
          Peabody Museum of Archaeology and Ethnology, Harvard University,
          Albuquerque and Cambridge, Mass.
    1988 The Sculptural Façade of Structure 9N-82: Content, Form and
          Significance. In *House of the Bacabs, Copán, Honduras* (David Webster,
          ed.): 41–72. Dumbarton Oaks, Washington, D.C.
Fash, William L., and Barbara W. Fash
    1996 Building a Worldview: Visual Communication in Classic Maya
          Architecture. *RES* 29–30: 127–147.
Fash, William L., and Kurt Z. Long
    1983 Mapa arqueologico del Valle de Copán. In *Introducción a la arqueología
          de Copán, tomo III* (Claude F. Baudez, ed.): 1–48. Secretaría de Estado
          en el Despacho de Cultura y Turismo, Tegucigalpa, Honduras.
Faust, Betty B., Eugene N. Anderson, and John G. Frazier
    2004 *Rights, Resources, Culture, and Conservation in the Land of the Maya.*
          Praeger, Westport, Conn.
Fedick, Scott L., and Anabel Ford
    1990 The Prehistoric Agricultural Landscape of the Central Maya Low-
          lands: An Examination of Local Variability in a Regional Context.
          World Archaeology 22: 18–33.
Ford, Anabel
    1996 Critical Resource Control and the Rise of the Classic Period Maya. In
          The Managed Mosaic: Ancient Maya Agriculture and Resource Use (Scott
          L. Fedick, ed.): 297–303. University of Utah Press, Salt Lake City.
French, Kirk D.
    2001 The Precious Otulum of Palenque. *PARI Journal* 2(2): 12–16.
    2007 Creating Space through Water Management at the Classic Maya Site
          of Palenque, Chiapas. In *Palenque: Recent Investigations at the Classic*

Maya Center (Damien B. Marken, ed.): 123–132. AltaMira Press, Plymouth, U.K.

French, Kirk D., David S. Stuart, and Alfonso Morales
    2006 Archaelogical and Epigraphic Evidence for Water Management and Ritual at Palenque. In *Precolumbian Water Management: Ideology, Ritual, and Power* (Lisa J. Lucero and Barbara W. Fash, eds.): 144–152. University of Arizona Press, Tucson.

Garvan, Beatrice
    1987 *Federal Philadelphia: 1785–1825: The Athens of the Western World.* University of Pennsylvania Press, Philadelphia.

Gillespie, Susan D.
    1989 *The Aztec Kings: The Construction of Rulership in Mexica History.* University of Arizona Press, Tucson.

Gliessman, Stephen R., Billie L. Turner, II, Francisco J. Rosado-May, and Manuel F. Amador
    1983 Ancient Raised Field Agriculture in the Maya Lowlands of Southeastern Mexico. In *Drained Field Agriculture in Central and South America.* BAR International Series 189 (J. P. Darch, ed.): 91–110. British Archaeological Reports, Oxford.

Grove, David C.
    1987 Chalcatzingo in a Broader Perspective. In *Ancient Chalcatzingo* (David C. Grove, ed.): 434–442. University of Texas Press, Austin.
    1999 Public Monuments and Sacred Mountains: Observations on Three Formative Period Landscapes. In *Social Patterns in Pre-Classic Mesoamerica* (David C. Grove and Rosemary A. Joyce, eds.): 255–299. Dumbarton Oaks, Washington, D.C.

Gunn, Joel D., John E. Foss, William J. Folan, Maria del Rosario Domínguez, and Betty B. Faust
    2002 Bajo Sediments and the Hydraulic System of Calakmul, Campeche, Mexico. *Ancient Mesoamerica* 13: 297–315.

Hansen, Richard D.
    1991 The Maya Rediscovered: On the Road to Nakbe. *Natural History* (May): 8–14.

Harrison, Peter D.
    1993 Aspects of Water Management in the Southern Lowlands. In *Economic Aspects of Water Management in the Prehispanic New World* (Vernon L. Scarborough and Barry L. Isaac, eds.): 70–119. JAI Press, Greenwich, Conn.

Harrison, Peter D., and Billie L. Turner II
    1978 Implications from Agriculture for Maya Prehistory. In *Pre-Hispanic Maya Agriculture* (Peter D. Harrison and Billie Lee Turner II, eds.): 337–373. University of New Mexico Press, Albuquerque.

Healy, Paul F., John D. H. Lambert, John T. Arnason, and Richard J. Hebda
    1983 Caracol, Belize: Evidence of Ancient Maya Agricultural Terraces. *Journal of Field Archaeology* 10: 397–410.

Hersch Martínez, Paul, Lilián Gonzálaez Chévez, and Andrés Fierro Alvarez

    2004 Endogenous knowledge and practice regarding the environment in a
           Nahua community in Mexico. *Agriculture and Human Values* 21(2–3):
           127–137.

Heyden, Doris

    1981 Caves, Gods, and Myths: World-View and Planning in Teotihuacan.
           In *Mesoamerican Sites and World Views* (Elizabeth P. Benson, ed.):
           1–39. Dumbarton Oaks Research Library and Collection, Washington
           D.C.

    2000 From Teotihuacan to Tenochtitlan: City Planning, Caves, and
           Streams of Red and Blue Waters. In *Mesoamerica's Classic Heritage:
           From Teotihuacan to the Aztecs* (Davíd Carrasco, Lindsey Jones,
           and Scott Sessions, eds.): 165–184. University of Colorado Press,
           Boulder.

Houston, Stephen, Karl Taube, Zachary Nelson, Ray Matheny, Gene Ware,
           Deanne Matheny, and Cassandra Messick

    2005 The Pool of the Rain God: An Early Stuccoed Altar at Aguacatal,
           Campeche, Mexico. *Mesoamerican Voices* 2: 37–62.

Hunt, Robert C.

    1988 Size and the Structure of Authority in Canal Irrigation Systems.
           Journal of Anthropological Research 44: 335–355.

Hunt, Robert C., and Eva Hunt

    1976 Canal Irrigation and Local Social Organization. *Current Anthropology*
           17: 389–411.

Knapp, A. Bernard, and Wendy Ashmore

    1999 Archaeological Landscapes: Constructed, Conceptualized, Ideational.
           In *Archaeologies of Landscape: Contemporary Perspectives* (Wendy
           Ashmore and A. Bernard Knapp, eds.): 1–32. Blackwell, Oxford.

Kunen, Julie L.

    2004 *Ancient Maya Life in the Far West Bajo: Social and Environmental Change
           in the Wetlands of Belize.* Anthropological Papers 69. University of
           Arizona Press, Tucson.

    2006 Water Management, Ritual, and Community in Tropical Complex
           Societies. In *Precolumbian Water Management: Ideology, Ritual, and
           Power* (Lisa J. Lucero and Barbara W. Fash, eds.): 100–115. University
           of Arizona Press, Tucson.

López Austin, Alfredo

    1997 *Tamoanchan, Tlalocan: Places of Mist* (Bernard R. Ortiz de Montellano
           and Thelma Ortiz de Montellano, trans.). University Press of Colo-
           rado, Niwot.

Lucero, Lisa J.

    1999 Water Control and Maya Politics in the Southern Maya Lowlands. In
           Complex Polities in the Ancient Tropical World (Elisabeth A. Bacus and
           Lisa J. Lucero, eds.): 34–49. Archeological Papers of the American
           Anthropological Association 9. Arlington, Va.

2006   *Water and Ritual: The Rise and Fall of Classic Maya Rulers*. University of
         Texas Press, Austin.

Lucero, Lisa J., and Barbara W. Fash (eds.)
2006   *Precolumbian Water Management: Ideology, Ritual, and Power*. University
         of Arizona Press, Tucson.

Luzzadder-Beach, Sheryl
2000   Water Resources of the Chunchucmil Maya. *Geographical Review* 90:
         493–510.

Mabry, Johnathan B. (ed.)
1996   *Canals and Communities: Small-Scale Irrigation Systems*. University of
         Arizona Press, Tucson.

Matheny, Ray T.
1978   Northern Maya Lowland Water-Control Systems. In *Pre-Hispanic
         Maya Agriculture* (Peter D. Harrison and Billie Lee Turner II, eds.):
         185–210. University of New Mexico Press, Albuquerque.

Maudslay, Alfred P.
1889–1902   *Biologia Centrali-Americana: Archaeology*, vol. IV. R. H. Porter,
         London.

Miller, Mary Ellen
1988   The Meaning and Function of the Main Acropolis, Copán. In *The
         Southeast Classic Maya Zone* (Elizabeth H. Boone and Gordon R.
         Willey, eds.): 149–194. Dumbarton Oaks, Washington, D.C.
2002   The Willfulness of Art: The Case of Bonampak. *RES* 42: 9–23.

Miller, Virginia
1991   *The Frieze of the Palace of Stuccoes, Acanceh, Yucatan, Mexico*. Dumbarton
         Oaks, Washington, D.C.

Neely, James
2001   A Contextual Study of the "Fossilized" Prehispanic Canal Systems of
         the Tehuacan Valley, Puebla, Mexico. *Antiquity* 75: 505–506.

Nichols, Deborah L.
1982   A Middle Formative Irrigation System near Santa Clara Coatitlan in
         the Basin of Mexico. *American Antiquity* 47: 133–144.
1987   Risk and Agricultural Intensification during the Formative Period in
         the Northern Basin of Mexico. *American Anthropologist* 89: 596–616.

Nichols, Deborah L., and Charles D. Frederick
1993   Irrigation Canals and Chinampas: Recent Research in the Northern
         Basin of Mexico. *Research in Economic Anthropology*, supplement 7:
         123–150.

Nuñez Chinchilla, Jesús
1966   Una cueva vitiva en la zona arqueológica de la ruinas de Copán. *Revista
         de la Sociedad de Geografía e Historia de Honduras* 18: 43–48.

Ortloff, Charles R.
1997   Hydraulic Analysis of the Kaminaljuyu Main Canal. In *Kaminaljuyu/
         San Jorge: Evidencia arqueológica de la actividad económica en el Valle
         de Guatemala, 300 A.C. a 300 D.C.* (Marion P. de Hatch, ed.): 22–27.
         Universidad del Valle de Guatemala, Guatemala City.

Palerm, Angel

    1955 The Agricultural Basis of Urban Civilization. In *Irrigation Civiliza-tions: A Comparative Study* (Julian H. Steward, ed.): 28–42. Pan American Union, Washington, D.C.

    1961 Distribución del regadío prehispánico en Teotihuacán y en el Pedregal. *Revista Interamericana de Ciencias Sociales* 1: 242–267.

    1973 *Obras hidráulicas prehispánicas en el sistema lacustre del Valle de México.* Seminario de Etnohistoria del Valle de México–Instituto Nacional de Antropología e Historia, México.

Parsons, Jeffrey R.

    1991 Political Implications of Prehispanic Chinampa Agriculture in the Valley of Mexico. In *Land and Politics in the Valley of Mexico: A Two-Thousand Year Perspective* (Herb Harvey, ed.): 17–42. University of New Mexico Press, Albuquerque.

Pope, Kevin O., and Bruce H. Dahlin

    1989 Ancient Maya Wetland Agriculture: New Insights from Ecological and Remote Sensing Research. *Journal of Field Archaeology* 16: 87–106.

Price, Barbara J.

    1971 Prehistoric Irrigation Agriculture in Nuclear America. *Latin American Research Review* 6(3): 3–60.

Puleston, Dennis E.

    1976 The People of the Cayman/Crocodile: Riparian Agriculture and the Origins of Aquatic Motifs in Ancient Maya Iconography. In *Maya Symposium of North America: An Interdisciplinary Conference on the Art and Civilization of the Ancient Maya: Aspects of Ancient Maya Civiliza-tion* (Francoise-Auguste de Montequin, ed.): 1–25. Hamline University, St. Paul, Minn.

    1977 Art and Archaeology of Hydraulic Agriculture in the Maya Lowlands. In *Social Process in Maya Prehistory; Studies in the Memory of Sir Eric Thompson* (Norman Hammond, ed.): 449–467. Academic Press, London.

Puleston, Dennis E., and Olga S. Puleston

    1971 An Ecological Approach to the Origins of Maya Civilization. *Archaeol-ogy* 24: 330–337.

Rands, Robert L.

    1955 *Some Manifestations of Water in Mesoamerican Art.* Smithsonian Bureau of American Ethnology, Anthropological Papers 48, Bulletin 157: 265–393. Smithsonian Institution, Washington, D.C.

Rice, Don S.

    1996 Hydraulic Engineering in Central Peten, Guatemala: Ports and Inter-Lacustrine Canals. In *Arqueología mesoamericana: Homenaje a William T. Sanders* (Alba Guadalupe Mastache, ed.): 109–122. Instituto Nacional de Antropología e Historia, Arqueología Mexicano, México.

Robertson, Merle Greene

    1993 *Sculpture of Palenque.* Princeton University Press, Princeton, N.J.

Rojas Rabiela, Teresa, Rafael Strauss, and José Lameiras

1974 *Nuevas noticias sobre las obras hidráulicas prehispánicas y coloniales en el Valle de México.* Seminario de Etnohistoria del Valle de México–Instituto Nacional de Antropología e Historia, Tlalpan, México.

Roys, Lawrence

1934 *The Engineering Knowledge of the Maya.* Contributions to American Archaeology 6. Carnegie Institution of Washington, Washington, D.C.

Sanders, William T.

1965 *The Cultural Ecology of the Teotihuacan Valley: A Preliminary Report of the Results of the Teotihuacan Valley Project.* Department of Sociology and Anthropology, Pennsylvania State University, University Park.

1973 The Cultural Ecology of the Maya Lowlands: A Reevaluation. In *The Classic Maya Collapse* (T. Patrick Culbert, ed.): 325–365. University of New Mexico Press, Albuquerque.

1976 The Agricultural History of the Basin of Mexico. In *The Valley of Mexico* (Eric R. Wolf, ed.): 161–178. University of New Mexico Press, Albuquerque.

Saturno, William A., Karl A. Taube, and David S. Stuart

2005 *The Murals of San Bartolo, El Petén, Guatemala,* part I: *The North Wall.* Ancient America 7. Center for Ancient American Studies, Barnardsville, N.C.

Scarborough, Vernon L.

1993 Water Management in the Southern Maya Lowlands: An Accretive Model for the Engineered Landscape. In *Economic Aspects of Water Management in the Prehispanic New World* (Vernon L. Scarborough and Barry L. Isaac, eds.): 17–69. JAI Press, Greenwich, Conn.

1996 Reservoirs and Watersheds in the Central Maya Lowlands. In *The Managed Mosaic: Ancient Maya Agriculture and Resource Use* (Scott L. Fedick, ed.): 304–314. University of Utah Press, Salt Lake City.

1998 Ecology and Ritual: Water Management and the Maya. *Latin American Antiquity* 9: 135–159.

2003a *The Flow of Power: Ancient Water Systems and Landscapes.* School of American Research Press, Santa Fe, N.M.

2003b Ballcourts and Reservoirs: The Social Construction of a Tropical Karstic Landscape. In *Espacios Mayas: Representaciones, usos, creencias* (Alain Breton, Aurore Monod Becquelin, and Mario Humberto Ruz, eds.): 77–92. Centro de Estudios Mayas, Instituto de Investigaciones Filológicas, Universidad Nacional Autónoma de México, Centro Frances de Estudios Mexicos y Centroamericanos, México.

Scarborough, Vernon L., and Fred Valdez, Jr.

2003 The Engineered Environment and Political Economy of the Three Rivers Region. In *Heterarchy, Political Economy, and Ancient Maya: The Three Rivers Region of the East-Central Yucatan Peninsula* (Vernon

L. Scarborough, Fred Valdez, Jr., and Nicholas Dunning, eds.): 3–13. University of Arizona Press, Tucson.

Scarborough, Vernon L., Robert P. Connelly, and Steven P. Ross
  1994   Pre-Hispanic Maya Reservoir Systems at Kinal, Peten, Guatemala. *Ancient Mesoamerica* 5: 97–106.

Schele, Linda, and David Freidel
  1990   *A Forest of Kings: The Untold Story of the Ancient Maya.* William Morrow, New York.

Schele, Linda, and Nikolai Grube
  1990   The Glyph for Plaza or Court. Copán Note 86. Copán Acropolis Archaeological Project and Instituto Hondureño de Antropología e Historia, Copan, Honduras.

Schele, Linda, and Peter Mathews
  1998   *The Code of Kings.* Simon and Schuster, New York.

Schele, Linda, and Mary Ellen Miller
  1986   *The Blood of Kings: Dynasty and Ritual in Maya Art.* Kimble Art Museum, Fort Worth, Tex.

Sharer, Robert J., Julie Miller, and Loa Traxler
  1992   Evolution of Classic Period Architecture in the Eastern Acropolis, Copán: A Progress Report. *Ancient Mesoamerica* 3: 145–160.

Sherbondy, Jeanette
  1992   Water Ideology in Inca Ethnogenesis. In *Andean Cosmologies through Time: Persistence and Emergence* (Robert V. H. Dover, Katherine E. Seibold, and John H. McDowell, eds.): 46–66. Indiana University Press, Bloomington.

Siemens, Alfred H.
  1978   Karst and the Prehispanic Maya in the Southern Lowlands. In *Prehispanic Maya Agriculture* (Peter D. Harrison and Billie Lee Turner II, eds.): 117–143. University of New Mexico Press, Albuquerque.

Siemens, Alfred H., and Dennis E. Puleston
  1972   Ridged Fields and Associated Features in Southern Campeche. *American Antiquity* 37: 228–239.

Spencer, Charles S.
  2000   Prehispanic Water Management and Agricultural Intensification in Mexico and Venezuela: Implications for Contemporary Ecological Planning. In *Imperfect Balance: Landscape Transformations in the Precolumbian Americas* (David L. Lentz, ed.): 147–178. Columbia University Press, New York.

Spinden, Herbert J.
  1913   *A Study of Maya Art: Its Subject Matter and Historical Development.* Memoirs of the Peabody Museum of Archaeology and Ethnology. Harvard University, Cambridge, Mass.

Stark, Barbara
  1999   Commentary: Ritual, Social Identity, and Cosmology: Hard Stones and Flowing Water. In *Social Patterns in Pre-Classic Mesoamerica* (David C. Grove and Rosemary A. Joyce, eds.): 301–317. Dumbarton Oaks, Washington, D.C.

Stephens, John L.

    1841 *Incidents of Travel in Central America, Chiapas, and Yucatan.* 2 vols. Harper, New York.

Stephens, Scott

    2006 The Essence of Life. *Cultural Survival Voices* 4(2): 1–2.

Stuart, David

    1997 The Hills Are Alive: Sacred Mountains among the Maya. *Symbols* (Spring): 13–17.

    2000 The Arrival of Strangers: Teotihuacan and Tollan in Classic Maya History. In *Mesoamerica's Classic Heritage: From Teotihuacan to the Aztecs* (David Carrasco, Lindsay Jones, and Scott Sessions, eds.): 465–513. University of Colorado Press, Boulder.

    2004 The Beginnings of the Copan Dynasty: A Review of the Hieroglyphic and Historical Evidence. In *Understanding Early Classic Copan* (Ellen E. Bell, Marcello A. Canuto, and Robert J. Sharer, eds.): 215–247. University of Pennsylvania Museum, Philadelphia.

    2005a A Foreign Past: The Writing and Representation of History on a Royal Ancestral Shrine at Copan. In *Copan: The History of an Ancient Maya Kingdom* (E. Wyllys Andrews and William L. Fash, eds.): 373–394. School of American Research Press, Santa Fe, N.M.

    2005b *The Inscriptions from Temple XIX at Palenque: A Commentary.* The Pre-Columbian Art Research Institute, San Francisco.

    2007 Reading the Water-lily Serpent as WITZ'. Electronic document, http://decipherment.wordpress.com/page/11/.

Stuart, David, and Stephen Houston

    1994 *Classic Maya Place Names.* Studies in Pre-Columbian Art and Archaeology 33. Dumbarton Oaks Research Library and Collection, Washington D.C.

Sugiyama, Saburo

    1993 Worldview Materialized in Teotihuacan, Mexico. *Latin American Antiquity* 4: 103–129.

Taube, Karl A.

    1992a The Iconography of Mirrors at Teotihuacan. In *Art, Ideology and the City of Teotihuacan* (Janet Berlo, ed.): 169–204. Dumbarton Oaks, Washington, D.C.

    1992b *The Major Gods of Ancient Yucatan.* Studies in Pre-Columbian Art and Archaeology 32. Dumbarton Oaks, Washington, D.C.

    1996 The Olmec Maize God. *RES* 29–30: 39–81.

    2004 Structure 10L-16 and Its Early Antecedents: Fire and Evocation and Resurrection of K'inich Yax K'uk' Mo'. In *Understanding Early Classic Copan* (Ellen Bell, Marcello Canuto, and Robert Sharer, eds.): 265–295. University of Pennsylvania Press, Philadelphia.

Thompson, J. Eric S.

    1952 Aquatic Symbols Common to Various Centers of the Classic Period in Meso-America. In *The Civilizations of Ancient America* (Sol Tax, ed.): 31–36. University of Chicago Press, Chicago.

1970   *Maya History and Religion*. University of Oklahoma Press, Norman.

Turner, Billie Lee, II, William Johnson, Gail Mahood, Fred Wiseman, and
     Jacke Poole

1983   Habitat y agricultura en la region de Copán. In *Introducción a la
       arqueología de Copán, Honduras, tomo I* (Claude F. Baudez, ed.): 35–142.
       Secretaria de Estado en el Despacho de Cultura y Turismo, Teguci-
       galpa, Honduras.

Uriarte, María Teresa

2006   The Teotihuacan Ballgame and the Beginning of Time. *Ancient
       Mesoamerica* 17: 17–38.

Valdés, Juan Antonio

1998   Kaminaljuyu, Guatemala: Descubrimientos recientes sobre poder y
       manejo hidráulico. In *Memorias del Tercer Congreso Internacional de
       Mayistas, 1995* (Juan Antonio Valdés, ed.): 752–770. Centro de Estudios
       Mayas, Universidad Nacional Autonoma de México, México.

Vogt, Evon Z.

1969   *Zinacantan: A Maya Community in the Highlands of Chiapas*. Harvard
       University Press, Cambridge, Mass.

1976   *Tortillas for the Gods: A Symbolic Analysis of Zinacanteco Rituals*. 1st ed.
       Harvard University Press, Cambridge, Mass.

1981   Some Aspects of the Sacred Geography of Highland Chiapas. In
       Mesoamerican Sites and World-Views (Elizabeth P. Benson, ed.): 119–142.
       Dumbarton Oaks, Washington, D.C.

1993   *Tortillas for the Gods: A Symbolic Analysis of Zinacanteco Rituals*. 2nd ed.
       University of Oklahoma Press, Norman.

Von Winning, Hasso

1985   *Two Maya Monuments in Yucatan: The Palace of the Stuccoes at Acanceh
       and the Temple of the Owls at Chichen Itzá*. Southwest Museum, Los
       Angeles.

Wilkerson, Jeffrey K.

1999   Public Buildings and Civic Spaces at Xochicalco, Morelos. In *Meso-
       american Architecture as Cultural Symbol* (Jeff Karl Kowalski, ed.):
       110–161. Oxford University Press, New York.

Wisdom, Charles

1940   *The Chorti Indians of Guatemala*. University of Chicago Press, Chicago.

Woodbury, Richard B., and James A. Neely

1972   Water Control Systems of the Tehuacan Valley. In *The Prehistory of the
       Tehuacan Valley*, vol. 4: *Chronology and Irrigation* (Frederick Johnson,
       ed.): 81–154. University of Texas Press, Austin.

NINE **SOCIAL IDENTITY AND COSMOLOGY AT EL TAJÍN**

Rex Koontz

NARRATIVE SCULPTURE AT EL TAJÍN

THE ARCHITECTURAL SCULPTURE of El Tajín, Veracruz, exhibits a rich corpus of figures, frames, and settings that repeat themselves in coherent groupings. The repetition across many of these images of figure and setting suggests that these images are narrative. Beginning with Ellen Spinden's (1933: 251) hypothesis that a group of ballcourt sculptures depicted the initiation of a young warrior into a warrior cult, most interpreters of Tajín sculpture have focused on deciphering the narrative logic of the sculptural groups. This focus has led to ever-refined narrative accounts, where current understandings of related lore (especially the ballgame and cosmology) have increased our understanding of the narrative elements and their relationships (García Payón 1959; Kampen 1972: 54–67; Tuggle 1968; Wilkerson 1984).

The search for narrative at El Tajín has often taken precedence over other iconographic problems, specifically, the question of who is acting and what sort of social world they inhabit. Kampen (1972: 55) first pointed out that assumptions about the narrative logic obscured the fact that we often did not know who was acting or how those actors were organized among themselves (see also Ládron de Guevara 1999: 75–79; Pascual Soto 1990). Important recent studies of Tajín (Castillo Peña 1995) and Classic Veracruz (Agüero Reyes n.d. [2004]) imagery have begun to address this problem through detailed analyses of discrete costume items and other features that distinguish the actors in these narratives.

This chapter recognizes the narrative content in its essentials as they are now understood, but it concentrates on distinguishing the different actors that made up Tajín monumental art. The iconographic study of the relationships among actors is developed here to shed light on how the patrons and designers of Tajín's imagery expressed their social organization. In short, in this chapter I tease out aspects of the social identities of Tajín elites as presented in the public sculpture. Social identity is used here in a broad sense that encompasses rank and office as well as more specific indigenous details of identity, such as deity associations and geographic or ethnic indices. Although the social identities depicted in the imagery and that seen in other material culture may not be perfectly congruent, analyzing these social identities in the imagery is an important step in documenting social practice at Tajín, as it has been for other areas of Mesoamerica (e.g., Carrasco 1971; Houston 1993: 127–136; Houston and Stuart 2001; Lind and Urcid 1983; Pohl 1994: 19–68; Ringle 2004).

A parallel approach, the worldview approach to Tajín imagery, privileges the analysis of motifs as elements in a coherent cosmology. Tuggle (1972) and Ladrón de Guevara (1999: 95–108) attempt to reconstruct the basic cosmological models operating at Tajín. This approach may be extremely productive when used in conjunction with an analysis of social identities, largely because these social identities were often embedded in cosmological models. I draw on this approach here and extend some prevalent ideas on Tajín cosmology, especially the place of the sacred mountain in that cosmology.

SINGLE-FIGURE FORMAT TO COMPLEX NARRATIVE

The creators of Tajín's public imagery were not always so interested in narrative. Before the apogee of Tajín in the Epiclassic (ca. A.D. 650–1000), the region's art showed more focus on single-figure compositions with much less narrative complexity (Proskouriakoff 1954: 89). Recent work by Pascual Soto (1998, 2000) has been instrumental in revealing these earlier tendencies. In the early (to A.D. 650) work, single figures are shown with elaborate costume and other signs of social identity, such as ceremonial pouches and staffs (Kampen 1972: fig. 18a–f; Pascual Soto 2000: 35). After ca. A.D. 650 Tajín art consistently depicts several differentiated characters in each composition. This is true for all media, including architectural sculpture (Kampen 1972: 55), decorated ceramics (du Solier 1945; Pascual Soto 2000), and painting (García Payón 1954; Ladrón de Guevara 1992). The development of multifigure compositions suggests that a chief function of Tajín art during its apogee was the communication of a host of social identities, clearly related to one another in complex narrative compositions.

DEITIES AND HUMANS AT EL TAJÍN

The basic distinction in Epiclassic Tajín iconography is between humans and the supernatural, indicated iconographically by the inclusion of a curving plate just above the eye of supernaturals, whereas the human eye is left unadorned. For example, in a scene from a key ballcourt panel (Figure 1), a principal deity is shown squatting, defined by the fang near the mouth,

FIGURE 1. El Tajín, South Ballcourt Panel 5, detail. Drawing by Daniela Koontz (after Kampen 1972: fig. 24).

FIGURE 2. El Tajín, South Ballcourt Panel 4, detail. Drawing by Daniela Koontz (after Kampen 1972: fig. 23).

the elongated upper lip, and the curving plate just above the eye (referred to as the "supraorbital plate" in this chapter). In another scene from the same ballcourt (Figure 2), two standing figures, both with unmarked eyes and therefore human, surround a central seated figure with eyes closed, the latter suggesting death. One would expect the participants of this rite to be human, as humans are also the participants in analogous presentations of the decapitation rite at the related Classic Veracruz site of Las Higueras (Sánchez Bonilla 1992: 149) and at the intriguingly similar presentation of the theme at Chichen Itza, Mexico (Taube 1994). In the midst of these humans is a supernatural, diving toward the sacrificial victim from the upper portions of the composition. This figure is fully skeletal, and therefore not human, and is marked by the supraorbital plate as a supernatural, as one would expect. Throughout Tajín imagery one finds other beings that are clearly not human, such as the disembodied eyes that fill many Tajín frames and friezes, are also given a supraorbital plate indicating their supernatural status. The same is true for many human-animal hybrids. In sum, the marking of Tajín supernaturals with a specific supraorbital plate and its absence on humans seems consistent throughout Tajín iconography.

SEVERED HEADS, DEITIES, AND HUMANS

If the iconographic markings around the eye are the chief way to differentiate between human and divine, then the severing of a human head in a ballcourt rite is the principal method of bridging the gap between these two states of being. This relationship can be seen most clearly by tracking the depiction of severed head offerings laid at the foot of rulers. In the image of the well-known scaffold sacrifice and beheading presided over by 13 Rabbit, a naturalistic human head is placed at the feet of the seated ruler (Figure 3). In another scene from that same program, two heads are laid at the feet of a personage seated on a bench (Figure 4). Although the ground line in the latter scene has been effaced, given the relationship of the heads to the seated figure, these must also be severed head offerings. Instead of a naturalistic rendering, however, these two heads are depicted with the supraorbital plate of supernaturals and a diagnostic hank of hair and extended upper lip. In a scene that serves to culminate the ballcourt decapitation sacrifice in the major ballcourt, this same supernatural with diagnostic hank of hair and extended upper lip is shown not as a disembodied head but as a full figure (Figure 5, lower center). Once again, the figure is placed at the feet of a seated figure. The wrapping around the mid-torso suggests this figure is somehow bundled, and the pose suggests a relation with the Chacmool figures found in several Mesoamerican contexts (García Payón 1973). Bundling and the Chacmool-related pose associate this figure with sacrificial imagery found across Mesoamerica

FIGURE 3. El Tajín, Mound of the Building Columns Sculpture 1, detail. Drawing by the author (after Wilkerson 1984: fig. 7).

FIGURE 4. El Tajín, Mound of the Building Columns Sculpture 5, detail. Drawing by the author (after Kampen 1972: fig. 33c).

FIGURE 5. El Tajín, South Ballcourt Panel 6, detail. Drawing by Daniela Koontz (after Kampen 1972: fig. 25, and on-site observations).

FIGURE 6. El Tajín, Mound of the Building Columns Sculpture 8, detail. Drawing by Daniela Koontz (after Castillo Peña 1995: pieza 017).

during this period (Miller and Samoya 1998: 60–67). More specifically, in the iconographic system of Tajín this supernatural is the transformed embodiment of the severed head offering, as seen above.

INVESTITURE AND DECAPITATION AT TAJÍN

This severed head offering and its transformed embodiment is placed in clear ritual and political contexts at the site. Specifically, the severed head is offered during rites of political investiture (Koontz n.d. [1994]). The iconographic case for investiture is complex and involves the narrative readings of several Tajín programs, but the basic iconographic data are these: as the culmination of two principal Tajín sacrificial narratives, the main deity at Tajín donates a baton and a piece of cloth to the human (Figures 5, 6). Using several Classic Veracruz images as well as general Mesoamerican patterns as analogs, this donation may be interpreted as the investiture into political power of the human supplicant. Decapitation sacrifice is clearly central to the rites necessary to obtain political power from the gods, as evidenced by the bundled severed head offering in Figure 5, among other evidence.

When decapitation sacrifice is located in a ballcourt, figures wearing yokes and *palmas* (vertically oriented stone objects attached to yoke) oversee the decapitation rite (Wilkerson 1984: figs. 13–15; see Figure 2). These

FIGURE 7. El Tajín, Mound of the Building Columns Sculpture 6, detail. Drawing by the author (after Castillo Peña 1995: pieza 011).

same yoke-wearing figures oversee or are chief participants in other rites surrounding power at El Tajín, both inside the ballcourt and out of it. In a sculpture (Figure 7) from the Mound of the Building Columns, yoke-wearers surround the figure 13 Rabbit at the left, who will eventually accede to political power in this sequence and here also sports a yoke-*palma* combination. Given that there are several individualized figures wearing yokes in all these scenes, it is not possible that only the paramount is depicted. Instead, the wearing of yokes must be a more general marking for an elite group that includes but is not limited to the ruler.

Earlier treatments of these Tajín yoke-wearing figures defined their social identity largely in relation to the ballgame. That these figures have a direct link to the Mesoamerican rubber ballgame is now beyond doubt (Ekholm 1946, 1949), although it is still unclear how yokes and other finely carved stone accoutrements would have functioned in an actual game (de Vries 1991; Scott 2001; Thompson 1941). The playing of the game by yoke-wearers is never illustrated in public imagery at Tajín, making it difficult to be specific about the type of ballgame played there or how the playing of the game was integrated with the ritualism of the yoke-wearers.[1] Instead, images of yoke-wearers in public space show them in sacrificial and other rites. Analyses of these rites are often placed in relation to current understandings of the Mesoamerican ballgame. An especially productive example of such an analysis is the identification of decapitation sacrifice in the Tajín imagery and its links to ballgame lore across Mesoamerica as well as to yoke-wearers at the site (Wilkerson 1984). Because here I am interested in the specific and perhaps distinct social practices that accompanied such ritualism at Tajín and not in widespread principles of ballgame iconography, the focus below is on the specific associations of ritual and identity embedded in Tajín's public imagery.

FIGURE 8. El Tajín, South Ballcourt Panel 5, detail of upper register. Drawing by Daniela Koontz (after Kampen 1972: fig. 24).

HORIZONTALLY POSED FIGURES AT EL TAJÍN AND THE MIXTEC *YAHA YAHUI*

To further delineate the social identity of the yoke-wearers, I turn to a figure that has been of interest to Tajín iconographers for some time. Directly above the central ballcourt panel and given its own frame is a prone figure, stomach down (Figure 8). The composition uses a form of split representation in which there are two bodies represented, one on each side of the central face.

This figure has long been identified as a supernatural because of the split representation and the buccal mask (García Payón 1973; Ladrón de Guevara 1999: 111–112). This form of buccal mask is an ancient motif in Classic Veracruz iconography, appearing on figures by the Late Formative (Medellín Zenil 1957). The bill is often identified with that of the duck but may be more cautiously characterized as a reference to the bill of any number of diving waterfowl (O'Mack 1991). The great majority of these early figures are humans wearing the deity mask, as in the Tajín example with the clearly marked almond eye (Figure 8), thus suggesting a deity impersonator rather than a deity. The Tuxtla Statuette, dated to ca. A.D. 162 and the most famous early example of this complex, is very likely also a masked and costumed human figure (Taube 2004: 72), as are several examples cited by Medellín Zenil (1957).

Ladrón de Guevara (1999: 104) associated this figure with the Late Postclassic deity Quetzalcoatl in his guise as Ehecatl because of the resemblance of the buccal masks that serve as a diagnostic trait for each figure. Ehecatl is widely recognized as a wind deity. Much closer in time to the Tajín example, a Western Maya noble is shown playing ball in the guise of the Wind Deity (Stuart et al. 1999), and this same Wind God, or more precisely a human impersonator, is shown wearing a heavy belt indicative of ballplayers in the Bonampak murals (Miller 2001: 86). This association of ballcourts and wind deities in Epiclassic Mesoamerica deserves further research, but for the purpose of this argument the Maya examples clearly show the impersonation of a wind god by a human. The same pattern of deity impersonation may be seen at Tajín and in other Classic Veracruz

FIGURE 9. El Tajín, panel from the area of the Pyramid of the Niches, detail. Drawing by the author (after Castillo Peña 1995: pieza 182).

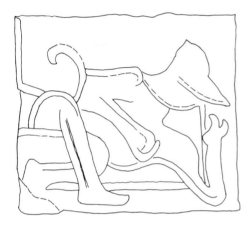

FIGURE 10. El Tajín, panel from the area of the Pyramid of the Niches, detail. Drawing by the author (after Castillo Peña 1995: pieza 182).

contexts, with the human eyes surmounting the waterfowl bill mask in numerous examples. Thus the Tajín figure is an impersonator of an age-old Classic Veracruz deity who is based on diving waterfowl and is somehow related to Classic Maya and Late Postclassic wind gods.

In addition to the general characteristics outlined above, several fundamental aspects of this horizontal figure emerge only through comparisons with other Tajín imagery. The figure is related to the composition below but is not part of it, as no part of this figure breaks the frame into the scene below. The element clearly connecting this upper figure with the lower scene appears rolled on the figure's arms. The same cloth object is also depicted as rolled over the arm of the deity in the scene of investiture immediately below the horizontal figure (see Figure 5). As discussed above, the cloth is one of two objects central to Tajín rites of political investiture, thus tying this upper figure directly to the rites of power transfer imaged below.

The Tajín ballcourt figure strikes a very specific pose—horizontal, with one leg bent and one leg straight—that may be found in other contexts at the site. As Ladrón de Guevara (1999: 116–117) has pointed out, another sculpture was recently unearthed at Tajín with a pose identical to the prone ballcourt figure (Figure 9). Here the horizontal figure, who is otherwise clearly human, is given claws on the hands and feet. Directly adjacent to this figure, on one of the short sides of the monument (Figure 10), is another carved figure, again anthropomorphic and again with claws instead of human hands. The face and any body detail on this latter figure have long been effaced. Instead of the horizontal posture seen on the long side of the monument, this figure is seated with one knee raised. This very particular seated posture is seen throughout Tajín, especially in a long frieze associated with the Pyramid of the Niches, a typical example of which is shown in Figure 11 (see also Kampen 1972: fig. 11c–k and Castillo Peña 1995: pieza 078). These seated figures are almost always anthropomorphic figures with zoomorphic heads. The horizontal figure above the ballcourt may then be

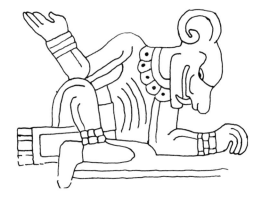

FIGURE 11. El Tajín, Pyramid of
the Niches frieze. Drawing by the
author (after Kampen 1972: fig. 11e).

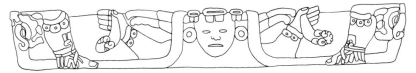

FIGURE 12. Santa Luisa, region of El Tajín, roll-out of carved yoke from Burial
15. Drawing by the author (after Wilkerson 1990: 166).

seen as part of a specific iconographic complex at Tajín that also includes
a seated figure with a raised knee and a zoomorphic aspect. There are
other examples of horizontal figures paired with the uniquely posed seated
figures in Tajín art (Kampen 1972: fig. 11i).

Importantly, this same combination of horizontal figure and seated
figure has been identified as a major motif on numerous Classic Veracruz
yokes. The horizontal figure, when seen on yokes, consists of the frontal
head shown at the center of the "U" shape, and the body in split representation (depicted or implied) on either arm of the yoke (Sarro n.d. [1995]:
144–152). The other element of the pair, the seated figure, is shown with
the particular raised-knee posture in the leg on the end of each yoke arm
(Proskouriakoff 1954: fig. 1; Figure 12). The example seen in Figure 12 is
one of a handful of yokes excavated from the Tajín region (Wilkerson n.d.
[1972]: 728–735), placing this imagery firmly in the time and place of the
Tajín ballcourt figure. Wilkerson (1984: 125) first noted that the compositional format of the horizontal figure above the ballcourt panel was similar
to the central figure found on numerous yokes. Sarro (n.d. [1995]: 144–152)
has greatly extended this insight to show that much of the imagery in the
smaller Tajín ballcourts is based on the prone figure and accompanying
yoke imagery. Sarro's important iconographic insight demonstrates that
the horizontally posed figure is a key iconographic element in several Tajín
ballcourts and the main figure on an important group of yokes.

Other Mesoamerican image systems depict an analogous recumbent
figure. The best documented of these is the Late Postclassic Mixtec, who

FIGURE 13. Codex Nuttall, p. 19,
detail. Drawing by the author
(after Pohl 1994: fig. 14).

depicted a horizontally posed figure with the same zoomorphic attributes
(claws) seen at Tajín (Figure 13; cf. Figure 9). Pohl (1994: 42–64), following
initial work by Smith (1973: 60–64), has identified this figure with a Mixtec
administrative office charged specifically with overseeing human sacrifice
and important aspects of the economy. In Mixtec, this office was called
yaha yahui, or "wizard or impersonator who flew through the air." The
emphasis on flying would explain the insistence on the horizontal position,
often hovering above the ground line, in the images from the Mixteca
(Smith 1973: 63) as well as those from Tajín. I think the similarity between
these figures may go even deeper, however, for the Mixtec definition insists
on the ability of this official to impersonate. In the Tajín examples shown
in the figures the human is often given animal traits (waterfowl bills, feline
claws) that likely indicate the impersonation of a supernatural power, and
thus I refer to this figure as the "flying impersonator."

The ability to impersonate these beings at Tajín may have been linked
to the ability to manifest relevant spirit entities. This linkage is likely the
meaning of the seated figure with raised knee, which is found directly
associated with the flying impersonator both in the architectural sculpture
of Tajín and on the yoke imagery (see Figures 9–12). That this leg pose
indicates another entity on the yoke, and not simply an attachment to the
central yoke figure, is strongly suggested by the close association of separate
raised-knee and flying-impersonator figures on several Tajín sculptures and
the independent existence of the former figure elsewhere. When shown
in full, Tajín imagery consistently depicts this figure as a composite of an
anthropomorphic body and zoomorphic head. The example in Figure 11
may be feline, but other zoomorphs abound (Kampen 1972: figs. 11c–k).
Although rare at Tajín outside of this raised-knee figure (but recall the

animal traits masked or worn by the flying figure above), composite human-animal figures are found in several areas and periods of Mesoamerican art, and most scholars agree they are somehow involved in the manifestation of supernatural entities or powers.

Mesoamerican ideas surrounding the manifestation of the supernatural in this context are necessarily complex, but I focus here on a single aspect that has been especially well documented for the Classic Maya: the intimate relationship between elite identity and the manifestation of the supernatural through these composite figures. In their account of the decipherment of the Classic Maya term for such manifestations, Houston and Stuart (1989) note that the inscriptions specify distinct supernatural entities were manifested by Maya lords and that these entities were "possessed" by the lord or the polity. For the Classic Maya, it seems that the ability to manifest these entities was directly tied to elite political power at a particular place. The Postclassic Mixtec *yaha yahui* officials were similarly concerned with manifesting supernatural entities, such as balls of light and other phenomena, as a direct corollary of their office (Pohl 1994: 44). In short, in Mesoamerica the manifestation of supernatural entities was sometimes considered a fundamental aspect of a particular political office. The flying impersonator at Tajín would be another of these offices, and the raised-knee posture and human-animal composite associated so closely with this figure acted as an index of the ability to manifest spirits.

Traditionally the raised-knee posture has been related to the batrachian earth monster depicted on numerous earlier yokes (Covarrubias 1957: 171–183; Wilkerson 1991: 56). The earliest firmly dated carved yokes (Cuevas 1975) show this creature with simplified but clearly legible toad-like hind legs in the same position as the later human leg with raised knee, while the frontal face of these early yokes is a generalized toad. It is likely that the root of the raised-knee posture may be found in these early batrachian yokes, and it may even be that the ability to manifest spirits was associated with the ritual ingestion of *Bufo marinus* toxins, as Kennedy (1982: 278) suggested, but the association with the batrachian does not fully explain the move to anthropomorphize this figure both in Classic Veracruz yokes and Tajín monumental architectural sculpture. A history of yoke form and function remains a desideratum of Classic Veracruz studies, but until one is produced any description of the differences between earlier batrachian and the later anthropomorphic iconography will remain a sketch. What is important to note here is that the relation between manifesting spirits and impersonation found in the Tajín flying-impersonator imagery is a close one in several areas of Mesoamerica. I have shown that the specific analogy that works best with the Tajín material is the Postclassic Mixtec *yaha yahui*, where flight, spirit manifestation, and impersonation are intimately intertwined and depicted in ways that closely parallel the Tajín imagery.

Just as important as the similarities in flight and impersonation is the sacrificial context in which these flying-impersonator figures appear in both the Tajín and Mixtec traditions. The key example of the flying impersonator at Tajín is placed in the ballcourt program that specifically outlines the rites of ballcourt decapitation sacrifice. The figure also appears on yokes that are main items of dress in the ballcourt decapitation ceremonies. Other flying impersonators at Tajín (see Figure 9) are marked by feline claws that are related to sacrifice and sacrificial offices across Mesoamerica. For the Mixtec *yaha yahui*, Pohl (1994: 44–51) has shown that a chief function of the group was to oversee sacrifice.

The control of sacrifice placed these flying-impersonator figures in a central political position in both the Tajín and Mixtec examples, even though in both cases they are not shown as the paramount ruler and their status is clearly that of secondary elites. Pohl (1994) discusses this point at length for the *yaha yahui*, noting that although the figure served as intercessor to the ancestral elite and was instrumental in the founding of discrete political territory, a *yaha yahui* was never shown ruling the territory.[2] The Tajín case is even more clear-cut: the figure controls one of the chief insignia of rulership in the cloth strip shown wrapped around the arm (see Figure 8) or held in the hands (Kampen 1978: 123–124), but the cloth is never received or worn by this figure.

YOKES, FLYING IMPERSONATORS, FINE CARVING, AND ELITE ADMINISTRATION

The yokes on which the flying impersonators are carved are some of the most intricately worked objects of fine stone produced in the Tajín realm specifically and in Classic Veracruz culture more generally. These objects are often characterized as much too bulky and heavy for the playing of the ballgame (de Vries 1991; Ekholm 1946; Thompson 1941), but whether they could be used in the ballgame may not have been the main point. Even today relatively little is known about the Classic Veracruz ballgame, given the paucity of active ballgame representations in the region. Instead of focusing on their use in the ballgame, Miller (2001: 79) points out that the objects associated with the ballgame focus to an unusual extent on precious, permanent materials and lavish carving, even when compared to other Mesoamerican elite markers. Although the attribution of most yokes to a particular region or time is notoriously complex, I would add that this is particularly true of yokes with a connection, either archaeological (Wilkerson 1971) or stylistic, to the Tajín realm.

It is their exorbitant value in both materials and craftsmanship that was an important—perhaps the crucial—aspect of the Classic Veracruz yoke tradition. These objects were heirloomed; buried with elite owners

(Lothrop 1923; Medellín Zenil 1960: 103; Palacios 1943; Wilkerson 1971); broken in dedication or termination rituals; produced in miniature replicas (Borhegyi 1969); and if Wilkerson (1990: 166) is right in assuming that some were recarved, kept for centuries and modified as changing style and subject warranted. When viewed from the spotty but consistent archaeological record, these portable stone works were treated as one of the most valuable elite commodities in Classic Veracruz.

What made these yokes so valuable? As is well known, the initial iconographic breakthrough on these objects came with their association to the ballgame, either as effigy sculptures of ballgame equipment or as actual ballgame gear (Ekholm 1946; Lothrop 1923). Although it is clear that the relation with the ballgame gave the objects some importance, it is doubtful that this tie fully explains the value accorded to these objects. No yoke-wearer at Tajín is ever represented playing the game, nor does yoke imagery show the game in action. The iconographic silence surrounding the game suggests that the objects designated more than ballplayers. I have argued above that yoke ownership indicated a particular social identity in an elite administrative class that probably played ball but certainly oversaw sacrifice and was responsible for performing certain spirit manifestations. Although admittedly little direct archaeological evidence exists for such a group, the only complete carved yoke found in situ in the Tajín region (see Figure 12) was in a burial of just such a regional elite personage (Wilkerson n.d. [1972]: 729–732). Here the bundled, flexed body of an adult male was seated directly on top of the yoke. The finely carved yoke depicts the figure of the flying impersonator, firmly tying not only yoke wearing but also the flying figure to the Tajín regional elite. Some jade and ceramic offerings were placed beside the figure, and the whole was covered with cinnabar.

The ownership of particular items as indicators of rank and office is certainly not foreign to Mesoamerica. In addition to the royal regalia found throughout the area as the sign of rulership, other offices could also be dependent on the acquisition of particular objects (Klein 1988). Given the value of the raw material from which these yokes were made, the significant investment in craftsmanship (especially those found near Tajín or with Tajín stylistic relations), their treatment in burials, and above all the iconographic associations they display, I would argue that yokes from the Tajín region are the material indicator or insignia of the sacrificial administrator class identified above with the flying impersonators.

The flying-impersonator iconographic complex outlined above for the yoke-wearers may now be seen in conjunction with the traditional view of these figures as ballplayers. The nexus of ballplayer and flying impersonator in this analysis is ballgame decapitation sacrifice, which could conceivably involve both ballplayers and the flying impersonators who oversaw sacrifice. Further, the yoke-wearers conceptualized as deity impersonators in addition to ballplayers may help explain the insistence throughout later Classic Veracruz art on the victims of ballcourt decapitation sacrifice being fully clothed in the yoke (and often an attached *palma*) as they are sacrificed. This elaborate costume cannot be ascribed simply to ballplaying. As shown above, it is unclear whether the decorated stone yoke was worn during the game, and all major commentators agree that the *palma* could not have been worn in play. Further, nearly all other sacrificial victims in this tradition are shown as stripped or with a minimum of clothing and adornment. However, Mesoamerican ritual practice is rife with examples of the sacrificial victim dressed with elements related to a deity before sacrifice (Klein 2000), especially if they were seen as manifesting that deity during ritual (López Austin 1993: 125). This practice would explain the need to elaborately dress the ballcourt sacrifice victim in the costume of a deity impersonator that also had associations with the ballgame.

In sum, Tajín yoke-wearers may now be directly related to the flying-impersonator figures through the latter's appearance on carved yokes, including an example known to be from the Tajín realm during this period. These flying impersonators could be interpreted as part of an elite administrative group, and the yokes the group wore and on which they were represented functioned as their insignia. The waterfowl-billed flying impersonator (see Figure 8) may be seen as a specific office inside this group, keeping the cloth so important to investiture rituals throughout Tajín; other flying impersonators with feline or other traits may have had associated roles overseeing sacrifice. It is in the role of sacrificer that the flying-impersonator and the ballplayer roles likely intersected for the yoke-wearers.

PALMA IMAGERY AND FLYING IMPERSONATORS

In nearly all cases, Tajín yoke-wearers are shown with a *palma* attached to the yoke. The imagery found on Classic Veracruz *palmas*, like that of the yokes, may be shown to relate directly to the office overseeing sacrifice and the transfer of power. A good example of sacrifice and investiture iconography may be found in the well-known *palma* from Coatepec, Veracruz (Figure 14). Like many *palmas*, this piece is carved on two sides that may be related to each other as a narrative. On one side (Figure 14, right) is the depiction of an avian impersonator holding a lanceolate blade of sacrifice in one hand and a severed head in the other. The beads that hang from the avian headdress identify this figure as a vulture impersonator seen throughout Classic Veracruz imagery (Kampen 1978). On the other side (Figure 14, left) a figure wears a cape and holds a baton. The investiture imagery of 13 Rabbit at El Tajín exhibits both the baton and cape (cf. Figure 6), strongly suggesting that this side of the Coatepec *palma* also illustrates

FIGURE 14. Coatepec, Veracruz, *palma* with scenes of decapitation sacrifice and investiture (from Proskouriakoff 1954: fig. 6, *palma* 5).

an investiture scene. When the two sides are taken together, the narrative resembles that of Tajín investiture: decapitation sacrifice leads to the investiture of the paramount. Further, the wearing of this *palma* with a yoke would mark the elite group that oversaw these ceremonies, as argued above. This *palma* iconography adds a social identity to our roster, one that is closely related to the flying impersonator: that of vulture impersonator and sacrificer, an office seen not only on this *palma* but also throughout the imagery of Tajín (see Kampen 1972: figs. 21, 34d; Wilkerson 1990: 171).

In addition to similarities in iconographic associations, *palmas*, like yokes, could be used as important dedicatory materials (Arellanos Melgarejo and Beauregard García 1981) and in elite burials (Wilkerson 1990: 171). Perhaps even more than the finely carved stone yokes, the extended shape and finely finished detailing of these objects do not lend themselves to ballgame play (Ekholm 1949) but instead suggest ritual use and indication of status and office. This is also the message of the inscribed imagery.

It is not surprising that *palma* iconography would follow Tajín convention rather closely, as the *palma* is specifically related to Tajín visual culture. Proskouriakoff (1954: 90) noted that Tajín art had an especially close relationship with the figural style of the *palma*, that the two shared a rather late position in the chronology, and that the distribution of the Classic Veracruz *palma* is restricted to the region of Xalapa north to Tajín.[3] The *palma* is thus more closely allied to Tajín visual culture in time and space, unlike the yoke, which is found throughout Classic Veracruz territory and history. Although *palmas* may contain heraldic single-figure compositions, numerous examples exhibit multifigure narrative, as seen in the abovementioned Coatepec *palma* as well as in numerous other examples of the form (Kampen 1978). This narrative structure is unlike the simpler yoke compositions. The tendency toward narrative is a characteristic of Tajín art in general and seems to be associated with the need to detail several social identities in important ritual and political contexts. The Coatepec *palma* may be interpreted as just such a mapping of social identities in relation to one another, specifically of the offices and rites that surrounded the transfer of power.

SKULL PLACE AND FLOWERING MAGUEY MOUNTAIN

A key group of social identities identified above are shown in direct relation to decapitation sacrifice and the transfer of political power. As I noted at the beginning of this chapter, the iconography of these figures consistently points to a larger context through the addition of architectural and landscape features. I now turn to the meaning of the natural and built landscape that framed the act and thus provided an important context for the yoke-wearers and other actors in the ballcourt. The ballcourt program locates the decapitation in the center of the court (Wilkerson 1984), as does a cognate image in the neighboring Central Plaza. Certainly the symbolic associations grouped around the center of the Tajín ballcourt played an important role in the meaning of the act.

In an earlier work (Koontz 2002) I argued that the numerous depictions of skulls around the center of the court identified that locale as a Place of the Skull. In addition to this motif, the center of the Tajín ballcourt is marked by an especially complex toponym seen in both central panels. Here a structure filled with liquid sits at the base of a mountain covered with maguey (*Agave* sp.) plants, many in full flower (see Figure 5). García Payón (1973: 34–53) associated these plants with the production of pulque, a mildly intoxicating beverage made from maguey sap that was used as an important feasting beverage in several areas of Mesoamerica by at least the Classic period (Miller and Taube 1993: 138). In an important discussion of the El Tajín mountain imagery, Wilkerson (1984: 126) extended the pulque reference by comparing the El Tajín Flowering Maguey Mountain to the Nahuatl Pozonaltepetl (Mountain of Foam), the place of pulque's origin in Late Postclassic narratives. Wilkerson viewed the El Tajín scene as the origin of a pulque cult that was crucial to El Tajín and Classic Veracruz culture. In both the García Payón and Wilkerson interpretations, the main meaning of the central scenes is the acquisition of pulque by humans, with the central liquid-filled structure identified as a pulque vat that was the original storehouse of the liquid.

Because these pulque interpretations are based largely on analogies with sixteenth-century central Mexican sources in Nahuatl, it may be helpful to examine those sources more closely and analyze the degree to which they relate to the much earlier El Tajín narratives. By far the most important Nahuatl narrative for my purpose is the origin of pulque recounted by central Mexican informants to Sahagún (1950–82, bk. 10: 194–195). In this passage Mayahuel (the Goddess of Pulque) and related deities prepare the first batch of pulque on Mount Chichinauhia, which is then renamed Pozonaltepetl in commemoration of the froth on the head of the drink. The informants seem to locate the discovery of pulque and Pozonaltepetl in Tamoanchan, a paradise founded after the building of the pyramids of Teotihuacan.

In a related version of the origin of maguey (*Histoyre du Mechique*), Ehecatl (Wind God; avatar of Quetzalcoatl) discovers Mayahuel in the sky and brings her to earth. Once on the ground the two deities transform into intertwined trees (Garibay 1965: 106–107). Relatives of Mayahuel (the Tzitzimime) find she is missing, descend from the sky, tear her apart, and eat her. The remaining bones of Mayahuel were collected by Ehecatl and buried at Tamoanchan, and from these bones maguey grew.

Most important for my purposes here, in the *Histoyre du Mechique* the origin of pulque is immediately preceded by the creation of humans by Ehecatl. Here Ehecatl perforates his tongue to let blood on the bones of a previous generation of humans (Garibay 1965: 106). In another variant of the creation of humans (*Leyenda de los Soles*), Quetzalcoatl bleeds not his tongue but his penis on the bones (Bierhorst 1992: 146), closely mirroring an El Tajín image of the deity perforating his penis to create humans (Delhalle and Luykx 1986; Taube 1986). The Tajín deity sacrifices at Flowering Maguey Mountain, but the location in the Nahuatl version is Tamoanchan.

FLOWERING MAGUEY MOUNTAIN
AS A PRE-COLUMBIAN PARADISE

The origins of pulque and humanity relate El Tajín's Flowering Maguey Mountain and Nahuatl narratives of Tamoanchan (Delhalle and Luykx 1986, 1998), although the resemblance is not exact. A major problem with the meaning of pulque in the El Tajín narratives is the insistence by the El Tajín artists on the flowering state of the major maguey plants. Flowering maguey is not suitable for pulque production—the budding flower of the plant must be cut just as it begins to sprout so that the sap may be harvested (Parsons 2001: 6). Although there are a few maguey plants in the El Tajín panels depicted without flowers—and thus are candidates for sap harvesting and pulque production—the central plants are shown with large, developed flower stalks. The flowering plants take up a majority of the compositional field inside the outlines of the mountain. Although some reference to pulque is probable, it is obvious that the designers of the El Tajín program were alluding to more than just the production of pulque by focusing on the flowering maguey.

Despite the problem with a pulque interpretation, the nature of the Nahuatl Tamoanchan may still help in the interpretation of El Tajín's Flowering Maguey Mountain. As discussed above, the El Tajín mountain and Tamoanchan environments are linked through their sharing of the episodes depicting the origin of pulque and the creation of humanity. More basically, however, they share a flowery, fecund nature. Tamoanchan is where the gods uncover human sustenance, in the form not only of maguey as in the versions above, but also of maize. Descriptions of Tamoanchan often emphasize the floral, paradisal nature of the place (López Austin 1997; Nicholson 1971: 403). Although the etymology of Tamoanchan itself has been debated and may be a loan from Huastec (Jiménez Moreno 1942: 132) or Western Maya (Thompson 1971: 115), other Nahuatl appellations for the place make clear its floral associations: Xochitl Icacan (Where the Flowers Arise), Xochincuahuitl (Flowering Tree), and Tonacaxochincuahuitl (Flowery Tree of Our Sustenance; López Austin 1997: 104). It is to this ideal "flowery" place, and not to pulque production, that the El Tajín designers are calling attention when they allow much of the maguey to flower promiscuously.

In an important statement on the iconography of this flowery Pre-Columbian paradise, Taube (2004) has shown that earlier Mesoamerican cultures developed the concept of a Flower Mountain as a core element of the paradisal environment. In Classic Teotihuacan as well as Classic Maya visual culture, this motif was often represented simply as a mountain with flowers emerging. More complex images included particular "breath" serpents emerging from the mountain or a floral headband attached to the personified mountain glyph. This paradise was the residence of the honored dead and the station of the breath soul, a crucial constituent of personhood (López Austin 1997: 163). López Austin (1997: 272–274) also identified flowering-tree imagery associated with a mountain or cave at Teotihuacan and convincingly linked these to later Nahuatl conceptions of Tamoanchan. What is important here is the presence of an earlier Classic tradition of flowering-mountain images that serve in much the same iconographic niche—that of a flowering, fecund paradisal mountain—as the Flowering Maguey Mountain at El Tajín. Thus El Tajín's Flowering Maguey Mountain takes its place between the earlier renditions of the paradisal flowering mountains identified by López Austin and Taube for the Classic cultures and Postclassic Nahuatl visions of Tamoanchan.

If the El Tajín mountain is a flowering mountain of paradise in the Mesoamerican tradition, then how does the structure full of liquid at the

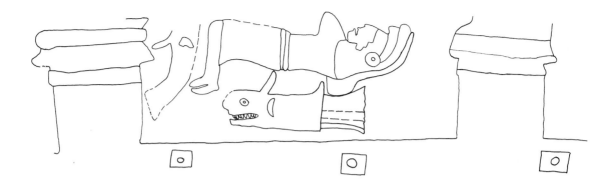

FIGURE 15. Las Higueras, Veracruz, Structure 1 murals, detail. Drawing by the author (after the photograph in Sánchez Bonilla 1993: 152).

base of the mountain fit into such an environment? There is no mention of such a structure in the Nahuatl narratives on Tamoanchan. Earlier, pulque-based interpretations of the scene identified the structure as a pulque vat. I (Koontz 2002) have argued that instead of pulque the structure contains water, consonant with the Place of the Skull associations for the center of this court (see also Taube 1986: 54). There are several other lines of evidence that suggest water is the liquid indicated, the first of which is the presence of the fish-man in the pool of liquid. Not only is the fish indicative of water, but also the related narrative in which humans are transformed into fish during a cataclysmic flood points to water as the liquid substance. Another argument for water is found in the imagery at Las Higueras, where a closely related Classic Veracruz mural program describes several of the same rites seen at El Tajín, including ballcourt decapitation (Sánchez Bonilla 1992: 152). Here a fish is associated with an anthropomorphic figure in a reclining position largely similar though not identical to the reclining figure in the El Tajín central panel (Figure 15). Further, reclining figure and fish are both framed by architectural forms not unlike the temple structure seen at El Tajín, and between the forms is clearly a mass of blue water. These examples suggest that the imagery at the center of Tajín's major ballcourt contains not only a flowering mountain but also pooled water.

The combination of flowering mountain and water source in the center of the ballcourt may have been reproduced monumentally in the plan of the central core. Cortés Hernández (1989) argued that a drainage system linked the modified hill on which Tajín Chico and the Mound of the Building Columns rest with the Great Xicalcoliuhqui below (Figure 16). The latter is a monumental construction based on the outline of the step fret. In the reconstruction of the drainage system by Cortés Hernández, the water emptied into the area of the Great Xicalcoliuhqui defined by the bottom corner of the fret. Water running off the hill was caught in this area by the barrier of the Great Xicalcoliuhqui, creating an artificial swamp. Earlier

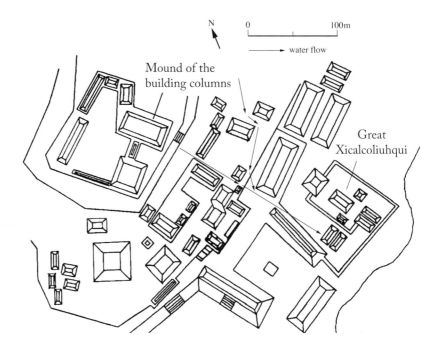

FIGURE 16. Map of
water drainage from
Tajín Chico to the
Great Xicalcoliuhqui.
Drawing by the author
(adapted from Cortés
Hernández 1989: fig. 2).

Veracruz cultures had long integrated springs or created artificial ponds
to serve as symbols of the sacrality and meaning inherent in the urban
landscape (Stark 1999: 308–309). At Tajín, a small ballcourt, too small to
be of any use except to mark the landscape, stood near the spot where
the water discharged into the lower area from above, perhaps to establish
this connection between the ballcourt and a water source. In this way the
ensemble of modified hill (Tajín Chico and the Mound of the Building
Columns) and water catchment complex (Great Xicalcoliuhqui) may be
seen as a monumental realization of the sacred geography described in the
center of the ballcourt, where the Flowering Maguey Mountain abutted a
structure filled with water and was directly associated with the ballcourt.
In short, the plan of a good portion of central Tajín may be structured by
this understanding of sacred mountains and water ballcourts, a variation
on the theme of pyramids and artificial ponds seen throughout ancient
Veracruz (Stark 1999: 304–305).

A final consideration regarding the Flowering Maguey Mountain at El
Tajín is the absence of maguey in the immediate El Tajín region. Although
a few species of agave may be found on the flanks of the Sierra Madre not
far from El Tajín, pulque-producing maguey is a Highland Mexican plant,
found above 1,800 m (El Tajín is at about 300 m). Let us assume for this
argument that the nonflowering maguey depicted is the pulque-producing
variety, a reasonable assumption that many previous researchers have made.
If so, then how did such an obvious exotic come to take a central role in El

Tajín's sacred landscape—specifically, the landscape of human origin and the place of political accession?

One important hypothesis accounts for the presence of maguey in El Tajín imagery by deriving it from Teotihuacan (Taube 1986). In this reading, other Mesoamerican elites used Teotihuacan-related elements (symbols and flora) as legitimating devices. Interestingly, an image has been unearthed recently at Teotihuacan that shows maguey ritualism similar to that found later at Tajín (Rivas Castro 2001). That said, little is known about the relationship of El Tajín and Teotihuacan. A particular foreign ceramic type popular at Teotihuacan, Lustrous Ware, has often been used to link the two sites, but the source of this type is not yet known and is probably not El Tajín itself (Cowgill 2003: 325; Daneels 1997: 149). Most elements of early El Tajín culture that do show some relation with Teotihuacan, such as tripod vases, seem to filter that relation through the regional Classic Veracruz culture (Pascual Soto 2000). In short, El Tajín as we know it is largely a post-Teotihuacan phenomenon and as such may have had less impetus to use Teotihuacan as a legitimator than earlier Maya regimes with direct connections to the metropolis (Stuart 2000).

Although the relation with Teotihuacan is still unclear and was probably not as strong as once believed, El Tajín at its apogee did have a relationship with highland peoples who could have provided a direct connection with maguey and pulque. The site of Yohualichan, in the Sierra de Puebla but only 60 km west of El Tajín, has long been linked to El Tajín through its strikingly similar use of the flying cornice, niche, and ballcourts (Palacios 1926) as well as strong similarities in fine ceramics (García Payón 1971: 532). These two sites were not interacting isolates, for the entire area between Tajín and Yohualichan exhibits the most homogenous material culture in the Classic Veracruz world (Daneels n.d.). Yohualichan sits at an elevation of only 600 m, but the region currently abounds in agave, the flowers of which are widely used in religious ritual in the area (Pascual Soto 1990: 155). Farther west in Puebla and squarely within the pulque- and maguey-producing region, García Cook (1981: 266) identified a site with strong connections to El Tajín that he dated to the apogee of El Tajín and Yohualichan. Napatecuhtlan (Medellín Zenil 1960: 112–113), also in a pulque-producing region in Puebla, is an important Tajín-related site with correspondences in all major ceramic types (Krotser 1981: 180) and clear links to Tajín sculptural style (Wilkerson 1990: 169–170). Farther north and east, Gaxiola González (1999: 55–59) has shown that the fine ceramics of Huapalcalco in the valley of Tulancingo, Hidalgo, are very similar to several of the most important elite types at El Tajín. These data, when taken together, suggest that El Tajín created a relationship with a string of sites west into the highlands of Hidalgo and Puebla (Pascual Soto 1998).

These areas would have produced pulque and other maguey products that could have been imported to the lowland center as trade or tribute items. The close similarities between the architecture and fine ceramics of El Tajín and Yohualichan may indicate that the latter was an El Tajín outpost and a staging area for these highland-lowland interchanges.

Given the extension of the El Tajín realm west into the Sierra de Puebla and onto the altiplano, the reference to a paradise of maguey-covered mountains could indicate these vital connections with the highlands (Pascual Soto 1990, 1998). Regions with maguey-covered mountains may have been at the edges of El Tajín's influence, and thus the Flowering Maguey Mountain could reference the boundaries of the El Tajín realm. It has long been known that mountains often served as the central foci not only of Pre-Columbian ritual but also of urban space and cosmology. Real mountains and their human-made cognates served as the central point of many, if not all, Mesoamerican urban spaces (Broda et al. 1987; Freidel et al. 1993; Tobriner 1972). Less attention has been paid to mountains as boundaries, although it is clear from contemporary analogies and ancient texts that they served this function as well (Freidel et al. 1993: 126–131; Monaghan 2000: 36; Stuart 1997). It is perhaps the function as polity boundary marker, as well as an advertisement for such exotics as pulque that came from these distant and different lands, that the El Tajín designers were referring to when they imaged a flowery paradise in which the ballcourt sacrifice was offered, humans were created, and the implements of human power were donated by the gods.

DISCUSSION: SOCIAL IDENTITY AT EL TAJÍN

The purpose of this chapter is to isolate certain social identities evident in the complex narrative imagery at El Tajín and to place these identities in relation to one another and their iconographic settings. Especially important to this system of social identities was a figure called here the flying impersonator, found in several prominent areas of public sculpture. This figure represented an elite administrative class that oversaw sacrifice, controlled key items of royal regalia, and manifested spirits. The flying impersonator was a key participant in ballgame decapitation sacrifice, and in this guise was linked directly to ballgame ritual, appearing as a major subject of yoke imagery. A closely related sacrificial office involved a vulture impersonator seen on *palma* imagery and in the architectural sculpture of Tajín. It was suggested that one of the key functions of complex narrative imagery at Tajín was to bring together these and other social identities in single compositions, thereby inscribing relative status and function through the relations set up in the imagery.

Not only were these social identities inscribed in relation to one another, they were also placed in a larger cosmology. Here a unique version of the Mesoamerican flowering mountain seems to reference the far reaches of the Tajín realm and the exotic maguey that flourished there. The ballcourt is both the home for and a key element in this paradisal imagery, which may have been replayed on a gigantic scale in the plan of the urban center itself by the pairing of the Mound of the Building Columns/Tajín Chico area with drainage systems that led into the Great Xicalcoliuhqui and its miniature courts. These courts must have been flooded periodically in Pre-Columbian times as they were in recent history, a fact that would have emphasized the aquatic, fecund nature of the ballcourt.

Acknowledgments

I began this study as a Dumbarton Oaks Summer Fellow in 2002. I thank Jeffrey Quilter, then director of Pre-Columbian Studies, for allowing me to present the kernel of this chapter to the assembled fellows and friends. Work was continued under a National Endowment for the Humanities Summer Stipend in 2003.

NOTES

1. The only extant representation at Tajín of a ballgame in progress shows the lower half of what appears to be a human figure striking the ball toward a skeletal figure (Ladrón de Guevara 1999: 89).

2. As Pohl (1994: 51) points out, *yaha yahui* could rise from that post to paramount ruler when the original ruling line expired.

3. *Palma*s are also found on the Pacific Coast of Guatemala and the surrounding area (Shook and Marquis 1996).

REFERENCES CITED

Agüero Reyes, Adriana
   n.d.   La función social de los personajes masculinos en el centro de Veracruz Durante el Período Clásico: Un estudio iconográfico. Tesis de licenciatura en Arqueología, Escuela Nacional de Antropología e Historia, México, 2004.
Arrellanos Melgarejo, Ramón, and Lourdes Beauregard García
   1981   Dos palmas totonacas: Reciente hallazgo en Banderilla, Veracruz. *La Palabra y El Hombre* 38–39: 144–160.
Bierhorst, John
   1992   History and Mythology of the Aztecs: The Codex Chimalpopoca. University of Arizona Press, Tucson.
Borhegyi, Stephan F. de
   1969   Miniature and Small Stone Artifacts from Mesoamerica. *Baessler Archiv* 17(2): 245–264.

Broda, Johanna, Davíd Carrasco, and Eduardo Matos Moctezuma

1987 *Great Temple of Tenochtitlan: Center and Periphery in the Aztec World.* University of California Press, Berkeley.

Carrasco, Pedro

1971 Social Organization of Ancient Mexico. In *Archaeology of Northern Mesoamerica*, part 1 (Gordon F. Ekholm and Ignacio Bernal, eds.): 349–375. Handbook of Middle American Indians, vol. 10 (Robert Wauchope, general ed.). University of Texas Press, Austin.

Castillo Peña, Patricia

1995 *La expresión simbólica del Tajín.* Instituto Nacional de Antropología e Historia, México.

Cortés Hernández, Jaime

1989 Elementos para un intento de interpretación del desarrollo hidráulico del Tajín. *Arqueología* 5: 175–190.

Covarrubias, Miguel

1957 *Indian Art of Mexico and Central America.* Alfred A. Knopf, New York.

Cowgill, George L.

2003 Teotihuacan and Early Classic Interaction: A Perspective from Outside the Maya Region. In *The Maya and Teotihuacan: Reinterpreting Early Classic Interaction* (Geoffrey E. Braswell, ed.): 315–336. University of Texas Press, Austin.

Cuevas, Bertha

1975 Problemas arqueológicos en Carrizal, Veracruz. *XIII Mesa Redonda de la Sociedad Mexicana de Antropología, Arqueología* 1: 315–322.

Daneels, Annick

1997 La relación Teotihuacan–centro de Veracruz: Una reevaluatión. *Revista Mexicana de Estudos Antropológicos* 42: 145–157.

n.d. Elite Interaction in Classic Period Central Veracruz. A paper presented at Symposium titled "Classic Veracruz" at the 66th Annual Meeting of the Society for American Archaeology, New Orleans, April 2001.

Delhalle, Jean-Claude, and Albert Luykx

1986 Nahuatl Myth of the Creation of Humankind: A Coastal Connection? *American Antiquity* 51: 117–121.

Du Solier, Wilfrido

1945 La cerámica arqueológica del Tajín. *Anales del Museo Nacional de Antropología e Historia*, quinta época 3: 147–192.

Ekholm, Gordon

1946 Probable Use of Mexican Stone Yokes. *American Anthropologist* 48: 593–606.

1949 Palmate Stones and Thin Stone Heads; Suggestions on Their Possible Use. *American Antiquity* 15: 1–9.

Freidel, David, Linda Schele, and Joy Parker

1993 *Maya Cosmos: Three Thousand Years on the Shaman's Path.* William Morrow and Company, New York.

García Cook, Angel
  1981 The Historical Importance of Tlaxcala in the Cultural Development of the Central Highlands. In *Archaeology* (Jeremy A. Sabloff, ed.): 244–276. Handbook of Middle American Indians, Supplement 1 (Victoria R. Bricker, general ed.). University of Texas Press, Austin.

García Payón, José
  1954 El Tajín: Descripción y comentarios. *Universidad Veracruzana* 3(4): 18–63.
  1959 Ensayo de interpretación de los tableros del juego de pelota sur de El Tajín. *El México Antiguo* 9: 445–460.
  1971 Archaeology of Central Veracruz. In *Archaeology of Northern Mesoamerica*, part 2 (Gordon F. Ekholm and Ignacio Bernal, eds.): 505–542. Handbook of Middle American Indians, vol. 11 (Robert Wauchope, general ed.). University of Texas Press, Austin.
  1973 *Los enigmas de El Tajín.* Colección Científica 3. Instituto Nacional de Antropología e Historia, México.

Garibay, Angel
  1965 *Teogonía e historia de los Mexicanos: Tres opúsculos del siglo XVI.* Editorial Porrúa, México.

Gaxiola González, Margarita
  1999 Huapalcalco y las tradiciones alfareras del Epiclásico. *Arqueología* 21: 45–72.

Houston, Stephen D.
  1993 *Hieroglyphs and History at Dos Pilas: Dynastic Politics of the Classic Maya.* University of Texas Press, Austin.

Houston, Stephen D., and David Stuart
  1989 *The Way Glyph: Evidence for "Co-Essences" among the Classic Maya.* Research Reports on Ancient Maya Writing 30. Center for Maya Research, Washington, D.C.
  2001 Peopling the Classic Maya Court. In *Royal Courts of the Ancient Maya*, vol. 1: *Theory, Comparison, and Synthesis* (Takeshi Inomata and Stephen D. Houston, eds.): 54–83. Westview Press, Boulder, Colo.

Jiménez Moreno, Wigberto
  1942 El enigma de los Olmecas. *Cuadernos Americanos* 1: 113–145.

Kampen, Michael E.
  1972 *The Sculptures of El Tajín, Veracruz, Mexico.* University of Florida Press, Gainesville.
  1978 Classic Veracruz Grotesques and Sacrificial Iconography. *Man,* new series 13: 116–126.

Kennedy, Alison
  1982 Ecce Bufo: The Toad in Nature and in Olmec Iconography. *Current Anthropology* 23: 273–290.

Klein, Cecelia
  1988 Tlaloc Masks as Insignia of Office in the Mexica-Aztec Hierarchy. In *Behind the Mask in Mexico* (Janet Brody Esser, ed.): 6–27. Museum of New Mexico Press, Santa Fe.

2000   Impersonation of Deities. In *The Oxford Encyclopedia of Mesoamerican Cultures* (Davíd Carrasco, ed.), vol. 2: 33–37. Oxford University Press, Oxford.

Koontz, Rex

2002   Terminal Classic Sacred Space and Factional Politics at El Tajín, Veracruz. In *Heart of Creation: The Mesoamerican World and the Legacy of Linda Schele* (Andrea Stone, ed.): 101–117. University of Alabama Press, Tuscaloosa.

n.d.   The Iconography of El Tajín, Veracruz, México. Ph.D. dissertation, Department of Art and Art History, University of Texas at Austin, 1994.

Krotser, Paula

1981   Veracruz: Corredor hacia el sureste. In *Interacción cultural en México central* (Evelyn C. Rattray, Jaime Litvak King, and Clara Díaz Oyarzabal, eds.): 175–186. Universidad Nacional Autónoma de México, México.

Ladrón de Guevara, Sara

1992   Pintura y escultura. In *Tajín* (Jürgen Brüggemann, Sara Ladrón de Guevara, and Juan Sánchez Bonilla, eds.): 99–131. El Equilibrista, México.

1999   *Imagen y pensamiento en El Tajín*. Universidad Veracruzana, Xalapa.

Lind, Michael, and Javier Urcid

1983   The Lords of Lambityeco and Their Nearest Neighbors. *Notas Mesoamericanas* 9: 78–111.

López Austin, Alfredo

1993   *The Myths of the Opossum* (Bernard R. Ortiz de Montellano and Thelma Ortiz de Montellano, trans.). University of New Mexico Press, Albuquerque.

1997   *Tamoanchan, Tlalocan: Places of Mist* (Bernard R. Ortiz de Montellano and Thelma Ortiz de Montellano, trans.). University Press of Colorado, Boulder.

Lothrop, Samuel

1923   Stone Yokes from Mexico and Central America. *Man* 23: 97–98.

Medellín Zenil, Alfonso

1957   La Deidad Ehecatl-Quetzalcoatl en el centro de Veracruz. *La Palabra y El Hombre* 2: 45–50.

1960   *Cerámicas del Totonacapan*. Universidad Veracruzana, Xalapa.

Miller, Mary Ellen

2001   Maya Ballgame: Rebirth in the Court of Life and Death. In *The Sport of Life and Death: The Mesoamerican Ballgame* (E. Michael Whittington, ed.): 78–87. Thames and Hudson, London.

Miller, Mary Ellen, and Marco Samoya

1998   Where Maize May Grow: Jade, Chacmools, and the Maize God. *RES* 33: 54–72.

Miller, Mary Ellen, and Karl Taube

    1993   *The Gods and Symbols of Ancient Mexico and the Maya: An Illustrated Dictionary of Mesoamerican Religion.* Thames and Hudson, London.

Monaghan, John D.

    2000   Theology and History in the Study of Mesoamerican Religions. In *Ethnology* (John D. Monaghan and Barbara W. Edmonson, eds.): 24–49. Handbook of Middle American Indians, Supplement 6 (Victoria R. Bricker, general ed.). University of Texas Press, Austin.

Nicholson, Henry B.

    1971   Religion in Pre-Hispanic Central Mexico. In *Archaeology of Northern Mesoamerica*, part 1 (Gordon F. Ekholm and Ignacio Bernal, eds.): 395–446. Handbook of Middle American Indians, vol. 10 (Robert Wauchope, general ed.). University of Texas Press, Austin.

O'Mack, Scott

    1991   Yacateuctli and Ehecatl-Quetzalcoatl: Earth-Divers in Aztec Central Mexico. *Ethnohistory* 38(1): 1–33

Palacios, Enrique Juan

    1926   *Youalichan y el Tajín. Monumentos arqueológicos en Cuetzalan descubiertos por la dirección de arqueología.* Secretaría de Educación Pública, México.

    1943   *Los yugos y su simbolismo: Estudio analítico.* Universidad Nacional Autónoma de México, México.

Parsons, Jeffrey R.

    2001   Agave. In *Archaeology of Ancient Mexico and Central America: An Encyclopedia* (Susan T. Evans and David L. Webster, eds.): 4–7. Garland, New York.

Pascual Soto, Arturo

    1990   *Iconografía arqueológica de El Tajín.* Universidad Nacional Autónoma de México, México.

    1998   *El arte en tierras de El Tajín.* Consejo Nacional para la Cultura y las Artes, México.

    2000   El Tajín en vísperas del Clásico Tardío: Arte y cultura. *Universidad de México* 590: 30–39.

Pohl, John M. D.

    1994   *The Politics of Symbolism in the Mixtec Codices.* Vanderbilt University Publications in Anthropology 46. Vanderbilt University, Nashville, Tenn.

Proskouriakoff, Tatiana

    1954   *Varieties of Classic Central Veracruz Sculpture.* Contributions to American Anthropology and History 58. Carnegie Institution of Washington, Washington, D.C.

Ringle, William M.

    2004   On the Political Organization of Chichen Itza. *Ancient Mesoamerica* 15: 167–218.

Rivas Castro, Francisco

    2001 El maguey y el pulque en Teotihuacan: Representación y simbolismo. *Arqueología* 25: 47–62.

Sahagún, Bernardino de

  1950–82 *General History of the Things of New Spain: Florentine Codex* (Arthur J. O. Anderson and Charles E. Dibble, trans. and eds.). 12 books in 13 vols. School of American Research and University of Utah, Santa Fe, N.M. and Salt Lake City.

Sánchez Bonilla, Juan

    1992 Similitudes entre las Pinturas de Las Higueras y las obras plásticas del Tajín. In *Tajín* (Jürgen Brüggemann, Sara Ladrón de Guevara, and Juan Sánchez Bonilla, eds.): 133–159. El Equilibrista, México.

Sarro, Patricia Joan

    n.d. The Architectural Meaning of Tajín Chico, the Acropolis at El Tajín Mexico. Ph.D. dissertation, Department of Art History and Archaeology, Columbia University, 1995.

Scott, John F.

    2001 Dressed to Kill: Stone Regalia of the Mesoamerican Ballgame. In *The Sport of Life and Death: The Mesaomerican Ballgame* (E. Michael Whittington, ed.): 50–63. Thames and Hudson, London.

Shook, Edward M., and Elayne Marquis

    1996 *Secrets in Stone: Yokes, Hachas and Palmas from Southern Mesoamerica.* American Philosophical Society, Philadelphia.

Smith, Mary Elizabeth

    1973 The Relationship between Mixtec Manuscript Painting and the Mixtec Language: A Study of Some Personal Names in Codices Muro and Sánchez Solís. In *Mesoamerican Writing Systems* (Elizabeth P. Benson, ed.): 47–98. Dumbarton Oaks, Washington, D.C.

Spinden, Ellen

    1933 The Place of Tajín in Totonac Archaeology. *American Anthropologist* 35: 225–270.

Stark, Barbara

    1999 Ritual, Social Identity and Cosmology: Hard Stones and Flowing Water. In *Social Patterns in Pre-Classic Mesoamerica* (David C. Grove and Rosemary A. Joyce, eds.): 301–318. Dumbarton Oaks, Washington, D.C.

Stuart, David

    1997 Hills Are Alive: Sacred Mountains in the Maya Cosmos. *Symbols* (Spring): 13–17.

    2000 "The Arrival of Strangers": Teotihuacan and Tollan in Classic Maya History. In *Mesoamerica's Classic Heritage* (Davíd Carrasco, Lindsay Jones, and Scott Sessions, eds.): 465–514. University Press of Colorado, Boulder.

Stuart, David, Stephen Houston, and John Robertson

    1999 Recovering the Past: Classic Maya Language and Classic Maya Gods. In *Notebook for the XXXIII Maya Hieroglyphic Forum at Texas* (Linda Schele, David Stuart, Stephen Houston, and John Robertson, eds.): (II)1–(II)80. Maya Workshop Foundation, Austin, Tex.

Taube, Karl

  1986 The Teotihuacan Cave of Origin. *RES* 12: 51–82.

  1994 Iconography of Toltec Period Chichen Itza. In *Hidden among the Hills: Maya Archaeology of the Northwest Yucatan Peninsula* (Hanns J. Prem, ed.): 212–246. Acta Mesoamericana 7. Verlag von Flemming, Möckmühl, Germany.

  2004 Flower Mountain: Concepts of Life, Beauty, and Paradise among the Classic Maya. *RES* 45: 69–98.

Thompson, J. Eric S.

  1941 Yokes or Ball Game Belts? *American Antiquity* 6: 320–326.

  1971 *Maya Hieroglyphic Writing: An Introduction.* 3rd ed. University of Oklahoma Press, Norman.

Tobriner, Stephen

  1972 The Fertile Mountain: An Investigation of Cerro Gordo's Importance to the Town Plan and Iconography of Teotihuacán. *Teotihuacán: XI Mesa Redonda, Sociedad Mexicana de Antropología:* 103–115.

Tuggle, H. David

  1968 The Columns of El Tajín, Veracruz, Mexico. *Ethnos* 33(1–4): 40–70.

  1972 Structure of Tajín World-View. *Anthropos* 67(3–4): 435–448.

de Vries, Reina

  1991 El yugo del juego de pelota como molde para cinturones de cuero. In *The Mesoamerican Ballgame* (Gerard W. van Bussel, Paul L. van Dongen, and Ted J. Leyenaar, eds.): 189–202. Rijksmuseum voor Volkenkunde, Leiden.

Wilkerson, S. Jeffrey K.

  1971 Un yugo 'in situ' de la region del Tajín. *Boletín del Instituto Nacional de Antropología e Historia* 41: 41–45.

  1984 In Search of the Mountain of Foam: Human Sacrifice in Eastern Mesoamerica. In *Ritual Human Sacrifice in Mesoamerica* (Elizabeth H. Boone, ed.): 101–132. Dumbarton Oaks, Washington, D.C.

  1990 El Tajín: Great Center of the Northeast. In *Mexico: Splendors of Thirty Centuries* (Octavio Paz, introduction): 155–185. Metropolitan Museum of Art, New York.

  1991 And Then They Were Sacrificed: The Ritual Ballgame of Northeastern Mesoamerica through Time and Space. In *The Mesoamerican Ballgame* (Vernon L. Scarborough and David R. Wilcox, eds.): 45–72. University of Arizona Press, Tucson.

  n.d. Ethnogenesis of the Huastec and Totonac: Early Cultures of North-Central Veracruz at Santa Luisa, Mexico. Ph.D. dissertation, Department of Anthropology, Tulane University, New Orleans, 1972.

TEN

FOUR HUNDRED YEARS OF SETTLEMENT AND CULTURAL CONTINUITY IN EPICLASSIC AND EARLY POSTCLASSIC TULA

Alba Guadalupe Mastache

Dan M. Healan

Robert H. Cobean

TULA, ALONG WITH TEOTIHUACAN and Tenochtitlan, was one of several large Pre-Hispanic cities that developed in the Central Mexican Highlands. This chapter summarizes recent archaeological investigations at Tula that, in conjunction with previous investigations, provide compelling evidence of a long and rich cultural tradition that exhibits striking continuity between the earliest settlement during the Epiclassic period and the dense, expansive urban settlement that characterized Tula during the subsequent Early Postclassic period. We proceed in reverse chronological order, considering first the Early Postclassic (Tollan phase) city, for which there is substantial information, before considering Tula's Epiclassic settlement, which has come to light relatively recently.

Tula is located in southwestern Hidalgo immediately north and west of the Basin of Mexico, where both Teotihuacan and Tenochtitlan are located. The core of the site is situated atop a hill or bluff overlooking the Tula River (Figure 1). The bluff is partially dissected by erosion, giving it the appearance of being two semi-distinct hills, atop which are situated two monumental complexes that are the most visible ruins at the site. The largest complex, situated on the southernmost hill, contains a large open plaza surrounded by monumental architecture that constituted Tula's political and religious center during its Tollan phase apogee (Figures 1, 2). Much of this monumental precinct was reconstructed by Jorge Acosta in the mid-twentieth century, and the associated architectural, sculptural, and other artistic elements compose the principal corpus of material traits most commonly associated with Tula.

FIGURE 1. Limits of Tula (heavy line) during its Late Tollan phase apogee
(ca. A.D. 1100). A, Tula Grande; B, Tula Chico; C, modern town of Tula; E,
University of Missouri excavations (Diehl 1983; Healan 1989); F, zones of
obsidian tool workshops; G, El Salitre swamp; H, Epiclassic site of Cerro
Magoni (ca. A.D. 550–650); I, Cerro La Malinche; J, Cerro El Cielito. Aerial
photograph courtesy of the Dirección General de Estudios del Territorio
Nacional, México.

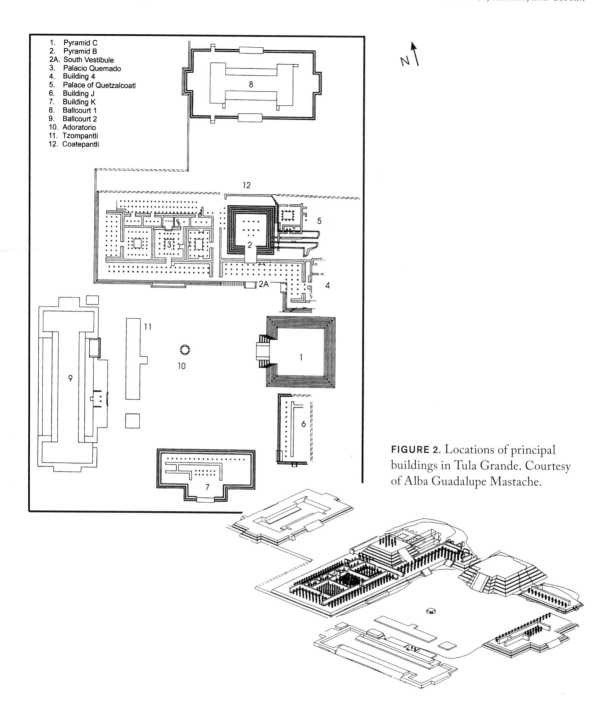

1. Pyramid C
2. Pyramid B
2A. South Vestibule
3. Palacio Quemado
4. Building 4
5. Palace of Quetzalcoatl
6. Building J
7. Building K
8. Ballcourt 1
9. Ballcourt 2
10. Adoratorio
11. Tzompantli
12. Coatepantli

FIGURE 2. Locations of principal buildings in Tula Grande. Courtesy of Alba Guadalupe Mastache.

The northernmost hill contains a somewhat smaller monumental precinct that has not been reconstructed but is notably similar in overall form to the larger monumental precinct immediately to the south. Surface survey and exploratory excavation revealed that this complex dates to Tula's earliest occupation, and it is interpreted to have been the political and religious center of Tula's earliest settlement. The similarity in layout led

Eduardo Matos Moctezuma (1974) and others to suggest that this smaller precinct served as the prototype for the later, Tollan phase monumental precinct on the other (southernmost) hill. For this reason Matos referred to this earlier monumental complex as Tula Chico, and by extension, the later and larger complex to the south as Tula Grande.[1]

THE EARLY POSTCLASSIC CITY

During the past several decades investigators from the Instituto Nacional de Antropología e Historia, Mexico City, and other institutions, including the University of Missouri, Columbia, and Tulane University, New Orleans, have conducted both excavations and surveys in diverse sectors of the ancient city. These investigations included independent surveys of Tula's urban zone conducted by Stoutamire (Healan and Stoutamire 1989; Stoutamire n.d. [1975]), Yadeun (1975), and Mastache and Crespo (1982). These and other investigations documented many aspects of the social, economic, and political complexity of this city (Charlton and Nichols 1997; Mastache and Cobean 1985; Sanders and Santley 1983; Sanders and Webster 1988; Sanders et al. 1979), as summarized in Healan (1989) and in Mastache et al. (2002).

During Tula's Late Tollan phase apogee (A.D. 1000–1150) it appears that the city covered an area of almost 16 km², with a maximum north-south dimension of 6 km and a maximum east-west dimension of 4 km.

Tula Grande

Much of the Tula Grande monumental precinct was excavated during the 1940s and 1950s by Jorge Acosta, Hugo Moedano, and other members of Acosta's staff (Figure 2). Some have criticized Acosta's work as containing misleading or false reconstructions of architectural features (Molina Montes 1982), but in fact Acosta's extensive and detailed published reports provide well-documented evidence for virtually all these features and the manner in which they were reconstructed (Cobean and Mastache 1988; Diehl 1989; Healan 2009).

The importance of Tula Grande as the city's symbolic axis and architectural center is manifested in its central location with respect to the extent of the Tollan phase city (see Figure 1). Its prominence is also evident in its location on one of the highest and most prominent points in the ancient city. Construction of Tula Grande involved considerable modification of the existing hilltop, including the building of an extensive system of terracing with fill up to a depth of 8 m beneath the plaza and overlying platforms that supported the monumental architecture of Tula Grande.

It seems obvious that the placement of Tula Grande was strategically motivated not only because it occupies an easily defended place, but also because its location at a centrally located, prominent point had considerable visual impact for inhabitants in virtually every part of the city. This prominence is evident even for the inhabitants of modern Tula. The placement of monumental precincts atop summits is common in many areas of Mesoamerica and the north of Mexico, of which an outstanding example is La Quemada, Zacatecas, which also shares with Tula a number of architectonic elements, including columned halls (Hers 1989; Nelson 1997). In central Mexico, sites having monumental centers placed on high elevations are common during the Late Classic and Epiclassic, and include Xochicalco, Teotenango, Cantona, and Cacaxtla-Xochitecatl (García Cook 2003; Hirth 2000; Piña Chan 1975; Serra Puche 1998), along with most Coyotlatelco sites in the Tula region (Mastache et al. 2002: 60–69).

Most monumental structures at Tula Grande were seriously damaged by Aztec period excavations apparently seeking sculpture and other relics that came to occupy honored places in Aztec centers in the Basin of Mexico. The *Historia de los mexicanos por sus pinturas* (García Icazbalceta 1941) describes a fifteenth-century king of Tlatelolco who sent an expedition to Tula to recover statues that were subsequently installed in the Tlatelolco precinct (Nicholson 1971). Moedano (1944) recovered several small *atlante* sculptures probably from Tula along with Aztec copies of them under modern streets near the Templo Mayor in Mexico City. During the 1990s Eduardo Matos and Leonardo López Luján (personal communications) found a basalt Chacmool sculpture that is surely from Tula in the Templo Mayor complex.

The Tula Grande monumental precinct is a great quadrangle measuring nearly 260 m east-west by 230 m north-south that is open on its northwest and southeast corners (Figure 2). It is composed of two architectural units forming opposing right angles that do not unite, leaving two open, diagonally opposed corners that formed the principal entrances to the plaza. The larger of these two units, measuring approximately 140 m on a side, is formed by Pyramids C and B and adjacent structures with columned halls. The other unit, approximately 120 m on a side, is formed by Building K and Ballcourt 2. The total number of monumental buildings in and immediately surrounding Tula Grande was probably between 50 and 60. By comparison, Bernardino de Sahagún's informants listed some 78 structures near the Templo Mayor of Tenochtitlan (Matos Moctezuma 2003: 143).

Pyramid C is clearly the most prominent architectural entity at Tula Grande, not only because it is the largest structure in the city but also because of its location and relationship to other buildings around the plaza. Pyramid C is seemingly the *axis mundi* on which the remaining elements of Tula Grande, and perhaps the rest of the city, were configured. Pyramid B occupies a secondary position, given its smaller size and less prominent

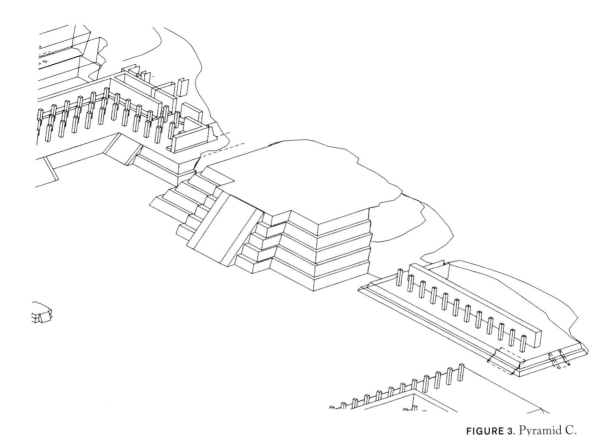

FIGURE 3. Pyramid C. Architectural drawing by Jesús Acevedo García and Alba Guadalupe Mastache.

setting in the precinct. These two pyramids are situated adjacent to each other at a 90-degree angle, each facing the plaza: Pyramid C toward the west and Pyramid B toward the south. This arrangement exhibits notable similarities to the Pyramids of the Sun and Moon at Teotihuacan, not only in the presence of two main pyramids, one larger than the other, but also in that the larger pyramid faces west and the smaller faces south. Another striking parallel between Tula Grande and Teotihuacan is their common spatial orientation, approximately 17 degrees east of astronomical north. It seems unlikely that such similarities are casual, and they may reflect an underlying cosmovision and perhaps fundamental ideological concepts that were shared by both cities.

Pyramid C consists of five sloping tiers. It has an abutting platform that supports a stairway that Acosta (1956: 55) called the *cuerpo adosado* (Figure 3), noting its similarity to abutting platforms for both the Sun and Moon pyramids of San Juan Teotihuacan. Indeed, Pyramid C closely resembles the Pyramid of the Moon in overall plan. In the vestibule flanking the northern side of Pyramid C, Acosta (1956: lámina 49) found a headless Chacmool, a small incomplete *atlante* sculpture, and a nearby fragment of another Chacmool sculpture, all of which he believed were originally atop Pyramid C.

FIGURE 4. Reliefs of felines and raptorial birds on the east facade of Pyramid B. Photograph by Robert H. Cobean.

FIGURE 5. Relief of composite being on the east facade of Pyramid B, identified as Tlahuizcalpantecuhtli by Jorge Acosta and Hugo Moedano. Photograph by Robert H. Cobean.

Pyramid B, situated immediately north of Pyramid C, also exhibits five sloping tiers and a square plan. Acosta (1956: 89) noted what appear to have been three principal construction stages for this building, based on partial superimposed platforms built only on one or two sides of the pyramid during different periods. Acosta clearly identified two interior substructures, the first of which was covered by unelaborated stone panels painted white. The second and third stages of the pyramid were faced with relief panels featuring processions of felines, canines, and eagles (Figure 4) and a composite creature having human, reptile, and avian attributes that both Acosta (1956) and Moedano (n.d. [1946]) considered to be a representation of Tlahuizcalpantecuhtli, the god Quetzalcoatl in his embodiment as the planet Venus (Figure 5).

The rich and diverse corpus of iconographic elements associated with Pyramid B has been described in detail by Acosta, Jiménez García (1998), and other scholars. Among the outstanding elements are the above-mentioned relief panels that covered the facades, along with other associated sculptural and architectonic features, including pillars, columns, and monumental sculptures, that were integral parts of both the pyramid and the temple that apparently surmounted it. The best-known sculptures at Tula are the so-called *atlantes* (or "caryatids") presently atop Pyramid B, which Acosta encountered in a Pre-Hispanic trench at the rear of the pyramid. These are anthropomorphic columns some 4.60 m in height that apparently supported the original temple roof and are believed to represent high-ranking Toltec warriors whose elaborate ceremonial costumes have been analyzed in detail by Acosta (1943, 1961b) and Kristan-Graham (n.d. [1989]). It is interesting to note that loose fragments, mainly feet and legs, of other *atlante* sculptures were previously encountered by Charnay and others at Tula that are quite similar to but larger than those from Pyramid B. Acosta (1944: 146) suggested that these may have been looted from Pyramid C.

Pyramid B Pillars

In addition to the cylindrical *atlante* columns, Pyramid B contains four square columns or pillars covered with reliefs on all four sides that apparently had originally been painted. On each pillar are four representations of human figures, each with two personages on the lower half and two on the upper half, totaling sixteen figures, although only twelve complete personages and fragments of two others are extant (Figures 6, 7). Alternating with the human figures are representations of spear or dart bundles on four sections of each pillar. An additional element is the *cipactli* symbol placed above and below each personage, in a sense framing these figures. This symbol often is linked to royal lineages, and it is significant that the

FIGURE 6. Pyramid B, Pillar 3: relief of bearded personage identified by Jorge Acosta as Topiltzin Quetzalcoatl. Drawing by Daniel Correa Baltazar and Elizabeth Jiménez García.

FIGURE 7. Pyramid B, Pillar 4: relief of armed personage with a large Venus glyph. Drawing by Daniel Correa Baltazar and Elizabeth Jiménez García.

date one *cipactli* constitutes the first day of the Mesoamerican 260-day calendar as well as the initial date of creation in myths of the creation of the universe (Taube 1993). One *cipactli* was also a favored date for the enthronement of Mexica Kings (Kristan-Graham n.d. [1989]: 236; Nicholson 1961). Elsewhere we have proposed that the temple atop Pyramid B functioned principally as a sanctuary or commemorative monument for Tula's royal dynasty (Mastache and Cobean 2000; Mastache et al. 2002: 96–106).

All extant personages possess attributes of warriors and other shared elements, including being depicted in profile and in the act of walking, but they also exhibit specific elements that differentiate each figure. Among these are glyphs or symbols that some personages have near the upper part of their heads that may refer to their name, position, or rank (see Figure 6). Some scholars have cited these glyphs as evidence that the pillars depict historical personages, perhaps rulers or high-ranking nobles who were members of Toltec dynasties (Acosta 1968; Jiménez García 1998; Kristan-Graham n.d. [1989]; Mastache and Cobean 2000). It is interesting to note an illustration from Book 8 of the Florentine Codex of the lords of Tenochtitlan (reproduced by Carrasco 1971: fig. 2), who are associated with glyphs notably similar to those on the Tula pillars.

Kristan-Graham (n.d. [1989]: 241, 317, 334), whose study of the Pyramid B pillars is the most rigorous to date, notes various similarities between the glyphs of some of the figures on the Pyramid B pillars and the symbols for various Mexica kings, especially Cuauhtemoc and Itzcoatl. She suggests that the Tula pillars could be commemorative monuments for the enthronement of rulers, some of whom may predate Tollan phase Tula. Pillars with similar personages are also common at Chichen Itza, Mexico. Noting the presence of personages at both sites possessing similar elements, such as a descending bird motif on helmets and headdresses, Kristan-Graham (n.d. [1989]: 251, 317) suggested that members of the same dynasties or even the same individuals could be represented at both sites. Some of the non-Maya glyphs depicted next to so-called Toltec personages on other columns at Chichen Itza are also quite similar to the glyphs on the Pyramid B pillars (Coe 1999; Mastache and Cobean 2000; Tozzer 1957).

Of particular interest is Pillar 3, which contains a personage that Acosta believed represented Topiltzin Quetzalcoatl (see Figure 6), presumably because the individual is bearded and has a feathered serpent glyph over his head (Martínez del Río and Acosta 1967: 38, fig. 14). This personage is shown in profile walking toward the left (from the observer's point of view) and, like the figures on the other pillars, is dressed as a warrior carrying a knife, a fending stick (*arma curva*), and a dart thrower (atlatl) and wearing a disk on his back, probably a back mirror (*tezcacuitlapilli*). The headdress or helmet has the form of an eagle's head topped by three large feathers. Other distinguishing costume elements include a noseplug and earplugs in the form of long cylinders; anklets similar to feline claws; and a semicircular pectoral made of rectangular plaques, perhaps of shell or turquoise, with a T-shaped motif in its center (Taube 1994: 233, 239). The other personage on the lower section of Pillar 3 is also depicted in profile, walking toward the right. He is also costumed as a warrior; wears a *tezcacuitlapilli;* and carries a knife, fending stick, and atlatl.

A Newly Discovered Pillar Section from Pyramid B

During the 1980s a conservation project directed by Roberto Gallegos at Tula Grande recovered an additional portion of a pillar from the north side of Pyramid B (Figures 8, 9). No report has been published on this find, and the exact location where it was found has not been specified, but

FIGURE 8. Pyramid B, Pillar 3: relief of personage with attributes of Tezcatlipoca. Drawing by Daniel Correa Baltazar and Elizabeth Jiménez García.

FIGURE 9. Pyramid B, Pillar 3: relief of personage with attributes of Tlaloc. Drawing by Daniel Correa Baltazar and Elizabeth Jiménez García.

0 [scale] 30 cm   0 [scale] 30 cm

it was apparently encountered near the large Pre-Hispanic trench where Acosta (1944, 1945) recovered the majority of the sculptures and pillars that are now atop the pyramid. Although incomplete, the newly found pillar is of great interest in terms of its iconography, because a relief on one side represents a personage having physical and costume elements of the god Tezcatlipoca, and a relief on the opposite side is a figure with attributes associated with Tlaloc. Mastache and Cobean (2000) have shown that this new pillar section constitutes the previously missing upper section of Pillar 3, seen in Figure 6, that is precisely the pillar believed to contain a depiction of Topiltzin Quetzalcoatl.

On the newly recovered section, as on the other sections, the two personages are represented in profile. The figure dressed as Tezcatlipoca (see Figure 8) walks toward the left; the other (Tlaloc) figure (see Figure 9) walks toward the right. The latter figure lacks the top of his head, but clearly wears the goggle-like accoutrements over the eyes that are characteristic of this deity. This personage is dressed as a warrior and carries two spears and a fending stick in his left hand and an atlatl in his right hand. On his chest is a disk with two perforations very similar in form to the plain pyrite mirrors found in the offerings of Sala 2 in the Palacio Quemado (Acosta 1964; Cobean and Mastache 2003), both of which possess perforations that suggest they were worn as pectorals.

The personage with attributes of Tezcatlipoca is dressed as a warrior with a butterfly pectoral, a *tezcacuitlapilli* on his back, a fending stick, an atlatl, and a knife sheathed in the cotton armor of his upper left arm, all elements typical of other warrior figures depicted at Tula. The most specific elements associated with Tezcatlipoca include a fleshless lower right leg with a smoking mirror in place of the foot, characteristics typical of Late Postclassic representations of the god. A double speech scroll is emerging from his mouth, and he wears a stepped helmet characteristic of other warriors depicted at Tula, although the upper section of the helmet is missing along with the upper section of the pillar where there might have been an identifying glyph for this personage. This depiction is the only clear-cut representation of Tezcatlipoca known for Tula and constitutes the oldest image of this deity identified in the Central Highlands.

The Tezcatlipoca personage on the newly found section is similar in several respects to the representations of Mexica kings depicted with Tezcatlipoca attributes in the Tizoc Stone, the commemorative stone for the emperor Axayacatl, and the recently recovered *cuauhxicalli* (sacrifical vessel) of Motecuhzoma I (Nicholson 1971; Pérez Castro et al. 1989; Wicke 1976). Many of the images of Mexica emperors on these monuments possess costume elements of Tula-style warriors (especially butterfly pectorals and stepped helmets) and have fleshless lower legs with smoke scrolls where the foot should be.

It is of considerable significance that the newly found section of Pillar 3 contains representations of individuals with diagnostic attributes of Tezcatlipoca and Tlaloc, particularly so if the bearded figure on the other section of Pillar 3 indeed represents Topiltzin Quetzalcoatl (see Figure 6). The placement of images of both Tezcatlipoca and Topiltzin Quetzalcoatl on the same column (and in one of the two principal monumental buildings at Tula Grande) suggests that the narratives in the indigenous chronicles concerning the ancient Tollan and the Toltecs may be represented in the iconography of Tula, regardless of whether these accounts describe historical events or are purely legendary (see Nicholson 2000: 233–244).

Building 4 (Palace to the East of the Vestibule)

On the east side of the Vestibule in front of Pyramid B is an entrance to a building complex that Acosta designated "Building 4, or the Palace to the East of the Vestibule" (Figure 10; see also Figure 2, no. 4). Based on partial excavation that exposed portions of four rooms, Acosta (1956: 44–46, 77–80) described the structure as an "enormous palace" of apparent grandeur: "The discovery of a wide entrance on the east side of the vestibule led us to an enormous and complicated system of rooms constructed with adobe having (preserved) walls that sometimes reached 4 m in height" (Acosta 1964: 60 [authors' translation]).

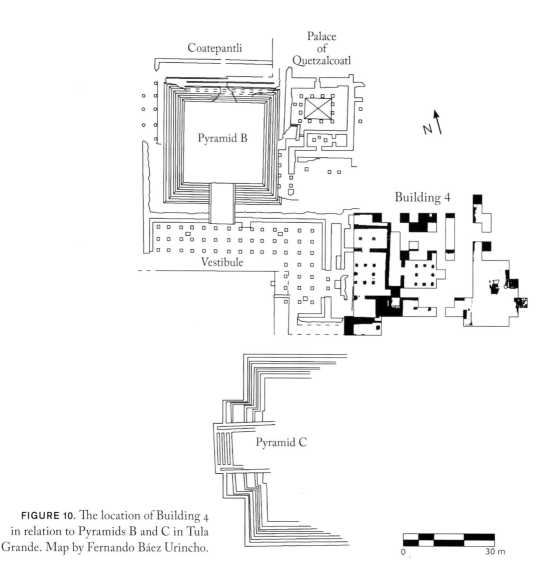

FIGURE 10. The location of Building 4 in relation to Pyramids B and C in Tula Grande. Map by Fernando Báez Urincho.

The "wide entrance" to this room complex measured almost 9 m in width and was subdivided by two pillars supporting lintels (Figure 10). This was clearly no ordinary entrance, but an access of considerable breadth divided into three sections similar to the entrance Acosta (1967) proposed for the temple on the summit of Pyramid B, as well as that to the Aztec period Temple of Huitzilopochtli at the Templo Mayor of Tenochtitlan (Matos Moctezuma 1988: 67, fig. 34). Acosta encountered in situ wooden beams for the entrances to some of the other rooms.

The remains of Building 4, still visible on the surface and documented in Acosta's field notes, consists of sections of four different rooms (Figure 10), including a gallery-like room spanning the entire building and the vestibule immediately in front. Embellishing the base of the interior wall of the west vestibule of Building 4 is a rectangular altar with a cornice.

FIGURE 11. Relief of the altar at the west entrance of Building 4 (from Acosta 1956 and Jiménez 1998: fig. 97). Reproduced courtesy of the Instituto Nacional de Antropología e Historia, Mexico.

Both the main body and the cornice of the altar were originally covered with reliefs, the surviving panels of which cover part of its main (west) and south faces (Figure 11). The extant reliefs depict a procession of richly attired persons walking toward a figure with his torso depicted frontally and his head facing left toward the procession (Figure 11). An undulating blue plumed serpent in the form of a capital "S" partially surrounds the central figure, whom Acosta (1956: 74–80, láminas 28, 29) called "el Gran Sacerdote Quetzalcoatl." Mastache and Cobean (2000) believe that, in the art of Tula, feathered serpents in the form of a capital "S" are symbols of royalty, possibly signifying a ruler, and that personages with whom they are articulated represent Toltec kings. Most of the relief panels to the left of this figure are missing, but his central location on the altar and the remnant feathers immediately to his left suggests that a comparable procession existed in that portion of the altar as well.[2] The costume, central placement, and other attributes of the central personage and his relationship to the other members of the procession scene suggest that this relief may depict an actual event or ceremony, such as the enthronement of a king or visiting dignitaries greeting or paying homage (see note 2). Additional fragments of relief sculptures were encountered elsewhere in Building 4 during the excavations described immediately below, including depictions of individuals with similar attire to the warrior figures on the Pyramid B pillars (Cobean, Mastache, Figueroa Silva, Suárez Cortés, Salazar, Martínez Landa, Báez Urincho, and Patiño n.d.).

During the field seasons of 2002, 2003, and 2004 of the current Instituto Nacional de Antropología e Historia (INAH) project at Tula, we excavated approximately 60 percent of the penultimate construction phase of Building 4 (see Figure 10), analysis of which is in progress (Báez Urincho 2007; Cobean, Mastache, Figueroa Silva, Suárez Cortés, Salazar,

Martínez Landa, Báez Urincho, and Patiño n.d.). The excavated remains probably date to the eleventh century A.D. The dimensions of Building 4 are approximately 60 m east-west by 45 m north-south. To the east of the grand entrance are two large columned halls, each measuring approximately 14 m by 15 m. These rooms are very similar to the large reception halls that Evans (2004) and others have described for the Late Postclassic royal palaces at Tenochtitlan. On the northern edge of the westernmost hall was a small room with several broken but complete ollas measuring more than 1.4 m in height. To the east of the two halls excavation encountered portions of several smaller rooms that may have been part of the royal living quarters. Unfortunately, there was extensive Aztec occupation in this sector of the building, which makes the original functions of the rooms difficult to interpret. The placement of two large columned halls and an adjacent storage area near the grand entranceway and the possible royal portraitures in the reliefs lend support to Acosta's interpretation that this building was one of Tula's royal palaces. Building 4 is placed adjacent to Tula's main pyramid, similar to the placement of Axayacatl's palace in relation to the Templo Mayor of Tenochtitlan (Evans 2004: 15).

The construction techniques and materials used in Building 4 are notably different from those of most other monumental buildings at Tula Grande. Most walls in Building 4 are of adobe rather than stone and are faced with mud rather than lime plaster, with little use of the decorative tabular stone facing commonly used on monumental architecture at Tula. It is interesting to note that some Aztec structures near Tenochtitlan's Templo Mayor also utilize adobe walls coated with mud (Leonardo López Luján, personal communication, October 2005). Its presence may constitute the intentional use of archaic elements that address the pretensions of both the Toltec and the Aztec to having northern origins.

Building 4 was damaged by fire, presumably during the Early Postclassic, as there appears to have been an overlying Late Tollan Phase (twelfth century A.D.) building that was subsequently almost completely dismantled, apparently by the Aztec.

Palacio Quemado

The Palacio Quemado, which along with Pyramid B forms the north side of Tula Grande, consists principally of three great quadrangular columned halls, or *salas,* each with a centrally located sunken patio (Figure 12; see also Figure 2, no. 3). As seen in Figure 12, the three *salas* do not interconnect; instead, each has its own entrance on different sides: Sala 1 on the east, Sala 3 on the west, and Sala 2 on the south. Hence only Sala 2 enjoyed direct access to the vestibule and the main plaza. The three are adjoined on the north by a row of six long, narrow rooms. Rooms 1, 5, and 6 on the eastern

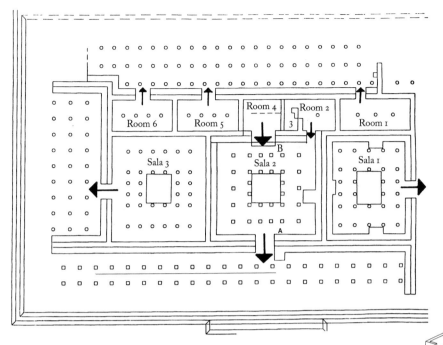

FIGURE 12. Plans of the Palacio Quemado. Drawings by Jesús Acevedo García and Alba Guadalupe Mastache.

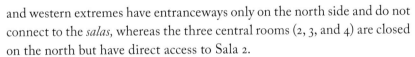

and western extremes have entranceways only on the north side and do not connect to the *salas,* whereas the three central rooms (2, 3, and 4) are closed on the north but have direct access to Sala 2.

The use of round columns versus square pillars in the Palacio Quemado is clearly patterned, as seen in Figure 12. Salas 1 and 3 on the extremes of the Palacio Quemado have circular columns, as do the north and west vestibules that communicate with them. In contrast, the centrally located Sala 2 and the south vestibule possess square columns. Thus two different categories of roofed-over space are delineated: those with direct access to the plaza (pillars) and those without (columns).[3]

Aside from the use of columns versus pillars, the three *salas* exhibit other differences as well. Salas 1 and 3 are slightly rectangular in form, whereas Sala 2 is square, measuring 26 m by 26 m. The central location of Sala 2, its accessibility from Rooms 2, 3, and 4 to the north, and it being the only *sala* with direct access to the plaza suggest, as Acosta (1961a: 56–57) observed, that Sala 2 was likely the most important space in the Palacio

FIGURE 13. Reconstruction of Sala 2 of the Palacio Quemado. Drawing by Fernando Getino Granados.

Quemado. Of particular importance is Room 4, located on a higher level than Sala 2, to which it had access via a small stairway situated on the Palace's north-south axis. Acosta (1961a: 34, 37) suggests that this small room constituted "a sanctuary where the most sacred rites were celebrated" and may have been a throne room for Toltec kings (Mastache et al. 2002: 117 [authors' translation]).

The three *salas* can be reconstructed in some detail on the basis of Acosta's excavation reports, in which he noted that he found evidence of destruction by burning. The roofs originally had a centrally located unroofed patio, or *impluvio*, that provided light to the interior of each *sala*. The patio floors were strewn with polychrome relief panels that had presumably been placed around the roof opening. The relief panels exhibited three principal motifs: representations of what Acosta (1956) interpreted as *cuauhxicalli*, or vessels containing sacrificed hearts (Figure 13); large solar disks like the *tezcacuitlapilli* worn by the *atlantes;* and reclining human figures. Other fallen sculpture included symbolic representations of precious stones or drops of water (*chalchihuites*), bundles of columns (*atados de columnillas*), and merlons (*almenas*) in the form of a capital "G" that Acosta (1956) interpreted as a representation of the cross-section of a conch shell—Venus-Quetzalcoatl symbol.

In Sala 1 Acosta (1956, 1957) recovered fragments of 8 solar disks, 4

FIGURE 14. Reliefs of reclining figures excavated by Jorge Acosta in the Palacio Quemado (from Jiménez García 1998). Reproduced courtesy of the Instituto Nacional de Antropología e Historia, Mexico City.

FIGURE 15. Drawing of a section of page 33 of the Codex Borgia showing ancestral deceased elite warriors (*huehueteteo*). Drawing by Héctor Patiño Rodríguez.

cuauhxicalli, and at least 20 panels with reclining personages, of which 7 of the last were reconstructed. Many of the reclining figures are armed (Figure 14) and exhibit other trappings of warriors. Some are surrounded by feathered serpents; others wear a large, transversely cut conch shell, or a half-star Venus war symbol, as a pectoral. As Kristan-Graham (1999: 171, 172) has noted, the various anatomical and costume attributes of the reclining figures in the Palacio Quemado suggest they may represent some of the same individuals depicted on the pillars of Pyramid B. Like the latter individuals, those on the Palacio Quemado panels may represent personages of two different categories: rulers and personages of a lesser status or function. Kristan-Graham (1999, n.d. [1989]) has also proposed that the reclining figures in the Palacio Quemado were commemorative monuments representing dead kings and noble warriors, which Mastache (n.d.) proposed were comparable to the *huehueteteo* (honored deceased ancestral warriors) depicted on page 33 of the Codex Borgia (Seler 1963; Figure 15).

Other relief sculptures from Sala 2 include panels that apparently

FIGURE 16. Part of the bench frieze on the south side of Sala 2 in the Palacio Quemado representing a procession warriors led by a personage with attributes of Tlaloc. Courtesy of Elizabeth Jiménez García.

FIGURE 17. Part of the bench frieze on the north side of Sala 2 in the Palacio Quemado representing a procession of elite personages. Photograph by Luis Gamboa Cabezas.

formed part of a continuous scene along the front of a bench that encircled the room. Along the east side of the principal entrance Acosta found a section of bench friezes representing a procession of six personages moving left to right, with three figures on the north face of the bench and three on the east face at the main entrance (Figure 16). The procession on the north face (location B in Figure 12) turned the corner at the entrance and is shown leaving the building on the east bench face (Acosta 1957: 131, 153, 168, láminas 8, 31). The personage leading the procession from the building possesses the goggles characteristic of Tlaloc (Figure 16) and is almost certainly the most important figure in the scene. The bench on the west side of the entrance to Rooms 2 and 3 likewise contained relief panels (location B in Figure 12) extending for more than 4 m (Figure 17), representing 13 personages moving from right to left, with 6 serpents on the overlying cornice moving in the same direction. Acosta (1957: 168–169) believed that the two processions extended in opposite directions on separate sides of the hall before converging at the main entrance along the south wall, where they presumably entered the south vestibule.

Acosta (1957) considered the personages in the two processions to be warriors, but only one figure in the north procession is armed, while the others carry what appear to be long banners or ceremonial staffs (scepters), decorated rattles, round banners (which may be shields), and at least one conch-shell trumpet. All of these objects are heavily ornamented with what appear to be feathers and scrolls. In contrast, all personages in the procession led by the Tlaloc-like figure on the south side of Sala 2 (Figure 16) carry weapons, some wear cotton armor, and almost surely represent warriors.

In our opinion, the two processions in Sala 2 involve wholly different individuals and activities. The figures in the north procession appear to represent high-ranking lords who are not warriors. These personages have the most sumptuous costumes depicted in any of Tula's friezes, and instead of weapons, they carry what appear to be musical instruments or noise makers. The south procession, however, is composed of warrior figures, and the speech scrolls coming from their mouths (including that of the leading individual dressed as Tlaloc) could well be symbols of song or of prayer. These friezes suggest a ritual similar to a ceremony for the sixth month of the Aztec calendar called Etzalqualiztli, as described by the informants of Sahagún, in which priests formed processions led by the high priest of Tlaloc (Sahagún 1956, vol. 1, Libro Segundo: 169).

The greater architectonic and symbolic importance of Sala 2 with respect to Salas 1 and 3 is also evident in the kinds of ritual contexts that have been identified there. It was precisely in the center of the patio of Sala 2 that we recently encountered a massive offering of marine materials that included an elaborate ceremonial garment (Figure 18) made of hundreds of finely carved shell plaques (Cobean and Mastache 2003). Above this offering was a later one consisting of a large pyrite mirror with turquoise mosaic fire serpents believed to represent a solar disk or *tezcacuitlapilli* like those on some of the fallen roof panels of Salas 1 and 2 (Cobean and Mastache 2003). In an analysis of these offerings, Taube (n.d.) considers the cut-shell garment offering to be a manifestation at Tula of the Teotihuacan-based cult of Tlaloc as a war god. This interpretation is supported by the procession in Sala 2 showing warriors being led by a personage with Tlaloc attributes (see Figure 16) and by the similarly attired individual on the newly discovered section of Pillar 3 from Building B (see Figure 9).

Besides the abovementioned turquoise mosaic mirror, an undecorated pyrite mirror was found overlying the shell garment in the earlier offering (Cobean and Mastache 2003). These mirrors are not the only ones found in Sala 2, however. During the 1950s, Acosta (1957) recovered a turquoise mosaic mirror and several small pyrite mirrors among a group of offerings beneath a Chacmool found in front of the eastern altar in Sala 2.

FIGURE 18. Shell mosaic
garment of Offering 2
in Sala 2 of the Palacio
Quemado. Photograph by
Salvador Guilliem Arroyo.

Discussion

We have noted that Tula Grande contained several distinct types of
buildings having functions that are not easily defined. Pyramids C and B,
adjacent and perpendicular to each other, were almost certainly the most
important architectonic elements at Tula Grande. Pyramid C was almost
certainly the principal structure, perhaps the *axis mundi* around which the
remaining elements of Tula Grande were planned. Pyramid B occupies a
secondary position as indicated by its smaller size and its location in the
precinct (but see Getino Granados and Cid Bezies [2000] for an alternative
interpretation of Pyramid B's role in the planning of the city).

Note that the differences between the two pyramids are not limited to
size and location. In a real sense Pyramid C is an entity unto itself, that is,
an autonomous architectural unit that was not articulated with the other
buildings. Even though Pyramid C was flanked by two structures, both
are separated from the pyramid by passageways, and they were dwarfed by
Pyramid C (see Figures 2, 3). Pyramid C is architecturally similar to the
Pyramids of the Sun and the Moon at Teotihuacan in possessing a *cuerpo*

adosado that abuts its frontal facade, thus constituting the same architectonic conception on a smaller scale. In this sense Pyramid C exhibits continuity with Teotihuacan, a conservative tradition that ties Tula to Classic Teotihuacan at least architecturally.

By contrast, Pyramid B is architecturally innovative, constituting a distinct entity that integrates in a single complex a pyramid-temple, a vestibule, and halls with benches and altars, thus uniting three distinct kinds of space and functions in a single structural unit. Just as Pyramid C links Tula with Teotihuacan, one can say that Pyramid B represents Tula's ties to northern architectonic traditions. The arrangement of pyramid and vestibule places a portico in front of a pyramidal structure, thus covering most of the pyramid's principal facade and obstructing its visual impact when seen from the plaza. The effect of this arrangement is to diminish the apparent volume and to some degree the grandeur of these structures (Hers and Braniff 1998).

Perhaps the existence of two principal but unequal pyramids at both Teotihuacan and Tula is related to the concept of duality. The image of the universe structured in pairs of opposing and complementary entities was a fundamental concept in the cosmovision of peoples in the Central Highlands (López Luján 1993: 95–101). At Teotihuacan the two pyramids occupy separate portions of the Street of the Dead, whereas at Tula the two occupy adjacent sides of the same plaza. Even at the Templo Mayor of Tenochtitlan, where two pyramids seemingly become one, the north (Tlaloc) temple was smaller than the south (Huitzilopochtli) temple, which possibly bespeaks a continuity in the cosmovision and the fundamental ideological concepts shared by these three cultures that endured for centuries (Mastache and Cobean 2000).

TULA CHICO AND THE EARLY SETTLEMENT AT TULA

Tula's earliest settlement corresponds to the Epiclassic Period Prado and Corral phases (A.D. 650–850), at which time it was centered around the Tula Chico monumental precinct located on a second prominence immediately north of Tula Grande (see Figure 1). Although smaller in scale, Tula Chico exhibits numerous similarities in its layout to Tula Grande (Mastache et al. 2002: fig. 4.12; Figure 19), suggesting the former may have served as a prototype for the latter (Matos Moctezuma 1974). One notable difference is that, in contrast to the approximately 17 degrees east-of-north orientation of Tula Grande, architectural remains at Tula Chico exhibit an approximately north-south orientation.

The early settlement is associated with Coyotlatelco ceramics that are characteristic of much of central Mexico during the Epiclassic period. The Prado complex (A.D. 650–750) is the diagnostic ceramic complex for the

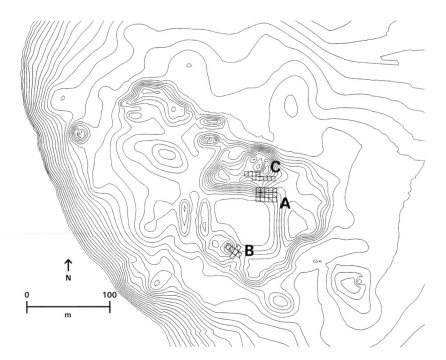

FIGURE 19. Topographic map of the plaza and adjacent structures at Tula Chico. Map by Jesús Acevedo García.

initial stage of settlement, but we do not know how large a settlement existed at that time. Prado complex ceramics were initially identified in exploratory excavations at Tula Chico (Cobean 1982; Cobean, Mastache, Figueroa Silva, and Suárez Cortés n.d.; Cobean and Suárez Cortés n.d.; Matos Moctezuma 1974), and as noted below have subsequently been associated with the oldest structural remains encountered to date at Tula Chico. Tula Chico also served as the monumental center for the succeeding Corral phase settlement (ca. A.D. 750–850). The surface distribution of Corral complex ceramics suggests a settlement core of at least 4 km^2 centered around Tula Chico (Healan and Stoutamire 1989: fig. 13.6).

The hill on which Tula Chico is situated appears to have been substantially modified by artificial terraces and platforms to accommodate the plaza and its constituent buildings. Tula Chico's plaza measures approximately 100 m east-west and is surrounded by several kinds of structures that appear to represent pyramids, ballcourts, and large platforms comparable to those of Tula Grande (cf. Figures 2 and 19). Exploratory excavations conducted over the past several decades (Cobean 1982; Cobean, Mastache, Figueroa Silva, and Suárez Cortés n.d.; Cobean and Suárez Cortés n.d.) indicate that some structures at Tula Chico have at least four construction stages.

The principal ballcourt at Tula Chico occupies the western side of the plaza, as does its counterpart at Tula Grande. In 2005, INAH excavated the northeast corner of this ballcourt, for which the best-preserved construction stage appears to date from the late Corral phase (ca. A.D. 800). Like those at Tula Grande, the Tula Chico ballcourt had stucco floors and the distinctive small tabular stone used as a decorative facade. A notable difference, however, is that the Tula Chico ballcourt is open ended, whereas the Tula Grande ballcourts are I-shaped (Ted Leyenaar, personal communication, October 2005).

In addition to its distinct north-south orientation, Tula Chico differs from Tula Grande and Teotihuacan in that its two principal pyramidal platforms are placed side by side on the northern side of the plaza. This arrangement is rather unusual. The closest parallel is perhaps the Templo Mayor of Aztec Tenochtitlan with its twin temples and stairways. Along the east side of the plaza, in the position corresponding to that of Pyramid C at Tula Grande, is a large rectangular platform somewhat similar in plan to the Palacio Quemado (Mastache et al. 2002: 75).

RECENT INVESTIGATIONS IN TULA CHICO

During 2002 and 2003, INAH conducted investigations at Tula Chico that included excavation of sections of the south facade of the larger (easternmost) of the two pyramids on the north side of the plaza (A in Figure 19). The lower facade of the pyramid has been badly damaged by Pre-Hispanic and modern looting. The summit of the pyramid has suffered less damage, where two hall-like rooms were partially excavated (C in Figure 19). Parts of the floors and walls of these halls had been destroyed and burned in Pre-Hispanic times. Although numerous carbon samples were recovered, no radiocarbon dates have yet been obtained, but the building is dated to the early Corral phase (ca. A.D. 750–800) based on associated ceramics (Cobean, Mastache, Figueroa Silva, and Suárez Cortés n.d.; Suárez Cortés et al. 2007).

Numerous fragments of relief sculpture were found on floors and in the rubble of the halls. These reliefs originally appear to have adorned benches and possibly the interiors of *impluvio*-like openings in the roofs. Several reliefs (Figure 20) depict richly attired reclining figures similar to those on panels that Acosta found in Salas 1 and 2 of the Palacio Quemado at Tula Grande (cf. Figures 20 and 14). Some of the Tula Chico figures wear stepped helmets, jade ear and nose plugs, cotton armor, *rodillera* knee protectors, and other dress elements that also appear in the Palacio Quemado reliefs. Several also have glyph-like elements near their heads (Figure 21).

Even earlier evidence of iconographic continuity between Tula Chico and Tula Grande comes from excavations conducted in the southwest corner of Tula Chico's plaza (B in Figure 19). Here a pure Prado phase (A.D. 650–750) deposit of sculptural fragments and other building rubble associated with a partially dismantled structure was encountered beneath rock fill underlying the present-day plaza surface (Figure 22). The most-intact sculptures include a relief of a raptorial bird and numerous bench

FIGURE 20. Reclining figure from the eastern pyramid at Tula Chico. Drawing by Daniel Correa Baltazar and Elizabeth Jiménez García.

FIGURE 21. Relief sculpture from the eastern pyramid of Tula Chico. Drawing by Bernabe Jiménez and Héctor Patiño Rodríguez.

cornices with vivid half-star motifs (A and B in Figure 22, Figures 23, 24). The sculptural style of the bird, the star motifs, and various triangle-shaped decorations from these Prado phase sculptures is similar to iconography from Xochicalco and Cacaxtla, Mexico (Foncerrada de Molina 1993: lámina IX; Smith 2000). The half-star element has been identified as a ritual war motif associated with the planet Venus (Baird 1989; Miller 1989; Smith 2000: 93). Miller (1989) eloquently documents images of "star warriors" at both Chichen Itza and Tula. The half-star element also is present in Classic Teotihuacan iconography (Baird 1989: 109–110).

Of particular interest is a fragment of a panel carved in relief showing the foot and lower leg of what was clearly a reclining personage (C in Figure 22). Although no other portion of this particular panel was encountered in the relatively small area excavated, its similarity to comparable portions of other depictions of reclining figures at Tula is striking (see Figures 14, 20). Hence this distinctive pose and sculptural style, certainly one of the most characteristic artistic elements of Tollan phase Tula, can be extended back at least as far as the Prado phase.

At some point Tula Chico appears to have been abandoned and its buildings burned and perhaps sacked. Excavations by Cobean and Suárez Cortés (n.d.) found evidence of burning in nearly all large buildings at Tula Chico. Austin Long of the Geosciences Laboratory of the University of Arizona, Tucson, dated five radiocarbon samples from these excavations, four from explorations of structural remains associated with the large platform along the east side of the plaza (see Figure 19, A and C). Two of these four samples (A-5852 and A-5853) are carbonized roof beams, whereas the other two (A-5856 and A-5855) are fragments of carbonized wood associated with two prior construction stages of the same structure (Figure 25). Calibrated to 2 standard deviations, these four samples range between A.D. 700 and 900, which does not allow for very precise placement of this particular structure in time. Considering, however, the stratigraphic

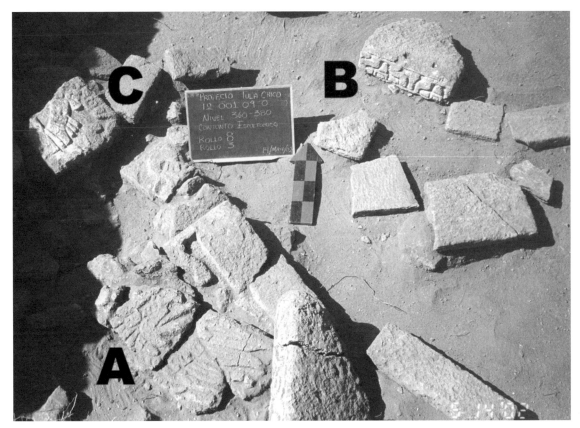

FIGURE 22. Sculptural elements of a Prado phase (A.D. 650–750) platform near the southwest corner of the Tula Chico plaza. Photograph by Dan M. Healan.

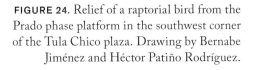

FIGURE 23. Bench cornice with Venus half-star motif from the Prado phase platform in the southwest corner of Tula Chico. Photograph by Elizabeth Jiménez García.

FIGURE 24. Relief of a raptorial bird from the Prado phase platform in the southwest corner of the Tula Chico plaza. Drawing by Bernabe Jiménez and Héctor Patiño Rodríguez.

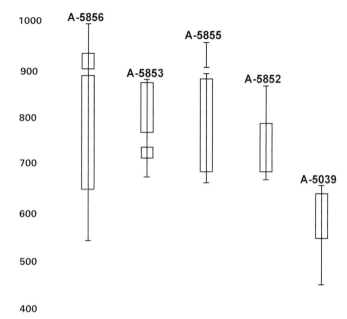

FIGURE 25. Radiocarbon dates: 2σ and 1σ (hollow) ranges for radiocarbon dates obtained for five carbon samples from Tula Chico. Data from Austin Long, Geosciences Laboratory, University of Arizona, Tucson. Calibration performed by CALIB (Stuiver and Reimer 1993).

data and the range of the dates obtained, it is reasonable to propose that (1) the earliest construction could have been around A.D. 700, because there is at least one construction stage prior to the dated context (A-5855), and (2) the abandonment and burning of the building likely occurred some time between A.D. 800 and 850. The fifth radiocarbon sample (A-5039) is a carbonized maize cob from the deepest levels of the ballcourt on the west side of the plaza and is presumably associated with the first construction stage, which may be as early as A.D. 600–650.

Despite its apparent destruction and abandonment, occupation of the area immediately surrounding the Tula Chico monumental precinct apparently continued and flourished as part of the subsequent Early Postclassic city. There is, however, no evidence of subsequent construction or occupation in Tula Chico itself, which apparently lay in ruins even as it was surrounded by the expanding urban settlement.

TULA CHICO, TULA GRANDE, AND THE TOLLAN PHASE CITY

The relocation of Tula's politico-religious core to Tula Grande at the end of the Corral phase was accompanied by growth that in the Late Tollan phase culminated in dense urban settlement that was perhaps three times the size of the Corral phase settlement (Healan and Stoutamire 1989; Figures 26–28). In this area, excavations conducted by a variety of projects over the past several decades have exposed remains of residential structures at at least 21 or more separate localities, revealing densely spaced and highly structured arrangements of residential compounds of various forms at every locality (Healan 1982, 2009; Paredes Gudiño 1992).

Of particular interest is that virtually all structural remains exposed to date at Tula exhibit one of three distinct spatial orientations: approximately north-south as in most of Tula Chico, roughly 17 degrees east of north as in most of Tula Grande, or roughly 18 degrees west of north. Moreover, the three orientations appear to exhibit spatial patterning: all exposed remains with a north-south orientation occur in the general vicinity of Tula Chico, those with an east-of-north orientation occur farther south around Tula Grande, and those with a west-of-north orientation are more widespread (Healan 2009: fig. 11). We assume, as did Mastache and Crespo (1982) that these represent three temporally distinct schemes of architectural orientation utilized at Tula over time. Given the relative ages of Tula Chico and Tula Grande, the north-south orientation is assumed to be the earliest, followed by the east-of-north orientation. The west-of-north orientation is assumed to be the latest of the three, given its association with structural remains that have been dated to the Late Tollan phase (Healan 1989: 163–167).

In virtually every case all structural remains exposed by excavation in a single locality, from the earliest to the latest, exhibit the same spatial orientation. Hence all construction within a given locality followed the same orientation over time, perhaps a reflection of enduring traditions or policies regarding construction at the local (neighborhood?) level. Alternatively, this consistency may simply represent the practice of incorporating existing platforms, foundations, and other walls into later building construction, as documented in several localities. Whatever the reason, its persistence through time in a given locality means that the orientation of a particular structure is an indication not of when the structure was built, but rather of when the locality was settled. As a result, all three orientations are visible on the surface today.

In a previous study, Mastache and Crespo (1982) identified numerous aligned, linear surface features on aerial photographs of Tula, which they interpreted as surface manifestations of terraces, platforms, walls, roadways, or other man-made features. In fact, three distinct alignments were identified, each of which corresponds to one of the three schemes of orientation exhibited by extant structural remains (Figures 26–28). This evidence not only provides additional support for the existence of multiple orientation schemes in the ancient city but also serves as a record of its growth over time. The earliest (or north-south) orientation is centered around and includes Tula Chico, the monumental center of Tula's initial (Prado–Corral phase) settlement (Figure 26), and corresponds rather well

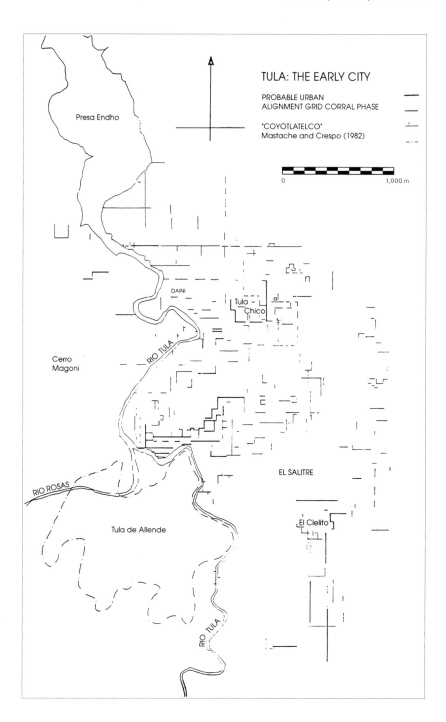

FIGURE 26. Epiclassic
Corral phase (A.D.
750–850) urban
alignment grid for Tula
(based on Mastache
and Crespo 1982).

to the surface distribution of Corral phase pottery (Healan and Stoutamire
1989: fig. 13.6). The subsequent, more extensive east-of-north orientation
is centered around and includes Tula Grande (Figure 27). It documents
the city's southward shift and realignment around its Tollan phase monumental center. The final (west-of-north) orientation is far more extensive

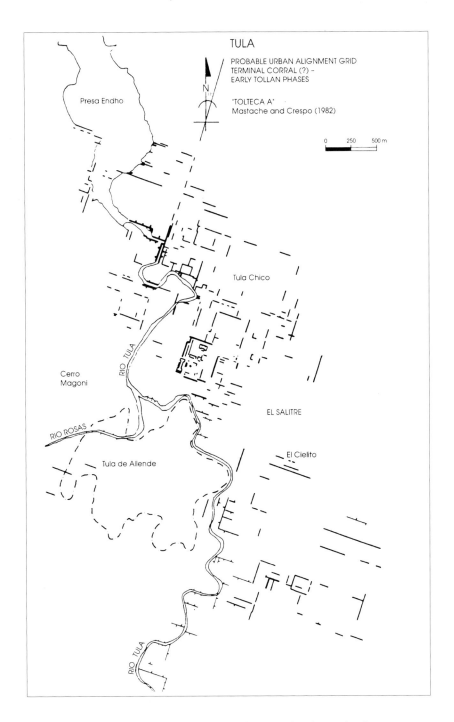

FIGURE 27. Early Tollan phase urban alignment grid for Tula (based on Mastache and Crespo 1982).

(Figure 28), representing additional settlement that brought the city to its maximum extent during the second half of the Tollan phase.

Evidence that Tula possessed internal planning—indeed, that the city possessed three different plans for construction during its existence—is as enigmatic as it is intriguing. Additional field research including ground-truthing of such features is clearly needed. However, it is apparent that

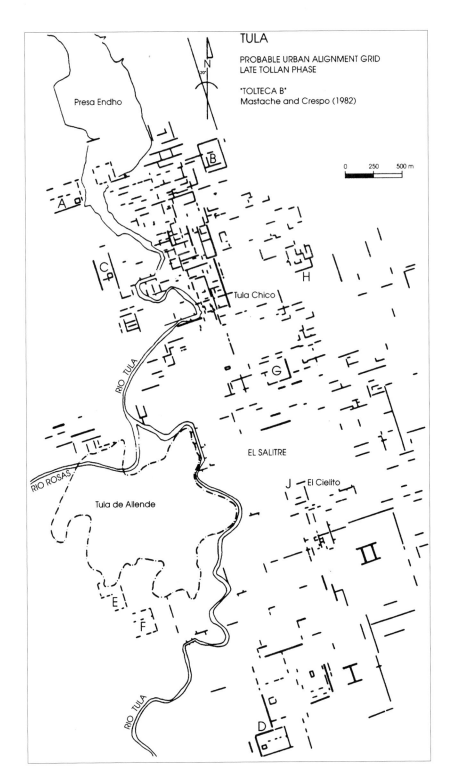

FIGURE 28. Late Tollan phase urban alignment grid for Tula (based on Mastache and Crespo 1982).

(1) all structural remains encountered to date at Tula correspond to one of three orientation schemes; (2) all remains in a single locality, from earliest to latest, exhibit the same orientation; and (3) localities with differing orientation schemes occur in close proximity to one another (e.g., Healan 2009: figs. 2a, 2g, 3b; Mastache et al. 2002: fig. 6.10). Getino Granados (2007) recently directed extensive salvage excavations in two northern sectors of the Tollan phase city, which uncovered barrios having their own local plazas and elite residences similar to the neighborhood structure proposed for Tula (Mastache et al. 2002: 170–176).

Of particular interest is the presence of what appears to be a system of north-south terraces and platforms partially surrounding the later monumental precinct at Tula Grande (see Figure 26), indicating monumental construction that may date from the Prado or Corral phase. Indeed, there is other evidence of Prado–Corral phase construction and occupation at Tula Grande, such as Acosta's (1945) discovery of what was described as "Coyotlatelco" occupation in several areas of the monumental precinct, including structural remains beneath the Palacio Quemado. More recently, Cobean (Mastache et al. 2002: 72, 128) encountered structural remains beneath Building K (see Figure 2) and in the vestibule south of the Palacio Quemado that probably correspond to platforms contemporary with those of Tula Chico. These early structures appear to have the same north-south orientation as Tula Chico, and they also have pure Corral phase ceramics.

The possible existence of Prado–Corral phase monumental construction at Tula Grande raises the intriguing possibility that early Tula had two monumental precincts, as some have previously suggested (Diehl 1983; Mastache and Crespo 1982: 23–24). Such a dual structure could indicate a settlement composed of two distinct ethnic or political factions, recalling the Quetzalcoatl-Tezcatlipoca duality recounted in legend and noted in the Pyramid B pillars. Alternatively, the two centers may represent wholly distinct polities, thus continuing what was in fact a widespread pattern of juxtaposed hilltop settlements in the Tula region in the immediately preceding La Mesa phase (ca. A.D. 550–650; Healan and Cobean n.d.; Mastache et al. 2002: 60–69).

One of the most enigmatic aspects of Tula's settlement history is the absence of construction or occupation of the Tula Chico monumental complex following the Corral phase, even as it was surrounded by the expanding Tollan phase city. This anomaly, not unlike the Acropolis surrounded by modern Athens, has been interpreted in various ways, including the notion that Tula Chico was hallowed ground for events known or believed to have occurred there at some time in the past (e.g., Mastache and Crespo 1982). Alternatively, noting the abovementioned possibility of independent but coexisting Prado–Corral phase settlements at Tula Chico and Tula Grande, the burning and destruction of Tula Chico may have been the result of conflict between competing polities that culminated in the incorporation of Tula Chico by Tula Grande, a situation not unlike what occurred between the neighboring settlements of Tenochtitlan and Tlatelolco in Aztec times.

The striking similarity of the recently recovered sculptures at Tula Chico to those of the Palacio Quemado at Tula Grande clearly shows that the roots of Early Postclassic Tula's distinctive corpus of art and iconography can be found at Tula Chico during the Corral and Prado phases. If, as Kristan-Graham (1999, n.d. [1989]) has proposed, reclining figures depicted at Tula are portraits of deceased kings or elite warriors in the tradition of the *huehueteteo*, or honored deceased ancestral warriors of the Codex Borgia (see Figure 15), then the roots of Tula's central institutions are to be found at Tula Chico as well (Mastache n.d.). Indeed, if even the earliest of these monuments are commemorations of already-deceased individuals, then we must ask where and when these institutions began. At the very least, it is obvious that, contrary to Coggins (2002: 45), if Early Postclassic Tula is Toltec, then Tula Chico is as well.

Acknowledgments

We thank the Foundation for the Advancement of Mesoamerican Studies, Crystal River, Florida, for financing some of the drawings of monuments at Tula as part of a grant to Elizabeth Jiménez García (Figures 6, 7, 8, 9, 20).

NOTES

1. We somewhat reluctantly utilize this terminology to facilitate comparison of the two precincts. We acknowledge, however, that this Tula Chico/Tula Grande dichotomy is somewhat simplistic: it underplays some notable differences in layout and other aspects, as discussed in the text, and may be misconstrued to mean that Tula consisted of two separate settlements.

2. If the remnant feathers immediately to the left of the central figure in Figure 11 are part of a feathered staff, which would presumably have been in front of the bearer, then the individuals in the missing portion are moving toward the central figure. If, however, they are part of a headdress, presumably situated behind the wearer, then the missing individuals are moving away from him. Given that all depictions of feathers in the extant procession are headdresses, it seems most likely that the individuals in the missing portion are moving away from the central figure and hence in the same direction as the extant procession. Thus the central figure would be greeting a line of individuals, whom he faces, as they file past him.

3. An exception is Room 2, which has a single column and connects to Sala 2.

REFERENCES CITED

Acosta, Jorge R.
    1943 Los colosos de Tula. *Cuadernos Americanos* 1(2): 133–146.

1944 La tercera temporada de exploraciones arqueológicas en Tula, Hgo. 1942. *Revista Mexicana de Estudios Antropológicos* 6: 125–164.

1945 La cuarta y quinta temporada de exploraciones arqueológicas en Tula, Hgo. *Revista Mexicana de Estudios Antropológicos* 7: 23–64.

1956 Resumen de los informes de las exploraciones arqueológicas en Tula, Hidalgo durante las VI, VII y VIII temporadas 1946–1950. *Anales del INAH* 8: 37–115.

1957 Resumen de los informes de las exploraciones arqueológicas en Tula, Hidalgo, durante las IX y X temporadas, 1953–54. *Anales del INAH* 9: 119–169.

1961a La doceava temporada de exploraciones en Tula, Hidalgo. *Anales del INAH* 13: 29–58.

1961b La indumentaria de los cariátides de Tula. In *Homenaje a Pablo Martínez del Río*: 221–228. Instituto Nacional de Antropología e Historia, México.

1964 La décimo tercera temporada de exploraciones en Tula, Hgo. *Anales del INAH* 16: 45–76.

1967 *Tula* (Guía). Instituto Nacional de Antropología e Historia, México.

1968 *Tula: Official Guide.* Instituto Nacional de Antropología e Historia, México.

Báez Urincho, Fernando
2007 El Edificio 4: Palacio del rey tolteca. *Arqueología Mexicana* 15(85): 51–54.

Baird, Ellen T.
1989 Stars and War at Cacaxtla. In *Mesoamerica after the Decline of Teotihuacan: A.D. 700–900* (Richard A. Diehl and Janet C. Berlo, eds.): 105–122. Dumbarton Oaks Research Library and Collection, Washington, D.C.

Carrasco, Pedro
1971 The Peoples of Central Mexico and Their Historical Traditions. In *The Handbook of Middle American Indians* (Robert Wauchope, ed.), vol. 11: 459–473. University of Texas Press, Austin.

Charlton, Thomas H., and Deborah H. Nichols
1997 Diachronic Studies of City-States: Permutations on a Theme: Central Mexico from 1700 B.C. to A.D. 1600. In *The Archaeology of City-States* (Deborah L. Nichols and Thomas H. Charlton, eds.): 169–207. Smithsonian Institution, Washington, D.C.

Cobean, Robert H.
1982 Investigaciones recientes en Tula Chico, Hidalgo. In *Estudios sobre la antigua ciudad de Tula* (Alba Guadalupe Mastache, ed.): 37–122. Colección Científica 121. Instituto Nacional de Antropología e Historia, México.

Cobean, Robert H., and Alba Guadalupe Mastache
1988 La excavación monumental en Tula. In *La antropología en México: Panorama histórico* (Carlos García Mora and María del Valle Berrocal, eds.), vol. 6. Colección Biblioteca. Instituto Nacional de Antropología e Historia, México.

2003 Turquoise and Shell Offerings in the Palacio Quemado of Tula, Hidalgo, Mexico. In *Latin American Collections: Essays in Honor of Ted*

J. J. Leyenaar (Dorus Kop Jansen and Edward K. de Bock, eds.): 51–66. Tetl, Leiden, The Netherlands.

Cobean, Robert H., and María Elena Suárez Cortés

    n.d. Informe de las excavaciones en Tula Chico, temporada 1989. Archivo de la Coordinación Nacional de Arqueología, Instituto Nacional de Antropología e Historia, México.

Cobean, Robert H., Alba Guadalupe Mastache, Javier Figueroa Silva, and María Elena Suárez Cortés

    n.d. Proyecto Tula: 2002–2003. Informe 2004. Archivo de la Coordinación Nacional de Arqueología Instituto Nacional de Antropología e Historia, México.

Cobean, Robert H., Alba Guadalupe Mastache, Javier Figueroa Silva, María Elena Suárez Cortés, Clemente Salazar, Blanca Estela Martínez Landa, Fernando Báez Urincho, and Hector Patiño

    n.d. Proyecto Tula: 2004. Informe 2005. Archivo de la Coordinación Nacional de Arqueología, Instituto Nacional de Antropología e Historia, México.

Coe, Michael D.

    1999 *Breaking the Maya Code Second Edition*. Thames and Hudson, London.

Coggins, Clemency Chase

    2002 Toltec. *RES: Anthropology and Aesthetics* 42: 35–85.

Diehl, Richard A.

    1983 *Tula: The Toltec Capital of Ancient Mexico*. Thames and Hudson, London.

    1989 Previous Investigations at Tula. In *Tula of the Toltecs: Excavations and Survey* (Dan M. Healan, ed.): 13–29. University of Iowa Press, Iowa City.

Evans, Susan Toby

    2004 Aztec Palaces and Other Elite Residential Architecture. In *Palaces of the Ancient New World* (Susan Toby Evans and Joanne Pillsbury, eds.): 7–58. Dumbarton Oaks Research Library and Collection, Washington, D.C.

Foncerrada de Molina, Marta

    1993 *Cacaxtla: La Iconografía de los Olmeca-Xicalanca*. Instituto de Investigaciones Esteticas, Universidad Nacional Autónoma de México, México.

García Cook, Ángel

    2003 Cantona: The City. In *Urbanism in Mesoamerica* (William T. Sanders, Alba Guadalupe Mastache, and Robert H. Cobean, eds.): 1: 311–344. Instituto Nacional de Antropología e Historia and Pennsylvania State University, México, and University Park.

García Icazbalceta, J. (ed.)

    1941 *Historia de los mexicanos por sus pinturas*. Salvador Chávez Hayhoe, México.

Getino Granados, Fernando

    2007 Los barrios de Tula: Estudios en la zona urbana norte. *Arqueología Mexicana* 15(85): 58–63.

Getino Granados, Fernando, and José Rodolfo Cid Bezies
    2000   Astros y montañas: Elementos rectores para el trazo urbano en
           Teotihuacan y Tula. *Arqueología* 24:87–106.
Healan, Dan M.
    1982   *Patrones residenciales en la antigua Ciudad de Tula*. In *Estudios sobre la
           antigua ciudad de Tula* (Alba Guadalupe Mastache, ed.): 123–148. Colec-
           ción Científica 121. Instituto Nacional de Antropología e Historia,
           México.
    1989   (ed.) *Tula of the Toltecs: Excavations and Survey*. University of Iowa
           Press, Iowa City.
    2009   House, Household, and Neighborhood in Ancient Tula. In *Domestic
           Life in Prehispanic Capitals: A Study of Specialization, Hierarchy, and
           Ethnicity* (Linda R. Manzanilla and Claude Chapdelaine, eds.).
           University of Michigan Museum of Anthropology, Memoir 46.
           Ann Arbor.
    n.d.   Acosta's Tula Grande: Fact or Falsification? A paper presented at
           the 66th Annual Meeting, Society for American Archaeology, New
           Orleans, 2001.
Healan, Dan M., and Robert H. Cobean
    n.d.   La interacción cultural entre el centro y el occidente de México.Vista
           desde la region de Tula. *Las Sociedades Complejas del Occidente de
           México en el Mundo Mesoamericano: Homenaje al Dr. Phil C. Weigand*
           (Eduardo Williams, ed.). El Colegio de Michoacán, Instituto Nacio-
           nal de Antropología e Historia, La Universidad de Guadalajara (in
           press).
Healan, Dan M., and James W. Stoutamire
    1989   Surface Survey of the Tula Urban Zone. In *Tula of the Toltecs: Excava-
           tions and Survey* (Dan M. Healan, ed.): 203–236. University of Iowa
           Press, Iowa City.
Hers, Marie-Areti
    1989   *Los toltecas en tierras chichimecas*. Instituto de Investigaciones Esteticas,
           Universidad Nacional Autónoma de México, México.
Hers, Marie-Areti, and Beatriz Braniff
    1998   Herencias chichimecas. *Arqueología* 19: 55–80.
Hirth, Kenneth G.
    2000   *Ancient Urbanism at Xochicalco*. University of Utah Press, Salt Lake City.
Jiménez García, Elizabeth
    1998   *Iconografía de Tula: El caso de la escultura*. Instituto Nacional de
           Antropología e Historia, México.
Kristan-Graham, Cynthia
    1999   Architecture of the Tula Body Politic. In *Mesoamerican Architecture
           as Cultural Symbol* (Jeff K. Kowalski, ed.): 162–175. Oxford University
           Press, New York.
    n.d.   Art, Rulership and the Mesoamerican Body Politic at Tula and
           Chichen Itza. Ph.D. dissertation, Department of Art History,
           University of California at Los Angeles, 1989.

López Luján, Leonardo

    1993 *Las ofrendas del Templo Mayor de Tenochtitlan.* Instituto Nacional de Antropología e Historia, México.

Martínez del Río, Pablo, and Jorge R. Acosta

    1967 *Tula (Guía).* Instituto Nacional de Antropología e Historia, México.

Mastache, Alba Guadalupe

    n.d. Notas acerca del Códice Borgia. Archivo del Proyecto Tula. México.

Mastache, Alba Guadalupe, and Robert H. Cobean

    1985 Tula. In *Mesoamérica y el centro de México* (Jesús Monjarás Ruiz, Rosa Brambila, and Emma Pérez-Rocha, eds.): 273–307. Colección Biblioteca. Instituto Nacional de Antropología e Historia, México.

    2000 Ancient Tollan: The Sacred Precinct. *RES: Anthropology and Aesthetics* 38: 100–133.

Mastache, Alba Guadalupe, Robert H. Cobean, and Dan M. Healan

    2002 *Ancient Tollan: Tula and the Toltec Heartland.* University Press of Colorado, Boulder.

Mastache, Alba Guadalupe, and Ana M. Crespo

    1982 Análisis sobre la traza general de Tula, Hgo. In *Estudios sobre la antigua ciudad de Tula* (Alba Guadalupe Mastache, ed.): 11–38. Colección Científica No. 121. Instituto Nacional de Antropología e Historia, México.

Matos Moctezuma, Eduardo

    1974 Excavaciones en la microarea: Tula Chico y la Plaza Charnay. In *Proyecto Tula: Primera Parte* (Eduardo Matos Moctezuma, ed.): 61–69. Colección Científica 15. Instituto Nacional de Antropología e Historia, México.

    1988 *The Great Temple of the Aztecs.* Thames and Hudson, London.

    2003 Buildings in the Sacred Precinct of Tenochtitlan. In *Urbanism in Mesoamerica* (William T. Sanders, Alba Guadalupe Mastache, and Robert H. Cobean, eds.), vol. 1: 119–147. Instituto Nacional de Antropología e Historia and Pennsylvania State University, Mexico City and University Park.

Miller, Virginia E.

    1989 Star Warriors at Chichen Itza. In *Word and Image in Maya Culture* (William F. Hanks and Don S. Rice, eds.): 287–305. University of Utah Press, Salt Lake City.

Moedano, Hugo

    1944 La diosa rapada. *Nosotros* 1–19: 24–26.

    n.d. Tollan. Master's thesis, Escuela Nacional de Antropología e Historia, Mexico, 1946.

Molina Montes, Augusto

    1982 Archaeological Buildings: Restoration or Misrepresentation. In *Falsifications and Misreconstructions of Pre-Columbian Art* (Elizabeth H. Boone, ed.): 125–141. Dumbarton Oaks Research Library and Collection, Washington, D.C.

Nelson, Ben A.

    1997 Chronology and Stratigraphy at La Quemada, Zacatecas, México. *Journal of Field Archaeology* 24: 85–109.

Nicholson, Henry B.

    1961 The Chapultepec Cliff Sculpture of Motecuhzoma Xocoyotzin. *El México Antiguo* 9: 379–444.

    1971 Major Sculpture in Prehispanic Central Mexico. In *Handbook of Middle American Indians* (Robert Wauchope, ed.): 10: 92–134. University of Texas Press, Austin.

    2000 *Topiltzin Quetzalcoatl: The Once and Future Lord of the Toltecs.* University Press of Colorado, Boulder.

Paredes Gudiño, Blanca

    1992 Unidades Habitacionales en Tula, Hidalgo. Colección Científica 210. Instituto Nacional de Antropología e Historía, Mexico.

Pérez Castro, Guillermo, Pedro Sánchez Nava, María Estefan, Judith Padilla y Yedra, and Antonio Gudiño Garfias

    1989 El Cuauhxicalli de Moctezuma I. *Arqueología* 5: 131–151.

Piña Chan, Roman

    1975 *Teotenango: El antiguo lugar de la muralla.* 2 vols. Gobierno del Estado de México, Toluca.

Sahagún, Bernardino de

    1956 *Historia general de las cosas de Nueva España* (Angel María Garibay, ed.). 4 vols. Editorial Porrua, México.

Sanders, William T., and Robert S. Santley

    1983 A Tale of Three Cities. In *Prehistoric Settlement Patterns* (Evon Vogt and Richard Leventhal, eds.): 243–291. University of New Mexico Press, Albuquerque.

Sanders, William T., and David Webster

    1988 The Mesoamerican Urban Tradition. *American Anthropologist* 90: 521–546.

Sanders, William T., Jeffrey R. Parsons, and Robert S. Santley

    1979 *The Basin of Mexico.* Academic Press, New York.

Seler, Eduard

    1963 *Comentarios al Códice Borgia.* 3 vols. Fondo de Cultura Económica, México.

Serra Puche, Mari Carmen

    1998 *Xochitecatl.* Gobierno del Estado de Tlaxcala, Tlaxcala, México.

Smith, Virginia

    2000 The Art and Iconography of the Xochicalco Stelae. In *Archaeological Research at Xochicalco* (Kenneth G. Hirth, ed.): 2: 83–101. University of Utah Press, Salt Lake City.

Stoutamire, James W.

    n.d. Trend Surface Analysis of Survey Data Tula, Mexico. Ph.D. dissertation, Department of Anthropology, University of Missouri, Columbia, 1975.

Stuiver, Minze, and Paula J. Reimer

    1993 Extended 14C Data Base and Revised CALIB 3.0 14C Age Calibration Program. *Radiocarbon* 35: 215–230.

Suárez Cortés, María Elena, Dan M. Healan, and Robert H. Cobean

    2007   Los origenes de la dinastía real de Tula: Excavaciones recientes en Tula Chico. *Arqueología Mexicana* 15(85): 48–50.

Taube, Karl A.

    1993   *Aztec and Maya Myths.* British Museum, London.

    1994   The Iconography of Toltec Period Chichen Itza. In *Hidden among the Hills: Maya Archaeology of the Northwest Yucatan Peninsula* (Hanns J. Prem, ed.): 212–246. Acta Mesoamericana 7. Verlag von Flemming, Möckmühl, Germany.

    n.d.   The Mirrors of Offerings 1 and 2 of Sala 2 in the Palacio Quemado at Tula: An Iconographic Interpretation. In *Ofrendas en un palacio Tolteca: Turquesa y concha en el Palacio Quemado de Tula, Hidalgo* (Robert H. Cobean and Alba Guadalupe Mastache, eds.). Instituto Nacional de Antropología e Historia, México (in press).

Tozzer, Alfred M.

    1957   *Chichen Itza and Its Cenote of Sacrifice.* Memoirs of the Peabody Museum of Archaeology and Ethnology, vols. 11 and 12. Harvard University, Cambridge, Mass.

Wicke, Charles R.

    1976   Once More around the Tizoc Stone: A Reconsideration. *Actas del XLI Congreso Internacional de Americanistas* 2: 209–222.

Yadeun, Juan

    1975   *El estado y la ciudad, el caso de Tula, Hgo.* Colección Científica 25. Instituto Nacional de Antropología e Historia, México.

THE FACE OF THE ITZAS

ELEVEN

William M. Ringle
George J. Bey III

IMPLICIT IN ANY ANALYSIS of how Mesoamerican cities presented themselves is the question of their audience. It is hardly to be doubted that the imagery and architecture of most Maya cities reflect the lifeways, beliefs, costume, and environment of a local, relatively homogenous population. In the Puuc region of northern Yucatan, for instance, this homogeneity rises almost to the point of monotony, with a few noteworthy exceptions. Apart from strong similarities in the decoration of facades—the use of mosaic masks, geometric stonework, colonnettes, and the like—instances in which architecture or individuals are represented appear to be self-reflexive. Rectangular thatch huts, for instance, are not uncommonly depicted on the facades of vaulted buildings and for the most part agree with what can be observed archaeologically. Murals and relief sculpture also generally reflect minor variations on regional conventions of dress and pose.

The faces presented by other cities in Mesoamerica are much more problematic in that references are made to a wider world. Many of these cities are under discussion in this volume, and several are candidates for the expanded definition of Tollan. One of these, Chichen Itza, has long been recognized as being "out of place," and not surprisingly early interpretations of that site tended to equate this difference with an occupation by foreigners. This history has been exhaustively and critically reviewed in recent years (Carrasco 1982; Gillespie 2007; Jones 1995, 1997) and need not be presented anew except to say that several investigators over the past two decades have failed to find evidence for an intrusive population and so argue for the essential "Maya-ness" of the city (Lincoln 1986, n.d. [1990]; Ringle 1990; Schele and Freidel 1990: 355). We find ourselves in general agreement with this last position, but as noted previously (Ringle 2004; Ringle et al. 1998), it fails to answer the question of why foreign references are so prevalent there.

This chapter is therefore an examination of how foreignness was incorporated and manifested at Chichen Itza. Our central thesis is that foreignness was mediated by the introduction of new forms of military organization, which in turn had implications for the construction of public spaces and the expression of individual identity. The imposition of novel forms of "discipline," in Foucault's (1979) sense, was but one aspect of wider changes during the Mesoamerican Epiclassic involving new, or renewed, forms of elite legitimacy centered about the Feathered Serpent.

RITUAL AT THE GREAT CENOTE, CHICHEN ITZA

Let us begin with a single artifact, a small jade head dredged from the Great Cenote by Edward Thompson (Figure 1a). Stylistically this head clearly came from elsewhere, almost certainly from a Late Classic workshop somewhere in the southern lowlands. Fortunately, an inscription on its reverse allows us to confirm its origin. The text makes undoubted reference to the Piedras Negras ruler K'inich Yo'nal Ahk II, who ruled from A.D. 687 to A.D. 729 (Martin and Grube 2000: 145; Proskouriakoff 1944, 1974: 205). The two dates include 7 Imix 14 Mac (9.13.7.13.1, A.D. 699), the thirteenth *tun* anniversary of his accession on 9.12.14.13.1 7 Imix 19 Pax (A.D. 687), and 5 Imix 19 Zac (9.13.14.13.1, A.D. 706), the completion of his first *k'atun* in office, probably a date then still in the future (Martin and Grube 2000: 145). Another inscribed jade from the cenote is its virtual contemporary. This jade (Figure 1b) mentions the Palenque ruler K'inich Kan B'alam II, who ruled from A.D. 684 to A.D. 702 and records the dates 13 Ahau 18 Kayab (A.D. 690), 2 Cib 14 Mol (A.D. 687), and 9 Manik 0 (or 20) Pop (probably A.D. 695). Although both jades could possibly have been heirlooms later tossed into the cenote, it is striking that both are portraits and date to within a decade of each other.

The dates are suggestive, because as noted by Osorio León and Pérez de Heredia (2001; Pérez de Heredia 1998), they are contemporary with the earliest ceramics present in the cenote in any quantity, sherds from the Late Classic Motul complex, which they date between A.D. 600 and A.D. 800. Elsewhere, excavation data from throughout "Old" and "New" Chichen Itza, as well as in peripheral groups, confirm a striking scarcity of ceramics antedating the Sotuta phase (A.D. 800–1050, in our view), the ceramics associated with the site's florescence. The only major exception is the earliest substructure of the Templo de la Serie Inicial, where relatively pure deposits of pure Motul phase pre-slate ceramics were recovered below sealed floors (Osorio León and Pérez de Heredia 2001; Schmidt 2003b: 1). To date this substructure is the earliest known masonry structure at the site. Osorio León and Pérez de Heredia suggest that its construction, the heightened offerings of Motul ceramics in the cenote, and the jades together suggest the cenote cult had its inception during the Late Classic, well before much else was constructed at the site. The jades may thus have

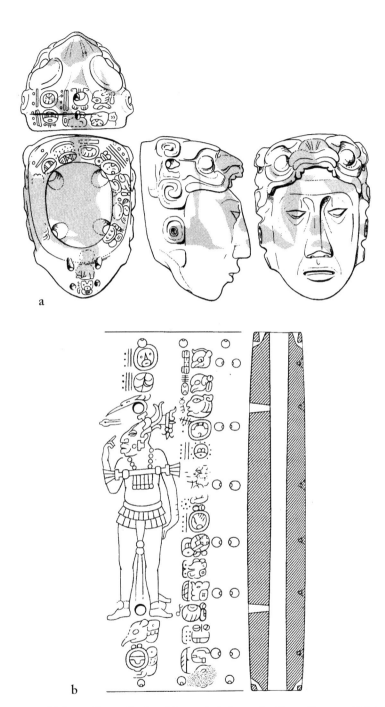

FIGURE 1. (a) Late Classic Piedras Negras jade from the Great Cenote, Chichen Itza (Coggins and Shane 1984: no. 53; from Proskouriakoff 1974: 205, plate 60.1, copyright 1974 by the President and Fellows of Harvard College); (b) Late Classic Palenque jade from the Great Cenote (from Proskouriakoff 1974: 204–205, plate 45.2, copyright 1974 by the President and Fellows of Harvard College).

FIGURE 2. Piedras
Negras Stela 7, a portrait
of Yo'nal Ahk II (Stone
1989: fig. 13, after
Spinden 1957: plate L,a)

been tossed in the cenote during or shortly after the lifetime of their wearers, perhaps at the same event and very close to A.D. 700.

In previous discussions (Ringle 2004; Ringle et al. 1998), we noted that the expansion of Feathered Serpent (FS) ideology involved place-making, either as the actual foundation of new centers or by the introduction of new dynasties legitimized by the institutions associated with the FS (see also Florescano 2004; López Austin and López Luján 1999). The overwhelming dominance of Sotuta pottery at Chichen Itza suggests that this city was also founded de novo not long before the beginning of the Sotuta phase. Undoubtedly a few modest structures had existed there before, but something else seems responsible for its explosive expansion in the following two centuries.

To return to the jade head, although its date of deposition can only be considered as conjectural, it is particularly interesting as a type of offering. Yo'nal Ahk I, grandfather and namesake of Yo'nal Ahk II, was apparently the dynastic founder of Piedras Negras (though not its first ruler). He is depicted on Piedras Negras Stelae 26 and 31 wearing the Teotihuacanoid War Serpent headdress and on Stela 26 holding a staff that terminates in an FS (Stone 1989) very much like the baton recently found beneath the Feathered Serpent Pyramid at Teotihuacan. He thus represents the introduction of the FS into Piedras Negras. Stone (1989: 162–163) demonstrates that this costume continued in full force through the reign of Yo'nal Ahk II on Stelae 7, 8, and 9 (Figure 2).

Dedicatory objects such as the jade are consistent with our previous arguments that Chichen Itza functioned as one of the Epiclassic Tollans, drawing offerings and perhaps supplicants from a wide periphery. It also functioned as something of an engine of investiture into military orders that were in some manner associated with the FS, its avatars, and associated deities. The headdress worn by this jade figurine again supports this idea, because it seems to be a variant of the animal-maw headdress so common on other jades and on the sculptures of Chichen Itza in later years (e.g., the *hombre-pajaro-serpiente* figures). If Chichen Itza became a Tollan ca. A.D. 700, then it would have been one of the initial wave of such centers emerging from the collapse of Teotihuacan a century earlier, as we have argued previously (Ringle et al. 1998).

The question is thus raised of the circumstances whereby the jades ended up in the cenote. The use of the cenote has received relatively little sustained interpretation by scholars, despite the wealth of published data (Coggins 1992; Coggins and Shane 1984; Lothrop 1952; Proskouriakoff 1974). On ethnohistorical grounds, Tozzer (1957: 200–205) argued it was used for rainmaking and divination. Piña Chan (1970: 56) accepted this interpretation for Late Classic Chichen Itza, but then saw a shift to human sacrifice during Chichen "Toltec" times. Coggins (cf. 1992: 236, 340) has suggested in several places that calendrics played a role, in particular the beginning and end of Baktun 10, whereas several of the contributors to Coggins's (1992) catalog contend that it was the receptacle for one or more termination rituals. These explanations do little to address the particular types of artifacts found in the cenote, however.

Miller and Samoya (1998) critiqued some of these earlier views and suggested that the cenote could instead be viewed as an otherworldly portal associated with the Maya Maize God. Furthermore, they identified the famous chacmool sculptures as associated with the theology of maize. Their arguments are based on a general association between jade, jade beads, and ears of corn, as well as a few figural jades they identify as representations of the Maize God, but again they do not deal with the entire assemblage of jades, much less the remainder of objects from the cenote.

In a short contribution such as this chapter, we cannot either, but a few points are in order. First, as Clemency Coggins has noted, the cenote rituals may well have changed over time. For instance, the offering of copal seems to be a late trait (Coggins and Ladd 1992: 352), as suggested by the form of copal nodules and the Postclassic vessels in which many were found, whereas lithics were primarily deposited during the florescence of Chichen Itza (Sheets et al. 1992: 174). We should therefore not be overly credulous with regard to Landa's description of sacrificial rites carried out at the cenote (Tozzer 1941: 19, 180), especially as models for events occurring 500 or 600 years earlier. As Hooton (1940: 272) and Hopkins (1992) emphasize, nonhuman far outnumber human bones in the cenote collections made by Thompson. More recent analyses of the cenote bodies (Anda Alanís 2007; Beck and Sievert 2005) demonstrate a variety of probable sacrificial treatments, including a substantial number of individuals who were killed prior to their deposition, rather than being thrown into the cenote alive, as Landa describes.

We have earlier (Ringle et al. 1998) presented evidence suggesting that a large fraction of the figural jades portray warriors costumed in headdresses were associated in some way with the FS. Such jades are consistently associated in caches elsewhere at putative Tollans, such as Tula, Xochicalco, and Monte Albán. Furthermore, some of the cenote jades portray the FS or one of his traits, such as wind. Other jades may well be costume ornaments associated with these warrior orders (Figure 3).

The other artifacts are likewise consistent with a military orientation. As Miller and Samoya (1998: 56) note, the lithics include no examples of groundstone manos or metates, surprising if the cenote was indeed consecrated to the Maize God. Instead the cenote collection contains a number of atlatl points, including several of foreign form (and some gold imitations; Sheets et al. 1992: 178), and large bifaces (Figure 4). Of a total of 250 artifacts reported, 13 were large bifaces (lance points or daggers), 12 tanged bifaces,

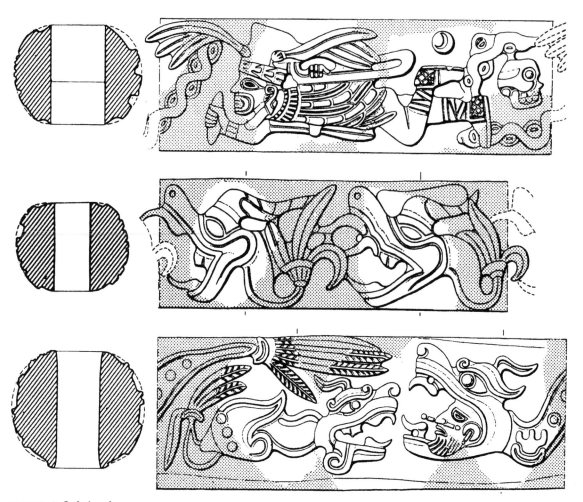

FIGURE 3. Jade beads from the Great Cenote with FS and warrior motifs (from Proskouriakoff 1974: plates 43.8, 42.3, 43.9, copyright 1974 by the President and Fellows of Harvard College).

23 side-notched bifaces, 33 corner-notched bifaces, 4 lanceolate bifaces, 59 bifacially flaked fragments of projectile points, 12 bifacial thinning flakes, 50 flakes, 17 obsidian flakes, 25 obsidian prismatic blades, and 2 obsidian cores. In addition another Peabody collection had 1 bifacial knife, 17 corner-notched bifaces, 4 lanceolate bifaces, and 2 corner-notched bifaces. Thus if debitage is excluded, virtually the entire assemblage (save for the obsidian blades) are projectiles, a conclusion reinforced by Sievert's (1992) study of edge wear.

Wooden objects include ear or lip ornaments, some bearing images of warriors (Coggins and Ladd 1992: figs. 8.1, 8.2, 8.5–8.7; Figure 5), atlatls, dart shafts, curved fending sticks like those held by "Toltec" warriors on stone reliefs (Figure 6), and various scepters (Figure 7). Noteworthy among the latter are those bearing images of serpents (see Coggins and Ladd 1992: figs. 8.38–8.44). Another group, perhaps Late Postclassic in date, depict seated rulers or descending gods, but again the association with rulership is significant. As for ceramics, most (92.3 percent) of the 104 whole or partially complete vessels from the cenote analyzed by Ball and Ladd (1992)

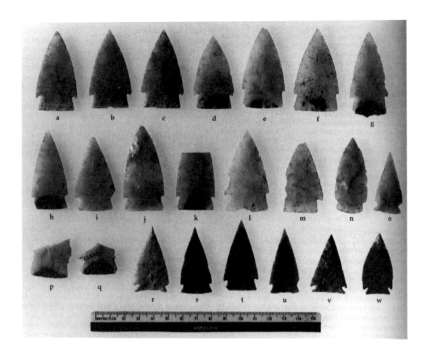

FIGURE 4. Lithics from the Great Cenote (from Coggins 1992: figs. 6.6 [top], 6.2 [center left], 6.1 [center], 6.8 [center bottom], 8.37a [lower right], copyright 1992 by the President and Fellows of Harvard College).

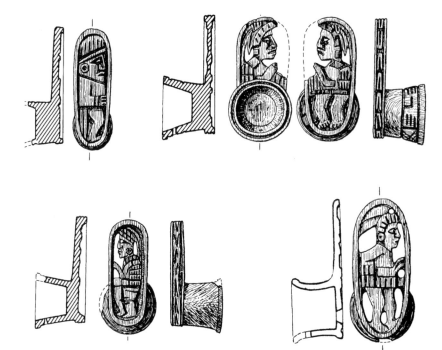

FIGURE 5. Wooden ear ornaments from the Great Cenote (from Coggins 1992: plates 8.7 [top left], 8.6 [top right], 8.5 [bottom left], 8.2 [bottom right], copyright 1992 by the President and Fellows of Harvard College).

are Late Postclassic in date and so may pertain to a later stage of cenote ritual. Noteworthy among the earlier vessels are two openwork censers, a thin-slate jar frescoed with FS imagery, and a Holtun Gouged-incised jar also with stylized FSs. Schmidt (1998: 426) illustrates an extraordinary vessel from the cenote that depicts a procession of individuals, two of whom are marked by vaguely Mixteca-Puebla–style face paint, one with that of Quetzalcoatl, the other with that of Mixcoatl (Figure 8). The vessel itself appears to be Maya and is classified in the Motul complex by Pérez de Heredia (1998: fig. 20). As argued in Ringle (2004), the feathered (Quetzalcoatl) and cloud (Mixcoatl) serpents at Chichen may represent dual offices within the overall Quetzalcoatl hierarchy; this vessel would argue for the early inception of this arrangement at Chichen Itza.

The most superficial review of metals from the cenote (Lothrop 1952) indicates that military themes are the almost exclusive concern of the famous gold disks. Furthermore, Lothrop (1952: 86, fig. 26) demonstrates that many of the other objects, such as the copper bells (Coggins and Shane 1984: no. 27), turn up as decorative elements on "Toltec" warrior costumes, while the symbolism of gold projectile points hardly needs comment. The gold "horse collar" (Lothrop 1952: fig. 56) mimics shell examples, such as those found in the famous Teotihuacanoid tombs from Kaminaljuyu, and is thus arguably associated with warrior orders. Finally, the well-known gold eye rings and mouth piece (Lothrop 1952: figs. 54, 55) carry explicit FS imagery and find counterparts in the relief sculpture and atlantean bench supports elsewhere on the Great Terrace (see Figure 12).

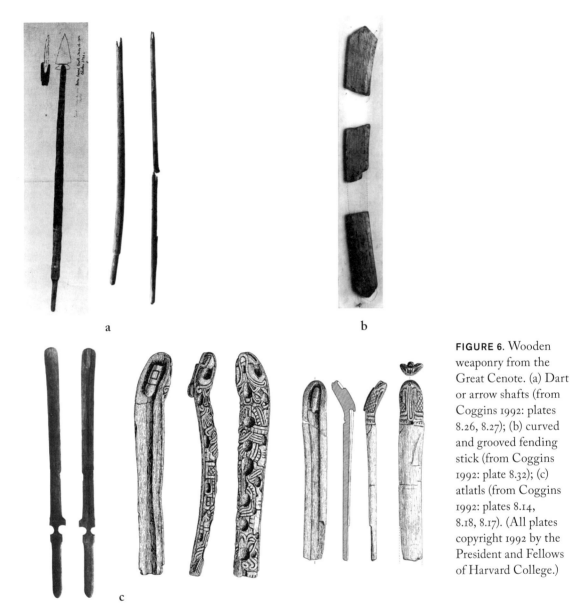

FIGURE 6. Wooden weaponry from the Great Cenote. (a) Dart or arrow shafts (from Coggins 1992: plates 8.26, 8.27); (b) curved and grooved fending stick (from Coggins 1992: plate 8.32); (c) atlatls (from Coggins 1992: plates 8.14, 8.18, 8.17). (All plates copyright 1992 by the President and Fellows of Harvard College.)

In short, cenote rituals, rather than being primarily associated with the forces of nature or agriculture, instead reflect the political rituals of Chichen's military orders. The Great Cenote was not a receptacle for a happenstance collection of surplus exotics from the far reaches of Mesoamerica. Instead its contents were structured by the military orders associated with the FS. The cenote was, in effect, a much-expanded version of the stone urn caches found around the Great Terrace (and at Tula), all of which are characterized by elements of the warrior's costume (see Ringle 2004; Figure 9). The early cenote jades suggest that from the outset foreignness was being incorporated in the context of these activities. Initially these reflect a neo-Teotihuacan

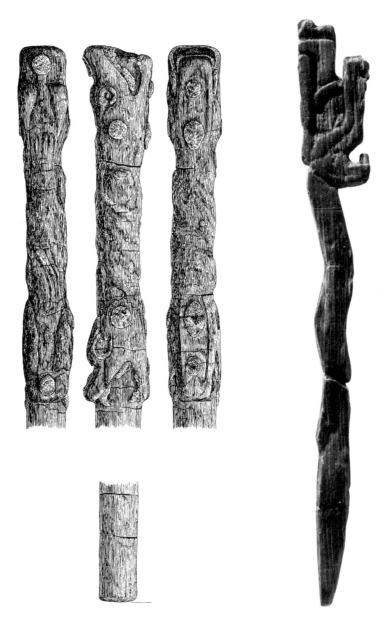

or pre-formal version of militarism, incorporating foreign imagery into a largely Maya symbol set, but then artifact styles shifted to more typically "Toltec" forms sometime during the Sotuta phase.

The recognition of the centrality of the warrior body to the rituals of Chichen Itza permits a revaluation of the symbolism of the chacmool. These sculptures have posed problems precisely because they have been assumed to be supernaturals, yet they lack the diagnostics that usually accompany such figures. Instead, their most identifiable aspects are those of the "Toltec" costume: pillbox hat, butterfly pendant, and the like. The chacmool is at base an effigy of a warrior whose reclining posture suggests that he is to

FIGURE 8. Polychrome bowl from the Great Cenote bearing two figures with Quetzalcoatl-related facial paint, possibly from the Motul phase (A.D. 600–800; from Schmidt 1992: 426).

receive whatever offerings were placed in the dish he usually holds. This interpretation thus fits nicely with our previous interpretation of the Great Terrace as a place of initiation.

CHRONOLOGY

For the past 25 years, debate has focused on the degree of overlap between the widespread Cehpech ("slateware") complex of northern Yucatan and the Sotuta complex of Chichen Itza, the ceramic complex associated with the vast majority of construction at the site. Now that most authorities accept at least some overlap between the two, attention has turned to Chichen itself, where recently several scholars have argued for early and late facets of the Sotuta ceramic complex (Cobos Palma n.d. [2003]: 385–433, 2004: 521–525; Cobos Palma and Winemiller 2001; Lincoln n.d. [1990]: 212–214, 219–221).

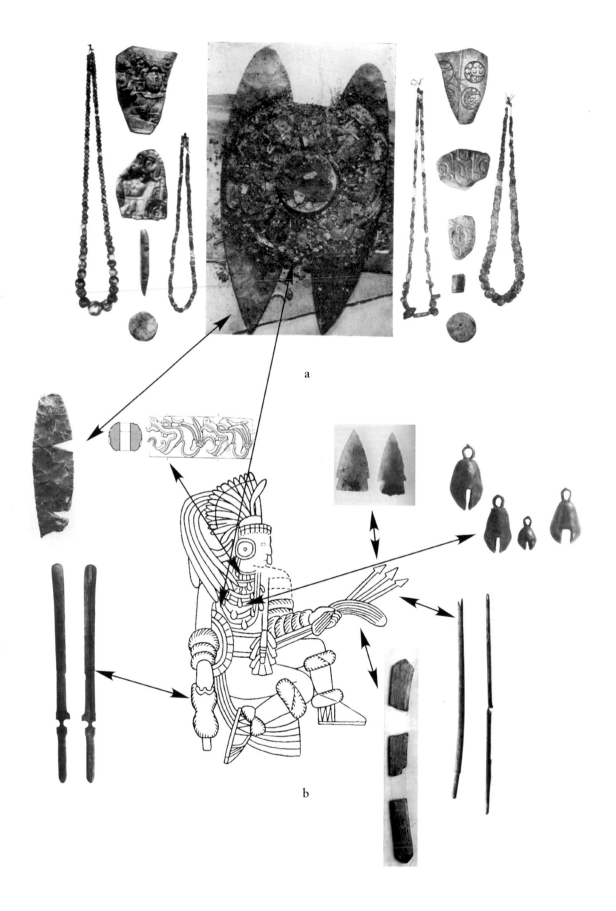

a

b

In contrast, early and late architectural phases at Chichen Itza have been recognized almost since the inception of organized fieldwork at the site. The Carnegie archaeologists developed a working definition of "Maya" versus "Toltec" architecture, which, although never formally expressed, clearly informed the studies of Ruppert (1935, 1943, 1952), Bolles (1977), and Morris et al. (1931). Formal definitions of the two styles may be found in Tozzer (1957), Marquina (1964), Kubler (1962: Chapter 9), E. Andrews (1965), Pollock (1965), and G. Andrews (1995). To avoid ambiguity as to how "Toltec" is being used, we here utilize E. Andrews's distinction between Florescent ("Puuc-like") and Modified Florescent ("Maya-Toltec") structures, with the caveats that these styles probably overlapped to some extent and that the division between the two did not necessarily correspond to changes in ceramic phases. Our use of "Toltec" refers to members of the military and priestly orders associated with any of the Tollans from the time of Teotihuacan onward, rather than just those from Tula.

G. Andrews (1995) makes several particularly valuable points with regard to the two architectural styles. First, Chichen's Florescent style is unlikely to have developed there, because there are no Proto-Puuc, Early Puuc, or Colonnette style structures at the site. Florescent architecture at Chichen Itza most resembles the late Mosaic style of the Puuc Hills, a style characterized by long-nosed mosaic masks. Yet Chichen Florescent structures lack the rows of colonnettes found in most Puuc buildings. Second and more importantly, there are significant differences in construction techniques. G. Andrews (1995: 305) notes that

> the stonework in walls of Maya-Chichen buildings is of the thick, semi-veneer block type, while all buildings in the late Puuc styles have thin veneer-over-concrete walls. For the most part vaults in Maya-Chichen buildings are slab-type corbelled vaults, whereas vaults of Classic Puuc Colonnette, Mosaic, and Late Uxmal style buildings feature concrete vaults faced with specialized wedge- and boot-shaped stones. Finally, some Maya-Chichen buildings . . . have pointed vaults . . . whereas no Classic Puuc buildings show this detail.

There is thus a puzzling disjunction between the use of the Puuc Mosaic style decoration on the facades of Florescent structures at Chichen Itza and the later adoption of Puuc construction techniques for Modified Florescent structures there. The Modified Florescent style is also characterized by a number of traits distinctive unto itself: colonnaded halls, radial pyramids,

(opposite) **FIGURE 9.** (a) Cache from the Castillo, Chichen Itza (Marquina 1964: foto 428), compared with (b) warrior costume artifacts from the Great Cenote (central figure from Tozzer 1957: fig. 574).

TABLE 1. Dates related to architecture at Chichen Itza and related Puuc sites

Long count	Calendar Round	Christian[1]	Style[2]	Location and comments
CHICHEN ITZA				
C-14[3]		A.D. 663	F	Iglesia
C-14[4]		A.D. 666/750	F	Casa Colorada
10.0.2.7.13	9 Ben 1 Zac	8-2-832	F-MF	Hieroglyphic Jambs (alternatively, 1 Calendar Round later)
10.1.15.3.6	11 Cimi 14 Pax	11-15-864	MF?	Great Ballcourt Stone
10.1.17.5.3	11 Ben 11 Cumku	12-22-866	F?	Water Trough (Cobos Palma n.d. [2003] suggests from Str. 5D2)
10.2.0.7.9	9 Muluc 7 Pop	1-11-870	F	Halakal Lintel
10.2.0.1.9	6 Muluc 12 Mac	9-13-869	F	Casa Colorada
10.2.0.15.3	7 Akbal 1 Chen	6-14-870	F	Casa Colorada
10.2.0.17.7	12 Manik 5 Zak	7-28-870	—	Chichen Stela 2: F-J; (near Casa Colorada, but freestanding): a dubious reading
10.2.1.0.0	(12 Ahau 18 Zac)	8-10-870	F	Casa Colorada 47
10.2.2.0.0	(8 Ahau 13 Zac)	8-5-871	F	Casa Colorada 51
10.2.3.0.0	(4 Ahau 8 Zac)	7-30-872	F	Casa Colorada 54
10.2.4.8.4	8 Kan 2 Pop	1-5-874	F	Yula Lintel 1
10.2.4.2.1	2 Imix 4 Mac	9-4-873	F	Yula Lintel 2
10.2.4.8.12	3 Eb 10 Pop	3-13-874	F	Yula Lintel 2
10.2.8.0.0	(10 Ahau 3 Yax)	4-4-887	F-MF	Caracol band fragment 9: debatable
10.2.9.1.9	9 Muluc 7 Zac	7-28-878	?	Initial Series Group (lintel reset, original location unclear)
10.2.10.0.0	2 Ahau 13 Chen	6-24-879	F	House of the Three Lintels
10.2.10.11.7	8 Manik 15 Uo	2-6-880	F	Monjas (several times)
10.2.11.0.0	11 Ahau 8 Chen	6-18-880	F	Akab Dzib
C-14[3]		A.D. 883	F	Iglesia
>10.2.0.0.0	3 Ahau 18 Mol	A.D. 869–889	MF	Temple of the Owls Capstone[5]
10.2.13.13.1	4 Imix 14 Zip	2-24-883	F	Monjas, East Annex, North Capstone, Room 2[6]
10.2.15.2.13	9 Ben 1 Zac	8-2-832	MF	Hieroglyphic Jambs (Kelley, Grube reading)
10.2.16.0.0	4 Ahau 3 Mol	5-23-885	F-MF	Caracol band fragment 17; Caracol Stela A1-B1
10.2.16.7.4	5 Kan 7 Muan	10-14-885	F-MF	Caracol band fragment 16: debatable

(continued)

battered lower wall zones, flat beam-and-mortar roofs, atlantean figures, chacmool statues, among others. For our purposes, another especially important trait is the use of square piers, often sculptured on all four sides (see, e.g., Figure 22).

The question then becomes when this transition took place. Cobos Palma (n.d. [2003]: 206) argues that Florescent architecture belongs primarily to the ninth century, whereas Modified Florescent structures primarily date to the tenth or later. Hieroglyphs are here of relatively little help in that no Modified Florescent buildings on the Great Terrace bear inscriptions. The same is true for most Mosaic-style Florescent structures from the Puuc Hills. In contrast, the prevalence of dedicatory dates on Chichen's Florescent buildings is a trait pointed to by Andrews (1995: 305) as further distinguishing Chichen and the Puuc zone. The narrow span covered by

Long count	Calendar Round	Christian[1]	Style[2]	Location and comments
10.2.17.0.0	13 Ahau 18 Yaxkin	5-18-886	F-MF	Caracol side Q10-R11; Caracol Stela C5
C-14[4]		A.D. 886/891	MF	Castillo
C14[4]		A.D. 891	MF	Monjas Complex east
10.3.0.8.4*	9 Kan 7 Muan	10-13-889	F-MF	Caracol band fragment 16: debatable
10.3.0.15.1	3 Imix 19 Zip	2-27-890	F-MF	Caracol band fragment 18: problematic[7]
10.3.1.0.0	10 Ahau 18 Xul	4-27-890	?	Chichen Stela 2: D10 (near Casa Colorada, but freestanding)
10.3.8.14.4	6 Kan 2 Pop	12-30-897	F?/MF?	Painted capstone, said to be from Halakal (Tozzer 1957: 156, fig. 540) or somewhere near the Mercado (Morley 1920: 520)
10.8.10.6.4	10 Kan 2 Zotz	2-4-998	MF	Osario (High Priest's Grave)
10.8.10.11.0	2 Ahau 18 Mol	5-11-998	MF	Osario (High Priest's Grave)
PUUC SITES				
10.1.10.0.11?	2 Chuen 3 Muan	10-18-859	F	Kabah Str. 2C6 Jambs (Codz Pop)
10.1.13.0.0	5 Ahau 18 Mac	9-21-862	F	Labna Mask snout
10.2.7.0.0	1 Ahau 8 Yax	7-9-876	F	Kabah Manos Rojas
10.3.6.0.0	(6 tun in 3 Ahau)	4-1-895	—	UXM St. 17
10.3.15.16.14	2 Ix 16 Pop	1-13-905	F-MF	UXM Ballcourt—North ring
10.3.15.16.15	3 Men 17 Pop	1-14-905	F-MF	UXM Ballcourt—South ring
10.3.17.3.19	12 Cauac 16 Xul	4-23-906	F	UXM Monjas South building (Schele and Mathews 1998: 287)
10.3.17.12.1	5 Imix 18 Kankin	10-2-906	F	UXM Monjas East structure, capstone[8]
10.3.18.9.12	4 Eb 5 Keh	8-9-907	F	UXM Monjas Y Capstone

Notes: Data principally from Graña-Behrens (n.d. [2002]); Grube (2003); Kelley (1982); Ringle et al. (1998); Stuart (1989). Architectural information from Ruppert (1952). Puuc dates from Kelley (1982), Kowalski (1987), Pollock (1980), and Thompson (1937). Calendar Round dates in parentheses are implied by k'atun-tun glyphs.

1. Christian dates are back-calculated in the Gregorian calendar.

2. F, Florescent; MF, Modified Florescent; F-MF, transitional Florescent-Modified Florescent.

3. Calibrated midpoint.

4. Calibrated midpoints.

5. Stuart's (1989) listing is in error, repeating the Monjas dates. Kelley (1982: 14) expresses doubt as to any verifiable date. The *tun* may have a coefficient of 13, so 10.2.13.0.0 is another possibility. Graña-Behrens (n.d. [2002]: 360) places it only in k'atun 10.2/1Ahau (A.D. 869–889).

6. Kelley (1982: 19) and Grube's (2003) reading. This capstone is partially eroded. Graña-Behrens (n.d. [2002]: 360) places it only in k'atun 10.2/1Ahau (A.D. 869–889).

7. The date, which reads "first *tun* of k'atun 12 Ahau," is preceded by the CR date 3 Imix 9/14 Yax. No occurrence of 3 Imix and either 9 or 14 Yax falls between 10.3.0.0.0 and 10.3.1.0.0.0, however (10.4.0.0.0 ending the k'atun 12 Ahau). Kelley (1982) amends this to 3 Imix 9 Zip, with the Long Count date given here.

8. Seven new radiocarbon dates for Uxmal have been published recently (Vallo 2003: 335–336). Four dates from the Chanchimez range from A.D. 736 to A.D. 877 (midpoint-to-midpoint). The three dates from the Monjas are inconsistent internally (ranging from A.D. 636 to A.D. 1163) and with the Monjas hieroglyphic dates.

these dates suggests that the Florescent occupation of Chichen Itza may have been relatively short, perhaps only A.D. 800–880, or even less.

We do have a few exceptions, however (Table 1). In the Puuc zone, perhaps the clearest date associated with a Mosaic-style structure is that placed on the nose of a mask on the west facade of the East Wing of the Labna palace (Pollock 1980: 10). This date reads 10.1.13.0.0 or A.D. 862 (Thompson 1937: 195). The jambs from the Codz Pop (Structure 2C6) of Kabah, a building in high Mosaic style, are also dated. Although the jambs are on the eastern side of the structure, Pollock (1980: 194) is of the opinion that if anything they are later than the famous masks of the western facade, although in all probability both sides were planned from the beginning. Despite alternative readings (Carrasco Vargas and Pérez de Heredia 1996: 302; Thompson 1954: 97), 2 Chuen 3 Muan (10.1.10.0.11, or A.D. 859) seems most satisfactory.[1] Because these dates are about 20 years before the dates on Florescent structures at Chichen Itza, they provide incontrovertible proof that the advanced Puuc stoneworking techniques, characteristic of Chichen's Modified Florescent architecture, were in existence when Chichen's technically cruder Florescent structures were built.

Four dates seem associated with the Modified Florescent style at Chichen Itza. One is the date on Structure 6E3, known as the Temple of the Hieroglyphic Jambs. It bears a Calendar Round (CR) date of 9 Ben 1 Zac that most authorities place at either A.D. 832 (Krochock 1995) or one CR later at 884 (Grube 2003; Kelley 1982). Formally, this building is a gallery-patio structure and so pertains to the Modified Florescent tradition. It would date the onset of this style before the end of the ninth century, either contemporary with or very shortly after the Florescent structures mentioned above.[2] Another date is carved on a stone purportedly from the Great Ballcourt depicting "Toltec" ballplayers much like those along the alley of the Great Ballcourt. Wren et al. (1989) argue for a date of 10.1.15.3.6 11 Cimi 14 Pax, or A.D. 864 (Wren et al. 1989). Dates from the Caracol (seeFigure 24), thought to be a transitional structure architecturally, range from A.D. 887 to A.D. 890. Finally, there is the Temple of the Owls (5C7). This building has several Modified Florescent architectural traits, including rectangular sculptured piers, basal batter, and "Toltec" iconography (Ruppert 1952: 124). A painted capstone from the building, now lost, has been argued to record a date that may be either A.D. 882 or 884 (Kelley 1982; Thompson 1937: 186). A late ninth-century advent of the Modified Florescent style would also be consistent with radiocarbon dates from the Castillo.

Another extremely important set of hieroglyphic dates associated with architecture come from Uxmal. These come from the ballcourt (January 13, A.D. 905, and one day later) and three capstones from the Nunnery (August 23, A.D. 906; October 2, A.D. 906; and August 9, A.D. 907) from the south and east ranges and Building Y, respectively.[3] These dates are important because the FS iconography at Uxmal is most evident in the Nunnery and the ballcourt, and it is generally assumed that such ideas were derived from Chichen Itza. Furthermore, some Modified Florescent architectural traits seem to be present in these groups, such as the carefully hewn sloping talus blocks of the Nunnery's supporting platform. Thus the development of the Modified Florescent style, as exemplified by the Castillo and Temple of the Chac Mool, and its subsequent spread to Uxmal, must have happened within the narrow window of A.D. 850–900, although better dating of substructures may push its inception back even further. The A.D. 998 date from the Osario of Chichen Itza, 3C1, indicates that this style flourished for another century, but from A.D. 1000 to A.D. 1200, the dates formerly favored for Chichen's apogee, we have nothing to guide us.

We therefore accept the slightly later onset of the Modified Florescent style (ca. A.D. 850–880) but would add that adoption of the style did not reflect an overall change in purpose of the site, but rather an intensification of the militarism that was increasingly transforming the landscape as a whole. Although in general the visible structures of the Great Terrace do slightly postdate the structures of the Monjas area (see Figure 12), substructures underneath many of the Great Terrace buildings must push initial construction of this area back to contemporaneity with the Monjas buildings. In our view both continued in use during the tenth century, although the Monjas area was increasingly colonized by Modified Florescent architecture, such as the Temple of the Wall Panels and several of the ballcourts. As we have argued on earlier occasions, this segregation of architectural styles may reflect a division between two types of leadership, that of the hegemonic empire on the one hand, centered on the Great Terrace, and the local polity on the other, within the Monjas area, much as Lind (n.d.) has argued for in Late Postclassic Cholula (see also López Austin and López Luján 1999: 42–43).

Although we are ignorant of its exact date, the Castillo-sub (Figure 10) is the major piece of evidence for militarism during the pre-Modified Florescent period on the Great Terrace. Architecturally and stratigraphically it predates all the buildings currently visible on the terrace (Bey and Ringle 2007) as well as the Temple of the Chac Mool, which actually postdates the final stage of the Castillo. Descriptions by Erosa Peniche (1939, 1948) and Marquina (1964) indicate that despite its decoration, architecturally the structure was Pure Florescent in style. The basal platform had nine terraces, like the final version, but the faces were undecorated *taluds* (Figure 10a). Only a single stairway ascended the front, and no sculptured piers were used in the entrance to the sanctuary. The walls of its superstructure also lack a basal batter, and its upper wall zone was delimited by simple three-part moldings (Marquina 1964: 852).

Several traits connect the Castillo-sub with the FS warrior complex, however, most notably the frieze of prowling felines and the twinned serpents and reed glyph over the doorway (Bey and Ringle 2007; Figure 10b). Inside a chacmool was discovered, although it could have been added some time after the dedication of the temple. Finally, several shields with pendant streamers were carved on the exterior facade. These have not been accurately drawn in past reproductions. A photograph by Ed Kurjack shows that the shield is decorated with crescents (Figure 11a). Similar shields are depicted on the north and west murals of the Upper Temple of the Jaguars (Figure 11b) and on its facade (Figure 11c), but the closest parallels are with two panels of unknown provenience from Tula (Figure 11d,e). A possibly related shield is also found in Aztec sources such as the Codex Mendoza. The meaning of the decoration is unknown, but its distribution strongly

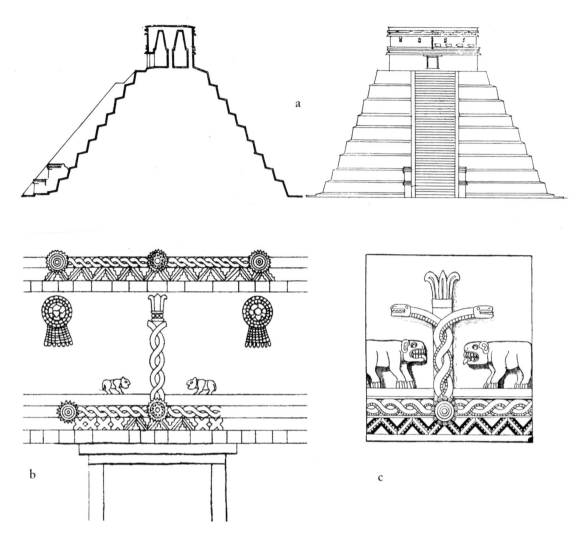

FIGURE 10. (a) Elevation of the Castillo-sub (Marquina 1964: lámina 263); (b) facade of the Castillo-sub (from Erosa Peniche 1939: fig. 1); (c) alternative reconstruction of the central element of the Castillo-sub facade (Tozzer 1957: fig. 86).

suggests it was in some way connected to the Toltec warrior costume and hence is another example of the early role specifically "Toltec" militarism had at Chichen Itza, here on its principle structure.[4]

MODIFIED FLORESCENT MILITARY ORDERS AT CHICHEN ITZA

Although asserting the importance of militarism at Chichen is hardly a novel proposition, the organization of its military was qualitatively different from that of other lowland Maya centers, and the profound manner in which it permeated the architecture of "New" (Modified Florescent) Chichen Itza has yet to be explored. In the following sections we trace the interlocking themes of the built environment and costume during the Modified Florescent period, two central devices in the presentation of the

a

b

c

d

e

FIGURE 11. (a) Shield from the facade of the Castillo-sub (photograph courtesy of Edward Kurjack); (b) same shield in the west mural of the Upper Temple of the Jaguars, Chichen Itza (from Coggins and Shane 1984: fig. 19 [detail]); (c) same shield from the exterior frieze of the Upper Temple of the Jaguars (from Seler 1998: fig. 89a); (d, e) identical examples from Tula (from Jiménez García 1998: figs. 145 [d], 144 [e]).

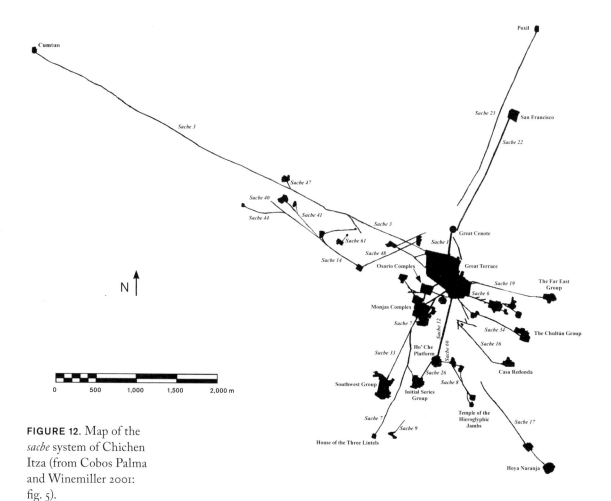

FIGURE 12. Map of the *sacbe* system of Chichen Itza (from Cobos Palma and Winemiller 2001: fig. 5).

city. We then conclude with an examination of peripheral settlement at Chichen to determine whether similar processes extended beyond the site center.

Circulation through the public space of Chichen Itza was controlled by a large number of *sacbes* (causeways) connecting a few large central terraces with one another and with outlying clusters of elite and residential architecture (Cobos Palma n.d. [2003]; Cobos Palma and Winemiller 2001; Schmidt 1998; Figures 12, 13). These central terraces were in effect extensive open-air stages, an architectural strategy held in common with most other large Maya centers, except that the relative extent and freedom of access to open plazas seem to be much greater at Chichen (Pollock 1965).

But the central innovation of Chichen's architects was the creation of significantly greater interior spaces by means of colonnades and innovations in roofing (Pollock 1965: 434). In no case were the interior spaces of any northern Maya building sufficient to have held more than a few dozen individuals, save for a few extraordinary exceptions. At Chichen Itza, the use of beam-and-mortar roofs or multiple parallel vaults supported

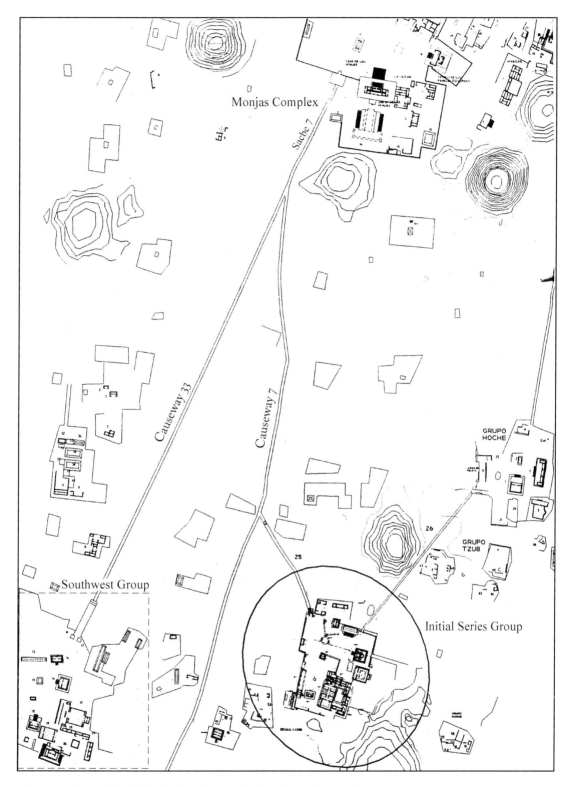

FIGURE 13. Map of the Initial Series Group, the Southwest Group, Sacbes 33 and 7, and the Monjas Complex, Chichen Itza (from Schmidt 2003b: III: fig. 2 [detail]).

by columns created much wider interior spaces. Columns allowed end walls to be opened up as well, greatly prolonging the length of rooms, although visibility must have been significantly impaired by these supports.

Doorways and piers provided new spaces for sculptural elaboration, to the extent that the majority of architectural sculpture on the Great Terrace was only visible from inside structures.[5] Although small depictions of deities occupy the upper or lower registers of piers and jambs, the much larger central register is almost invariably occupied by a human, warriors for the most part but also several individuals generally lumped together as "priests." Although many structures at Chichen are referred to as temples, in no case do their carved piers represent priests exclusively. In fact, warriors are a consistent majority in all cases, and when priests are present, they are often depicted on some of the most peripheral faces.

These sculptured supports created interior spaces dramatically different from those found at other sites in Yucatan. Whereas in traditional Maya sites sculpture either provided an image of the king or served as a backdrop to focus attention on the king's body (throne backdrops, canopies, wall panels, and so on), the use of sculptural piers created in effect a three-dimensional representation of spectator space. In such rooms the spectator was surrounded by images of warriors much like himself, and as in many Tollans, the image of the leader is notable chiefly by its absence. Instead, only a vacant bench or table throne provided a focal point to the room.[6]

One of the striking differences between Chichen Itza and other Maya sites is that although representations of a few ranks of society are given in great detail at southern sites, at Chichen there are dozens. These have conventionally been lumped as either "Maya" or "Toltec," but this scheme is a gross oversimplification of a truly extraordinary repository of information about Pre-Hispanic costume. A working premise of this chapter is that the internal order of these images reflects in some manner the organization of elite life. A promising early start on interpreting these patterns was made by Ann Morris and Jean Charlot (Morris et al. 1931) using the piers and benches of the Temple of the Warriors and the Northwest Colonnade. The far larger sample made available by the work of Merle Greene Robertson (1995, 1996) now makes it possible to extend this methodology to other structures, but as Morris and Charlot found, the patterns are rarely clear cut. In fact, it might be said that the piers are consistently inconsistent, in that very often three sides of a pier will be virtually identical but differ completely from the fourth, or two sides of a building will present a clear contrast except for a few individuals. For example, on the jambs and pilasters of the Upper Temple of the Jaguars, every individual (n = 16) but one carries an atlatl, darts, and a curved stick. The lone exception (H6) has two curved sticks, yet he is not otherwise differentiated, nor is he in a particularly significant position.

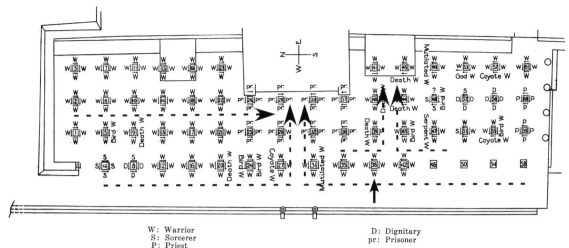

W: Warrior
S: Sorcerer
P: Priest

D: Dignitary
pr: Prisoner

FIGURE 14. The directed gazes of the sculptures of the Northwest Colonnade, Chichen Itza (from Morris et al. 1931: fig. 171).

Within the colonnades, space is organized in two principal fashions. One is by the gaze of the sculpted warriors. Almost every figure faces toward the centerline of the building or toward the rear. The figures are rigidly and stereotypically posed as if in attendance to whatever activity is being carried out at the center rear of the room. This arrangement creates a simple axis of mirror symmetry about the central axis, directing attention toward the principal entrance or bench. In larger structures, secondary foci can interrupt this simple ordering. As Charlot and Morris noted (Morris et al. 1931: fig. 171), a secondary axis in the Northwest Colonnade, which fronts the Temple of the Warriors, led up to the carved bench south of the main stairway (Figure 14). However, it was deemed more important on the exterior piers to follow the main axis, and so the figures of pier 38 (arrow in the figure) face north instead of south. Note that both patterns reflect the perspective of a person entering the structure, not that of the presumed paramount seated on the interior throne. It is the perspective of the many witnessing the one, whose return gaze is only implied.

Space was also orchestrated by the arrangement of costumes on the piers, jambs, and columns, again drawing upon axes of symmetry and complementarity (i.e., consistent differences across an axis). Some of these patterns are illustrated in Figure 15. Again the importance of the midline is clearly emphasized by the distribution of costumes but in a more complicated fashion. Costume is sometimes ranked by distance to the midline, for instance, rather than being dichotomized. There is also very often an inner-outer complementarity in which the outer portico figures differ from those within (e.g., the Temple of the Chac Mool). A variant concerns the front (facing toward the outside or toward the midline) versus back (facing toward the rear or away from the midline) faces of square piers. The faces paralleling the midline were often of particular importance, especially of jambs and pilasters.

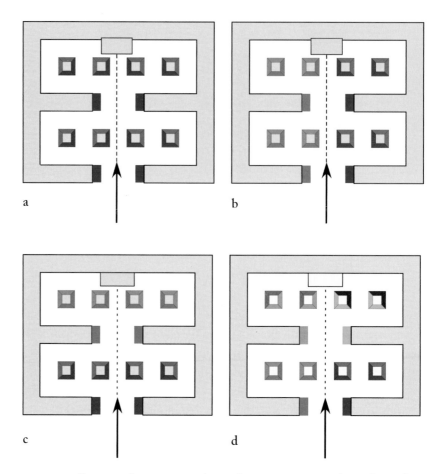

FIGURE 15. Patterns of symmetry and complementarity among the sculptured piers of Chichen Itza. (a) Mirror symmetry/front-back complementarity; (b) mirror complementarity/front-back complementarity; (c) mirror symmetry/inner-outer complementarity/front-back complementarity; (d) mirror complementarity/inner-outer complementarity/front-back complementarity.

To examine the patterning of dress, the distributions of several costume elements in the sanctuaries of six "temples" have been tabulated: the Temple of the Warriors (and the associated Northwest Colonnade), the Castillo, the Temple of the Big Tables, the Northeast Colonnade, the Osario (also known as the High Priest's Grave), and the Upper Temple of the Jaguars (Figures 16–21). Two conclusions are immediately apparent. One is that costume elements do not pattern consistently with respect to one another. In other words, there is no single "Maya" or "Toltec" costume. Second, certain traits that would seem to connote high rank or ethnic identity in fact do not. The butterfly pectoral, for instance, is found only sporadically and not at all in the Osario or the Northeast Colonnade (Figures 16, 20a). It is prominent in the innermost room of the Big Tables but is much more so

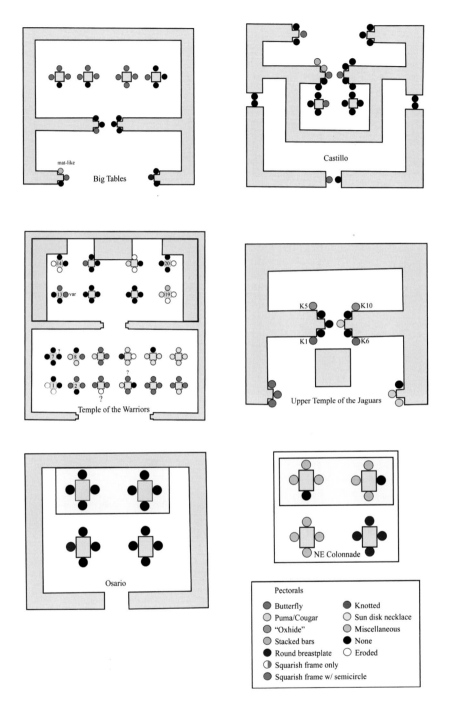

FIGURE 16. Distribution of pectorals in six Modified Florescent "temples."

in the exterior portico of the Temple of the Warriors and in the Northwest Colonnade that stands before it. The peaked *xiuhuitzolli* diadem was the typical crown of the Aztec emperors and is worn by the central FS in the frieze of the Lower Temple of the Jaguars, yet in our sample of temples it is worn by several individuals in the same structure, in positions both central and peripheral (Figure 17). It is particularly common on the piers

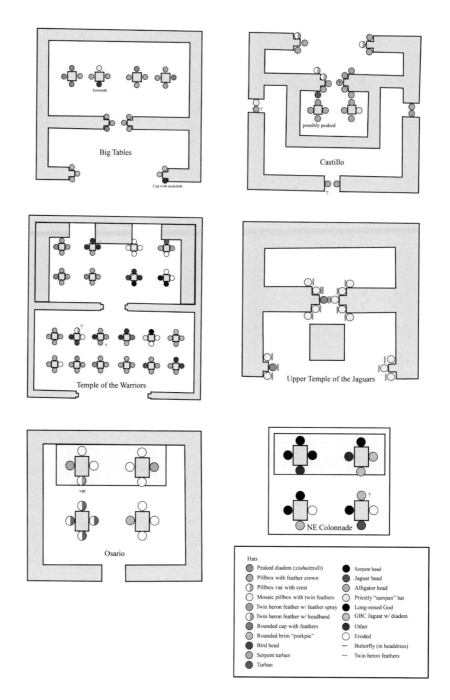

FIGURE 17. Distribution
of hats in six Modified
Florescent "temples."

of the Northwest Colonnade, where 19 examples occur (Figure 20b). A
given pier never has more than one example, however, suggesting it did
mark rank of some kind, yet 2 of the 32 prisoners (if that is what they are)
at the base of the stairway leading up to the Temple of the Warriors also
have this crown.

Nevertheless, it is also apparent that the interiors of these structures

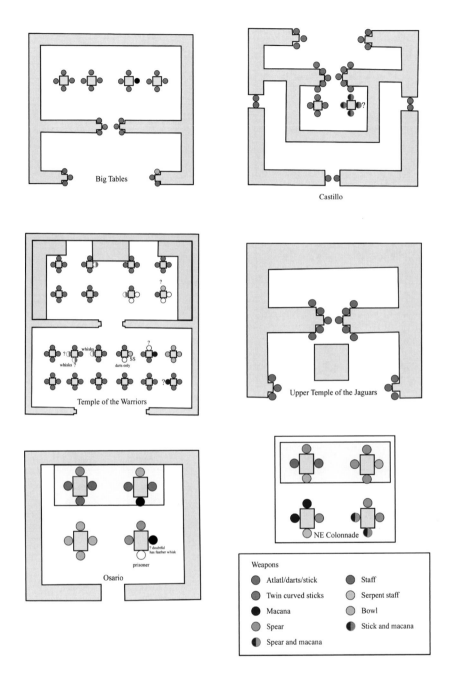

FIGURE 18. Distribution of weapons in six Modified Florescent "temples."

were ordered according to patterns of symmetry and complementarity that could combine and intersect to create a variety of complicated results. For instance, in the Upper Temple of the Jaguars, in the outer portico and on the central jamb faces there seems to be a strong contrast along the central axis between warriors with butterfly pectorals versus warriors with feline pectorals (Figure 16). The major exception is K6, a butterfly warrior

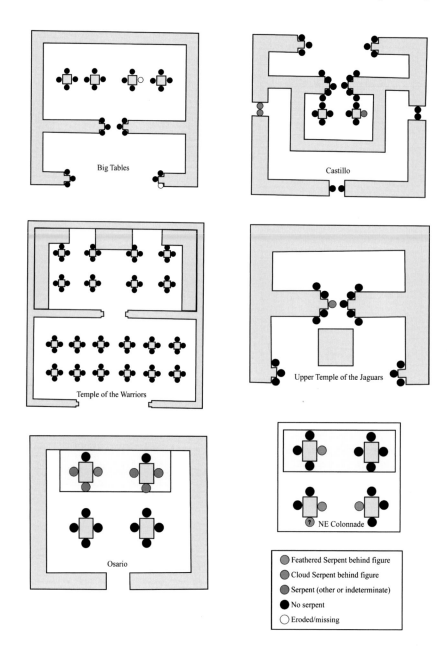

on the feline side. This jamb is otherwise identical to K1 on the opposite side, however, including the name glyph and star motif above the warriors' heads. Since these two make up the exterior face of the inner entrance, it seems that here the desire was to signal something about the interior sanctum (inner-outer complementarity). In support of this argument note that the interior jamb faces (K5 and K10) are also identical, again down to the name glyph and pectoral. These two pairs of identical figures each bracket three warriors who differ in costume.

A somewhat similar pattern can be seen in the Castillo, where the four

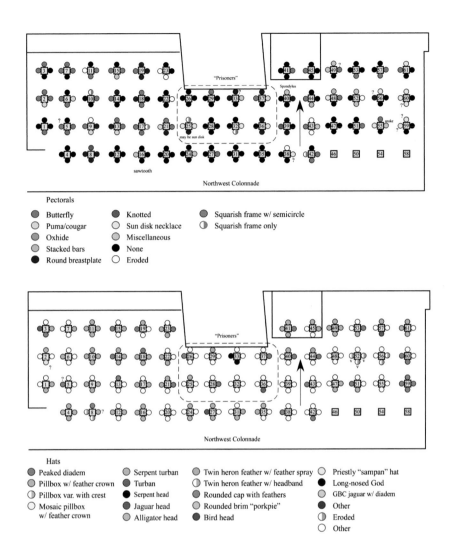

Northwest Colonnade

Pectorals
- ⬤ Butterfly
- ○ Puma/cougar
- ◐ Oxhide
- ◑ Stacked bars
- ⬤ Round breastplate
- ⬤ Knotted
- ○ Sun disk necklace
- ◐ Miscellaneous
- ⬤ None
- ○ Eroded
- ◐ Squarish frame w/ semicircle
- ◑ Squarish frame only

Northwest Colonnade

Hats
- ⬤ Peaked diadem
- ◐ Pillbox w/ feather crown
- ◑ Pillbox var. with crest
- ○ Mosaic pillbox w/ feather crown
- ○ Serpent turban
- ◐ Turban
- ⬤ Serpent head
- ◐ Jaguar head
- ◑ Alligator head
- ○ Twin heron feather w/ feather spray
- ◑ Twin heron feather w/ headband
- ◐ Rounded cap with feathers
- ○ Rounded brim "porkpie"
- ⬤ Bird head
- ○ Priestly "sampan" hat
- ⬤ Long-nosed God
- ◐ GBC jaguar w/ diadem
- ⬤ Other
- ◑ Eroded
- ○ Other

FIGURE 20. Distribution of pectorals and hats in the Northwest Colonnade, Chichen Itza.

faces closest to the left side of the midline all have individuals wearing butterfly pectorals (Figure 16). Two figures on the exterior west side of the inner doorway also wear a pectoral that is perhaps a variant of the butterfly design. This neat patterning is broken by the figure on the center of the inner east jamb, who also wears the butterfly pectoral. So again perhaps the desire was to have a pair of butterfly-wearing warriors flank the entrance to the inner sanctum.

Weapons seem to provide one reasonably strong means of differentiating warriors and are again strongly patterned (Figure 18). The atlatl–darts–curved stick complex is by no means ubiquitous, but it is dominant in the Temple of the Warriors–Northwest Colonnade (Figure 21) and the Upper Temple of the Jaguars. In contrast, they are only present on warriors on the outer jambs of the Castillo. The Osario warriors with these weapons occupy only the piers around which the main bench was built, but pride of

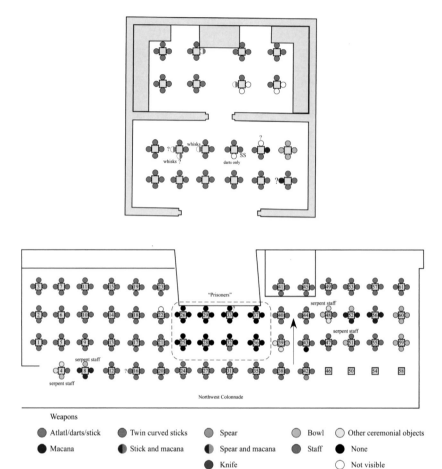

FIGURE 21. Distribution of weapons in the Temple of the Warriors–Northwest Colonnade complex.

place is given to individuals holding staffs. Atlatls and darts are found not at all on the piers of the Big Tables or the Northeast Colonnade, where paired curved sticks or spears and *macanas* are prominent (as they are in the interior of the Castillo).

Although further analysis is needed, it would seem that these buildings and the piers within them reflect different military orders and ranks. For instance, the twin-heron-feather ornament (Nahuat *aztaxelli*) is found on all figures of the Upper Temple of the Jaguars and seems to be presented to an initiate on the badly destroyed interior bench (Ringle 2004; Figure 17). It is also prominent in the upper register of the rear wall of the North Temple of the Great Ballcourt. In contrast, the entrance to the patio of the gallery-patio structure 3D11 (the Mercado) is guarded by figures who wear an unusual alligator-like headdress. The close-but-not-perfect patterns of complementarity and symmetry may also suggest that different orders were included as token outside attendants in these sculptural audiences. The patterning of the Castillo in particular seems to play off such minor deviations.

One prominent marker of rank—that of figures who have feathered serpents curling behind them—has a puzzling distribution (Figure 19). Such figures are invariably the central individuals in the warrior processions illustrated on carved benches, and confrontations between paired FS warriors may be found on the Temple of the Wall Panels and the murals of the Upper Temple of the Jaguars. Yet among the pier sculptures, they are surprisingly rare. The only unambiguous examples occur on the Northeast Colonnade piers. Three others are less certain because the serpents are not clearly feathered. One is located on the east face of the east pier inside the Castillo sanctuary, and the other two are on piers from the Northwest Colonnade (37E, 38E). The serpent figures from the Osario are also too eroded to be certain. Feathered serpent warriors are totally absent from the Upper Temple of the Jaguars, the Big Tables, the North Colonnade, and the Temple of the Warriors. One explanation might be that the benches, being the seats of the paramount(s), naturally depicted the FS insignia of that rank. The piers depicted only those of lesser rank but permanently in attendance on their leaders on the benches. This, however, does not explain the few exceptions just noted.

In addition to reflecting rather complicated patterning, the piers of the Northeast Colonnade also provide an interesting insight into the type of activities carried out in such rooms (Figure 22). One contrast between the front and rear piers is that several of the individuals on the rear piers hold ceremonial objects. The 3S priest holds a dish with jade tubes, 3W a staff terminating in a feline(?) head and a feathered scepter of some sort, 3E a long staff (like those from the Lower Temple of the Jaguars and the North Temple) and a feather whisk, 4W a pouch of some sort, and 4E another bowl with copal or tamales and perhaps more jade tubes. Such objects are strongly reminiscent of the objects presented to the initiate in the North Temple of the Great Ballcourt and so may be insignias of command.

MILITARY TRANSFORMATION OF THE MODIFIED FLORESCENT

This military face of Chichen is so familiar from publications and photographs that it is easy to forget that these sculptures accompanied an unprecedented restructuring of public space. Although military iconography can be found in preceding Florescent structures, some of foreign inspiration, not a single warrior image is known from building facades. The Akab Dzib and Water Trough[7] lintels depict generic lords, unarmed and sitting on pillows and without any clothing that would identify them as other than Maya (Figure 23). The Halakal lintel may be an exception, as it is probably from a Florescent structure (Ruppert 1952: 155), but its warriors

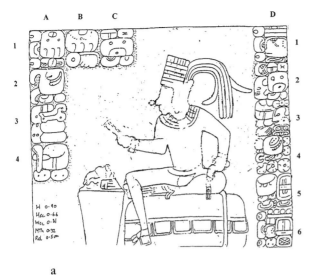

a

b

c

FIGURE 23. Florescent images of lordship. (a) Akab Dzib (from Maudslay 1974: III: plate 19); (b) Water Trough Lintel (from Robertson 1995: rubbing T15923); (c) Halakal Lintel (preliminary drawing courtesy of the Corpus of Maya Hieroglyph project).

(opposite) FIGURE 22. Sculptured piers of the Northeast Colonnade, Chichen Itza (piers from Ricketson 1927: 11).

differ significantly from the Modified Florescent warriors depicted in the site center.

In contrast, the Modified Florescent style marks a significant shift in both militarism and the incorporation of outside influence. The sculpted piers served not only as supports but as important visual cues concerning rank and status. The axes of symmetry and complementarity of the piers develop complicated interior spatial grids and sight lines, positioning spectators in a well-defined social space. In stark contrast to the glorified Maya ruler accompanied by a few supporters, here the emphasis is on the mass, on military order and discipline, consistent with depictions of warfare in the murals of the Upper Temple of the Jaguars, the Temple of the Warriors, and the East Annex of the Monjas complex. In contrast to the emphasis on personal heroics found in most scenes of Late Classic lowland warfare, in these murals the emphasis is on a bird's-eye view of the engagement as a whole. Leaders can be picked out, but the composition of the picture does not naturally direct the eye toward them. Here too the details of costume are faithfully recorded, just as they are on the columns.

Foucault (1979) provides some tools for thinking about the expression of order during the transition from a soldiery composed of individual warriors to one of trained regiments. The second half of *Discipline and Punish* in fact begins with a consideration of a similar transition in Enlightenment France. As military discipline became internalized by the soldiery, it resulted in very different dynamics of the presentation of power, one with direct application to Chichen Itza:

> Hitherto the role of the political ceremony had been to give rise to the excessive, yet regulated manifestation of power; it was a spectacular expression of potency, an "expenditure," exaggerated and coded, in which power renewed its vigour. It was always more or less related to the triumph. The solemn appearance of the sovereign brought with it something of the consecration, the coronation, the return from victory; even the funeral ceremony took place with all the spectacle of power deployed. Discipline, however, had its own type of ceremony. It was not the triumph, but the review, the "parade," an ostentatious form of the examination. In it the "subjects" were presented as "objects" to the observation of a power that was manifested only by its gaze. They did not receive directly the image of the sovereign power; they only felt its effects—in replica, as it were—on their bodies, which had become precisely legible and docile [Foucault 1979: 187–188].

Foucault's intent is to show that such changes were but one facet of a web of related strategies of power that began to penetrate ever deeper into society. These strategies succeeded not by an increase in overt repressiveness, but on the contrary by differentiating and categorizing people, and training individuals to the demands of the industrial age.

According to Foucault, among the great innovations of this period was the classificatory grid, the basis for new academic disciplines as well as changes in production and social control. By these disciplines the individual was made known and accessible to the "microphysics" of power. But the grid was hardly an invention of the eighteenth century; it was the basis for the accounting sheets organizing the political economy of Old Kingdom Egypt and the town layouts of the Middle Kingdom (Kemp 1989)—and, nearer to this discussion, the foundation for the massive experiment in residential reorganization at Teotihuacan. It is therefore tempting to see a rather similar process occurring at Chichen Itza. Another comment of Foucault's regarding the reasons for the division of interior space during the late Enlightenment is relevant:

> Disciplinary space tends to be divided into as many sections as
> there are bodies or elements to be distributed. . . . Its aim was to
> establish presences and absences, to know where and how to locate
> individuals, to set up useful communications, to interrupt others, to
> be able at each moment to supervise the conduct of each individual,
> to assess it, to judge it, to calculate its qualities or merits. It was
> a procedure, therefore, aimed at knowing, mastering and using
> [Foucault 1979: 143].

At Chichen Itza, the regulatory grid finds expression in the horizontal emphasis of its architecture and the division of its interiors by colonnades. The vertical dimension of Chichen is only modestly expressed. The Castillo, at 31 m in height, is less than half the height of Tikal Temple 1, and rather than the vertical triangle of authority symbolized in typical Late Classic temple construction, here hierarchy was expressed by explicitly positioning sculptured individuals in this grid. At Chichen not only do the colonnaded halls represent a frozen parade, but the figures depicted on the piers also betray a quite different attitude toward the warrior than that seen elsewhere in the Maya area. The presentation of the latter, sometimes in the company of a very few others, is aptly characterized by the beginning of Foucault's first quote above. Furthermore, individual expression and distinctiveness of posture are defining characteristics of southern lowland sculpture. At Chichen, however, apart from a few individuals who are clearly elderly, physical features and postures are almost invariant. Difference is instead conveyed by means of costume and ornament, consistent with our argument that the individuality of these piers is not unlike the disciplinary individuality set forth by Foucault—paradoxically an individuality created to better control the masses.

SETTLEMENT BEYOND THE GREAT TERRACES

To understand the full context of this process of militarization, some attention must be given to evidence from the rest of the city. The palaces of many elite families were located throughout the city, often at *sacbe* termini, and the modifications they underwent provide another perspective on the manner in which foreign ideas penetrated Chichen Itza. One of the areas where it is possible to trace the incorporation of foreignness into the lives of the inhabitants of the city is the Initial Series Group (Grupo de la Serie Inicial; Ruppert 1952; Schmidt 2003a,b, 2005, 2007; von Winning 1985; Figure 24). Schmidt's recent detailed excavations of this complex of temples, palaces, and plazas suggest the direction by which new foreign elements made their way into the lives of this elite unit. The Initial Series Group, which is surrounded by a wall, is best considered as a single palace group or the expression of an elite Maya court, in which the wide range of social, religious, and political activities that formed the life of an elite Chichen extended family and their entourage was carried out. The palace or main residence was formed by the three buildings (Casa de los Falos [5C14], Casa de los Caracoles [5C5], and Casa de las Columnas Atlantes [5C15]). Surrounding this palace were administrative and religious structures as well as nonelite residences and buildings used for food preparation and other domestic activities.

When the group actually began to take shape is not clear, although a lens of Middle/Late Formative ceramics found directly above bedrock attests to its antiquity (Osorio León 2003: 97). Some of its basic outlines were laid down during the early Motul phase (A.D. 600–800), as reflected in the first construction stage of the Templo de la Serie Inicial (5C4-I). Two broad periods of construction followed during the Sotuta phase, and it is to this time that all the visible architecture is dated (Figure 25).[8] The first is associated with Florescent architecture, as reflected in the Casa de los Falos and, somewhat later but still in this first period, the second construction stage of the Templo de la Serie Inicial. (Stage 5C4-II of the Templo de la Serie Inicial is dubbed the Templo de los Sacrificios by its excavators.) Architecturally 5C4-II can be characterized as transitional to the Modified Florescent but still reflects pre-formal sensibilities. It consisted of two rooms, the outermost a very narrow gallery with an entry divided by two piers. Between them lay a trapezoidal stone "en la típica forma de un altar de sacrificios [in the typical form of a sacrificial altar]" (Osorio León 2003: 98), a form that was, however, non-Maya. The second room was larger and defined by a stucco *zocalo* (plinth) running along the base of the three sides of the interior.

The second major period of Sotuta activity is associated with the construction of architecture, architectural spaces, and iconography consistent

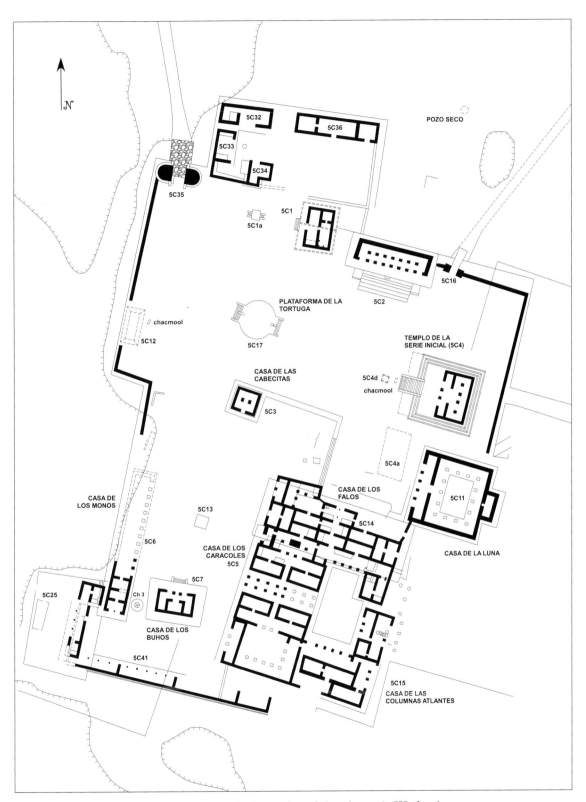

FIGURE 24. Plan of the Initial Series Group (redrawn from Schmidt 2003b: III: fig. 3).

a

b

c

d

e

FIGURE 25. (a) Structure 5C4 the Templo de la Serie Inicial; (b) Construction stage 5C4-I (from Schmidt 2003b: III: fig. 9); (c) stage 5C4-II, the Templo de los Sacrificios (from Schmidt 2003b: III: fig. 10); (d) stage 5C4-III, the Templo de los Atlantes (from Schmidt 2003b: III: fig. 11); (e) stage 5C4-IV, the Templo del Dintel (from Schmidt 2003b: III: fig. 12). Thick black lines denote construction during that stage.

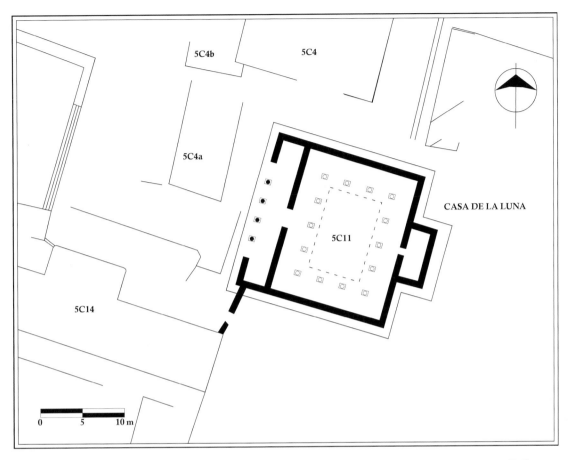

FIGURE 26. Gallery-patio structure 5C11 (Casa de la Luna), Initial series Group (after Schmidt 2003b: III: fig. 17).

in style with the Modified Florescent structures of ceremonial center. The third construction phase of 5C4(-III), the Templo de los Atlantes, marked a decisive shift in this direction, as reflected in the two atlantean figures that probably stood at its doorway and were later reutilized in its final configuration (5C4-IV). A chacmool at the front of the temple stairway is thought to also belong to this stage and, if true, would further support a Modified Florescent date for 5C4-III. A fourth and final stage of this structure (5C4-IV, Templo del Dintel) is dated to the Postclassic. Construction is limited to a small room at the summit constructed from a number of reutilized stones, among them the atlantean supports and the famous hieroglyphic lintel from which the entire court complex draws its name. The original location of the lintel is, however, unknown.

Contemporary with 5C4-III and separated from it by a narrow passageway was 5C11, a gallery-patio structure also known as the Casa de la Luna (Figure 26). As Schmidt (2003b: I: 12) notes, this building is very similar to other gallery-patio structures, such as the Mercado (3D11), and is thus Modified Florescent in style. Facing the same direction as 5C4, it consists of a large north-south gallery (originally vaulted), which one entered through a series of round columns, the center two of which were decorated with armed warriors (atlatls and darts) enveloped by plumed serpents. The interior patio is a smaller version of the patio of 3D11 in the Mercado. A set of columns surrounding a *pluvium* or open interior court would have supported a roof of perishable material.

A dismantled bench was found in the passageway between 5C4 and 5C11 (Figure 27a). It is likely that this bench is from 5C11 and perhaps was located in its gallery, as were the benches from 3D11 and the North and Northwest Dais of the Court of a Thousand Columns south of the Temple of the Warriors. Iconographically and stylistically this bench is a virtual duplicate of the North Dais (Figure 27b). It depicts two warriors enveloped by plumed serpents flanking a sacrificial vessel of tamales or copal with banners stuck in it. A procession of warriors in turn flanks each of these figures. There is little doubt that these two "serpent" warriors are the ones depicted on the columns of 5C11 (see Figure 29), indicating that the procession depicted on the bench probably was directed through those columns into the gallery and patio.

Just south of the 5C4 and 5C11 is the main palace of the group (Figure 28) where the juxtaposition of Florescent and Modified Florescent architecture is also evident. As noted above, it consists of three wings (Los Falos [5C14], Los Caracoles [5C5], and Las Columnas Atlantes [5C15]). In essence, though, there are really two major architectural stages here, 5C14 and 5C5/5C15, because 5C14 is a Florescent range structure consisting of vaulted rooms oriented east-west, while the rooms of 5C5/5C15 behind it are of a very different sort. The latter are characterized by a mix of smaller vaulted rooms combined with the extensive use of columns and square piers to create large vaulted spaces. Furthermore, the plan of 5C5 is reminiscent of patio-gallery buildings, such as 5C11, and so this half is Modified Florescent in style.

We can thus see an evolution similar to that observed in 5C4. The scale and interior layout of the Casa de los Falos indicate it was likely the first phase of the palace's construction. A range structure consisting of two rows of vaulted rooms, the Casa de los Falos had a vertical lower wall zone (no basal batter), lacked columned entrances, and its north portico was decorated with a diamond mosaic pattern like that of the House of the Three Lintels (see Figure 12). It is Maya in its sensibilities and echos quite clearly the Monjas, albeit on a smaller scale (Schmidt 2003b: I). It is likely that this part of the palace was built at the same time as, or perhaps somewhat before, the Templo de los Sacrificios (5C4-II) and thus can be identified as a Florescent construction prior to the introduction of the full Modified Florescent architectural and iconographic complex.

a

FIGURE 27.
(a) Dismantled bench
between 5C4 and 5C11
(from Schmidt 2003b:
III: fig. 16); (b) central
section of the bench
from the North
Colonnade (from Morris
et al. 1931: fig. 257).

b

Regarding the facade of this structure:

What is interesting is how here a Classic Maya concept, that referred
to as the "vision serpent," is expressed in the typical style of Chichen
Itza, which is customarily called "Maya-Toltec." This is good evidence
that with respect to the history of Chichen Itza, these two phenomena (Maya-Toltec) should no longer be explained only as the supposed
opposition between ethnic groups and/or a sequence of phases
[Schmidt 2003b: I: 14].

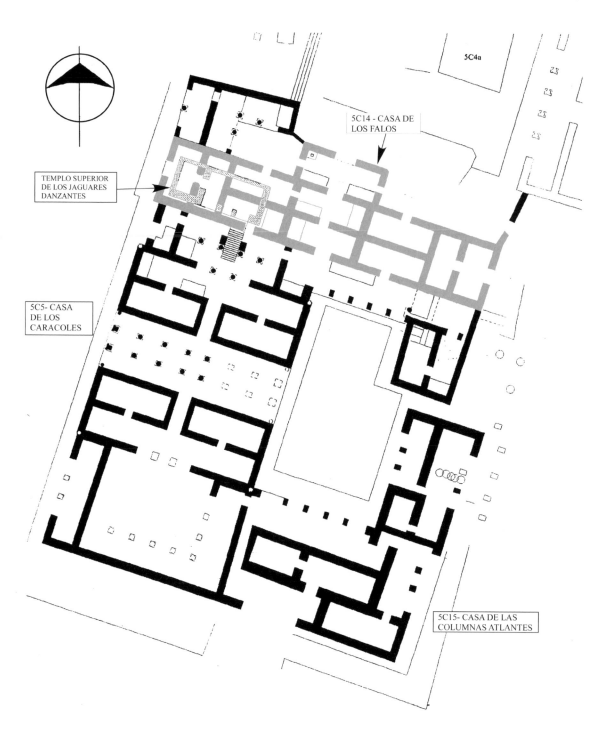

5C4a

5C14 - CASA DE
LOS FALOS

TEMPLO SUPERIOR
DE LOS JAGUARES
DANZANTES

5C5- CASA
DE LOS
CARACOLES

5C15- CASA DE LAS
COLUMNAS ATLANTES

0   5   10 m

FIGURE 28. Palace, Initial Series Group (Casas de los Falos, Templo los
Caracoles, and Casa de las Columnas Atlantes, from Schmidt 2003b: III: fig. 21).

FIGURE 29. The two sculptured columns from the entrance to 5C11 (from Schmidt 2003b: III: figs. 18, 19).

Like some of the Florescent constructions already mentioned, we see here the adoption of some aspects of the FS complex in the iconography of the wall panels but still in a style in which Maya elements predominate. Even these, however, are not direct quotes of images from other sites on the northern plains, but evidence a local filter (e.g., the preoccupation with *bakabs* and *pawahtuns*). Echoing our earlier point, the foreignness that becomes so evident in the Modified Florescent city is part of a process that began significantly earlier.

The additions of 5C5 and 5C15 on the south side of 5C14, based on our interpretation, took place during the Modified Florescent and were contemporary with the construction of 5C11, 5C4-III, and the developments in the city's site center outlined above. These additions emphasize the opening up of space through the use of columns to create galleries, patios, and passageways. These later additions focus around interconnecting interior courtyards that direct the flow of people from one section to another without the necessity to go outside. The main entry into this space was via a columned gallery entered from the west through two atlantean figures not unlike those of the gallery-patio building 5C11 (Figure 29). Continuing forward led to the main sunken patio, surrounded by a series of columned rooms, some of which are marked with square piers of warriors similar to those from the Great Terrace colonnades. The use of patio-gallery units, atlantean figures, square carved columns depicting warriors, and interior courtyards clearly express the rise of new kinds of military orders and associated types of behavior.

Schmidt (2003b: I: 18) argues that the iconography covering the west facade of the Casa de los Caracoles (5C5) expresses ideas about descent, lineage, and genealogy, which leads him to conclude that the structure served as a *popol na,* or lineage house. It may also be a statement legitimizing the authority of the elite family that occupied this central palace in the court of the Initial Series Group. We are probably looking at the way a particular elite family incorporated the new ideas of foreignness into their family's sociopolitical structure. But it also seems to mark a redefinition of how elites articulated with the center. Prior the Modified Florescent, elites functioned as lesser lords much like those elsewhere across the peninsula. The Modified Florescent transformation suggests their role was now formalized and constrained. Those that adapted now seem to have been defined as leaders of military orders, having specific emblems of rank and living in compounds with specific structures associated with such orders, especially the gallery-patio, the warrior temple, and the ballcourt, all of which bore "Toltec" imagery.

The Southwest Group (Grupo del Suroeste), although unexcavated, is another group which seems to follow a similar dynamic (Figures 13, 30a). Consisting of structures 5B11–5B25, in addition to several not numbered, this is another large terrace like the Initial Series Group. Again several of its structures were probably early. Structures 5B22 and 23 are range structures with vertical lower walls. Ruppert (1952: 114–116) notes that the vault stones of 5B22 and 5B25, another range structure, are not veneer types and thus were probably Florescent in style. Structure 5B23, built against 5B22, may have been slightly later, as it did have veneer vault stones and a columned entrance, but it was not Modified Florescent in style.

Three separate clusters involve Modified Florescent construction, two with gallery patios and all three with "temples" (5B16, 18, and 21). Structure 5B16 has sculptured square piers with "human figures" (Figure 30b), 5B18 (the "Castillo of Old Chichen") has piers with floral motifs (Ruppert 1952: fig. 142d) and a sculptured eagle on the west side of the pyramid (Figure 30c). Finally, 5B21, known as the Temple of the Jaguar Atlantean Columns, has a serpent band around it and warrior atlantean figures emerging from the mouth of a jaguar. The one illustrated in Ruppert (Figure 30d) also wears a butterfly pectoral. These sculptures suggest that all three clusters were involved with at least one of the later warrior orders. Whether the groups represent a time series or whether more than one group utilized this terrace remains to be determined.

One interesting facet of the group is that it is connected by Sacbe 33 to the Monjas platform (Cobos Palma n.d. [2003]; Cobos Palma and Winemiller 2001; Schmidt 2003a,b). This *sacbe* intersects Sacbe 7, which connects the Monjas platform with the Florescent Temples of the Three and Four Lintels. Cobos Palma and Winemiller (2001) cogently argue that the meandering Sacbe 7 was an early causeway on the basis of the structures it links and because of parallels with other Florescent causeways at such

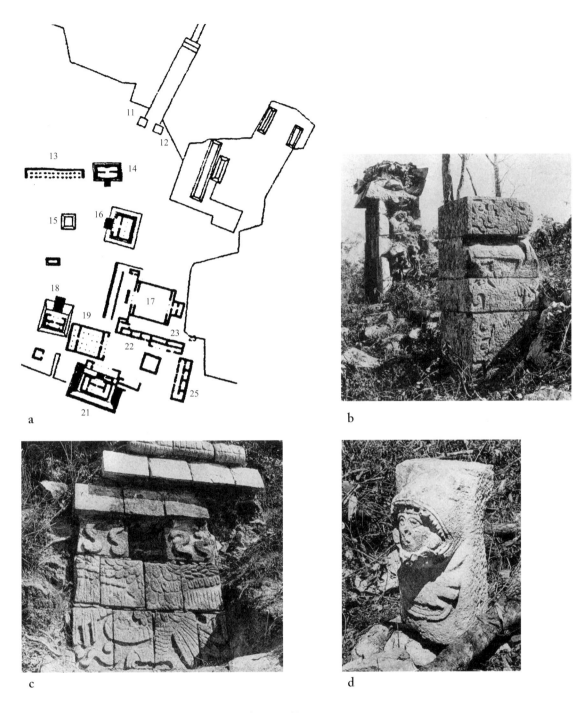

FIGURE 30. (a) Plan of the Southwest Group (detail of Figure 13: structures are all in Quad 5B). The numbers correspond to the structure numbers mentioned in the text (e.g., 13 is structure 5B13); (b) Carved rectangular pier with warriors, 5B16 (from Ruppert 1952: fig. 142a); (c) Eagle panel, 5B18 (from Ruppert 1952: fig. 142e); (d) "Jaguar Atlantean," 5B21 (from Ruppert 1952: fig. 142a).

sites as Sayil. They also identify Sacbe 33 as early because they believe it was
part of an initial network centered on the Monjas platform. Inspection of
Cobos Palma's *sacbe* map (see Figure 12) strongly suggests that it was part
of a later network of roadways, however. In contrast to Sacbe 7, Sacbe 33
runs almost perfectly straight. Furthermore, it is almost exactly aligned
with Sacbe 22 in the northern section of the site. Sacbe 22 runs between the
Great Cenote north to a radial temple in the San Francisco Group and so
is late (Cobos Palma and Winemiller 2001). We argue therefore that Sacbe
33 was built at the same time that Modified Florescent architecture was
introduced into the Southwest Group.

A definite subset of the *sacbes* identified by Cobos Palma and Winemiller
as part of the late system are quite straight and lead directly to the Great
Terrace. This may then mark a change in the use of causeways. Cobos
Palma and Winemiller (2001; see also Cobos Palma 2007) suggest it was
related to a change from *multepal* (rule by council) to centralized authority
but do not speculate further. We suggest that the later *sacbes* were designed
for the conduct of troops in and out of the city, both for display purposes
and to facilitate the marshaling of forces in the site center or their easy
egress for the city's defense. These later *sacbes* may have accompanied a
change in the form of government, as Cobos Palma and Winemiller suggest, but certainly paralleled a reorganization of the military.

CONCLUSIONS

To reiterate the general thrust of this chapter, foreignness at Chichen was
mediated by militarism, specifically the form of militarism institutionalized
within the leadership of the FS. Participation would seem to have been initiated by a local elite who added modest tokens of this new ideology, especially
in association with the Castillo-sub and the initiation of cenote rituals, to
what were otherwise architectural and ceramic styles common elsewhere in
northern Yucatan. Sometime between A.D. 850 and A.D. 900 participation
in this ideology became dramatically more evident in the increased number
of emblems from elsewhere in Mesoamerica and in the reorganization of
public space. These changes, we argue, reflected a shift in leadership from
the traditional one of a paramount lord supported by lesser nobles (reflected
in the radial *sacbe* networks and outlying elite complexes) to one that recast
these supporting groups in the form of military orders.

Chichen Itza remained grounded in Maya culture, as the persistence
of long-nosed masks on Modified Florescent facades attests. Chichen
seems to have made no attempt to reproduce itself regionally with regard
to architecture or sculpture, and so it is doubly striking that its closest
parallel was Tula, Hidalgo. We attribute this similarity not to a population
exchange but to their roles as regional Tollans and their subscription to a

common military ideology. In our view, it is perhaps the strongest evidence of an overarching institutional base for the Tollans of Mesoamerica, one that apparently underwent a concerted formalization toward the end of the ninth century.

In Yucatan, the direct heirs to this tradition only appear well after the abandonment of Chichen, including some of the Late Postclassic centers of the East Coast (e.g., Tulum) and of course Mayapan. Mayapan, as we have argued elsewhere (e.g., Ringle et al. 1998: 222), may have resulted from a political detente between the Cocoms of Chichen and the leading dynasty of the other major competing Terminal Classic Tollan, Uxmal. As the details of history began to fade, this relationship was remembered as the League of Mayapan.

Barry Kemp (1989) has argued that urbanism during the Old and Middle Kingdoms of Egypt was an evolving experiment in total control. Cities were laid out in grids and cells, art styles were formalized, and attempts were made to exhaustively account for economic transactions. The New Kingdom marked a significant shift from such an all-encompassing attempt at state supervision to more indirect methods of control. At this time we also see a great flowering of personal expression among the nobility and a much greater range of personal wealth.

It is tempting to see a somewhat similar process with regard to the various cities claiming the mantle of Tollan. If indeed these sites were in some way part of an overarching and evolving institution, it would seem that Teotihuacan marked the great experiment in societal regulation. The hieratic art style, the apartment complexes, and the existence of state workshops suggest intensive governmental involvement in all facets of society. This regulation seems to have relaxed and concentrated mostly in the organization of the elite and military in those Tollans of the Epiclassic, although Tula itself was apparently reorganized by a new street grid. This new form of control seems to have involved a proliferation of ranks that, while promoting individual visibility, also deftly managed to confine individuals within those roles.

In conclusion, we cannot understand the spread of FS iconography simply as the diffusion of religious or mythic ideas, or as the expected outcome of generalized models of exchange. None of these models help us understand the specific choices made by the elites of Chichen Itza—or the other Tollans of Mesoamerica, for that matter. In our view, the expansion of Chichen depends on particular historical circumstances and the prior formation of specific institutions associated with the FS, institutions which then incorporated and were incorporated by the leadership of the city. Only now are we beginning to realize that Mesoamerica, rather than being just a term of convenience used by archaeologists, may well have been the result of broader institutional processes. The "superstates" model of the southern

Maya lowlands is one step in this direction (Martin and Grube 2000). A growing realization of how FS ideology was employed is, we believe, another, although we are far from fully understanding this process.

Acknowledgments

We thank several colleagues now working at Chichen for their generosity in sharing information and for conversations over the years. Chief among these is Dr. Peter Schmidt, director of the Proyecto Chichen Itza for the past several years. His recent reports have been especially helpful to our thinking, and we also thank him for permission to reproduce several of his illustrations and to visit areas presently closed to visitors. Raphael Cobos Palma has also been most generous; his recent settlement survey analysis has provided a means of linking a wide variety of changes at Chichen, though not necessarily in the ways we have suggested, and provides a number of key insights into architecture and chronology. Other colleagues at Chichen, especially Pepe Osorio León and Eduardo Pérez de Heredia, have also provided critical data. Tomas Gallareta Negrón and Jeff Kowalski also provided us the benefit of their experience, for which we are thankful.

NOTES

1. This date is in the aberrant Puuc system, in which the month coefficient is usually one less than expected. Note that both south jambs begin with a coefficient of 11, which may represent the number of days between the CR date and the lahuntun.

2. Cobos Palma (2003) argues that this gallery-patio structure lacks several diagnostic traits, such as the basal batter of the lower wall zone, and so may predate the full Modified Florescent style. Krochock's early date is based on a reading of C3-C4 on the jambs as the third tun of 5 Ahau. This passage is highly eroded, however, and therefore not wholly secure.

3. For the history of interpretation of most of these dates, see Kowalski (1987: 34–37). Thompson and Kelley originally proposed the dates listed in Table 1. Schele and Mathews (1998: 287–288) present the date on the capstone of the south range of the Nunnery, but do not illustrate it or reference previous studies.

4. Schmidt's (2007: 163–165) recent overview of his work at Chichen indicates that the substructure of the Temple of the Big Tables was supported by typical square pillars bearing typical "Toltec" warriors, although its facade appears to be Florescent. Iconographically it is said to be close to the Temple of the Chac Mool and the Lower Temple of the Jaguars. Fuller publication will determine whether this substructure violates the patterns claimed herein.

5. Except for the substructure of the Temple of the Big Tables (note 4), sculptured piers are characteristic only of the Modified Florescent structures of Chichen, although they are by no means confined to the Great Terrace. Carved columns can be found in the Initial Series and Southwestern Groups, for instance. Many of these remain unpublished, unfortunately. Structures whose piers or columns have been published in full include the Temple of the Warriors complex (including the Temple of the Chac

Mool and the Northwest Colonnade; Morris et al. 1931), the Northeast Colonnade (Ricketson 1927; Robertson 1995), the Temple of the Big Tables, the Castillo, the Osario, the Xtoloc Temple, and the Upper Temple of the Jaguars, all by Robertson (1995), and mostly recently the Palace of the Sculpted Columns (Robertson 1996).

6. There are too many benches in too many contexts at Chichen to assume that all were thrones for a single sovereign. We will not take up this complicated question further except to say that in our opinion these benches were probably the seats of the leaders of various military orders who were subservient to a central authority. That central authority may have been invested in a dual leadership (see Ringle 2004).

7. Cobos Palma (2003: 245, 2004: 526) has suggested this lintel may come from the range structure 5D2. Ruppert (1952) states this structure did not employ veneer vault stones, had a vertical lower wall zone, and had a basement with rounded quoins. It thus is Florescent in style.

8. To Cobos Palma (2003) we owe the crucial observation that range structures seem to go out of use during the Modified Florescent. He, however, seems to view the Templo de la Serie Inicial group as belonging to a single early construction stage and thus argues that 5C11 is an early form of the gallery-patio. His published views antedate the recent reports on the group by Schmidt, however.

REFERENCES CITED

Anda Alanís, Guillermo de
2007　Sacrifice and Ritual Body Mutilation in Postclassical Maya Society: Taphonomy of the Human Remains from Chichén Itzá's Cenote Sagrado. In *New Perspectives on Human Sacrifice and Ritual Body Treatments in Ancient Maya Society* (Vera Tiesler and Andres Cucina, eds.): 190–208. Springer, New York.

Andrews, E. Wyllys, IV
1965　Archaeology and Prehistory in the Northern Maya Lowlands: An Introduction. In *Handbook of Middle American Indians*, vol. 2 (Robert Wauchope and Gordon R. Willey, eds.): 288–330. University of Texas Press, Austin.

Andrews, George F.
1995　*Pyramids and Palaces, Monsters and Masks: The Golden Age of Maya Architecture*, vol. 1: *Architecture of the Puuc Region and the Northern Plains*. Labyrinthos, Lancaster, Calif.

Ball, Joseph W., and John M. Ladd
1992　Ceramics. In *Artifacts from the Cenote of Sacrifice, Chichen Itza, Yucatan* (Clemency C. Coggins, ed.): 235–344. Memoirs of the Peabody Museum of Archaeology and Ethnology, vol. 10, no. 3. Harvard University, Cambridge, Mass.

Beck, Lane A., and April K. Sievert
2005　Mortuary Pathways Leading to the Cenote at Chichen Itza. In *Interacting with the Dead: Perspectives on Mortuary Archaeology for the New Millennium* (Gordon F. M. Rakita, Jane E. Buikstra, Lane A. Beck, and Sloan R. Williams, eds.): 290–304. University Press of Florida, Gainesville.

Bey, George J., III, and William M. Ringle

2007   From the Bottom Up: The Timing of the Tula-Chichen Itzá Exchange.
        In *Twin Tollans: Chichen Itza, Tula, and the Epiclassic to Early Postclassic
        Mesoamerican World* (Jeff K. Kowalski and Cynthia Kristan-Graham,
        eds.): 377–427. Dumbarton Oaks Research Library and Collection,
        Washington, D.C.

Bolles, John S.

1977   *Las Monjas.* University of Oklahoma Press, Norman.

Carrasco Vargas, Ramón, and Eduardo Pérez de Heredia

1996   Los Ultimos Gobernantes de Kabah. In *Eighth Palenque Round
        Table 1993* (Martha J. Macri and Jan McHargue, eds.): 297-308.
        Pre-Columbian Art Research Institute, San Francisco.

Carrasco, Davíd

1982   *Quetzalcoatl and the Irony of Empire: Myths and Prophecies in the Aztec
        Tradition.* University of Chicago Press, Chicago.

Cobos Palma, Rafael

2004   Chichen Itza: Settlement and Hegemony during the Terminal
        Classic Period. In *The Terminal Classic in the Maya Lowlands: Collapse,
        Transition, and Transformation* (Arthur A. Demarest, Prudence M.
        Rice, and Don S. Rice, eds.): 517–544. University Press of Colorado,
        Boulder.

2007   Multepal or Centralized Kingship: New Evidence on Governmental
        Organization at Chichén Itzá. In *Twin Tollans: Chichen Itza, Tula, and
        the Epiclassic to Early Postclassic Mesoamerican World* (Jeff K. Kowalski
        and Cynthia Kristan-Graham, eds.): 315–343. Dumbarton Oaks
        Research Library and Collection, Washington, D.C.

n.d.   The Settlement Patterns of Chichen Itza, Yucatan, Mexico. Ph.D.
        dissertation, Department of Anthropology, Tulane University, New
        Orleans, 2003.

Cobos Palma, Rafael, and Terence L. Winemiller

2001   Late and Terminal Classic-Period Causeway Systems of Chichen Itza,
        Yucatan, Mexico. *Ancient Mesoamerica* 12: 283–291.

Coggins, Clemency C. (ed.)

1992   *Artifacts from the Cenote of Sacrifice, Chichen Itza, Yucatan.* Memoirs of
        the Peabody Museum of Archaeology and Ethnology, vol. 10, no. 3.
        Harvard University, Cambridge, Mass.

Coggins, Clemency C., and John M. Ladd

1992   Copal and Rubber Offerings. In *Artifacts from the Cenote of Sacrifice,
        Chichen Itza, Yucatan* (Clemency C. Coggins, ed.): 345–358. Memoirs
        of the Peabody Museum of Archaeology and Ethnology, vol. 10, no. 3.
        Harvard University, Cambridge, Mass.

Coggins, Clemency C., and Orrin C. Shane, III

1984   *Cenote of Sacrifice: Maya Treasures from the Sacred Well at Chichen Itza.*
        University of Texas Press, Austin.

Erosa Peniche, José A.

1939   Descubrimientos y exploración arqueológica de la subestructura del Castillo en Chichén Itzá. *Actas del la Primera Sesion del XXVII Congreso Internacional de Americanistas* II: 229–248.

1948   *Guia para visitar las ruinas de Chichen-Itza.* 4th ed. Editorial Yikal Maya Than, Mérida, Yucatán.

Florescano, Enrique

2004   *Quetzacóatl y los Mitos Fundadores de Mesoamérica.* Taurus, México.

Foucault, Michel

1979   *Discipline and Punish.* Vintage Books, New York.

Gillespie, Susan D.

2007   Toltecs, Tula, and Chichén Itzá: The Development of an Archaeological Myth. In *Twin Tollans: Chichen Itza, Tula, and the Epiclassic to Early Postclassic Mesoamerican World* (Jeff K. Kowalski and Cynthia Kristan-Graham, eds.): 85–127. Dumbarton Oaks Research Library and Collection, Washington, D.C.

Graña-Behrens, Daniel

n.d.   Die Maya-Inschriften aus Nordwestyukatan, Mexiko. Inaugural Ph.D. dissertation, Rheinischen Friedrich-Wilhems-Universität zu Bonn, Bonn, Germany, 2002.

Grube, Nikolai

2003   Hieroglyphic Inscriptions from Northwest Yucatán: An Update of Recent Research. In *Escondido en la selva* (Hanns J. Prem, ed.): 339–370. Universidad de Bonn and Instituto Nacional de Antropología e Historia, Bonn and México.

Hooton, Earnest A.

1940   Skeletons from the Cenote of Sacrifice at Chichen Itzá. In *The Maya and Their Neighbors:* 272–280. Appleton-Century, New York.

Hopkins, Mary R.

1992   Mammalian Remains. In *Artifacts from the Cenote of Sacrifice, Chichen Itza, Yucatan* (Clemency C. Coggins, ed.): 369–385. Memoirs of the Peabody Museum of Archaeology and Ethnology, vol. 10, no. 3. Harvard University, Cambridge, Mass.

Jiménez García, Elizabeth

1998   *Iconografía de Tula: El caso de la escultura.* Colección Científica. Instituto Nacional de Antropología e Historia, México.

Jones, Lindsay R.

1995   *Twin City Tales: A Hermeneutical Reassessment of Tula and Chichén Itzá.* University Press of Colorado, Niwot.

1997   Conquests of the Imagination: Maya-Mexican Polarity and the Story of Chichén Itzá. *American Anthropologist* 99: 275–290.

Kelley, David H.

1982   Notes on Puuc Inscriptions and History. Supplement to *The Puuc: New Perspectives* (Lawrence Mills, ed.). Central College, Pella, Iowa.

Kemp, Barry J.

1989 *Ancient Egypt: Anatomy of a Civilization*. Routledge, London.

Kowalski, Jeff K.

1987 *The House of the Governor*. University of Oklahoma Press, Norman.

Krochock, Ruth J.

1995 A New Interpretation of the Inscriptions on the Temple of the Hiero-glyphic Jambs, Chichén Itzá. *Texas Notes on Precolumbian Art, Writing, and Culture 79*. Austin.

Kubler, George

1962 *The Art and Architecture of Ancient America*. Penguin Books, Baltimore.

Lincoln, Charles E.

1986 The Chronology of Chichen Itza: A Review of the Literature. In *Late Lowland Maya Civilization* (Jeremy A. Sabloff and E. Wyllys Andrews V, eds.): 141–198. School of American Research and University of New Mexico Press, Albuquerque.

n.d. Ethnicity and Social Organization at Chichen Itza, Yucatan, Mexico. Ph.D. dissertation, Department of Anthropology, Harvard University, Cambridge, Mass., 1990.

Lind, Michael

n.d. The Great City Square: Government in Ancient Cholula. Manuscript in possession of the author (1992).

López Austin, Alfredo, and Leonardo López Luján

1999 *Mito y realidad de Zuyuá*. El Colegio de México and Fondo de Cultura Económica, México.

Lothrop, Samuel K.

1952 *Metals from the Cenote of Sacrifice, Chichen Itza, Yucatan*. Memoirs of the Peabody Museum of Archaeology and Ethnology, vol. 10, no. 2. Harvard University, Cambridge, Mass.

Marquina, Ignacio

1964 *Arquitectura Prehispánica*. Instituto Nacional de Antropología e Historia and Secretaría de Educación Pública, México.

Martin, Simon, and Nikolai Grube

2000 *Chronicle of the Maya Kings and Queens*. Thames and Hudson, New York and London.

Maudslay, Alfred P.

1974 [1889–1902] *Biologia Centrali-Americana. Archaeology*. 4 vols. (Francis Robicsek, ed.). Facsimile of the 1889–1902 edition. Milpatron Publishing, New York.

Miller, Mary E., and Marco Samoya

1998 Where Maize May Grow; Jade, Chacmools, and the Maize God. *RES* 33: 54–72.

Morley, Sylvanus G.

1920 *The Inscriptions at Copan*. Publication 219. Carnegie Institution of Washington, Washington, D.C.

Morris, Earl H., Jean Charlot, and Ann A. Morris

1931 *The Temple of the Warriors at Chichen Itzá, Yucatan*. Publication 406. Carnegie Institution of Washington, Washington, D.C.

Osorio León, José

2003   Excavación de la Estructura 5C4, Templo de la Serie Inicial. *Proyecto Chichen Itza: Informed de actividades julio de 1999 a diciembre de 2002* (Peter J. Schmidt, ed.): 95–104. Mérida, México.

Osorio León, José, and Eduardo Pérez de Heredia

2001   La arquitectura y la cerámica del clásico tardío en Chichén Itzá: Excavaciones en el edificio de la Serie Inicial. In *Los Investigadores de la Cultura Maya 9: Tomo II:* 327–334. Universidad Autónoma de Campeche, Campeche, Yucatán.

Pérez de Heredia, Eduardo

1998   Proyecto Chen K'u: La cerámica del Cenote Sagrado exploraciónes de los Años 60's. Report submitted to the Foundation for the Advancement of Mesoamerican Studies. Electronic document, http://www .famsi.org/reports/97061es/index.html, accessed September 14, 2005.

Piña Chan, Román

1970   *Informe preliminar de la reciente exploración del Cenote Sagrado de Chichén Itzá.* Investigaciones 24. Instituto Nacional de Antropología e Historia, México.

Pollock, H. E. D.

1965   Architecture of the Maya Lowlands. In *Handbook of Middle American Indians*, vol. 2 (Robert Wauchope and Gordon R. Willey, eds.): 378–440. University of Texas Press, Austin.

1980   *The Puuc.* Memoirs of the Peabody Museum of Archaeology and Ethnology, vol. 19. Harvard University, Cambridge, Mass.

Proskouriakoff, Tatiana

1944   *An Inscription on a Jade Probably Carved at Piedras Negras.* Notes on Middle American Archaeology and Ethnology 47. Carnegie Institution of Washington, Cambridge, Mass.

1974   *Jades from the Cenote of Sacrifice, Chichen Itza, Yucatan.* Memoirs of the Peabody Museum of Archaeology and Ethnology, vol. 10, no. 1. Harvard University, Cambridge, Mass.

Ricketson, Edith B.

1927   Sixteen Carved Panels from Chichen Itza. *Art and Archaeology* 23: 11–15.

Ringle, William M.

1990   Who Was Who in Ninth-Century Chichen Itza. *Ancient Mesoamerica* 1: 233–243.

2004   On the Political Organization of Chichen Itza. *Ancient Mesoamerica* 15: 167–218.

Ringle, William M., Tomás Gallareta Negrón, and George J. Bey, III

1998   The Return of Quetzalcoatl: Evidence for the Spread of a World Religion during the Epiclassic Period. *Ancient Mesoamerica* 9: 183–232.

Robertson, Merle Greene

1995   *Merle Green Robertson's Rubbings of Maya Sculpture.* CD-ROM set. Pre-Columbian Art Research Institute, San Francisco.

1996   Chichén Itzá: The Palace of the Sculptured Columns. Report submitted to the Foundation for the Advancement of Mesoamerican Studies.

Electronic document, http://www.famsi.org/reports/95001/index.html, accessed September 14, 2005.

Ruppert, Karl

    1935 *The Caracol at Chichen Itza, Yucatan, Mexico*. Publication 454. Carnegie Institution of Washington, Washington, D.C.

    1943 *The Mercado, Chichen Itza, Yucatan*. Contributions to American Anthropology and History 43. Publication 546. Carnegie Institution of Washington, Washington, D.C.

    1952 *Chichen Itza: Architectural Notes and Plans*. Publication 595. Carnegie Institution of Washington, Washington, D.C.

Schele, Linda, and David Freidel

    1990 *A Forest of Kings: The Untold Story of the Ancient Maya*. William Morrow, New York.

Schele, Linda, and Peter Mathews

    1998 *The Code of Kings*. Scribner, New York.

Schmidt, Peter J.

    1998 Chichén Itzá: Los contactos con el centro de México y la transición al periodo Posclásico. In *Los Mayas* (Peter J. Schmidt, Mercedes de la Garza, and Enrique Nalda, eds.): 426–449. Conaculta and Instituto Nacional de Antropología e Historia, México.

    2003a Siete años entre los itzá. Nuevas excavaciones en Chichén Itzá y sus resultados. In *Escondido en la selva* (Hanns J. Prem, ed.): 53–63. Universidad de Bonn and Instituto Nacional de Antropología e Historia, Bonn and México.

    2003b *Proyecto Chichen Itza: Informe de actividades julio de 1999 a diciembre de 2002*. 3 vols. Report submitted to the Instituto Nacional de Antropologia e Historia, México.

    2005 Neuvos hallazgos en Chichén Itzá. *Arqueología Mexicana* 76: 48–55.

    2007 Birds, Ceramics, and Cacao: New Excavations at Chichén Itzá, Yucatan. In *Twin Tollans: Chichen Itza, Tula, and the Epiclassic to Early Postclassic Mesoamerican World* (Jeff K. Kowlaksi and Cynthia Kristan-Graham, eds.): 151–203. Dumbarton Oaks Research Library and Collection, Washington, D.C.

Seler, Eduard

    1998 The Ruins of Chichen Itza in Yucatan. In *Collected Works in Mesoamerican Linguistics and Archaeology*, vol. 6 (J. Eric S. Thompson, Francis B. Richardson, and Frank E. Comparato, eds.): 41–165. Labyrinthos, Culver City, Calif.

Sheets, Payson D., John M. Ladd, and David Bathgate

    1992 Chipped-Stone Artifacts. In *Artifacts from the Cenote of Sacrifice, Chichen Itza, Yucatan* (Clemency C. Coggins, ed.): 153–189. Memoirs of the Peabody Museum of Archaeology and Ethnology, vol. 10, no. 3. Harvard University, Cambridge, Mass.

Sievert, April K.

    1992 Appendix 6.C: Use-Wear Analysis of Chipped-Stone. In *Artifacts from the Cenote of Sacrifice, Chichen Itza, Yucatan* (Clemency C. Coggins, ed.): 182–187. Memoirs of the Peabody Museum of Archaeology and Ethnology, vol. 10, no. 3. Harvard University, Cambridge, Mass.

Spinden, Herbert J.

1957   *Maya Art and Civilization.* Falcon's Wing Press, Indian Hills, Colo.

Stone, Andrea

1989   Disconnection, Foreign Insignia, and Political Expansion: Teotihuacan and the Warrior Stelae of Piedras Negras. In *Mesoamerica after the Decline of Teotihuacan, A.D. 700–900* (Richard A. Diehl and Janet C. Berlo, eds.): 153–172. Dumbarton Oaks Research Library and Collection, Washington, D.C.

Stuart, George E.

1989   *Introduction: The Hieroglyphic Record of Chichén Itzá and Its Neighbors.* Introduction to Research Reports on Ancient Maya Writing 23–25. Center for Maya Research, Washington, D.C.

Thompson, J. Eric S.

1937   *A New Method of Deciphering Yucatecan Dates with Special Reference to Chichen Itza.* Contributions to American Archaeology 22. Publication 483. Carnegie Institution of Washington, Washington, D.C.

1954   *The Rise and Fall of Maya Civilization.* University of Oklahoma Press, Norman.

Tozzer, Alfred M. (ed. and translator)

1941   *Landa's Relación de las cosas de Yucatán.* Papers of the Peabody Museum of American Archaeology and Ethnology 18. Harvard University, Cambridge, Mass.

Tozzer, Alfred M.

1957   *Chichen Itza and Its Cenote of Sacrifice: A Comparative Study of Contemporaneous Maya and Toltec.* Memoirs of the Peabody Museum of Archaeology and Ethnology, vols. 11 and 12. Harvard University, Cambridge, Mass.

Vallo, Michael

2003   Xkipché Ceramics. On Current Data, Methods, Results, and Problems. In *Escondido en la selva* (Hanns J. Prem, ed.): 309–338. Universidad de Bonn and Instituto Nacional de Antropología e Historia, Bonn and México.

von Winning, Hasso

1985   *Two Maya Monuments in Yucatan: The Palace of the Stuccoes at Acanceh and the Temple of the Owls at Chichén Itzá.* Anniversary Publication Fund XII. Southwest Museum, Los Angeles.

Wren, Linnea H., Peter J. Schmidt, and Ruth J. Krochock

1989   The Great Ball Court Stone of Chichén Itzá. *Research Reports on Ancient Maya Writing 25.* Center for Maya Research, Washington.

TWELVE

THE MEXICA IN TULA AND TULA IN MEXICO-TENOCHTITLAN

Leonardo López Luján

Alfredo López Austin

THE TOLLAN-QUETZALCOATL DYAD IN THE POLITICAL HISTORY OF MEXICO-TENOCHTITLAN

THE AUTHORS OF THIS CHAPTER share an interest regarding a crucial dyad in Mesoamerican history: that of Tollan-Quetzalcoatl. A book on the nature of men-gods appeared more than 30 years ago (López Austin 1973); since then, another has recently been published examining the Tenochca imitation of Toltec art (López Luján 2006). More than three decades separate one study from the other, and during this time, we have left the subject and returned to it, both individually and together. There is nothing unique about our keen interest in revealing the mysteries of the Feathered Serpent, the legendary ruler, and the city that oscillates between ecumenical and anecumenical.[1] For centuries, countless authors, intrigued by similar enigmas, have come before us, and clearly many will follow us with their inquiries on this interplay of myth, legend, and history.

Saying that the Tollan-Quetzalcoatl dyad is complicated because of the impact of politics does not fully explain this concept. The dyad was the ideological basis of a widespread political project in Mesoamerica, one that had been in operation for centuries. We dealt with this subject together in our essay *Mito y realidad de Zuyuá* [*The myth and reality of Zuyuá*] (López Austin and López Luján 1999, 2000), where we focus on the double figure of Tollan (as an anecumenical dwelling place, where the distinction was produced between men prior to their appearance on the surface of the earth and as a prototypical earthly capital), which is a parallel to the double figure of Quetzalcoatl (as a generic creator of humanity and as a legendary ruler). During the Epiclassic (A.D. 650–900) and Postclassic (A.D. 900–1521), these double figures served to lay down a political order that justified the nascent power of multiethnic, hegemonic, militarized states, capitals of regional systems competing with one another for control of trade routes. This order—which we have designated by the term "Zuyuan"[2]—did not

CHARACTERIZATION AS A SOCIOPOLITICAL ORGANIZATION
- ☐ exercised control as part of a complex, hegemonic organ
- ☐ governed populations of different ethnic groups inhabiting a given region
- ☐ assigned each subordinate political entity a political-economic role

DIFFERENCES IN TRADITIONAL FORMS OF CLASSIC PERIOD POLITICAL ORGANIZATION
- ☐ *Type of multiethnic structure*
  The old heathen order was based on the premise that each human group had been created by a patron god who gave them their ethnic identity, religious focus, language, tradition, and profession. There was a shared essence between the patron god and the human group. The sovereign was a human being connected to the patron god and regarded as his intermediary, so he was considered the elder brother of his subordinates. The new, multiethnic order preserved this relationship but imposed a collective, supraethnic governing body over it.
- ☐ *Type of influence and hegemonic domination of some political units over others*
  There was a shift from relative disintegration based on alliances among the different political entities to the imposition of a highly formalized political-economic structure.
- ☐ *Type of bellicose action*
  The political emphasis changed to an aggressive militaristic system with a well-developed military class.

IDEOLOGY
The function of the regime was to maintain peace and harmony among the disparate groups that were a reflection of universal order. In reality, it was an expansionist military system based on the forced imposition of harmony.

RELATIONS WITH TRADITIONAL FORMS OF ORGANIZATION THAT IT HAD SUBORDINATED
- ☐ preserved the traditional ethnic internal political order of each unit
- ☐ respected the ideological power bases in each unit
- ☐ superimposed a multiethnic apparatus as the head of the global organization

SOME SETTINGS IN WHICH ZUYUAN REGIMENS APPEARED
- ☐ Central Mexico: Tula, Cholula, and the Basin of Mexico
- ☐ Michoacán: Tarascan state
- ☐ Oaxaca: Mixtec chiefdoms
- ☐ Guatemala Highlands: the Quiches, Cakchiquels, and Rabinals
- ☐ Northern Yucatán: Chichen Itza

FIGURE 1.
The Zuyuan regimen.

destroy ancestral political configurations, which were structured around ethnicity and lineage; on the contrary, it grouped them into larger territorial units, delegating to them specific governmental functions that pertained to a more complex state formation. It was an imposed reconstitution—by military force—of the archetypical, globalizing, and legitimating peace and harmony of the Feathered Serpent and his primordial city (Figure 1).

The Zuyuan system differed from the Classic forms of political organization in at least three ways: (1) multiethnic structure; (2) hegemonic influence and dominion of some political units over others; and (3) bellicose action. The first difference resulted from the combination of two classes of government: the traditional or gentillic, based on the kingship ties of the community with their patron deities (in each of the units in the political system), and the global, based on territory. By means of the traditional one, power was exercised over individuals by their ethnic identities, independent of where they were located; in the global one, power was exercised over all settlements of a territory, independent of their ethnicities. The Zuyuan system, as discussed below, also tried to resolve the problem of the integration of diverse ethnic groups; but this was done by reducing diversity ideologically, using the conception of the essential unit of humankind under a divine order that had produced several different human groups. The second difference came about because the Zuyuans, in contrast to those preceding them, attempted regional dominion through the imposition of a thoroughly formalized politicoeconomic structure. Their confederations of hegemonic capitals were not merely military alliances, but jurisdictional organs of great administrative complexity. The third difference was that the Zuyuan system exceeded the limits of Classic period bellicosity, largely because it was not only a warrior regime but also a militaristic one.

In summary, the Zuyuans constructed a system whose cohesion was based on two apparently contradictory principles. On the one hand, they followed an ideological path that was reinforced by maintaining peace and harmony among peoples that supposedly was a reflection of universal order. On the other hand, Zuyuan states developed powerful military bodies of control and undertook aggressive campaigns of expansion against weaker polities. The Zuyuan system was an enterprise of enforced harmony.

Significantly, the most numerous and important written and pictographic testimonies on the Tollan-Quetzalcoatl dyad come from the Basin of Mexico, a region profoundly influenced by the Mexica-Tenochcas. This group was immersed in such an accelerated political transformation that the successive periods of their history substantially affected their mythical and religious paradigms, and that of their neighbors. Broadly speaking, this political transformation may be divided into three successive phases. In the first, from the foundation of Mexico-Tenochtitlan until the victory over Azcapotzalco in A.D. 1430, changes were focused primarily on the consolidation of the figure of patron god Huitzilopochtli and the transformation of the offering he made to his people during the search for the promised land. The great power of the god Tezcatlipoca must have fused in the patron god with fiery, celestial, astral, solar, and warrior attributes; the original gifts of the *minacachalli* and the *chitatli* used by lake fishermen and hunters[3] must have been exchanged for the darts of warfare and the dreams of glory, power, and wealth of those who wield arms on a divine mission (López Austin 1973: 176–177).

In the second phase, from the victory over Azcapotzalco and the reconstitution of the Triple Alliance (*excan tlatoloyan*) until the establishment of supremacy over their allies around A.D. 1486, the Mexica fully embraced the Zuyuan ideological context with supreme status as heirs to historical Tula in Hidalgo:[4] with their allies Tetzcoco and Tlacopan, they were privileged to receive the power of Quetzalcoatl. In the third phase, from the beginning of their exclusive hegemony to the Spanish conquest of A.D. 1521, they turned their backs on the Zuyuan order. The proud Mexica recovered supreme control for their god Huitzilopochtli, and they put an end to Tetzcocan aspirations, subjecting this powerful ally to the new victorious ideology of the patron god of Tenochtitlan.

As is well known, ideology responds at each moment in history to the specific needs of political action, consolidation, and justification. However, when historical transformations are sudden, both ideological adjustment and reconfiguration are complex—even more so if the ideological base is composed of deeply rooted ancient traditions, religious dogmas, and mythical accounts. Following the ideas of Fernand Braudel (1974: 60–106) on this point, the historical rhythms governing politics, morality, religious beliefs, and myths are different; the lag brought about by distinct levels of resistance to change often produce a breakdown between political action and its intellectual underpinning (López Austin 1992).

Another problem faces societies that must adapt their ideologies as a result of sudden transformations of their historical-political contexts. The new ideology must convince all members of an increasingly heterogeneous society in which there are diverse interests, tendencies, and plans in life. The degree of penetration of the new ideas varied among the privileged and the dispossessed, the cultivated and the uncultivated, and young and old: some were more profoundly immersed in traditional discourse, in created interests, or in consolidated beliefs, and others were more hopeful at the prospect of favorable transformation.

However, the ideological discourse was not uniformly embraced in time, as it was unable to completely replace what had been proclaimed in earlier times. Even in texts from the corpus of official history, ideas from different ideological eras overlapped, replete with incongruities, contradictions, and anachronisms. The rapid transformation of the Mexica—from immigrants in a highly complex political scene to their swift ascent to hegemonic preeminence—produced great difficulties in generating a seamless adjustment between politics and ideology. The historiographic inconsistencies of Mexica documentary sources are a field ripe for modern researchers, because they facilitate heuristic study. Thus reinterpretations and modifications of historical discourse at times are conspicuous as touched-up patches that affect the coherence of the exposition, providing clues that shed light on the time frames of revisions. Reading Mexica historical texts, one can perceive the different faces of the patron god, the various promises at the outset of the migration, or the disparate lines of reasoning used to justify their subjugation and domination of other groups.

In this chapter we analyze the ideological relations between the mythical and legendary images of Tollan and the reality of Tenochtitlan as a capital that needed to provide justification for its hegemony at the end of the Late Postclassic. For purposes of the present discussion, we first adopt a list of ideological complexes as a guide that in our opinion is prominent throughout Mexica history. These are then related to the activities undertaken by the Mexica in the ruins of Tula and at their own capital, actions with great political weight and by which they attempted to link the images of anecumenical Tollan and those of archaeological Tula with the reality and representations of Tenochtitlan.

IDEOLOGICAL COMPLEXES

Without attempting to provide an exhaustive list of the different aspects of the Tollan-Quetzalcoatl dyad in the history of Tenochtitlan, we now enumerate the main ideological complexes to properly contextualize the problem at hand. In this case, an ideological complex is a structured group of ideas, beliefs, principles, and values used independently of its origins or character as a basis to justify, consolidate, or legitimate a political action.

Mythical Origins of the Human Race

Mesoamerican cosmovision was developed over the centuries until the Late Postclassic, when it was converted into a complex of central, structuring components highly resistant to change, and they served as a basis for actions and conceptions more susceptible to social and political transformations. These elements formed part of what we have referred to in other works as the *núcleo duro,* or "resistant core" (López Austin 2001). Based on this nucleus, one of the fundamental contradictions concerning the origins and nature of humans was effectively resolved, for paradoxically the human race was unitarily conceived as one species, yet diversified because of its ethnic differences. As the essential unity and diversity of man, the solution was the interplay of two successive processes of mythical birth: a unitary god by the name of Quetzalcoatl created all of humanity; but the division of the god, conceived of as different deities, produced the protagonists of a second type of origin myth. This type of creation gave particular characteristics to each human group at the time of their appearance in the world (Figure 2). Thus the god Quetzalcoatl was the creator of humans in general, and Tollan, his anecumenical kingdom, was the dwelling place where humans to be born were transformed into their diverse ethnic identities. When the different groups of people had to leave the mythical city to populate the

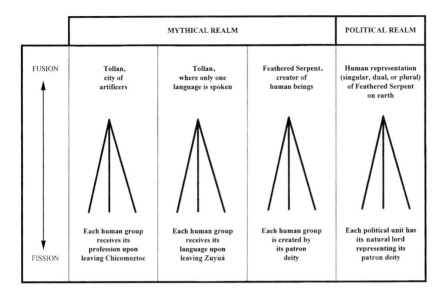

	MYTHICAL REALM			POLITICAL REALM
FUSION	Tollan, city of artificers	Tollan, where only one language is spoken	Feathered Serpent, creator of human beings	Human representation (singular, dual, or plural) of Feathered Serpent on earth
FISSION	Each human group receives its profession upon leaving Chicomoztoc	Each human group receives its language upon leaving Zuyuá	Each human group is created by its patron deity	Each political unit has its natural lord representing its patron deity

FIGURE 2. Transition between unity and diversity in divine and earthly realms.

world, they left at the instructions of Quetzalcoatl (sometimes in his guise as Nacxitl), presided over by their respective patron gods and endowed with languages, customs, and crafts that from that time forward would distinguish them (see Sahagún 2000, bk. VI, chap. xxix, par. 1: 949–954; *Popol Vuh* 1964: 107–112; *Título de Totonicapán* 1983: 174–175; *Memorial de Solalá* 1950: 47–57; López Austin and López Luján 1999: 51–55, 2000).

Earthly Prototype

The myths of a creator god of humanity and of an anecumenical kingdom from which the diversity of humankind was brought forth provided the necessary elements to forge the legend of the ruler Quetzalcoatl and his earthly Tula. Thus, in the transition from myth to legend, the idea of a prototypical city arose, a city that was a marvelous place, inhabited by the totality of human races, who spoke the same language and were skilled in all mechanical arts (Sahagún 2000, bk. X, chap. xxix, par. 1: 949–953), for these crafts had been invented by Quetzalcoatl himself (Sahagún 2000, bk. III, chap. iii: 308). The texts tell of the legendary Tula as a place of abundant fertility and wealth (*Anales de Cuauhtitlán* 1945: 8; Sahagún 2000, bk. III, chap. iii: 308–309, bk. X, chap. xxix, par. 1: 949–952). The biography constructed of its ruler Quetzalcoatl portrayed him as full of virtues, and at his dwelling place, four palaces were erected of precious materials; their role as cosmic trees was revealed through their four colors (Sahagún 2000, bk. X, chap. xxix, par. 1: 950–951; *Anales de Cuauhtitlán* 1945: 8).

The exuberance and splendor of the Toltecs described in these sources have given rise to highly diverse interpretations. Even in the sixteenth century, Sahagún stated that Quetzalcoatl was a figure akin to King Arthur of English legends (2000, bk. VIII, prologue: 719–720), and the Toltecs were the Trojans of the New World (2000, bk. X, chap. xxix, par. 1: 949). Today some authors see more of a historical description than a legendary construction in these texts (e.g., Diehl 1983: 60; Feldman 1974: 140–141, fig. 39). There are even those who believe that Toltec exuberance is an idealized reflection of the fertile lowlands of eastern Mexico, inhabited by the Olmec-Xicalanca (Duverger 1983: 212–224). Davies (1974: 111, 1977: 14–18), one of the most meticulous historians of the Toltecs, sees a generalized conception in descriptions of Tollan as Chicomoztoc or Quinehuayan, the universal point of origin of all peoples, which was transformed into an abstraction that may be found not only at Tula in Hidalgo but also anywhere in Mesoamerica. In our opinion the marvelous city and its ruler must be sought in the imagining of an otherworld.

According to legend, harmony and wealth came to an end: in the beginning of this world, in the light of the dawn, before the sun rose, humanity had to abandon the city and splintered into multiple groups, each one distinguished by its language, patron god, and a specific trade among the diversity of arts.

Sacred Character of the Abandoned Cities

In the Mesoamerican past, archaeological sites seem to reflect the supernatural force of its former inhabitants, beings of an earlier world that gave rise to the present one, one that remains latent beneath the worked surfaces of stones. Teotihuacan was the most conspicuous case, and its ceremonial center was regarded as the setting for the creation of the sun and the moon and a burial place worthy of kings (López Luján 1989: 43–49; Matos Moctezuma and López Luján 1993: 157–159; Sahagún 2000, bk. 10, chap. 29, par. 14: 974–975). Archaeological Tula, although much later and quite modest in comparison to the great capital of the Classic period, was also regarded as a site charged with divine power. We know of its fame in the Late Postclassic, but most likely in its own time Tula fulfilled the function of a sacred city, a mundane replica of the anecumenical Tollan, just as Cholula in Puebla and other cities did in their respective eras. Its ruins were occupied, and its monuments were exhumed and new offerings were deposited in them, all as recognition of having been the home of the portentous ruler Quetzalcoatl.

Transfer of the Sacred Character

The image of anecumenical Tollan imbued sacred character to its earthly replicas. Therefore, in its capacity as mundane Tollan, Cholula was converted into a sacred city with sufficient divine faculties to sanctify recently elected rulers, who turned to it in search of confirmation of their authority

(Rojas 1985: 130–132). After their decline the Tollans of this world retained the hierophantic power that permeated their archaeological remains. Those who kept the memory of the glory of these cities of yore in their tradition tended to visit ruins imbued with supernatural power, and there they performed cult acts demanded by their devotion (e.g., Castañeda 1986: 235–236). There was another method of harnessing that force: by taking control of the sacred matter. Each object that had been used in the city's heyday had absorbed sacred power, and thus it became a highly prized object that could be transported and reused (López Luján 1989: 25–36, 2002: 24–27; López Luján et al. 2000; Matos Moctezuma and López Luján 1993: 161–165). Therefore the ruins of the legendary Tula were stripped of many of its ancient objects. Charged with numinous power, they were transported to different locations, where their function as offerings was rehabilitated in new contexts.

Sacred character cannot be reduced to relics that had once formed part of the setting of a hierophany. According to Mesoamerican belief, the forms of the divine attract gods lodged in what they identified as similar. This principle determined the value of sculptural images (López Austin 1993: 137–139). Therefore the images exhumed in the Late Postclassic in what was by that time the archaeological zone of Tula were considered archetypes of the sacred, and they were reproduced or partially imitated in objects that would become gifts for the gods and liturgical components of consecrated settings (López Luján 1989: 19, 32–33, 37–42, 2002: 27–29; Matos Moctezuma and López Luján 1993: 160–161).

Source of Rulers' Powers

For the Mexica, the legitimacy of power was based on two postulates: on the one hand, the ruling lineage claimed to have been created by the god Quetzalcoatl (Sahagún 1979, bk. VI: 7r–68v); on the other, this same lineage was the legitimate heir of Toltec nobility, thanks to Acamapichtli's blood ties. Shortly after they settled on the island in Lake Tetzcoco, the Mexica launched a search for a ruling lineage that would allow them to incorporate themselves into the political hierarchy of the region, because they lacked sufficient legitimacy to be ruled by their own lords. After some failed attempts, they received a noble, Acamapichtli, from the reigning lineage in Culhuacan whom they made *tlatoani* (king) in 1376. As in other historical passages referring to crucial ideological moments, there are highly disparate versions of the ascent of this first ruler (e.g., Durán 1984, *Historia*, chap. vi, v. 2: 52–56; Benavente 1971, epístola proemial: 8); however, without a doubt, beginning in his reign all the Mexica sovereigns and nobles proudly flaunted their Culhua ancestry, which was linked with ancient Tula, because Culhuacan was a Toltec settlement in the Basin of

Mexico (Davies 1984: 209). The quest for ties of legitimation coalesced in a series of marriage alliances that culminated in the Colonial period with the marriage of Don Pedro Tlacahuepan, son of Motecuhzoma Xocoyotzin, to a noble from Tula-Xicocotitlan (see Alvarado Tezozómoc 1949: 136, 144, 151–152, 156–157; Davies 1977: 42, 1984: 209; *Relación de la genealogía* 1991).

Underpinning of the Zuyuan System

In Central Mexico, Yucatan, the Guatemala Highlands, Michoacán, Oaxaca, and other regions of Mesoamerica, from at least the Early Postclassic there were political movements aimed at the forced inclusion of ethnic rulers in a regional regime encompassing many ethnic groups. Each political unit that was included took on a specific administrative function in the group. An example of this form of imposition and distribution of functions is found in the Acolhua politics of Techotlalla (Torquemada 1975–83, bk. II, chap. 8, v. 1: 127–128). The ideological foundations of these movements referred to the mythical figures of the creator god of mankind and to his anecumenical city, Tollan. As discussed above, the myth was complemented by the legend of an earthly city, Tula, and its wise, mundane ruler, Quetzalcoatl. In the anecumenical city, groups of people had existed without ethnic and linguistic distinctions, and only at their departure from Tollan, to go out into the world, had they received their definitive characteristics. Those who militarily promoted regional regimens of multiethnic unity attempted to establish the model of anecumenical Tollan on earth, an order that presumed that all ethnic groups had to remain under the direction of the representatives of Quetzalcoatl (López Austin and López Luján 1999: 59–71).

One of the tools of domination employed in Zuyuan politics was a Triple Alliance composed of the strongest states in the region. The institution had to maintain order by means of a tribunal with three headquarters, known as the *excan tlatoloyan*. According to historian Chimalpain Cuauhtlehuanitzin (1991: 12–15), the legendary Tula had belonged to this institution, together with Otompan and Culhuacan. This last group managed to preserve its position in the alliance, despite the fall of its ancient allies. In the end, in 1430, the Mexica asserted their supposed right to remove Culhuacan when they won the war against Azcapotzalco. Then they reconstituted the *excan tlatoloyan* with Texcoco and Tlacopan, and they used it as a tool of domination to extend their control over their entire known world.

Transfer of Toltec Power

Because Tenochtitlan was in charge of directing military activities in the Triple Alliance, very soon the city surpassed its allies in power and attempted to elevate itself politically over them. For this purpose, it reclaimed the glory of Tula and the direct link with Quetzalcoatl for itself. Among the numerous testimonies of this appropriation, we cite only three by way of example. The first is a speech given in Tetzcoco after the death of Nezahualpilli by the *cihuacoatl* (viceroy) of Tenochtitlan to Quetzalacxoyatl, son and successor to the deceased. The *cihuacoatl* acknowledged the power of sovereigns is derived from Ce Acatl Nacxitl Quetzalcoatl. However, by referring to Quetzalcoatl, he stated that he was "lord of Aztlan Chicomoztoc," thus appropriating the legendary ruler by converting him into the lord of the birthplace of the Mexica (Alvarado Tezozómoc 2001, chap. ciii: 444).

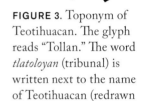

FIGURE 3. Toponym of Teotihuacan. The glyph reads "Tollan." The word *tlatoloyan* (tribunal) is written next to the name of Teotihuacan (redrawn from *Códice Mapa Quinatzin* 2004: 2).

According to the second legend, King Huemac of Tula played the sacred ballgame against the rain gods. The king won the game, and the gods wished to give him tender ears of maize and corn husks as payment for the wager. However, Huemac rejected this payment, demanding instead that they give him greenstone beads and quetzal feathers. Offended by the scorn of the Toltec *tlatoani*, the gods sent a terrible frost and then a drought that lasted four long years (*Leyenda de los Soles* 1992: 126–127). An original account, didactic in nature, seems to end with this story. However, in the version we know, there is a sudden twist in the narrative that breaks the canonical account and introduces an incongruent episode, a strong indication of the political alteration of this account. In fact, in an unjustifiable addition, it is said that the Mexica offered a human sacrifice to the rain gods. After this act of devotion, the gods made it known that the end of the Toltecs had arrived and they made it rain, but now for the benefit of the Mexica. In this way, the Mexica were portrayed as worthy successors to the ancient people (Broda 1987: 237–238; Graulich 1988: 217, 233–234; Olivier 2003: 141).

The third testimony refers to the adjudication of the title of Tollan. In some documentary sources, it is said that Tenochtitlan was founded "in the rushes, in the reeds" (*in toltzallan, in acatzallan*) (Alvarado Tezozómoc 1949: 3–4), a metaphor that connects the Mexica capital with ancient Tula, a city whose name indicates it is a place of abundant rushes (Davies 1980: 192). However, the explicit recognition of the projection of Tollan on earth is iconographic in character. In fact, toponyms of sacred cities that were projections of the anecumenical city tended to include the glyph of rushes. This may be seen in codices referring to Teotihuacan (Figure 3), Tula-Xicocotitlan (Figure 4), the city that the Mixtecs called Frieze of Rushes (Figure 5), and Cholula (Figure 6). In the particular case of Tenochtitlan, the *Códice Sierra* (1982) attributes to it the name of Tollan through the use of a rectangle decorated with a stepped fret, from which some rushes grow (López Austin and López Luján 1999: 71–72; Figure 7).

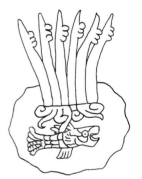

FIGURE 4. Toponym of Tula-Xicocotitlan (redrawn from *Códice Boturini* 1964).

FIGURE 5. The city that the Mixtecs called Frieze of Rushes. The ruler 9 Deer underwent a nose-piercing rite here (redrawn from *Códice Colombino* 1966: 13).

FIGURE 6. Toponym of Cholula (redrawn from Rojas 1985: n.p.).

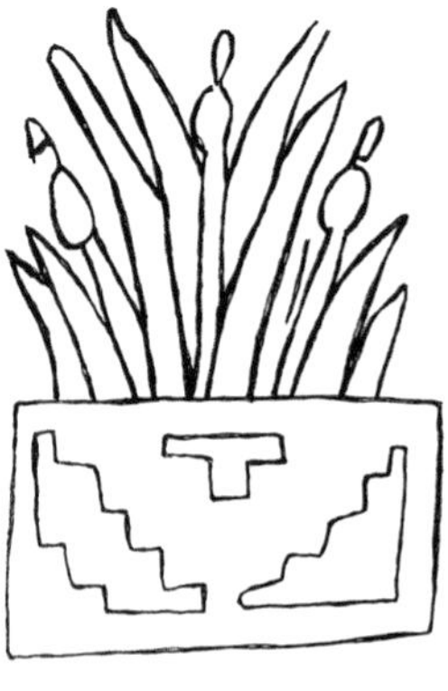

Rejection of Zuyuanism

Ideological complexes may also refer to the abandonment of an earlier political proposal. In our particular case, the force acquired by the Mexica state during the reigns of Ahuitzotl (A.D. 1486–1502) and Motecuhzoma Xocoyotzin (A.D. 1502–1520) made it possible for Tenochtitlan to proclaim itself the center of the universe, without the need to refer to the *excan tlatoloyan* or to the Zuyuan regime of Tollan and Quetzalcoatl. Now the mission entrusted to them by Huitzilopochtli to continue expanding and looting was more than sufficient. The Mexica, based on their military victories and an ideological rationalization, broke the equilibrium of the alliance. Tenochtitlan invoked a new justification for its destiny: the gods had entrusted Huitzilopochtli with domination of the known world, and the proof was the very power of its armies. With this brutal justification,

FIGURE 7. Toponym of Mexico-Tenochtitlan (redrawn from *Códice Sierra* 1982).

the god remained as the generous "adoptive father," prepared to receive under his protection all people who recognized his superiority (Alvarado Tezozómoc 2001, chap. xxiii: 115–117; López Austin 1992: 57). The official histories state that in the times of Ahuitzotl, the Mexica were already invoking in Xoconochco the power that their patron god Huitzilopochtli had granted to them to conquer faraway peoples (Alvarado Tezozómoc 2001, chap. lxxxi: 347–348). It also tells us that Motecuhzoma Xocoyotzin, instead of being considered the ruler of one of the three states of the *excan tlatoloyan*, received the title of *Cemanahuac tlatoani*, a term that Alvarado Tezozómoc (2001, chap. xcvii: 428) translates as "the emperor of the world."

Return of the Disavowed Idea

However, the new ideology did not crystallize completely, so the figure of Quetzalcoatl persisted as a source of power, at least in a surreptitious and frightening form. It was said that Huitzilopochtli had received the throne of Quetzalcoatl on loan for an undetermined length of time (Alvarado Tezozómoc 2001, chap. lviii: 249), but the arrival of the Spaniards filled Motecuhzoma Xocoyotzin with doubts. In 1519 the Mexica sovereign received from Hernán Cortés a gift of wine and biscuits. Motecuhzoma refused to ingest the food, claiming that "it belonged to the gods and that to eat it would be a sacrilege." He then ordered his priests to take the offering to the ruins of Tula "to bury it in the temple of Quetzalcoatl, for those who had arrived here were his sons" (Durán 1984, *Historia*, chap. lxix, v. 2: 511). Shortly thereafter Motecuhzoma became fully convinced the Europeans were the envoys of the displaced god (Alvarado Tezozómoc 2001, chap. cix: 470–471; Carrasco 2000: 205–240; Graulich 1991; Nicholson 2001b: 13–14).

THE MEXICA AND OTHER CENTRAL MEXICAN GROUPS AT TULA-XICOCOTITLAN

The nine ideological complexes analyzed above are fundamental for an understanding of the activities that the Mexica and other peoples in Central Mexico undertook in the ruins of ancient Tula-Xicocotitlan (Figure 8). Numerous pieces of archaeological evidence indicate that ca. A.D. 1150, the main buildings of Tula were consumed in flames (Acosta 1956a: 67; Mastache et al. 2002: 42, 129). As a consequence of this disaster, considered by modern archaeologists to have been a deliberate burning, it is unclear whether the city remained completely uninhabited or if it managed to retain some sectors of its population. What is certain is that the population in the region sooner or later managed to grow until the arrival of the Spaniards (Diehl 1974: 190–192, 1983: 166–168; Healan et al. 1989: 247), at which time it is estimated that the number of inhabitants was slightly higher than that of

1.   **Building C**
2.   **Building B**
2A. **South vesitbule**
3.   **Palacio Quemado or Burnt Palace**
4.   **Palace to the east**
5.   **Palace of Quetzalcoatl**
6.   **Building J**
7.   **Building K**
8.   **Ballcourt 1**
9.   **Ballcourt 2**
10. **Central adoratory**
11. **Tzompantli**
12. **Coatepantli**

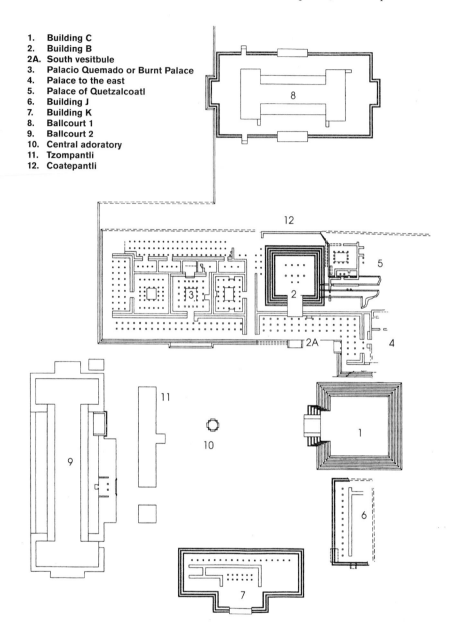

FIGURE 8. Location of the principal buildings in Tula's sacred precinct (from Mastache et al. 2002: fig. 92).

the site at the time of its maximum splendor (Stoutamire n.d. [1975]: 80–81; Yadeun 1975: 24, 28–29). However, according to several authors (Diehl 1974: 191; Healan and Stoutamire 1989: 209, 213, 235–236; Healan et al. 1989: 247; Mastache and Crespo 1974: 76–77), the occupation during the Palacio phase (A.D. 1350–1521) was never as dense or urban as that of the Tollan phase (A.D. 900–1150). Instead it was composed of small villages and hamlets in alluvial lands and of a settlement around Tula Grande that could have been associated with the veneration of the ruins.

The excavation seasons conducted by Jorge R. Acosta in the Great Plaza of the Tollan phase resulted in enormous quantities of Aztec II (A.D. 1200–

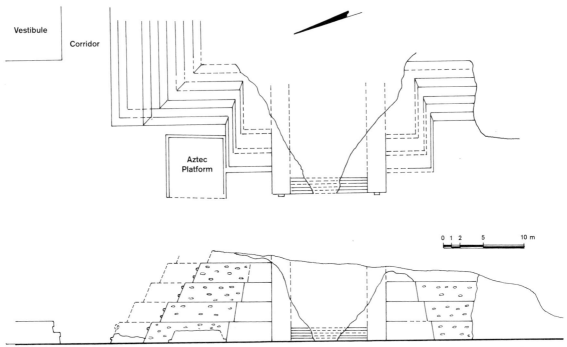

Vestibule

Corridor

Aztec
Platform

0 1 2   5   10 m

1400/1450), III (A.D. 1300/1350–1521), and IV (Final Late Postclassic–Early
Colonial) ceramics. These materials are indisputable proof of the three
long centuries of human activity on the ruins of the ancient city (Acosta
1956–57: 75–76, 92). Unfortunately, it has not yet been possible to determine the identity of the bearers of these ceramics, because types Aztec III
and IV were manufactured in at least four zones of the Basin of Mexico:
Tenochtitlan, Texcoco, Chalco, and the western end of the Peninsula of
Ixtapalapa (Hodge et al. 1993: 138–150).

FIGURE 9. Late Post-
classic platform attached
to the northwest corner
of Building C, Tula
(redrawn from Acosta
1956a: pl. n.p.).

However, what can be determined with exactitude are the sorts of
activities usually carried out in the ruins of Tula between the thirteenth
and sixteenth centuries. There are those actions that added the imprint of
the Late Postclassic on the already archaeological city. What stands out is
the construction of religious buildings, sumptuous residences, and simple
rooms on top of the vestiges of the ancient ceremonial center. We recall
in this regard the spaces with traces of ceremonial, domestic, and craft
activities erected on top of Building K (Getino Granados n.d. [2000]: 137–
144, 181–182; Mastache et al. 2002: 128–129; see Figure 8); the quadrangular
structure found in the interior of Ballcourt 1 (Acosta 1941: 239–240); the
temazcal (sweat bath) built in the center of Ballcourt 2 (Eduardo Matos
Moctezuma, personal communication, December 2005); the rectangular
platform attached to the northwest corner of Building C (Acosta 1956a:
83, 107–112, 114, 1957: pl. 13–14; Figure 9); and the pyramidal platforms
situated on top of Room 1 (Acosta 1956a: 95–96) and Room 2 (Acosta 1957:

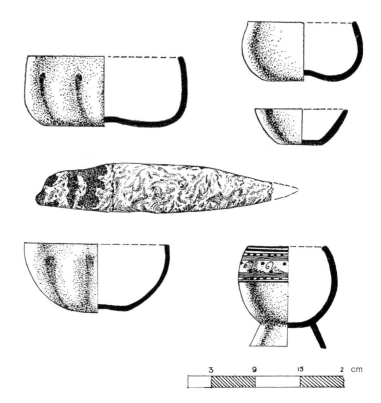

FIGURE 10. Artifacts that formed part of the three Late Postclassic offerings deposited at the northwest corner of Building C, Tula (redrawn from Acosta 1956a: fig. 13).

146–147, 164–166, 1960: 42–43, 1964: 53–54) of the Burnt Palace (Palacio Quemado).[5]

Beyond the Great Plaza but still in its surroundings there are other examples of Late Postclassic architecture, for example Building D (Acosta 1957: 142); Mound I of Cerro de La Malinche (Rodríguez 1995: 131–134); Building 2 (Acosta 1942–44: 148–149); the structure added onto a Toltec temple at the locality of El Canal (Diehl 1989: 27; Stocker and Healan 1989: 152); the Palace of El Cielito (Acosta 1941: 245–246); and the possible elite residence at the foot of El Cielito next to the Tula–San Marcos highway (Diehl 1974: 192, 1989: 18–19).

The burial of corpses and the internment of offerings in old monuments may also be included in this group of additive activities. The mortal remains of individuals of all ages have been discovered, almost always accompanied by extremely humble funerary offerings. For instance, there are the simple, individual sepulcher in the vestibule of Building B (Acosta 1945: 44–45) and the mass burial in Building "4,"[6] which contained a bowl, nine Black/ Orange Aztec III vessels, and a reused Toltec spindle whorl (Acosta 1964: 66–71). The masonry tomb of a possible dignitary also appeared in Room 2 of the Burnt Palace, but unfortunately it was destroyed (Acosta 1964: 53–55).

In comparison to the sepulchers, Late Postclassic offerings are much more abundant at Tula. They have been discovered in pits excavated in the bedrock and in the interior of the fill of buildings, most notably from the Tollan phase: in the Central Adoratory (Acosta 1945: 47–48, 1956a: 50–53, 56); in the vestibule of Building B (Acosta 1945: 45–46); at the northwest corner, the balustrades, and stairway of Building C (Acosta 1956a: 49, 84–87, 92–93, 108–112, 114–115, 1957: 136, 139, 145; Figure 10), and in Rooms 1 and 2 of the Burnt Palace (Acosta 1956a: 73–76, 1957: 147–148, 164). This phenomenon not only indicates intense ritual activity in the Great Plaza but also emphasizes the sacred character of its ruins (Acosta 1956a: 93).

Generally speaking, Late Postclassic offerings have contents similar to those from Tenochtitlan, Tlatelolco, and other contemporary capitals in the Basin of Mexico. Among the items exhumed by archaeologists are all sorts of Aztec II and III containers; Texcoco White and Black/Red cups; Texcoco Compuesto incense burners; ceramic braziers decorated with Tlaloc or Mictlantecuhtli faces; a ceramic temple model and a vertical drum; flint sacrificial knives; ceramic, travertine, and greenstone human figurines; shell and greenstone beads; and a sculpture of a serpent with a human face emerging from its open jaws (Figure 11).

FIGURE 11. Late Postclassic sculpture representing a serpent with a human face emerging from its jaws. Found near two monochrome Aztec ceramic vessels near the south wall of Building C, Tula (from Acosta 1956a: pl. 7).

What should be added to this list are the celebrated reliefs from Cerro de la Malinche, carved at the end of the fifteenth century in pure Mexica style (Navarrete and Crespo 1971: 15; Nicholson 2001a: 234–236). This complex is composed of two figures: that of Topiltzin Quetzalcoatl doing penitence next to the glyph 1 Reed and that of the goddess Chalchiuhtlicue next to the glyph 8 Flint (Figure 12, the goddess to the left). These reliefs have been convincingly interpreted as the Mexica paying homage to the two deities inherited from their Toltec forebears (Fuente 1990: 39), and as a "retrospective historical" image of Ce Acatl Topiltzin, which served to validate the Mexica tradition of sculpting effigies of their rulers on the cliffs of Chapultepec (Pasztory 1983: 125–127; Quiñones Keber 1993: 153).

FIGURE 12. Reliefs from Cerro de la Malinche. Drawing by Fernando Carrizosa.

TRANSPORTING TOLTEC SCULPTURES TO LATE POSTCLASSIC CITIES

Sixteenth-century historical sources offer equally valuable testimonies on the activities we have classified as a second group. We refer specifically to the excavation of buildings to extract sculptures, burials, and offerings, actions that many modern authors have referred to using such pejorative terms as "looting" and "pillaging." However, the individuals involved were not seeking profit or gain, but rather the recovery of aesthetically prized objects—above all those objects that were regarded as magical, given that they were the work of a powerful people (López Luján 1989: 73; Matos Moctezuma and López Luján 1993: 162–163). A passage from Sahagún (2000, bk. X, chap. xxix, par. 1: 949) tells of both the profound knowledge that the Mexica and their contemporaries had of the surface vestiges of the city of Quetzalcoatl and the exploration of the subsoil in search of antiquities:

> and having dwelled and lived there together [the Toltecs in Tula-Xicocotitlan], there are traces of the many works they made there, among which they left a work that is there and that may be seen today, although they did not finish it, which they call coatlaquetzalli, which are some pillars in the form of a serpent that has its head on the ground, standing, and with its tail and rattles above. They also left a mountain or a hill that these Toltecs began to make and did not finish, and the old buildings of their houses and the surfacing that can be seen today. Nowadays, it is also worth mentioning beautifully made things that can be found: pieces of pots or clay, and vessels or wide bowls, and pots. They also take precious stones and jewels and fine turquoise from the earth.

One can imagine how the religious fervor and admiration for the beauty of the ancient works devastated the sacred city. The loss of reliefs and facing stones was massive. On the long list of monuments that were affected were Ballcourt 1 (Acosta 1940: 173, 187, 1941: 240); Building 4 (Acosta 1956a: 78); Building B (Acosta 1941: 241–244, 1942–44: 128, 132–135, 1945: 27–28, 1956a: 74; Diehl 1983: 61);[7] Building C (Acosta 1942–44: 146, 1945: 46, 61, 1956a: 46–48; Diehl 1983: 60, 1989: 27); and Building K (Getino Granados n.d. [2000]: 110, 120, 137, 141). In general, the damaged areas yield considerable volumes of Aztec ceramics, a fact that suggests the cause of the destruction (e.g., Acosta 1940: 172–173, 187). An extreme case was discovered in Room 2 of the Burnt Palace, where there was an offering box with Late Postclassic materials that was covered with a Toltec slab showing a jaguar in procession (Acosta 1957: 147, 164).

Not all acts were carried out with fervor and admiration. In the same period 9 Chacmools—of the 10 known today from this site—were mutilated for unknown reasons. They were violently decapitated, and the heads of eight of them have never been found (Acosta 1941: 241, 1942–44: 147, 1956a: 70, 80–84, 1956b: 159–160, 1957: 160, 163, 169; Castillo Tejero and Dumaine 1986: 223–224; Fuente et al. 1988: 53–59; Jiménez García 1998: 70, 72–78). The remaining one, from Room 2 of the Burnt Palace, was found buried in a trench, and the head was deposited in the fill of the platform built in the same room in the Late Postclassic.

However, we know that several groups from Central Mexico were involved in obtaining and reusing Toltec antiquities. There is convincing historical and archaeological evidence that following their exhumation, monoliths from Tula were taken to diverse destinations. One of them was the city of Tlaxcalla, capital of the principal enemies of the Mexica. According to Motolinía (Benavente 1971: 78), a mask and a small image from Tula were worshipped at the main pyramid of the city together with the sculpture of Camaxtle:

> Then they dressed the statue of their god Camaxtle, which was three *estados* tall, as mentioned above, and they had a small idol that they said had come from the old first people who inhabited this land; they put the idol next to the great statue of Camaxtle. . . . Then they said "today Camaxtle comes out as his son Quezalcovatl." They also put a mask on him, that this and the small idol had come from Tulla and Puyahutla, from where it is said Camaxtle himself was from, and also these Tlaxcaltecs, who are from here at that place about twenty-eight leagues from there.

Another destination was Tlatelolco, as first noted by Barlow (1989: 20–21). A brief fragment of the *Historia de los mexicanos por sus pinturas* (1965: 60) states that the people of Tlatelolco made a journey to the city of Quetzalcoatl to bring a cult image back to the island: "In the year 99 [A.D. 1422] those from Tlatilulco went to Tula and as [the Toltecs] had died and left their god there, which was called Tlacahuepan, they took it and brought it to Tlatilulco."

Finally, we refer to the sacred precinct of Tenochtitlan, where the decapitated image of a Chacmool was uncovered recently (Figure 13). Found as part of the Colonial foundations of the House of the Marquis del Apartado, this sculpture displays typical Toltec traits (see Acosta 1956b; Castillo Tejero and Dumaine 1986: 223–224, 247–248; Fuente et al. 1988: 51–59; Jiménez García 1998: 69–77) in terms of raw material, size, proportions, and iconographic elements (Table 1), so there seems to be no doubt as to its origins (López Luján 2002: 26–27).

TABLE 1. The Toltec Chacmools

Provenience	Discovery	State of conservation	Orientation of face	Bracelet	Pectoral	Dress	Size of pedestal (cm)	Height of plate (cm)
Central Shrine	1942	Without head/legs	Left	Without	Without	Apron/?	? × 72 × 13	32
Burnt Palace	1947	Only torso	Left	?	Triple necklace	?/?	? × ? × 9	?
Building C	1947	Without head	Left	Band/knife	Triple necklace	Apron/loincloth	109 × 46 × 10	42
Building C	1947	Without head	Left	Band/?	Triple necklace	Apron/loincloth	102 × 37 × 6	40
Building C	1947	Only torso	?	?	?	?/?	? × ? × 8	28
Burnt Palace	1954	Complete	Left	Band/knife	Butterfly	Apron/loincloth	109 × 51 × 8	35
Burnt Palace	1954	Without head	?	?	Without	Apron/loincloth	117 × 58 × 6	38
Ballcourt 2	1981	Without head/legs	?	?	Without	?/loincloth	? × ? × ?	35
?	? .	Without head/legs	Left	Band/knife	Butterfly	Apron/loincloth	? × ? × ?	41
?	?	Only torso	?	?	?	?/?	? × ? × ?	42
Apartado	1995	Without head	Left	Band/knife	Without	Apron/loincloth	106 × 47 × 09	34

Note: ?, unknown.

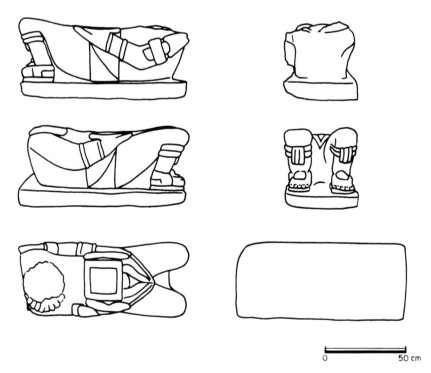

FIGURE 13. The six sides of the Toltec Chacmool found in 1995 in the colonial foundations of the House of the Marquis del Apartado, Mexico City. Drawing by Fernando Carrizosa.

0   50 cm

MEXICA IMITATION OF TOLTEC SCULPTURE

The recovery of the Toltec past found its best expression in imitation. Mexica artists copied practically all types of remains that passed before their eyes: free-standing sculptures of atlantean figures, standard bearers, colossal serpents, and Chacmools;[8] reliefs of so-called "bird-serpent-men," processions of armed figures, undulating serpents, birds of prey, and felines; large-scale braziers with the effigy of Tlaloc or protuberances; and multicolored borders painted on earth and stucco surfaces (Beyer 1955; Fuente 1990: 48–52; Nicholson 1971: 118, 131; Nicholson with Quiñones 1983: 78–79; Pasztory 1983: 90–91, 144–146, 173–178; Umberger 1987: 74–82). The unusual quantity and quality of these imitations suggest the profound effect and appreciation of the value and meaning of the art of Tula. The observation made by Octavio Paz (1989: 77–78) is not inappropriate: "if Tula was a rustic version of Teotihuacan, Mexico-Tenochtitlan was an imperial version of Tula."

In certain visual complexes, the overwhelming reuse of themes is so strong that we might surmise a sort of neo-Toltecism in the art of the island of Tenochtitlan-Tlatelolco. Such is the case of the sculptural group discovered in 1944 at number 12 on the street of República de Guatemala, Mexico City, today occupied by the celebrated Pasaje Catedral or "Cathedral Passageway," an arcade through a building joining Guatemala and Donceles streets (Moedano Koer 1944a–1944e; Rosado Ojeda 1944).[9] On this lot, Hugo Moedano Koer, Rafael Orellana, Juan Valenzuela, and Antonieta Espejo uncovered stairways (Espejo 1996: 179)[10] and a total of 75 complete and incomplete archaeological objects associated with them, including an unusual number of archaist images (Mateos Higuera 1979: 213–214; Navarrete and Crespo 1971; Nicholson 1961, 1971: 111, 119; Solís 1997; Umberger 1987: 75–76, 96). Among these are eight handsome slabs representing birds of prey and felines, the latter roaring and seated on their hindquarters. Based on the position of their bodies, these felines evoke free-standing sculptures found by Acosta in different parts of Tula (Moedano Koer 1944d) and indirectly, animal processions decorating the facades of Building B (Solís 1997: 84–85). This fact and the existence of the stairway lead one to believe that the Mexica sculptures were originally tenoned into the walls of a building that could be considered neo-Toltec in style, which would have been located just north of the main ballcourt.

Another set of sculptures found in the Pasaje Catedral is composed of four males and one female dressed in Toltec garb; they recall the colossal figures discovered by Acosta in Tula's Building B. They depict a spectacular group of divine warriors displaying the butterfly emblem on forehead and chest and armed with spearthrowers and darts. The male figures have a sacrificial knife bound to their arm, and they wear a triangular apron over their loincloths; in contrast, the female figure has a *tzotzopaztli* (weaving

FIGURE 14. Mexica sculpture of a figure dressed as a Toltec warrior. Found in the Pasaje Catedral, Mexico City. Photograph by Michel Zabé.

batten) tied to her arm and wears a skirt in the form of interlaced arrows. Their provenance is subject to debate, because one of the five sculptures, singled out by a small beard like that of Quetzalcoatl, is ostensibly distinguished from the rest by more detailed technical execution and by its greater anatomical realism (Figure 14). Based on these differences, Navarrete and Crespo (1971: 13–15), Nicholson (1971: 111, 119), and Townsend (1979: 17–18) believe that the bearded image is a Mexica copy of the other four, which are originally from Tula. However, Fuente (1990: 46–48) and Umberger (1987: 75–76) are of the opinion that all of them are Mexica imitations and that the contrasts in sculptural quality arise because four of them date to an earlier period. A hypothesis that strikes us as more plausible has been proposed by Solís (1997: 90–93), who suggests that the five images were carved in the same workshop in Tenochtitlan. Following this logic, the intention was to highlight iconographically the bearded figure, in addition to the fact that it is evident that the creator of this image was more skilled than the sculptor who executed the other four. Whatever the explanation, the fundamental point here is that these small "colossal figures" were associated with the slabs of animals and they must have formed part of the sculptural program of an archaist building in the sacred precinct of the Mexica capital.

According to Felipe Solís (personal communication, May 2007), Hugo Moedano Koer's team detected several large-scale ceramic roof ornaments representing *tecciztli* shells in the same spot; two of these pieces are currently in the Museo Nacional de Antropología in Mexico City. This detail is of extreme importance for our study, because seven virtually identical roof ornaments (measuring 230 cm × 100 cm × 8 cm) were recovered in 2007 at Donceles 97, a property located only 20 m to the east of the Pasaje Catedral. According to recent research conducted by Raúl Barrera Rodríguez and Gabino López Arenas (2008), the architectural and sculptural vestiges found on this property were part of the *calmecac*, the temple-school dedicated to Quetzalcoatl. Among other pieces of evidence supporting their proposal there is the image of the sacred precinct of Tenochtitlan from the *Primeros memoriales* (Sahagún 1993: 269r), showing the relative position of the *calmecac*, and the drawing of this school in the *Codex Mendoza* (1992: 61r), where it is shown as topped by roof ornaments in the shape of *tecciztli* shells. In sum, it would be of enormous importance if the archaist sculptures of the Pasaje Catedral that we have described belong to a neo-Toltec style building and if this building was indeed the *calmecac*, an institution for nobles protected by Quetzalcoatl.

HOUSE OF EAGLES

The best example of the neo-Toltec style in Tenochtitlan is doubtless the House of Eagles, a religious building dating to the fifteenth century

that also formed part of the sacred precinct and was located
a few meters north of the Great Temple (Figure 15). Its
iconographic and decorative program brings Tula
back to life in all its splendor three centuries
after its turbulent collapse. In the second
constructive stage of the House of
Eagles (ca. A.D. 1469), allusions
to Toltec civilization were
everywhere to transmit to
the faithful the idea of the
glorious past.[11] Particularly
surprising in this body of material are eight large biconical braziers,
whose surfaces were decorated with appliquéd

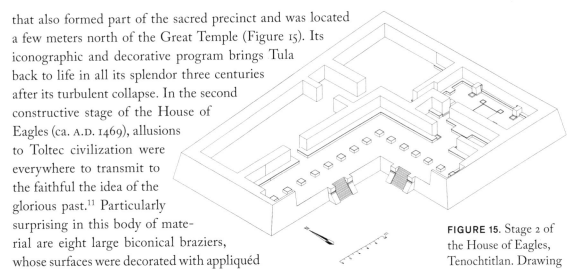

FIGURE 15. Stage 2 of
the House of Eagles,
Tenochtitlan. Drawing
by Tenoch Medina.

faces of the Rain God streaming tears (Figure 16). These braziers, found
opposite the altars in the inner rooms of the Mexica building, are copies
of braziers of type Abra Café Burdo, Variedad Tláloc known from Tula
(see Acosta 1956a: 110–111, 114–115, pl. 52; Cobean 1974: 35, 1990: 421–426,
pl. 196d, 198; Diehl 1983: figs. 39–40; Stocker 1974: 29–30, fig. 12a; Stocker
and Healan 1989: 152–154; Figure 17). Although these Mexica imitations
are fairly faithful to the Toltec originals, they betray their distinct origin in
their smaller dimensions and in certain stylistic details, above all in the way
the appliqué details were added. This observation has been corroborated
by the petrographic analysis carried out by Jaime Torres and the neutron
activation analysis conducted by Hector Neff, experts whose results consistently identify the temper and clay of the eight braziers as coming from
Tenochtitlan and its vicinity (López Luján 2006: 96–100).

The walls of the House of Eagles also bear the unmistakable Toltec
stamp. Mexica artists followed technical and stylistic solutions that were
in vogue during the Tollan phase, as shown by the discoveries of Acosta
(1945: 38, 1956–57: 82–83, 1960: 42, pl. VI, 1961: 32, 1964: 60) and Moedano
Koer (1947: 113). One of these solutions consists of applying the pictorial
layer on walls combining stucco and earth surfaces. The smooth, whitish
stucco surface was placed on the lower third of the wall, followed by a
surface made of rough, dark earth up to the roof. While the latter was still
moist, pigments, mixed with lime water, were applied, resulting in opaque
colors with great chromatic saturation.

In the House of Eagles, Toltec ornamental motifs were also copied,
such as multicolored borders (López Luján 2006: 120; López Luján et al.
2005). These motifs were composed of four horizontal bands that always
follow the same color sequence: black, blue, red, and yellow from bottom
to top. Each band measures between 9 and 11 cm in height, totaling an
approximate height of 40 cm. The horizontal borders decorate the entire

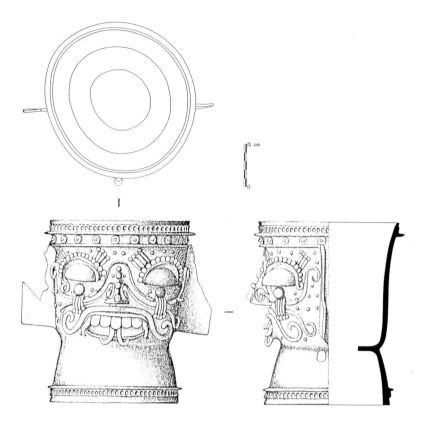

FIGURE 16. Mexica
Tlaloc brazier, imitation
of ceramic type Abra
Café Burdo, Variedad
Tláloc. From the
House of Eagles,
Tenochtitlan. Drawing
by Fernando Carrizosa.

FIGURE 17. Toltec Tlaloc braziers. Ceramic type Abra Café
Burdo, Variedad Tláloc. Drawing by Fernando Carrizosa.

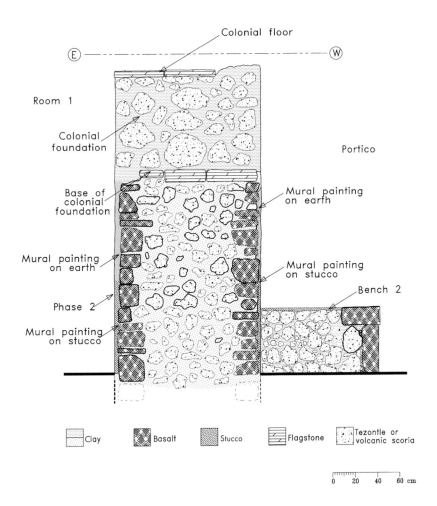

Colonial floor

Room 1

Colonial foundation

Base of colonial foundation

Mural painting on earth

Phase 2

Mural painting on stucco

Portico

Mural painting on earth

Mural painting on stucco

Bench 2

Clay Basalt Stucco Flagstone Tezontle or volcanic scoria

0 20 40 60 cm

FIGURE 18. Mexica bench construction system. Portico, bench 2, from the House of Eagles, Tenochtitlan. Drawing by Tenoch Medina.

wall, reaching several meters in length. On the walls without benches, the border is about 80 cm above the floor. What is interesting for our purposes is that Acosta found the same type of border at Tula in the passage running from Building B to the Burnt Palace (Acosta 1956a: 44, fig. 3, 1956–57: 82–83). It is surprising that the Toltec borders measured 38 cm in height and were 79 cm above the floor. They were composed of four bands: yellow, blue, red, and black from top to bottom. Just as in the House of Eagles, below the border, the wall was painted white, and above the border it is red.

The final touch to the neo-Toltec program of the House of Eagles was an impressive sequence of bench reliefs. To date, 86 linear m have been excavated from the fill (López Luján 2006: 102–116). Each bench is composed of two panels roughly carved. The upper part is a frieze with images of serpents with undulating bodies. The lower panel shows a procession of figures coming together on both sides of a *zacatapayolli*, a grass ball into which the bloody perforators from auto-sacrifice were inserted.

Over time numerous authors have proposed that the benches found at Tenochtitlan were obtained by the Mexica at the ruins of Tula (Figures 18,

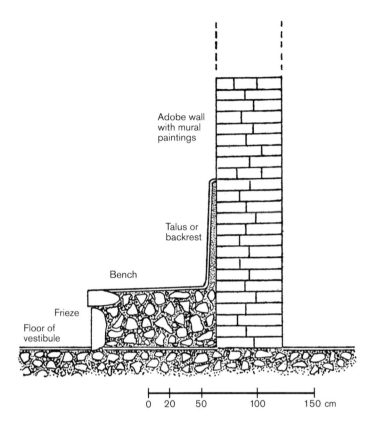

Adobe wall
with mural
paintings

Talus or
backrest

Bench

Frieze

Floor of
vestibule

FIGURE 19. Toltec bench construction
system. Vestibule of Building B, Tula
(redrawn from Acosta 1945: fig. 21).

0   20   50   100   150 cm

19). However, this suggestion is far from the case. Petrographic, technological, and stylistic analysis of the benches at the House of Eagles indicate
that without a doubt they are archaist copies (López Luján 2006). In effect,
Mexica artists imitated the Tula benches, employing local raw materials
and their own construction techniques. They used earth and large, irregular
tezontle (volcanic scoria) stones as fill—unlike the Toltecs, who used earth
and smaller sedimentary rocks. In addition, they utilized thick slabs of
tezontle and pyroxene basalt carved on five sides, which contrast with the
thin Toltec pieces of limestone worked on six sides (Acosta 1956–57: 81–82;
Jiménez García 1998: 23). In the House of Eagles, they built up a first row
measuring 41–45 cm in height with these slabs; on top of this row they
placed a second row 16–18 cm tall. In contrast, the artists of Tula used slabs
slightly less high (35–37 cm on the first row and 15–16 cm on the second),
often using plaster to adhere them. Another interesting difference has to
do with the angle of the first row of the stones carved with the figures in
procession. In the House of Eagles, these slabs are in a perfectly vertical
position, just as in the vestibule of Building B at Tula (Moedano Koer 1947:
115); however, in the Burnt Palace and in Building 4 of that same city, the
slabs were placed in a sloping position (Acosta 1956a: 77–78, 1957: 132–133).

Iconographically the bas-reliefs at the House of Eagles, just like their

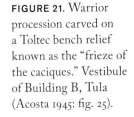

FIGURE 20. Warrior procession carved on a Mexica bench relief. Portico, bench 2, from the House of Eagles, Tenochtitlan. Drawing by Fernando Carrizosa.

FIGURE 21. Warrior procession carved on a Toltec bench relief known as the "frieze of the caciques." Vestibule of Building B, Tula (Acosta 1945: fig. 25).

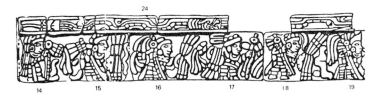

models, represent individuals dressed in Toltec garb and bearing defensive and offensive weapons, although always in a noncombative stance (Figures 20, 21). None of the 201 figures discovered to date bear the complex insignia of the officials of the Mexica military that were rendered in such documents as *Primeros memoriales* (Sahagún 1993: 68r–69r, 72r–80r), *Codex Mendoza* (1992), and *Lienzo de Tlaxcala* (1983). It is significant that the bench bas-reliefs in the House of Eagles do not depict those offensive weapons that were absent from the Toltec military inventory but were used extensively by Mexica armies, such as the bow-and-arrow combination, and particularly to the *macuahuitl* (a wooden club edged with obsidian blades). The latter instrument, so feared by the Spanish invaders, was represented profusely in pictographic documents of Mexica tradition and somewhat rarely in the sculptures of this civilization (e.g., Gutiérrez 1983: 142–144, figs. 124, 125). On the benches of the House of Eagles, no elements suggest a specific event from Mexica history. The bas-reliefs completely lack calendrical signs, name glyphs, place names, and allusions to the reasons underlying the auto-sacrifice represented. The images only seek to record in stone the sacrifices performed by high dignitaries without time references.

Since its discovery, the House of Eagles has often been compared with different hypostyle halls at Tula (e.g., Klein 1987: 307; Mastache et al. 2002: 111–114; Molina Montes 1987: 102; Solís 1997: 91).[12] Some authors have suggested the configuration of the Mexica building is similar to that of the Burnt Palace, because the House of Eagles also has a portico supported by pilasters, rooms decorated with bench reliefs, and a patio with an impluvium. Nevertheless, we have reached the conclusion that there is no such analogy between the two buildings (López Luján 2006: 262–265). The hypostyle halls at Tula were composed of an entrance portico and an extremely large, rectangular hall that always exceeded 500 m² in area. Their shapes and dimensions implied that their interiors were used for activities involving large groups of people. In contrast, the inner rooms of the House of Eagles display a much more complex spatial configuration and all are smaller than 72 m² (Table 2). In other words, these small, barely illuminated rooms that were isolated from the outside are spaces more in tune with prayer, meditation, and penitence. This suggestion is confirmed by the iconography and the chemical remains recovered from the stucco floors of the building, which indicate that oblation and auto-sacrifice were the principal rites that took place there (Barba et al. 1996; López Luján 2006: 260–262). Complementing these data, a study of the historical sources has determined with a fair degree of certainty that this neo-Toltec building served as a setting for rites of dynastic transition: a wake was held there over the body of the dead king, and a few days later in the same location the successor to the throne conducted rites of death and rebirth prior to ascending the throne (López Luján 2006: 271–291).

In conclusion, the House of Eagles did not have the same functions as its Toltec predecessors or models. Physical similarities were simply the result of an architectural revival that lacked specific connotations but took on the quality of a sacred symbol alluding to a grandiose past. From this perspective, it is worth asking: what was the meaning of evoking the Toltec past in a structure destined for rituals surrounding the major rites

TABLE 2. Comparison of the halls in the Burnt Palace, Tula, and the rooms in the House of Eagles, Tenochtitlan

Inner space	Area (m²)
Burnt Palace, Tula	
Hall 1	537
Hall 2	657
Hall 3	518
House of Eagles, Tenochtitlan	
Room 1	72
Room 2	28
Room 3	28

of passage of Mexica kings? In general, we can state that the neo-Toltec iconographic and decorative program transmitted the idea of prestigious ancestry, an established means of legitimating the supremacy of the king, heir, and indisputable successor to the great Quetzalcoatl.

CONCLUSIONS

We can surmise that the attitude of the Mexica toward the archetypical image of Tollan and Quetzalcoatl—toward the ruins of the legendary Tula and the figure of their own patron god, Huitzilopochtli—can be characterized as variable over time. This was the case in different periods of their history and in terms of the different components of society and their diverse ideologies. Nonetheless, an ongoing, generalized belief seems to have been the sacred character of the site, which was visited, honored, and deprived of the vestiges of its ancient glories by the Mexica and their contemporaries. Nevertheless, beyond the widespread admiration of the peoples of the Central Highlands, there is the need (evident in the Mexica attitude) to transform their capital, first into the successor of the legendary Tula, and later in the new projection of the anecumenical Tollan.

Once the Mexica reached their maximum power and domination, they may have had pretensions of removing any legitimating references to Tollan and to archaeological Tula. It is difficult to derive this idea from extant material testimonies, but if true, the pride of the sons of Huitzilopochtli was demolished by the impact of the Spanish conquest and the cosmological interpretation given to the European invasion: Quetzalcoatl had returned because of Huitzilopochtli's arrogance, and the latter god had to recognize his true stature.

Tula, its architecture, sculptures, paintings, and ritual objects were models for Tenochtitlan. There is evidence that one incentive for copying

FIGURE 22. Dedication Stone of the
Inauguration of the Great Temple.
Drawing by Fernando Carrizosa.

Tula must have been political: the ostentatious display showing that the
Mexica capital was the successor of the former city's power and held an
unbroken legitimacy. However, other evidence suggests much more profound causes: the use of forms that invited divine beings to occupy their
space. Beyond ideological adaptations to the vagaries of history, the figure
of Tollan as an anecumenical place and the place of origin for humans
had penetrated rituals connected to power and became rooted in these
rituals independent of ideological changes. The liturgy linked to the most
important political acts had created a mundane projection of Tollan on
religious architecture. The penetration of the faithful in neo-Toltec precincts launched a mystical journey to another time-space, and there, they
fulfilled high-level rituals for the transfer of rulership. The recently elected
sovereign had to visit the House of Eagles through a ritual death, and there
he received his new being and the responsibility of his future power (López
Luján 2006: 291–293). He had to journey to anecumenical Tollan, because

this place was the threshold of the other time-space, the antechamber of the creation of humans (see *Memorial de Sololá* 1950: 47–57; *Popol Vuh* 1964: 107–112; *Título de Totonicapán* 1983: 174–175). To become king the elected ruler came to Tollan; perhaps he gave offerings there to the god Nacxitl-Quetzalcoatl, who bestowed distinctive characteristics on different ethnic groups, and the elected ruler crossed the limits between this and the other world to take on power. Later, in a complementary ritual, the deceased king returned his gift to the place of origin of power. In this celebration, the *zacatapayolli* must have had the symbolic value of the sacred place where Quetzalcoatl intervened to bestow his legitimation. We can see this symbolism in the relief known as the Dedication Stone commemorating the inauguration of the Great Temple (Figure 22), a monument in which Tizoc and Ahuitzotl let blood as they flank a *zacatapayolli* in the year 8-Reed (A.D. 1487). According to Townsend (1979: 40–43; cf. Klein 1987: 318–324), the celebrated scene represented Tizoc legitimizing the ascent to the throne of his brother and successor, Ahuitzotl, a ceremony that took place at the navel of the universe, the place of the earth's reproductive and alimentary forces. Nicholson with Quiñones Keber (1983: 54) emphasize that the date that appears above the *zacatapayolli*, 7-Reed, is one of the archetypical names of Topiltzin Quetzalcoatl, inventor and patron of auto-sacrifice carried out by both *tlatoque*. The parallel would seem to confirm our interpretation that those who attended the ritual in the House of Eagles were mystically situated in the anecumenical Tollan, precisely at the axis mundi in the mythical realm governed by Quetzalcoatl, where the transfer of political authority was carried out.

Acknowledgments

We thank our friends Jai Alterman, Davíd Carrasco, Fernando Carrizosa, Robert Cobean, William L. Fash, Laura Filloy, Joyce Marcus, Eduardo Matos Moctezuma, Tenoch Medina, Debra Nagao, Joanne Pillsbury, and José Ramírez for their support.

NOTES

1. In this chapter, ecumenical (from *oikos*, house) is defined as the world inhabited by natural and supernatural beings, and anecumenical as the space exclusive to supernatural beings.

2. The designation is conventional (see López Austin and López Luján 1999: 38–40).

3. The *minacachalli* was the dart used in lake hunting, propelled with the *atlatl* (spearthrower); the *chitatli* was the net bag used to collect game.

4. To distinguish anecumenical Tollan from its earthly manifestation, we reserve the original name for the former and use Tula to refer to the archaeological city.

5. According to Diehl (1989: 26), the small size, crudeness, and lack of decoration of these constructions suggest that they were erected by small, disorganized groups of individuals.

6. Acosta's Building "4" is to the northeast of Ballcourt 1 (see Diehl 1989: 23). It should not be confused with Building 4, located in the Great Plaza. About the latter, see note 12.

7. A huge trench was dug during the Late Postclassic on the north side of Building B; it had a volume of 2,600 m^3 (Acosta 1961: 29, 1964: 46). The colossal figures, columns, and piers that held up the roof of the temple were violently cast into this pit.

8. The enormous formal, stylistic, and iconographic differences between the Chacmools from Tula and those from Tenochtitlan lead us to think that, beyond mere imitation, these are two sculptural expressions extremely different from a pan-Mesoamerican tradition of great temporal depth (López Austin and López Luján 2001).

9. Unfortunately, this important discovery was publicized only through the local newspapers. Apparently a technical report was never submitted to the authorities at the Instituto Nacional de Antropología e Historia, Mexico City (José Ramírez, personal communication, August 2005).

10. These stairways were dismounted at the end of November 1944 and were taken to Tlatelolco under the orders of Pablo Martínez del Río (Espejo 1996: 179).

11. The second construction stage of the House of Eagles is contemporary with Stage IVb of the Great Temple. Stage IVa of the Great Temple was characterized by the presence of two chambers on its front platform that were decorated with benches imitating the Tula bench reliefs (López Luján 2006).

12. Some of these authors (Francisco Hinojosa, personal communication to Molina Montes 1987: 102; Mastache et al. 2002: 113–114; Molina Montes 1987: 102; see also Chapter 10 in this volume) have made reference to certain spatial analogies between the House of Eagles and Building 4 at Tula. The latter is a complex of adobe rooms connected directly to Pyramid B via the Southern Vestibule. Building 4, also known as "Palace to the East" (see Figure 8), was partially excavated in the 1950s by Acosta (1956a: 44–46, 77–80), and today it is being explored by Robert H. Cobean (personal communication, October 2005). On the one hand, the House of Eagles differs from Building 4 in construction materials and finishes, in the precise distribution of pilasters and benches, and in that it is not articulated to the north with any pyramidal structure. On the other hand, the Toltec building and the Mexica one display interesting similarities in the relative positions of their first rooms and interconnecting doors.

REFERENCES CITED

Acosta, Jorge R.

    1940   Exploraciones en Tula, Hgo., 1940. *Revista Mexicana de Estudios Antropológicos* 4: 172–194.

    1941   Los últimos descubrimientos arqueológicos en Tula, Hgo., 1941. *Revista Mexicana de Estudios Antropológicos* 5: 239–248.

1942–44   La tercera temporada de exploraciones arqueológicas en Tula, Hgo., 1942. *Revista Mexicana de Estudios Antropológicos* 6: 125–160.

    1945   La cuarta y quinta temporadas de exploraciones arqueológicas en Tula, Hgo., 1943–1944. *Revista Mexicana de Estudios Antropológicos* 4: 23–64.

1956a   Resumen de los informes de las exploraciones arqueológicas en Tula, Hgo. durante las VI, VII y VIII temporadas. 1946–1950. *Anales del INAH* 8: 37–115.

1956b   El enigma de los chac mooles de Tula. In *Estudios antropológicos publicados en homenaje al doctor Manuel Gamio:* 159–170. Universidad Nacional Autónoma de México and Sociedad Mexicana de Antropología, México.

1956–57 Interpretación de algunos de los datos obtenidos en Tula relativos a la época tolteca. *Revista Mexicana de Estudios Antropológicos* 14: 75–110.

1957   Resumen de los informes de las exploraciones arqueológicas de Tula, Hgo., durante las IX y X temporadas. 1953–1954. *Anales del INAH* 9: 119–169.

1960   Las exploraciones arqueológicas en Tula, Hgo., durante la XI temporada, 1955. *Anales del INAH* 11: 39–72.

1961   La doceava temporada de exploraciones en Tula, Hgo. *Anales del INAH* 13: 29–58.

1964   La decimotercera temporada de exploraciones en Tula, Hgo. *Anales del INAH* 16: 45–75.

Alvarado Tezozómoc, Hernando de

1949   *Crónica mexicáyotl* (Adrián León, trans.). Universidad Nacional Autónoma de México and Instituto Nacional de Antropología e Historia, México.

2001   *Crónica mexicana* (Gonzalo Díaz Migoyo and Germán Vázquez Chamorro, eds.). Dastin, Madrid.

Anales de Cuauhtitlán

1945   In *Códice Chimalpopoca* (Primo Feliciano Velázquez, trans.): 1–118, 145–164. Universidad Nacional Autónoma de México, México.

Barba, Luis, Agustín Ortíz, Leonardo López Luján, Karl F. Link, and Luz Lazos

1996   Chemical Analysis of Residues in Floors and the Reconstruction of Ritual Activities at Templo Mayor. In *Archaeological Chemistry. Organic, Inorganic and Biochemical Analysis* (Mary Virginia Orna, ed.): 139–156. American Chemical Society, Washington, D.C.

Barlow, Robert H.

1989   Cuauhtlatoa: El apogeo de Tlatelolco. In *Tlatelolco: fuentes e historia* (Jesús Monjarás-Ruiz, Elena Limón, and María de la Cruz Paillés H., eds.): 31–57. Instituto Nacional de Antropología e Historia and Universidad de las Américas, México.

Barrera Rodríguez, Raúl, and Gabino López Arenas

2008   Hallazgos del recinto ceremonial de Tenochtitlan. *Arqueología Mexicana* 93: 18–35.

Benavente o Motolinía, Toribio de

1971   *Memoriales*, 2nd ed. (Edmundo O'Gorman, ed.). Universidad Nacional Autónoma de México, México.

Beyer, Hermann

1955   La 'Procesión de los señores.' Decoración del primer teocalli de piedra en Mexico-Tenochtitlán. *El México Antiguo* 8: 8–42.

Braudel, Fernand

    1974   *La historia y las ciencias sociales.* Alianza Editorial, Madrid.

Broda, Johanna

    1987   The Provenience of the Offerings: Tribute and Cosmovision. In *The Aztec Templo Mayor* (Elizabeth H. Boone, ed.): 211–256. Dumbarton Oaks Research Library and Collection, Washington, D.C.

Carrasco, Davíd

    2000   *Quetzalcóatl and the Irony of Empire. Myths and Prophecies in the Aztec Tradition,* revised ed. University Press of Colorado, Boulder.

Castañeda, Francisco de

    1986   Relación de Tequizistlán y su partido. In *Relaciones geográficas del siglo XVI, México, I* (René Acuña, ed.): 211–251. Universidad Nacional Autónoma de México, México.

Castillo Tejero, Noemí, and A. Dumaine L.

    1986   Escultura en piedra procedente de la zona arqueológica de Tula, Hidalgo, México. *Beiträge zur Allgemeinen und Vergleichenden Archäologie* 8: 213–282.

Chimalpain Cuauhtlehuanitzin, Domingo de San Antón Muñón

    1991   *Memorial breve acerca de la fundación de la ciudad de Culhuacan* (Víctor M. Castillo F., ed. and trans.). Universidad Nacional Autónoma de México, México.

Cobean, Robert H.

    1974   The Ceramics of Tula. In *Studies of Ancient Tollan: A Report of the University of Missouri Tula Archaeological Project* (Richard A. Diehl, ed.): 32–41. Department of Anthropology, University of Missouri-Columbia, Columbia.

    1990   *La cerámica de Tula, Hidalgo.* Instituto Nacional de Antropología e Historia, México.

Codex Mendoza

    1992   (Frances F. Berdan and Patricia Rieff Anawalt, eds.). University of California Press, Berkeley.

Códice Boturini

    1964   In *Antigüedades de México, II* (Edward King, ed.): 7–29. Secretaría de Hacienda y Crédito Público, México.

Códice Colombino

    1966   (Alfonso Caso and Mary Elizabeth Smith, eds.). México, Sociedad Mexicana de Antropología, México.

Códice Mapa Quinatzin

    2004   *Códice Mapa Quinatzin. Justicia y derechos humanos en el México antiguo* (Luz María Mohar Betancourt, ed.). Comisión Nacional de los Derechos Humanos, Centro de Investigaciones y Estudios Superiores en Antropología Social, and Miguel Ángel Porrúa, México.

Códice Sierra

    1982   (Nicolás León, trans.). Editorial Innovación, México.

Davies, Nigel

1974 Tula: Realidad, mito y símbolo. In *Proyecto Tula (1a Parte)* (Eduardo Matos Moctezuma, ed.): 109–114. Instituto Nacional de Antropología e Historia, México.

1977 *The Toltecs Until the Fall of Tula.* University of Oklahoma Press, Norman.

1980 *The Toltec Heritage. From the Fall of Tula to the Rise of Tenochtitlan.* University of Oklahoma Press, Norman.

1984 The Aztec Concept of History: Teotihuacan and Tula. In *The Native Sources and the History of the Valley of Mexico* (Jacqueline de Durand-Forest, ed.): 207–214. British Archaeological Reports, Oxford.

Diehl, Richard A.

1974 Summary and Conclusions. In *Studies of Ancient Tollan: A Report of the University of Missouri Tula Archaeological Project* (Richard A. Diehl, ed.): 190–195. Department of Anthropology, University of Missouri-Columbia, Columbia.

1983 *Tula. The Toltec Capital of Ancient Mexico.* Thames and Hudson, London.

1989 Previous Investigations at Tula. In *Tula of the Toltecs. Excavations and Survey* (Dan M. Healan, ed.): 13–33. University of Iowa Press, Iowa City.

Durán, Diego

1984 *Historia de las Indias de Nueva España e islas de tierra firme,* 2nd ed., 2 vols. (Ángel Ma. Garibay K., ed.). Editorial Porrúa, México.

Duverger, Christian

1983 *L'origine des aztèques.* Éditions du Seuil, Paris.

Espejo, Antonieta

1996 Las ofrendas halladas en Tlatelolco. In *Tlatelolco a través de los tiempos, cincuenta años después (1944–1994), 1, Arqueología* (Francisco González Rul, ed.): 171–184. Instituto Nacional de Antropología e Historia, México.

Feldman, Lawrence H.

1974 Tollan in Hidalgo: Native Accounts of the Central Mexican Tolteca. In *Studies of Ancient Tollan: A Report of the University of Missouri Tula Archaeological Project* (Richard A. Diehl, ed.): 130–149. Department of Anthropology, University of Missouri-Columbia, Columbia.

Fuente, Beatriz de la

1990 Escultura en el tiempo. Retorno al pasado tolteca. *Artes de México,* nueva época 9: 36–53.

Fuente, Beatriz de la, Silvia Trejo, and Nelly Gutiérrez Solana

1988 *Escultura en piedra de Tula. Catálogo.* Universidad Nacional Autónoma de México, México.

Getino Granados, Fernando

n.d. El Edificio K de Tula, Hidalgo. Licenciate thesis in Archaeology, Escuela Nacional de Antropología e Historia, México, 2000.

Graulich, Michel

    1988 *Quetzalcóatl y el espejismo de Tollan*. Instituut voor Amerikanistiek V.Z.W., Antwerp.

    1991 Les signes avant-coureurs de la chute de l'empire aztèque. In *Apparitions et miracles* (Alain Dierkens, ed.): 139–151. Editions de l'Université de Bruxelles, Brussels.

Gutiérrez Solana, Nelly

    1983 *Objetos ceremoniales en piedra de la cultura mexica*. Universidad Nacional Autónoma de México, México.

Healan, Dan M., and James W. Stoutamire

    1989 Surface Survey of the Tula Urban Zone. In *Tula of the Toltecs. Excavations and Survey* (Dan M. Healan, ed.): 203–236. University of Iowa Press, Iowa City.

Healan, Dan M., Robert H. Cobean, and Richard A. Diehl

    1989 Synthesis and Conclusions. In *Tula of the Toltecs. Excavations and Survey* (Dan M. Healan, ed.): 239–251. University of Iowa Press, Iowa City.

Historia de los mexicanos por sus pinturas

    1965 In *Teogonía e historia de los mexicanos. Tres opúsculos del siglo XVI* (Ángel Ma. Garibay K., ed.): 21–90. Editorial Porrúa, México.

Hodge, Mary G., Hector Neff, M. James Blackman, and Leah D. Minc

    1993 Black-on-Orange Ceramic Production in the Aztec Empire's Heartland. *Latin American Antiquity* 4(2): 130–157.

Jiménez García, Elizabeth

    1998 *Iconografía de Tula. El caso de la escultura*. Instituto Nacional de Antropología e Historia, México.

Klein, Cecelia F.

    1987 The Ideology of Autosacrifice at the Templo Mayor. In *The Aztec Templo Mayor* (Elizabeth H. Boone, ed.): 293–370. Dumbarton Oaks Research Library and Collection, Washington, D.C.

Leyenda de los soles

    1945 In *Códice Chimalpopoca* (Primo Feliciano Velázquez, trans.): 119–164. Universidad Nacional Autónoma de México, México.

Lienzo de Tlaxcala

    1983 (Alfredo Chavero, ed.). Cartón y Papel de México, México.

López Austin, Alfredo

    1973 *Hombre-dios. Religión y política en el mundo náhuatl*. Universidad Nacional Autónoma de México, México.

    1992 La religión y la larga duración: Consideraciones para la interpretación del sistema mítico-religioso mesoamericano. *Journal of Latin American Lore* 18: 53–62.

    1993 *The Myths of the Opossum. Pathways of Mesoamerican Mythology*. University of New Mexico Press, Albuquerque.

    2001 El núcleo duro, la cosmovisión y la tradición mesoamericana. In *Cosmovisión, ritual e identidad de los pueblos indígenas de México* (Johanna Broda and Félix Báez-Jorge, eds.): 47–65. Conaculta and Fondo de Cultura Económica, México.

López Austin, Alfredo, and Leonardo López Luján

 1999 *Mito y realidad de Zuyuá. Serpiente Emplumada y las transformaciones mesoamericanas del Clásico al Posclásico.* El Colegio de México and Fondo de Cultura Económica, México.

 2000 The Myth and Reality of Zuyuá: The Feathered Serpent and Meso-american Transformations from the Classic to the Postclassic. In *Mesoamerica's Classic Heritage: From Teotihuacan to the Aztecs* (Davíd Carrasco, Lindsay Jones, and Scott Sessions, eds.): 21–84. University Press of Colorado, Boulder.

 2001 El *chacmool* mexica. *Caravelle. Cahiers du Monde Hispanique et Luso-brésilien* 76–77: 59–84.

López Luján, Leonardo

 1989 *La recuperación mexica del pasado teotihuacano.* Instituto Nacional de Antropología e Historia and GV Editores, México.

 2002 The Aztecs' Search for the Past. In *Aztecs* (Eduardo Matos Moctezuma and Felipe Solís, eds.): 22–29, 89, 500–509. Royal Academy of Arts, London.

 2006 *La Casa de las Águilas: Un ejemplo de la arquitectura religiosa de Tenoch-titlan.* 2 vols. Fondo de Cultura Económica, Instituto Nacional de Antropología e Historia, and Harvard University, México.

López Luján, Leonardo, Giacomo Chiari, Alfredo López Austin, and Fernando Carrizosa

 2005 Línea y color en Tenochtitlan. Escultura policromada y pintura mural en el recinto sagrado de la capital mexica. *Estudios de Cultura Náhuatl* 36: 15–45.

López Luján, Leonardo, Hector Neff, and Saburo Sugiyama

 2000 The 9-Xi Vase: A Classic Thin Orange Vessel Found at Tenochtitlan. In *Mesoamerica's Classic Heritage: From Teotihuacan to the Aztecs* (Davíd Carrasco, Lindsay Jones, and Scott Sessions, eds.): 219–249. University Press of Colorado, Boulder.

Mastache de E., Alba Guadalupe, and Ana María Crespo O.

 1974 La ocupación prehispánica en el área de Tula, Hgo. In *Proyecto Tula (1a Parte)* (Eduardo Matos Moctezuma, ed.): 71–103. Instituto Nacional de Antropología e Historia, México.

Mastache, Alba Guadalupe, Robert H. Cobean, and Dan M. Healan

 2002 *Ancient Tollan: Tula and the Toltec Heartland.* University Press of Colorado, Boulder.

Mateos Higuera, Salvador

 1979 Herencia arqueológica de Mexico-Tenochtitlan. In *Trabajos arque-ológicos en el centro de la ciudad de México (antología)* (Eduardo Matos Moctezuma, ed.): 205–268. Instituto Nacional de Antropología e Historia, México.

Matos Moctezuma, Eduardo, and Leonardo López Luján

 1993 Teotihuacan and Its Mexica Legacy. In *Teotihuacan, Art from the City of the Gods* (Kathleen Berrin and Esther Pasztory, eds.): 156–165. Thames and Hudson and Fine Arts Museums of San Francisco, San Francisco.

Memorial de Solalá. Anales de los cakchiqueles
    1950   (Adrián Recinos, ed. and trans.). Fondo de Cultura Económica,
             México.

Moedano Koer, Hugo
    1944a Las cariátides de Tula y los hallazgos de Guatemala 12. *El Nacional* 24
             August: 3, 10.
    1944b La diosa raptada. *Nosotros* 26 August: 24–26.
    1944c Tula y sus problemas. *El Nacional* 10 September: 3, 5.
    1944d El nexo cultural entre los aztecas y los toltecas. *El Nacional* 4 Novem-
             ber: 2, 5.
    1944e ¿La cultura azteca es realmente azteca? Significación de los últimos
             hallazgos arqueológicos en la ciudad de México. *Hoy* 4 November:
             54–57.
    1947   El friso de los caciques. *Anales del INAH* 2: 113–136.

Molina Montes, Augusto F.
    1987   Templo Mayor Architecture: So What's New? In *The Aztec Templo
             Mayor* (Elizabeth H. Boone, ed.): 97–107. Dumbarton Oaks Research
             Library and Collection, Washington, D.C.

Navarrete, Carlos, and Ana María Crespo
    1971   Un atlante mexica y algunas consideraciones sobre los relieves del
             Cerro de la Malinche, Hidalgo. *Estudios de Cultura Náhuatl* 9: 11–15.

Nicholson, H. B.
    1961   An Outstanding Aztec Sculpture of the Water Goddess. *The Masterkey*
             35(2): 44–55.
    1971   Major Sculpture in Pre-Hispanic Central Mexico. In *Handbook of
             Middle American Indians*, vol. 10: *Archaeology of Northern Mesoamerica*,
             part 1 (Gordon F. Ekholm and Ignacio Bernal, eds.): 92–134. University
             of Texas Press, Austin.
    2001a *Topiltzin Quetzalcoatl. The Once and the Future Lord of the Toltecs.*
             University Press of Colorado, Boulder.
    2001b *The "Return of Quetzalcoatl"; Did It Play a Role in the Conquest of Mexico?*
             Labyrinthos, Lancaster, Calif.

Nicholson, H. B., with Eloise Quiñones Keber
    1983   *Art of Aztec Mexico. Treasures of Tenochtitlan.* National Gallery of Art,
             Washington, D.C.

Olivier, Guilhem
    2003   *Mockeries and Metamorphoses of an Aztec God. Tezcatlipoca, "Lord of the
             Smoking Mirror."* University Press of Colorado, Boulder.

Pasztory, Esther
    1983   *Aztec Art.* Harry N. Abrams, New York.

Paz, Octavio
    1989   *Arte antiguo y moderno.* Los privilegios de la vista. Arte de México 3,
             no. 1. Fondo de Cultura Económica, México.

Popol Vuh
    1964   (Adrián Recinos, trans.). Fondo de Cultura Económica, México.

Quiñones Keber, Eloise

1993 Quetzalcoatl as Dynastic Patron: The "Acuecuexatl Stone" Reconsidered. In *The Symbolism in the Plastic and Pictorial Representations of Ancient Mexico* (J. de Durand-Forest and M. Eisinger, eds.): 149–155. Holos Verlag, Bonn.

Relación de la genealogía

1991 Relación de la genealogía y linaje de los señores que han señoreado esta tierra de la Nueva España. In *Relaciones de la Nueva España* (Germán Velázquez, ed.): 101–125. Historia 16, Madrid.

Rodríguez, María J.

1995 Sistema constructivo en un palacio tolteca. In *Arqueología del norte y del occidente de México. Homenaje al Doctor J. Charles Kelley* (Barbro Dahlgren and Ma. de los Dolores Soto de Arrechavaleta, eds.): 131–145. Universidad Nacional Autónoma de México, México.

Rojas, Gabriel de

1985 Relación de Cholula. In *Relaciones geográficas del siglo XVI: Tlaxcala, II* (René Acuña, ed.): 120–145. Universidad Nacional Autónoma de México, México.

Rosado Ojeda, Vladimiro

1944 El reciente e interesante descubrimiento de la calle de Guatemala. *El Nacional* 10 August: 3, 6.

Sahagún, Bernardino de

1979 *Códice Florentino. Manuscrito 218-20 de la Colección Palatina de la Biblioteca Medicea Laurenziana.* 3 vols. Archivo General de la Nación, Secretaría de Gobernación, México.

1993 *Primeros memoriales.* University of Oklahoma Press, Patrimonio Nacional, and Real Academia de la Historia, Norman.

2000 *Historia general de las cosas de Nueva España.* 3 vols. (Alfredo López Austin and Josefina García Quintana, eds.). Consejo Nacional para la Cultura y las Artes, México.

Solís, Felipe

1997 Un hallazgo olvidado: Relato e interpretación de los descubrimientos arqueológicos del predio de la calle de Guatemala núm. 12, en el Centro Histórico de la Ciudad de México, en 1944. In *Homenaje al doctor Ignacio Bernal* (Leonardo Manrique and Noemí Castillo, eds.): 81–93. Instituto Nacional de Antropología e Historia, México.

Stocker, Terrance L.

1974 A Small Temple in the Tula Residential Zone. In *Studies of Ancient Tollan: A Report of the University of Missouri Tula Archaeological Project* (Richard A. Diehl, ed.): 25–31. Department of Anthropology, University of Missouri-Columbia, Columbia.

Stocker, Terry, and Dan M. Healan

1989 The East Group and Nearby Remains. In *Tula of the Toltecs. Excavations and Survey* (Dan M. Healan, ed.): 149–162. University of Iowa Press, Iowa City.

Stoutamire, James W.

    n.d.   Trend Surface Analysis of Survey Data, Tula, Mexico. Ph.D. dissertation, Department of Anthropology, University of Missouri, Columbia, 1975.

Título de Totonicapán

    1983   (Robert M. Carmack and James L. Mondloch, eds. and trans.). Universidad Nacional Autónoma de México, México.

Torquemada, Fray Juan de

    1975–83 *Monarquía indiana. De los veinte y un libros rituales y monarquía indiana, con el origen y guerras de los indios occidentales, de sus poblazones, descubrimiento, conquista, conversión y otras cosas maravillosas de la mesma tierra*, 8 vols. Universidad Nacional Autónoma de México, México.

Townsend, Richard Fraser

    1979   *State and Cosmos in the Art of Tenochtitlan.* Dumbarton Oaks Research Library and Collection, Washington, D.C.

Umberger, Emily

    1987   Antiques, Revivals, and References to the Past in Aztec Art. *RES: Anthropology and Aesthetics* 13: 63–105.

Yadeun, Juan

    1975   *El Estado y la ciudad: el caso de Tula, Hgo. (Proyecto Tula).* Instituto Nacional de Antropología e Historia, México.

THIRTEEN

CONFIGURATION OF
THE SACRED PRECINCT
OF MEXICO-TENOCHTITLAN

Eduardo Matos Moctezuma

THE SACRED PRECINCT OR CEREMONIAL PLAZA at Tenochtitlan displays characteristics also found in more ancient Mesoamerican cities. In this chapter I discuss this convergence by emphasizing certain components of other sacred precincts, such as those of Teotihuacan and Tula, to show how they later resurfaced in the Aztec city. Three fundamental aspects are considered in each of these sacred precincts: the presence of a building that acts as the center of the universe, the ceremonial precinct itself, and its relationship to the city in which it is found. Using this framework, I address the symbolic traits and urban characteristics of the earlier precincts, and the elements later incorporated by the Aztec into their own precinct.

BACKGROUND

In the Basin of Mexico, the inhabitants of Cuicuilco made the first known attempt to construct a monument modeled after the surrounding mountains. I refer to the famous circular building that retains a similarity to the volcanic cones found toward the south of what is now Mexico City. In fact, these small volcanoes left a deep imprint on local cultures: especially Xitle, which covered Cuicuilco in lava and compelled the population residing there to abandon the site and settle in more auspicious zones. One such zone was Teotihuacan. The importance of the volcano and its devastating effect was manifest in the worship rendered to the Old Fire God, Huehueteotl, in the form of an old man hunched over with a brazier on his back or head. Represented in this manner, the god symbolizes a volcano with the smoke characteristic of said volcano rising from the brazier (Matos Moctezuma 2002). The fact that the volcano is represented in human form is an indication that it had life within and could trigger earthquakes, launch columns of smoke, and spurt lava (represented by a red stream). In contrast, there are mountains with the beneficial capacity

FIGURE 1. Building of the Altars, Moon Plaza, Teotihuacan. Architectonic structure represents the universe concept.

to act as deposits of water (blue stream) and grain, providing sustenance to humankind. This deity is later found in the ancient city of Teotihuacan in the shape of an ancient god who displays characteristics similar to those found in Cuicuilco and Copilco. He was also worshipped in Tenochtitlan, where he was known by the names Xiuhtecuhtli, Ixcozauhqui, Cuezaltzin, or Huehueteotl. Bernardino de Sahagún (1956: 56) calls him the "other Vulcan" and describes him as follows: "He is also called Huehuetétole, which means 'the ancient god,' and they all consider him a father given the effects he produced because the flame burns, it illuminates and scorches, and these are effects to be feared."

However, it is in Teotihuacan that many additional aspects emerge that would also appear in later cultures in central Mexico. Thus the conceptualization of the universe and its characteristics may be perceived both in the layout of the city toward all four directions of the universe and in the architectural structure found at the foot of the Pyramid of the Moon (Figure 1). This structure is clearly worthy of interest, given that its architectural distribution already manifests concepts regarding the configuration of the universe that bear similarity to the first plate of the Codex Fejérváry-Mayer

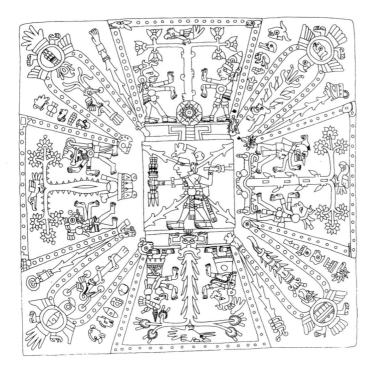

FIGURE 2. The four routes of the universe (from the Codex Fejérváry-Mayer, plate 1: drawing after page 1).

(Figure 2) and those found on pages 75–76 of the Madrid or Tro-Cortesian Codex. These concepts can also be noted in the solar trajectory and westward orientation of such buildings as the Pyramid of the Sun and the Feathered Serpent Pyramid in the Citadel. Both symbolized the center of the universe and represented sacred mountains and their potential as *altepetl* ("water-mountain"), positioned within the community as deposits of water and grain to be used for sustenance. However, the *altepetl* is considered the basic political and territorial unit in Central Mexico related to the social division of work, both economically and politically. This unit consisted of one or several more-or-less compact civic and ceremonial centers, including temples and palaces, where the governing body resided (it was considered a political unit only if it was governed by a *tlatoani* ["he who speaks" or "supreme ruler"]) and of a series of rural settlements mostly populated by tributary peasants. Below I carry out a more detailed analysis of these elements.

CEREMONIAL PRECINCT AT TEOTIHUACAN

In this section I list the components present in both of the complexes at Teotihuacan that displayed the characteristic of acting as the center of the universe or axis mundi (Figure 3). There were two of these: the Pyramid of the Sun found in the Great Plaza, which is formed by a platform nearly 35 m wide that surrounds the pyramid on three of its sides (south, east,

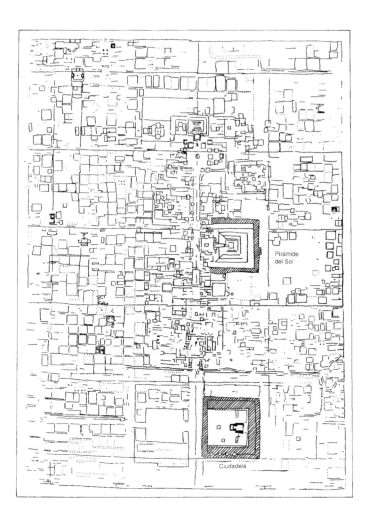

FIGURE 3. Map of Teotihuacan showing the platform around the Pyramid of the Sun and the Citadel, Teotihuacan's axis mundi.

and north). The Pyramid of the Sun was built during the Tzacualli phase (A.D. 1–150), which I have therefore called the "old city." In ca. A.D. 250 for reasons still unknown but that seem to indicate an internal power struggle, the center was displaced to the south, to the site occupied by the Citadel and the Feathered Serpent Pyramid within it. Let us examine the characteristics present in both plazas and their constructions.

Platforms Surrounding the Buildings That Act as Centers of the Universe

These platforms form the Great Plaza, in which are found buildings that act as centers of the universe, such as the Pyramid of the Sun and, in the case of the Citadel, the Feathered Serpent Pyramid. There are constructions on the upper surface of these platforms, and access to the plaza is restricted—it can only be entered via a stairway leading to the Street of the

Dead, ensuring its privacy. I believe that these platforms acted as boundaries separating a highly sacred space in a city of other spaces that were residential or not as sacred.

In the Great Plaza formed by this platform other constructions are found. In the case of the Pyramid of the Sun, there are several buildings across from its main facade, whereas in the case of the Citadel, in addition to the Feathered Serpent Pyramid, there are such buildings as the shrine located in the center of the plaza.

Orientation of Main Buildings toward the West

The Pyramid of the Sun and the Feathered Serpent Pyramid (as well as the building covering it) face to the west. They are all oriented according to the path of the sun through the heavens from east to west.

Presence of Streams

A few stone channels are found in the cave underneath the Pyramid of the Sun. Another 3-m-wide channel has been found surrounding the three sides of the pyramid. On the Feathered Serpent Pyramid, the same element is depicted in the form of wavy serpents surrounded by marine elements, such as snails and shells.

Human Sacrifice

In the Pyramid of the Sun, at each corner of the four superimposed structures that make up the construction there are skeletons of infants (Batres 1906: 22). In the Citadel there are individuals sacrificed with their hands tied behind their backs in groups of 1, 2, 4, 9, and 18 skeletons surrounding the Feathered Serpent Pyramid; in addition a burial mound of 20 individuals is located inside this temple. It is thought that the presence of these bodies is somehow related to agricultural cycles.

Life-Death Duality

The concept of the duality of life and death is present in certain elements, such as water and human sacrifice. It is also manifested in the very character of the cave as a space used to enter the underworld, as the womb from which people are born, and as the place where grain and water are kept to feed humankind. It is important to remember that the Mictlan, as the ninth and deepest bank of the underworld, displays the characteristics of a womb.

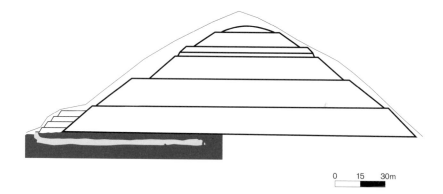

FIGURE 4. Pyramid
of the Sun (a sacred
mountain) with the
cave beneath it.

Sacred Mountains and Caves

Teotihuacan is where the relationship between sacred mountains and caves appears for the first time in ancient Mesoamerica, as seen in the Pyramid of the Sun (Figure 4). This mountain-cave relationship reappeared centuries later, as seen in pictograms like those of Culhuacan or Teoculhuacan-Chicomoztoc. In both cases, the mountain-cave is the womb where the grain and water destined for humankind is kept by the gods.

Some caves have already been excavated in the city of Teotihuacan. In two of them, astronomical markers have been found in the form of slabs driven into the ground, in addition to other artifacts left by the inhabitants of Teotihuacan. In other caves are the most recent burials yet found for the ancient city.

At any rate, we have encountered some natural references, such as mountains with caves, already known to the inhabitants of Teotihuacan. According to reports by scholars, around 144 caves have been found in the Hill of the Star in Culhuacan, Iztapalapa, some of which exhibit archaeological vestiges, such as petroglyphs, walls, and stuccos in addition to having been used as astronomical observatories (Montero 2002; Wallrath 2002). Their studies indicate that the caves were occupied for rituals during the Classic and Postclassic periods, when they were used by the inhabitants of Teotihuacan, as shown by the presence of stone engravings and a Teotihuacan settlement nearby (Montero 2002; Wallrath 2002). Something similar took place on the hill of Chapultepec with its springs, where Teotihuacan remains have been detected by Raúl García.

In Teotihuacan, the mountain-cave binomial appears in paintings in several cases: one of these is in the Tlalocan mural of Tepantitla (Figure 5), where it can be observed that the deity presiding over the mural is located on a mountain with plants and grain stored inside; at the same time, the deity showers water down onto the earth. Esther Pasztory (1993)

FIGURE 5. Tepantitla Painting Mural, Teotihuacan, showing the god Tlaloc throwing water on the earth. The god has a womb within a mountain to keep the grain that feeds humankind.

has interpreted this element as a womb. In the lower section of the same mural, where ground level is represented with men amusing themselves and there are land parcels with sown plants, a current of water passes in and out of a mountain. In other sites at Teotihuacan there are mural paintings of what I believe could be a mountain-cave, as in the case of La Ventilla, where this motif can be observed with the symbol of Venus inside one of the chambers.

The presence of the sacred mountain can also be seen in other Pre-Hispanic cities, as in the case of Cholula (Figure 6). In effect, in the *Historia Tolteca-Chichimeca* (1976) the symbol of the city is represented by a mountain with aquatic symbols, such as the frog found in the upper section accompanied by the name Tlachihualtepetl, or "Constructed Mountain."

CEREMONIAL PRECINCT AT TULA

Let us now briefly analyze the ceremonial chamber at Tula. First and foremost, the city does not have the same kind of layout as that of Teotihuacan, or later, Tenochtitlan. Tula does not share most of the similarities found in the layouts of Teotihuacan and Tenochtitlan. However, the ceremonial precinct of the plaza in Tula presents certain similar characteristics (Figure 7). For example, the Great Plaza is bordered by a platform with construc-

FIGURE 6. Sacred mountain with the cave-womb (from *Historia Tolteca-Chichimeca* 1976: 11).

tions on its upper surface, as in both cases found at Teotihuacan. On the northern side is Building B, or Tlahuizcalpantecuhtli, and beside it is the so-called Burnt Palace. The western side is blocked by a large ballcourt. In the plaza are a central altar, the *tzompantli,* and some remains of what was once a temple, possibly dedicated to the planet Venus. The main building is oriented toward the west, just like those already mentioned in Teotihuacan.

In general the components of the Great Plaza in Tula are similar to those already described in Teotihuacan: a ceremonial precinct framed by a great platform with constructions on the upper surface, a main building oriented toward the west following the path of the sun, and a shrine—as well as other constructions—in the center of the plaza. The elements not found in Teotihuacan that emerge for the first time among the Toltecs in the city of Tula include the structure of a ballcourt oriented from north to south blocking off the plaza on its western side and the Tzompantli, or Place of Skulls. Also above the great platform on its northern side there are three rooms with columns; walkways with a parade of warriors; the warrior figures of the *atlantes* in Building B (the Tlahuizcalpantecuhtli); and the sculpture of the Chacmool, a stone figure of a semi-reclined character that, in the case of Tula, is apparently associated with sacrifice and war.

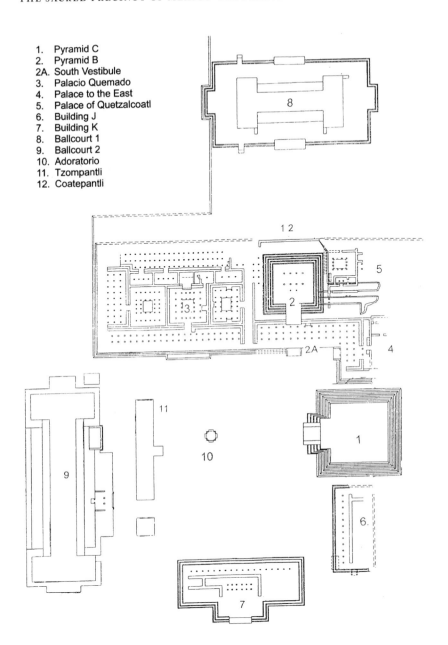

1. Pyramid C
2. Pyramid B
2A. South Vestibule
3. Palacio Quemado
4. Palace to the East
5. Palace of Quetzalcoatl
6. Building J
7. Building K
8. Ballcourt 1
9. Ballcourt 2
10. Adoratorio
11. Tzompantli
12. Coatepantli

FIGURE 7. Precinct of the city of Tula.

CEREMONIAL PRECINCT AT TENOCHTITLAN

Let us now turn our attention to Tenochtitlan. In this case, the images of the city handed down to us are useful, such as plate 1 from the Codex Mendoza (1992: plate 1; Figure 8) and the Cortés map published in Nuremberg in 1524 (Figure 9). The map from Sahagún's (1993) *Primeros memoriales* is also useful for studying the precinct (Figure 10).

In the first two abovementioned texts are representations of the city.

FIGURE 8. Representation of
Tenochtitlan. Drawing based on
plate 1 of the Codex Mendoza.

The Codex Mendoza shows the symbol of the eagle standing on the prickly
pear cactus growing out of a rock in an aquatic environment (Figure 8).
Underneath these figures are the *chimalli*, or coat of arms, with seven
plumes or tassels alluding to the seven tribes that left the mythical city
of Chicomoztoc. A bundle of darts crosses the coat of arms, and the
word "Tenochtitlan" beneath all these symbols leaves no room for doubt
regarding the identity of the city. Two diagonal bands intersect as streams,
indicating the city's lacustrine nature. These streams divide Tenochtitlan
into four quadrants or neighborhoods, immediately bringing to mind the
aforementioned division of Teotihuacan. This division with streams placed
diagonally is reminiscent of the image in the Codex Fejérváry-Mayer (see
Figure 2), in which diagonals are present with each end ruled over by a
different bird. At the center of each bird are yellow circles with four glyphs
representing the different paths of the universe. Counterclockwise from
the top are: east, a reed; north, the *tecpatl*, or sacrificial knife; west, a *calli*,

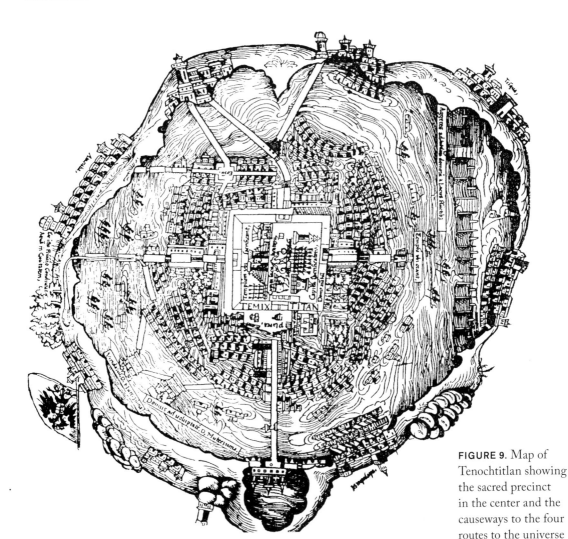

FIGURE 9. Map of Tenochtitlan showing the sacred precinct in the center and the causeways to the four routes to the universe (map of Tenochtitlan published along with a Latin version of Hernán Cortés's letters, Nuremberg, 1524).

or house; and south, a *tochtli*, or rabbit. Each one is found to the left of its corresponding universal path, as indicated by trapezoids that contain a plant growing from a like element, such as a bird over the plant with deities on either side. At the center is Xiuhtecuhtli, Lord of the Year and of fire, armed with an atlatl and three darts and intersected by red streams (blood) pointing diagonally toward the edges.

I have already discussed the symbolism of the ceremonial precinct and Great Temple in many publications (e.g., Matos Moctezuma 1988), therefore I only summarize them briefly here, following the same order used to list the characteristics observed above for Teotihuacan and Tula.

Platform Surrounding the Ceremonial Precinct

A striking feature of the sacred precinct at Tenochtitlan is the large number of temples, shrines, and the like found there. According to Bernardino de

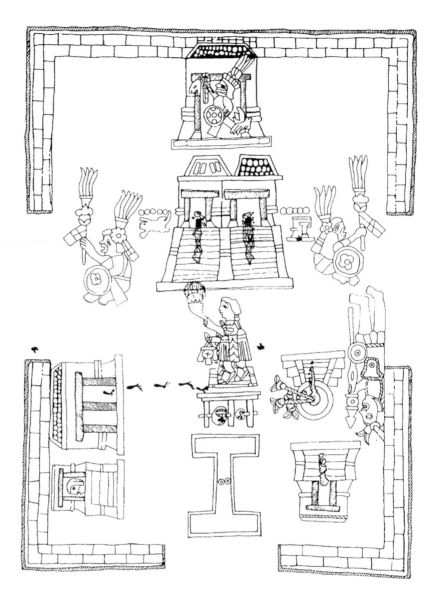

FIGURE 10. Sacred
precinct of Tenochtitlan
showing the Great
Temple, which
represents the two
sacred mountains
at the center of the
Aztec universe (from
Sahagún 1993: 269r).

Sahagún (1956: 232), there were 78 buildings; however, the actual number
must have been lower, given the evident repetition of some of these in
the text. This contrasts with the plazas or precincts of Teotihuacan and
Tula, where fewer structures are found. Such is not the case, however,
in Tlatelolco, twin city and contemporary to Tenochtitlan, which also
contains a large number of buildings. Of the 78 buildings mentioned by
Sahagún, partial or complete archaeological remains have been found
of more than 40. Most of these were located by the Great Temple Project (Proyecto Templo Mayor) and by the Urban Archaeology Program
(Programa de Arqueología Urbana), both under the auspices of the Great
Temple Museum in Mexico City.

Just as in the cities of Teotihuacan and Tula, the main precinct or plaza was surrounded by a platform approximately 30 m wide, as is seen behind the Great Temple, where part of this platform was encountered with a few shrines and altars on its upper surface. Toward the interior of the plaza, the platform has stairways alternating with walls, as found in the ceremonial enclosure of Tlatelolco. The belief that a wall bordered the ceremonial enclosure, called by some authors of chronicles (e.g., Acosta 1962: 237) a *coatepantli*, or wall of serpents, is unwarranted. The platform, like those of earlier cities, ensures the privacy of the plaza: it could only be entered by one of the four gateways that led to the highways of Tepeyac to the north, Iztapalapa to the south, Tacuba to the west, and a lesser highway to the east. These highways divided the city into four quadrants, or *barrios*, and were oriented according to the four paths of the universe, as in Teotihuacan.

Orientation of the Main Building toward the West

The main building was the Great Temple, or Hueyteocalli. It was facing west just as do the Pyramid of the Sun and the Feathered Serpent Pyramid in Teotihuacan and the main temple in Tula. However, unlike these structures, the Great Temple was accessed by two stairways in its upper section that led to the shrines of Tlaloc and Huitzilopochtli; that is, the building was divided into two clearly differentiated parts, each with its own characteristics. The building formed a unit—the Great Temple—while acting as two distinct places of worship dedicated to the deities of water and war, respectively.

Presence of Streams

On several occasions chroniclers mention springs of water inside the ceremonial precinct where various ceremonies were enacted (e.g., Sahagún 1956: 1: 241). Their presence on the side of the temple dedicated to Tlaloc makes reference to water as a vital element, just as do the serpents depicted in the temple, especially those descending the *alfardas*, or balustrades.

Human Sacrifice

Human sacrifice is evident in the Great Temple, especially on the side dedicated to Huitzilopochtli. Several historical sources recount that during the festival of Panquetzaliztli, for example, a large number of slaves and captive warriors were sacrificed to honor the god of war (e.g., Sahagún 1993: 252v). Thus they commemorated what the god did to his enemies, the *centzohuitznahuas*, or four hundred southerners, on Coatepec Hill. Evidence for human sacrifice also exists on the side dedicated to Tlaloc.

Life-Death Duality

The duality of life and death was fully expressed in the Great Temple by the presence of both gods on its upper section. On one hand was Huitzilopochtli, God of War and therefore of imposition on other groups, as well as of the death that war brings. On the other hand was Tlaloc, God of Rain, who gave life to plants and made it possible to feed humankind. In this fashion, the life-death duality was present through the attributes of the two numens that occupied the upper part of the building and the myths they were immersed in. In addition, this duality becomes even more evident if we recall how, upon dying, warriors were destined to accompany the sun—another aspect of Huitzilopochtli—from the east to its zenith. Therefore the sacrifice of captured warriors on that side of the Great Temple is reminiscent of the same act performed by the God of War on his sister, Coyolxauhqui, whom he killed by throwing her down into the depths of Coatepec Hill.

Another interesting aspect related to this duality is the manner in which deities were accompanied by the deceased, depending on the manner of their death: all those whose deaths were related to water inhabited Tlalocan (an eternally green place), the dwelling place of Tlaloc, whereas the dead warriors accompanied the sun—Huitzilopochtli—during part of the latter's journey. Also recall that one of the first steps to reach Mictlan was by crossing two mountains that come together. The two sacred mountains represented in the Great Temple might have symbolized this place.

Sacred Mountains and Caves

Since 1980, I have suggested (Matos Moctezuma 1980) that the Great Temple represents two mountains, each corresponding to a specific myth: on Huitzilopochtli's side, a mountain is depicted and the myth is represented once again during the Panquetzaliztli festival. The different components of the Great Temple on the side of the God of War were related to the myth: the sculpture of the goddess Coyolxauhqui, decapitated and dismembered at the foot of the Hill-Temple after warring against her brother Huitzilopochtli. Eight figures of characters that I believe represent the *centzohuitznahua* against whom the Sun God fought were found placed on the stairway of the third stage of building construction. Some of these have their hands on their chests to protect their hearts, while others display cavities in their chests with green stones representing their hearts. This image is reminiscent of the words Diego Durán (1951: 25) used to describe the combat on Coatepec Hill: "once dawn came, they found the main forces behind that rebellion, together with the lady we said was called Coyolxauh, and all of their chests were opened and only their hearts were taken."

In contrast, Tlaloc's side is the mountain of sustenance, or Tonacatepetl, also mentioned in myths—in particular the one in which Quetzalcoatl must enter the mountain to steal the corn stored there to be given to men. As for the caves, some chroniclers have related how different peoples, including the Aztec or Mexica, originally came from these caves or the mythical city of Chicomoztoc. However, in the ceremonial precinct these caves are mentioned as a place to deposit the skins of those who had been flayed. In the Great Temple itself there are the chambers of offerings I and II, positioned in the middle of the two stairways that led to the upper part of each building. Given their position and characteristics, they could symbolize caves. The one on Huitzilopochtli's side (Chamber I) had as its main figure an earth deity, identified by López Austin as Mayahuel, surrounded by a large number of green stones. The chamber on Tlaloc's side (Chamber II) is dedicated to the Rain God. The chamber is presided over by a sculpture in green stone and has an inclined clay pot with the figure of Chalchiuhtlicue that appears to cast water toward the entrance of the room.

The Aztec possessed very important natural references: the above-mentioned Hill of the Star in Culhuacan and the Hill of Chapultepec, where flowing springs supplied the city of Tenochtitlan with water. There was a cave there related to the *cincalco*, or house of corn, related once again to the sacred mountain in which water and grains of corn are stored.

To conclude the topic of the ceremonial precinct of Tenochtitlan and its components, I list the elements that were incorporated both from Teotihuacan and Tula:

From Teotihuacan. City has a layout of four quadrants or *barrios* marked by the great causeways according to solar movement, orienting the city toward the west and highlighting the presence of the four universal paths. The main precinct or plaza is surrounded by a great platform dividing the sacred spaces from the rest of the city. This platform has buildings on its upper surfaces. Positioned on both sides of the Great Temple are shrines of inclined planks, in some cases decorated with painting, in which half-eyes are found in the Teotihuacan style, as occurs also in the Red Temple of Tenochtitlan (Figure 11). There are sculptures imitating the gods of Teotihuacan, such as the Old Fire God, Huehueteotl (Figure 12), as well as possible masks (Figures 13, 14). In different offerings of the Aztec Great Temple, pieces from Teotihuacan have been found, doubtless brought from that city (López Luján 1989). The Nahua myths establish the appearance of the Fifth Sun in Teotihuacan.

From Tula. There is a grand plaza bordered by the platform and a ball-court. The *Tzompantli* or Place of the Skull is present. Benches are depicted with processions of warriors exactly like the Burnt Palace of Tula, with

FIGURE 11. Red Temple
of Tenochtitlan, built in
Teotihuacan style.

FIGURE 12. Huehueteotl sculpture found near the
Great Temple of Tenochtitlan. It is an imitation of
the images of the Old Fire God of Teotihuacan.

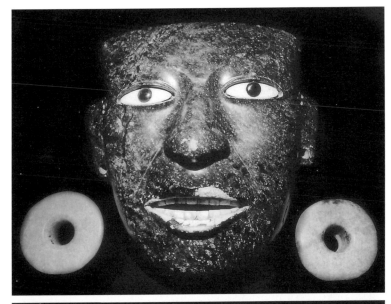

FIGURE 13. Teotihuacan mask from offering 78 in the Great Temple of Tenochtitlan.

FIGURE 14. Teotihuacan mask from offering 20 in the Great Temple of Tenochtitlan.

zacatapayolli as an element of convergence in the procession. There is a circular temple dedicated to Ehecatl-Quetzalcoatl, which in Tula is not found in the ceremonial precinct but in another part of the city. Sculptures of Chacmool, *atlantes,* and caryatids made from stone are present (Figures 15, 16). In the House of Eagles north of the Great Temple of Tenochtitlan braziers are found with Tlaloc's face painted in white, just as in Tula (Figure 17). In the myths there are found red and blue streams, as mentioned in the *Historia Tolteca-Chichimeca* (1976). Everything related to whiteness (the symbol of mythical geographic origin and temporal beginnings)—such as serpents, frogs, fish, junipers, bulrushes, reeds—is also mentioned in the

FIGURE 15. Toltec Chacmool found in front of the Great Temple of Tenochtitlan.

FIGURE 16. Aztec Chacmool found in front of the shrine of Tlaloc at the Great Temple.

same chronicle and incorporated by the Aztec into their own myths, as expressed in the founding myths of their city, Tenochtitlan.

CONCLUSIONS

Teotihuacan is doubtless the first city in which a pyramid representing a sacred mountain has been found associated with a cave as a symbol of an entrance into the underworld or womb. Is this not what we find centuries later in the figure on the mountain—Culhuacan or Teoculhuacan—regarding the seven caves or Chicomoztoc where humankind was born, as painted and told in the *Historia Tolteca-Chichimeca* (1976) as well as other

FIGURE 17. Brazier from the House of Eagles at the north of the Great Temple. Similar braziers have been found in Tula.

codices and documents? By transferring this concept to Tenochtitlan, we can see how the Great Temple represented two mountains conjoined. In addition the temple had the character of an axis mundi that some buildings representing mountains possess, as is the case of the Pyramid of the Sun and the Feathered Serpent Pyramid in the Citadel and Great Temples of Tula and Tenochtitlan. Thus we find a tradition that dates back to a very early era in Central Mexico and was present until the time of the Spanish conquest.

REFERENCES CITED

Acosta, Joseph de
>   1962   *Historia natural y moral de las Indias, en que se tratan de las cosas notables del cielo, elementos, metales, plantas y animales dellas, y los ritos y ceremonias, leyes y gobierno de los indios.* Fondo de Cultura Económica, México.

Batres, Leopoldo
>   1906   *Teotihuacan.* Imprenta de Fidencio Soria, México.

Codex Mendoza
>   1992   (Frances F. Berdan and Patricia Rieff Anawalt, eds.), 4 vols. University of California Press, Berkeley.

Durán, Diego

    1951 *Historia de las Indias de Nueva España e islas de la tierra firme.* Editorial
          Nacional, México.

Historia Tolteca-Chichimeca

    1976 (Paul Kirchhoff, Lina Odena Güemes, and Luis Reyes García,
          eds.). Centro de Investigaciones Superiores del Instituto Nacional de
          Antropología e Historia, México.

López Luján, Leonardo

    1989 *La recuperación mexica del pasado teotihuacano.* Instituto Nacional de
          Antropología e Historia and GV Editores, México.

Matos Moctezuma, Eduardo

    1980 El Templo Mayor de Tenochtitlan: Economía e ideología. *Boletín de*
          Antropología Americana (series 2) 1: 7–19.

    1988 *The Great Temple of the Aztecs. Treasures of Tenochtitlan.* Thames and
          Hudson, London.

    2002 Huehuetéotl-Xiuhtecutli en el centro de México. *Arqueología Mexicana*
          56: 58–63.

Montero, Ismael Arturo

    2002 El sistema cavernario del Huizachtepetl. In *Huizachtepetl, geografía*
          sagrada de Iztapalapa (Ismael Arturo Montero García, ed.): 171–209.
          Delegación Iztapalapa, México.

Pasztory, Esther

    1993 Teotihuacan Unmasked: A View through Art. In *Teotihuacan, Art from*
          the City of the Gods (Kathleen Berrin and Esther Pasztory, eds.): 44–62.
          Thames and Hudson and the Fine Arts Museum of San Francisco, San
          Francisco.

Sahagún, Bernardino de

    1956 *Historia general de las cosas de la Nueva España.* Editorial Porrúa,
          México.

    1993 *Primeros memoriales.* University of Oklahoma Press, Patrimonio
          Nacional, and Real Academia de la Historia, Norman.

Wallrath, Mateo

    2002 Los petroglifos hallados en el Cerro de la Estrella. In *Huizachtepetl,*
          geografía sagrada de Iztapalapa (Ismael Arturo Montero García, ed.):
          205–209. Delegación Iztapalapa, México.

CITIES AS COSMOLOGICAL ART

The Art of Politics

David Carrasco

The question of the character of the place on which one stands is the fundamental symbolic and social question. Once an individual or culture has expressed its vision of its place, a whole language of symbols and social structure will follow [Smith 1970: 457].

A culture, we all know, is made by its cities [Walcott 2007: 197].

TWO OF THE MOST PERPLEXING QUESTIONS facing Mesoamerican studies have been: What was the social order of complex Mesoamerican settlements? To what extent did religious symbolism play a primary role in their urbanization processes? Concerning the first question, it was not so long ago that scholars and the public alike were confused about whether Mesoamerican settlements fit into the evolving categories of "city," "civilization," "urbanism," and sometimes "empire." To put it another way, we were puzzled as to what extent and in what cases these terms and their definitions were appropriate and applicable to the complex and sometimes contradictory archaeological data from various sites. To further complicate the matter, Mesoamerican studies have, when exploring these questions, periodically suffered a partitioning (without good comparative scholarship) of Maya lowlands settlements versus Central Highlands sites in Mexico while relegating other significant regions to peripheral significance. The problem of religious symbolism and aesthetics has also challenged scholars, leading some to argue that Mesoamerican cities were primarily sacred precincts and others to see religiosity as an illusion with no useful future in our areas of study.

The organizers of this volume—and the conference that motivated it—approached these two questions of settlements and symbolism, city and aesthetics by choosing the very useful title of *The Art of Urbanism: How Mesoamerican Kingdoms Represented Themselves in Architecture and Imagery*. This substantial and metaphorical title invited the contributing authors to consider the art and architecture of Mesoamerican urbanism in at least two major ways. First, the title invited us to consider how Mesoamerican peoples built and ornamented their towns and cities with artistic expressions telling of the mythical and historical origins of a place, representing their own social hierarchies and celebrating the prodigious powers of their divinities while also using art and architecture to assist in the management of their dynamic natural landscape. In this view of the topic the chapters in this volume reflect on art *in* the city. What becomes clear is that an enormous amount of thought and effort went into creating urban landscapes and physiognomies that turned politics into artistic spectacle and utilized design, color, ritual, and symbol as political instruments. Second, the title suggested another powerful dimension of the art of urbanism—namely, how certain cities and sacred places were themselves political, aesthetic, and cosmological symbols. As several of the chapters demonstrate, many Mesoamerican cities not only contained great art and architecture, but they were also as a whole constructed, imagined, and remembered as prodigious forms of religious and political art. In this view, the physiognomies of urban landscapes become entire performances and texts telling, reshaping, persuading, and celebrating the cosmology, natural landscape, and/or royal histories of the place: in other words, the city *as* art. The suggestion here is that the rulers and designers of each of these civic-ceremonial cities achieved a bird's-eye or cosmic view of their settlement and were able to design its layout (or at least the central ceremonial core) as a holistic replica of the cosmovision.

The authors contributing to this volume were asked to consider how various ceremonial cities used their art and architecture to establish themselves as places of political and cosmological centering or orientation in space and time—locally, regionally, historically, and mythically. Drawing on advances in ecological studies of urban places combined with the methods that specialists in various regions of Mesoamerica have used to study art, archaeology, religion, and social settlements, the authors explore, among other issues, how the reorganization and integration of the natural landscape, imagery, color, and miniature and monumental art functioned as forms of political narratives, ritual celebration, and the imposition of power and authority in various areas of Mesoamerica. These chapters also benefit from recent studies in Mesoamerican political, ecological, and religious history that have shown how powerful material and symbolic exchanges across certain regions of Mesoamerica shaped and reshaped the identities of peoples, the power of goods, and the complexity of religious ideas (see especially Carrasco et al. 2000).

It should be noted that these patterns of center and periphery, settlement and symbolism, and the dynamics among various capitals and competing civic-ceremonial cities were symbolized, in part, at the very site of the conference: which was the Auditorio Eduardo Matos Moctezuma at the

Museo del Templo Mayor in Mexico City. For it was at this archaeological site under the brilliant guidance of Eduardo Matos Moctezuma that Mexican archaeologists discovered and deciphered the myriad ways that the Aztec designed, imagined, and performed their capital city as the axis mundi of their empire and universe. The very productive Proyecto Templo Mayor and the Museo del Templo Mayor have shown us how Tenochtitlan and its central ceremonial precinct served not only as a material and symbolic container of many other regions and competing ceremonial cities but also as a nexus of several historical periods and aesthetic traditions that preceded the Aztec empire.

In what follows I highlight several themes that are woven through the excellent chapters to aid the reader to see some of the deeper meanings of this volume. Returning to the opening epigraph, we see how specific and regional cities answered the question of the "place on which" their symbolic and social worlds were established and developed. We see, in ways not addressed in previous publications, how art, architecture, myth, and ritual were employed to elevate the prestige of certain sites to the status of "centers of the world" that integrated time and space, the time of the gods and the struggles of humans, sky, earth and underworld, local knowledge and distant kingships, and natural and cultural landscapes into socially cohesive worlds.

THREE THEMES AND THEIR REPRESENTATIONS

Beyond the many particular contributions of the individual chapters in this volume, summarized in the Introduction, readers will note several shared and contested concerns and problems crucial to contemporary Mesoamerican studies. These include three themes: the settlement and symbolism of the center and the imitation/renovation of the archetype; the art of politics; and the management and symbolism of the natural landscape, especially water. In some—if not all—chapters, recent scholarship showing the persistent and widespread devotion of the ancient Mesoamericans to the concept of *altepetl* ("mountain of water") informs the ways that the *arts of the city* and the *city as art* are presented. In recent years investigators have been revealing or in some cases returning to what Alfredo López Austin (1997) wrote about persuasively in his book *Tamoanchan/Tlalocan: Places of Mist*—that an agricultural mentality organized by myths of Tamoanchan and the *altepetls* of creation stories was joined with regional political ideologies that structured a widely shared Mesoamerican religious tradition. From reading the rich series of chapters in the present volume it appears that very similar cosmological models, with regional variations, concerning the creation of life and the designation of the center of the world were used in widespread parts of Mesoamerica to bring settlement and aesthetics into a coherent expression.

Theme 1: Settlement and Symbolism of the Center and Imitation/ Renovation of the Archetype

The volume as a whole reflects intensely on the indigenous pride of place that was worked, ritualized, imagined, and memorialized by each of the societies discussed. In some cases the authors, striving to mirror the social pride and cosmological significance of a specific city's builders and celebrants, elevate the status of a city to the level of a Mesoamerican archetype. Ann Cyphers and Anna Di Castro (Chapter 1, this volume) reflect that the inhabitants of the early site of San Lorenzo created "lasting Mesoamerican concepts closely implicated in later sociopolitical developments [that] can be perceived in their material culture, . . . thus giving shape to a composite heritage that would enrich the cosmologies of later civilizations." In a few cases, the authors do not argue that their particular site, say Chalcatzingo, was an archetypal settlement imitated by subsequent communities but rather that elements of natural landscape and social settlement were creatively fused together, establishing a pattern that was shared or repeated, though not necessarily copied, by other communities. Many chapters argue that the site(s) in question not only expressed, through art and architecture (and often social order and social identity), celestial and terrestrial archetypes and powers but also that the particular sites became aesthetic—and sometimes cosmological—models for neighboring and faraway settlements. In the cases of Tula, Teotihuacan, and Cholula, it appears that their prestige as centers of the world blossomed during their historical apogees and continued on through history, inviting other cities to copy them or at least integrate part of the older symbolic order into their local ceremonial aesthetics and politics.

What is significant to me as a historian of religions is that these chapters, sometimes without full awareness, echo what a group of historians of religions have debated since the publication more than 50 years ago in French (and subsequently in more than a dozen other languages) of Mircea Eliade's *Cosmos and History,* later published as *The Myth of the Eternal Return* (Eliade 1954). Eliade claimed, borrowing in part from Paul Mus's work on Southeast Asian cities, that traditional cities in various parts of the world were constructed around the symbolism of the center as manifested in sacred mountains, cosmic trees, and ritually constructed pyramids or monumental temples. Eliade's work led to international scholarship about the ways sacred mountains, both real and imagined, stood at the axis of theologies, cosmologies, and historical cities and empires. Scholars, including Charles H. Long (e.g., 1986; Africa and Mesoamerica) Jonathan Z. Smith (e.g., 1978; ancient Near East), Paul Wheatley (e.g., 1971; China), Lindsay Jones (e.g., 1995, 2000; Mesoamerica), and Joseph Rykwert (e.g., 1988; Italy), have amply illustrated a general human interest in constructing monumental settlements that serve, in Wheatley's (1971) felicitious phrase, as "the pivot of the four quarters." In Wheatley's prose we find the most succinct statement yet on what kind of coordination between sky, earth, and society had to be achieved for a specific city to rise to the level of what Fash and López Luján (Introduction, this volume) call iconic Mesoamerican centers. Wheatley referred to this coordination as "cosmo-magical thinking," operative, in his view, in China and Mesoamerica. In his chapter "The Ancient Chinese City as a Cosmo-Magical Symbol," he wrote:

> Underpinning urban form not only in traditional China but also throughout most of the rest of Asia, and with somewhat modified aspect in the New World, was a complex of ideas to which René Berthelot has given the name astro-biology. . . . This mode of thought presupposed an intimate parallelism between the mathematically expressible regimes of the heavens, and the biologically determined rhythms of life on earth, as manifested conjointly in the succession of the seasons and the annual cycles of plant regeneration [Wheatley 1971: 414].

Many chapters in this volume confirm and innovate on this view of how an "intimate parallelism" between the worlds of the gods and the struggles of humans was understood and expressed in the aesthetics of Mesoamerican urbanism. This theme of archetypal cities—or cities that came to be valued as models for other communities—is one that has long been a deep concern in Mesoamerican studies, though usually without the emphasis on religious and artistic symbolism that appears in the present volume. Readers may recall the powerful debate in the 1940s about whether the Tollan of the texts was equivalent to the historical Tula in Hidalgo or to the grandiose Teotihuacan. It is useful to recall the equally important debate between Alfonso Caso and Wigberto Jiménez Moreno about whether there was one underlying religion (an archetypal religion) for all of Mesoamerican urban history or many different religious visions that contributed to the multitude of types of ritual practices and complex pantheons. This volume gives various answers to the question: when and where did these archetypal concepts and exemplary places (the *altepetl* and Tollan, to name just two) become most powerfully represented in art and architecture? Some chapters discuss the ways that one urban place or mythic space became historically, regionally, or interregionally valued, copied, or innovated on by its builders and neighbors, resulting in something like what Italo Calvino calls in his *Invisible Cities* "the sum of all wonders."

Outstanding candidates to fulfill this archetypal prestige where settlement and natural symbolism, cosmological models, and social identities fused together in exemplary ways include the watery hill of San Lorenzo as interpreted by Ann Cyphers and Anna Di Castro (Chapter 1, this volume);

the "foot of the mountain" of Chalcatzingo as surveyed by David C. Grove and Susan D. Gillespie (Chapter 2); and Teotihuacan with its mountain gods as deciphered by Zoltán Paulinyi (Chapter 6) and as an interactive model with Copan by William L. Fash, Alexandre Tokovinine, and Barbara W. Fash (Chapter 7). We also learn a great deal about the powerful evolution of Tula's several parts, described by Alba Guadalupe Mastache, Dan M. Healan, and Robert H. Cobean (Chapter 10), as well as the grand design of Monte Albán, outlined by Joyce Marcus (Chapter 3). Barbara W. Fash (Chapter 8) points out the quatrefoil designs and water management at Copan, and Cholula achieves monumental status in the work of the longevity and resettlement near the "man-made mountain" in the chapter by Gabriela Uruñuela y Ladrón de Guevara, Patricia Plunket Nagoda, and Amparo Robles Salmerón (Chapter 5). We see the complexity of the historical problem of archetypal sites echoed in the ways that William M. Ringle and George J. Bey III (Chapter 11) illustrate how exemplary warfare and foreignness were literally represented in the many faces of the Itzas in Chichen Itza. The evolution of art, settlement organization, and warfare appears in Eduardo Matos Moctezuma's (Chapter 13) evaluation of the "hearts of heaven" and the deep tradition of mountain and pyramid representations linking the Templo Mayor to Teotihuacan and Tula. Flowering Maguey Mountain, the ballcourt, and the distinctions and closeness of deities and humans at El Tajín lead Rex Koontz (Chapter 9) to observe that "here a unique version of the Mesoamerican flowering mountain seems to reference the far reaches of the Tajín realm." Leonardo López Luján and Alfredo López Austin (Chapter 12) suggest another version of a grand Mesoamerican model when they focus on the Tollan-Quetzalcoatl dyad, because in their view it "was the ideological basis of a widespread political project in Mesoamerica, one that had been in place for centuries" before the rise of Tenochtitlan. Perhaps the clearest statement of a settlement and its art as an imitation of archetypes, in this case celestial ones, is found in the astonishing murals of San Bartolo. Contrasting these murals with those at Bonampak, William A. Saturno (Chapter 4) writes "in contrast, at San Bartolo all of the action [in the murals]—including the coronation of the historical [king]—takes place above the skyband in the realm of the gods. In this way the [king] ties his legitimacy not to his mortal ancestry but to his direct association with the divine."

Theme 2: The Art of Politics—Center and Periphery

The above observation about the coronation of a king in the realm of the gods points to a second powerful theme in these chapters: the art of politics—especially royal politics—in Mesoamerican cities. Even when rulers are barely mentioned in a chapter, it is clear that the work of integrating the social settlement and local history with the natural landscape and its mythologies required skillful, imaginative, and potent political leadership throughout Mesoamerican history. As readers discover in this volume, the architectural evidence from Cuicuilco to Chalcatzingo and San Lorenzo, from El Tajín to Monte Albán and Cholula, from Teotihuacan to Tula to Chichen Itza and Copan and well beyond shows that political leadership was expressed through art and architecture but also that rulership was a form of cultural performance art that depended on and was expressed by monumental aesthetics. The art of Mesoamerican politics is especially evident in the grand urban designs, individual buildings, and intercity relationships found among the Zapotec, Toltec, Maya, Olmec, and Aztec. And several chapters show, from Chichen Itza to El Tajín and on through Tula and Tenochtitlan, that ritual sacrifice—including human sacrifice—was a particularly potent form of political performance art. Many chapters suggest that numerous Mesoamerican cities were cities of sacrifice, and the overall impression is that Mesoamerica evolved, from Teotihuacan on, into a dominion of sacrifice as one of the primary models in the art of politics.

A powerful and related issue in these chapters about sacrifice in the art of politics is the style of management of center and periphery; that is, the effective ways that a local capital influences, controls, and interacts with its dependent polities and sometimes competing city-states. The dynamics of center and periphery is a theme addressed in such works as Richard Townsend's (1979) *State and Cosmos in the Art of Tenochtitlan*, Davíd Carrasco's (2001) Tollan-oriented *Quetzalcoatl and the Irony of Empire*, and Michael E. Smith's (2001) writings on regional polities and their competing dynamics. What the social theorist Edward Shils (1970: 7–8) wrote about great centers ruled by elites seems to be at work in numerous Mesoamerican cities:

> authority has an expansive tendency . . . a tendency to expand the order it represents towards the saturation of territorial space. Rulers, simply out of their possession of authority and the impulses which it generates, wish to be obeyed and they wish to obtain assent to the order they symbolically embody.

Keeping this expansive tendency in mind, it is interesting to ask the following questions in relation to these chapters: Why does ritual killing and its artistic representations become such an important expression of authority, obedience, and the "saturation of territorial space" in Mesoamerican politics and aesthetics? Are we faced with a political ordering of consciousness and settlement that echoes Clifford Geertz's (1980) contention that religious spectacle with its lavish aesthetics is in fact the state, what the state was really for? If that is the case in Mesoamerica, then perhaps the ritual and aesthetics of sacrifice was what the state was really for. Why do Mesoamerican theater states depend on ritual violence to such a degree and at times with such intensity? Could it be that Mesoamerican rulers believed that they were residing at the center of something akin to what Stanley Tambiah (1985) claimed about the kingdoms of Southeast Asia, namely, that they were "pulsating galactic polities"? These were kingdoms in which the capital cities were in constant tension and periodic antagonism with surrounding allied and enemy settlements, resulting in enormous resources, aesthetic and military, dedicated to persuading competitors, enemies, and allies that the avenue to agricultural and trade prosperity as well as cosmic stability was located in the capital where the watery mountain stood. Arthur Demarest (1992) sustained that the same held true for Classic Maya polities and regional politics, although more recently he has conceded that the political economies of Southeast Asia and the Maya lowlands had significant differences. Nonetheless several chapters in this volume suggest that when Monte Albán, Tula, Xochicalco, and Chichen Itza are viewed as military centers, something like a "galactic polity" mentality and set of rivalries was at work (see, e.g., Marcus 1992). The control of vast human resources and their production was unquestionably a central motivating force in the nucleation of peoples into towns, cities, and imperial capitals in ancient Mesoamerica. But art, ideology, and performance were what sustained the most successful civic-ceremonial centers through good times and bad for centuries, in the face of intense competition from rival kingdoms. What this volume makes clear, regardless of whether some Mesoamerican states at certain periods were organized in a fashion similar to galactic designs, is that our scholarship now faces new opportunities to understand the material-symbolic nexus that integrated city-states, regions, and struggling empires.

This volume enlarges our knowledge of center-periphery dynamics in the cases of Cholula, Tula, Monte Albán, El Tajín, and especially Teotihuacan. In fact the notion of center-center and center-periphery dynamics is expanded through time and space in two chapters, one linking Teotihuacan to Tula and Tenochtitlan (Chapter 12, this volume) and another linking Teotihuacan to Copan as well as other kingdoms in the Classic Maya world (Chapter 7). These and other chapters discuss in cogent terms the several ways in which one city worked to appropriate artistic and architectural traditions of other sites and how other sites were driven to integrate Teotihuacan into their own aesthetic and political programs. These chapters push us toward future work with the archaeological, iconographic, and textual records to see to what extent Teotihuacan functioned as the archetypal city or as a competing archetypal city challenging and challenged by places and kingdoms both nearby and far away (in time and space).

Theme 3: Management and Symbolism of the Natural Landscape

A third theme that flows through several chapters is the religious power and social management of hills, mountains, fire, caves, sky, and especially water. Many of these natural elements were valued for their physical powers and became royal symbols of authority and place. In this volume, water moves to center stage. There are insightful explorations of local and regional "water mountains" and several remarkable variations on the theme of the *altepetl*. Water rituals, rain gods, cenote rites, water channels, and especially water management are analyzed from a variety of disciplinary perspectives that reveal the fundamental social and symbolic role of water in Mesoamerican history. Rex Koontz (Chapter 9) shows how El Tajín was, in part, built around permanent springs so that the ballcourt could be periodically flooded in a rite of mythic regeneration. His chapter opens up our thinking about the role of water in ritual renovation and political symbolism in new ways. Barbara Fash's (Chapter 8) comments summarize well the overall significance and power of water and can serve as a guide for the reader in exploring this theme and its gendered associations throughout the volume. She writes:

> the nature of water as a fundamental resource with both benevolent and malevolent aspects, with life-giving and life-taking properties, reinforced its spiritual potency. Water's birthing and nurturing characteristics most commonly become naturally linked with female roles, fertility, and growth, whereas its opposite, fire and solar heat, generally becomes associated with male qualities.

Perhaps the richness of the water theme in this volume points to a future conference on the "Waters of Mesoamerica" in which we give as much attention to the water side of the notion of the *altepetl* as we have given to the mountain side of this *difrasismo*.

Thankfully, this excellent volume shows that there were numerous moments and places where the wonders and uses of place, mountains, ritual, water, hierarchy, warfare, and myths were crystallized into the sums of regional struggle, competition, collapse, and renewal. There is a sense of deep historical respect for what went on before the florescence of individual powerful cities as well as for what went on, geographically and politically, in between various powerful, often competing ceremonial cities. There is also a sense that we today benefit greatly from the symbolic, ritual, and technological efforts of Mesoamerican peoples who for millennia strove to configure their own complexities into attractive, magnetic images and places. And it was fortunate indeed that Mexico City and Washington, D.C., the Museo del Templo Mayor and Dumbarton Oaks, joined together and organized the conference on which this volume is based at the archetypal place—the site of the Great Aztec Temple. More than once during the proceedings and while reading this volume I was reminded of the work of the urban ecologist Paul Wheatley, and it is to him I give the last word about cities that were symbols that generated us and our inquiries. Toward the end of his magisterial *The Pivot of the Four Quarters: A Preliminary Inquiry into the Nature and Character of the Ancient Chinese City*, Wheatley (1971: 473) translated an ode from the Shih-Ching, a royal text, as follows. I wonder at how it resonates with this volume:

> The capital of Shang was a city of cosmic order
> The pivot of the four quarters
> Glorious was its Renown
> Purifying its Divine Power
> Manifested in longevity and tranquility
> And the protection of us who come after.

REFERENCES CITED

Calvino, Italo
    1978 *Invisible Cities.* Harvest Books, New York.
Carrasco, Davíd
    2001 *Quetzalcoatl and the Irony of Empire.* University Press of Colorado, Boulder.
Carrasco, Davíd, Lindsay Jones, and Scott Sessions (eds.)
    2000 *Mesoamerica's Classic Heritage: From Teotihuacan to the Aztecs.* University Press of Colorado, Boulder.
Demarest, Arthur A.
    1992 Ideology in Ancient Maya Cultural Evolution: The Dynamics of Galactic Polities. In *Ideology and Pre-Columbian Civilizations* (Arthur A. Demarest and Geoffrey W. Conrad, eds.): 135–157. School of American Research, Santa Fe, N.M.
Eliade, Mircea
    1954 *The Myth of the Eternal Return.* Pantheon Books, New York.
Geertz, Clifford
    1980 *Negara: The Theatre State in Nineteenth-Century Bali.* Princeton University Press, Princeton, N.J.
Jones, Lindsay
    1995 *Twin City Tales: A Hermeneutical Reassessment of Tula and Chichén Itzá.* University of Colorado Press, Niwot.
    2000 *The Hermeneutics of Sacred Architecture: Experience, Interpretation, Comparison.* Harvard University Press, Cambridge, Mass.
Long, Charles H.
    1986 *Significations: Signs, Symbols, and Images in the Interpretation of Religion.* Fortress Press, Philadelphia.

López Austin, Alfredo

    1997   *Tamoanchan/Tlalocan: Places of Mist.* University of Colorado Press, Niwot.

Marcus, Joyce

    1992   Dynamic Cycles of Mesoamerican States. *Research and Exploration* 8: 392–411.

Rykwert, Joseph

    1988   *The Idea of a Town: The Anthropology of Urban Form in Rome, Italy and the Ancient World.* MIT Press, Cambridge, Mass.

Shils, Edward

    1970   Center and Periphery. In *Selected Essays:* 7–8. Center for Social Organization Studies, Chicago.

Smith, Jonathan Z.

    1970   The Influence of Symbols upon Social Change: A Place upon Which to Stand. *Worship* 44(8): 457.

    1978   *Map Is Not Territory: Studies in the Histories of Religions.* E. J. Brill, Leiden.

Smith, Michael E.

    2001   Urbanization. In *The Oxford Encyclopedia of Mesoamerican Cultures: The Civilizations of Mexico and Central America*, vol. 3 (Davíd Carrasco, general ed.): 290–294. Oxford University Press, New York.

Tambiah, Stanley

    1985   *Culture, Thought, and Social Action: An Anthropological Perspective.* Harvard University Press, Cambridge, Mass.

Townsend, Richard F.

    1979   *State and Cosmos in the Art of Tenochtitlan.* Studies in Pre-Columbian Art and Archaeology 20. Dumbarton Oaks Research Library and Collection, Washington, D.C.

Walcott, Derek

    2007   The Antilles: Fragments of Epic Memory. In *Nobel Lectures: From the Literature Laureates 1986 to 2006.* New Press, New York.

Wheatley, Paul

    1971   *The Pivot of the Four Quarters: A Preliminary Inquiry into the Nature and Character of the Ancient Chinese City.* Aldine, Chicago.

CONTRIBUTORS

George J. Bey III is a member of the Department of Anthropology and Sociology of Millsaps College, Jackson, Mississippi. His archaeological work, carried out in collaboration with William M. Ringle and Tomás Gallareta Negrón, currently focuses on the eastern Bolonchén District of the Puuc Hills. Previously he and Dr. Ringle co-directed long-term research at Ek Balam, Yucatán, Mexico.

Davíd Carrasco is the Neil L. Rudenstine Professor of the Study of Latin America at Harvard Divinity School and also holds a joint appointment with the Department of Anthropology in the Faculty of Arts and Sciences. He received his B.A. at Western Maryland College, and his Th.M., M.A., and Ph.D. at the University of Chicago. Dr. Carrasco is a historian of religions specializing in hermeneutics in the study of religion, Mesoamerican religions, and the Mexican-American borderlands. His work has been focused on the symbolic nature of cities in comparative perspective, utilizing his 20 years of research in the excavations and archives associated with the sites of Teotihuacan and Mexico-Tenochtitlan in Mexico. This work has resulted in publications on ritual violence and sacred space, the Great Aztec Temple, the myth of Quetzalcoatl, the Feathered Serpent, and the history of religions in Mesoamerica. He is editor-in-chief of the award-winning three-volume *Oxford Encyclopedia of Mesoamerican Cultures*. Dr. Carrasco has received the Mexican Order of the Aztec Eagle, the highest honor the Mexican government gives to a foreign national.

Robert H. Cobean is an archaeologist at the Instituto Nacional de Antropología e Historia, Mexico City. His research interests include the study of urbanism processes at the ancient city of Tula, Hidalgo; obsidian mining and trade in Pre-Hispanic Mesoamerica; and regional studies concerning the Olmec civilization.

Ann Cyphers is a senior research scientist at the Instituto de Investigaciones Antropológicas, Universidad Nacional Autónoma de México, Mexico City. She has conducted research in the San Lorenzo Tenochtitlan region of southern Veracruz for the past 19 years.

Anna Di Castro is a doctoral candidate at the Facultad de Filosofía y Letras, Universidad Nacional Autónoma de México, Mexico City, and collaborator in the San Lorenzo Tenochtitlan Archaeological Project.

Barbara W. Fash is director of the Corpus of Maya Hieroglyphic Inscriptions Program, Peabody Museum, Harvard University, Cambridge, Massachusetts. She has directed or participated in a number of multinational efforts to record and conserve the monolithic and stone mosaic sculpture in Copan, Honduras, culminating in the creation of the Copan Sculpture Museum, for which she designed and installed the exhibitions and completed the museum's catalog. She has published extensively on Maya iconography, Mesoamerican water management, and the conservation and curation of archaeological and archival collections, and she has curated several exhibitions. Her archaeological fieldwork extends to the Basin of Mexico and the valleys of Morelos and Puebla as well as Copan.

William L. Fash is Bowditch Professor of Central American and Mexican Archaeology and Ethnology and William and Muriel Seabury Howells Director, Peabody Museum, Harvard University, Cambridge, Massachusetts. He received his Ph.D. in Anthropology from Harvard University in 1983. He has participated in and/or directed a series of multi-institutional, multinational, and interdisciplinary research efforts devoted to illuminating all aspects of ancient Maya lifeways and cultural history in the Copan Valley, Honduras, and to conserving its cultural patrimony. He was awarded the Order of José Cecilio del Valle by the president of Honduras in 1994. Outside Copan his Mesoamerican fieldwork includes research at Chalcatzingo, Morelos; Cuahtinchan, Puebla; and Teotihuacan, Mexico.

Susan D. Gillespie, an archaeologist and ethnohistorian, is associate professor of anthropology at the University of Florida, Gainesville. She has directed archaeological projects in Oaxaca and Veracruz. She is the author of *The Aztec Kings*.

David C. Grove is professor emeritus of anthropology at the University of Illinois at Urbana-Champaign. He has carried out over three decades of archaeological research at Chalcatzingo, Morelos, as well as undertaken investigations in Veracruz, Guerrero, Oaxaca, and the Basin of Mexico. He is presently affiliated with the University of Florida as courtesy professor.

Dan M. Healan is professor of anthropology at Tulane University, New Orleans. He has directed archaeological field projects in Tula, Hidalgo, and Zinapecuaro, Michoacan. His interests and areas of specialization include lithic technology, quantitative analytical methods, Pre-Columbian urbanism, and prehistoric household organization.

Rex Koontz teaches art history at the University of Houston. Dr. Koontz is a student of Classic Veracruz art and civilization. He has studied and published on the site of El Tajín for more than a decade. More general interests include the aesthetics of non-Western art and its relation to power, as well as the history and historiography of Mesoamerica. *Landscape and Power in Ancient Mesoamerica*, edited with Kathryn Reese-Taylor and Annabeth Headrick, addresses aesthetics and power, and *Mexico* (fifth edition) with Michael D. Coe is a general treatment of Mesoamerican history.

Alfredo López Austin is emeritus professor and researcher of history at the Instituto de Investigaciones Antropológicas, Universidad Nacional Autónoma de México, Mexico City. He received his Ph.D. in History at the Universidad Nacional Autónoma de México. Most of his work has been devoted to the study of Central Mexican religion, magic, medicine, and politics. He has published many books, among them *Human Body and Ideology; The Myths of the Opossum; The Rabbit on the Face of the Moon; Tamoanchan, Tlalocan: Places of Mist*, and *Mexico's Indigenous Past* (with Leonardo López Luján).

Leonardo López Luján is senior professor and researcher of archaeology at the Museo del Templo Mayor, Instituto Nacional de Antropología e Historia, Mexico City. He received his Ph.D. in Archaeology at the Université de Paris X, Nanterre. He has excavated in the ruins of Tenochtitlan, Mexico, since 1980 and has directed several projects in Central Mexico. Among his publications are *The Offerings of the Templo Mayor of Tenochtitlan* (revised edition), *La Casa de las Águilas*, and *Aztèques: Sculptures de la collection du Musée du quai Branly* (with Marie-France Fauvet-Berthelot).

Joyce Marcus is the Robert L. Carneiro Distinguished University Professor at the University of Michigan, Ann Arbor. She has worked in North, Middle, and South America. Among her recent books are *San José Mogote 1: The Household Archaeology* (co-authored with Kent V. Flannery) and *The Ancient City* (co-edited with Jeremy A. Sabloff).

Alba Guadalupe Mastache (1942–2004) was an archaeologist at the Instituto Nacional de Antropología e Historia, Mexico City, for more than 40 years. She directed projects investigating the Toltec state and the anthropology of Guerrero. In collaboration with Professor William T. Sanders, she directed the multidisciplinary project "Urbanism in Mesoamerica," sponsored by the Instituto Nacional de Antropología e Historia and Pennsylvania State University, College Park.

Eduardo Matos Moctezuma is emeritus researcher, Instituto Nacional de Antropología e Historia, Mexico City. He graduated as an archaeologist from the Escuela Nacional de Antropología e Historia and received his M.A. in anthropological sciences from the Universidad Nacional Autónoma de México, Mexico City. Prof. Matos also holds an honorary doctorate from the University of Colorado, Boulder. His other honors include the Palmes Académiques; Ordre National du Mérite; Officier de l'Ordre des Arts et des Lettres de la Republique Francaise; and the Henry Nicholson Medal, Harvard University. He is a member of El Colegio Nacional, the Academia Mexicana de la Historia, and the Seminario de Cultura Mexicana, Mexico City. He is a member of the German Archaeological Institute, and has published more than 400 titles, including books, articles, catalogs, and guides.

Zoltán Paulinyi has lectured since 1996 in the Department of Theory and History of Art of the Facultad de Artes, Universidad de Chile, Santiago. He received his undergraduate degree and Ph.D. in history and archaeology at Eötvös Lóránd University, Budapest. After conducting ethnohistorical research on the Pre-Hispanic Central Mexican Highlands, his interest turned to the iconography of Teotihuacan art, now his principal field. He has also entered the field of the iconography of Moche art of Peru.

Patricia Plunket Nagoda is chair of the anthropology department at the Universidad de las Américas, Cholula, Puebla. After completing her doctoral dissertation at Tulane University, New Orleans, on the Mixteca Alta of Oaxaca, she has focused on the archaeology of southwestern Puebla and has published on domestic ritual, abandonment processes, ceramics, and the impact of volcanism on Pre-Hispanic communities of Central Mexico. She is currently co-director of the Tetimpa Project.

William M. Ringle is a member of the department of anthropology, Davidson College, Davidson, North Carolina. His archaeological work, carried out in collaboration with George J. Bey and Tomás Gallareta Negrón, currently focuses on the eastern Bolonchén District of the Puuc Hills. Previously he and Dr. Bey co-directed long-term research at Ek Balam, Yucatán.

Amparo Robles Salmerón received her B.A. in archaeology at the Universidad de las Américas, Cholula, Puebla. She has participated in fieldwork with the Tetimpa Project and the Coordinación de Apoyo Arqueológico of Universidad de las Américas and with the CEMCA in both the Bajío and the Maya areas. Ms. Robles's thesis deals with the first three building stages of the Great Pyramid in Cholula, where she has been in charge of mapping for the past two years.

William A. Saturno is assistant professor of archaeology at Boston University. He received his Ph.D. in anthropology from Harvard University, Cambridge, Massachusetts. A specialist in Mesoamerican civilization and archaeological remote sensing, he has conducted fieldwork in the southwestern United States, Bolivia, Cambodia, Mexico, Belize, Honduras, and most recently Guatemala. In March 2001, while exploring in northeastern Guatemala for Harvard's Peabody Museum of Archaeology and Ethnology (Cambridge, Massachusetts), he discovered the remote archaeological site of San Bartolo and the oldest intact murals ever found in the Maya world. He directs the San Bartolo Regional Archaeology Project, the multinational interdisciplinary research effort dedicated to the excavation and conservation of these spectacular murals and to understanding San Bartolo's role in this largely unexplored region of the Maya area during the period when Maya civilization itself was just forming.

Alexandre Tokovinine is a research associate of the Corpus of Maya Hieroglyphic Inscriptions, Peabody Museum, Harvard University, Cambridge, Massachusetts. He is a Maya epigrapher and archaeologist who has participated in several projects in Guatemala, including the Holmul Archaeological Project and Proyecto Arqueológico de Investigación y Rescate Naranjo. He received his Ph.D. degree in anthropology at Harvard University, and his dissertation centered on Classic Maya place names. Dr. Tokovinine was a junior fellow of Pre-Columbian Studies at Dumbarton Oaks in 2008.

Gabriela Uruñuela y Ladrón de Guevara is professor of anthropology, director of the Museum of the City of Cholula in the Casa del Caballero Aguila, and head of the Coordinación de Apoyo Arqueológico at the Universidad de las Américas in Cholula, Puebla. She received her Ph.D. in anthropology from the Universidad Nacional Autónoma de México, Mexico City. In addition to her work on human osteological collections from the Sayula Basin in Jalisco, Dr. Uruñuela has published on mortuary practices, domestic household organization, abandonment processes, and the impact of volcanism on Pre-Hispanic communities of Central Mexico. She is currently co-director of the Tetimpa Project.

INDEX